Also by Joseph E. Persico

My American Journey (collaboration with General Colin Powell)

Nuremberg: Infamy on Trial

Casey: From the OSS to the CIA

Edward R. Murrow: An American Original

The Imperial Rockefeller: A Biography of Nelson A. Rockefeller

The Spiderweb

*Piercing the Reich: The Penetration of Nazi Germany
by American Secret Agents During World War II*

My Enemy, My Brother: Men and Days of Gettysburg

ROOSEVELT'S SECRET WAR

ROOSEVELT'S SECRET WAR

FDR and World War II Espionage

JOSEPH E. PERSICO

Random House / New York

LIBRARY OF CONGRESS CATALOGING-IN-PUBLICATION DATA
Persico, Joseph E.
Roosevelt's secret war: FDR and World War II espionage / Joseph E. Persico.
p. cm.
Includes bibliographical references and index.
ISBN 0-375-50246-7
1. World War, 1939–1945—Secret service—United States.   2. Roosevelt,
Franklin D. (Franklin Delano), 1882–1945   3. United States. Office
of Strategic Services—History.   4. Intelligence service—
United States—History—20th century.   I. Title.

D810.S7 P45 2001
940.54'8673—dc21   2001019106

Printed in the United States of America on acid-free paper
Random House website address: www.atrandom.com

6 8 9 7 5

Book design by Gabriel Levine

To the next generation,
Amanda, Joshua, and Georgia,
and my literary agent,
Clyde Taylor

If you know the enemy and know yourself, you need not fear the result of a hundred battles. If you know yourself but not the enemy, for every victory gained you will also suffer a defeat. If you know neither the enemy nor yourself, you will succumb in every battle.

Sun-tzu
The Art of War

Foreword

THE genesis of this book lies in my lifelong fascination with Franklin D. Roosevelt. As a boy growing up in New York State, it seemed to me that the nation was governed by a triumvirate as immutable as the heavens. Fiorello La Guardia was New York City's mayor, Thomas Dewey was the state's governor, and Roosevelt was the president. Subsequent ascendents to these offices seemed, to an immature mind, unwelcome interlopers. The brightest star in this constellation was, of course, FDR.

Most of my previous books have dealt, in whole or in part, with espionage and World War II. After a search of some six hundred Roosevelt entries in the Library of Congress, I was surprised to find that none covered specifically the President's involvement in World War II intelligence. I saw an opportunity to fuse my interests in the man, the field, and the era.

Few leaders have been better suited by nature and temperament for the anomalies of secret warfare than FDR. "You know I am a juggler, and I never let my right hand know what my left hand does," he once confessed. "I may be entirely inconsistent, and furthermore I am perfectly willing to mislead and tell untruths if it will help me win the war." His style of leadership bears out this admission. FDR compartmentalized information, misled associates, manipulated people, conducted intrigues, used private lines of communication, scattered responsibility, duplicated assignments, provoked rivalries, held all the cards while showing few, and left few fingerprints. His behavior, which fascinated, puzzled, amazed, dismayed, and occasionally repelled people, parallels many of the qualities of an espionage chief.

FDR's talent for intrigue was merely another weapon in the Rooseveltian arsenal, along with vision, courage, charm, and unquenchable spirit, that he employed toward laudable ends—combating the Depression, seeking social justice, and winning the war. As for the last objective, his benign duplicity was best captured by his son James. "I had a conversation with father," the young Marine officer writes, "in which I discussed the dishonesty of his stand on war." "Jimmy," FDR explained, "I knew we were going to war. . . . But I couldn't come out and say a war was coming, because the people would have panicked and turned from me. . . . If I don't say I hate war, then people are going to think I don't hate war. If I say we're going to get into this war, people will think I want us in it. If I don't say I won't send our sons to fight on foreign battlefields, then people will think I want to send them. . . . I couldn't take every congressman into my confidence because he'd have run off the Hill hollering that FDR is a war monger. . . . So you play the game the way it has been played over the years, and you play to win."

Still, the President took almost childish delight in subterfuge for its own sake. Roosevelt loved being told secrets and retailing gossip. He was accused by enemies and friends alike of being devious and lacking in candor, and justly so. He dangled people like puppets on the string of his whims. He would fool those who thought they could predict his moves by changing course. His early New Deal ally Rexford Tugwell observed, "He deliberately concealed the processes of his mind." His vice president Henry Wallace concluded that the only certainty in dealing with the man was the uncertainty of "what went on inside FDR's head." As one scholar put it, "Nothing would have pleased him more than to observe historians arguing passionately about what constituted the 'real Roosevelt.' " His inscrutable nature found full play when America went to war. The man with the instincts of a spymaster now had a war in which to indulge his attraction to the clandestine.

Wars are won by superior might wedded to military performance. Espionage is a handmaiden, not the instrument of victory. But a war's outcome is affected by the genius or ineptitude, the coups or blunders, the measures and countermeasures of secret warriors. How FDR performed on that clandestine front is the story that follows.

Albany, New York
July 19, 2001

A Note to Readers

THERE exists, for intelligence practitioners and scholars, precise distinctions between codes and ciphers, cryptology and cryptanalysis, coding and encryption, decoding and decryption. However, in the interest of reducing confusion for the general reader, these terms are used here in their broader colloquial sense. Were purist rules to be followed, the Hugh Whitemore play about Alan Turing's role in Ultra would have to be entitled *Breaking the Ciphers,* not *Breaking the Code.* This is a linguistic straitjacket that I have hoped to avoid.

Acknowledgments

WRITERS of history and of historical figures must stand on the shoulders of numerous others in order to tell their story. This book could not have been written without the unstinting cooperation of the staff of the Franklin D. Roosevelt Library in Hyde Park, New York. At the time I began, the library's director was Verne W. Newton, who, in addition to steering me initially in wise directions, read my final manuscript with great care and to the author's profit. I especially benefited from the assistance of the library's supervisory archivist, Raymond Teichman, and Lynn Bassanese was unfailingly helpful and imaginative in handling my queries. Others who aided me at Hyde Park were Robert Parks, Nancy Snedeker, Alycia Vivona, and Mark Renovitch, who was especially helpful in finding photographs. Verne Newton's successor, Cynthia Koch, continued to provide the backing of her staff.

At the National Archives I relied on William Cunliffe, Larry Macdonald, John Taylor, and Sidney Shapiro. At the Library of Congress, I was assisted by Margaret Krewson, former chief of the European Division, Mark Matucci, and Marvin Kranz. I thank Meredith Butler, director of libraries at my alma mater, the State University of New York at Albany, and among her staff I am deeply indebted to William Young for tracking down my endless queries. I have been well served by a talented reference team at the

Guilderland, New York Library who researched numerous matters for me. That staff, under the library's director, Carole Hamblin, included Margaret Garrett, Gillian Leonard, Maria Preller, Eileen Williams, Joseph Nash, and Thomas Barnes. At the New York State Library, I was assisted by Jean Hargrave and Eileen Clark.

I received valuable help from the Truman Library in Independence, Missouri, beginning with the library's director, Larry Hackman, and particularly from Randy Sowell. The Truman scholar Robert Ferrell was extremely generous to me. Duane A. Watson of Wilderstein Preservation Incorporated opened for me the files of FDR's confidant Margaret Suckley. I was measurably helped by two noted historians of intelligence, Michael Warner of the Central Intelligence Agency and Robert L. Benson of the National Security Agency. Five other accomplished writers in the intelligence field, Thomas Troy, David Kahn, Hyden Peake, Arnold Kramish, and Rick Russell, also provided me with invaluable help. Nicholas B. Sheetz, manuscripts librarian at Georgetown University, generously opened his collection to me. Several of my requests dealing with military matters were filled by the staff of retired General Colin Powell, including his chief aides, William Smullen, Peggy Cifrino, and Larry Wilkerson. Derek Blackburn provided useful Churchill material.

I benefited enormously from the time and freedom provided by fellowships to the Rockefeller Institute Study Center at Bellagio, Italy, and the Bogliasco Foundation, also in Italy. My daughter, Vanya Perez, ably prepared the manuscript. And I thank Edwin Sours, Henry Jurenka, John Foley, and Michael Mattioli, each of whom knows what he did to keep this project moving.

Others who read the manuscript and provided invaluable guidance included my wife, Sylvia LaVista Persico, and fellow writers Bernard Conners and Tanya Melich. I further want to recognize the valued role of my late agent, Clyde Taylor, in the publication of this and my other works. Finally, I was the fortunate author guided by the sure hand of Robert Loomis, my editor, who supplied enthusiasm, judgment, and encouragement throughout this project.

Contents

Prologue

THE President had been awake since eight-thirty this Sunday morning, December 7, 1941. He sat in bed flipping through the thick Sunday editions of *The New York Times,* the *Herald Tribune,* the two Washington papers, even the hateful *Chicago Tribune,* snapping the pages with a rapidity that created a breeze; yet he would later be able to recall what he read with a retentiveness that daunted his aides. His valet, Navy Petty Officer Arthur Prettyman, helped FDR out of bed and into his wheelchair, a makeshift affair adapted from a kitchen chair with the legs cut off and the seat mounted onto a metal frame. Prettyman wheeled FDR into the bathroom, where the President began shaving himself with a straight razor. He dressed casually this morning, finishing his attire with a baggy sweater that belonged to his son Jimmy. He was looking forward to a day of rest. The night before Mrs. Roosevelt had arranged dinner for thirty-four guests, an eclectic list including relatives, friends, White House aides, middle-ranking government officials, and military officers. To one guest, the ensemble suggested an exercise in social catch-up. The President had excused himself early and left before the musicale led by the violinist Arthur LeBlanc, not precisely FDR's cup of tea. One guest, Bertie Hamlin, whom FDR had known since his youth, thought the President "looked very worn. . . . He had an unusually stern expression."

His mood was explained by intercepted and decoded Japanese messages reaching his desk in recent weeks which suggested a Japan bent on war. Back in his room the President took a pad and began drafting in his bold hand an appeal to Emperor Hirohito to join him in a statesman-to-statesman effort to stave off disaster. But within a half hour of dispatching this olive branch to the emperor, FDR's hopes were dampened. A young naval aide, Lieutenant Lester R. Schulz, just two days on the job, brought to the President the latest decrypted message from Tokyo, instructions to the Japanese ambassador in Washington spelling out what the President regarded as intolerable demands. It was near midnight before Prettyman lifted a drained FDR into bed.

The next morning, the world looked brighter as the President breakfasted on his customary orange juice, coffee, toast, soft-boiled eggs, and bacon. The sun rose in a clear sky bathing the East Wing of the White House in pale gold light. The weather, for December, was glorious, cool, heading toward a high of forty-three degrees. Golfers were getting ready to tee off at Washington's Burning Tree course, among them CBS's broadcast star, thirty-three-year-old Edward R. Murrow, just back from London. The President had invited Murrow for supper that evening to learn firsthand how the British were bearing up under the Blitz and Hitler's string of unbroken conquests. "Wild Bill" Donovan, just six months into his job as Roosevelt's spy chief, veiled by the opaque title Coordinator of Information, had gotten away from the capital for a late-season football game between the Brooklyn Dodgers and the New York Giants at the Polo Grounds.

As Prettyman removed the debris of the President's breakfast, FDR called for his doctor. His chronic sinusitis was acting up, but otherwise he appeared to have shed the cares of the night before.

Admiral Ross McIntire left his dispensary on the first floor and strode through the unaccustomed Sunday-morning stillness of the White House, his heels echoing hollowly up the stairway. Outside, the capital's streets were deserted and traffic sparse. Washington was a sleepy, middle-class city populated by middle-class government workers who abandoned downtown on the weekend. The silence was broken only by the peal of the bells of St. John's Church across Pennsylvania Avenue on Lafayette Square, summoning worshippers to morning services. As McIntire entered FDR's study, the President reflexively rolled back his large, handsome head, and the doctor administered nose drops. FDR blinked, sat up, and launched into one of his anecdote-strewn monologues. Roosevelt and

McIntire had first met aboard a cruiser when FDR was assistant secretary of the Navy and the doctor a young medical officer. Roosevelt remembered the affable MD thereafter and brought McIntire into the White House, where he began his heady ascent to his present rank. The President and his doctor swapped stories for almost two hours before FDR prepared himself for his only official appointment that Sunday, a visit by the Chinese ambassador, Hu Shih. Then he could do what he really wanted, which was to work on his stamp collection, his passion since he was eight years old.

At 12:30 P.M., the ambassador was ushered into the White House. In tune with the leisurely day he had in mind, the President chose to see Hu Shih in his upstairs study rather than in the more formal Oval Office below, though both rooms reflected FDR's casual disarray. Stacks of books, piles of yellowed papers tied with string carpeted the floor, and FDR's ship models sailed along the tops of bookcases. Portraits of the President's mother and wife studied each other across opposite walls. Hu Shih found himself assigned a role familiar to Roosevelt's visitors, serving as a sounding board for whatever popped into the President's mind. This day FDR wanted the ambassador to listen to what he had cabled to Hirohito the night before. He read with relish from his literary handiwork. "I got him there; that was a fine, telling phrase," he exclaimed. "That will be fine for the record," he added, punctuating the point with a stab of his cigarette in its ivory holder. Hu Shih left the President's study a half hour later, having heard much and said little.

As his guest departed, FDR turned eagerly to the manila envelope sent over the day before from the State Department. His hobby had prospered mightily after he became president. Mail came into the department from all over the world, and every Saturday a messenger delivered a batch of the most interesting stamps to him. He asked his valet to bring him the tools of his avocation—his album, magnifying glass, scissors, packet of stickers, and the collector's bible, *Scott's Stamp Catalogue*.

Harry Hopkins, FDR's gaunt constant confidant, padded down the hall from the bedroom he occupied next to the Lincoln study. Another large list of guests had been invited for lunch this Sunday, though, as Eleanor later recalled, "I was disappointed but not surprised when Franklin sent word a short time before lunch that he did not see how he could join us. . . . The fact that he carried so many secrets in his head made it necessary for him to watch everything he said, which in itself was exhausting." Instead, the President had chosen to have lunch alone with Hopkins. They ate off trays, Roosevelt's set on a removable rack affixed to his wheelchair. FDR stabbed desultorily at his food. The White House chef, Henrietta Nesbitt, was notorious for dull menus. Eleanor had met her through Hyde Park politics and, for some unfathomed reason, had decided the woman would make a good housekeeper. FDR's son Jimmy found Mrs. Nesbitt "the worst cook I ever encountered."

While the President munched on an apple and flipped through his album, Hopkins stretched out on a couch. Their conversation was light, bantering, with serious concerns set aside this day. At 1:47 P.M., the phone rang. FDR picked it up. The White House operator apologized for intruding, but she had Navy secretary Frank Knox on the line, and he insisted on speaking to the President.

"Put him on," FDR said. "Hello, Frank." His voice took on its habitual gaiety.

Knox's voice was choked. "Mr. President," he said, "it looks as if the Japanese have attacked Pearl Harbor!"

"No!" Roosevelt gasped.

Knox said that he had no further details, but would keep the President advised. Hopkins, learning what had happened, was incredulous. There must be some mistake, he said. Japan would not attack Honolulu. FDR quickly regained his composure. His wife had long ago observed, "His reaction to any great event was always to be calm. If it was something that was bad, he just became almost like an iceberg, and there was never the slightest emotion that was allowed to show." To Hopkins's doubts that the Japanese would make such an attack, the President responded that this was just the kind of thing they would do, talk peace while plotting war.

The United States had fallen victim to the most stunning failure of intelligence in the country's history, likely in the entire history of warfare. What happened that tranquil Sunday had been preceded by and would be followed by fluctuating triumphs and failures in something relatively new to Franklin Roosevelt, the sub rosa battlegrounds of espionage. The story began in 1938.

ROOSEVELT'S
SECRET WAR

★

Chapter I

————— ★ —————

Gentleman Amateurs

THE DATE was May 12, 1938. With three bells announcing his arrival, trailed by trotting Secret Service agents lugging wire baskets of official papers, FDR propelled his wheelchair from the first-floor elevator into the Oval Office where he summoned Missy LeHand. As she came in, the President greeted his secretary with a blinding smile and an expression that said, what does the world have in store for Franklin Roosevelt today?

It was nearly 11 A.M. as the softly attractive LeHand sat down and propped her steno pad on her knee. By now, eighteen years at his side, through his glowing early promise, the catastrophe of polio, the slow resuscitation of his spirits and ambitions, she could read FDR's every mood and need instantly. The President took from a can on his cluttered desk one of the forty-odd Camel cigarettes he would smoke that day and inserted it into a nicotine-stained holder. He chose from a wire basket a letter delivered personally to the White House the day before by Uncle Ted's son Kermit Roosevelt. It was from Vincent Astor. Before he began dictating, FDR reread the nineteen handwritten pages in the familiar script. The letterhead read simply *Nourmahal,* the name of Astor's yacht. The very word suffused FDR with warm memories. He had first sailed the *Nourmahal* in 1932 while still president-elect. The luxurious oceangoing vessel, manned by a crew of forty-two, recalled America's Cup races off Newport watched from her deck, fishing trips off Long Island Sound, cruises in the Caribbean, card games, drinking, and, for some of Astor's pals, occasional amorous adventures on board.

It was to the *Nourmahal,* tied up in Miami, that FDR had retreated in February 1933 after an incident that nearly ended his presidency before it began. He had been seated in the back of an open car after addressing a crowd when, as he later described the moment, "A man came forward with a telegram about five or six feet long and started telling me what it contained. Just then I heard what I thought was a firecracker: then several more." Roosevelt saw a Secret Service agent wrestle the man to the ground. The assailant was Giuseppe Zangara, an unemployed bricklayer and political malcontent whose shots had miraculously missed Roosevelt, but struck Anton Cermak, the mayor of Chicago then visiting Miami, a woman, and a policeman. Roosevelt accompanied Cermak to the hospital, where the fifty-nine-year-old mayor's wound proved fatal. The other victims survived. The president-elect then joined Astor and other friends aboard the *Nourmahal,* grateful for a respite from the horrors of the day.

Subsequently, FDR had sailed the *Nourmahal* every year, enjoying himself tremendously, especially his fellow passengers' sophomoric hijinks. He got a kick out of the mock bills Astor sent after each cruise—"Expenses incurred for alcoholic stimulants and repeated correctives, $37.50 per diem. (Note: the Chief Steward reports that consumption of the above stores was so vast as to overwhelm his accounting system.) With a further $1.90 for chipping Mother-of-Pearl surfaces of bell contacts through impatient punching of the above, to hasten the arrival of correctives. Seventeen cigars, Profundo Magnifico, $.90 each." And always the appended note, "The President is exempt."

The letter from Honolulu now in Roosevelt's hands did not, however, recount shipboard capers. Rather, it was Astor's report of an espionage mission the President had entrusted to the yachtsman. This deep trust, granted by a president to a private citizen, had equally deep roots. The names Roosevelt and Astor had echoed down Hudson Valley history since colonial times. The Roosevelts of Hyde Park and the Astors up the road at Rhinebeck stood at the heart of the Dutchess County gentry, their lives a weave of family, professional, and commercial interests. Franklin's much older half brother, James, was close to Vincent's father, Colonel John Jacob Astor IV, heir to the vast fortune founded by a once penniless fur-trading German immigrant, the first John Jacob Astor. Vincent's grandmother was the grande dame who defined New York society by the four hundred guests who could fit into her Fifth Avenue ballroom. When Vincent's father went down with the *Titanic* in 1912, the son dropped out of Harvard to assume control of the family's holdings, inheriting $75 million and tagged by gossip columnists as "the richest boy in the world." James Roosevelt became executor of the Astor estate and continued as a trusted advisor to Vincent, who prized his counsel and always referred to FDR's brother as "Uncle Rosey."

Franklin and Vincent had known each other as boys, but were not then close since FDR was eight years older. As Astor put it, much later "we grew to be the same age." The two avid sailors met again during the First World War while Franklin was serving as President Woodrow Wilson's assistant secretary of the Navy. They had met to consider how yacht owners and powerboat sailors might organize their vessels into a Volunteer Patrol Squadron, an idea that ultimately became the Naval Reserve. Later, FDR received an urgent appeal from his brother, James, to help locate Ensign Astor. The young scion had donated an earlier yacht, the *Noma,* to the Navy and was serving aboard her on anti-submarine patrols off the French coast. James Roosevelt, possessing Astor's power of attorney, needed to determine if the young officer was still alive before signing documents affecting Astor business interests, principally huge chunks of Manhattan real estate.

Providing such constituent services was among Assistant Secretary Roosevelt's least demanding duties. What genuinely engaged him was what later drew him closest to Astor, the netherworld of espionage. The clandestine had captivated Franklin Roosevelt from his youth. The first recorded signs of his bent for the covert surfaced while he was a student at Harvard. He had devised a code, numerals substituting for vowels, and symbols, such as an asterisk, substituting for consonants, all run together giving no hint of where words started or ended. Though child's play for a serious cryptanalyst, the code nevertheless served Franklin's need for and pleasure in secrecy. He had developed a crush on a beautiful Bostonian named Alice Sohier, not yet sixteen. One coded entry in his diary, dated July 8, 1902, at the end of his sophomore year, raises curious speculation. "Alice confides in her doctor," he wrote. The next day's coded entry read, "Worried over Alice all night." A half century later the subject of his concern would explain only, "In a day and age when well brought up young men were expected to keep their hands off the persons of young ladies from respectable families, Franklin had to be slapped—*hard.*"

Doris Kearns Goodwin, chronicler of Roosevelt's wartime years, has explored the roots of FDR's character that may explain his attraction to the secret and covert. Franklin had been an intuitive child, Goodwin writes, who "learned to anticipate the desires of his parents even before he was told what to do." She quotes Franklin's mother, Sara Delano Roosevelt, saying that her boy rarely required disciplining: "We took secret pride in the fact that Franklin instinctively never seemed to require that kind of handling." Franklin's childhood compulsion to please his parents had grown into an adult reflex to charm and ingratiate, to turn every encounter into a personal triumph, sacrificing candor to achieve likability. By the time FDR became president, dissimulation had become second nature, and subterfuge cloaked in geniality became his stock-in-trade. Harold Ickes, his interior secretary, as crusty and blunt as Roosevelt was smooth and impenetrable, once complained, "You keep your cards up close to your belly."

Franklin D. Roosevelt had first entered upon the national consciousness on March 17, 1913, at the age of thirty-one, with his appointment by President Woodrow Wilson as the youngest person ever to become assistant secretary of the Navy. Franklin particularly savored the moment since his distant cousin and Eleanor's uncle Theodore Roosevelt had held the same position before going on to become, at forty-two, the country's youngest president. FDR's boss, the secretary of the Navy, was fifty-one-year-old Josephus Daniels, former editor and publisher of the Raleigh (North Carolina) *News & Observer.* This prohibitionist/pacifist/populist could not have been more unlike his urbane, elegant deputy. Daniels, with his string ties, somber suits, and small-town manners and morals, was a figure out of the departed nineteenth century. Roosevelt was a man of the emerging twentieth century. At times, with the nakedly ambitious Roosevelt under him, Daniels must have felt as if he were sitting on a volcano. On one occasion, FDR looked over a site for building barracks for eleven thousand sailors. The next day, he let the construction contract. Four months later, the work completed, he went to Daniels for permission to carry out the project. The secretary had been forewarned. When Daniels initially went to New York's Senator Elihu Root to clear Roosevelt's appointment, Root had asked him if he really understood the Roosevelts. "Whenever a Roosevelt rides, he wishes to ride in front," Root warned, "they like to have their own way." For all his homespun manner, Josephus Daniels was no fool. He knew that a northern aristocrat would complement his southern folksiness, and he possessed that rare quality in a leader—he was not afraid to hire a subordinate who might be smarter than he was.

The component of the Navy Department that quickly captured the assistant secretary's imagination was the Office of Naval Intelligence. ONI, at that point, was the closest equivalent to an American central intelligence agency. In its thirty-first year when FDR came to the department, ONI was a small, elite subempire, one that had planted naval attachés in all significant world capitals, poking into the secrets of foreign powers. ONI's chief, Captain James Oliver Harrison, unhappily observed that Roosevelt and his political mentor and private secretary, an untidy, irreverent man named Louis Howe, were poaching on his turf, organizing their own secret intelligence cell. FDR's amateurs, Harrison complained to the Chief of Naval Operations, were interfering with his professionals. Soon after America entered World War I in April 1917, Harrison was replaced by a more pliant ONI chief, Captain Roger Welles. Welles happily commissioned FDR's socialite pals into naval intelligence, young men who shared the right schools, clubs, and connections, among them FDR's onetime law partner, Alexander Brown Legare, who founded the Chevy Chase Hunt Club; Lawrence Waterbury, star polo player; and Steuart Davis, a Harvard classmate and commander of the Volunteer Patrol Squadron. ONI's roster soon began to resemble the Social Register.

Roosevelt's intelligence priority had been set before the United States entered World War I. German saboteurs were suspected of blowing up the National Storage Plant on Black Tom Island in Jersey City, New Jersey, on July 30, 1916, a blast that killed seven men, injured thirty-five more, and destroyed millions of dollars' worth of munitions intended for the Allies. FDR became obsessed by the threat of internal subversion, a concern that was to dominate his intelligence thinking for years. No rumor was too wild to enlist his attention. One ONI informant reported that a German-American colony in New Hampshire was plotting to acquire a plane to bomb the Navy yard at Portsmouth. Roosevelt sent out investigators. In October 1917 a friend returned from a visit to Block Island with a possible explanation as to why the battleship *Texas* had run aground there. Visibility at the time was an ample six hundred yards, his friend told FDR. A sailor who had earlier lived on Block Island with Germans suspected of spying had been the forward lookout on the *Texas* when she struck the beach. FDR ordered another investigation. ONI personnel, quickly grasping the boss's prejudices, began feeding him what he wanted to hear. A typical report to the assistant secretary on the Krantz Manufacturing Company of Brooklyn noted, "The employees are almost German to a man. Every official has a German appearance . . . and [they] always converse in German." With FDR's fervent support, ONI hired hundreds of new investigators, the rapid expansion justified by threats, fanciful or hypothetical, against Navy installations.

The spy thriller atmosphere pleased Roosevelt to the point of apparently producing spy fiction. FDR later liked to tell how "the Secret Service found a document in the safe of the German consul in New York entitled: To Be Eliminated." The first name on the list was Frank Polk, intelligence coordinator at the State Department. "Mine was the second," Roosevelt would inform rapt listeners. The Secret Service, he maintained, then provided him with a revolver and holster. He wore the gun for only a few days, Roosevelt claimed, then left it in his desk drawer. No evidence supports any part of this story.

On July 9, 1918, the assistant secretary boarded the USS *Dyer,* the Navy's newest destroyer, to witness the war in Europe. Upon his arrival in England, FDR met his first grownups in the espionage game and was suitably dazzled. He spent two hours in London with Admiral Sir Reginald Hall, director of Britain's Naval Intelligence, known as Blinker for the rapid batting of his eyes, especially when he was excited. Blinker Hall had already influenced American history. It was Hall who created Room 40, the Royal Navy's codebreaking arm, and it was Room 40 that decoded the Zimmerman telegram, which revealed a German plot to induce Mexico and Japan to go to war against the United States. Hall had leaked the telegram to Washington, significantly affecting President Wilson's decision to enter the war. Dr. Walter Page, America's ambassador to Great Britain, said of Hall: "Neither in fiction or fact can you find any such man to match him. . . . The man is a genius—a clear case of genius."

Blinker Hall, in a wing-tipped collar, his head haloed in a ring of frizzy white hair, his eyes batting with anticipation, warmly admitted Roosevelt into the inner sanctum of British espionage. He had been describing German troop movements to his guest when he suddenly broke off and pointed across the room. "I am going to ask that youngster at the other end of the room to come over here," Hall said. "I will not introduce him by name. I want you to ask him where he was twenty-four hours ago." The officer approached, and Roosevelt put the question to him. He had been on enemy soil, inside Germany, "[I]n Kiel, sir," he replied to an astonished FDR. Blinker Hall brushed the feat aside. He had spies passing back and forth between the German-Danish border and England practically every night, he said.

The young agent's tale of derring-do was a charade concocted by Hall precisely to impress Roosevelt. Hall's fiction was the first time, but not the last, in which British intelligence would employ ruses and outright fabrications to bend FDR to its ends—and succeed. In a journal FDR kept, he wrote of this encounter: "Their Intelligence Department is far more developed than ours and this is because it is a much more integral part of their Office of Operations." This failing in U.S. naval intelligence, he added, "will be eliminated." Indeed, by the end of the war, the ONI, led by Roosevelt, could boast an intelligence network spread across Europe, Latin America, and the Far East, employing hundreds of agents and informants.

★

Vincent Astor had reentered Roosevelt's life as a result of the disaster that struck in 1921, FDR's crippling attack of polio. With Franklin rendered near helpless by the disease, his brother, James, went to Astor for a favor. Swimming had become part of Franklin's long, painful, largely unsuccessful rehabilitation. Ferncliff, the thousand-acre Astor estate near Hyde Park, had an indoor heated pool. Vincent readily agreed to let Franklin use it. Astor now saw an FDR cruelly reduced from the suave charmer, the tall, confidently striding naval official, the avid golfer, and skilled sailor who had raced boats off Campobello Island. As Roosevelt began using the Astor pool, what previously had been mere acquaintance with Vincent ripened into deep friendship. After FDR had made a partial recovery from the near death of body and soul, and reentered politics, Astor came even more closely into his life. While the political views of the liberal Democrat and the multimillionaire real estate magnate, publisher, and sportsman were not always in alignment, Astor nevertheless generously backed FDR's successful bids for governor of New York in 1928 and 1930 and made a then substantial $25,000 contribution to FDR's 1932 presidential campaign.

The affection between the two men deepened. Franklin sent Vincent a pair of engraved cufflinks and called Astor "a dear and perfect host" after one *Nourmahal* voyage. Vincent sent Franklin a Chris Craft catalogue and asked him to pick the yacht he wanted. It would be Astor's gift. After Roosevelt became president, Astor observed a decorum that FDR much appreciated. Whenever the President entered a room, Vincent always rose. Only when they were alone did he address FDR as "Franklin." Otherwise, it was "Mr. President," with "Sir" tacked on to his comments. Doubtless the friendship also worked because, like FDR, Astor was not consumed wholly by the pleasures of his class. Along with his yacht, plane, clubs, and café society pursuits, the man had a social conscience. Astor backed reform movements, underwrote scientific explorations, and stayed atop world affairs. It was this last passion of Astor's that was to shape Roosevelt's early involvement in espionage in the years before World War II.

As far back as 1927, Astor and a circle of friends had rented a nondescript apartment at 34 East Sixty-second Street in New York where they set up a mail drop and installed an unlisted telephone. The group met monthly in secret and traded gossip and informal intelligence. They had a name for their tight little society, The Room. Astor's fellow members included Theodore Roosevelt's son Kermit; Winthrop W. Aldrich, banker; David K. E. Bruce, sometime diplomat; Nelson Doubleday, publisher; William Rhinelander Stewart, philanthropist; Marshall Field, journalist; and fewer than a dozen other eminences.

Astor, a man with a large, square, roughly handsome head, his resemblance to an aging pug relieved only by his upper-class speech, presided over The Room. On returning from their frequent globe-trotting, over dinner, members reported the world leaders they had met with and what they had learned that was not to be found in newspapers. Distinguished figures were invited to speak to them, the polar explorer Commander Richard E. Byrd on one occasion, Somerset Maugham on another, not so much for his prominence as a novelist and playwright, but because Maugham had been a secret agent in World War I, a role for which The Room members felt a keen affinity. With their love of secrecy, shared confidences, and clandestine trappings, The Room might easily be dismissed as dilettante amateurs, grown men enjoying boys' games of secret codes and invisible inks. To an extent this impression was accurate. Yet, their elevated professional and social positions did place valuable intelligence at their fingertips.

With the inauguration of FDR as president on March 4, 1933, The Room now had a friend at the top and an eager consumer for its insider information. While Roosevelt was never formally a member of The Room, he knew them all through the Groton, Harvard, society, and professional fraternity. They were his people. For as much as FDR, in his public life, associated with the crusty, the earthy, the humbly born—political cronies like a Louis Howe, a Jim Farley, or an Ed Flynn—when the moment was purely social, he chose to spend it with his fellow patricians. Intelligent, trusted, patriotic friends like Vincent Astor could straddle both spheres, hence the dispatching of the *Nourmahal* on a secret mission to the Pacific.

By the mid-thirties, Japan's belligerence was beginning to alarm FDR.

In 1937, Japanese planes had sunk the American gunboat *Panay* in Chinese waters. Within a year, a militarist regime, led by Prince Fumimaro Konoye, took power. Japan, as it had since 1932, continued biting off pieces of China. By the end of 1938, the Japanese would occupy Nanking, Canton, and Hankow. Japan would quit the League of Nations and warn the United States to recognize its "New Order" in East Asia.

Though FDR had carried his keenness for espionage into the White House, a nation sunk in the slough of the Depression had scant resources to invest in spy games. Since money was short, overseas intelligence assignments tended to go to officers of independent means serving as military attachés. Dwight Eisenhower, then an Army lieutenant colonel, described the attachés as ". . . estimable, socially acceptable gentlemen; few knew the essentials of intelligence work. Results were almost completely negative and the situation was not helped by the custom of making long service as a military attaché, rather than ability, the essential qualification for appointment as head of the Intelligence Division in the War Department." Since the military had few sources to obtain the information that Roosevelt wanted on Japan's movements in the Pacific, he had turned to the loyal, resourceful, well-connected Vincent Astor.

On that morning of May 12, 1938, as FDR dictated his reply to Astor's report from the *Nourmahal,* domestic problems were uppermost in his mind. He was trying to get a twenty-five-cent-an-hour minimum wage bill through Congress, fighting conservatives who opposed more money for public works, and hoping the Supreme Court would not strike down his latest bill to support farm prices, as it had the last one. Dealing with Astor's spy mission offered a welcome diversion from the crushing, if more prosaic, burdens of his office.

Earlier in the year, FDR had written to Astor giving him his confidential instructions. While sailing the *Nourmahal* in the Pacific, the yachtsman was to seek out signs of a military buildup—any bases, ports, airfields, or fueling facilities in the Marshall Islands, then ruled by Japan under a League of Nations mandate. Astor's cover story was to be that he and Kermit Roosevelt were conducting an oceanic expedition. Astor had written back assuring FDR that his instructions "could not be more clear." Prior to Astor's departure, FDR smoothed the mission's way at his old haunt, the Navy Department. ONI loaned Astor a transmitter and receiver that could communicate on frequencies not available on the *Nourmahal*'s radio. In return, Astor would use the vessel's sophisticated direction-finding apparatus to ferret out the location of Japanese radio stations for the Navy. Astor wrote to FDR that he preferred not to follow the President's precaution that the Navy "keep a security watch on me," which would only arouse suspicion. Besides, he had used his connections to obtain letters of introduction from Prince Konoye to remove any questions about his presence in the Marshalls. Nevertheless, Astor did arrange a contingency in the event that he needed help. A message to his New York office reading, "Many happy returns of the day," meant that the Navy should start tracking the *Nourmahal* by radio. "My deportment in the Marshalls," he assured the President, "will be perfect. When and if, however, there is something that deserves taking a chance—or if I notice increasing suspicion or resentment, I would like to be able to send a 'standby' message to Samoa and Hawaii." The radioed word "automobile" would signal an emergency. Astor assured the President he would never sound this alarm "unless completely up against it." He ended confidently, "I may be able to do a job in a way that the regular service never could." On the eve of his departure, Astor wrote FDR once more, "I don't want to make you jealous, but aren't you a bit envious of my trip?" The mission was indeed right up FDR's alley, skipping formal channels, employing his own agents, using secret signals, making it completely his baby, much the way he ran the administration.

Now, months later, the mission completed, Roosevelt finished dictating his reply to Astor's report. Missy LeHand had to concentrate intently. The President spoke quickly, rarely at a loss for what he wanted to say. He complimented Astor on completing his assignment and concluded, "I will not say more until I see you." FDR rarely committed anything to paper that he could handle face-to-face.

In truth, Astor's report had proved a disappointment. Despite the promise from Prince Konoye, the Japanese had suddenly retracted permission for the yachtsman to visit the Marshall Islands. After that, despite his claim that he would not be afraid to take chances, Astor had not pushed hard. British intelligence agents in the Pacific had told him that their two attempts to penetrate the Marshalls had been thwarted. Astor meekly reported to FDR that had he tried where the British failed, he would have achieved only "a 100% probability of making serious trouble for you and the State and Navy Departments."

He had subsequently reduced his mission to cruising the nearby Gilbert and Ellice Islands, where he did manage to intercept messages revealing Japanese actions in the Marshalls and pick up secondhand intelligence from the British. He learned that Eniwetok appeared to be the principal Japanese naval base in these islands and Bikini the secondary position. An airfield was under construction on Wotje and six submarines had been spotted in a nearby lagoon. It was, on the whole, thin stuff. The most encouraging personal intelligence Astor reported was that FDR's worrisome distant cousin Kermit, a heavy drinker, had sipped "only beer and sherry" on the voyage "and is in the best shape in years." Roosevelt had gratefully observed the change when Kermit had shown up at the White House to deliver Astor's report.

While the Astor mission had provided the minutest of triumphs, FDR still nourished a preference for private channels and personal friends as his eyes and ears rather than technical codebreaking. Intelligence from the latter source was becoming available, thanks largely to a cryptanalyst who had entered the field from an unlikely start. William F. Friedman was a Cornell graduate in genetics who as a young man had been employed by a rich eccentric to apply analytic techniques to determine if Francis Bacon had written the dramas attributed to William Shakespeare. Literary puzzles led to code cracking, and the intense, bespectacled Friedman was hired by the Army, eventually heading the Signal Intelligence Service during the 1930s. A small but zealous Friedman team, led by Frank Rowlett, had for years been attacking the Japanese diplomatic cipher, designated Red, and by 1936, had broken the code. This breakthrough meant that Roosevelt had a foreign power's secret diplomatic cables delivered directly to his desk. It meant that the President knew what Japanese ambassadors were reporting to Tokyo from Berlin, Rome, Moscow, and Washington at roughly the same time the Japanese foreign minister did. It meant that Roosevelt knew that Germany, Italy, and Japan were sealing their Axis partnership six months before the State Department picked up this intelligence from its sources.

At about the time that Astor completed his mission to the Marshalls, the Japanese began phasing out the Red code and using a new cipher, one the American cryptanalysts designated Purple. FDR could no longer read the emperor's mail. Friedman's codebreakers, however, were already mounting as vigorous an attack on Purple as they could, given their niggardly peacetime resources.

While the President cast an uneasy eye over the Pacific, he found the situation in Europe more immediately troubling. With the horrors of the last war only twenty years behind, Britain and France hoped against hope to perpetuate a tenuous peace. Unknown to the World War I Allies, Adolf Hitler, by 1937, had already declared his intentions to his inner circle. At a secret Berlin meeting held on November 5, he had gathered the Nazi leadership, led by his heir apparent, Hermann Göring, to proclaim Germany's destiny. Deutschland represented Europe's purest folk, Hitler claimed. Yet its present borders were insufficient to provide the country's eighty-five million people with the living standard they deserved. "The German future," Hitler stated, was "therefore dependent exclusively on the solution of the need for living space." And since Germany's neighbors were unlikely to give up their soil willingly, Germany must take it. Within a year of this pronouncement, Hitler had annexed his native Austria, seized one slice of Czechoslovakia, and by March 1938, had swallowed the rest. Whatever public noises Hitler might make to appease Britain and France, Europe's great states appeared to be on a collision course.

The Nazi military buildup had already thrown the arms restrictions imposed on Germany at Versailles after the last war onto the trash heap. The expansion included an increased espionage campaign against America, particularly to obtain its technology. The mission proved surprisingly simple, and in most cases, spies were not even necessary. American salesmen, throughout most of the thirties, pressed their "Made in the USA" products onto eager German customers—automatic pilots, gyro compasses, even control systems for anti-aircraft guns. Du Pont sold information on explosives to German munitions makers. Sperry Gyroscope licensed a German company to manufacture instruments enabling aircraft to fly blind. Pratt & Whitney sold the Germans aircraft engines. U.S. industry was willingly helping to bring the Wehrmacht and Luftwaffe to a state of readiness, making the efforts of German agents almost redundant.

Still, the President could presume that one of the most prized secrets in America's aerial arsenal would remain inviolable. A plant located at 80 Lafayette Street in Manhattan produced a bombsight, the product of the genius of Carl L. Norden, believed to be the most accurate such instrument in the world. The boast among Army fliers was that the Norden sight could guide a bomb from a plane into a pickle barrel. Working at the plant as an inspector was a thirty-five-year-old German immigrant, Hermann W. Lang, blond, with a broad, pleasant face and a quiet, agreeable manner. On a Sunday afternoon in the fall of 1937, Lang met, at the home of a friend, forty-year-old Nikolaus Ritter, a major in the Abwehr, German military intelligence, posted to America. Lang's loyalty to his homeland proved stronger than his affection for his adopted land. He unhesitatingly told Ritter about his work, how he had access to blueprints for an extraordinary bombing device. He was supposed to return the plans to a safe at the end of the day, but instead took them home. After his wife went to sleep, he set the blueprints on the kitchen table and traced them. Lang volunteered to give a copy to Ritter. When Ritter offered to pay, Lang looked hurt. "I want to do something for the Fatherland," he said. "I want Germany to have this bombsight. If you gave me money I would throw it away. It would be dirty money." Ritter was overjoyed. He had been in the United States less than two weeks and had scored an espionage coup. On November 30 a steward from the Hamburg-Amerika Line's *Reliance,* who doubled as an Abwehr courier, limped aboard the ship, leaning on a furled umbrella. Rolled inside the umbrella were Lang's partial plans for the Norden bombsight. Over succeeding months, Lang continued to supply the rest of the copied blueprints, smuggled aboard planes and ships between the pages of newspapers. Piece by piece the tracings found their way into the hands of Luftwaffe engineers, who constructed their own version of America's air war secret.

Paradoxically, British prime minister Neville Chamberlain was to ask Roosevelt, just days before war broke out in Europe, for the plans for the Norden bombsight for use by the Royal Air Force. Roosevelt, not wanting to give American isolationists an issue with which to attack him, turned down the request from a likely ally for a weapon that had already been stolen by a likely enemy. The British were not to obtain the Norden bombsight until well into the war.

Roosevelt would soon have reason to regret American industry's eager commerce with Germany and the poor security afforded military secrets. At 2:50 A.M. on September 1, 1939, he was wakened by a call from a close associate whom he had named ambassador to France, William C. Bullitt. Bill Bullitt was FDR's kind of guy—rich, ebullient, charming, bursting with energy and ideas. He had been Roosevelt's choice in 1933 as the first American ambassador to the Soviet Union. FDR had then shifted the bald, blue-eyed dynamo to Paris in 1936 where, for his lavish parties, Bullitt became known as the "Champagne Ambassador." It was a somber Bullitt who interrupted the President's sleep this night to tell FDR that he had just talked to the U.S. ambassador in Warsaw, Anthony Drexel Biddle Jr. The German army, Biddle had reported, was attacking Poland with a force building to sixty divisions and over a thousand aircraft. "Then it's happened," Roosevelt told Bullitt. Within days, Europe's major powers were again at war.

The outbreak of hostilities brought Vincent Astor and The Room more closely into FDR's orbit. Astor's Pacific mission may have been a letdown, and The Room, whose members had now reconstituted themselves as The

Club, still behaved somewhat as adventure-seeking dilettantes. Despite the sophomoric antics, however, their powerful positions in the American establishment continued to offer ideal listening posts. In the fall of 1939, Astor wrote FDR, "Tomorrow I am starting to work on the banks, using the Chase as a guinea pig. . . . Espionage and sabotage need money, and that has to pass through banks at one stage or another." Club member Winthrop Aldrich, who directed the Chase National, New York's leading bank, proved Astor's point. He informed Roosevelt that Amtorg, the Soviet Union's trading corporation in America, was spending over $2 million a week, much of it in its role as an espionage front.

Astor himself was a director of the Western Union Cable Company. Snooping into international cables was a federal crime, but Astor happily ran the risk. He was able to apprise FDR of intercepted telegrams revealing foreign agents operating out of Mexico and spying on the United States. Cables to and from Spanish embassies in the Americas exposed Spain's increasing ties to Nazi Germany. FDR further learned that a Brazilian naval mission buying arms in America was a gang of grafters. The President actively promoted this eavesdropping. On October 20, 1939, Astor reported that he had arranged to listen in on foreign radio transmissions, "in accordance with your wishes. . . ."

While the activities of The Club provided peripheral excitement, what Astor hankered for was to become FDR's chief of a future American intelligence service. With Europe at war, and given Astor's connections in Britain, especially through the English branch of his family, the opportunity might well be on the horizon. Undeniably, an intelligence vacuum had to be filled. Even before the war, FDR had expressed his exasperation to his secretary of state, Cordell Hull. The Federal Bureau of Investigation, the Army's Military Intelligence Division, and the Office of Naval Intelligence were "constantly crossing each other's tracks," he complained to Hull. This duplication was wasteful, expensive, and inefficient, the President charged. He wanted the activities of the three agencies sensibly coordinated.

This sudden passion for administrative efficiency must have come as a shock to Hull, for a hallmark of the Roosevelt administration was bureaucratic anarchy. FDR disdained organization charts, created competing offices without warning those running the old offices, and blithely broke the chain of command to deal with whomever he pleased. Responsibilities he assigned were vague and the authority to fulfill them murky. As an observer put it, the President handed one job to several men and several jobs to one man. Textbook administrative concepts such as a manageable "span of control" meant nothing to Roosevelt. At one point, nearly one hundred associates could bypass his secretaries and phone the President directly. Few, however, abused this privilege more than once. The shrewder of his associates did not see FDR's style as the mark of a poor administrator, but as a deliberate device for keeping everyone else off balance while he alone maintained control. In a rare burst of poetic imagery, Secretary of War Henry Stimson once observed, "His mind does not easily follow a consecutive chain of thought but he is full of stories and incidents and hops about in his discussions from suggestion to suggestion and it is very much like chasing a vagrant beam of moonshine around a vacant room." By forcing people who often held contrary views to work together, FDR ran the short-term risk of causing conflict, confusion, and injured feelings. But over the long term his dispersal of authority acted as a brake against the commission of major blunders. If FDR's leadership was chaotic, it was inspired chaos.

Nevertheless, the President was genuinely displeased with the disjointed, overlapping, shotgun conduct of intelligence. On June 26, 1939, two months before the war erupted in Europe, he had ordered the heads of the FBI, MID, and ONI to start synchronizing their actions. He handed responsibility for this thankless task to the assistant secretary of state for administration, George S. Messersmith. Roosevelt, at this stage, had no thought of creating a central intelligence service. He was not yet ready, nor was the country. As *The New York Times* editorialized: "No secret police is needed or wanted here." He simply needed someone to knock heads together. Messersmith was wise enough to recognize the rivalries and jealousies among federal fiefdoms, particularly endemic among those trafficking in secrets. He thus sought to put a civilized tone on his first attempt to bring together the competing agencies by inviting their chiefs to his Georgetown home for dinner. Afterward, over port and cigars, they could figure out a way to stop stepping on each other's toes. The dinner was hardly a success. The figure then with the major counterespionage role was FBI director J. Edgar Hoover, and Hoover did not deign to show up at Georgetown. He attended Messersmith's next meeting only when ordered directly to do so by the President.

Espionage involves peeking at the other fellow's hand, marking the cards, cooking the books, poisoning the well, breaking the rules, hitting below the belt, cheating, lying, deceiving, defaming, snooping, eavesdropping, prying, stealing, bribing, suborning, burglarizing, forging, misleading, conducting dirty tricks, dirty pool, skulduggery, blackmail, seduction, everything not sporting, not kosher, not cricket. In short, espionage stands virtue on its head and elevates vice in its stead. As Europe went to war and America clung to the slope of a slippery peace, the country essentially lacked the back alleys, the counterfeiters, the potions, all the implements of deceit necessary to conduct what has aptly been called the game of the foxes. All FDR had, at this point, was a clique of gentleman amateurs, equally amateurish military attachés abroad, an underfunded codebreaking service, and an empty intelligence center with rivals messily competing around the edges for supremacy.

Chapter II

———═★═———

Spies, Saboteurs, and Traitors

ON A gray London morning, May 20, 1940, four men approached a flat at 47 Gloucester Place. Behind the door, a young man, clean-cut and studious-looking, sat amid the remains of his breakfast. He did not respond to the knocking even when a booming voice shouted, "Police!" Instead he bolted the door and called out coolly, "No, you can't come in." A Scotland Yard detective rammed his shoulder against the door and it burst open. The others filed in, a second detective, an officer from MI5, the British domestic military intelligence service, and the second secretary of the American embassy. The man they had broken in on was Tyler Kent, a code clerk also attached to the embassy. One of the detectives produced a search warrant, and Kent stood by, unruffled, as his visitors rummaged through his apartment. They found 1,929 U.S. embassy documents, including secret correspondence between Franklin Roosevelt and Winston Churchill. The content of these messages was such that their exposure to the public could harm the President and the Prime Minister, and jeopardize America's presumed neutrality in the European war. What they revealed could also influence the upcoming U.S. presidential election.

Though they had been corresponding for months, Roosevelt and Churchill had met only once twenty-one years before, an unsatisfactory encounter from FDR's viewpoint. Roosevelt confided to Joseph P.

Kennedy, his ambassador to Britain, his initial reaction to Churchill: "I have always disliked him since the time I went to England in 1918. He acted like a stinker at a dinner I attended, lording it all over us." Roosevelt was not alone in his distaste. The novelist-physicist C. P. Snow observed that Churchill was "widely and deeply disliked," and had been so for most of his life. During the thirties, Churchill was viewed as brilliant, but a burnt-out case, a has-been who sought refuge in drink. The American undersecretary of state, Sumner Welles, in recalling a visit to Churchill's office, noted, "Mr. Churchill was sitting in front of the fire smoking a 24-inch cigar, and drinking whiskey and soda. It was quite obvious that he had consumed a good many whiskies before I arrived." Yet, Felix Frankfurter, appointed to the Supreme Court by Roosevelt, who also visited Churchill just before the war, came away glowing. Meeting the man, Frankfurter wrote, "was one of the most exhilarating experiences I had in England—it made me feel more secure about the future." A Frankfurter opinion counted with FDR. And so, when Prime Minister Neville Chamberlain took Churchill into his government as First Lord of the Admiralty, FDR made a risky overture for the head of a presumably neutral nation toward the naval chief of a belligerent country. Eight days after war was declared, FDR instituted a secret correspondence recalling their common naval experience. "It is because you and I occupied similar positions in the World War that I want you to know how glad I am that you are back again in the Admiralty," Roosevelt began. He went on, "What I want you and the Prime Minister to know is that I shall at all times welcome it, if you will keep me in touch personally with anything you want me to know about. You can always send sealed letters through your pouch or my pouch." He later explained to Joe Kennedy as his reason for initiating the contact, ". . . [T]here is a strong possibility that he [Churchill] will become the prime minister and I want to get my hand in now." FDR's expectation had been borne out on May 10, 1940, when Churchill moved into 10 Downing Street, replacing Chamberlain. The day before, Hitler had declared, "The decisive hour has come for the fight today decides the fate of the German nation for the next 1000 years." He then unleashed the Luftwaffe, the Wehrmacht, all of Germany's might against Holland, Luxembourg, Belgium, and France, simultaneously and with stunning effect. Roosevelt was relaxing in his upstairs study in his favorite red leather Jefferson chair, when he learned that eight months of not-quite-war yet not-quite-peace—the "phony war"—had been shattered. His envoy to Belgium, John Cudahy, telephoned him to describe the German Blitzkrieg under way. Hitler had earlier seized Denmark and

Norway. Within the next five days the Low Countries and Luxembourg were defeated and France was reeling.

From Paris, Bill Bullitt sent a message to Washington stamped PERSONAL AND SECRET FOR THE PRESIDENT. Bullitt judged Britain's situation hopeless, and he proposed a desperate strategy. "I should like to speak what follows into your most private ear at the White House and to have no record of it," Bullitt's cable began. France, he predicted, "will be crushed utterly." More alarming, "The British may install a government of Oswald Mosley and the union of British fascists which would cooperate fully with Hitler. That would mean the British navy would be against us." In case the war went that badly, he urged that "the British fleet would base itself in Canada in defense of that dominion which might become the refuge for the British crown." FDR, however, was not yet ready to write off the British navy in its home waters or the king in Buckingham Palace. He ignored Bullitt's proposal.

One American vigorously disapproved of the collusive nature of the secret correspondence passing between FDR and Churchill, the code clerk Tyler Kent, who had access to these messages. The reserved twenty-nine-year-old lone wolf was a deeply discontented man. Kent believed that he was working well below his station. He possessed all the WASP credentials favoring a successful diplomatic career. Tyler Gatewood Kent descended from an old Virginia family that dated to the 1600s. His father, William Patton Kent, had been a career officer in the U.S. Consular Service. Tyler had been born during his father's posting to Manchuria and thereafter traveled with the family to subsequent assignments in China, Germany, Switzerland, England, and Bermuda. He had received a first-class education, St. Albans, Princeton, the Sorbonne, and spoke French, Greek, German, Russian, Italian, and Spanish. Still, Kent had been hired by the State Department in 1934 not as a fledgling diplomat but as a clerk. He had come to London in October 1939 after serving at the American embassy in Moscow, where he had been assigned to the code room. His political ideas had begun to take shape at that time, characterized by a visceral hatred of communism.

A code clerk was essentially a technician, and Kent's fellow clerks encoded and decoded messages that were shaping history with the indifference with which bank tellers handle bundles of money. Kent, on the contrary, read, reread, and thought deeply about the secrets that passed through his hands. For him, the FDR-Churchill exchanges had taken on an alarming turn from the very first. In a dispatch dated October 5, 1939,

Churchill, then First Lord of the Admiralty, asked FDR to have American warships alert the British navy to any German ship movements in the Atlantic. "The more American ships cruising along the South American coast the better," Churchill observed, "as you, sir, would no doubt hear what they saw or did not see." He began signing his dispatches "Naval Person," chummily underlining his present and FDR's former navy affiliation. Roosevelt readily complied with Churchill's request. Admiral John Godfrey, director of British Naval Intelligence, reported on February 26, 1940: ". . . [T]heir [U.S.] patrols in the Gulf of Mexico give us information, and recently they have been thoroughly unneutral in reporting the position of the SS *Columbus,*" a German merchant vessel subsequently captured by the British.

Another secret exchange further punctured the thin membrane of neutrality. American shipowners complained bitterly to the President that the Royal Navy was forcing their vessels into British ports to be searched. The British, seeking to maintain a blockade against shipments that might aid their enemies, believed themselves within their rights in detaining any vessels, including American. Roosevelt told Churchill of the American shipowners' discontent. Churchill made a swift exception. He responded, "I gave orders last night that no American ship under any circumstances be diverted into the combat zone around the British Isles declared by you. I trust this will be satisfactory."

Roosevelt's breaches of neutrality drove Tyler Kent to a desperate act. The American people, he was convinced, did not want to be enmeshed in Europe's fight. A Roper public opinion poll taken immediately after the war began indicated that less than 3 percent of Americans wanted their country to enter the war on the Allied side. The largest percentage, 37.5 percent, preferred to "Take no sides and stay out of the war entirely." Yet, here was an American president, in Kent's view, conniving with the British, risking America's entanglement in a conflict his people decidedly did not want. There could be little doubt of what Churchill wanted; as the Prime Minister put it to an Admiralty official, "Our objective is to get the Americans into the war. . . . We can then best settle how to fight it afterwards."

In another message to Roosevelt, Churchill dangled tempting bait before the President. FDR had earlier turned down Prime Minister Chamberlain's request for the Norden bombsight. Now Churchill offered a quid pro quo: "We should be quite ready to tell you about our ASDIC methods whenever you feel they would be of use to the United States Navy" and added that FDR could be ". . . sure the secret will go no further." Churchill was offering a new sound wave technique able to detect submerged submarines, later called, in the American version, sonar. The British would trade ASDIC for the Norden bombsight. Roosevelt responded that he would consider the deal, and it was consummated while the United States was still technically neutral.

Tyler Kent, as he brooded in the airless silence of the code room translating messages into the State Department's Gray code, fretted that FDR was "secretly and unconstitutionally plotting with Churchill to sneak the United States into the war." He had developed a corollary obsession: "All wars are inspired, fomented, and promoted by the great international bankers and banking combines which are largely controlled by the Jews." He had, he later admitted, "anti-Semitic tendencies for many years." Kent finally decided where his duty lay. He had to gather evidence that he could place into the hands of the U.S. Senate and the American press to expose Roosevelt's duplicity and keep the United States out of the war. Roosevelt, Kent believed, had to be stopped, especially since, it was rumored, he might run for an unprecedented third term. And so Kent began to steal and copy documents from the code room which he hid in his flat in a brown leather bag, a crate, and in the cupboard. He also managed to secure duplicate keys to the code room so that he could conduct his pilfering anytime day or night.

Early in 1940, Kent had met thirty-seven-year-old Anna Wolkoff, not particularly attractive, but vivacious, witty, and worldly, the daughter of czarist émigrés. Her father had been an admiral in the czar's navy and an attaché assigned to London at the time of the 1917 Russian Revolution. Anna's mother had served as a maid of honor to the czarina. The revolution was the Wolkoffs' undoing. The admiral and his wife had fled to London and now ran the Russian Tea Room, renowned for serving the best caviar in town. Anna owned a fashionable dress shop. She had a simple explanation for the Wolkoffs' social dethronement, the gang of Communists, Jews, and Freemasons who had instigated the revolution. Tyler Kent had found a soul mate.

Anna took her new friend to Onslow Square to meet a man who immediately impressed Kent. Captain A.H.M. Ramsay was a Sandhurst graduate, a wounded and decorated soldier in the First World War, a Tory member of Parliament, and a distant relative of the royal family. Further, he was a man convinced that his country was being taken over by a vast Jewish conspiracy. Ramsay had fought back by founding the Right Club, whose members blamed the world's woes on Wolkoff's villainous trio of Bolsheviks, Jews, and Masons.

Though recognizing a kindred spirit, Kent found the old soldier politically naïve. The embassy clerk determined to enlighten Ramsay. He took him to his flat and spread before him a feast of classified documents. Ramsay was dazzled to be reading in a London bed-sitting room secret exchanges between Roosevelt and Churchill. Kent explained their underlying meaning, Churchill's desire to draw America into this "Jew's War" and Roosevelt's obvious connivance in the scheme.

On a visit to Kent's room in March 1940, Anna Wolkoff asked him if she might borrow some of the purloined documents. Kent, knowing of Captain Ramsay's interest, assumed she wanted to show them to the Englishman again, and agreed. Instead, she took the papers to a photographer friend of her father, who copied them. Wolkoff, of the aristocratic past, then gave the photos to a fellow patrician, Don Francesco Maringliano, duke of Del Monte, a lieutenant colonel in the Italian army posted to his country's London embassy. The duke knew that what Churchill and the supposedly neutral FDR were secretly telling each other could prove invaluable to Italy and its Axis partner, Germany. The stolen information that he relayed to Rome was about to be intercepted itself by means the duke could not have predicted.

Bletchley Park had been built nearly seventy years before by Sir Herbert Leon, a Victorian businessman. Sir Herbert evidently possessed more commercial acumen than aesthetic judgment. One architect described his estate as ". . . a maudlin and monstrous pile probably unsurpassed . . . in the architectural gaucherie of the mid-Victorian era . . . altogether inchoate, unfocused and incomprehensible." Bletchley Park's sole redeeming virtue was its location roughly midway between Oxford and Cambridge. This position attracted the Government Code and Cypher School, Britain's codebreaking agency, which moved to Bletchley Park just before the war started. There a clutch of mathematicians, linguists, academics, and eccentrics, recruited largely from universities, labored over foreign codes with considerable success, though the cryptographers were having a deuce of a time with one seemingly unbreakable German cipher encrypted on a machine called the Enigma.

Among codes the British were able to break was one used by the German foreign ministry. Soon after Maringliano's delivery of the Kent messages to Rome, the codebreakers intercepted cables sent by Hans Mackensen, the German ambassador to Italy, to the foreign ministry in Berlin. One report demonstrated that Mackensen knew all about Churchill's assurances to Roosevelt that American merchant vessels would not be forced into British ports to be searched. This intelligence played right into Germany's hands. Hitler's foreign office now tipped off other neutrals, who quickly bombarded the British Admiralty, complaining about the favoritism shown the Americans.

More explosive was a message FDR sent on May 16, six days after Churchill took over as prime minister, which Tyler Kent had stolen. As Nazi military victories began swallowing up the European continent, Churchill knew that the key to Britain's survival lay in keeping the sea lanes open, free of German submarines. He asked FDR to spare fifty old moth-balled American destroyers to bolster his thinly stretched fleet. The Bletchley cryptanalysts were shocked to find Roosevelt's response to this request reported nearly verbatim in a dispatch sent from Ambassador Mackensen to the German foreign minister, Joachim von Ribbentrop. The secret FDR cable now available in Berlin read, "It would be possible to hand over 40 or 50 destroyers of the old type, but this is subject to the special approval of Congress, which would be difficult to obtain at present."

That Roosevelt was even considering giving fifty ships to Britain would raise Cain among American isolationists. Almost from the moment he had become president, FDR had been struggling inside a straitjacket of neutrality. In the mid-thirties, the U.S. Senate's Nye Committee held hearings that concluded the United States had been sucked into the First World War by international bankers, munitions manufacturers, and war profiteers, a consortium branded in the shorthand of the day the "Merchants of Death." In 1934, 1935, and 1936, Congress enacted laws deliberately intended to keep America out of Europe's congenital squabbles. This legislation prohibited loans to any government in default on its war debts, barred even private loans to warring governments, and outlawed arms shipments to any belligerent. In 1938 a proposed amendment to the Constitution would have required a nationwide vote before the country could go to war, except if invaded. The measure was narrowly defeated in the House of Representatives only after strenuous lobbying by the White House.

FDR believed that the politicians were making the mistake usually attributed to generals—fighting the last war. Nineteen thirty-nine was not 1917. Hitler had reneged on his promise that if given Czechoslovakia's Sudetenland his appetite would be appeased. Instead, in March 1939, he seized the rest of Czechoslovakia. Next he began threatening Poland over the Polish Corridor, the strip of land separating East Prussia from the rest of Germany. The hounding of the Jews in Germany—the gradual stripping away of their citizenship, their property rights, their very right to earn a livelihood—was in full flood well before the war broke out. And Hitler had turned Germany into the most powerful military force in Europe. Roosevelt accepted what the isolationists did not, that Britain's fight was the good fight and vital to all democracies. Even before the war, he had begun to nudge his nation away from purist neutrality. His Treasury secretary, Henry Morgenthau Jr., recorded in his diary what FDR told his staff in confidence on April 20, 1939: "He . . . says that he is going to have a patrol from Newfoundland down to South America and if some submarines are laying there and try to interrupt an American flag and our Navy sinks them, it's just too bad. . . . If we fire and sink an Italian or German . . . we will say it the way the Japs do, 'So sorry. Never happen again.' Tomorrow we sink two."

The President repeated his intention in a private conversation with Britain's King George VI during a visit to the United States in June 1939, an occasion now remembered more for the hot dogs served to the royal couple at Hyde Park than for strategies discussed. The king later wrote of his visit that FDR had promised full support if Britain went to war against Germany. Roosevelt also repeated his covert plan for a naval patrol in the Western Hemisphere, "about which he is terribly keen," the king wrote. "If he saw a U-boat he would sink her at once and wait for the consequences."

Roosevelt's subsequent redefining of the frontiers of the Western Hemisphere was mind boggling. In an age of airplanes and swift ships, he claimed, having the traditional three-mile limit define the hemisphere's extent was obsolete. He summoned the State Department's geographer to the White House to consider a more up-to-date sphere within which the Monroe Doctrine would prevail—that is, where no foreign intrusion would be tolerated. The geographer watched stunned as the President drew a north-south line on a map on his desk running from Iceland to the Azores. Henceforth, FDR said, these Portuguese islands should be considered part of the Western Hemisphere.

Still, as he leaned toward Britain, the President was constantly looking over his shoulder. Every pro-British move needed to be cloaked by stealth and subterfuge. A perception that he was a war lover could prove politically lethal, especially as he wrestled over the decision as to whether to break the two-term tradition and run for a third term. He liked to say that he was weary of the killing burdens of his office and longed for the tranquility of Hyde Park. He told Senator George Norris, who had stopped by to see him, "People come in here day after day, most of them trying to get something from me, most of them things I can't give them, and wouldn't if I could. You sit in your chair in your office too, but if something goes wrong or you get irritated or tired, you can get up and walk around, or you can go into another room. But I can't, I am tied down to this chair day after day, week after week, and month after month. And I can't stand it any longer. I can't go on with it." But Eleanor Roosevelt read her husband better than he read himself. She told an interviewer, "When you are in the center of world affairs, there is something so fascinating about it that you can hardly see how you are going to live any other way. In his mind, I think, there was a great seesaw: on one end, the weariness which had already begun, and the desire to be at home and his own master; on the other end, the overwhelming interest which was the culmination of a lifetime of preparation and work, and the desire to see and to have a hand in the affairs of the world in that critical period."

Should he choose to run again, the last thing FDR needed was premature disclosure that he was considering turning over fifty American ships to one side in a war his countrymen hoped to avoid. Yet, even Berlin knew that he was contemplating the destroyer transfer. From the time Bletchley Park detected the leak, MI5 and Scotland Yard had begun to investigate its source. Since Roosevelt's dispatches to Churchill came to London and since Ambassador Mackensen's dispatches originated in Rome, the British suspected that the link was the Italian embassy in England. Their search led to Don Francesco Maringliano, who was followed to the Russian Tea Room, which in turn pointed the investigation toward Anna Wolkoff and Tyler Kent. Kent's behavior may have been more perverted patriotism than deliberate treachery, but the outcome was the same. What Roosevelt and Churchill told each other in their most confidential communications passed from Kent to Wolkoff to Maringliano, to the Italian foreign ministry, to Ambassador Mackensen, and to the Nazi foreign office. By May 20, British officials believed they had more than enough evidence to arrest Wolkoff and to search Kent's lodgings. It was then that they had found the extraordinary cache of pilfered documents, duplicate keys to the code room, and a steel cabinet plastered with stickers proclaiming, THIS IS A JEW'S WAR.

Kent, as an American citizen employed by the State Department, should have enjoyed diplomatic immunity. Nevertheless, the British police took him into custody and brought him to Joe Kennedy at the ambassador's residence. There the clerk from the code room found himself facing not only the American envoy, but also an immensely rich, politically powerful figure. Kennedy later described his fifteen minutes with Kent: ". . . I asked him how on earth he could break trust with his country and what he must be thinking about in its effects on his parents. Kent never batted an eye. He played up and down the scale of an intense anti-Semitic feeling, showed no remorse whatever except in respect to his parents and told me to 'just forget about him.' It was a tragic scene." After Kennedy had finished with him, the British police locked up Kent in Brixton Prison.

More than a little irony and some hypocrisy pervades this scene. Kennedy had amassed a formidable fortune in banking, shipbuilding, motion pictures, and, reportedly, bootlegging during Prohibition. Like many men who have made money, he wanted to prove he could shine in other circles. He contributed substantially to FDR's national campaigns, thus winning appointments as head of the Securities and Exchange Commission and then the U.S. Maritime Commission. Still he was hungry. Kennedy next had his eye on the Treasury Department. However, FDR was not about to dislodge his old friend Henry Morgenthau Jr. The President knew that he owed Kennedy something more, and he used his eldest son, Jimmy, as his go-between. Young Roosevelt made so many journeys to Marwood, Kennedy's Maryland estate, that he and the older man became friendly. On one such occasion Kennedy confessed that if he could not have Treasury he was "intrigued by the thought of being the first Irishman to be ambassador from the United States to the Court of Saint James's." Jimmy later recalled, "I really liked Joe, but he was a crusty old cuss and I couldn't picture him as an ambassador, especially to England." Nevertheless, young Roosevelt relayed Kennedy's wish to FDR. "When I passed it on to father," Jimmy subsequently wrote, "he laughed so hard he almost toppled from his wheelchair." But as time went on, Roosevelt was taken by Kennedy's audacity. As Jimmy described a conversation with the President, "he was kind of intrigued with the idea of twisting the lion's tail a little. . . ." FDR summoned Kennedy to the White House, and young Roosevelt has described a moment, if believed, surely unique in the screening of potential ambassadors. "Father said to him, 'Joe, would you mind stepping back a bit, by the fireplace perhaps, so I can get a good look at you?' Puzzled, Kennedy did so. Then father said, 'Joe, would you mind taking your pants down?' I was as surprised as Joe was. We couldn't believe our ears. Joe asked father if he'd said what he thought he'd said, and father said he had indeed. I guess it was the power of the presidency, because Joe Kennedy undid his suspenders and dropped his pants and stood there in his shorts, looking silly and embarrassed. Father said, 'Someone who saw you in a bathing suit once told me something I now know to be true. Joe, just look at your legs. You are just about the most bowlegged man I have ever seen. Don't you know that the ambassador to the Court of Saint James's has to go through an induction ceremony in which he wears knee britches and silk stockings? Can you imagine how you'll look? When photos of our new ambassador appear all over the world we'll be a laughingstock. You're just not right for the job, Joe.' " "All you had to say was something was impossible for Joe to want it," Jimmy recalled. Kennedy then asked, if he could persuade the British to allow him to wear a cutaway coat and striped pants to the ceremony, would the President then appoint him? The relentless Kennedy won the protocol point with Britain and the ambassadorial appointment from FDR.

The President may have had an ulterior motive. Joe Kennedy had proved something of a misguided missile in Washington. The right wing saw him as a renegade, a businessman who attacked his own kind. The left painted him as a man who could be troublesome for labor. Within the administration, he was counted a power-hungry publicity hound, a harsh critic of the administration when it suited him, and a man whose business dealings might not stand up to close scrutiny. Henry Morgenthau met with the President shortly before Kennedy's appointment became official and recorded in his diary a presidential display that astonished him. "I have made arrangements to have Joe Kennedy watched hourly," FDR said, "and the first time he opens his mouth and criticizes me, I will fire him." He repeated several times, Morgenthau remembered, "Kennedy is too dangerous to have around here." Thus the bootstraps Irishman, snubbed while a student at Harvard, still socially banging on society's door, attained the most prestigious American appointment in international diplomacy.

Kennedy turned out to be a smash choice from the moment of his arrival in 1938 at the palatial thirty-six-room embassy residence on Grosvenor Square. The British public embraced Kennedy, his appealing wife, Rose, and brood of nine handsome children. The luck of the Irish held as the ambassador scored a hole in one on his first round of golf at the Stoke Poges course in Buckinghamshire. Joe Kennedy's London life appeared charmed.

He may have been a favorite of the British people, but Joe Kennedy was not popular in government circles. Early in 1939 he angered FDR by attempting to consort with Nazis. Helmuth Wohlthat, an economic advisor to Reichsmarschall Hermann Göring, wanted to meet with Kennedy to consider an American gold loan to Germany. Kennedy's request to see the man was instantly turned down by a horrified FDR. Unabashed, Kennedy repeated the request, and again the President refused. Kennedy then, in direct contradiction of FDR's orders, allowed Wohlthat to come see him in London. Learning of the ambassador's insubordination, Roosevelt put a stop to any further encounters.

In December, after the war had begun, Kennedy returned temporarily to Washington, where he delivered to the President his blunt opinion of Churchill. The then First Lord of the Admiralty, he told FDR, was "ruthless and scheming." The man, he claimed, was in touch with an American clique eager to embroil the United States in Europe's war, "notably, certain strong Jewish leaders." During this Washington sojourn Kennedy stopped by the State Department, on February 1, 1940, to see another visiting ambassador, Bill Bullitt, FDR's envoy to France. There, Kennedy blithely interrupted an interview that Bullitt was having with Joseph M. Patterson and Doris Fleeson, respectively publisher and Washington reporter of the New York *Daily News*. Bullitt later described his astonishment at Kennedy's bad manners to Interior secretary Harold Ickes. As Ickes summarized Bullitt's account, "Before long he [Kennedy] was saying that Germany would win, that everything in France and England would go to hell, and that his one interest was in saving his money for his children. He began to criticize the President very sharply, whereupon Bill took issue with him." The argument became so heated that Patterson and Fleeson discreetly withdrew. "Joe continued to berate the President," Ickes's account went on, and "Bill told him that he was disloyal and that he had no right to say what he had before Patterson and Fleeson." Kennedy's language offended Bullitt, to which Kennedy responded, according to Ickes, "[H]e would say what he Goddamned pleased before whom he Goddamned pleased. . . ."

Churchill's son, Randolph, remarked of the American ambassador's defeatism: "We had reached the point of bugging potential traitors and enemies. Joe Kennedy, the American ambassador, came under electronic surveillance." Ironically, during that May 20 encounter between Tyler Kent and Kennedy, an American ambassador who himself did not believe in the war, who ridiculed Britain's chances of survival, and who practiced his own brand of anti-Semitism berated a lowly code clerk who shared both his politics and his prejudices. Kennedy treated the matter as he always did when his principles collided with his survival. He pulled the rug on Kent. Two days after his talk with the ambassador, Kent was fired by the State Department, Kennedy denied him diplomatic immunity, and the code clerk remained in the custody of the British. In this matter, at least, the President showed no disagreement with his ambassador's conduct. Kent's loss of immunity was instantly approved in Washington. Kennedy declared that if the United States had been at war during Kent's betrayal, he would have recommended that he be sent home and shot by a firing squad.

FDR had just returned from a dip in the White House pool when he received a transatlantic phone call from an uncharacteristically contrite Kennedy. Because of Tyler Kent's treachery, the Gray code, through which the President and Churchill communicated, had been compromised, the ambassador informed FDR. An American assistant secretary of state, Breckinridge Long, reckoned the cost of Kent's disloyalty in his diary: "Appalling . . . it means that not only are our codes cracked a dozen different ways, but that our every diplomatic maneuver was exposed to Germany and Russia. It is a terrible blow—almost a major catastrophe."

Tyler Kent was tried in secret in the Old Bailey on October 23, 1940, charged with violating Britain's Official Secrets Act and the Larceny Act for stealing the documents. Kent's defense attorney, a London barrister, Maurice Healy, argued that this court had no jurisdiction over an American whose arrest and trial were "entirely contrary to the general principles of international law and the comity of nations." After four days of testimony, however, it took the jury of twelve Englishmen only twenty-five minutes to find Kent guilty of endangering their country. He was sentenced to seven years and, with equal secrecy, packed off to the windswept Isle of Wight, to a camp for political prisoners. In a separate trial, Anna Wolkoff received ten years.

The Churchill government found in the Kent-Wolkoff scandal just the provocation it wanted. Within forty-eight hours of Kent's arrest a massive roundup of British fascists took place, including the Jew-baiting Captain Ramsay. The Low Countries had fallen to Germany within days, and on June 20, France surrendered after only a shocking six weeks' struggle. Obviously, British leaders believed, Poland, Luxembourg, Belgium, Denmark, the Netherlands, Norway, and France could not have fallen under Hitler's heel simply because they were weak. Fifth columnists had to be the answer. The British were convinced that Norway had been flooded with German "tourists" before the invasion. German parachutists who dropped into the Netherlands were rumored to have been guided by enemy agents signaling them from the ground. The contagion of suspicion crossed the Atlantic, and FDR eagerly embraced the conspiracy rationale. Even before the fall of France, he had shared his preoccupation with the American people. On May 26, 1940, FDR was wheeled into the White House's first-floor diplomatic cloakroom to deliver a fireside chat. He stubbed out his cigarette, squared the pages of his text, faced the three microphones of the major networks, and told the country, "Today's threat to our national security is not a matter of military weapons alone. We know of new methods of attack. The Trojan Horse. The fifth column that betrays a nation unprepared for treachery. Spies, saboteurs, and traitors are the actors in this new tragedy."

FDR's fear of subversion had been deeply planted during his World War I experience with the Navy Department, especially a shock like the Black Tom explosion. More searing, on a June evening in 1919, Franklin and Eleanor had experienced terrorism firsthand. They were parking their car on R Street in Washington when a deafening explosion tore off the front of the residence of Attorney General A. Mitchell Palmer, who lived across the street from their home. Palmer had made himself the scourge of radicals and Communists and was zealously hunting them down to combat the "Red Scare." An assassin, out to kill Palmer, had instead blown up himself. Pieces of the corpse landed on the Roosevelts' front steps. Concern over saboteurs and terrorists persisted after FDR became president. He told reporters at a press conference that Americans had to "protect this country against . . . some of the things that happened over here in 1914 and 1915 and 1916 and the beginning of 1917, before we got into the war."

★

In June 1940, practically on the eve of the Republican convention, FDR pulled off a master stroke that could well abet his designs on a third term. His secretary of war, Henry Woodring, stuck in FDR's craw like a fish bone. He had appointed Woodring, a former Kansas governor, in 1936 more to placate economically depressed midwest farmers than for military views congruent with his own. Woodring was an isolationist who had sought to block FDR's effort to ship munitions to Britain. The President dreaded firing anybody and welcomed an excuse that would justify ejecting an unwanted subordinate. Woodring's attempted obstruction of the arms shipments handed FDR the perfect opportunity to unload the secretary. But he went further. With the potential for war mounting, he seized the moment to make his cabinet bipartisan and thus less politically assailable.

Frank Knox was a self-made multimillionaire who had risen from grocery clerk to cub reporter, eventually to publisher of the *Chicago Daily*

News. He was a veteran of that legendary band the Rough Riders, who had charged San Juan Hill with Teddy Roosevelt. Knox, a visceral foe of the New Deal, had actually hoped to oppose Roosevelt in 1936 as the Republican presidential candidate. Instead, he had had to settle for the vice presidential nomination, going down to defeat with the head of the ticket, Alf Landon. What Knox did have in common with Roosevelt was a rejection of isolationism as illusory and an acceptance of interventionism as a necessity.

On an afternoon in December 1939, FDR invited Knox to the White House for a free-ranging view of the world situation. Knox was still with the President as six o'clock approached, and FDR suggested that he stay for dinner. Afterward, they could watch the movie *Drums Along the Mohawk.* Knox declined, though he found himself increasingly seduced by the Roosevelt magnetism. Before he left, FDR tested on him a plan of breathtaking boldness. He wanted the defeated 1936 Republican ticket, Landon and Knox, to come into his cabinet, filling the two military secretaryships, war and Navy. Indicative of Roosevelt's sinuous style, the very day before, he had instructed his press secretary, Stephen Early, to tell reporters, "I don't think it is likely the President will put a Republican as a member of his cabinet." Landon subsequently made known that he was not interested in the War Department post, fearing Roosevelt intended merely to exploit him. FDR then turned to a quintessential establishment American.

Henry Stimson was a product of Phillips Academy at Andover, where, in his day tuition was sixty dollars a year and students cut their own firewood. He went on to Yale, joined Skull and Bones, and later graduated from Harvard Law School. His roots in the country were deep. He could recall stories his great-grandmother had told him of her conversations with George Washington. Stimson had previously served as President William Howard Taft's secretary of war, Calvin Coolidge's governor general of the Philippines, and Herbert Hoover's secretary of state, in all serving every president since William McKinley in one key post or another. At seventy-three, lean, tall, with his steel gray hair and erect posture, Stimson was the soul of rectitude and enjoyed as well a reputation as an able administrator. To the grumbling of disappointed Democratic office seekers and the cries of betrayal from fellow Republicans, Stimson and Knox were enlisted in FDR's coalition cabinet just before the Republican convention, the former as secretary of war, the latter as secretary of the Navy.

Chapter III

———— ═ ★ ═ ————

Strange Bedfellows

F DR'S CONCERN over a secret and silent invasion of the United States by fifth columnists and saboteurs allied him with one of the canniest players on the Washington scene. In June 1939 the President had given the leading espionage role to J. Edgar Hoover and his FBI in an attempt to impose order on the jerry rig that passed for intelligence operations in the United States. J. Edgar, self-elevated from plain old John Hoover, had started his career as a file clerk in the Department of Justice. There, through his appetite for work and talent for accumulating dossiers on people, he caught the eye of Attorney General Mitchell Palmer and moved up quickly. Hoover made his first major strike in 1920, as Palmer's chief lieutenant during the Red Scare, rounding up nearly ten thousand suspected radicals and subversives. By 1924, at age twenty-nine, Hoover had become director of the department's Bureau of Investigation, which by 1935 metamorphosed into the Federal Bureau of Investigation. Ed Tamm, number three man at the bureau behind Hoover's constant companion, Clyde Tolson, had first suggested the name. Hoover was not immediately taken by the initials FBI until Tamm pointed out a bonus. They could also stand for Fidelity, Bravery, and Integrity. During the thirties Hoover gained national fame for the astutely publicized battles his "G-men" waged against gangsters. In 1939, when the war broke out, the director, with his instinct for the main chance, shifted the bureau's principal mission from fighting crime to hunting subversives, spies, and saboteurs.

On May 20, 1940, the President's aide Major General Edwin M. "Pa" Watson poked his head into the Oval Office to tell FDR that Treasury secretary Morgenthau had just phoned with a problem normally outside Treasury's province. Hoover had gone to Morgenthau complaining that he was being thwarted in his counterespionage work by Attorney General Robert H. Jackson, his nominal boss and a staunch civil libertarian. Congress had outlawed wiretapping in the Communications Act of 1934, and in 1939 the Supreme Court upheld the ban. Citing this decision, Jackson had issued an order barring the FBI from wiretapping. Publicly at least, Hoover paid the order lip service. "I do not wish," he said, "to be the head of an organization of potential blackmailers." But the FBI chief was a far shrewder and tougher player than Robert Jackson. To enlist support, Hoover had taken his problem first to Morgenthau, the President's Hudson River neighbor and confidant, rather than directly to FDR. Morgenthau noted in his diary on May 20: "I spoke to J. Edgar Hoover and asked him whether he was able to listen in on spies by tapping the wires and he said no; that the order given him by Bob Jackson stopping him had not been revoked. I said I would go to work at once. He said he needed it desperately."

Prior to Jackson's tenure, Hoover's agents had been wiretapping for years, and with Roosevelt's blessing. FDR had given Hoover an off-the-cuff order to track "Communist and fascist activities." Thereafter Hoover located a loophole in the 1934 act to legitimatize the President's wishes. The Justice Department had ruled that wiretapping per se was not outlawed, but only the *disclosure* of wiretapped information. The FBI, in the name of national security, then began tapping the phones and bugging the rooms of diplomats, journalists, labor leaders, and political activists. Jackson's ruling had been designed precisely to plug that hole. It was this ban, Hoover complained, that handcuffed him in his battle against foreign agents. He told Morgenthau that the Royal Canadian Mounted Police had asked his help in surveilling four Nazi spies "working in Buffalo across the Canadian borders," but Jackson's order had stymied any investigation. Consequently, the frustrated Hoover had gone to ask Morgenthau to intervene at the White House. Pa Watson told the Treasury secretary that it was his understanding that wiretapping was illegal, but he promised to take Hoover's complaint to the President. FDR's answer was instantaneous: "Tell Bob Jackson to send for J. Edgar Hoover and order him to do it and a written memorandum will follow." The memorandum went out the next day. Roosevelt's reasoning revealed a supple legal mind. "I have agreed with the broad purpose of the Supreme Court decision relating to wiretapping in investigations," FDR declared, "wiretapping should not be carried out for the excellent reason that it is almost always bound to lead to abuse of civil rights. However, I am convinced that the Supreme Court never intended any dictum in the particular case which it decided to apply to grave matters involving the defense of the nation. It is, of course, well known that certain other nations have been engaged in the organization of so-called 'fifth columns' in other countries and in preparation for sabotage, as well as in actual sabotage. . . . You are, therefore authorized and directed in such cases as you may approve, after the investigation of the need in each case, to authorize the necessary investigating agents that they are at liberty to secure information by listening devices direct to the conversation or other communications of persons suspected of subversive activities against the government of the United States, including suspected spies." In short, never mind Congress, the Supreme Court, or the attorney general's qualms. The nation was in peril.

FDR was not yet done. He asked Attorney General Jackson later that May if there existed "any law or executive order under which it would be possible for us to open and inspect outgoing . . . or incoming mail to and from certain foreign nations" to uncover "Fifth Column activities—sabotage, antigovernment propaganda, military secrets, etc." Jackson responded with the answer the President did not want to hear. Opening mail was illegal. Nevertheless, Hoover, who by now well understood his president, began training FBI agents in mail-opening techniques.

The furtive and dour Hoover and the gregarious and charming Roosevelt developed a surprising rapport, something approaching friendship. Whenever he arrived at the President's office, Hoover experienced the arms thrown up in welcome and the flattering use of his first name. As Sam Rosenman once described a Roosevelt greeting, "[H]e could make a casual visitor believe that nothing was so important to him that day as this particular visit, and that he had been waiting all day for this hour to arrive." Ed Tamm recalled accompanying his boss to the White House as many as thirty times, and the director and FDR, Tamm said, "got along very, very well. There was always an obvious manifestation of friendship and admiration. Of course, Mr. Roosevelt had the ability to give that impression to everyone he dealt with, but he was *very, very* friendly to Mr. Hoover." As Hoover himself put it, "I was very close to Franklin Delano Roosevelt personally and officially."

Hoover was already the scourge of liberals that he would remain for the rest of his life. His wiretapping, bugging of rooms, surreptitious break-ins, "black bag jobs" in bureau parlance, outraged champions of civil liberties in Congress. None of the disapproval hurt him at 1600 Pennsylvania Avenue. On May 16, 1940, FDR was guest of honor at the annual black-tie White House Correspondents dinner. Spotting Hoover among the guests, Roosevelt called out from the dais, "Edgar, what are they trying to do to you on the Hill?" "I don't know, Mr. President," Hoover answered. FDR made a thumbs-down gesture, and added with a voice loud enough for all to hear, "That's for them." Of course, the two men were using each other. But, there was more to it than mutual exploitation. Francis Biddle, who by then had succeeded Robert Jackson as attorney general, and who had known Roosevelt at Groton as the most patrician of Grotonians, commented, almost in disbelief, "The two men liked and understood each other."

Why should the President not have appreciated his federal police chief? Hoover appeared to be doing a splendid job, particularly at spy catching. German intelligence agents in the United States had been communicating with the Abwehr through a shortwave radio station on Long Island. Hoover's men uncovered the operation and, instead of shutting it down, took it over. Their informant had been William Sebold, a German-born naturalized American citizen. During a visit to Germany, Sebold had been contacted by Abwehr agents who threatened the lives of his family still living in Germany if he did not spy for them. He agreed, but immediately upon his return to the United States reported the contact to the FBI, which took him on as a double agent at fifty dollars per week. He was to pretend to be working loyally for the Fatherland by radioing intelligence via the Long Island station. Sebold's phony messages were exploited by the Departments of State, War, and Navy to feed false information to the Nazi regime. The flow of traffic coming from Germany tipped off the FBI to Abwehr intelligence targets and revealed new agents who had been recruited in America.

So complete was the President's confidence in Hoover that the relationship began to move into areas testing legitimacy. Earlier on the day that he had attended the White House Correspondents dinner, FDR had addressed a joint session of Congress hammering at his pet theme, "the treacherous use of the fifth column" and the necessity for America to strengthen its national defense. The speech was blatantly interventionist, and its isolationist critics were swift in counterattacking. Two days after addressing

Congress, FDR brandished a sheaf of telegrams before his press secretary, Steve Early. The senders, he told Early, were opponents of a strong national defense. He wanted Early to give the telegrams to J. Edgar Hoover to "go over" the names and addresses. Whatever "go over" meant, Hoover had the senders checked against the FBI's dossiers and promptly reported his findings back to the President. Three days later, Roosevelt sent Early another batch with a note reading, "Here are some more telegrams to send to Edgar Hoover." By the end of May, Hoover had checked out 131 of the President's critics, including two senators, Burton K. Wheeler and Gerald Nye, and America's aviator hero, Charles Lindbergh.

The President and Lindbergh, the Lone Eagle who flew the Atlantic solo in 1927, had met once, on April 20, 1939. Lindbergh, convinced of Germany's bright future and fast becoming the darling of the isolationists, was determined not to be taken in by Roosevelt's charm. At the end of fifteen minutes, he left the White House feeling that the President was "a little too suave, too pleasant, too easy." Later Lindbergh told friends that the experience had been like talking to a man wearing a mask. From behind that mask, the President had studied America's boyish paragon of Yankee virtue with a measuring eye. He was aware of an incident five months before at which Lindbergh had accepted from the number two Nazi, Hermann Göring, the Service Cross of the Order of the German Eagle with Star. With Germany having sliced itself a piece of Czechoslovakia only two weeks before and with Nazi persecution of the Jews intensifying, acceptance of the medal had tainted Lindbergh in the judgment of many Americans including the President. Lindbergh's defense, that the medal had been sprung on him without warning, that the presentation had taken place at a dinner given by the American ambassador, and that to have refused it would have been an offense further straining U.S.-German relations, did not wash with Roosevelt.

Then, on May 19, 1940, two days before FDR was to deliver a speech on military preparedness to Congress, Lindbergh openly unfurled his own isolationist banner. In a nationwide Sunday night broadcast, he charged the Roosevelt administration with creating "a defense hysteria." Nobody was threatening to invade the United States unless the "American people bring it on through their own quarreling and meddling with affairs abroad," he warned. The only danger of war, Lindbergh claimed, came from "powerful elements in America who desire us to take part. They represent a small minority of the American people, but they control much of the machinery of influence and propaganda." If a fifth column threatened the United States,

Lindbergh said, it lay in Roosevelt's belligerence. After hearing the speech, FDR told Henry Morgenthau, "If I should die tomorrow, I want you to know this. I am absolutely convinced that Lindbergh is a Nazi." He wrote Henry Stimson, who was about to join his cabinet, "When I read Lindbergh's speech, I felt that it could not have been better put if it had been written by Goebbels himself. What a pity that this youngster has completely abandoned his belief in our form of government and has accepted Nazi methods because apparently they are efficient." Lindbergh's name entered the President's list of foes. J. Edgar Hoover was only too ready to maintain a watch on him for FDR, but not necessarily because of Lindbergh's politics. The FBI director already had a thick file on the flier hero, started after Lindbergh supposedly credited the Treasury Department, rather than the FBI, with solving the kidnapping and murder of his infant son.

FDR was sufficiently pleased with Hoover's zeal in monitoring Lindbergh and other administration critics that he sent the director an artfully vague note of gratitude. "Dear Edgar," it began, "I have intended writing you for some time to thank you for the many interesting and valuable reports that you have made to me regarding the fast moving situations of the last few months." Hoover's response bordered on the mawkish. "The personal note which you directed to me on June 14, 1940," he wrote back, "is one of the most inspiring messages which I have ever been privileged to receive; and, indeed, I look upon it as rather a symbol of the principles for which our Nation stands. When the President of our country, bearing the weight of untold burdens, takes the time to express himself to one of his Bureau heads, there is implanted in the hearts of the recipients a renewed strength and vigor to carry on their tasks." The letter contained an enclosure, the latest information on FDR's enemies.

The President's actions in employing his chief spy catcher against enemy agents and potential saboteurs were legitimate. His siccing Hoover on what he saw as opponents of military preparedness was, if less defensible, at least politically explainable. But the next use to which FDR put Hoover clearly breached an ethical wall. On June 25, 1940, Vincent Astor, conducting another off-the-books operation in New York, gave FDR some curious political intelligence. Wendell Willkie, liberal businessman and political neophyte, had been nominated as the Republican presidential candidate that month in Philadelphia. "Within the last few days," Astor wrote, "Wendell Willkie has asked J. Edgar Hoover to run on his Vice Presidential ticket. Hoover's reply to this was that, in view of the many fine things that you had done for him and the FBI, he would consider anything of the sort an act of great disloyalty to you, and therefore would not entertain any such proposition." Encouraged by Hoover's fealty, FDR had a little matter that he wanted the director to tend to, keeping an administration skeleton securely in the closet. Vice President Henry Wallace, possessed of an interest in mysticism and the occult, had corresponded with a White Russian spiritualist with whom he traded utopian plans for world peace. Wallace's handwritten letters to the Russian also supposedly contained disparaging observations about FDR. Wallace claimed that the correspondence was false. Nevertheless, the treasurer of the Republican National Committee had managed to obtain copies, and the RNC had a press release prepared to make public Wallace's indiscreet comments. Hoover was able to obtain the correspondence and the Republican release, which he showed to FDR, and which indeed brimmed with potential embarrassment for the President.

How Roosevelt handled the potential threat is now known because of the discovery in recent years of a secret device he had concealed in his office. Inside a drawer of FDR's desk was a panel with buttons reading Record, Pause, Rewind, Idle, and Playback. They controlled a recording system in place since August 1940. The year before, FDR had been badly burned when he was misquoted after a private meeting in the Oval Office with a group of senators. Word had leaked out that the President had said America's defense perimeter began at the Rhine. The implication was that the United States would go to war if German troops crossed their own river. A White House stenographer, Henry Kannee, subsequently came up with a solution to avoid repetitions of such distortions—a secret record of what exactly was said inside the Oval Office. Kannee took the technical challenge to the RCA Corporation. Several months later, J. Ripley Kiel, an RCA inventor, found himself in the Oval Office while the President was away vacationing in New England. Under the scrutiny of Secret Service agents, Kiel drilled holes through the President's desk drawer and through the floor to a basement storage area. He concealed a small microphone in a lamp on the desk, then ran a wire from the lamp through the drilled holes to a machine in the basement. There a rudimentary tape recorder captured the spoken word onto a motion picture film's sound track.

On August 22, with the President back from his vacation, the hidden recording system was tested during a press conference in the Oval Office. As soon as the conference ended and the last reporter had filed out, the President asked a new staffer, Lowell Mellet, a former newspaperman himself, to close the door. FDR knew that his opponent Willkie, still married, was rumored to be involved with another woman, Irita Van Doren, a prominent literary critic in New York. Roosevelt began to speak in a conspiratorial tone, either forgetting or not caring that the recorder was running. "Ah, Lowell," he began, "now, I agree with you that there is, so far as the old man goes [presumably himself], we can't use it publicly. . . . You can't have any of our principal speakers refer to it, but people down the line can do it properly. (Raps desk for emphasis.) I mean the Congress speakers and state speakers, and so forth. They can use your material to determine the fact that Willkie left his old . . . (inaudible whisper). All right. So long as it's none of us people at the top. Now, all right, if people try to play dirty politics on me, I'm willing to try it on other people. Now, you'd be amazed at how this story about the gal is spreading around the country." The President mentioned a parallel, New York's former mayor Jimmy Walker, who, Roosevelt said, had an "extremely attractive little tart" but hired his estranged wife, for $10,000, to appear at his side during a corruption trial. "Now, Mrs. Willkie may not have been hired," the machine recorded FDR saying, "but in effect she's been hired to return to Wendell and smile and make his campaign with him."

As it turned out, the Republicans never issued the release about Wallace and the potentially damaging letters. Willkie may have been too principled to stoop to base tactics, or as has been suggested, a deal was struck—no mention of the Wallace correspondence by the Republicans in exchange for no mention of Willkie's extramarital affair by the Democrats.

On another occasion, FDR's secretary of the interior, Harold Ickes, went to J. Edgar Hoover asking that he run a check on Willkie's ethnic roots. FDR recognized that in Willkie he was up against no Depression-haunted Herbert Hoover, no insular Alf Landon. Wendell Willkie was a six-foot, 220-pound bear of a man, a fresh, appealing star in the Republican firmament, a candidate possessing solid business credentials as president of the huge Commonwealth and Southern utilities corporation, yet a man of liberal bent, indeed a former Democrat. FDR looked across the ring to the other corner and saw his match. Willkie was, Ickes recalled FDR as saying, "the most formidable candidate for himself that the Republicans could have named." At the time, a rumor was circulating that Willkie had changed his name from Wulkje. Ickes, acting for the President, asked the FBI to check out this story. If it proved true and it became known to the public, it could cost Willkie the Polish-American vote. This time, Hoover's trusted number three, Ed Tamm, advised his boss that carrying out the administration's political mischief would be "a serious mistake." Hoover agreed, drew the line, and said no to Ickes.

The President, who publicly said he "had no wish to be a candidate" for a third term, was, however, moving energetically behind the scenes. On the same day that Ickes sought out Hoover, FDR had dispatched another close aide on a related mission. Adolf Berle typified the tough, brainy breed drawn to the New Deal. He had been the youngest graduate ever of Harvard Law School, then served as an intelligence officer in World War I. He later went into private practice, taught at Columbia, and became a member of Roosevelt's legendary Brain Trust. By 1938, the stocky, square-faced, stern-visaged Berle at age forty-three was appointed assistant secretary of state. So comfortable was he with the President that Berle addressed memos to FDR as "Dear Caesar." The practice temporarily ended when Roosevelt directed an aide to "Get hold of Berle and tell him to be darn careful in what he writes me because the staff see his letters and they are highly indiscreet." But soon, Berle resumed using the imperial salutation, which seemed not to displease the President all that much.

On the strength of his slender World War I experience, Berle had been assigned by FDR, along with a grab bag of other duties, to succeed George Messersmith in the hapless job of coordinating intelligence among the FBI, Army, and Navy. Temperamentally, he hardly seemed an ideal choice. As a strong civil libertarian, Berle found the assignment odious, referring to "this infernal counterespionage which I inherited from Messersmith." His juggling act, he noted in his diary, "is to prevent a 'fifth column' . . . trying to commit crimes; at the same time to prevent this machinery from being used hysterically, in violation of civil liberties. . . ."

The President now had another uncongenial task for Berle. The journalist Marquis Childs, FDR said, had tipped him off that former president Herbert Hoover, whom Roosevelt had defeated in 1932, might have behaved inappropriately during the Republican convention in Philadelphia that nominated Wendell Willkie. The ex-president, supposedly, had sent cablegrams to the former French premier Pierre Laval asking him to substantiate a report that Roosevelt once made a firm commitment to send American troops to fight in France. With the 1940 election approaching, with the President walking a narrow path between intervention and neutrality, this issue could prove a political land mine. FDR instructed Berle to go to the FBI and find out what messages Herbert Hoover might have exchanged with Laval. He did not care, Roosevelt claimed, about the man's personal political opinions or actions. But when he intruded himself into matters bearing on the foreign policy of the United States, that became the President's business. This time the FBI willingly accommodated FDR. J. Edgar Hoover had his staff run down the rumor and reported back that no Herbert Hoover correspondence with Laval had turned up.

Clearly, in using the FBI to dig into the comportment of Willkie and former president Hoover, FDR had used an ambitious FBI director to commingle foreign intelligence with domestic spying. His behavior exposed the steel underneath the sheath of patrician geniality. He was a Hudson River gentleman willing to employ the tactics of a street fighter. As one observer put it, Roosevelt gave "a carefully measured appearance of friendly irresolution." But the man had not risen from a wheelchair to the presidency through lack of grit. Once he decided to run for a third term, FDR would unhesitatingly stomp on any hand reaching for his power.

★

What J. Edgar Hoover knew, but was not about to reveal to the President, was that the United States faced no serious threat of internal subversion. Adolf Hitler had specifically ordered Admiral Wilhelm Canaris, chief of the Abwehr, not to conduct sabotage against the United States. No cargoes in American ships bound for Britain and no British properties in the United States were to be attacked, even though Britain was Germany's enemy. Hitler wanted no Black Tom provocations. The objective of German diplomacy in 1940 was to keep America out of the war. Hoover knew this and at one point noted that Germany "today relies far more on propaganda than on espionage and uses the mails and cables little for the latter purpose." Even the spying that Germany thought it was carrying out in America was largely under Hoover's control through double agents. But if the President's belief that America faced sabotage and internal subversion would cause him to depend increasingly on Hoover, the director was all too willing to indulge the presidential prejudices.

One sensitively placed German officer was actually supplying rather than stealing secrets in America. At 1439 Massachusetts Avenue in Washington stood a gloomy pile of brown-red brick, its outer perimeter bristling with parapets and cast-iron railings, the German embassy. On the second floor, behind heavy velvet draperies, was the office of General Friedrich von Boetticher, a short, thick-bodied figure sporting a monocle, his red hair standing up in a stiff brush cut, his bull neck creased at the nape, his whole presence suggesting a Prussian in a B movie. Boetticher had been in

Washington for seven years, sent there in Hitler's defiance of the Treaty of Versailles barring the posting of German military attachés abroad. Beginning in August 1940, Boetticher supplied U.S. War Department intelligence officers with bundles of sensitive information—German aircraft strength, operational plans, maps, and damage assessment reports on the bombing of Britain during the Blitz. Boetticher provided this intelligence, not through secret drops, codes, or cutouts, but by striding through the front entrance of the War Department's Munitions Building on Constitution Avenue in full uniform—riding breeches and boots, his barrel chest bursting with medals and Nazi insignia. The familiar figure was allowed to pass by the guards, his briefcase unsearched.

Boetticher knew exactly what he was doing. The Germans were aware that Churchill supplied Roosevelt with reports of British military operations. Boetticher's deliberate revelation of German secrets to the American military served two ends: to establish unmistakably the power of German arms and to contradict any of Churchill's reports unfavorable to Germany. In one pointed example, on September 15, 1940, the hottest day of the Blitz, the Luftwaffe sent 200 bombers protected by 300 fighters over England. The Royal Air Force claimed 180 kills. The Germans wanted the Roosevelt government to know that they had suffered only 60 aircraft lost. Hence, General von Boetticher's campaign of espionage in reverse.

The Germans did have one concealed objective in 1940, the defeat of Franklin Roosevelt. They had launched a two-pronged enterprise backed by secret funds. The operation had begun as early as September 14, 1939, when the President received a phone call from John L. Lewis, the powerful union leader, asking him to see a man named William Rhodes Davis. FDR's relations with Lewis had gone sour the year before, when Roosevelt bucked Thomas Kennedy, the candidate of the United Mine Workers for governor of Pennsylvania. Instead, FDR had supported Charles A. Jones, the State Democratic Committee's choice. In a close primary, the Lewis candidate won anyway. Still the President had offended a proud man. Thus when Lewis called a year later, Roosevelt chose not to alienate the labor leader any further and agreed to see the unknown Davis the next day.

William Rhodes Davis was an oil operator whose most spectacular deal to date had been to persuade the Mexican government to ship millions of dollars' worth of oil to the fuel-short German navy. However, this lucrative arrangement had ended when the war broke out and Mexican suppliers faced the British naval blockade. The resilient Davis hoped to resume the sale of oil by engineering a peace plan. Just before noon on September 15,

FDR greeted a well-dressed, white-haired, ruddy-faced visitor oozing the manners of the Old South. Davis had expected to see Roosevelt alone, but found him with Adolf Berle. FDR had called Berle the day before, as soon as Lewis had hung up, and told him to be on hand so that "a careful record be had of the conversation" with Davis. Berle had already warned Roosevelt that he considered Davis a Nazi agent and the State Department had a dossier on the man dating back to 1928. Still, FDR listened to Davis's proposal. Through his overseas contacts, the oilman explained, he had become close to Hermann Göring. In fact, just days before, the Führer's deputy had cabled him to sound out the President about a peace proposal. "The Germans desire to make peace," Davis told FDR, "provided certain of their conditions were met." The President nodded in rhythm with his visitor's words, a gesture commonly misinterpreted to mean agreement, when it signaled only that he was listening. The Hitler regime wanted to know, Davis explained, "whether the President might not either act as arbitrator or assist in securing some neutral nation who might so act?"

It was not FDR's style to turn off any source of information; and so he led Davis on, telling him that he already had "various intimations that he might intervene in the European difficulty," but he would have to be invited officially by a government before acting. Davis saw an opportunity to meet that condition. He told the President that the Germans wanted to confer with him again within the next eleven days. Would the President want him to report back when he returned from Europe? "Naturally, any information that would shed light on the situation would interest me," the President answered, and the meeting ended.

Given his tainted credentials, Davis's peace mission, not surprisingly, withered. The indefatigable finagler, however, simply altered course 180 degrees. He knew that the Nazis loathed Roosevelt. In his meeting with Göring, he assured him that, through his influence with the powerful John L. Lewis, any bid by Roosevelt for a third term could, with enough money, be defeated. Göring liked that. Roosevelt might throw an occasional bone to American neutralist public opinion, but his anti-Nazi sentiments were all too obvious and their depth confirmed by the secret FDR-Churchill correspondence known to the Germans through Tyler Kent's leaks. Goering estimated that, should Roosevelt decide to run, it would cost up to $150 million to defeat him. The blustering Reichsmarschall told Davis that he was prepared to spend whatever it took. Göring next brought the scheme to Hitler and won the Führer's enthusiastic consent. In a final meeting with Davis, Göring promised to send soon the first installment of cash to defeat a Roosevelt reelection bid. Germany clearly lacked the foreign exchange to provide anything like the sums that Göring mentioned. Yet, he did manage to scrape together enough for the first gambit. The sum of $160,000 was funneled through Davis to an unidentified Pennsylvania Democratic politician who was to use the money to bribe his state's delegates to the July Democratic convention to oppose FDR.

Right until the convention, Roosevelt had continued to remain coy about his intentions regarding a third term, keeping even his closest intimates guessing. He stayed at the White House during the sweltering humidity of a Washington heat wave and listened, no doubt with a certain bemusement, as Senator Alben Barkley of Kentucky read the message he had sent to the delegates in Chicago. He had, FDR said, "no wish to be a candidate again," and "all the delegates to this convention are free to vote for any candidate." Of course, they nominated Roosevelt, including the supposedly bought-off Pennsylvania delegation, which went solidly for him.

The second prong of the Beat Roosevelt strategy was masterminded by General von Boetticher's colleague in the German embassy in Washington, the chargé d'affaires, Dr. Hans Thomsen, a tall, handsome, blond-haired, exquisitely mannered German of Norwegian ancestry. The clever Thomsen and his glamorous wife, Bebe, managed to soften the appearance of serving a vile regime by playing the good Germans. After Nazi storm troopers smashed 815 Jewish shop windows, burned 76 synagogues, and murdered 36 Jews in 1938, a moment burned into history as Kristallnacht, Bebe would burst into tears at diplomatic receptions, almost on cue, to bewail the awful things the Nazis were doing.

The ambitious Thomsen nevertheless continued to serve his Führer with shrewdness and style. He intended to operate with a good deal less money than Göring had proposed to beat FDR, but with more finesse. In April 1940, even before the party conventions, he received $50,000 from Berlin to covertly underwrite American isolationism as a prelude to driving Roosevelt out of the White House. Thomsen engaged George Sylvester Viereck, an American public relations counselor, to devise the strategy. With Viereck's scheme in hand, Thomsen described for the foreign office his opening tactic: "to invite fifty isolationist Republican Congressmen on a three-day visit to the Party convention, so that they may work on the delegates of the Republican Party in favor of an isolationist foreign policy." The cost he estimated at a modest $3,000.

The day before the Republican convention was slated to adopt its platform, a full-page ad addressed to the delegates and to "American mothers, wage-earners, farmers, and veterans" appeared in *The New York Times.* "Stop the war machine!" it read. "Stop the interventionists and war mongers. Stop the Democratic Party which we believe is the war party. . . ." Ostensibly, the ad had been placed and paid for by the National Committee to Keep America Out of Foreign Wars. Thomsen had kicked in another $3,000 toward its cost.

Not only did these interventions have no effect on FDR's fortunes, but the outcome of the Republican convention was hardly good news in Berlin. On June 28, Thomsen cabled the foreign office, "Willkie's nomination is unfortunate for us. He is not an isolationist . . . he belongs to those Republicans who see America's best defense in supporting England by all means 'short of war.' " The resourceful Thomsen, however, was not yet out of tricks. He went to North Dakota's Senator Gerald P. Nye, who had delivered a speech that Thomsen rated a masterpiece of isolationist reasoning. In a July 18 cable to Berlin, Thomsen boasted that "after lengthy negotiations," Nye had been persuaded to distribute his speech "to 200,000 especially selected persons. This undertaking," he added, "is not altogether easy, and is particularly delicate since Senator Nye, as a political opponent of the President, is under the careful observation of the secret state police here." Ultimately, Thomsen boasted that more than a million copies of isolationist speeches and articles, printed in *The Congressional Record,* were mailed at public expense, using the franking privileges of twenty-four sympathetic members of Congress. These tracts, Thomsen claimed, though presumably authored by congressmen, had actually been written by Viereck as part of the anti-Roosevelt strategy.

While FDR was chronically criticized for being opportunistic and devious, other facets of his intricate character surged to the fore in the 1940 campaign, his statesmanship and boldness. On September 16 the draft, vigorously promoted by FDR and lukewarmly passed by Congress, became law. The timing could not have been worse. The President's political sachems pleaded with him to hold up conscripting men at least until after the election. Sam Rosenman observed, "[A]ny old-time politician would have said [it] could never take place." But Roosevelt insisted that the country's preparedness took precedence over politics. On October 29 a dubious secretary of war, Henry Stimson, stood blindfolded before a huge fishbowl full of cobalt-colored capsules, each containing a number assigned to young men of draft age. Stimson's blindfold had been cut from the cloth of a chair used at the signing of the Declaration of Independence. He reached his hand into the bowl, pulled out a capsule, and handed it to the President. "The first number," Roosevelt announced soberly into the network microphones, "is one-fifty-eight." The six thousand registrants across the country holding that number were to report for military duty.

The President pledged, in a fervent speech at the Boston Garden in the last days of the campaign, "I have said this before, but I shall say it again and again: Your boys are not going to be sent into any foreign wars." Chatting privately with his speechwriter Robert Sherwood, Roosevelt observed afterward, "If we're attacked, it's no longer a foreign war." How close the President believed the country was to being drawn into the conflict is revealed in a transcript of a conversation with his staff captured by the concealed Oval Office recorder. It took place in the late afternoon of October 8, a time of day when the President liked to relax and ruminate. He spoke of a telegram that Roy Howard, of the Scripps-Howard newspaper chain, had received from a Japanese named Mitsunaga, chief of the Japanese press association. "Now this Mitsunaga fella wires to Roy," the President began, "and says, 'there will be no war with the United States'—I'm quoting from memory—'on one condition, and one condition only' (slams the desk), and that is that the United States will recognize the new era in not the Far East, but the East, meaning the whole of the East. Furthermore . . . and the only evidence of this recognition the United States can give is to demilitarize all its naval and air and army bases in Wake, Midway and Pearl Harbor! God! That's the first time that any damn Jap has told us to get out of Hawaii!" The President paused theatrically, then made a comment that rang with premonition: ". . . [T]he only thing that worries me is that the Germans and the Japs have gone along, and the Italians, for, oh, gosh, five, six years without their foot slipping. Without their misjudging foreign opinion. They've played a damn smart game. [But] the time may be coming when the Germans and Japs will do some fool thing. That would put us in! That's the only real danger of our getting in, is that their foot will slip."

On November 5, FDR won his precedent-shattering third term. Soon after, the clumsy and intrusive Oval Office eavesdropping device was shut down. The fourteen press conferences, together with several private conversations recorded, were not discovered until found accidentally by a historian, Robert J. C. Butow, while researching at the FDR Library in Hyde Park in 1978. After hearing them, the historian Arthur Schlesinger Jr. observed, "With all their technical imperfections, the tapes add a fascinating dimension to our sense of the Roosevelt presidency. They offer the historian the excitement of immediacy: FDR in casual, unbuttoned exchange with his staff. One is struck by how little the private voice differs from the public voice we know so well from the speeches. The tone is a rich and resonant tenor. The enunciation is clear, the timing is impeccable. The voice's range is remarkable, from high to low in register and from insinuatingly soft to emphatically loud in decibel level."

After Roosevelt's reelection, Hans Thomsen, ever the realist, cabled Berlin, "The supreme law of his actions—and we shall have to adapt ourselves to that during the coming four years—is his irreconcilable hostility to the totalitarian powers."

Chapter IV

———=★=———

Spymaster in the Oval Office

VINCENT ASTOR wanted to be Franklin Roosevelt's chief intelligence operative, and through his associates in The Club, his tentacles extending into business, broadcasting, journalism, and international society, he appeared to be succeeding. So comfortable was he in his association with FDR that he used White House stationery when communicating with the President. He enjoyed Roosevelt's trust to an extent that he occasionally went ahead with his schemes and told FDR later. On April 18, 1940, he informed the President that "British intelligence in this area [New York City] is in charge of Sir James Paget, assisted by a Mr. Walter Bell, who conduct the so-called British Passport Control Office, although passports occupy but little if any of their time. . . . It occurred to me that Paget and Bell might from time to time obtain leads useful to us. I therefore arranged a meeting with Paget, at which I asked for unofficial British cooperation, but made it clear that we, for obvious reasons, could not return the compliment in the sense of turning over to them any of our confidential information. This somewhat one-sided arrangement was gladly accepted." Of course, the arrangement was accepted, since it wove another strand in the net designed to pull the United States into the war on Britain's side. FDR did not resist this outcome and consequently did not object to his old sailing mate's espionage freelancing.

Two days later, Astor was back to the President with what he regarded as an intelligence opportunity presented on a silver platter. The Japanese ambassador to the United States had recently called a member of The Club, Winthrop Aldrich, chairman of the Chase National Bank, and assured him that "his government was preparing to liquidate the Chinese war as rapidly as adequate policing arrangements could be made." At that point, the ambassador claimed, the Japanese could start paying more attention to their domestic economy. They wanted the Chase bank to send a commission to Japan to advise them. Here was a chance to penetrate Japanese intentions far more deeply than having the *Nourmahal* poke around remote Pacific atolls. Astor told the President, "It seems to me that such a commission might be of great value to us in obtaining valuable information, provided that certain individual members were wisely chosen and adequately educated in advance as to what to look for." At this point, FDR was preoccupied with what he could do to keep a beleaguered Britain afloat. What he did not want was to do anything that might provoke the already wary Japanese into darker suspicions of U.S. intentions. He turned Astor down.

Astor's arrangement with Sir James Paget produced the socialite spy's first great triumph. Confidential correspondence of all governments sent between the Western Hemisphere and the rest of the world had to be routed, via diplomatic pouch, through two central points, Bermuda and Trinidad, both British Crown colonies. In his courtship of the Americans, Paget had let Astor rummage through these presumably inviolate mailbags. As Astor explained to the President on March 14, "In regard to the opening of diplomatic pouches in Bermuda and Trinidad, I have given my word never to tell anyone—with always you excepted. The fear of the British is that if the facts become known, the writers would exercise greater caution or send their letters via a different route." Thanks to this snooping, FDR could now read the secrets of a Japanese attaché, a German chargé d'affaires, a Brazilian foreign minister, or a Soviet ambassador. Astor alerted FDR that the American, George Sylvester Viereck, who was working with Hans Thomsen to defeat Roosevelt's renomination, had sent twenty-seven intelligence reports to the German embassy. The same batch of violated pouches revealed to Roosevelt that the Spanish foreign minister, Ramón Serrano Súñer, had sent a dispatch to Spain's embassies worldwide urging closer cooperation with the Nazis. An intercepted memorandum from Hervé Alphand, then Vichy France's financial attaché in Washington, must have given FDR both mingled pause and pride. Alphand reported to Vichy that the United States was woefully understrength in aircraft, tank, and artillery production. Still, he respected the latent power of America. "We will be making a great mistake if we think the sad example of our country is going to be followed by American democracy," Alphand concluded.

The President threw Astor assignments both strategic and mundane. On May 7, FDR received a letter from a Betty Lawson Johnson. Every day, letters from ordinary citizens poured into the White House mail room, but Mrs. Johnson rang the right bell to get hers before the President. She claimed a connection to the British royal family, and FDR had a soft spot for royals. Her husband, Mrs. Johnson said, had it on reliable authority that the Germans had stolen the Norden bombsight and had smuggled it into Germany aboard the SS *Bremen*. Consequently, King George wanted her to advise the President of this loss. "Knowing your affection for the Royal family, and England's great struggle," her letter went on, "I have come to you, Mr. President, realizing you are the only great man in our America who realizes and sees the dangers to our America if the Allies are beaten. . . ." Mrs. Johnson sealed her bona fides by mentioning, "I had the honor of being at the White House, and meeting with your dear mother the night your son, Franklin, invited us to see *Gone With the Wind*." The President told Missy LeHand to forward Mrs. Johnson's letter to Vincent Astor in New York and have him look into her claim.

Within days, Astor was back with his answer. "The story about the theft of the bombsight, and its having been hidden aboard the BREMEN is the same old song and dance which has cropped up repeatedly in the past. It always comes in the same form, and seems to be regarded as of great importance by the same type of people; the sort that Cholly Knickerbocker calls Café Society. In my opinion, there is little to it. . . ." Astor was both right and wrong. The Norden bombsight's plans had not been aboard the *Bremen*. But they had been stolen and had reached Germany aboard the Hamburg-Amerika Line's *Reliance* three years before, thanks to Hermann Lang. This head start speeded production of the Luftwaffe's own bombsight, which fit neatly into Hermann Goering's plan for a major air offensive against Britain timed for that fall.

His successes so far merely whetted Astor's appetite. To him, the capital of espionage in America should be New York City, as the major U.S. port and the heart of commerce, finance, and communication. Thus, early in June 1940, Astor asked to come to the White House. The courtly multimillionaire stopped by Missy LeHand's desk, charming her, as was his custom, with gallant compliments and invitations to sail on his yacht. Once ensconced privately with the President, Astor explained the tangle of intelligence in New York. J. Edgar Hoover's people, the Office of Naval Intelligence, and the Army's Military Intelligence Division were tripping all over each other and the lines had to be disentangled. He could do it, Astor explained, but the Navy chief, Admiral Harold Stark, kept putting him off. Could the President instruct Stark to see him? Roosevelt, ever disposed to accommodate Astor, called in his naval aide, Captain D. J. Callaghan. He told Callaghan to make sure that Admiral Stark saw his friend. FDR then alerted Stark, prior to the appointment, saying, "I simply wanted you to know that I have requested him [Astor] to coordinate work in the New York area and, of course, want him given every assistance. Among other things, I would like to have great weight given his recommendation on the selection of candidates because of his wide knowledge of men and affairs. Please pass this on to Walter Anderson." Admiral Anderson was director of naval intelligence and a politically attuned sailor. He urged the Navy's office of personnel to arrange a commission for Astor, as a commander at the very least. The personnel staff balked. It took regular Navy officers years to make commander, they argued. Anderson was adamant. The President wanted it done, and that was that. As one participant in the process explained to a colleague, "Astor must have a job. . . . Vincent Astor, for your information, stands very close to the great white father, so proceed with caution."

By the time Astor received his commission, Sir James Paget had been replaced as British espionage chief in America. His successor was a diminutive Canadian, William Stephenson. Diminutive, perhaps in stature, Stephenson was in all other respects a formidable character. His life is worth lingering over, since it would play a pivotal role in Roosevelt's involvement in World War II espionage. William Samuel Stephenson had been born on January 11, 1896, and raised on the bone-chilling plains of western Canada. From his earliest school days, the boy exhibited that rare and admirable combination, depth of intellect and a taste for action. In high school, the "wee fellow," as he was called, became both a bookworm and an athlete. With the outbreak of World War I, he marched straight from high school into the trenches, with the Royal Canadian Engineers. At age eighteen, he won a battlefield commission. Between his unit's heavy losses and his natural leadership, he was promoted to captain by age nineteen. During his twentieth month at the front, Stephenson was felled in a gas attack and invalided back to England. His lungs, the doctors said, could not stand up to front-line conditions in the trenches. He was considered "disabled for life."

For most soldiers his situation would have marked an honorable end to war. Stephenson, instead, turned to the air campaign, volunteering for the Royal Flying Corps. He became an ace, scoring twenty-six kills. On July 28, 1918, Stephenson's Camel was mistakenly shot down by a French observer aircraft. Wounded in the leg, the flier landed behind enemy lines and was taken prisoner, but managed to escape. Stephenson later became a boxer, earning the world amateur lightweight championship title. He settled in Britain, where twin talents for invention and commerce made him a millionaire before he was thirty. One of his companies, Pressed Steel, coincidentally drew Stephenson into espionage. Steel-buying missions brought him into Germany, where he found the pace of military production alarming. What he learned he fed back to Winston Churchill, who, in the years before the war, had made himself a Cassandra by warning his resistant countrymen that Germany was rearming and that Britain must be prepared to fight.

As soon as Churchill became prime minister, Bill Stephenson was summoned to 10 Downing Street. He was to move to the United States and take Paget's place under cover of the Passport Control Office, Churchill directed. His mission was to protect British property from sabotage, thwart German clandestine operations in the Western Hemisphere, but above all, to draw the United States into the war. Ian Fleming, the future creator of James Bond, and a Stephenson subordinate, described the man at the time as "very tough, very rich, single-minded, patriotic, and a man of few words." Stephenson, upon his arrival in the United States that same May, set up shop in Room 3603 Rockefeller Center, and looked up Paget's accomplice, Vincent Astor. Astor insisted that Stephenson stay at what he called his "broken-down boarding house," the swank St. Regis Hotel.

As his undercover activities began to stretch the thin disguise of a passport-control office, the U.S. State Department demanded that Stephenson register his organization. He acquiesced, identifying the operation as the inscrutable British Security Coordination. Later legend would have it that Churchill personally assigned Stephenson the code name Intrepid. The truth is rather more prosaic. Intrepid was the cable and telegraph address Stephenson's BSC used over the wires of Western Union.

Vincent Astor quickly reestablished with Bill Stephenson the cozy arrangement he had enjoyed with Sir James Paget. Indeed, it was from

Stephenson that he learned of a cloud forming on his horizon. Late in 1940, the President allowed Admiral Anderson, as director of naval intelligence, to make an unusual covert appointment. Wallace Banta Phillips was a bald-headed, hunchbacked businessman with a mysterious past. Phillips claimed to have been an intelligence officer with the American Expeditionary Force in World War I. He thereafter settled in London, heading a rubber products company called Pyrene. During the years of peace, he conducted an industrial spy service and boasted that he had agents on his payroll stretching from the Soviet Union to Mexico, including seven former prime ministers. He had volunteered his services to his native land and was taken on by Anderson as a dollar-a-year man working out of New York City and given the title representative of the Special Intelligence Service of the Office of Naval Intelligence. In this position Phillips enjoyed unrestricted access to ONI's secret files and funds.

Several months later, on March 19, 1941, FDR finally formalized Vincent Astor's nebulous role. He informed ONI, MID, the State Department, and the FBI that "As Area Controller for the New York area, Commander Vincent Astor, U.S.N.R. is designated." Astor was given an office at 50 Church Street and lofty-sounding authority. He was to assign intelligence priorities, resolve conflicts, act as a clearinghouse, and be informed before the other four agencies could make any new espionage contacts. His authority had been granted without the President's first consulting the military intelligence chiefs or J. Edgar Hoover, omissions that would scarcely ensure Astor of a warm welcome into the field.

For all his newfound authority and intimacy with FDR, Astor was about to experience what all Roosevelt associates eventually learned: He was privy to only part of the total man. No sooner did he assume his new mandate when someone he described as the "number one man" in British intelligence, doubtless Stephenson, tipped him off about the emergence of a potential rival in Wallace Phillips. On April 20, Astor dispatched a car and driver from New York to hand-deliver a letter to Hyde Park, where the President was spending the weekend. In it he begged for "just 5 minutes worth" of the President's time the next day. He appended a note asking FDR's other secretary, Grace Tully, if the President might send his reply back via the driver on his return to the city. In the meantime, he said, he would wait at home for a phone call. Taking no chances, should the requested meeting or call fall through, he appended a six-page longhand letter that began, "Dear Mr. President, One might suppose that I would leave you in peace while trying to get a rest in Hyde Park. However, here is a situation which I do not feel justified in keeping from you, for if it went wrong I believe it could result in a real scandal and be just what the isolationists would like. The situation concerns a Mr. Wallace Phillips." Astor went on to inventory Phillips's sins. "He claims to be very rich and to be a great friend of Churchill and most of his war cabinet. . . . He claimed that he a) had frequent contacts with you, b) was a great friend of J. Edgar Hoover who gave him the run of F.B.I. files, c) had access to MID, ONI and FBI files in New York." Astor revealed that he had already confronted Phillips personally, and that the man appeared unabashed and unapologetic about his behavior. "Since then I have discovered the following from P. himself," Astor went on, "a) he has entire charge of expenditures of the Navy's 'secret' fund (about $100,000), b) he alone selects agents to be sent abroad, c) he refuses to allow the FBI to check these men, d) in my opinion he pays his agents exorbitantly ($4,000–6,000 per year) plus $10 per day plus travel expenses. . . . Furthermore, in my opinion, for what it's worth, Mr. P. is unreliable in his statements, indiscreet, and a social climber, which is a dangerous combination for one in his position." Astor's final comment reveals FDR as the master manipulator looking down from above onto his subordinates scurrying around like mice in a maze. "I have reported the whole matter to Admiral Anderson (3rd Dist.) who is just as worried as I am," Astor closed. Yet, it was Anderson who had hired Phillips in the first place, with FDR's approval. Astor's torpedo had misfired before it was launched. Phillips continued his services for ONI.

Not only did Vincent Astor face rivals in Phillips, the ONI, MID, and FBI, but a new competitor was about to enter FDR's clandestine service. John Franklin Carter had first met Roosevelt in January 1932 after writing a profile of the then New York governor for *Liberty* magazine. The piece prompted an impressed FDR to invite Carter to Albany just as the governor was beginning to emerge as a Democratic candidate for the presidency. Carter told FDR, "You're going to be elected President." Roosevelt, he later recalled, "wasn't quite as sure as I was."

Carter had been born in Fall River, Massachusetts, in 1897, one of seven children of an Episcopalian minister. He attended Yale with Stephen Vincent Benet, Thornton Wilder, Archibald MacLeish, and Henry Luce and thereafter was rarely out of sparkling company. Carter worked for just one month on a new magazine called *Time,* launched by his classmate Henry Luce, before he left to join *The New York Times.* Carter became an ardent New Dealer and in 1936 went to work as a speechwriter and idea man for Henry Wallace, then secretary of agriculture. He was described by a colleague as "brilliant, cynical, occasionally cockeyed and always exciting." After leaving government, Carter started a syndicated column, "We the People," written under the pen name Jay Franklin. His office in the National Press Building was just blocks from the White House.

Early in 1941, Carter tested out on undersecretary of state Sumner Welles a scheme that had been percolating in his mind as America seemed fated for war. He told Welles that the various intelligence services were "pretty well loused up and floundering around. There might be a use for a small and informal intelligence unit operating out of the White House without titles without any bullshit. . . ." Besides, Carter believed that since he had worked hard to get FDR elected for the controversial third term, he deserved something. Welles passed Carter's idea along to the President, who immediately asked the columnist to stop by the White House. Carter had a head start before he even met with the President. He did not like the State Department, nor did FDR. Roosevelt found its policy guidance rigid and excessively neutral. State, in his judgment, was defeatist, reflected in the pessimism of his envoy to Britain, Joe Kennedy. He suspected department careerists of leaking secrets to the isolationists, and he had distrusted State's notoriously porous Gray code even before the Tyler Kent episode. The President was aware of the old story that as far back as the 1920s the American consul in Shanghai made his retirement speech to the diplomatic community in this code, his remarks understood by all. More important, FDR believed the department was poorly equipped to conduct intelligence abroad. A young Dean Acheson, who would one day rise to secretary of state, noted, "Techniques for gathering information differed only by reason of the typewriter and the telegraph from the techniques which John Quincy Adams used in St. Petersburg and Benjamin Franklin was using in Paris."

Carter made his pitch to the President for the informal White House intelligence ring and found FDR receptive. Roosevelt was aware that during World War I President Wilson had been secretly advised by a body called The Inquiry. At its peak, The Inquiry numbered 126 scholars, scientists, and literary figures, including the historian Samuel Eliot Morison and the journalist Walter Lippmann, currently writing for *The New Republic*. Its members worked out of anonymous quarters in Manhattan and prepared confidential peace terms and redrawn maps of Europe for Wilson to pursue in the postwar era. To FDR, what Carter was proposing had the ring of The Inquiry. The man seemed to know everybody—officials, diplomats, the entire press corps domestic and foreign, and corporate executives all over the globe. He also had access to the National Broadcasting Company's worldwide shortwave network. And FDR grasped that Carter's profession offered the perfect cover for delivering intelligence, a Washington journalist coming to the White House occasionally to interview the President.

On February 13 the President approved the establishment of "a small special intelligence and fact finding unit" under Carter. He also arranged for plausible deniability. As Carter described FDR's terms, "The overall condition was attached to the operation by President Roosevelt that it should be entirely secret and would be promptly disavowed in the event of publicity." It was left to Adolf Berle at State, FDR's intelligence handyman, to implement the Rube Goldberg apparatus the President had concocted. That year's military appropriations act included an "Emergency Fund for the President," from which FDR transferred $10,000 to the State Department. State was then to finance Carter, ostensibly by buying from him surveys on conditions in various countries, with Germany leading the list.

On February 20, a week after FDR had approved Carter as his newest spy, Berle described to his superior, Sumner Welles, his less than impressive first encounter with the columnist. "Jay Franklin (J.F. Carter) came in to see me today. He stated as a result of his conversation with the President and with you, and preparatory to the work he had been asked to do, he had spent some seven hundred dollars, and that he would be broke by the end of this week. . . . He wanted an advance of some kind against the compensation which he would eventually receive for his work. Accordingly I lent him seven hundred dollars." Berle concluded, "I am not, of course, familiar with what the President has asked him to do, nor do I wish to be. . . ."

Carter was cast in the Roosevelt mold—quick, bright, bold, passionate in his beliefs, with the passion leavened by practicality and a sense of humor. The new spy's assignments roved indiscriminately. Besides collecting intelligence, FDR wanted Carter to do political analysis, evaluate new weapons, troubleshoot military bottlenecks, and monitor other intelligence operations. It would no doubt have surprised and saddened Vincent Astor to learn that the President specifically asked Carter to keep an eye on his old friend's operation.

After several months, Carter had only eleven full-time agents on the payroll in his determination to keep the operation compact. He managed a clever multiplier effect by obtaining from the U.S. Passport Division the names of persons given visas for travel to foreign countries and those of foreigners coming into the United States. Carter's operatives would then coach willing outward-bound travelers in what to look for abroad, and would question arriving foreigners willing to describe military and industrial conditions, particularly in the Axis countries.

★

The boldest covert operation that FDR had been pursuing, while America was still technically neutral, was unknown to either Carter or Astor, the FBI, or the military intelligence branches. Back in July 1940, Treasury secretary Henry Morgenthau had dined with the British ambassador, Lord Lothian, Henry Stimson, and Frank Knox. Lothian had conducted a clever campaign of ingratiating himself with Americans, among whom Morgenthau, because of his closeness to FDR, had become a prime target. The British peer, born Philip Henry Kerr, was fifty-eight at the time, a tall, big-boned man with a high brow and Roman nose, every bit the lord. Despite his rank and wealth, Lothian had quickly grasped that Americans were much taken with bluebloods exhibiting a just-plain-folks demeanor. Thus he wore a battered gray fedora, drove his own car, and bought his own train tickets when traveling in the United States.

That July evening, during an after-dinner conversation, Lothian pointed out to Morgenthau that though Japan's belligerency and territorial ambitions were obvious, the United States was still selling fuel to the Japanese. Lothian then dropped a bombshell: "If you will stop shipping aviation gasoline to Japan," he offered, "we will blow up the oil wells in the Dutch East Indies so that the Japanese can't come down and get [them]. . . . At the same time the Royal Air Force could concentrate its bombing attacks on German plants producing synthetic gasoline." Caught in this three-way squeeze, the Axis powers would simply run out of gas. The United States was not at war with Japan, nor was Britain. The ambassador's proposal could be seen as nothing less than blatant aggression against the Japanese. The scheme, Morgenthau later confided to his diary, left him with his "breath . . . taken away." If the British "would blow up the wells, it would simply electrify the world and really put some belief in England. . . . [I]f we don't do something and do it fast, Japan is just going to gobble up one thing after another."

The next day, Morgenthau went to the White House to test Lothian's idea on FDR. The Treasury secretary, a Jew, had become a hard-line interventionist, prompted in part by what Hitler was doing to his co-religionists in Europe. He later told FDR, "[T]his thing might give us peace in three to six months." The President thereupon launched into a monologue lasting half an hour, during which he astonished Morgenthau with his pinpoint knowledge of oil deposits around the world. FDR also told him that he had been thinking for months of blockading all of Europe, "just leaving a small channel open directly to England through which all ships would have to pass. . . ."

Morgenthau's visit had run overtime, and Stimson, Knox, and Sumner Welles were outside the office waiting to see the President. FDR asked Morgenthau if he minded if they came in. "By all means, they are great guys," he answered. With the others ushered in, the President casually floated the Lothian proposal, without mentioning Morgenthau's role. To the Treasury secretary's delight Stimson favored taking a hard line against Japan. But Welles was aghast and warned that so rash a move would cause Japan to declare war on Great Britain. The meeting had been vintage Roosevelt—elicit several opinions, the more contrary the less likely FDR was to go off on a wrongheaded course. The debate over Lothian's proposed swap, an American fuel embargo for British destruction of the Dutch East Indies oil fields, ended in an Oval Office stalemate.

Still, the President hankered after the near impossible, hurting Japan without provoking war. The next opportunity rose in December 1940. Roosevelt was outraged by Japan's indiscriminate bombing of Chinese cities and the aerial machine-gunning of helpless civilians. Morgenthau wrote in his diary: ". . . [H]e [FDR] has mentioned it to me that it would be a nice thing if the Chinese would bomb Japan." China's leader, Generalissimo Chiang Kai-shek, had sent Morgenthau a plea for five hundred U.S. aircraft. With airpower, Chiang argued, he could retake Canton and Hankow. He could threaten bases on Hainan and Formosa, even Japan itself. Chiang's request had been delivered to Morgenthau by the generalissimo's American air advisor, Claire Chennault, a former U.S. Army Air Corps captain. As Chennault explained to Morgenthau, the objective was to "burn out the industrial heart of the [Japanese] Empire with firebomb attacks on the teeming bamboo ant heaps of Honshu and Kyushu." The Treasury secretary had close ties to the Chinese ambassador to Washington, T. V. Soong, Chiang's brother-in-law. Soong wanted Morgenthau to sell Chiang's proposal to FDR. Morgenthau leveled with the ambassador. "Well, his asking for 500 planes is like asking for 500 stars." Still, he took the Chinese proposal to the President, who put one question about Chiang to Morgenthau: "Is he still willing to fight?" Yes, Morgenthau assured him, "that is what the message is about." "Wonderful," the President replied. "That's what I've been talking about for four years."

Five hundred planes were out of the question, but Roosevelt offered a compromise. He asked what the Chinese might think of obtaining a few long-range American bombers, with the understanding that they would be used to firebomb Tokyo and other Japanese cities. When Morgenthau relayed this proposal to T. V. Soong, the Chinese ambassador was ecstatic. "This would give us a chance to hit back," he answered.

On the morning of December 19 the President held a cabinet meeting after which he asked Morgenthau, Hull, Stimson, and Knox to stay behind. They retreated to the Oval Office, where they debated the practicality of giving China bombers to attack Japan. The President ran his finger over a map that T. V. Soong had provided showing Chinese air bases only a tantalizing 650 miles from Tokyo. He appeared to give his approval to Morgenthau's idea when he said, "The four of you work out a program."

FDR's swings, from cautiously scotching a chance for Astor's Room to spy inside Japan to endorsing an outright act of belligerency against that country, reflect the multiplicity of the Roosevelt character. His biographer James MacGregor Burns observes: "As war administrator, as businessman, as president he liked to try new things, to take a dare, to bring something off with a flourish." A clandestine strike against Japan fitted that definition perfectly.

Two days after the meeting with the President, Morgenthau invited Soong, General Mow, of the Chinese air force, and Claire Chennault to his elegant three-story home at 2201 R Street near Washington's Embassy Row. Over drinks they estimated the number of bombers, pursuit planes, and logistical support required to hit Tokyo. Chennault raised a problem. They could not expect barely trained Chinese pilots simply to hop into B-17s and make for Japan. Only American pilots backed by American flight and ground crews could currently perform such a mission. That was no problem, Morgenthau said. The U.S. Army Air Corps would release men from active duty who could then volunteer to fly for China. Morgenthau's brainstorm—American planes, flown by American pilots, firebombing Japanese cities—remained a rashly belligerent act. He believed, nevertheless, that he had the President's proxy to go forward.

Secretary of War Stimson began having second thoughts. On Sunday, December 22, he invited the Treasury secretary, Knox, and the Army chief, General George C. Marshall, to his home "to try to get some mature brains into [the plan], before we got committed to it." General Marshall doubted the Army could spare any planes for China. His massive authority carried weight. Morgenthau agreed to scale down the program and drop the request for bombers. He asked instead for a hundred pursuit planes. Stimson approved the compromise. When informed of the deal, Soong and Chennault, having started from zero, were delighted to get any planes. FDR unhesitatingly approved a scheme under which an initial hundred pilots resigned from the Army Air Corps and volunteered to fly P-40 pursuit aircraft, presumably financed by the Chinese, but secretly paid by the U.S. government. They would receive $600 a month plus $500 for every Japanese plane destroyed. Thus was born a World War II legend, the American Volunteer Group, more colorfully, the Flying Tigers, led by Claire Chennault.

Months after the December White House meeting, Chennault was still pushing for China-based air raids against Japan, and the President was still interested in providing the bombers. But the sober-minded Marshall first asked if he might send General John Magruder to China to evaluate Chiang's forces and to weigh the potential political fallout of American-engineered bombing of Japan. Magruder came back warning that Chennault's proposition could lead the Japanese to attack the United States. Roosevelt was by now providing military aid to the Chinese; he was willing secretly to sponsor the firebombing of Tokyo from China; and on July 26, 1941, he clamped an embargo on the shipment of American oil to fuel-hungry Japan. Doubtless the President's antagonistic actions influenced a Japanese decision that was to explode over Pearl Harbor in less than five months.

Chapter V

———═★═———

The Defeatist and the Defiant

HOW WILLIAM J. Donovan entered the Roosevelt intelligence universe is a sinuous tale. Soon after Frank Knox had been lured into the Roosevelt administration in June 1940, and before Henry Stimson had been appointed secretary of war, Knox called the President from his *Daily News* office in Chicago. He had heard rumors, he said, that FDR was thinking of putting another Republican into the cabinet, namely William J. Donovan. More likely, Knox was floating an idea, rather than checking a rumor, since he and Donovan were thick. Donovan, at the time, was an immensely successful lawyer, a former acting attorney general, and an authentic World War I hero. He had been Knox's close political ally, hosting dinners at his duplex apartment on fashionable Beekman Place in Manhattan to raise money for the publisher's ill-fated 1936 presidential bid. When that effort failed, Donovan's shrewd behind-the-scenes politicking won Knox second place on the Republican ticket.

Knox told FDR, "[F]rankly, if your proposal contemplated Donovan for the War Department and myself for the Navy, I think the appointments could be put solely upon the basis of a nonpartisan nonpolitical measure of putting our national defense departments in such a state of preparedness as to protect the United States against any danger to our security. . . ." Roosevelt replied smoothly, "Bill Donovan is also an old friend of mine—we were in law school together—and frankly, I should like to have him in the Cabinet, not only for his own ability, but also to repair in a sense the very great injustice done him by President Hoover in the winter of 1929." FDR had again demonstrated what one aide called a "fiendish memory." In 1928, Donovan had been acting attorney general in the Coolidge administration. When Herbert Hoover became president in 1929, it was assumed that Hoover would appoint him attorney general. Hoover did not do so because, it was rumored, powerful Republicans did not want a Catholic in the cabinet. His rejection, at that point, had been the bitterest disappointment in Bill Donovan's life.

The Columbia Law School class of 1907 comprised only twenty-one members. Yet, for all FDR's avowal of friendship, Donovan always denied that he and Roosevelt had been close there. And despite his response to Knox, FDR evinced no further enthusiasm for Donovan as his secretary of war. "I fear that to put two Republicans in charge of the armed forces might be misunderstood in both parties," he explained. The only close personal exchange between himself and Donovan occurred on April 9, 1940, when Roosevelt sent a telegram of condolence on the death in an automobile accident of Donovan's adored twenty-two-year-old daughter, Patricia. Donovan wrote back the next day: "That you took the time from many and pressing duties makes me doubly grateful. . . ."

Soon after his conversation with Knox the President did exactly what he said he would not do. He named another Republican to a defense portfolio in his cabinet, Stimson, not Bill Donovan, as secretary of war. Still, Knox was not finished with promoting his friend. On July 9, at the White House, he agreed with what the President had been saying all along—that the swift collapse of France, the Low Countries, and Norway could be explained only by fifth column subversives operating from within. The Navy secretary proposed having a correspondent from his Chicago *Daily News,* Edgar Mowrer, already in Britain, study methods for detecting fifth columnists that the United States might adopt. And he wanted someone else to join Mowrer, Bill Donovan.

To the President, the possibility of internal subversion appeared only too credible. Over a quarter-million residents in America were, like Hermann Lang, who had stolen the Norden bombsight, German-born. In 1939 the FBI received sixteen hundred reports of alleged sabotage. But on a single day in May 1940, with Hitler's forces overrunning Europe and with Churchill rounding up suspected subversives in droves, the FBI received over twenty-nine hundred reports of suspected sabotage. FDR not only seized on Knox's idea, but took it a step further. Why not also have Donovan form a judgment of Britain's capacity to stand up to Germany? Could the British stop the Germans in the air? Could they withstand an invasion? There was no point in pouring aid down a rathole, the President believed.

The next day Knox asked Lord Lothian to smooth the path for Donovan in Britain. Nothing could have pleased Lothian more. He had earlier described to London the American mood as "a wave of pessimism passing over this country to the effect that Great Britain must inevitably be defeated, and that there is no use in the United States doing anything more to help it and thereby getting entangled in Europe. . . . There is some evidence that it is beginning to affect the President. . . ." Donovan's findings might reverse that pessimism.

Secretary of State Cordell Hull cabled the American ambassador in Britain, Joe Kennedy, "We would appreciate any arrangements and preparations which could facilitate Colonel Donovan's mission." Kennedy greeted this news with the enthusiasm of someone handed a dead rat. He shot back a reply to Hull that Donovan's and Mowrer's prying would amount to "the height of nonsense. We are already making an investigation here on this [fifth columnists] subject and [Harvey] Klemmer of my office is handling it." Rather than paving the way, he intended to tell the British that Edgar Mowrer was just a reporter and not "entitled to confidential files and discussions with government officials. If Colonel Knox does not stop sending Mowrers and Colonel Donovans over here," he concluded, "this organization is not going to function effectively." Unsure that this cable alone would scuttle the mission, Kennedy called Sumner Welles the same day on the transatlantic phone. He wanted Welles to take to the President the cable he had received from Hull along with his own vigorous protest. Welles dutifully did so, encountering Roosevelt just returning from a rubdown by the White House physician. FDR read the correspondence and then followed a vintage Rooseveltian course, handing a squabble to his subordinates. He wrote Knox, "Please take this up with Secretary Hull and try to straighten it out. Somebody's nose seems to be out of joint." The displaced nose obviously belonged to Joe Kennedy and what had dislocated it was the prospect of someone arriving in London too much like the ambassador for comfort, another wealthy, forceful, energetic, self-made Irish American burning with ambition, William J. Donovan.

Kennedy's counterattack failed, and Donovan prepared to set off for England. If anything could warm his reception by the British, it was the ambassador's opposition to his trip. Kennedy was a man predicting

Britain's defeat. Donovan was a man who might be persuaded the country could survive. Another ally assured a cordial welcome. As soon as William Stephenson had arrived in New York to take charge of British intelligence, he had phoned Donovan at his law office on Wall Street. Donovan said, "Stay where you are." Within twenty minutes, he was in the Canadian's suite. The two men had met occasionally during the thirties in London while Donovan was traveling on business. They instantly renewed a kindred spirit. Stephenson was soon convinced that his friend was a figure of power and influence in Washington. When he learned that the President was sending Donovan to Britain, it appeared that he had bet on a winner. Stephenson alerted the British secret service to open every door for his friend.

On the morning of July 15, 1940, Donovan's wife, Ruth, received a terse phone call from her husband in New York alerting her that he would be gone indefinitely, embarked on a secret mission. Donovan then boarded a Pan American flying boat, the *Lisbon Clipper,* for the flight to England via Portugal. On reaching London, he checked into Claridge's, his favorite hotel. The uncertainty of Britain's survival and Ambassador Kennedy's pessimism were understandable at the time of Donovan's arrival. All of Britain's allies on the Continent had fallen. Germany controlled the Atlantic coast from Scandinavia to Spain. Mountains of British military equipment lay smoldering and abandoned on the beaches at Dunkirk. Germany had gathered the world's largest concentration of armor and airpower, poised for an invasion of Britain. Yet, Donovan found British grit still intact. That June, the Foreign Office undersecretary, Sir Alexander Cadogan, wrote in his diary, "We have simply got to die at our posts—a far better fate than capitulating to Hitler as these damned frogs had done." A sign at a London newsstand read: FRENCH SIGN PEACE TREATY: WE'RE IN THE FINALS!

The British embraced Donovan. He spent a whirlwind two and a half weeks moving atop the peaks of British power and society. The American-born Lady Astor arranged for him to meet King George and Queen Mary at Astor's home at 4 St. James Square. On July 23, Robert Vansittart, chief diplomatic advisor to the foreign secretary, told Churchill, "There is at the present moment over here a Colonel William Donovan (he is staying at Claridge's). . . . He is a Republican, but he is a friend of Roosevelt and has been sent over here on a mission by consent of the two political parties in the United States, his real object being to collect as much information as would be useful in the event of America coming into the war. . . . I think in any event you should see him for a short while. He is an important person, and will be still more important to us in the future." Churchill saw Donovan at 5:30 P.M. on July 25.

Three days later, Lady Diana Cooper invited Donovan to Sunday dinner to meet Churchill again. Donovan discreetly chose not to knock Joe Kennedy's nose further out of joint and instead accepted a dinner invitation from the ambassador. He reluctantly declined Lady Diana and sent her a dozen yellow roses. She later responded with a thank-you note, adding, "I am happy to tell you that Winston was in his most engaging and invigorating form and I am sure you would have enjoyed it enormously. . . . I hope you had a hideous evening with Joe and I hope that you will lunch or dine another day."

Donovan's most prophetic English encounter, as far as America's entry into the realm of espionage, took place not with monarchs or prime ministers, but in a grimy, nondescript office building at 52 Broadway opposite the Saint James underground station late on a Sunday morning just prior to his departure for home. The only hint of the building's official character was the posting of two elderly guards in blue uniforms with brass buttons who listlessly admitted the American visitor. Inside, Donovan met a Scot whose unaffected manner belied his position at the pinnacle of British society. Donovan's host was fifty-year-old Colonel Stewart Menzies, wealthy heir to a Scottish distillery fortune and a soldier who had won the Distinguished Service Order during the Great War as a member of the prestigious Household Cavalry. Menzies's parents had been close friends of Edward VII. Menzies's mother, Lady Holford, served as lady-in-waiting to Queen Mary, and her son was rumored to be the illegitimate offspring of the king. Menzies used his elevated connections skillfully and shamelessly to become Britain's chief spymaster as head of MI6. He was a man of charm but not warmth. The wife of one of his subordinates described him as "hard as granite under a smooth exterior." Inside intelligence circles, he was referred to simply as "C." Menzies had been alerted to Donovan's arrival by his American operations chief, William Stephenson. What Menzies and Donovan discussed at 52 Broadway is nowhere recorded. Like Blinker Hall captivating FDR in 1918, "C" may have given Donovan heady glimpses into British spycraft. That he received more than a cursory *tour d'horizon* seems premature, given that Donovan, however sympathetic, was still a civilian, held no office, and represented a neutral nation.

On August 3, eighteen days after his arrival in England, Donovan boarded the *Clare,* a four-engine British flying boat, camouflaged with green and blue patches, for his return flight to America. The Royal Air Force delivered champagne, and Brendan Bracken, Churchill's protégé, provided books to relieve the tedium of the crossing. Donovan arrived in New York at 7 P.M. Sunday, August 4. His wife, Ruth, met him at the airport, still no wiser as to why or where her husband had gone.

The attitude of the British toward Donovan's visit was rather like that of a couple much relieved at having made a good impression after inviting the boss over for dinner. Admiral John H. Godfrey, director of Britain's naval intelligence, whom Donovan had also seen, writes in his memoirs that the unspoken object of the American's mission "was to discover if we were worth supporting." The answer was to become clear in Donovan's actions upon his arriving home.

On August 9, FDR left the White House for a vacation in New England. He invited Donovan along, as he told reporters, "so he can tell me what he found on the other side when he went over." Donovan caught up with the presidential party at the Hyde Park railroad station, and accompanied FDR for a two-and-a-half-day swing through the New England countryside, their most intimate association thus far. Since his return, Donovan had run into increasing pessimism in the administration over Britain's fate. Joe Kennedy, he told friends, could take much credit for this defeatism. The President wanted to know, could England hold out against an invasion? Donovan described what British leaders had shown him—well-organized air defenses, airfields wisely dispersed and cunningly camouflaged, and planes safely sheltered. He painted a picture of the English coast bristling with barbed wire and machine guns, just the first line of a deep defensive deployment. The British still stood in mortal peril, Donovan told the President, but with America's backing, they could make it. They needed immediately a hundred Flying Fortresses and a million rifles for the Home Guard to stave off an invasion.

During the two days that Donovan had the President's ear, they pursued FDR's favored pastimes, long drives through glorious foliage and frequent stops for roadside picnics. Donovan continued to tell the President what he wanted to hear, reversing the gloom and doom prophecies of Kennedy. He had a recommendation as well: that the United States start collaborating with British intelligence by creating its own centralized espionage service.

Donovan was soon demonstrating a budding influence on FDR's decisions. Lord Beaverbrook, Britain's minister of aircraft production, had pleaded with Donovan to persuade America to give the British the Norden bombsight. Through their own sources, they knew that the Germans already had obtained the American design. Within weeks Bill Stephenson was able to cable his London superiors, "President has sanctioned release to us of the bombsight, to be fitted henceforth to bombers supplied to us." It was Donovan who had convinced FDR. Churchill had begged for old American destroyers to replace the Royal Navy's heavy losses in Norwegian sea battles. Donovan began lobbying Secretary of War Stimson and influential senators to back a counterproposal FDR had made to Churchill, destroyers for naval bases to be leased to the United States for ninety-nine years. When FDR finally went ahead with the deal on September 3, without the blessing of a balky Congress, he gave Donovan substantial credit.

Ambassador Kennedy had sought to torpedo Donovan's mission and failed. In the marketplace of FDR's esteem, Donovan's fortunes were on the rise and Kennedy's stalemated. The ambassador longed to quit the Court of Saint James's because he could not believe in the policies he had been sent there to represent—Roosevelt's strategies to prop up Britain. The President shrank from firing anybody, but Kennedy had long been skating on thin ice. His womanizing was flagrant, including an open affair with the movie star Gloria Swanson. His slanderous private comments about the President leaked to the media. His blaming the war on "the Jewish conspiracy" was disgraceful. James Reston, the *New York Times* London correspondent, said of Kennedy, "He couldn't keep his mouth shut or his pants on." Still, FDR did not want the ambassador to leave his post yet. He feared having Kennedy shooting off his mouth in the United States during an election year. In the end, Kennedy broke the stalemate; he simply announced his retirement and headed home on October 23, 1940. Two years and nine months of the impetuous Irishman's outrages had ended for FDR.

Meanwhile, though Bill Donovan's stock was rising, he was still dissatisfied. What he hankered for, above all, was what he had done so valorously twenty-two years before, to lead American troops. Two days after his return from England, he had dined with Henry Stimson, and as the evening was about to end, the secretary of war dangled a tantalizing prospect before Donovan. How would he like to head one of the training camps the Army was reviving? "I wouldn't say no," a grinning Donovan replied. Stimson later wrote of his guest's reaction in his diary: "He was determined to get into the war some way or other and was the same old Bill Donovan that we have all known and been so fond of." Promisingly, General Marshall invited Donovan to visit training camps and mobilization centers. He spent ten days in October touring Fort Benning, Fort Sam Houston, and Fort Sill. He wrote to Robert Vansittart at the British Foreign

Office that he had also been offered the Republican Senate nomination from New York State. But that was not what he wanted: "I intend to go with the troops, and as it looks now I shall probably spend the winter in Alabama training a division."

It was not to be. His hopes began to wither as no call to arms came to him from the White House.

★

On December 22, 1940, a quiet Sunday, Missy LeHand interrupted the President's rest to inform him that the journalist Fulton Oursler had just called from New York pleading for a confidential meeting as soon as possible. FDR knew Oursler well, a reporter, lecturer, biographer, playwright, a writing jack-of-all-trades who had often come to the White House. If Oursler, no political ally, was eager to meet with the President in secret, FDR was curious enough to accommodate him. LeHand called Oursler back, telling him to present himself anonymously at ten-thirty the following morning at the front door with the other tourists, rather than through the official guests' entrance.

Oursler took the train to Washington and, after a fifteen-minute wait in the Red Room, was ushered to FDR's second-floor study. There the President cheerily introduced him to a Scotch terrier given to him five months before by a distant cousin and close Hudson Valley friend, Margaret "Daisy" Suckley. The dog's full name, bestowed by FDR, was Murray, the Outlaw of Falahill, though he was called simply Fala. The President asked about Oursler's young daughter, April, surprising the journalist with his detailed recollection of the girl's schooling. He chattered on about whatever subject caught his fancy that afternoon, seemingly oblivious of the fact that Oursler had come to him with a certain urgency. Finally, Oursler seized on a brief pause in the monologue. He began to explain that he had just returned form the Bahamas on assignment from *Liberty* magazine. The Bahamas' present governor, the Duke of Windsor, formerly England's Edward VIII, who had abdicated his throne to marry the American divorcée Wallis Simpson had previously refused interviews. Oursler had scored a scoop, not only getting an interview, but also stumbling into something that could shake the warring world.

To Americans, Windsor was the ever-boyish prince charming who had enchanted the country during his 1924 visit to the United States. A popular song of the day ran, "I danced with a man who danced with a girl who danced with the Prince of Wales." America's affection had been increased by the sheer romance of a monarch who chose love over power. To British insiders, however, beginning with the Prime Minister, the duke's behavior since departing the throne was embarrassing, possibly treasonous. After his abdication, Windsor had gone to live with his wife in France, and while there he made a visit to Germany in October 1937, ostensibly to study housing and working conditions. He wanted to learn, he said, how Britain could benefit from what he considered a model Nazi program. What particularly pleased him during this tour was that German officials referred to his wife as "Her Royal Highness," words she would never hear in the British Isles. The high point of the trip had been an invitation to Berchtesgaden to spend the day with Hitler, who impressed the duke with what he had done to root out communism in Germany.

When the war broke out, Windsor was chagrined to be appointed only a major general with vague liaison duties at French army headquarters. As king, he had carried the rank of field marshal. Winston Churchill, a cultural, if not always a political Tory, had staunchly stood by Edward VIII during the abdication crisis. But as prime minister, knowing the duke's admiration for Germany, even with Britain now at war, Churchill found Edward troublesome. After France fell, the former king expected the Prime Minister to offer him a position of real substance back home, which Churchill knew was impossible. His presence in England would prove awkward for the present king, Edward's brother, George VI.

On July 9, 1940, through the "former Naval person" channel established between Churchill and Roosevelt, the Prime Minister notified FDR of how he proposed to handle the sensitive royal. He wanted the President to know his solution before it became public. "The position of the Duke of Windsor on the Continent in recent months," Churchill wrote, "has been causing His Majesty and His Majesty's government some embarrassment as, though his loyalties are unimpeachable, there is always a backwash of Nazi intrigue which seeks now that the greater part of the Continent is in enemy hands to make trouble about him. There are personal and family difficulties about his return to this country." Churchill had a solution. He had offered Edward the governorship of the Bahamas, and "His Royal Highness has intimated that he will accept the appointment." Privately, the Prime Minister was more blunt. His intention was to keep Windsor "out of Hitler's grasp," which was not proving easy. The duke and duchess had gone to Lisbon in preparation for their departure to the Bahamas and showed scant inclination to leave. The Germans were just as eager to keep

Windsor in Europe, assigning a key intelligence officer, Walter Schellenberg, this mission. The objective was to have this friend of Germany returned to the British throne that he had abdicated. The Germans made clear that, unlike the British, they were ready to recognize Wallis as queen. While the duke dithered in Lisbon as the guest of a rich Portuguese banker, Ricardo Santo Silva, German intelligence agents filed back to Berlin every anti-war, anti-Churchill, even anti–royal family remark that Windsor made. Finally, and reluctantly, the duke and his wife boarded a British warship for the Bahamas. Prior to leaving, he gave his Portuguese host, Silva, a code word to be used when the time was ripe for him to return to Europe.

Upon his arrival in his much reduced realm, Windsor began pestering Churchill, a man leading a nation at war, about perquisites for his new office. With millions of Britons answering the colors and falling in battle, Edward insisted on draft exemptions for his servants. He wanted a Navy ship assigned for his personal use. Churchill, his patience stretched thin, telegraphed the duke that even major generals could be court-martialed.

Franklin Roosevelt still felt warmly toward British royals. He once confided to a friend that he had been hurt when, in his visit to England during the First World War, he had not been invited to Buckingham Palace. He considered it one of his social peaks when King George and Queen Mary accepted his invitation to visit the Roosevelt family seat, at Hyde Park. Eleven days before Fulton Oursler's arrival at the White House, FDR had himself entertained the Duke of Windsor. The President had boarded the USS *Tuscaloosa* at Miami for a ten-day pleasure cruise, and was joined briefly by Edward, who had accompanied his wife to Florida for her dental work. Windsor met a fit, beaming FDR, relieved of burdens and refreshed by days of fishing, nights of poker, and watching movies aboard ship. FDR saw a smiling, sleek Edward, well garbed and well tanned, a startling contrast to his beleaguered countrymen still undergoing the Blitz. As Daisy Suckley described the duke, "Windsor is completely insignificant looking but charming and quick. . . . You can't help liking him and feeling sorry because he is an exile from home and country. . . . His wife, a completely unscrupulous woman, as is proved by her past life, does, however, seem to keep his devotion and make him happy."

Now, days later, Oursler was in the White House, uneasy but convinced that he must tell the President about his own encounter with Windsor. "Mr. President," Oursler said, "I am perfectly aware that there is more than a slight air of the preposterous about what I have to tell you, but it is all factual." The story had begun on December 13 with Oursler's arrival with his wife, Grace, and daughter, April, at the British Colonial Hotel in the Bahamas. After initially being turned down, the journalist finally won an interview with the duke. Oursler received word to present himself at Government House in Nassau at 6 P.M. the next day. Upon his arrival, he was led up a wooden stairway and through a large ballroom whose sole contents appeared to be mountains of luggage that the duke and duchess had brought from Europe. Windsor, in a checked sportcoat, received Oursler in a recently refurbished drawing room. He spoke amiably of how splendid it had been to be back, however briefly, in the United States. Life in Nassau, he said, was like living in a village.

Oursler was not long into his interview before the duke began asking *him* questions. He wanted to know if the journalist thought America should get into the war. Oursler, at that stage an isolationist, answered no. The duke's expression seemed to suggest that Oursler had passed a test, and he began to speak more openly. He warned his visitor, "there was no such thing in modern warfare as victory," for one side. "The German armies," he went on, "had never been defeated in 1914–1918." The home front had collapsed behind them. He next explained to a stunned Oursler, "[I]t would be a tragic thing for the world if Hitler were overthrown. Hitler was the right and logical leader of the German people." He considered Adolf Hitler a great man. The duke leaned forward, shooting his head out like a turtle's from its shell, close to Oursler's face. "Do you suppose that your President would consider intervening as a mediator when, and if, the proper time arrives?" he asked. Britain was being destroyed, and the time was coming, he said, "when a man like your President must stop this war. I am not a defeatist but I am realistic." The duke mentioned his recent visit with FDR on the *Tuscaloosa,* but told Oursler that he had said nothing to Roosevelt of what they were now discussing. Instead, he and the President had talked of economic development for the Caribbean islands.

After two hours, a shaken Oursler left the duke. The next morning, as he was packing to return home, Windsor's aide-de-camp, Captain Vyvyan Drury, phoned asking if he might come to Oursler's hotel. Upon his arrival, Drury began a recitation of the duke's sad plight. Anthony Eden, Churchill's foreign minister, hated him. So did Lord Halifax, Eden's predecessor, and Lord Lothian as well. Drury asked Oursler, "Would you enter into a Machiavellian conspiracy?" Oursler nodded noncommittally, not wanting to turn off a source. "Tell Mr. Roosevelt," Drury went on, "that if he will make an offer of intervention for peace, that before anyone in England can oppose it, the Duke of Windsor will instantly issue a statement supporting it and that will start a revolution and force peace." Drury warned Oursler that if he should betray the duke's confidences to him in print, "the lid would be blown off the British Empire."

Oursler recognized that Windsor had used Drury as a mouthpiece to provide himself a wall of deniability. What the aide had passed along was obviously what the duke wanted Oursler to tell FDR. Thus, upon his return to New York, the journalist had asked for the White House appointment.

Oursler had barely begun reciting his experience in the Bahamas to the President when FDR broke in. "Fulton," he said, "nothing can surprise me these days. Why, do you know that I am amazed to find some of the greatest people in the British Empire, men of the so-called upper classes, men of the highest rank, secretly want to appease Hitler and stop the war." The President's knowing smile told Oursler that Roosevelt knew all about his conversation with the duke. British agents in the Bahamas, well aware of Windsor's defeatist sympathies, had eavesdropped on the talk, reported it to the British embassy in Washington, which in turn informed FDR. The President continued to monopolize the conversation, surprising Oursler with the depth and strength of his opinions about the duke and the British peace crowd. He finally stopped long enough to let Oursler tell what had happened to him in Nassau. Though he already knew the content of the duke's tête-à-tête with the journalist, the very mention of the ex-monarch's machinations rekindled FDR's wrath. "He could barely listen to the words that I spoke," Oursler recalled. "He looked away. His hands trembled. His whole body shook." "When Little Windsor says he doesn't think there should be a revolution in Germany, I tell you, Fulton," FDR exploded, "I would rather have April's opinion on that than his."

When he calmed down, the President suggested to Oursler how he should handle the duke's request that he intervene. "Why don't you just be a good come-on guy? That's good Americanism," the President advised. He lit a cigarette and, to the journalist's surprise, tilted back the great, handsome head and began to dictate exactly what Oursler should reply to Captain Drury for the duke's benefit. He should say, "On my way home from Florida, I stopped off in Washington and had a talk with my friend. His answer to my conversation was that in Washington today everything is on a twenty-four-hour basis and no man has the gift of being able to read the future. If you have anything else in mind, let me know." FDR wanted this intelligence source to keep pumping. When he finished dictating, Oursler asked the question that had gone begging. Why had not Windsor himself asked the President to broker a peace when the two were together

on the *Tuscaloosa*? FDR laughed and explained that during the visit he had
employed his tactic for not hearing what he did not want to hear by domi-
nating the conversation. "I would not let him," he told Oursler. "The nearest we came to discussing the War was when I praised the courage and
fighting spirit of the British people. . . ." The President then repeated to
Oursler the one thing he had told Windsor: "You know your father was a
Navy man. You ought to have heard him express his opinion of the Germans. He used every short word known to a sailor." The duke made a feeble attempt to answer, then trailed off, FDR recalled.

Roosevelt then revealed how well aware he was of Windsor's indiscretions. "Everyday from the offices of the Prime Minister in Downing Street,
there would be brought to the King a dispatch box," he told Oursler. "It
was the same thing as a briefcase except that it was made of wood and lacquered and locked. These were the most confidential papers of the Empire." FDR told how one day when the Prime Minister came to the king's
retreat at Fort Belvedere, he found Britain's topmost secrets strewn about
the piano for anyone to see, "especially," the President added with a jaundiced eye, "Mrs. Simpson," at the time the king's mistress. Wallis, FDR
pointed out, was regarded as chummy with Joachim von Ribbentrop,
Hitler's ambassador to Britain. The President also knew all about the
duke's behavior while serving as a liaison officer between the British and
French forces. "He was there at the most intimate councils of the com-
manders-in-chief of these two armies." Noting that Windsor passed back
and forth from the front to Paris, FDR said, "Now I have nothing to prove
what I am going to say, but I do know that there were nine shortwave wireless sets in Paris constantly sending information to the German troops, and
no one has ever been able to decide how such accurate information could
be sent over these wireless stations." Oursler, already reeling from the
President's confidences, now had heard FDR virtually brand the former
king of England as a German spy. Roosevelt added with amused contempt,
"They couldn't send him to the Fiji Islands because he wouldn't go
there. . . . Then [the Windsors] wouldn't go to Jamaica; too far away. But
the Bahamas were close to the United States. Now and then they could go
over to Miami and mingle with the night club crowds they so enjoy."

Whether Oursler ever dispatched the President's suggested message or
any other reply to the Bahamas is unknown. He did publish an article in
Liberty magazine, quoting the duke as saying, "You cannot kill eighty million Germans and since they want Hitler, how can you force them into a
revolution they don't want?" But Oursler never mentioned a word of

Windsor's peace overture, fearing that knowledge of their former king's German sympathies would sow serious upheaval in Britain, as Captain Drury had warned. His sixteen-page account of his meeting with the duke and FDR was tucked away and not published until fifty years later by his son, Fulton Oursler Jr.

The Oursler episode reveals several strands in the President's makeup: his spongelike absorption of information, his highly personal reactions to the players in the drama, his disinterest in supporting anything short of the defeat of Hitler, even while America was neutral, and the clear distinction he drew between the symbolic role of those who wore the ermine and their actual character. Though his contempt for "Little Windsor" as a royal twerp was obvious, he rarely passed up an opportunity to consort with him. Nearly a year later, on October 21, 1941, with all his other appointments canceled because of the death the day before of Eleanor's brother Hall Roosevelt, the President nevertheless entertained the Duke and Duchess of Windsor at lunch in the White House. He then took them on a tour of the second-floor living quarters. The duke's sympathies had not altered. At about the time of this visit, he wrote his friend Silva back in Lisbon, "Britain has virtually lost the war already and the U.S.A. would be better advised to promote peace not war." The duke was to be a guest of the President at the White House or Hyde Park on eight more occasions before FDR's death. On none of these visits, however agreeable the company, did Roosevelt allow any serious conversation to intrude.

Chapter VI

"There Is No U.S. Secret Intelligence Service"

FRANK KNOX'S championing of Bill Donovan continued. In December 1940, while FDR was hosting the Duke of Windsor and listening to Fulton Oursler's startling account of the duke's peace meddling, Knox was asking the President to approve a second Donovan mission abroad. The idea's origins are clouded by counterclaims. Donovan would later maintain that the President "asked me if I would go and make a strategic appreciation from an economic, political, and military standpoint of the Mediterranean area." This stretches the President's approval of the trip to initiation of it. The seed was more likely sown by Bill Stephenson of British intelligence. The trail leading to the second journey appears to have run from Stephenson urging Donovan, to Donovan persuading Knox, to Knox convincing FDR. Supporting this explanation is the fact that Donovan's way was paid for by the British secret service. Early in December, Ruth Donovan again said good-bye to her peripatetic husband as he and Stephenson boarded a plane for London. He would be gone, Bill told her, over Christmas and New Year's and likely for months.

Donovan at the time was fifty-seven and Stephenson forty-four. As fellow heroes of the first war, they scarcely felt the age difference, and the two men had grown close. Donovan was tall, approaching the portly, and Stephenson short and slight. Their associates thus began to refer to "Big

Bill" and "Little Bill." They stopped en route at Bermuda, where Stephenson brought Big Bill into the secret operation that Vincent Astor had shared in, the opening of pouches of presumably inviolable diplomatic mail from dozens of countries. In pursuit of his assignment to draw the United States into the war, Stephenson showed Donovan an intercepted message supposedly revealing that Nazi fifth columnists were preparing to seize the southern half of the Western Hemisphere.

Thanks to Stephenson's preparing the way, Donovan arrived in England with his stock soaring. On December 17, the permanent undersecretary of state, Sir Alexander Cadogan, wrote to the Foreign Office: "[Colonel Stewart Menzies] tells me that Mr. Stephenson, who travelled over with Colonel Donovan, has impressed upon him that the latter really exercises a vast degree of influence in the administration. He has Colonel Knox in his pocket and, as Mr. Stephenson puts it, has more influence with the President than Colonel House had with Mr. [Woodrow] Wilson." The latter claim no doubt would have amazed FDR.

Given his inflated rapport with the President, Donovan had no trouble securing another appointment with Winston Churchill. Almost immediately upon his arrival, the Prime Minister invited Donovan to lunch at 10 Downing Street. On the night before, and on the day of their luncheon, the Prime Minister ordered RAF strikes on the German industrial center of Mannheim. The message was not lost on Donovan. Britain could dish it out as well as take it. During their talk, however, Churchill stated that Britain could not survive bloodletting on the scale of the first war, which had cost the empire over a million dead. He took Donovan to a map and pointed out what he described as Germany's soft underbelly, the Mediterranean and the Balkans, where he preferred to fight. Donovan, who during World War I had witnessed the slaughter Churchill described, was sympathetic if not necessarily in agreement. Before leaving, he explained that MI6 had asked him to make a tour of the Middle East. Splendid idea, Churchill agreed. No sooner had Donovan left Downing Street than the Prime Minister instructed his field commanders and overseas intelligence stations to open all doors to their American visitor. Donovan was to be "taken fully into our confidence," he ordered, as he had "great influence with the President."

On New Year's Eve 1940, Donovan, wearing a long sheepskin trench coat he had bought at Cordings in Piccadilly, boarded a four-engine Sunderland reconnaissance flying boat at Plymouth Sound. As he settled in, a crewman presented him with a hamper of delicacies that defied wartime rationing—fresh lobster, cold pheasant, Stilton cheese, turtle soup, three bottles of Moselle, all courtesy of Lord Louis Mountbatten, to mark Donovan's fifty-eighth birthday. He was off to a glowing start. He had won Churchill's confidence. Admiral Godfrey, the director of British naval intelligence, advised Admiral Andrew Cunningham, commander in chief of the Mediterranean Fleet, concerning his imminent guest, "It was Donovan who was responsible for getting us the destroyers, the bombsight and other urgent requirements. . . . There is no doubt that we can achieve infinitely more through Donovan than any other individual. . . ."

His Mediterranean odyssey took Donovan to Spain, Malta, Egypt, Palestine, Iraq, Bulgaria, Yugoslavia, Libya, and, on his way home, to the land of his forebears, Ireland. He had listened with his steady, blue-eyed gaze to generals, admirals, princes, sheikhs, spies, kings, and politicians during seventy-eight days of near-constant motion, exhausting much younger escorts. He was back in America on March 18, 1941. Frank Knox immediately called the White House and spoke to the President's aide Pa Watson. He wanted to make sure that FDR saw Donovan before Roosevelt left the next day for a cruise on the presidential yacht, *Potomac*. By now, FDR had also received a cable from Churchill that read, "I must thank you for the magnificent work done by Donovan in his prolonged tour of Balkans and Middle East. He has carried with him throughout an animating, heart-warming flame." Despite this endorsement, FDR told Watson to schedule only fifteen minutes for Donovan to report on his two-and-a-half-month journey.

At nine-thirty the next morning, Donovan, accompanied by Knox, arrived at the White House. They joined FDR and his alter ego, Harry Hopkins, a man so pale and fleshless, yet so lively in spirit, that he resembled an animated corpse. Hopkins, the onetime social worker and New Deal troubleshooter, lived in the White House, occupying a large bedroom with a huge four-poster bed, the room in which Abraham Lincoln had signed the Emancipation Proclamation. His presence suggested that the President had given the meeting a certain weight. Yet, while Donovan was bursting to tell what he had learned in the Mediterranean war zone, the President launched into what an aide described as "wildly irrelevant" talk. The fifteen-minute session grew into a full hour. Still, Donovan managed to report little as the meeting petered out in FDR's ramblings. Though it appeared that Roosevelt was only talking and not listening, another level of that multi-tiered mind had been hatching an idea.

On April 4, two weeks after seeing Knox and Donovan, the President summoned his cabinet. He was still unhappy with the muddled state of U.S. intelligence. "Disputes were settled in Great Britain," he noted, "by a gentleman known as 'Mr. X,' whose identity was kept a complete secret." He was contemplating "a similar solution for our country in case we got into war." FDR had confused the code names. Rather than Mr. X, he was actually referring to "C," Stewart Menzies, head of Britain's MI6. The cabinet members could only guess at who the President had in mind for his "C"—Vincent Astor, J. Edgar Hoover, Adolf Berle, possibly another recent candidate, New York City's Mayor Fiorello La Guardia, or Bill Donovan? Of John Franklin Carter, they knew nothing.

Donovan, though his earlier dream to train troops had aborted, still insisted that his only wish was to command "the toughest division in the whole outfit." But when Frank Knox suggested after the cabinet meeting that Donovan write out his ideas about how American intelligence should be organized, the man leaped to the task. By April 26, Donovan had delivered to Knox a four-page memorandum laying out how a spy service should operate, the first enunciation of an American central intelligence agency. He made no claim to originality. His model was based on the way "the British government gathers its intelligence," he admitted. Donovan urged an organization above partisan politics to be headed by "some one appointed by the President directly responsible to him and to no one else," and secretly funded. He was sufficiently sensitive to prevailing turf wars to add that the proposed agency should not "take over the home duties now performed by the F.B.I., nor the intelligence organizations of the Army and the Navy." Yet, he wanted to confine them and urged that his envisioned agency have "sole charge of intelligence work abroad." A pleased Knox forwarded Donovan's plan to FDR.

During the cabinet meeting at which the President had favored centralizing intelligence under a "Mr. X," Henry Stimson had taken notes that he later showed to General Marshall. Marshall, in turn, asked General Sherman Miles, his assistant chief of staff for intelligence, his opinion of the President's idea. Miles's riposte was swift. He had already learned from a London source that while in England, Donovan had inquired of British intelligence officials how they dealt with the constitutional and legal quandaries raised by clandestine operations, how secret enterprises were financed, in short, how a nation spied. Miles advised Marshall, "In great confidence O.N.I. tells me . . . there is a movement afoot, fostered by Col. Donovan, to establish a super agency controlling *all* intelligence. This would mean that such an agency, no doubt under Col. Donovan, would collect, collate and possibly evaluate all military intelligence that we now gather from foreign countries. From the point of view of the War Department, such a move would appear to be very disadvantageous, if not calamitous." Miles had no immediate cause for concern. In the Roosevelt fashion, it would take a ferment of circumstances, time, place, and his own mood before the President would act.

In the meantime, the British mounted an intense campaign to enlist the United States in an intelligence partnership. Along with Little Bill Stephenson, Donovan had made another friend as a result of his efforts to get the overage American destroyers for the Royal Navy, the director of British naval intelligence, Admiral John Godfrey. In late May the admiral, accompanied by Commander Ian Fleming, the future creator of James Bond, left England on a secret mission to draw America into Britain's intelligence web. They arrived in civilian dress aboard the commercial aircraft *Dixie Clipper,* hoping to make an anonymous entrance. They were appalled to be greeted by a horde of reporters, cameramen, and popping flashbulbs. They were much relieved to find that all the attention was meant for Elsa Schiaparelli, the fashion designer. Admiral Godfrey then proceeded to an elegant address on New York's Sutton Place, where he was to be the guest at the home of the man he intended to use as his instrument in forging a British-U.S. espionage alliance, Bill Donovan.

Later, when the admiral and Fleming moved from New York to Washington, they were appalled to discover the low state of American intelligence. After dealing with the fragmented bureaucracies, Godfrey reported to London, "Even the more senior U.S. Navy, Military and State Department officials . . . prefer their intelligence to be highly coloured. For instance, the Navy Department's estimate of the size of the German U-boat fleet is higher than our own by approximately one third, while the War Department's estimates of the first line strength and first line reserves of the German Air Force are higher than ours by 250%. This predilection for sensationalism hinders the reasoned evaluation of intelligence reports." As for cooperation between ONI, MID, and the FBI, it was, he noted, practically nonexistent. "These three departments showed the utmost goodwill towards me and Ian Fleming but very little towards each other." Jealous and competitive, the Americans operated on the premise that knowledge is power, but that knowledge shared is power diluted. Godfrey's final verdict: "There is no U.S. Secret Intelligence Service. Americans are inclined to refer to their 'S.I.S.,' but by this they mean the small and uncoordinated force of 'Special Agents' who travel abroad on behalf of one or another of the Governmental Departments. These 'Agents' are, for the most part, amateurs without special qualifications and without training in Observation. They have no special means of communication or other facilities and they seldom have clearer brief than 'to go and have a look.' " Godfrey agreed with those Americans he met who said that a better source of intelligence was *The New York Times,* which was faster, better informed, more accurate, more objective, and cost, at the time, pennies a copy. Godfrey decided that he must ring an alarm directly in the Oval Office. But gaining entry proved a problem.

While Admiral Godfrey was trying to see Roosevelt, FDR was looking for an opportunity to alert the nation that he intended to bring the United States a giant step closer to alliance with Britain. He had been moving in that direction from the day the war began, largely through his secret correspondence with Churchill. Eight months after hostilities started, he had used a commencement address at the University of Virginia in Charlottesville to make clear where he stood. Before a jammed Memorial Gymnasium, wearing an academic gown and a mortarboard at a jaunty angle, he condemned Hitler's ally, Benito Mussolini, for declaring war on a collapsing France. "On this tenth day of June, 1940," he intoned, "the hand that held the dagger has struck it into the back of its neighbor." Churchill, listening to the radio in the Admiralty, was struck by the President's political courage. "I wondered about the Italian vote in the approaching presidential election," he later wrote; "but I knew that Roosevelt was a most experienced American party politician. . . ." More gratifying to Churchill was what Roosevelt said next: "We will extend to the opponents of force the material resources of this nation." *Time* magazine reported afterward: "With this speech, the U.S. had taken sides. Ended was the myth of U.S. neutrality." But these had been only fine words from a nation whose own defenses were still puny, and by a president who did not know exactly how far he dared get ahead of public opinion. At the time he addressed the Virginia graduates, the U.S. Army ranked eighteenth in the world. It was not only weaker than the major powers—Germany, France, Britain, Russia, Italy, Japan, and China—but outstripped by Belgium, the Netherlands, Portugal, Spain, Sweden, even tiny Switzerland. Germany had 6.8 million men under arms, the United States 504,000. The country lacked an arms industry. Its productive capacity was invested in the output of cars, washing machines, and refrigerators, in all of which it was the world leader.

However relatively weak the nation, FDR was determined to share whatever he could to shore up Britain. To him, England's plight was not something discovered solely in Churchill's cables or the cold assessments of his military analysts, but a highly personal matter. He had an English friend who dated back to his youthful trips abroad, Arthur Murray, a business executive and former member of Parliament. The two regarded themselves as distantly related. During the Blitz, Murray's wife wrote, "Dear Mr. President (Cousin Franklin) . . . I am going this afternoon to sort out . . . bundles of warm clothes for the children and women who have been evacuated. . . . This is the first few names on my list; John Hodson (aged 10) one parent killed in air raid, other missing; George Elton (aged 12) mother killed, father in army abroad; Elsie Burrey (age 7) both parents killed; Harry Young, mother missing, father killed at Dunkirk. And the list goes on."

His visceral conviction that Britain's fight was America's fight had led FDR to take the daring step in September of giving the British the fifty old destroyers before Congress had a chance to say no. But it was not enough. As 1940 drew to a close, Churchill had sent FDR a letter arriving on December 9 that spelled out Britain's peril. After a depressing inventory of British losses from the Blitz—the plants destroyed, the arms lost, the ships sunk by U-boats—he laid bare his country's plight: Britain was going broke. "The moment approaches where we shall no longer be able to pay cash for shipping and other supplies." Roosevelt wanted both to save Britain from collapse and buy time for the United States to rearm. But, as a neutral, how did he surmount the tangle of obstacles, the reluctance of commercial interests to loan money to a sinking ship, the congressional resistance to outright gifts? The answer came about in Rooseveltian fashion, in another gestation discernible nowhere but in the President's mind. As Harry Hopkins put it, "I began to get the idea that he was refueling, the way he so often does when he seems to be resting and carefree. . . . Then, one evening, he suddenly came out with it—the whole program. He didn't seem to have any clear idea how it could be done legally. But there wasn't a doubt in his mind that he'd find a way to do it." FDR would simply circumvent the obstacles in his path through a device of ingenious simplicity. The United States would send Britain weapons and supplies without charge. Then, after the war, the British could pay for them or return them. The program, passed by Congress and signed by the President on March 11, 1941, was called lend-lease.

An impatient President next wanted to press aid to Britain beyond lend-lease. The only question was how rapidly he dared move. On April 11, with Hitler's Wehrmacht triumphing in Yugoslavia, Greece, and North Africa,

Roosevelt initiated a secret operation. He informed the man who held the purse strings for him, budget director Harold Smith, to find money to covertly finance American patrols to protect British shipping in the Atlantic. He shared his intentions with only four members of his cabinet because, as he put it, the rest "could not keep their mouths shut." On April 10, Henry Stimson, among those trusted, confided to his diary that he had spent "a very long day at the White House. . . . The President had evidently been thinking," he wrote, "how far he could go toward the direction [of] the protection of the British transport line. He had made up his mind that it was too dangerous to ask the Congress for the power to convoy." Roosevelt feared that if such a resolution were pressed now it would probably be defeated. From the heaps of books and papers cluttering his office, the President asked Stimson to hand him his favorite atlas. He opened it to the Atlantic, and drew a pencil down a vertical line between the easternmost bulge of Brazil and the westernmost bulge of Africa, at roughly longitude 25 degrees. "He is trying to see how far over in the direction of Great Britain we could get," Stimson later wrote in his diary. "His plan is then that we shall patrol the high seas west of this median line, so that they will be within our area." In the President's scheme, American planes and ships would accompany the British convoys and alert them to the presence of German raiders or submarines. Soon after the meeting with Stimson, FDR quietly informed a delighted Churchill of this extended support for Britain. And a stretch it was. By executive fiat, FDR had swept Iceland and Greenland, over twenty-one hundred miles from the U.S. border, into the Americas, no different from Cuba, Argentina, or Peru, just as he had done earlier with the Azores.

Admiral Harold Stark, the Chief of Naval Operations, had become accustomed to being summoned to the White House at odd hours. FDR's performance invariably mesmerized him. He once told an interviewer: "When we were squidging as far as we could in North American waters," FDR produced books "to prove that Iceland was in the western hemisphere. . . . I don't think anyone could equal him. He could sit and plot all the towns that would be passed on a flight down Brazil and over to India." When the Navy, on FDR's flimsy authority, was ordered to build a chain of offshore bases, Stark complained to Roosevelt, "I'm breaking all the laws." Roosevelt replied, "That's all right Betty [Stark's unlikely nickname], we'll go to jail together."

On April 24 the President closeted himself with Stimson and Knox to consider how best to explain his increasingly bellicose posture to the

American people. Stimson was struck by the sinuosity of the President's thought processes. FDR kept referring to the new patrol policy as "principally a defensive measure," saying that the force in the Atlantic was merely going to patrol, looking out for any aggressors and reporting them. After hearing this semantic wiggle several times, Stimson interjected with a bemused smile, "But you are not going to report the presence of the German fleet to the Americas. You are going to report it to the British fleet." After leaving the White House that day, Stimson wrote in his diary of the President's latest gambit, "He seems to be trying to hide it into the character of a purely reconnaissance action which it really is not."

The next day, the President had a press conference scheduled, and Stimson urged him to level with the reporters if the patrol issue came up. When the question was indeed raised, FDR stuck by his story. "Now this is a patrol, and has been a patrol for a year and a half, still is, and from time to time has been extended," the President explained, "for the safety of the Western Hemisphere." He made no mention of the patrols passing intelligence on German naval movements to British warships.

Henry Stimson had one constituency and one duty, the country's armed forces and their state of preparedness. FDR had a nationwide constituency that ran from isolationists to interventionists, and he had to gauge just how far he dared get ahead of the public. Indeed, when a month after the press conference, a German submarine sank an American freighter, the *Robin Moor,* in the South Atlantic but outside the patrol zone, the President made the required rhetorical fuss, branding the attack piracy, demanding compensation from Germany, and kicking German consular staffs out of the country. But he did not make of the matter another *Lusitania.*

On May 24 an event at sea forced FDR's combative streak back to the surface. He was informed that the German pocket battleship *Bismarck* had escaped British attackers and was headed toward the Americas. FDR considered the maneuver a threat to U.S. security. His aide Sam Rosenman has described the President's quandary regarding the *Bismarck:* "Should he order submarines to attack it? What would the people say if he did? There would obviously not be enough time to ask Congress." The British navy solved the President's dilemma when, on May 26, it sank the *Bismarck* far closer to France than to the United States.

The President, however, was not appeased. To him, the incident underscored the *potential* of Nazi aggression against the Americas. He summoned Rosenman and Robert Sherwood, a three-time Pulitzer Prize–winning dramatist, and said that he wanted them to help him write a tough speech to be delivered at the Pan American Union, where he was scheduled to speak on May 27, commemorating Pan American Day. One day after the *Bismarck* went to the bottom, FDR, in black tie, his brow moist with sweat on one of the steamiest days of the year, was wheeled into the East Room of the White House to address an audience of Latin American diplomats and their spouses. The occasion was customarily marked by boilerplate paeans to hemispheric solidarity. It quickly became apparent that this speech, which only the trusted Grace Tully had been allowed to type, was not primarily intended for the Latin Americans seated on gilded chairs in the room. The Roosevelt voice, at once commanding yet intimate, was being heard by some eighty-five million people over radio. FDR came quickly to the point. "[W]hat started as a European war has developed, as the Nazis always intended it should develop, into a world war for world domination. No, I am not speculating about this," he went on. "I merely repeat what is already in the Nazi book of world conquest. They plan to treat the Latin American nations as they are now treating the Balkans. They plan to strangle the United States." He portrayed a Nazi octopus, its tentacles already enveloping Europe, now stretching across North Africa toward the Suez Canal and capable of reaching the Azores and Cape Verde Islands in the Atlantic only "seven hours distance from Brazil" for modern bombers.

The President shared with his audience an intense debate going on behind the scenes. In their secret correspondence, Churchill had confided to Roosevelt that German submarines were sinking ships faster than Britain could replace them. American military chiefs had been dead set against FDR's revealing to the Germans how well their wolf pack strategy was working. Furthermore, they feared that by publicly discussing German naval operations, British codebreaking successes might be compromised. FDR overruled his chiefs. He assumed that German submariners kept a fairly accurate tally of their scores. More important than protecting secrecy was to substantiate his claim that the wolf packs were a menace to the United States and to arouse the American people from their complacency. And so he told his perspiring, brow-mopping audience, "The blunt truth is this—and I reveal this with the full knowledge of the British government, the present rate of Nazi sinking of merchant ships is more than three times as high as the capacity of British shipyards to replace them; it is more than twice the combined British and American output of merchant ships today. . . . We shall give every possible assistance to Britain and to all who, with Britain, are resisting Hitlerism." He continued, "Our patrols are helping now to insure delivery of the needed supplies to Britain. All additional measures necessary to deliver the goods will be taken." America's situation had changed, the President declared. Until now, the war in Europe had required only a "limited" national emergency. That stage was over. He now proclaimed, "an unlimited national emergency exists."

After the speech, FDR retreated to the Monroe Room, where he was joined by Harry Hopkins and Robert Sherwood, who had brought along the songwriter Irving Berlin. Sam Rosenman had always been impressed by FDR's capacity to shift gears instantly. "The President was able to relax completely, or the job would have killed him earlier," Rosenman noted. "He was an expert at dividing his day into periods of work and play, of excitement and relaxation, of importance and minutiae." That evening, setting aside the significant step he had taken with his speech, FDR asked Berlin to play the piano for him. He wanted to hear the composer's first big hit, "Alexander's Ragtime Band." Berlin complied, continuing with an impromptu concert of his other favorites. Afterward, a beaming President retired to his bedroom. Sherwood popped in to say good night and found FDR still in high spirits. He was blanketed under almost a thousand telegrams. "They're ninety-five per cent favorable," he grinned. "And I figured I'd be lucky to get an even break on this speech." In Vichy France, FDR's ambassador, Admiral William Leahy, saw the speech as more than increased preparedness. To the admiral, whose association with FDR preceded World War I, the President had declared war against Hitler.

For all FDR's charges of a German threat, the truth was that Hitler still hoped to avoid a conflict with America. He had issued his navy strict orders against sinking American ships. He had no intention of attacking either North or South America. That spring, his eye had turned in the opposite direction, toward the East. Nevertheless, FDR continued to believe in the genuineness of a Nazi threat. One consequence was his warming to the idea of an American intelligence agency, thus far the unsuccessful objective of Admiral Godfrey. The admiral had spent two weeks in Washington plotting how to place his case before FDR. Finally, he found an opening wedge. A fellow Briton, Sir William Wiseman, who had been chief of British intelligence in America during World War I, knew the publisher of *The New York Times,* Arthur Hays Sulzberger, who was persuaded to intercede on Godfrey's behalf. Thereafter, the admiral was invited to dinner at the White House, and promised an hour alone with the President afterward.

Godfrey and Ian Fleming had been doing their homework, meeting with Bill Donovan at his Georgetown townhouse to help him draft a "Memorandum of Establishment of Service of Strategic Information." The draft began: "Strategy, without information upon which it can rely, is helpless. Likewise, information is useless unless it is intelligently directed to the strategic purpose." The United States clearly lacked an instrument to implement this logic of warfare. "Our mechanism of collecting information is inadequate," the paper continued. The potential enemy surely did not make that mistake: "It is unimaginable that Germany would engage in a $7 billion supply program without first studying in detail the productive capacity of her actual and potential enemies. It is because she does this that she displays such a mastery in the secrecy, timing and effectiveness of her attacks." The United States must establish "a coordinator of strategic information, who would be responsible directly to the President." The plan also heeded Donovan's earlier concern: ". . . [T]he proposed centralized unit will neither displace nor encroach upon the FBI, Army and Navy Intelligence, or any other department of the Government." Again, aping the British pattern, Donovan's draft noted: ". . . [T]here is another element in modern warfare, and that is the psychological attack against the moral and spiritual defenses of a nation. In this attack, the most powerful weapon is radio."

Donovan was later to claim that he had submitted his ideas for an intelligence agency at Roosevelt's request. However, he had a penchant for making stories come out the way he wanted, ex post facto. Frank Knox was still Donovan's eager advocate and continued to bewail the failure of the administration to use his friend's talents. He told Supreme Court Justice Felix Frankfurter, "I am getting to be a little sensitive about urging him because it looks as if I were trying to find something for him to do, which is not the case." FDR continued to perpetuate the notion that he had been close to Donovan; but Knox's failure thus far to win a substantial berth for the man stemmed from a long ago collision. In 1932, Donovan had been the unsuccessful Republican candidate to succeed FDR as governor of New York while Roosevelt was running for the presidency. Donovan had vigorously attacked FDR during the campaign and became a vocal critic of the New Deal afterward.

The Donovan memorandum reached the President's desk with exquisite timing, on June 10, the very day that Admiral Godfrey was urging FDR both to get into the intelligence game and to name Donovan America's spymaster. Sir William Wiseman had warned Admiral Godfrey about FDR's conversational ploys. Godfrey went to the White House knowing that Roosevelt "would almost certainly pull my leg and make some provocative remark about the British, or Imperialism, and that I must on no account allow myself to get cross (or 'mad' as the Americans say)." FDR lived up to his billing. During dinner, he asked how Godfrey had traveled to the United States. When the admiral answered that he had come via Bermuda, Roosevelt retorted, "Oh yes, those West Indies Islands. We're going to show you how to look after them, and not only you but the Portuguese and Dutch. Every nigger will have his two acres and a sugar patch." Godfrey was known to have a short fuse, but managed to ignore the taunt and "mustered up the semblance of a laugh." Dinner was followed by what Godfrey described as "a rather creepy, crawly film" about snakes.

The admiral did get his private hour with the President. FDR began by reminiscing about his visit to London in the last war and his admiration for Blinker Hall, Godfrey's predecessor. Again the President jabbed: "Hall had a wonderful intelligence service but I don't suppose it's much good now." Godfrey bit his tongue, and listened while Roosevelt nostalgically recalled Blinker Hall's revealing to him the exploits of British spies sneaking in and out of Germany. Godfrey was astonished to find that after nearly a quarter of a century, Roosevelt still swallowed the concoctions that Hall had fed him. When he finally had a chance to get in a word, he urged FDR to create "one intelligence security boss, not three or four." And the person most qualified, he said, was William J. Donovan. FDR noncommittally resumed his reminiscing, and Godfrey left the White House doubtful that he had made a sale.

The President had already offered Donovan a job before Godfrey's visit, not as America's intelligence chief, but a position that had to have offended that proud, ambitious man. On June 5, while Donovan, with Ian Fleming, had been designing an American espionage agency, Henry Morgenthau Jr. and FDR discussed making Donovan the New York State chairman of the Defense Savings Program. Donovan had received a letter from Morgenthau that read, "This would be a full time job," and FDR agreed that it presented "an unusual opportunity for public service in these critical times." Twelve days after the offer, on June 17, an impatient Morgenthau told his secretary to get hold of Donovan on the phone. "I want to have him give me a yes or no on whether he is going to take the Chairmanship in New York State," he fussed. "I am not going to wait any longer." During their subsequent phone conversation, Donovan was evasive. War bond salesman was hardly the role in which he saw himself. The call ended with Morgenthau demanding Donovan's answer by sunset.

Donovan did not call Morgenthau back. Instead, he was summoned to the White House the next day, where he met the President, along with his champion, Knox, and Ben Cohen, a trusted New Deal aide who drafted much legislation for Roosevelt. By then FDR had had eight days to study Donovan's proposal for a coordinator of intelligence. Donovan was primed. He waxed eloquently and persuasively, urging that America catch up with other major powers in the intelligence field. FDR was impressed by Donovan's energy, ideas, and conviction. Here was the man who had told him that Britain would survive after Dunkirk, who had assured him that the RAF would prevail in the air war, and that the British could not only take it, but hand it out. Thus far, he had proved right.

After leaving the White House, Donovan finally got around to calling Morgenthau, who was out of the office. He left a message that he was not going to become New York chairman of the Defense Savings Program, for he had at last been offered an appointment commensurate with his ambition and talents. After the meeting with Donovan, FDR had scrawled across the bottom of the espionage agency proposal, "JBJr. Please set this up *confidentially* with Ben Cohen, military not O.E.M.," signed "FDR." JBJr. was John B. Blandford Jr., assistant director of the budget. What FDR meant was that this latest federal agency was to be placed under the military and its creation kept quiet by not making it part of the Office of Emergency Management. In these ten words scribbled on an interoffice memo, the President created America's first central intelligence service.

Ben Cohen went to see Blandford's boss, Harold Smith, the director of the Bureau of the Budget, in the Executive Office Building, the gloomy stone heap to the west of the White House, to figure out how to translate FDR's note into a government entity. Cohen and Smith came up with possible titles for Donovan, Coordinator of Strategic Information or Coordinator of Defense Information, and tested them with the military. The chiefs balked. They did not want "strategic" or "defense" in Donovan's title. They compromised finally on the nebulous Coordinator of Information. Since the organization would be under the military, Donovan, the President's aides suggested, should be commissioned a major general. Again the officers balked. However, they said, he could use the honorific "colonel," his World War I rank. Donovan was not to be salaried but would be reimbursed only for "transportation, subsistence and other expenses incidental to the performance of your duties." He himself would have to pay for the scrambler phones to be installed in his homes. The first draft of a proposed press release announcing Donovan's appointment had repeated from his proposal that he could "undertake activities helpful in securing of defense information not available to the government through existing agencies and departments." The sentence meant that Donovan could initiate espionage. This clause was knocked out by the military.

Donovan later described to a friend his terms for taking the job: "It is sufficient to say that I told the President that I did not want to do it and that I would only do it on three conditions: 1. That I would report only to him. 2. That his secret funds would be available. 3. That all the Departments of the government would be instructed to give me what I wanted." Donovan, unconvincingly, wanted it understood that he had not reached out for the job; the President had reached out to him.

On July 14, nearly a month after FDR had picked Donovan as his intelligence chief, word went out to relevant federal agencies, announcing fuzzily, that Colonel William J. Donovan, as coordinator of information, would be "assembling and correlating information which may be useful in the formulation of basic plans for the defense of the nation." The Office of the Coordinator of Information became the latest of 136 emergency agencies that FDR had created. News of Donovan's appointment earned a third of a column on page 5 of *The New York Times*. Guesses by journalists as to what the coordinator's duties actually meant ranged from espionage to controlling the gasoline supply. It seemed a thin start for a spy service, but as a colleague observed of Donovan, he had the "power to visualize an oak where he saw an acorn." Despite their past political differences, the new coordinator fit a profile visible in many of the people surrounding FDR. Like Roosevelt, Donovan was a magnetic personality, full of charm, brimming with ideas and energy, possessed of an irrepressible optimism. Both men had faced acid tests of courage and prevailed—Roosevelt overcoming the crippling effects of polio, and Donovan displaying a bravery in combat that scoffed at death. The two men differed in politics, not in character. Bill Donovan was FDR's kind of man.

On June 18, William Stephenson, the BSC chief, cabled London, "Donovan saw President today and after long discussion where in all points were agreed, he accepted appointment. He will be coordinator of all forms [of] intelligence including offensive operations . . . you can imagine how relieved I am after three months of battle and jockeying for position in Washington that our man is in such a position of importance to our efforts." The jubilation reached even higher and prompted an astonishing claim. Major Desmond Morton, Churchill's liaison officer with the British secret service, wrote after Donovan's COI had been in existence for two months, "[A] most secret fact of which the Prime Minister is aware but not all other persons concerned, is that to all intents and purposes U.S. Security is being run for them at the President's request by the British. A British officer [Stephenson] sits in Washington with Mr. Edgar Hoover and General [*sic*] Bill Donovan for this purpose and reports regularly to the President. It is of course essential that this fact should not be known in view of the furious uproar it would cause if known to the Isolationists."

Who was this "Wild Bill" whom Roosevelt had made the country's first spymaster? He had been born to first-generation Irish Catholic parents on New Year's Day 1883 in Buffalo, New York, the first of nine children, of whom five survived to adulthood. Young Donovan was a natural athlete with a bookish bent. He began keeping notebooks, in one of which he copied a revealing passage attributed to Ralph Waldo Emerson: "He had read the inscription on the gates of Busyrane—'Be bold'; and on the second gate—'Be bold, be bold, and evermore be bold'; and then again had paused well at the third gate—'But not too bold.' "

Donovan first enrolled in Niagara University because it was affiliated with a diocesan seminary, and he wanted to become a Dominican priest. At the end of his third year, after quarterbacking the football team, he decided that he lacked the calling for the priesthood and transferred to Columbia University to study law. He did not cut much of an academic swath, but won campus glory as the star quarterback for the Columbia Lions. Donovan scraped through law school with nary an A or a B. His single distinction outside sports was as a debater. He won the George William Curtis Medal for Public Speaking with a talk prophetically entitled "The Awakening of Japan." Franklin Roosevelt had indeed been a law school classmate, but he and Donovan moved in separate social orbits.

After Columbia, Donovan returned to Buffalo and was soon asked to join one of the city's leading firms, followed by an invitation to the exclusive Saturn Club. In 1912, hungry for adventure beyond the decorous walls of a law office, he organized a cavalry troop of forty-two socially prominent Buffalonians. The unit, christened the Silk Stocking Boys, was accepted into the National Guard, and his comrades elected Donovan their captain.

At age thirty, still a bachelor, he met Ruth Rumsey, a diminutive stunner, platinum blonde, slim, smart, and aristocratic from head to toe. They were married on July 14, 1914. The descendant of starving Irish peasants had made it. He was a leader in his profession, belonged to the best clubs, and had married into the town's Protestant elite, though he insisted that he and Ruth must marry and rear their children in the Catholic faith.

In 1916, Donovan's Silk Stocking Boys were called to active duty under General John "Black Jack" Pershing to help capture the Mexican revolutionary General Pancho Villa. The expedition never caught Villa, but Donovan had the time of his life, driving his men and himself mercilessly, sitting around the campfire at night, singing and swapping tales. The Silk Stocking Boys returned to Buffalo on March 12, 1917. Three days later, Donovan had to tell a disbelieving Ruth that he was off again. He had orders to report to the New York National Guard armory in Manhattan. Less than a month later, on April 6, the United States entered the war in Europe, and Donovan was given command of the 1st Battalion of the 69th Infantry Regiment, the fabled "Fighting Irish."

The 69th Regiment sailed for France on October 24, 1917, and, on its arrival, went directly to the front. The bloodying of the regiment was swift. At the Battle of Ourcq, in Donovan's battalion of approximately 1,000 men, 600 were killed, wounded, or missing. Donovan appeared to lack a fear nerve, exposing himself repeatedly to enemy fire in what seemed to his men a contempt for death. He was awarded the Distinguished Service Cross at Ourcq, the nation's second highest medal.

The regiment's chaplain, Father Francis P. Duffy, recalled how after the battle he heard one of Donovan's men exclaim, "Wild Bill is a son of a b———, but he's a game one." Thus, according to Father Duffy, "Wild Bill" Donovan was born. An earlier version, however, had it that while Donovan was chasing Pancho Villa, his men complained about the exhausting pace he set. "Look at me," their commander taunted them, "I'm not even panting. If I can take it, why can't you?" From one of the tired troopers came a plaintive cry, "We ain't as wild as you are, Bill," and the name apparently stuck.

On October 19, in the Meuse-Argonne sector, Donovan's battalion was ordered to advance against a strong German position. Wearing dress uniform, waving his pistol aloft, Donovan rose from a shell hole to lead the attack. He fell, seriously wounded, the nerves and blood vessels in his knee shattered. He refused to be taken from the field. Soon, gray-clad figures of German infantry emerged from the smoke of an artillery barrage. The American line began to sag. Donovan shouted to his men, "They can't get me and they can't get you." Inspired, the Fighting Irish rose up and repulsed the Germans. For this performance, Wild Bill was awarded the Congressional Medal of Honor.

After the war Donovan returned to Buffalo and the law. He was first drawn into public service as U.S. attorney for the Western District of New York in 1922. In that era of Prohibition, he authorized a raid on his own Saturn Club, outraging his fellow members who denounced him as "a common mick" and who expected him to resign from the club. "The law is the law," he told reporters, "and I have sworn to uphold it." And, seeing no reason to deprive himself of the pleasures of membership, he remained in the Saturn Club.

In 1924, Donovan was promoted to assistant attorney general and went to Washington, where he became nominal boss of the rising J. Edgar Hoover, a relationship that fit poorly from day one. It was during this period that Donovan experienced the rebuff that FDR later recalled, the refusal of President Herbert Hoover, after making him acting attorney general, to appoint Wild Bill to the full post.

In 1932 politics beguiled him, and Donovan won the Republican nomination as candidate for governor of New York. But that year, with the Depression deepening, was a lean season for Republicans. Donovan was pulled under by the same voter tide that swept FDR into the White House.

His political ambitions frustrated, Donovan returned to New York and established a Wall Street law firm, heavy with international clients. While becoming rich at the law, he still retained his avidity for public issues. In 1936 he left the practice to his partners and went off to observe firsthand the fighting between Italy and Ethiopia. His wife by now accepted, if she did not embrace, his absences. Thus far, in their marriage, eighteen months was the longest period during which he had stayed at home.

This was the man who had come into FDR's orbit in 1940, a multimillionaire Wall Street lawyer, globe-trotting student of world affairs, a mover at the summit of society with connections to practically everyone who mattered. Now in his late fifties, the man still retained a restless, curious, devouring mind that leaped from enthusiasm to enthusiasm, giving ideas, the brilliant and harebrained, an equal hearing. A colleague remembered of Donovan, "He was soft-spoken, but determined. He would persuade you with logic, charm, and presence, but always persuade you." Indeed, he had persuaded FDR that America needed an intelligence service and that the obvious choice to head it was himself.

★

A president turning to espionage to strengthen his country's defenses followed in a long tradition. Phillip Knightley writes in *The Second Oldest Profession:* "The spy is as old as history. . . . The Old Testament names the twelve spies Moses sent on a mission to the land of Canaan. . . . Alfred the Great was always interested in the Danish threat . . . he went into the enemy encampment himself disguised as a bard." The fourth-century B.C. Chinese general and military thinker Sun-tzu writes: "One good spy is worth a regiment of troops." Roosevelt was also pursuing the path of his earliest predecessor. George Washington, "first in war, first in peace," was also early to engage in espionage. In 1753, just turned twenty-one, Washington entered the Ohio wilderness to ascertain for the British if any French had penetrated British colonial soil. He managed to dine with French officers at a fort called Venanges. Washington merely sipped while the Frenchmen "dos'd themselves pretty plentifully," he later wrote. He went on, "The Wine . . . soon banished the restraint which at first appeared in their Conversation, and gave license to their Tongues to reveal their Sentiments more freely. They told me it was their absolute Design to take Possession of the Ohio. . . ."

When in 1775 Washington became commander of American Revolutionary forces, he declared that gaining intelligence about the British was one of his "immediate and pressing Duties." He paid over three hundred dollars to an undercover agent who entered British-occupied Boston "to establish a secret correspondence for the purpose of conveying intelligence on the Enemy's movements and designs." The amount was substantial at the time, but as King Frederick II of Prussia once noted, "A man who risks being hanged in your service merits being well paid," which was precisely the risk run by Nathan Hale, America's first national hero, hanged regretting only that he had but one life to spy for his country. Hale's statue today stands in front of the headquarters of the Central Intelligence Agency.

President Abraham Lincoln had no formal espionage service during the Civil War, but he did engage Allan Pinkerton's detective agency to spy for the Union. The Confederates employed women, including Belle Boyd, who outwitted Pinkerton, and Rose O'Neill Greenhow, a rich Washington hostess who gathered intelligence at parties she gave and passed it along to Confederate agents, including Lincoln's assassin, John Wilkes Booth.

The first country to create a permanent, publicly funded spy service had been Great Britain in 1909, although British espionage dates back to Queen Elizabeth's secretary of state, Sir Francis Walsingham. Sir Francis developed an organization that ran agents into France, the Low Countries, Italy, Germany, even Turkey, and penetrated the Spanish Armada, costly operations paid for out of his own pocket. England's lead in entering the permanent spy business was soon followed by Germany in 1913, Russia in 1917, and France in 1935.

America's Office of Naval Intelligence was founded in 1882. It was followed soon after by the Army's Military Intelligence Division, which was largely a housekeeping service, running loyalty checks on War Department personnel, protecting government buildings, bridges, and other facilities, and conducting meager intelligence.

During World War I the United States entered the codebreaking field when a short, balding, brilliant, fanatic poker player named Herbert O. Yardley launched a cryptographic service that came to be known as the Black Chamber. But in the era of peace that followed, Yardley found his chamber choked for funds. In 1929, when Henry Stimson became President Hoover's secretary of state, Stimson was appalled to have deciphered Japanese messages delivered to his desk. He shut down the Black Chamber for engaging in what he regarded as unethical conduct. As he famously notes in his memoirs, "Gentlemen do not read each other's mail."

By the 1930s, the Army's foreign intelligence branch had fewer than seventy agents to cover the world. When war broke out in Europe, America's Office of Naval Intelligence reported "a real undercover foreign intelligence service, equipped and able to carry on espionage, counterespionage, etc. does not exist." Now, with creation of Donovan's COI, America was in the game. How this official entry would mesh with Roosevelt's informal rings of agents, led by Vincent Astor and John Franklin Carter, remained to be tested.

One point was clear. Few leaders were better adapted temperamentally to espionage than Franklin Roosevelt. No one, not even his closest associates, ever fully penetrated the President's core being. His speechwriter, the insightful Robert Sherwood, admitted, "I could never really understand what was going on in Roosevelt's heavily forested interior." Information was compartmentalized according to unfathomable boundaries existing only inside FDR's mind. Henry Stimson did not always know what Pa Watson knew. Watson did not know what Harry Hopkins knew. And Hopkins, closer to FDR than anyone else, did not necessarily know what FDR told Henry Morgenthau Jr. Secretary of State Hull might not have so hated his undersecretary, Sumner Welles, if FDR had not given secret assignments to Welles behind Hull's back. Blunt-speaking Harold Ickes, secretary of the interior, once told FDR, "You are one of the most difficult men to work with that I have ever known." "Because I get too hard at times?" Roosevelt asked. "No," Ickes answered, because ". . . you won't talk frankly even with people who are loyal to you."

What had produced a character that suggested Machiavelli in Byzantium? In his *Roosevelt in Retrospect,* John Gunther attempts to decipher

FDR, calling him a "cryptic giant." "The central point of his character as a youth was that he was a 'good boy,' " Gunther observes. "Later, as the psychologists would say, he overcompensated for this by being unconventional and daring, by upsetting applecarts." Gunther concluded that FDR "went north by going south and loved it. He was tricky for fun." The novelist John Steinbeck, whom the President once asked to do some spying in Mexico, concurred, noting, "[H]e simply liked mystery, subterfuge, and indirect tactics . . . for their own sake." Steinbeck also offered an ironic but shrewd perception. He believed that deviousness usually derives from cowardice, but, Gunther knew, "Roosevelt had the courage of a lion. Why, then, should he have been so fond of techniques and maneuvers that, to put it bluntly, verged on deceit?" Gunther concluded that Roosevelt was so clever and confident that he thought people would never catch on to him. Unwelcome petitioners to his office were not even given the chance to present their case, but were overcome by a flood of FDR meanderings, then ushered out, before they realized what had happened. Others, encouraged by a nodding and smiling FDR, believed that they had won his agreement, when all he meant was, I hear what you are saying. Yet, this master of dissembling and deception was no warped personality. Sherwood concluded, "[A]lthough crippled physically and prey to various infections, he was spiritually the healthiest man I have ever known. He was gloriously and happily free of the various forms of psychic maladjustment. . . ." His personal physician, Admiral Ross McIntire, said of his patient in 1940, that his health was "the best in many years." The President ate heartily, drank temperately, slept soundly, exercised regularly by swimming, and kept his weight at a steady 187½ pounds.

Franklin Roosevelt was the architect who sat above, looking down onto a cross section of the compartments he had created, the only one who knew what was going on in all of them, while his subordinates could barely see beyond the walls surrounding them.

Chapter VII

———=★=———

Spies Versus Ciphers

FDR WAS the first world figure to learn one of the great strategic secrets of the war. He came to know it, not through Donovan, Carter, Astor, the FBI, or the military intelligence branches, but from an unlikely source.

Sam E. Woods was something of a good-time Charley assigned to the U.S. embassy in Berlin in 1940 as the commercial attaché. His job was to help American firms conduct business efficiently and profitably in Germany. William L. Shirer, in Berlin as a correspondent at the time, noted that Woods "seems to those of us who knew him and liked him the last man in the American Embassy in Berlin likely to have come by such crucial intelligence." Genial Sam Woods, however, had a German friend with connections in government ministries, the Reichsbank, and the Nazi Party. His friend was a covert anti-Nazi, eager to pass along to the attaché intelligence about the regime he reluctantly served. They had worked out a system. Woods would reserve two seats at a movie theater and send one ticket to his friend, who would meet him there and pass along his latest secrets as they sat in the dark. In early August 1940, as the Germans were preparing to smash Britain from the air, as Operation Sea Lion was being organized for the invasion of England, when it was rumored that Hitler might invade Spain, with the Führer and Stalin joined in a peace pact that left Britain to fight Germany alone, Woods's source passed along a scribbled note pointing in the opposite direction: Hitler and his generals were plotting the invasion of their presumed ally, the Soviet Union.

Woods was no political seer. As Shirer put it, his "grasp of world politics and history was not striking." Yet, he was sufficiently respectful of what he was learning to keep a file of the movie theater gleanings over the next five months. Then his informant gave him a Christmas present—precise details from a directive, dated December 18, describing Operation Barbarossa, Hitler's plan for invading Russia. Woods concluded it was time to act.

In early January 1941 the State Department informed the President that it had received a startling report from its Berlin embassy. The disbelieving secretary of state, Cordell Hull, had already asked J. Edgar Hoover to evaluate the information provided by Sam Woods. FBI agents checked the names Woods had mentioned in various German ministries and on the General Staff. They were, the bureau reported back, men in a position to know what was going on, and some were believed to be anti-Nazi. Woods's intelligence appeared authentic.

Roosevelt's quandary now was how best to handle this information vis-à-vis the Soviet Union. FDR chose to be direct. He would simply have the American ambassador in Moscow, Laurence Steinhardt, inform Stalin. However, Steinhardt advised against this course. He was well aware that Stalin distrusted Churchill and Roosevelt. Britain and the United States had both sent troops to Russia in 1918–19, after the revolution, to try to strangle the Bolshevik regime in its cradle. The Soviet dictator was convinced that the capitalists would spread any canard to drive a wedge between him and his new ally, Germany. This partnership, he believed, would keep his country safe from attack while Hitler went about swallowing up the rest of Europe.

Finally, on March 1, nearly two months after FDR had first seen Woods's report, Sumner Welles was dispatched to sound the alarm to the Soviet ambassador in Washington, Konstantin Oumansky. An encounter with Oumansky was not something looked forward to with pleasure. The Russian's background was in Soviet police work and capitalist-baiting journalism. His manner was universally characterized as boorish. Still, Welles did his duty and reported the impending danger to the Soviet Union. In describing the meeting he recalled, "Mr. Oumansky turned very white. He was silent for a moment and then merely said: 'My government will be grateful for your confidence and I will inform it immediately of our conversation.' " What Oumansky actually did was to follow the Stalin line. He called Hans Thomsen, the chargé d'affaires at the Germany embassy, and told him that the Americans were spreading vicious rumors to undermine the friendship between their two countries.

Reports of a German invasion, however, began to reach Moscow in a crescendo. Even before Welles's warning, on February 18, Sir Stafford Cripps, Britain's ambassador to Moscow, had held a press conference and declared that Germany would attack Russia before the end of June. On April 3, Churchill asked Cripps to deliver his personal note to Stalin warning of a German troop buildup in the East, information based on intercepted codes, the source, however, not revealed to Stalin. From Tokyo, the Soviets' legendary spy, the German Richard Sorge, pinpointed the invasion date. The hard-drinking, womanizing Sorge, working undercover as a journalist, had the run of the German embassy, where he was treated like a fellow staff member and made privy to the choicest secrets. On May 15, Sorge cabled his Moscow controllers that the invasion would begin on June 22. The Soviets' best source in Switzerland, a well-connected publisher, Rudolf Roessler, code-named Lucy, confirmed that date and, in addition, provided the Wehrmacht's order of battle.

On May 16, FDR had in hand a memorandum on the letterhead of "John Franklin Carter, 1210 National Press Building," relaying a report from a Swedish member of parliament "who has a record of being 60% right . . . on all developments since Munich." The Swede reported that millions of German troops were massing on the Soviet border, and "maps of Russia [were] being printed in huge quantities." Carter's source also predicted the invasion toward the end of June. "The Germans are reported confident that they can beat Russia in one or two months," the source added. Secretary of War Stimson's outlook was even bleaker. He predicted that Russia would surrender even before being attacked.

The Soviet Union was the beating heart of world communism, as feared by most Americans as it was loathed by Churchill. Yet, the Prime Minister knew where Britain's advantage lay. As the rumored invasion date approached, he told his dinner guests at Chequers—Anthony Eden, John Colville, his private secretary, and John Winant, the American ambassador who had replaced Joe Kennedy—what he intended. "Hitler was counting on enlisting capitalist and Right Wing sympathizers in this country and the U.S.A.," Churchill said. But Hitler was wrong. If the anticipated attack did occur, "We should go all out to help Russia." Winant now felt free to reveal earlier guidance he had received from FDR: Roosevelt would support "any statement Churchill might make welcoming Soviet Russia as an ally." After dinner, with the other guests gone, Colville tweaked Churchill about the arch anti-Communist making favorable noises about the Soviet Union. It was on this occasion that Churchill made his memorable response: "Not at all. I have only one purpose, the destruction of Hitler, and my life is much simplified thereby. If Hitler invaded Hell I would make at least a favorable reference to the Devil in the House of Commons."

Over a hundred warnings of the pending invasion are estimated to have reached the Kremlin. Operation Barbarossa had become the worst-kept secret of the war. Why, when it appeared that every Moscow factory worker had heard of the threat, was it disregarded by Stalin? Whatever else he may have been, the Soviet leader was no naïf. As late as May 1941, Stalin addressed graduates of the Soviet military academies in the Kremlin. Almost certainly, he told them, there would be war with Germany by 1942, even possibly with the Soviet Union taking the initiative, since "Nazi Germany as the dominant power in Europe is not normal," he warned. But the Red Army currently was not strong enough either to repel or launch an attack. Therefore, Russia had to try by diplomacy to stall German aggression. Besides, Stalin did not believe that Hitler was mad enough to start fighting Russia before he had defeated England and thus saddle himself with a two-front war. He did not deny that German armies were massing on his border. But that was only Hitler's way of pressuring him to give in to Germany's economic demands. All these reports that Hitler planned to invade, loot his country, enslave his people, and crush communism were capitalist provocations designed to goad him into a conflict against Germany while Russia was still unprepared. Then the British would make peace with Germany, and he would be left to fight the Nazis alone.

On the night of June 21, a German soldier deserted to the Russian army and told his interrogators that an attack would take place at 3 A.M. the next morning. Within three hours Stalin had the report, but rejected it and supposedly ordered the bearer of the news shot. The invasion that FDR had known about for over five months began when the deserter said it would. Like the husband who is the last to know that his wife is faithless, Stalin was stunned by the invasion. As the depth of Hitler's deceit and his country's debacle sank in, Stalin went into a depression approaching a nervous breakdown. For several days, at the moment of its greatest peril, Russia was leaderless.

★

FDR had been the first major world leader to learn of the pending Nazi attack on Russia from the serendipitous source of Sam Woods in Berlin. At the same time, a much more systematic enterprise was extracting secrets for him from the other side of the globe. Until the spring of 1938, FDR had been able to read Japan's diplomatic traffic between Tokyo and its embassies worldwide after American cryptanalysts broke the Japanese Red code. Then Japan switched to a new, thus far impenetrable code, labeled Purple. Deliveries to the White House stopped.

On the afternoon of September 20, 1940, customary quiet prevailed at Arlington Hall, a former girls' school in the northern Virginia suburbs where the Army had quartered its codebreaking Signal Intelligence Service. Frank B. Rowlett, a usually reserved, scholarly former schoolteacher, now working for SIS, suddenly let out a war whoop. "That's it!" Rowlett shouted, jumping up and down. His two assistants, Robert O. Ferner and Albert W. Small, joined in the shouting and began dancing around the office. The elation among men who ordinarily spent their days in gnomelike absorption in their work was occasioned by the fact that, after eighteen months, they had broken Purple. The team celebrated this landmark in American espionage by sending out for bottles of Coca-Cola, which they downed, and then went back to their offices. Their superior, Major General Joseph Mauborgne, the Army's chief signals officer, started referring to Rowlett and his team as "magicians" and the Japanese traffic they decrypted as "Magic." Magic meant, once again, that the Tokyo foreign office might as well have placed FDR on its distribution list, since he could read what Japanese diplomats were telling each other almost as soon as they could.

Rivalry between American Army and Navy cryptanalysts, however, was to produce a bizarre system for delivering Japan's diplomatic secrets to the President. The flood of messages intercepted daily was too great to be handled by the Army alone. Thus, the naval codebreaking unit, OP-20-G, shared the workload. Each service had its own officer who decided which intercepts were sufficiently significant to be seen by the nation's leaders. This judgment was made for the Army by Colonel Rufus S. Bratton of G-2 and for ONI by Lieutenant Commander Alwin D. Kramer. Distribution was limited to the President, the secretaries of state, war, and navy, the Army Chief of Staff, the director of military intelligence, the director of naval intelligence, and the chiefs of naval operations and war plans. Messages selected were delivered in locked pouches to these officials, each of whom had his own key. But who should deliver the pouch containing the cream of decrypts to the President, a task that would reflect prestige and credit on the service chosen? After protracted wrangling, the Army and Navy came up with a solution. In odd-numbered months, such as January, March, and May, his military aide would deliver Magic to the President, and in even-numbered months his naval aide would do so. No provision was made in this jerry rig for delivering Magic to the President in the evening or on Sundays. Intelligence that could determine war or peace was handled as a nine-to-five job.

The inanity increased in July 1941 when Colonel Bratton noticed a copy of a Magic decrypt that the President's aide Pa Watson had thrown into his wastebasket. Watson was a big, florid-faced, good-natured Virginian who had come to the White House as the President's military aide. He now held one of the most difficult jobs in the administration, presidential secretary in charge of appointments. He determined who got to see FDR. Pa Watson was liked by all and underrated by some as a simple soul. He was, in fact, unusually astute and not above allowing others to underestimate him, since they would then lower their guard to his advantage. When Colonel Bratton informed the Army intelligence chief, General Sherman Miles, of Watson's carelessness with the decrypt, Miles decided that Magic could no longer be entrusted to the White House. Throughout June, Roosevelt continued to receive Magic decrypts from his current naval aide, Captain John R. Beardall. But in July, an Army month, no decrypts appeared. FDR asked Beardall what had happened. Fearing to contradict General Miles's order, the Navy thereafter worked out an arrangement under which Beardall could read the decrypts during an Army month and then summarize them for FDR; but he could not show the actual messages to the President of the United States.

In spite of this triumph of red tape over sanity, the Magic channel began proving its worth. Decryption was analogous to seeing one's opponent's hand in a card game, rather than guessing at it. It was the equivalent of listening in on a telephone conversation, as contrasted to a hearsay report of it. Signal intelligence delivered exactly what an adversary was saying, unfiltered by any third party. A spy's reporting could be twisted by prejudice or hidden agendas, or deliberately distorted by a double agent. Yet, signal intelligence had its limitations as well. The thousands of intercepted and decrypted messages yielded raw information, often unanalyzed and lacking context. But a spy's report, at its best, could present intelligence filtered through analysis and placed in context. The recipients of the broken code or the spy's report, however, could never be sure that they were receiving the virtues of one or the failings of the other.

FDR retained his penchant for the melodramatic, for spies over electronic espionage. At roughly the same time that Rowlett and his crew were breaking Purple, Captain James Roosevelt, the President's eldest son, who had entered the Marine Corps in 1940, was called to the White House. As he later described the occasion, "[F]ather summoned me for a secret mission." Jimmy was to accompany an Army major, Gerald Thomas, on a trip through the Philippines, China, Burma, India, Iraq, Egypt, Crete, Palestine, and Africa. As far as Major Thomas knew, their mission was to report any military buildup and gauge the adequacy of U.S. supply lines to these places. But FDR had another assignment for Jimmy. Behind closed doors in his private study he told his son, "This must be completely confidential. The Congress, the press and the public would never approve my message, but I consider it critical to the morale of countries we must support." Jimmy was to give ceremonial gifts to the leaders of the nations he visited, then take these people aside and deliver a confidential message from the President. They were to be told that while the United States was still officially neutral, Roosevelt "would do everything he could to help those who were at war" fighting the fascists. Jimmy was also to convey a pledge that would certainly have rattled isolationist Americans. He was to confide to his hosts FDR's belief "that we might well be at war before long and that we then would pitch in with both hands to help them." In effect, Jimmy was to tell these leaders, "Hang on until we get in."

The President had a final warning before his son's departure: "If you speak publicly of it, I'll deny it and disown you. If you get in any trouble, you'll have to get out of it on your own. There will be times when you will leave Major Thomas and go off on your own to see who I want you to see. I can't provide you government planes or anything like that . . . you'll have to make your own arrangements as you go along. We can't take the chance of having you communicate with me formally while you're gone, but report to me the moment you return." Codes snatched from the air were all well and good; but this was what FDR enjoyed masterminding, with Vincent Astor, John Franklin Carter, and now his son, secret capers sidestepping government channels.

Secretary of War Stimson, now a convert to codebreaking, worried that the President failed to appreciate Magic adequately. On January 2, 1941, he asked Pa Watson for an appointment with FDR. He found Roosevelt still in bed at 10:30 A.M., working his way through a basket of pending business. He wanted the President to understand, he said, that Magic offered a window not only on what the Japanese were up to, but also on what was happening inside Germany. The Japanese ambassador to Berlin, General Hiroshi Oshima, was close to Hitler, and proudly and thoroughly reported his conversations with the Führer to his superiors in the Tokyo foreign office through the Purple code. Of this conversation with FDR, Stimson later wrote: "First, I told him that he should read certain of the important reports which had come in from Berlin giving the summary which the Japanese ambassador there had made of the situation and others like it. He hadn't read them."

FDR began giving greater attention to the Magic intercepts, and through them glimpsed the gulf between what Japan said publicly and what it was doing secretly. Five months after Purple had been broken, on February 14, 1941, Roosevelt welcomed the new Japanese ambassador to Washington, Admiral Kichisaburo Nomura, whom he had known since World War I. As old friends, the two men agreed that they should speak candidly to avert a collision between their nations. But when FDR read the intercepted instructions sent to Nomura by the Japanese foreign minister, Yosuke Matsuoka, he wondered how any honest exchange was possible. He described Matsuoka's messages as "the product of a mind which is deeply disturbed. . . ."

The Japanese had reason to believe that their code had been broken. Dr. Hans Thomsen, the German chargé d'affaires in Washington who had tried to fix the 1940 election, had a line into the State Department's code room. According to the Magic rules, only the secretary, Cordell Hull, was to receive intercepts at State. Hull, however, shared this intelligence with at least six of his top subordinates. One of them, in turn, allowed four more officials in the Far Eastern Division to see the intercepts. With so many recipients, multiple copies had to be run off on a mimeograph machine in the code room. The room's chief was Joseph P. Dugan, an isolationist. What Dugan saw of the Magic intercepts he discussed, even showed, to a like-minded friend. This friend, unknown to Dugan, was in Thomsen's pay. Thus the German diplomat was able to cable Berlin, "As communicated to me by an absolutely reliable source, the State Department is in possession of the key to the Japanese coding system and is, therefore, able to decipher telegrams from Tokyo to Ambassador Nomura. . . ."

On May 6 the Magic codebreakers decrypted a message from Oshima in Berlin relaying what Thomsen had discovered. Thomsen had also alerted Nomura in Washington, and on May 20 the Japanese ambassador reported to Tokyo, "I have discovered that the United States is reading some of our codes though I do not know which ones." Astonishingly, after a perfunctory investigation, the Japanese concluded that their top ciphers were still unbreakable. Only some of their less important and less secure systems, they concluded, had been penetrated. They continued to send their top-secret diplomatic traffic via Purple, and the President continued to read it via Magic. After the Japanese invaded Indochina in mid-July, FDR slapped an oil and cotton embargo on the country. And because the Japanese continued to use the compromised Purple, he knew almost immediately how far he had pushed Japan. In another intercepted cable to Ambassador Nomura, dated July 31, Tokyo warned, "There is more reason than ever before for us to arm ourselves to the teeth for all-out war."

Relations between the United States and Japan continued to deteriorate. On October 16 the Konoye government was displaced by the even more bellicose regime of General Hideki Tojo. That October, a Navy month, the Magic decrypts continued to arrive at the President's desk. But in November, an Army month, the traffic stopped, except for Captain Beardall's secondhand summaries. FDR, a man dismissive of bureaucratic channels, particularly foolish contortions generated by interservice rivalries, had had enough. He now demanded to see the full text of Magic intercepts, a seemingly reasonable request by the commander in chief of the nation's armed forces. Beardall uneasily pointed out that November was an Army month in which he was only to give the President summaries. An exasperated FDR told him to bring him all the Magic traffic. After hurried consultations between the Army and Navy, General Miles reluctantly agreed that his service, during its delivery months, would allow the President to see the decrypts. But by now, Roosevelt had tired of the internecine nonsense of Army months and Navy months. Henceforth, he ordered all Magic traffic, in the original, to be delivered to him by Captain Beardall, his naval aide.

While FDR was just beginning to appreciate the value of signals intelligence, Winston Churchill had displayed an absolute hunger for it from the start. The Prime Minister grabbed the red lacquered boxes from his courier's hand and devoured the decrypts inside which were stamped across the top in bold red letters, ULTRA. While American cryptographers at Arlington Hall had been wrestling with Purple, eccentrics and a smattering of geniuses at Bletchley Park, Sir Herbert Leon's sprawling estate, had succeeded in breaking the traffic in a cipher system that the Germans considered impenetrable. The radio transmissions of the German military and government ministries were encrypted on a machine called the Enigma. Superficially, the Enigma resembled a portable typewriter with a standard keyboard. The machine had been invented in the 1920s by two German engineers, Arthur Scherbius and Boris Hagelin, for use by business firms wanting to conceal their trade secrets. The name reportedly derived from the convoluted *Enigma* Variations by the English composer Sir Edward Elgar. The machine was first used by German banks and the national railway system; but by 1928, the German army and navy were employing the Enigma to encode classified messages. The Luftwaffe adopted the system in 1935.

The Enigma machine had a space where three or more removable rotors could be placed. In addition, movable wire plugs ran from the machine to an electrical plugboard. Thus, as each letter of a plain language message was being typed, the rotors and the settings of the plugboards caused a different letter to emerge. These settings could be changed, even several times a day, which meant that the possible permutations for each letter became astronomical. With five rotors they reached six sextillion. The Germans calculated that it would take 1,000 codebreakers 900 million years to figure out all the potential key combinations.

The Poles, ever distrustful of their German neighbor, had been attacking the system for years, and in 1932 broke their first Enigma message. However, the ability of the Germans to keep changing rotors and plugboard settings made cracking the Enigma an endless challenge. After Poland was defeated in the fall of 1939, a few Polish cryptanalysts managed to flee to Britain, where they shared their knowledge of Enigma with the Government Code and Cypher School at Bletchley Park. The British quickly took the lead, and by 1940 the park's stately lawns and croquet course had sprouted utilitarian Nissen huts, where mathematicians, physicists, linguists, novelists, chess champions, and Oxford and Cambridge dons labored over Enigma. Among them was Alan Turing, King's College mathematician, whose attack on the system planted the seed for the modern-day computer. One of Turing's colleagues offered a striking definition of the man's genius. Upon hearing an idea hatched by one of his other colleagues, he would say to himself, why hadn't he thought of that? But upon hearing one of Turing's ideas, he concluded that he could never have thought of it. Among Turing's associates were Leonard Palmer, decoder of ancient Minoan and Mycenaean inscriptions, and the offbeat novelist Angus Wilson, once sighted frolicking about the Bletchley swan pool at midnight stark naked.

Ultra was the designation chosen for Enigma messages intercepted and decrypted at Bletchley, the arrival of which so stirred Churchill's anticipation. Wrens, members of the Women's Royal Naval Service, performed most of the work. Eventually, over a thousand of these young women labored among the "bombes," huge (eight- by eight-foot) electronic contraptions of lights, plugs, wires, and whirring wheels that could solve the Enigma rotor and plugboard settings, and thus enable the cryptanalysts to break the messages. It was a convent-like life for these young women and almost equally monastic for the Bletchley men. The staff, which by war's end, numbered over ten thousand, were quartered in two adjacent RAF bases or crowded into nearby village boardinghouses. So paramount was secrecy that once assigned to Bletchley one could virtually abandon all hope of being reassigned elsewhere. At its peak, the Bletchley staff was decrypting over eighty-four thousand messages every month that the Germans regarded as unbreakable. Churchill demanded to see so much of this traffic that a Mrs. Owens of the Women's Auxiliary Air Force, was assigned full time to do nothing but oversee the PM's Ultra deliveries.

The British were prepared to go to extraordinary lengths to safeguard the secrecy of Ultra. The ultimate example, claimed by writers after the war, supposedly occurred when Churchill, knowing through Ultra that Coventry had been targeted by Luftwaffe bombers, declined to warn the city. Coventry's air defenses, by being ready for an attack, might tip off the Germans that their codes were being broken. Better to sacrifice a city than to compromise Ultra, the reasoning went. Coventry was indeed raided on November 14, 1940, during which the city's center was leveled, its magnificent cathedral destroyed, and over five hundred civilians killed. But the story of Churchill's alleged coldhearted calculus in leaving the city unprepared was untrue. Three days before the raid, Ultra had indeed identified a major Luftwaffe strike, code-named Moonlight Sonata. But the decryption yielded neither the date nor the target. Churchill's intelligence analysts first led him to think that London was to be attacked, and in this mistaken belief, he canceled a trip to the country and ordered his staff to take shelter in a nearby underground station. "You are too young to die," he told them. Coventry was discovered to be the target just four hours before the Germans struck, but not through Ultra. The RAF had learned how to intercept the Luftwaffe's system for guiding bombers to their destination via radio beams. What doomed Coventry was that the RAF's countermeasure—jamming the beams, thus misleading the German bombers—had used the wrong frequency. Nevertheless, secrecy was a fanatic obsession at Bletchley Park, and the Churchill/Coventry story provided an apocryphal example.

The Americans were eager to share in Britain's codebreaking feats. The British, in the sphere of cryptanalysis, however, believed it better to receive than give. In February 1941 a team of four American cryptographers, led by William Friedman, the dean of U.S. codebreakers, was driven through blacked-out London accompanied by four crates in the back of a truck. The crates contained the components to construct a copy of the machine on which the Japanese enciphered messages in the Purple code. It was a gift for the Government Code and Cypher School. In exchange, their Bletchley counterparts provided the Americans with a few secrets, but revealed nothing of the bombes that enabled them to break into Enigma.

Two reasons account for Britain's unwillingness to be more forthcoming. First, "C," Stewart Menzies, head of MI6, told Churchill that the Americans "were not as security minded as one would wish." Thus, while Roosevelt was putting U.S. neutrality on the line by having American ships patrol for British convoys, Menzies was advising the PM against "divulging to the President the information regarding U.S. Naval Units being chased by U Boats." If the Americans were told which U-boats were pursuing them, they might well deduce that the source of this intelligence was British penetration of German naval codes. It was impossible, Menzies claimed, to "devise any safe means of wrapping up the information in a manner which would not imperil this source [Ultra]. . . ." The second reason the British were reluctant to make the Americans full cryptanalytic partners was more cunning. Among the decrypts delivered daily by Mrs. Owens to Prime Minister Churchill were not only German secrets, but also broken American codes. Britain's eavesdropping on a friend had been going on since the First World War, and it was not something that Churchill could comfortably risk having Roosevelt discover.

Chapter VIII

———=★=———

Donovan Enters the Game

B ILL DONOVAN, the man who would see an acorn and envision an oak, took his meager mandate as coordinator of information and quickly began to build the kind of espionage service inspired by his British mentors. His charter, in the numbing prose of federal bureaucrats, to "collect and analyze all information and data which may bear upon national security . . . and to make the same available to the President . . . and other Federal agencies," made the COI sound like a paper-shuffling mill. But a subsequent FDR instruction gave Donovan pliable authority that he could stretch into an intelligence agency closer to his ambitions. He was "to carry out when requested by the President such supplementary activities as may facilitate the securing of information for national security not now available to the government." In short, he could spy.

It reflects Donovan's sophistication that he did not turn immediately to shady foreigners, private detectives, or cast-off intelligence operatives from the military, FBI, or State Department to staff his nascent organization. Almost the first person he sought out was Archibald MacLeish, the poet-intellectual librarian of Congress. Despite the public's movie screen image of espionage as shadowy, slouch-hatted figures writing in invisible ink and stealing secret plans, Donovan recognized that 95 percent of intelligence involved conventional research. MacLeish's library offered a mother lode of information to be mined from the world's largest collection of books, man-uscripts, periodicals, films, and maps. Donovan's first recruits went to work, at MacLeish's invitation, in an annex of the Library of Congress. Ignoring civil service hiring procedures, Donovan also enlisted an impressive array of scholarly talent: James Phinney Baxter, president of Williams College and a leading authority on Germany; William Langer, Harvard professor of European history; Sherman Kent, Yale professor; Conyers Read of the University of Pennsylvania; James L. McConaughy, president of Wesleyan University and subsequently governor of Connecticut. McGeorge Bundy, later to become President John F. Kennedy's national security advisor and president of the Ford Foundation, wrote, "It is a curious fact of academic history that the first great center of area studies in the United States was not located in any university, but in Washington, during the Second World War. . . ." Donovan had created, Bundy observed, "a remarkable institution, half cops and robbers and half faculty meeting."

Beyond the academic enlistees, other early recruits suggested the breadth of Donovan's ambitions for the COI. He signed up to head a Field Photographic branch John Ford, the Hollywood director whose credits included *Young Mr. Lincoln, Drums Along the Mohawk, How Green Was My Valley,* and two films for which he won Oscars as best director, *The Informer* and *The Grapes of Wrath.* Gregg Toland, arguably the best cameraman in American filmmaking, with screen credits including *Citizen Kane, Wuthering Heights,* and *The Grapes of Wrath,* also joined the COI film unit.

Later chroniclers who worked with Donovan, Stewart Alsop and Thomas Braden, found him "not a first rate administrator." Stanley Lovell, a businessman-chemist picked to head the Research and Development branch, was more blunt: "All who knew him and worked under him recognized that Donovan was the worst organizer of all." Wild Bill drove the professionals in the Bureau of the Budget mad. After only three weeks of COI's existence, detecting early chaos, bureau officials drafted a memorandum asking the President to clarify for them just what this new agency was supposed to do. In the end, the budget chiefs recognized that kindred souls like FDR and Donovan did not bend to organization charts, fixed expenditures, or rules. The bureau initially earmarked $450,000 for a COI payroll of ninety-two employees. Within months the staff had ballooned to 596 people and kept growing. The joke in government circles was that a COI employee who missed a day was likely to return to find two new employees sitting at his desk. Most repellent to budget officials, who worshipped financial accountability, Donovan had, in effect, managed to receive a blank check from the President. Most of his funds were to be "unvouchered"; they could be spent secretly for whatever purpose Donovan deemed in the national interest.

His staff first occupied a run-down apartment house at Twenty-third and E Streets, N.W. Washington, but soon spread like lava to engulf a complex of redbrick buildings originally belonging to the National Institutes of Health, then flowed over bleak temporary frame buildings in back of a brewery, all collected under the mailing address 2430 E Street, N.W. Donovan, who understood the power of first impressions, commissioned the noted architect Eero Saarinen to design, for visiting VIPs, the most impressive briefing room in Washington. It was equipped with air conditioning against the tropical Washington weather, sliding wall panels for map displays, fluted wooden room dividers, a revolving globe five feet in diameter, and a theater. Colonel Edwin L. Sibert, an Army intelligence officer, visited Donovan's burgeoning empire and said it "closely resembled a cat house in Laredo on a Saturday night, with rivalries, jealousies, mad schemes, and everyone trying to get the ear of the director. But I felt that a professional organization was in the making. . . ."

Bill Donovan, perhaps a managerial calamity, was, more importantly, a natural leader, a master of theater, a man who floated above the mundane, much like the President he served. He managed to have Marine Captain Jimmy Roosevelt assigned as his liaison between COI and all federal agencies. When young Roosevelt called, Donovan knew, his calls would be taken. As *Life* magazine put it, "[T]o get Jimmy Roosevelt into your show is as good as a seat at the White House breakfast table." Donovan also hired Estelle Frankfurter, sister of Felix Frankfurter, the Supreme Court justice and FDR confidant. Donovan intuitively understood the strategies of success, even if he could not concentrate on an organization chart if someone held a gun to his head. The man's brain was fertile, not orderly.

In August 1941, Donovan had a visitor, Wallace Banta Phillips, whom Vincent Astor had tried unsuccessfully four months before to have FDR dump. Phillips was running a string of agents abroad for ONI, the "K Organization," operating in twelve countries, he told Wild Bill. Though technically under the Navy, the K Organization reported to a committee representing State, War, Navy, and the FBI. This hydra-headed arrangement was not working, Phillips said, and he wanted Donovan to take it over. Instead of trying to crush a potential rival, as Astor had done, Donovan looked closely into the mouth of this gift horse and saw opportunity.

He pressured the Bureau of the Budget to come up with $2.5 million for him to absorb the K Organization, thus buying himself an existing espionage unit for COI.

Phillips's uncontested divorce from ONI and remarriage to the COI was symptomatic of a discomfort that the Army and Navy intelligence branches felt toward spying. An Army attaché spotting the latest tank model at a military parade or a naval attaché learning of a potential adversary's battleship strength while watching foreign fleet maneuvers was their concept of espionage. Still, the services saw an opportune solution to their need for better intelligence, despite their reluctance to collect it. Let Bill Donovan and his new COI do the shady stuff. Donovan saw the opening and scooted through it like the college quarterback he had been. By October 11, he could inform FDR, "By joint action of the Military and Naval Intelligence Services there was consolidated under the Coordinator of Information the undercover intelligence of the two services." His organization had been handed this assignment, he said, because "A civilian agency has distinct advantages over any military or naval agency." He moved quickly to send COI personnel abroad. Their function was to recruit secret agents and conduct espionage even after "diplomatic relations are severed." He was further preparing to conduct clandestine communications "both by radio and other means that will endure after the particular country has been closed to us diplomatically." Roosevelt could admire the man's bold maneuvering, as long as he himself still held the leash, which was not always visible to the person at the other end.

Just two days later, on October 13, FDR seemed to put his stamp of approval on Donovan's swelling authority. Adolf Berle informed the President that something was bothering the FBI, and he too was concerned. The bureau operated a shortwave station between the United States and England, and British intelligence in America had been permitted to use this link to transmit hundreds of messages to London, all in code. The FBI had not the foggiest idea of what was being sent over its own circuit, and was uncomfortable with the arrangement. FDR sent a memorandum giving Donovan responsibility to unsnarl the problem: "This seems to be a matter which you ought to look into, will you handle it with Berle, FBI and the British intelligence?"

Donovan's standing also received a backhanded boost from an unexpected source. Later that month, the COI director brought to the White House a cable from the American embassy in Berlin that seemed certain to interest FDR. The embassy had forwarded press accounts from the

Nazi Party newspapers, the *Angriff* and the *Völkischer Beobachter,* reporting Donovan's appointment. The latter paper's headline read, THE JEW-ROOSEVELT NAMES WAR MAKER DONOVAN AS SUPER-AGITATOR. The purpose of Donovan's COI, both papers reported, was "making the American people ripe for war." These stories, the embassy noted, marked an advance in Nazi vituperation: ". . . [S]ince the appearances of articles in several German newspapers some months ago on the alleged Jewish ancestry of the President, this is the first time he has been referred to as a Jew in German newspaper headlines." A subsequent story in the Nazi press reported, "Roosevelt has named the Colonel Coordinator of Information. Hiding behind this title he is brewing a Jewish-Democratic crisis which is directed at all of Europe. Colonel Donovan's office . . . has grown into the largest espionage and sabotage bureau that has so far been seen in any Anglo-Saxon country." This Nazi ranting delighted both Donovan and the President who had appointed him.

Not everyone saw the COI as a welcome answer to the gap in America's intelligence defenses. Senator Burton K. Wheeler of Montana, a New Deal friend but isolationist foe of FDR's, complained one month after the creation of the agency, "Mr. Donovan is now head of the Gestapo in the United States. That is the proper place for him, because he knows how such things should be done. . . ." Wheeler then ticked off a list of senators whose offices had supposedly been raided by Donovan when he was with the Justice Department in the twenties. "So he is a fitting man to head the Gestapo of the United States," the senator concluded.

Donovan, however, would have to contend with rivals with far sharper fangs than the gaseous Wheeler. The COI director and J. Edgar Hoover had crossed paths nearly twenty years before when both were on a different footing. Donovan was then assistant attorney general and Hoover, as acting director of the then Bureau of Investigation, was his subordinate. To Donovan, in those days, Hoover seemed a plodding bureaucrat mired in administrative trivia. To Hoover, Donovan was a dilettante who stuck his nose where he had no business and failed to act when he should. Hoover was angered to find his orders inexplicably countermanded or his disciplinary actions reversed. When he took his complaints to Donovan, the assistant AG was always too busy to see him. Later, as Donovan began to understand Hoover's power, he suspected that the FBI director had played a part in President Hoover's failure to appoint him as attorney general. Indeed, J. Edgar Hoover liked to boast: "I stopped him from becoming AG in 1929. . . ."

By the time FDR had appointed Donovan to run the COI, Hoover had a substantial head start in the intelligence field. A full year before, in one of his instant, inexplicable decisions, Roosevelt had ordered that "Edgar" was to have "foreign intelligence work in the Western Hemisphere," and MID and ONI "should cover the rest of the world." Given the President's nod, Hoover had moved swiftly. Well before Donovan signed up his first college professor, the FBI already had 150 secret agents, the Special Intelligence Service, working to combat Nazi influence in Latin America. For Hoover, his initial bureaucratic victory was just the first step in an intelligence strategy that suggested, today Latin America, tomorrow the world. Running this worldwide network, Adolf Berle reported to the President, was Hoover's ultimate goal for the FBI.

In his naked ambition, the man had his critics. Secretary of War Stimson wrote in his diary of the FBI chief: "[H]e goes to the White House . . . and poisons the mind of the President." General Marshall found Hoover puerile and petulant, "more of a spoiled child than a responsible officer." Still, he had provided useful, if questionable, services to FDR during the 1940 election and continued to do so. Hoover was not only personally helpful to FDR, but was apparently doing a splendid job of spy catching. The FBI still controlled the Abwehr's shortwave station on Long Island and continued to feed bogus intelligence back to Germany over this circuit. The penetration was so complete that even funds sent for the salaries and expenses of the compromised agents were intercepted by the FBI. And then, on July 30, 1941, Hoover practically shut down German espionage in the United States overnight. The FBI arrested thirty-three Nazi agents. William Sebold, the German-born double agent working against the Abwehr and for the bureau, helped finger the suspects, including one seemingly innocuous figure. It was Sebold who tricked the simple Hermann Lang into admitting that he had stolen the plans for the Norden bombsight. These triumphs, which Hoover described over lunches with FDR, could not fail to impress.

In the summer of 1941, the President was approached by the distraught wife of Kermit Roosevelt, his distant cousin and Eleanor's first cousin, the member of The Club who had accompanied Vincent Astor aboard the *Nourmahal* on the 1938 spying expedition to the South Pacific. The heavy-drinking Kermit, already plagued with a venereal disease, had strayed again. He had run off with a masseuse named Herta Peters, their whereabouts unknown. Kermit's wife pleaded with the President to find him and end the scandal. FDR asked Vincent Astor, now coordinating intelligence in the New York City area, to get help from the FBI.

Astor made an immediate blunder. He went to the FBI, but at the wrong level. Since he was operating out of New York, Astor contacted Thomas Donegan of the bureau's office in that city and conveyed the President's desire for assistance in finding Kermit. Astor then called Director Hoover, annoyed by the bureau's slow pace in handling the case. On learning that Astor had talked to his New York subordinate first, Hoover became furious. The wellborn amateur was about to get a lesson from the humbly born Hoover in how these games were played. The director explained icily, "[A] thing like that ought not be given directly to our New York office. As a matter of fact if you'd called me . . . in the first instance, I would have arranged to put a special on right away . . . so that nobody in our New York office would necessarily know about it. . . . I know how a story like this if it got out by any chance would just be terribly embarrassing to the big boss. It's a kind of case that we usually handle in a little different way, that is, where there is a personal angle involved I generally will send some personal representative directly from Washington so he can go ahead and handle it without anybody locally knowing what it is all about you see. . . ." Astor's mistake was that he had failed to bring a scandal in the President's family directly to Hoover. The director's expertise at such matters would not only increase Roosevelt's indebtedness to him, but Hoover's awareness of this presidential dirty linen would make FDR wary of ever attacking him. That was how Hoover's dossiers worked from the President on down. Hoover also used the conversation with Astor to jab an emerging rival as America's spymaster. He accused Astor of supporting Bill Donovan and said, "Now I don't know anything about the Colonel Donovan situation and I, of course, care less. But the point about it is if they want Colonel Donovan to come in or if they want you to come in or they want Smith or Brown . . . hell, I'll wire my resignation tonight if that's the way the President feels about it. . . . The job doesn't mean enough to me." Astor backed down, and responded meekly, "Anything that I said which may have been improper, I was mad that night myself, all I can do, I apologize to you in blank. . . ." In the end, Hoover got a personal plea for help with Kermit's disappearance from the White House, but not directly from the President.

By now, FDR's adoring and adored secretary, Missy LeHand, was no longer on the scene. The month before, June 4, 1941, she had been felled by a stroke in front of the President at a White House party, an affliction that ultimately killed her. In the meantime, her premier position in the President's office was assumed by Grace Tully, perhaps lacking Missy's innate femininity, but a first-rate executive secretary. Tully has been vividly sketched by Sam Rosenman: "She was Irish, very devout Catholic. She had an Irish temper, and one of her virtues, as well as one of her faults, was her directness with people. . . . She was militant in her devotion to Roosevelt; she had a very good humor and was good company, inclined to drink a little too much on occasion and show it, nothing really disreputable, but if she had two or three drinks, she'd get very loquacious." FDR referred to Tully as "The Duchess." It was Tully whom the President told to call Hoover and ask him to handle the search for Kermit personally. By having her call Hoover, FDR managed to keep himself one layer removed from direct intervention in a mess. It was a tactic that Hoover, a fellow adept, could not fail to admire.

The FBI found Kermit Roosevelt and kept him under surveillance for a month, especially since his inamorata was believed to be German and a potential spy. Vincent Astor learned from the episode both that J. Edgar Hoover was no man to have as an enemy and that the director bitterly resented Bill Donovan. What he could not know was that his role, indeed the whole treatment of this embarrassing incident involving the President's family, was placed in Hoover's personal files. Astor's conversations with the director had been recorded by a listening device on Hoover's phone. Bill Donovan might have once dismissed Hoover as a mere clerk, but a critic once described the FBI chief as America's "most dangerous file clerk." Hoover's final judgment on Donovan's COI was equally harsh: He described its creation as "Roosevelt's folly."

It was in the realm of political intelligence that Hoover continued to be most useful to the President. In September 1941, at FDR's direction, Adolf Berle contacted Ed Tamm, Hoover's number three aide, to ask the bureau to provide inside information on any congressional opponents of the administration's foreign policy. Within a day, the director himself got back to Berle. "There was no indication," Hoover said, "of any revolt on matters relating to the foreign policy. The President can have anything and everything he wants, at least through the present term of Congress. . . . Opposition to appropriation bills will probably depend upon how specifically these bills provide for British aid, since there seems to be a growing anti-British sentiment." The director gave no hint of how his organization managed to penetrate the confidential councils of Congress. Hoover was further able to tip off the President to an upcoming congressional investigation "into the entire motion picture industry in order to show that the Administration had been using the movies as a vehicle to propagate information about the War."

In October, Bill Donovan lost another turf battle, along with yielding intelligence operations in Latin America to Hoover. Nelson Rockefeller, the
thirty-three-year-old grandson of the richest American, John D. Rockefeller, and himself an aficionado of Latin America, persuaded FDR to create still another agency, the Office for Coordination of Commercial and
Cultural Relations Between the American Republics. The energetic and
ambitious Rockefeller became head of the new agency, which was subsequently more trimly renamed the Office of the Coordinator of Inter-
American Affairs. Donovan had managed to add to his COI charter
psychological warfare to be conducted via radio. He and Rockefeller were
thus running overlapping broadcasting operations to win the hearts of
Latinos. To trump Donovan, Rockefeller used a tactic that he picked up
from Henry Wallace while playing tennis with the Vice President. Wallace
had advised "what you ought to do is . . . give him [FDR] something that's
ready to be signed." Rockefeller, a quick study, presented just such a pre-
emptive letter to the President on October 15. FDR read it, made a few
minor changes, and sent it that day to Bill Donovan. The letter began: "It
appears that some question has been raised as to the fields of responsibility of your work and that of Nelson Rockefeller's organization. . . . Propaganda by radio or any other media directed at Latin America should be
handled exclusively by the Coordinator of Inter-American Affairs. . . ."
Donovan had now been kicked out of the Western Hemisphere on the
ground by Hoover and in the air by Rockefeller.

He was in for one more stumble. Donovan wanted to recruit Henry
Field, a leading anthropologist and Middle East expert. He invited Field to
his Georgetown home and began his soft-spoken, persuasive sales pitch.
Much to his astonishment and annoyance, he failed to make a sale. He already had a job in the government, Field explained. As he later described
Donovan's reaction to this rare rejection, "Wild Bill's face got red, his eyes
blazed and he drew a letter from his pocket signed 'Franklin D. Roosevelt,'
authorizing him to recruit anyone, anywhere, for his mission." Field then
pulled out his own letter, demonstrating that he was already working for an
intelligence operation run directly by the President. Donovan, as Field recalled, "was very amazed. . . ." Thus the director of the COI learned of the
existence of John Franklin Carter's ring and that his agency was not the
only espionage fiefdom spawned in the Oval Office.

Chapter IX

―――――――★―――――――

"Our Objective Is to Get America into the War"

ALL THAT the White House staff, including the Secret Service detail, was told on August 3, 1941, was that FDR was boarding the presidential yacht, *Potomac,* for a ten-day fishing trip off Cape Cod. Before leaving, the President had written his mother, Sara, "The heat in Washington has been fairly steady and I long to sleep under a blanket for the first time since May." Washington mythology had it that the British, who knew something about torrid outposts, paid a tropical supplement to their diplomats posted to the American capital and that the ambassador performed his duties in khaki shorts and a pith helmet.

The composition of the small presidential party appeared to confirm the purpose of the boat trip. Pa Watson, Admiral Ross McIntire, FDR's physician, and Captain John Beardall, his naval aide, were all avid fishermen. To McIntire, "There was nothing about the start of the trip to make us think it was other than the usual thing." Just prior to their departure, FDR "told me that he was going to take a little trip up through the Cape Cod Canal," Eleanor Roosevelt recalled. "Then he smiled and I knew he was not telling me all that he was going to do."

On August 4 the President's party did put into the New Bedford Yacht Club for some fishing and a picnic. There, Roosevelt welcomed aboard the attractive and amiable Princess Martha of Sweden. After her brief visit, he changed the flashy shirts he favored when fishing for a white shirt and tie. The final sartorial touch was the regulation Navy cape with velvet collar and braid frogs given to him by his cousin Colonel Henry Roosevelt, who was now serving, in the family tradition, as assistant secretary of the Navy. Getting a man confined to a wheelchair in and out of an overcoat was a clumsy business, and the cape had been an inspired alternative. As the vessel steamed out of New Bedford harbor, a flotilla of five destroyers and the heavy cruiser USS *Augusta* rose over the horizon. The *Potomac* came alongside the cruiser and the President was piped aboard. He was greeted on the quarterdeck by the leadership of the American armed forces: General George Marshall, Army Chief of Staff; Admiral Harold Stark, Chief of Naval Operations; Admiral Ernest King, commander in chief of the U.S. Fleet; and General Henry Arnold, commander of the Army Air Forces. The flotilla then swung north, headed toward rough seas off Newfoundland. The sea was FDR's element, and he tended to gather around him seafaring men whom he had known when he served as assistant secretary of the Navy. He had first met Stark as a young lieutenant commanding a destroyer. Once, while aboard another destroyer, the *Flusser,* Roosevelt had offered to take the ship between the narrow strait separating Campobello Island and the Maine coast. He knew these waters well, he said. The *Flusser*'s skipper, Lieutenant William F. Halsey Jr., suspected there was a difference between handling a sailboat and piloting a warship. But he later wrote of the incident: "As Mr. Roosevelt made his first turn, I saw him look aft and check the swing of our stern. My worries were over; he knew his business." Years earlier, when FDR visited the Pan Pacific Exposition in San Francisco, his personal aide had been Husband E. Kimmel, now commanding naval forces at Pearl Harbor.

Steaming toward the *Augusta,* aboard the Royal Navy's new battleship, the *Prince of Wales,* rode Winston Churchill, eager to find out what Franklin Roosevelt was really like. What stuff was he made of? How deep was his abhorrence of Hitler? How likely was he to join Britain in fighting Nazism? The month before, the President had delivered a strong message to Congress that had heartened Churchill. The sea lanes from the United States to Iceland, Roosevelt had declared, had to be kept open and protected against even a "threat of attack." He had then left it to the Navy to figure out what constituted a threat. Admiral Stark was called to the White House, where he hoped for clarification. Just what did the commander in chief expect of the Navy? "To some of my very pointed questions," Stark later wrote a friend, "which all of us would like to have answered, I get a smile or 'Betty, please don't ask me that.' " What Stark guessed, and what FDR was not eager to spell out, was that he wanted the U.S. Navy to patrol four fifths of the Atlantic Ocean for the British. Admiral Ernest King, the fleet commander, was careful not to underestimate the President's intentions. King simply ordered the fleet to go after any German submarine or raider close by or at "reasonably longer distances. . . ." This long arm of the American naval patrol served Britain well, but Churchill, as he approached the American ships, wanted more.

On Saturday morning, August 9, the *Augusta* and *Prince of Wales* came alongside each other. On the deck of the American warship stood Franklin Roosevelt, supported on the arm of his son Elliott, who had been waiting aboard the cruiser. Elliott, the first Roosevelt son to enter the military, had by then been on active duty almost a year, and had made a small declaration of independence by joining the Army Air Forces rather than his father's favored Navy, and without FDR's knowledge. A cosmetic ruse had been employed on this trip to minimize the President's handicap. His metal leg braces had been painted black to blend with dark shoes and socks.

As Churchill strode up the gangway to the upper deck the *Augusta*'s band struck up "God Save the Queen." The two leaders beamed and shook hands warmly. As they chatted, Ed Starling, chief of the White House Secret Service detail, was sitting in a deck chair on the *Potomac*'s fantail, headed back to the mainland. A battered fedora was perched on Starling's head, the trademark FDR cigarette holder clamped between his teeth, and a cloak like the President's draped over his shoulders. Starling's impersonation was the first time that a double had been used to conceal FDR's whereabouts. Roosevelt had taken great delight in the deception. The year before, he had boasted to his confidant Daisy Suckley of how he had fooled the press while making a secret tour of Atlantic defense zones. He had told his press officer to release in advance his itinerary before he boarded the *Tuscaloosa* out of Pensacola, Florida. From the ship he wrote Suckley, "We have all been laughing at the complete ignorance and gullibility of the press! They fell for the visit to the Andaman Islands (Indian Ocean), Celebes (North Pacific) and South Hebrides (Antarctic) and believe it or not, the Cherubic Isles from Edward Lear's *Book of Nonsense!*"

FDR mentioned to Churchill that they had met before at Gray's Inn during Roosevelt's 1918 visit to England. The Prime Minister said that he had no recollection of the occasion, which took the proud President aback. Reading the disappointment in FDR's face, Churchill quickly refreshed his memory and claimed, yes, he vividly remembered Roosevelt's "magnificent presence in all his youth and strength."

The Churchill whom FDR was meeting, essentially for the first time, was a man straddling two centuries in age and manner. He was now sixty-six. He had stood in the crowd celebrating Queen Victoria's Golden Jubilee in 1887. He became a national hero at age twenty-five after his well-publicized escape from the Boers in South Africa during their failed struggle against the British. He entered Parliament at age twenty-seven. He subsequently held an impressive array of posts—undersecretary for colonies, privy councillor, home secretary, First Lord of the Admiralty, minister of munitions, and chancellor of the Exchequer. The Admiralty post had nearly been his undoing when, after the bloody disaster in the Dardanelles in 1915, he had been relieved. He thereafter went into the trenches in France with the Grenadier Guards. He took to soldiering much as he had as a young man and seemed heedless of death. He was a man of fleeting moods, shifting from bursts of euphoria to bouts of depression that he called his "black dog." While still in the trenches and contemplating his political future, he wrote his wife, Clementine: "I am so devoured by egoism." Yet, he confessed to his physician, Lord Moran, a latent self-destructive impulse. "I don't like standing near the edge of a platform when an express train is passing through," he told Moran. "I don't like to stand by the side of a ship and look down into the water. A second's action would end everything, a few drops of desperation."

FDR could let his hair down with Daisy Suckley, whom he once told, with unintended callousness, that he could tell her anything because she didn't know anything. She was fifty years old at the time of FDR's meeting with Churchill, a maiden lady only distantly related but always introduced by Roosevelt as his "Cousin Daisy." She was genteel, prudish, and judgmental. Fortunately, a basic decency and kindness counterbalanced her inclination to brand people too quickly as "common" or "coarse," terms she applied especially to Jews. It was to Daisy that FDR wrote his first impression after lunching alone with Churchill aboard the *Augusta*. "He is a tremendously vital person and in many ways is an English Mayor La-Guardia. Don't say I said so!" he told her. "I like him and lunching alone broke ice both ways."

Churchill, like FDR, had a taste for the clandestine. The historian Ronald Lewin writes: ". . . [A]ll that was romantic in [Churchill] . . . thrilled to the excitement of intercepted signals, delphic reports from agents, broken code. . . . the same impulse drew him to mavericks and buccaneers, unorthodox figures who defied convention. . . . they appealed to his craving for the flamboyant, the adventuresome, the unusual, the unconventional; cloaked in secrecy, their attraction was doubly potent." The description could just as easily have mantled FDR.

Almost daily, British aircraft dropped Ultra decrypts for the Prime Minister onto the deck of the *Prince of Wales*. The box they came in was weighted so that if the plane crashed and sank the box would sink too. Churchill did not share all these secrets with FDR. By now, American and British codebreakers had supposedly reached an agreement for a "free exchange of intelligence." But with Britain's cryptanalysts so far ahead, Churchill felt that too free an exchange might become a one-way street. He had recently roared at one of his aides, "Are we going to throw all our secrets into the American lap? If so, I am against it. It would be very much better to go slow, as we have far more to give than they."

When the President and Prime Minister finally sat down to work at the *Augusta*'s wardroom table, first on the agenda was Japan. The month before, forty thousand Japanese troops had seized Indochina with its vast rubber resources. FDR had retaliated by freezing Japanese assets in the United States and cutting off the sale of high-octane airplane fuel to Japan. Still, as the President had told his interior secretary, Harold Ickes, at the time, his goal was not war in the Pacific: "I simply have not got enough Navy to go around—and every little episode in the Pacific means fewer ships in the Atlantic." He said to Churchill that a fight with Japan would be "the wrong war in the wrong ocean at the wrong time." The PM agreed. Their first objective must be to defeat Hitler.

All that the public was later told of the secret meeting at sea was that it had produced a ringing declaration, the Atlantic Charter, released to the press on August 14. Roosevelt and Churchill had agreed that their nations sought no other country's territory, nor any changes in other territories without the freely expressed wishes of their inhabitants. They supported the right of all peoples to choose their own form of government, and they pledged to promote free trade, disarmament, and a permanent system of security for the world. These goals were to follow "the final destruction of the Nazi tyranny," the continuing priority. Churchill was only too delighted to wed Britain publicly to the United States in these lofty sentiments. But it was his private agenda that had dominated his sessions with FDR on the *Augusta*. Britain's sea losses had so far totaled a nearly fatal fifteen hundred ships sunk by mid-1941. FDR promised the PM that American warships would not only protect British convoys, but that they would patrol as far as three hundred miles into the Atlantic *to seek out and attack* German submarines.

Upon his return to London, Churchill told Sir Dudley Pound, First Sea Lord, "Our objective is to get the Americans into the war. . . . We can settle best how to fight it afterwards." He assured his cabinet that Roosevelt "was obviously determined to come in." He further reported, "The President had said that he would wage war but not declare it, and that he would become more and more provocative. If the Germans did not like it, they could attack the American forces." As far as Churchill was concerned, FDR had all but declared war against Germany, at least on the high seas.

Three weeks after the Atlantic conference, the USS *Greer,* a destroyer of World War I vintage, camouflaged in shades of gray, was sailing from Boston to Iceland to deliver mail to the forty-four hundred American Marines FDR had sent there nearly eight weeks before. Off Iceland, a British patrol plane signaled the *Greer* that a U-boat lay ten miles ahead. The destroyer began tracking the German sub, reporting its position back to the plane. The plane dropped four depth charges without scoring a hit and left to refuel. The *Greer* continued to pursue the submarine. The U-boat's captain, believing the depth charge attack had been made by the destroyer, then fired torpedoes at the *Greer,* unsuccessfully. The *Greer* then fired several depth charges with equal lack of success before breaking off the engagement. Since the U-boat had remained submerged throughout the fight, its skipper never knew who had attacked him first, aircraft or ship, British or American.

Roosevelt chose a fireside chat on September 11 to exploit the incident. He had intended to make the radio talk sooner, but his beloved mother, Sara, had died four days before. Her influence on his life was incalculable. She was a physically imposing woman, almost five feet ten, a great beauty in her day, and with a character to match her stature. Even after FDR became president, she still controlled his money. She always sat at the head of the family table, a grande dame, imperious and accustomed to reign. When her sister was stranded in Europe by the outbreak of war in 1939, she simply could not understand why Franklin did not send a battleship to fetch his aunt. The loss of his mother struck FDR hard, and he remained in seclusion at his home in Hyde Park for several days before returning to Washington for the radio address.

Wearing a light gray seersucker suit and a black mourning band, the President was wheeled into the East Room to a clutch of microphones next to a poster proclaiming, KEEP 'EM FLYING. An estimated sixty million

Americans were listening as he began. "The United States destroyer *Greer*, proceeding in full daylight toward Iceland, . . . was flying the American flag," Roosevelt intoned somberly. "Her identity as an American ship was unmistakable. She was then and there attacked by a submarine. . . . I tell you the blunt fact that the German submarine fired first upon this American destroyer without warning, and with deliberate design to sink her." Technically, yes, the submarine had fired first at the *Greer*, but only after having been depth-charged by the British plane. "It is clear," the President continued, "Hitler has begun his campaign to control the seas by ruthless force. From now on," he warned, "if German or Italian vessels of war enter the waters the protection of which is necessary for the American defense, they do so at their own peril." He meant that American warships would shoot on sight. FDR would later say that he was perfectly willing to tell untruths to win a war. At this point, he was willing to bend the truth about the attack on the *Greer* to prepare the country to accept war. He justified his stance with a simple homily, ". . . [W]hen you see a rattlesnake poised to strike, you do not wait until he has struck before you crush him. . . ." He had proof, FDR said, that Hitler was not only a threat at sea, but a danger to the American landmass. Bill Stephenson's British Security Coordination had provided him with a letter from the Bolivian military attaché in Berlin reporting a plot to create a Nazi government in that South American country. Stephenson's information enabled FDR to state in his broadcast that this attempt "to subvert the government of Bolivia" proved Hitler's designs on Latin America.

Churchill, upon hearing the President speak, instantly understood the Nazi dilemma. "Hitler will have to choose between losing the Battle of the Atlantic," he said, "or coming into frequent collision with United States ships." The Germans also now recognized that, at least on the Atlantic, they faced two enemies. The German navy chief, Admiral Erich Raeder, advised Hitler, "There is no longer any difference between British and American ships."

Six weeks later, on October 27, a rainy evening in Washington, Secret Service agents carried the President from his limousine into the shelter of the Mayflower Hotel. The first time that his secretary, Grace Tully, had seen the President of the United States hoisted like a sack of flour out of the car and into a wheelchair, she had turned away and cried. But since the President never showed the slightest embarrassment at this handling, she and the rest of the staff became accustomed to it. FDR was already late for one of the premier events of the Washington social season, the annual

Navy Day dinner. The performer in him knew that his late arrival would only heighten his audience's anticipation. Waiting in the flag-draped ballroom under a canopy of blazing chandeliers were the capital's powers—cabinet members, congressional leaders, Supreme Court justices, the nation's military chiefs, and their spouses, everybody who was anybody.

On the dais, the President, smiling and exuberant, looked splendid in black tie, especially after being seen so often in the gray suits he favored. As the Marine Corps band finished "Hail to the Chief," a new star in the federal constellation, William J. Donovan, rose to introduce the President. Roosevelt maintained a magisterial silence until the audience became hushed, and then began his remarks. A little over a month after the *Greer* incident, on October 16, a brand-new $5 million destroyer, the USS *Kearney,* had been torpedoed while patrolling off Iceland with the loss of eleven American lives. The President seized on the incident this evening to denounce Germany. "We have wished to avoid shooting," he said. "But the shooting has started. And history has recorded who fired the first shot. In the long run, however, all that will matter is who fired the last shot." He then traced a threat that ran from land to sea. "Hitler has often protested that his plans for conquest do not extend across the Atlantic Ocean." He paused for effect before unleashing his shocker. "I have in my possession a secret map, made in Germany by Hitler's government—by planners of the New World Order. . . . It is a map of South America and a part of Central America as Hitler proposes to reorganize it. . . . The geographical experts of Berlin have ruthlessly obliterated all the existing boundaries; they have divided South America into five vassal states. . . . And they have also so arranged it that the territory of these new puppet states includes the Republic of Panama, and our great lifeline—the Panama Canal. This map, my friends, makes clear the Nazi design not only against South America but against the United States as well."

Fear of a Nazi end run through South America and into the United States had long preoccupied the President. He had directed Adolf Berle to instruct all American embassies in Latin America to spy on German companies, German immigrant clubs, and just plain suspicious Germans south of the border. Berle had quickly been inundated with the effluvia of amateur informants. From Cuba came a list of schoolteachers, students, and an unemployed sixty-two-year-old mulatto, all described as "persons believed to hold pro-German sympathies." A thick dossier compiled in Mexico would surely have astonished the popular café society pianist José Iturbi. Iturbi was, according to this file, "a principal agent for Germany in Latin America."

The British had long been feeding FDR's fears. An MI6 report forwarded to the President nearly a year and a half before warned him that German troops were headed for Dakar, Senegal, just 1,900 miles across the South Atlantic from Natal, Brazil. These troops, the British claimed, were the vanguard of a far larger force that would cross this narrow neck of the ocean and set up bases in Brazil within striking distance of the Panama Canal. The British report had six thousand German troops already there prepared to join pro-Nazi Brazilians to overthrow the pro-American regime of President Getulio Vargas. FDR ordered the Navy to come up with a plan to thwart the takeover. The Navy devised "Pot of Gold," an operation to transport over a hundred thousand American troops to Brazil. However, the plan had a flaw. The American military, at that point, had neither the ships nor the men to carry it out.

The American press was instantly suspicious of the map FDR described in his Navy Day speech. At a press conference the next day, a reporter asked Roosevelt if he might see the map. Oh, he could not do that, the President explained in horror. It "has on it certain manuscript notations, which if they were reproduced would in all probability disclose where the map came from." And disclosure, he went on, would "dry up the source of future information." Another reporter pressed ahead: "What would you say to the charge of the suspicion that the map . . . had been foisted on you in some way? That it was also a forgery or a fake of some sort?" FDR smiled complacently. He had acquired the map from "a source which is undoubtedly reliable," he said. "There is no question about that!"

FDR's isolationist nemesis, Senator Burton K. Wheeler, learned that the unidentified source of the map was Little Bill Stephenson, who gave it to Big Bill Donovan, who passed it on to the President. Wheeler's suspicions had immediately been aroused. "Where did it originate?" he asked on the Senate floor. "It originated in the office of Colonel Donovan. . . . Perhaps I should say it originated in New York, in the minds of gentlemen closely associated with the British government. . . ." The map's provenance was indeed cloudy. The British had an explanation as to how they had acquired it, another tale of derring-do. Their secret agents had snatched it from a German courier, Gottfried Sandstede, who thereafter "met with an accident" arranged by the Gestapo for his carelessness. Sandstede, however, was not murdered by the Gestapo in 1941; he died on the Russian front in 1944. The map of South America that FDR had refused to share with the press did not outline a Nazi partition. Rather, it was entitled, in German, "Air Traffic Grid of the United States of South America's Main Lines," and showed straight line routes connecting major cities and contained long-hand notes, also in German, referring to the production, storage, and shipment of airplane fuel to these sites.

Not only was the map spurious, but the Nazi plot to take over Bolivia that FDR had warned of in his earlier fireside chat was an outright British fabrication. The letter from the Bolivian attaché alleging the plot had been forged by the BSC and swallowed whole at the White House. Even before FDR had used this information in his speeches, Adolf Berle had warned Secretary of State Cordell Hull that British intelligence agents were "manufacturing documents detailing Nazi conspiracies in South America." He cautioned, "I think we have to be a little on our guard against false scares."

The intriguing question is why all this suspect intelligence—reports of Nazi troops in South America, a forged letter predicting a Nazi takeover in Bolivia, a suspicious map, a manipulated version of the *Greer* incident—found its way into the speeches of the President of the United States. The answer clearly lies in FDR's underlying objective. He wanted U-boats attacked. He wanted America in the fight. And if someone handed him documents that strengthened his case, he was not about to scrutinize them to death. The truth was that since June 1941 the British had learned from Ultra decrypts that German U-boat commanders had received frequent instructions to avoid clashes with American vessels. Further, Hitler had not the slightest intention of invading the Western Hemisphere. But these facts stood in the way of what FDR wanted—to stand by Britain in the defeat of Nazism. His proselytizing appeared to be working. On November 8, after a close House tally and a thirteen-vote margin in the Senate, Congress amended the Neutrality Act to allow the President to arm U.S. merchant ships. That same month a Gallup poll revealed that if the Nazis attacked South America, two thirds of Americans were willing to go to war.

★

As 1941 drew to a close, FDR's newest intelligence creations, headed by Astor, Carter, and Donovan, vied for the President's favor. Bill Donovan, with the largest, most visible apparatus, rushed ahead with indiscriminate energy, for Wild Bill was a man to whom motion equaled progress. He began to bombard FDR with memoranda churned out by his ever-growing staff. A November 12 report from the coordinator of information quoted a supposedly confidential remark by Churchill to the effect that after the war both "German *and* Russian militarism must be destroyed." With Britain's best hope of survival at this point resting on Russia's recent entry into the war, it must have surprised FDR to be told that Churchill would make so rash a comment. Five days later, Donovan delivered to the President intelligence purportedly from within the Third Reich that the Germans were filled with "despair" and "misery," that morale was sinking fast, and that a single major setback would leave the Nazi regime hanging "dangerously in the balance." Such errant nonsense at a time when Hitler had yet to taste defeat somehow drew no rebuke from FDR, and Donovan's stock seemed unaffected. The COI chief's access to the White House continued, totaling nine meetings with the President in 1941.

FDR's least recognized agent, John Franklin Carter, who was now operating with $54,000 from the President's emergency funds, also continued to enjoy easy access to the Oval Office, thanks to his cover as a columnist friendly to the administration. Some assignments that FDR gave Carter were straightforward espionage, in one instance, having an agent investigate a suspected fifth column operation on the French island of Martinique in the West Indies. Others skirted the defensible. Charles Lindbergh continued to infuriate FDR, especially after the aviator became the crown jewel in the isolationist America First movement. In late April 1941, days after Lindbergh gave his first speech as a member of the organization, the President called Carter into his office and began speaking in his elliptical fashion, leaving the journalist mystified as to where he was headed. FDR finally got around to the Civil War and the Copperheads, northerners who sympathized with the South. The President wanted Carter to look into present-day Copperheads. Carter now understood what was expected of him. Within days, he delivered a fifty-page report for placement in the President's nighttime reading file. Thus armed, FDR was able to fire back when a reporter at a press conference asked him why Colonel Lindbergh had not been called to active duty. That was simple. Lindbergh, the President explained, was the equivalent of the arch–Civil War Copperhead Clement L. Vallandigham. The thrust drew blood. Lindbergh wrote FDR three days later resigning his commission as a colonel in the Army Air Corps Reserve. In Roosevelt's mind, his assignment to Carter had not been prompted by personal animus. Lindbergh, in FDR's eyes, was an enemy of his country, as dangerous as any fifth columnist, and had to be exposed.

Perhaps the oddest—or given FDR's multi-layered thought processes, a typical—assignment was the one he had given Carter to take a discreet look into the effectiveness of his dear friend Vincent Astor's operation in New York. On completing the assignment, Carter could barely wait to phone his conclusion to FDR. He told the President that Astor was confused "about the whole problem of investigation in the New York district." This verdict was merely a preliminary jab presaging a full-scale attack on a rival whom Carter believed was clearly out of his depth.

★

To the President, what was happening in Europe was vital to America, what was happening in the Pacific a distraction. Seen from the Japanese perspective, however, the United States had become an obstacle to Japan's grand strategy for creating the Greater East Asia Co-Prosperity Sphere, a union, with their country at its heart, freed of Western colonialists. The United States was aiding the empire's enemy through its extension of lend-lease to China, embargoing vitally needed fuel—in short, attempting to block Japan's imperial destiny. China had become the major sticking point between the United States and Japan. After nine years of unofficial and four years of full-scale war, the Japanese dared not lose face by a withdrawal from China, yet could not defeat it as long as Chiang Kai-shek continued to be propped up by American military aid. The emperor's government had been willing to placate the Americans by trimming back its ambitions in Southeast Asia. But Roosevelt demanded an impossible price, Japan's complete withdrawal from China.

Through Magic decrypts, FDR knew of the Japanese frustration. One broken cable dated November 4, 1941, and marked "urgent" from Tokyo's foreign minister, Matsuoka, to the ambassador in Washington, Nomura, warned: "Conditions both within and without our Empire are so tense that no longer is procrastination possible, yet, in our sincerity to maintain pacific relationships between the Empire of Japan and the United States of America, we have decided, as a result of these deliberations, to gamble once more on the continuance of the parleys, but this is our last effort. . . . We gambled the fate of our land on the throw of this die."

In the face of intensifying mutual mistrust, the President sought to strengthen security at home by dealing with his customary bugaboo, fifth column infiltration, particularly by Japanese living on the West Coast, whether American citizens or aliens. Carter employed in his ring a Chicago businessman, Curtis B. Munson, a levelheaded operator not easily stampeded into herd judgments. With FDR's blessing, Carter had sent Munson to the West Coast to gauge the loyalty of Japanese residents. Munson reported, "There are still Japanese in the United States who will tie dynamite around their waist and make a human bomb of themselves." But American-born Japanese were "universally estimated from 90 to 98 percent loyal to the United States. . . . They are very American and are of a proud, self-respecting race suffering from a little inferiority complex and a lack of contact with the white boys they went to school with. There is no Japanese 'problem' on the coast, there will be no armed uprising of Japanese." FDR glanced at these findings and quickly dismissed them as "nothing much new." What caught his eye, however, was a later Munson paragraph: "Your reporter . . . is horrified to note that dams, bridges, harbors, power stations etc. are wholly unguarded everywhere. The harbor of San Pedro could be razed by fire completely by four men with hand grenades. . . . Dams could be blown and half of lower California might actually die of thirst. . . ." An alarmed FDR moved quickly. Memories of smoldering Black Tom munitions storehouses in 1916 were still alive in his mind. On November 11 the President directed Carter, Donovan, the FBI, and the Army to protect these sites. In Roosevelt's shotgun style of delegation, the four parties could sort out their respective roles themselves. He further told Carter, "[I]mmediate arrests may be required."

Was the United States facing an attack, overt or covert by Japan? In mid-November, Britain's Joint Intelligence Committee issued its assessment. Yes, Japan and the United States were approaching a crisis. But above all, the British analysts concluded, the Japanese would never risk war with the United States. If negotiations between America and Japan broke down, the Japanese might well attack, but in Southeast Asia, and their first target would likely be Thailand.

★

That fall, the President received a document of such sensitivity that its exposure could provoke an international crisis. Its thudding title, "Army and Navy Estimate of United States Over-All Production Requirements," masked its significance. Within the War Department, the plan had been shorthanded to "Rainbow Five." The previous July, the President had asked General Marshall to prepare an estimate of what it would take, should America enter the war, to defeat Germany. By September 25, the top-secret seventeen-page Rainbow Five report, was on the President's desk. The plan projected the full productive capacity of a great industrial nation—its manpower, machinery, and matériel—to achieve the objective. Rainbow Five predicted the need for 216 infantry divisions, 51 motorized divisions, and a vastly expanded Navy, all at a projected cost of $150 billion. Given the secrecy of the document, only thirty-five copies were made.

However aggressive the President himself felt, the debate between interventionists and isolationists went on and extended into the War Department. Though involved in devising a contingency plan for war with Germany, some members of Marshall's staff were unhappy at considering the Third Reich even as a theoretical enemy. Officers who thought, with the President, that the United States could wage a successful war against Germany, or that it should do so, were put down by their isolationist colleagues as "soreheads."

On the evening of December 3, Senator Burton K. Wheeler received a surprise visit from an unidentified officer in the Army's War Plans Division. The officer had with him a copy of the Rainbow Five plan. "Aren't you afraid of delivering the most secret document in America to a senator?" Wheeler is supposed to have asked. His visitor was unfazed, replying that Congress had "a right to know what's really going on in the executive branch when it concerns human lives." The next day, Wheeler leaked the Rainbow Five plan to Chesley Manly, the Washington correspondent of FDR's fiercest journalistic critic, the *Chicago Tribune*.

J. Edgar Hoover was tasked to investigate the leak. Suspicion fell instantly on an officer in the War Plans Division, Colonel Albert C. Wedemeyer, a soldier of partly German extraction and a warm friend of General Ludwig Beck, chief of the German General Staff. Hoover's report to the attorney general, marked "strictly personal and confidential," was emphatic but circumstantial. "Wedemeyer spent two years in Germany attending the German War College," the FBI chief noted. "He is reported to be most pro-German in his feelings, his utterances and his sympathies. He personally travelled through Germany with Colonel Lindbergh. . . ." On September 21, "Wedemeyer took four days' leave for the purpose of going to New York to attend a banquet or dinner with Colonel Lindbergh. . . . Colonel Wedemeyer engaged in rather heated discussions with fellow officers at the War Department concerning his lack of sympathy with the Administration's international program. . . . He advocates a 'hands off' policy toward Japan. . . . He is otherwise very isolationist in his statements and sympathies." However, neither the FBI nor the Army was able to connect Wedemeyer directly to the leak.

Rainbow Five was a major military secret, and its disclosure likely violated the Espionage Act of 1917. The attorney general, Francis Biddle, thought that the *Chicago Tribune*'s publisher, Colonel Robert McCormick, could be prosecuted under the act. Printing the story had, in fact, troubled the *Tribune*'s managing editor, J. Loy Maloney, who bucked the decision up to McCormick. If FDR had a premier hater, it was the tall, stern, sixty-one-year-old conservative publisher of the *Tribune*. Given his rigid tory views, one wit called McCormick "the greatest mind of the fourteenth century." McCormick told Maloney that he wanted the story to run, and on page one. It appeared on December 4 under a headline that shouted, FDR'S WAR PLANS! GOAL IS TEN MILLION ARMED MEN, PROPOSED LAND DRIVE BY JULY, 1943. The body of the story read: ". . . President Roosevelt calls for American Expeditionary Forces aggregating five million men for a final land offensive against Germany and her satellites. . . . Germany and her European satellites cannot be defeated by the European powers now fighting against her. . . . If our European enemies are to be defeated, it will be necessary for the United States to enter the war. . . ." July 1, 1943, was the date set for America's presumed entry.

No matter that Secretary Stimson pointed out to the press that Rainbow Five was a *contingency* plan, not what the United States would do, but what the country might have to do. "What would you think of a general staff," he lectured the reporters, "which did not investigate every conceivable type of emergency which might confront it?"

Though a contingent plan, Rainbow Five was the most provocative jab yet at Hitler. It dealt not only with estimates of guns, ships, and men that the United States might raise, but its dense appendices contained maps of Germany, potential targets, and made estimates of the strength of the prospective enemy. The explicitness of the plan would inevitably affect Hitler's strategic thinking, and it had to alarm Americans who wanted to keep the United States out of war. Rainbow Five, blown in a major American newspaper and its Washington affiliate, the *Times-Herald,* might have been a bombshell of international magnitude if its occurrence was not so totally obliterated by what was to happen in America on a peaceful Sunday afternoon just three days later.

Chapter X

———═★═———

Catastrophe or Conspiracy

I
T WAS just past 1:30 P.M. when FDR heard Frank Knox's voice over the phone telling him, "Mr. President, it looks as if the Japanese have attacked Pearl Harbor." Soon a Signal Corps enlisted man was patching a line into the President's phone to take a call from Governor Joseph Poindexter in Honolulu. Listening hard through the static, the President exclaimed, "My God, there's another wave of Japanese over Hawaii right this minute!" A Secret Service man on duty remembered, "His chin stuck out about two feet in front of his knees, and he was the maddest Dutchman anybody ever saw."

A stream of generals, admirals, and aides filed in and out of the office throughout the afternoon. At 8:30 P.M., members of the cabinet, summoned by the President, began arriving as stewards lugged in extra chairs, forming them into a horseshoe around the President's desk. At 9 P.M., FDR met with the leaders of Congress. Through the window facing south over the Ellipse the moon could be glimpsed riding in a haze over a capital that had started the day at peace. In front of the White House, a crowd milled about, the stunned, the curious, and the angry. A stenographer took notes as FDR began addressing the arc of grave faces. At the root of the Japanese attack, the President said, he detected machinations of the Axis partnership: ". . . [W]e received indications from various sources—Europe and Asia—

that the German government was pressing Japan for action under the Tripartite Pact. In other words, an effort to divert the American mind, and the British mind from the European field, and divert American supplies from the European theater to the defense of the East Asia Theater." FDR told his listeners, who leaned forward to catch his somber delivery, that his administration had reluctantly reached the conclusion that the ongoing negotiations with Japan were a sham, particularly the sticking point concerning the U.S. demand for Japan's withdrawal from China. ". . . [T]hey were to agree to cease their acts of aggressions, and that they would try to bring the China war to a close," he said. He returned to the theme of Axis conniving: "And so the thing went along until we believed that under the pressure from Berlin the Japanese were about to do something. . . ." The sneak attack had a historical parallel in the Russo-Japanese war, FDR noted. Pearl Harbor was "equalled only by the Japanese episode of 1904, when two squadrons, cruisers . . . without any warning—I think on a Sunday morning, by the way—Japanese cruisers sank all of them. . . ."

As the President spoke, military aides continued to set fresh bulletins before him. He looked up from one to announce, "It looks as if out of eight battleships, three have been sunk, and possibly a fourth. Two destroyers were blown up while they were in dry-dock. Two of the battleships are badly damaged. Several other smaller vessels have been sunk or destroyed. . . . I have no word on the Navy casualties, which will undoubtedly be very heavy, and the best information is that there have been more than one hundred Army casualties and three hundred men killed and injured." His labor secretary, Frances Perkins, the only woman in the cabinet, recalled, "The President could hardly bring himself" to describe the slaughter and had physical difficulty in getting the words out. Another eyewitness, however, Undersecretary of State Sumner Welles, observed how FDR "demonstrated that ultimate capacity to dominate and control a supreme emergency which is perhaps the rarest and most valuable characteristic of any statesman."

Senator Tom Connally of Texas, chairman of the Senate Foreign Relations Committee, sat close to the President, his face red with rage as he bellowed, "How did it happen that our warships were caught like lame ducks at Pearl Harbor?" Connally slammed his fist down hard on the President's desk. "How did they catch us with our pants down?" "I don't know, Tom," FDR answered. "I just don't know." After the cabinet and congressional leaders left, Treasury secretary Henry Morgenthau returned to his office and told his staff gathered there, "They will never be able to explain it." Adolf Berle wrote in his diary: ". . . If there is anyone I would not like to be it is the Chief of Naval Intelligence."

Aides, couriers, and secretaries continued to enter the President's study all evening. At twenty-five minutes past midnight FDR received his last visitors. He had summoned the COI chief, Bill Donovan, and the CBS broadcaster Edward R. Murrow, recently back from covering the war from London, who had been invited for Sunday supper. Earlier that day, Donovan had been at a football game at the Polo Grounds, watching the Brooklyn Dodgers pummel the New York Giants 21 to 7, when a voice announced over a loudspeaker, "Colonel William Donovan, come to the box office at once. There is an important phone message." The message was from the President's son Captain Jimmy Roosevelt, telling Wild Bill that the President needed him in Washington at once.

Now, some eleven hours later, the parade of officials finally ended, Donovan and Murrow found FDR alone sitting in semi-darkness, his face illuminated by a pool of light from a desk lamp. The room was still cluttered with the extra chairs. Stacks of books, piles of yellowed papers tied with string rested alongside the bookcases, and FDR's ship models cast their shadows against the walls. Gathering dust in one corner stood an incongruous pipe organ. Removed from the President's desk were the stamp album, magnifying glass, scissors, and stickers he had been working on when Knox's call turned his world upside down. The reporter in Murrow noted that the President was now wearing a shapeless gray "sack jacket" and munching a sandwich washed down with a beer. FDR's ashen pallor matched the jacket, and he appeared drained of energy. Still, Murrow remembered, "Never have I seen one so calm and so steady." The President asked Murrow about morale in bomb-blasted London. Murrow's response that Britain would hold out clearly pleased FDR. He had received a call earlier from Churchill and told the PM, "We're all in the same boat now."

FDR had before him the latest damage assessments from Pearl Harbor delivered by Admiral Stark. Over 350 Japanese torpedo and dive bombers had struck in three waves. Casualties were heavy and would ultimately total 2,403 Americans dead and 1,178 wounded. Much of the Pacific Fleet lay at the bottom of Pearl Harbor or in disemboweled ruin, the decks running red and strewn with bodies. The Navy's losses totaled eighteen vessels, including the battleships *Arizona, West Virginia,* and *California* sunk, the *Oklahoma* capsized, and the *Nevada* run aground. The President turned to Donovan, speaking in cold rage, "They caught our ships like lame ducks! Lame ducks, Bill! . . . We told them at Pearl Harbor, and everywhere else, to have the lookouts manned. But they still took us by surprise." The ship losses seemed particularly personal to him. He still liked to refer to his years as assistant secretary as, "When I was in the Navy." The losses suffered by the Air Corps were almost as staggering as the fleet's. Nearly 350 planes had been destroyed or damaged. FDR pounded his fist on the desk. "They caught our planes on the ground, by God, on the ground!"

Pearl Harbor was an intelligence failure of stunning magnitude. Not only naval intelligence but all military intelligence had failed abysmally. The FBI failed. The fledgling Donovan organization failed, though on that night FDR never criticized Donovan's performance. Rather, he told Donovan, "It's a good thing that you got me started on this [intelligence business]. . . ." When, through Magic, the President, the secretaries of war and state, and the service chiefs were able to read what the Japanese ambassador and foreign minister were saying up to the moment the first torpedo struck the first American warship, with broken codes revealing that the Japanese had spies reporting on the fleet's deployment at Pearl Harbor, how could the imminence of the attack have been missed? Why had both signal and human intelligence failed so totally?

The answer can be found only by examining how the intelligence available to the President was used, misused, or unused. In hindsight, a fairly straight line can be traced from clue to clue to an inevitable attack. If one seeks perhaps the earliest warning it was the message Ambassador Joseph Grew transmitted from Tokyo to Secretary Hull on January 27, 1941, over eleven months before the attack. "A member of my Embassy," Grew cabled, "was told by my . . . colleague that from many quarters, including a Japanese one, he heard that a surprise mass attack on Pearl Harbor was planned by the Japanese military forces, in case of 'trouble' between Japan and the United States. . . . My colleague said that he was prompted to pass this on because it had come to him from many sources, although the plan seemed fantastic." On the other hand, a Magic intercept of a Japanese transmission from Pearl Harbor to Tokyo dated February 15, just nineteen days after Grew's message, predicted an American, not a Japanese threat: "Indications seem to be that the U.S. has decided to declare war on Japan within the next three weeks."

China had continued to remain the sore point between the United States and Japan. The Japanese, as late as September 1941, continued to demand first, that the United States and Britain not increase their military position in the Far East; second, that the United States lift its embargo on oil; and third, that America stop aiding Chiang Kai-shek. The State Department had advised the administration "that adoption and application of a policy of imposing embargoes upon strategic exports to Japan would be . . . likely to lead to this country's becoming involved in war." War could likely have been averted since the United States could have lifted the oil embargo at no cost to itself. But FDR had stuck to the position that Japan must leave China; and this demand the Japanese could not abide. Thus, something of a diplomatic Kabuki dance leading inexorably toward war had followed.

By November, Japan had two key emissaries in Washington, the regular ambassador, Kichisaburo Nomura, and a special envoy, Saburo Kurusu. Kurusu had earlier served in the Japanese consulate in Chicago, where he married an American, Alice Little. At a press conference on his most recent return to the United States, Kurusu had sought to ingratiate himself with an American audience by saying, "I fully realize the difficulty of my task, making a tight scrum, I wish I could break through the line and make a touchdown." Kurusu's aide had to explain to baffled American reporters that "scrum" was a rugby term, and that the envoy had meant to say "huddle."

Every communication, however secret, between the two diplomats and Tokyo during the buildup to Pearl Harbor was available to the President. A November 5 message classified "of utmost secrecy," from the foreign office to the Washington embassy carried instructions in the event that a long-shot pending accord between Japan and the United States could be approved. This message, broken and translated the same day, set a suspiciously rigid deadline. "It is absolutely necessary that all arrangements for the signing of this agreement be completed by the 25th of this month," the dispatch read. Behind this message, and unknown even to Nomura and Kurusu, was a decision reached by the Japanese cabinet, headed now by the tough new premier, General Hideki Tojo, to go to war if the Americans failed to meet the deadline.

FDR might have been warned of what was coming if one of his chief intelligence sources had possessed more imagination. During the late summer of 1941, the FBI chief in New York, Percy E. "Sam" Foxworth, arranged a meeting between his boss, J. Edgar Hoover, and a Yugoslav named Dusko Popov, recently arrived in the United States. Popov came from a wealthy family with far-flung business connections, which allowed him to pursue his burning passion, café society high life. In 1939, Johann Jebsen, with whom Popov had attended school in Germany and who now worked for the Abwehr, recruited the Yugoslav playboy as an agent. Popov was sent to spy in England, where he promptly revealed his Abwehr role to MI6. The British happily recruited him as a double agent. Abwehr officials were so pleased with the intelligence Popov fed them, fabricated by MI6, that they decided to send him to America to establish a spy network.

Popov arrived in the United States via neutral Portugal aboard a flying boat in August 1941. In order to carry out his double agent role without being arrested as an actual German spy, Popov would have to get Hoover's approval to operate a bogus espionage ring. It was then that Sam Foxworth arranged for Hoover to meet Popov. What Popov had already revealed to Foxworth was extraordinary. He told him that his friend Jebsen and Baron Gronau, the German air attaché in Japan, had escorted Japanese naval officials to Taranto, Italy, to study one of the war's most effective air raids. The Japanese wanted to learn how the British, in November 1940, had practically destroyed the Italian fleet in Taranto harbor by using torpedo planes launched from the aircraft carrier *Illustrious*. If that intelligence did not suggest Japanese interest in Pearl Harbor, Popov had stronger evidence. Before leaving Lisbon, the Abwehr gave him a lengthy list of questions to pursue while he was in America. Much of the questionnaire was general and predictable: He was to report on American troop movements, war production, shipping activity, and military base locations. But his most specific instructions, covering a third of the questionnaire and given "the highest priority," dealt with Pearl Harbor. Popov was to travel to Hawaii to answer these queries: "Details about naval ammunition and mine depot on Isle of Kushua [Pearl Harbor]. . . . Is the Crater Punch Bowl [Honolulu] being used as an ammunition dump? . . . How far has the dredger work progressed at the entrance and in the east and southeast lock? Depth of water? . . . The pier installations, workshops, petrol installations, situation of dry dock No. 1 and of the new dry dock which is being built. . . . Reports about torpedo protection nets newly introduced in the British and USA Navy." The Abwehr also wanted, clearly at the behest of the Japanese, sketches and the exact location of "Wickham" (Hickam), Wheeler, Luke, and "Kaneche" (Kaneohe) airfields.

J. C. Masterman, who headed the British XX (Double Cross) Committee that handled double agents like Popov, had also been given a copy of the questionnaire. Masterman concluded, ". . . [I]n the event of the United States being at war, Pearl Harbor would be the first point to be attacked. . . ." However, he did not report this conclusion to U.S. authorities because he did not want to appear to be another Briton nudging America toward war. The Americans, he believed, upon seeing this extraordinary document, would draw their own conclusion.

Just as extraordinary as Popov's instructions was the form in which they had been communicated. The entire questionnaire had been reduced four hundred times normal to the size of a period by the microdot process developed by a German professor, Arnold Zapp.

Prior to meeting with J. Edgar Hoover, Foxworth warned Popov, "Mr. Hoover is a very virtuous man." The New York chief believed the warning necessary because in the weeks that Popov had been waiting to see Hoover, he had used Abwehr money to indulge his pleasures to the hilt. He rented a penthouse apartment on Park Avenue and resumed an affair with the French actress Simone Simon. Another FBI report had Popov with a girlfriend in Florida, where the bureau threatened him with prosecution for violating the Mann Act in taking a woman across state lines for immoral purposes. Popov complained to a British intelligence agent, "If I bend over to smell a bowl of flowers, I scratch my nose on a microphone."

For Hoover the meeting was hate at first sight. He disliked Slavs, along with Jews, Catholics, and blacks. Further, Hoover distrusted double agents. Popov was tall, handsome, suave, glib, high living, flashy, and a foreigner, everything that Hoover detested. The director had been shown the reports of Popov's sexual escapades and, perhaps even more damning, learned that Popov had dared stray into Hoover's favored night spot, the Stork Club in Manhattan. Here was a man who could commit, in Hoover's eyes, the ultimate sin: He might embarrass the bureau. Under no circumstances would Hoover allow Popov to establish even a fake German spy ring in the United States. And he certainly was not going to let the man go to Pearl Harbor. Of all that Popov told him, the only thing that caught Hoover's attention was revelation of the microdot process. The mechanics rather than the substance of Popov's Abwehr instructions seized Hoover's imagination. He cut short the meeting with the Yugoslav and told him, "I can catch spies without your or anyone else's help. . . ." Like all double agents, "you're begging for information to sell to your German friends so that you can make a lot of money and be a playboy." Not only did Hoover dismiss Popov, but the competitive director refused to inform his intelligence rivals, MID, ONI, and COI, of what the Yugoslav had been told to look for at Pearl Harbor.

What Hoover did, on September 3, just days after seeing Popov, was to send a letter marked "strictly confidential," through Pa Watson to FDR. It began, "I thought the President and you might be interested in the attached photographs which show one of the methods used by the German espionage system in transmitting messages to its agents." Hoover had attached a copy of a telegram with two tiny smudges, which were the microdots. He also provided the President with a sampling of the questions contained in Popov's instructions. Hoover made no mention that Popov had revealed the secret to him, making it appear that the microdot process had been discovered "in connection with a current investigation being made by the FBI." The part of the microdot enlarged and translated for the President included questions about total U.S. monthly production of fighter planes, planes delivered to Britain, even "the air-training plan being followed in Canada." But, astonishingly, Hoover included none of the pointed inquiries about Pearl Harbor, not a word about the numerous specific questions that would have alerted the President that the Japanese had an alarming interest in America's major naval bastion in the Pacific. It was as if a lookout on the *Titanic* had alerted the captain to a rowboat to port while ignoring the iceberg to starboard. As for Dusko Popov, Hoover kicked him out of the country. He was allowed to go to Rio de Janeiro to carry on his double life there for MI6.

Bill Donovan, prior to Pearl Harbor, did forward to the President one item of critical intelligence. Malcolm R. Lovell, one of Donovan's early recruits, reported to his chief a statement made to him by Dr. Hans Thomsen, the German chargé d'affaires in Washington. The diplomat had told Lovell, "If Japan goes to war with the United States, Germany will immediately follow suit." Thomsen also told him, "Japan knows that unless the United States agrees to some reasonable terms in the Far East, Japan must face the threat of strangulation. . . . If Japan waits, it will be comparatively easy for the United States to strangle Japan. Japan is therefore forced to strike now. . . ." On November 13, Donovan had Thomsen's statement hand-delivered to the President. Further evidence of Japan's intent came in a Magic intercept of message Number 812, dated November 22, from Tokyo to Nomura and Kurusu in Washington, noting that the Japanese had extended their deadline for signing the agreement with the United States from November 25 to November 29. The foreign minister added, "The deadline absolutely cannot be changed. After that things are automatically going to happen."

Admiral Stark, the Navy chief, sent a message to the Pacific Fleet on November 24, reading: "A surprise aggressive movement in any direction including attack on Philippines or Guam is a possibility." At noon the next day, FDR called together his War Council in the Oval Office, including Hull, Stimson, Knox, Marshall, and Stark. The President, according to Stimson's diary, predicted, "We were likely to be attacked perhaps (as soon as) next Monday [December 1], for the Japanese are notorious for making an attack without warning." Stimson's entry went on, "The question was how we should maneuver them into the position of firing the first shot without allowing too much danger to ourselves."

Two days later, FDR obtained intelligence that a Japanese fleet was moving south from Shanghai. The same day the President received a memorandum from Admiral Stark classified "Secret" that warned, "Japan may attack: The Burma Road; Thailand; Malaya; the Netherlands East Indies; the Philippines; the Russian Maritime provinces." That same November 27, Stark radioed the Pacific Fleet one of the key messages sent prior to the Pearl Harbor attack: "This dispatch is to be considered a war warning," it read, "an aggressive move by Japan is expected within the next few days. The number and equipment of Japanese troops and the organization of Naval Task Forces indicates an amphibious expedition against either the Philippines, Thai or Kra Peninsula or possibly Borneo."

Along with the near certainty of attack, the American codebreakers now produced proof of breathtaking Japanese duplicity. In a rush translation, Magic revealed that on November 28 the new Japanese foreign minister, Shigenori Togo, was telling his Washington negotiating team, "Well, you two ambassadors have exerted superhuman effort but, in spite of this, the United States has gone ahead and presented this humiliating proposal." Togo referred to a ten-point plan submitted by Stimson that included a Japanese pullout from China. The foreign minister then coached the ambassadors: "However, I do not wish you to give the impression that the negotiations are broken off. Merely say to them that you are awaiting instructions. . . ."

While Japan and America appeared on a collision course, Churchill's communications to Roosevelt indicated clearly that the Prime Minister did not want to see the United States distracted from the conflict in Europe by a diversion in the Pacific. On November 26 he sent a message via their private channel using his favored form of address, "Personal and secret for the President from Former Naval Person," that read: ". . . [W]e certainly do not want an additional war."

On November 30 the President was in Warm Springs, where he had gone to celebrate a belated Thanksgiving with fellow polio victims being treated there. The hiatus was abruptly ended by a desperate call from Stimson. A

Japanese attack seemed imminent, the secretary of war warned. The President should return to Washington at once, which he did on December 1.

On the very day that FDR returned to Washington, Premier Tojo sought an audience with Emperor Hirohito to ask his permission to implement the plan for war against the United States. The emperor nodded his assent. A Japanese task force under radio silence—six aircraft carriers, two battleships, two cruisers, and nine destroyers—had already steamed out of Kure naval base four days before destined for Pearl Harbor with orders, once the emperor's agreement was obtained, to deal the American Pacific Fleet "a mortal blow."

Among the Magic decrypts shown to FDR by his naval aide, Captain Beardall, one particularly captured his interest. The Japanese foreign office had sent Japan's ambassador in Berlin, General Oshima, a message to deliver to Hitler and his foreign minister, Joachim von Ribbentrop, that read: ". . . Say very secretly to [the Germans] that there is extreme danger that war may suddenly break out between the Anglo-Saxon nations and Japan through some clash of arms and add that the time of the breaking out of this war may come quicker than anyone dreams. . . ." The usual Magic procedure was for FDR to return decrypts. But a day later, for the first time, the President asked Beardall to retrieve a copy of this transmission for him to keep.

Besides the unmistakable content of the diplomatic traffic, other intelligence sources pointed to a Japanese attack. An eye-opener was a September 24 message from Foreign Minister Togo to the consul general in Honolulu, Nagao Kita, telling him to divide Pearl Harbor into five sectors and report on ship moorings and other activities in each sector. The message went on: "With regard to warships and aircraft carriers, we would like to have you report on those at anchor (these are not so important) tied up at wharves, buoy and in docks."

Kita had a sharp-eyed agent to fulfill Tokyo's requests. Ensign Takeo Yoshikawa had been assigned to Hawaii by the Third Bureau, the intelligence branch of the Japanese Naval General Staff, to serve undercover as vice consul. He had arrived in Honolulu on March 26, 1941. Yoshikawa's assignment was to provide intelligence on U.S. Pacific Fleet activity in Pearl Harbor for Admiral Isoroku Yamamoto, then masterminding the strike against this target. Yoshikawa led a deceptively leisurely life. He hung around a Japanese-owned restaurant, the Shunchu-ro, located conveniently on a hill overlooking Pearl Harbor. It had two telescopes for sightseers to enjoy the magnificent view. Yoshikawa took girlfriends on boat rides around Kaneohe Bay. He rented a Piper Cub at John Rodgers Airport and cruised above the harbor. All the while, this apparently indefatigable tourist was taking pictures, making notes, and preparing reports for Kita to send to Tokyo. He also sent home postcards of aerial views which were used to construct a mock-up of Pearl Harbor to train Japanese torpedo bomber pilots for the strike.

Captain Theodore S. Wilkinson, about to be named as chief of naval intelligence and described as "one of the best brains in the armed forces," huddled with Lieutenant Commander Alwin D. Kramer, the Navy's chief Japanese translator, over the September 24 message dividing Pearl Harbor into sectors. Kramer's responsibility was to choose which messages to distribute to senior officials. The two officers concluded that Togo's interest in ship locations did not mean that the Japanese intended to attack Pearl Harbor; that was too farfetched. Rather, they concluded that the Japanese wanted to know in what order and how quickly American warships might sortie from the harbor to prevent or retaliate against an attack by Japan in Southeast Asia. The significance attached to this message is indicated by the fact that the Army did not translate it for over two weeks. The President was shown only those intercepts deemed worth his attention, and no evidence exists that FDR was shown this particular message which, after the fact, became known as "the bomb-plot message." The decrypt was not even forwarded to Admiral Husband Kimmel, commander of naval forces at Pearl Harbor. In retrospect, Wilkinson and Kramer's misreading of the bomb-plot message appears obtuse. Yet, this particular decrypt would not have stood out as unique at the time. Tokyo was demanding similar information from its agents throughout Southeast Asia, the Philippines, Panama, and even San Francisco, San Diego, Seattle, and Vancouver. On November 19, Tokyo had alerted several diplomatic posts, including Washington, of a special signal to be inserted into the daily radio weather forecast: "In case of emergency (danger of cutting off our diplomatic relations)." If the threatened break involved the United States, the weather report would say, "Higashi No Kazeame," meaning "East Wind Rain." "When this is heard," Tokyo instructed its envoys, "please destroy all code papers, etc."

On December 1, the day FDR returned from Warm Springs, Tokyo told Nomura and Kurusu: "[T]o prevent the United States from becoming unduly suspicious we have been advising the press and others that though there are some wide differences between Japan and the United States, the negotiations are continuing."

The cascade of clues pointing to an imminent attack continued. On December 2, Foreign Minister Togo asked Consul General Kita for more pinpoint intelligence on Pearl Harbor: ". . . [T]he presence in port of warships, airplane carriers, and cruisers is of utmost importance. . . . [L]et me know day by day. Wire me in each case whether there are any observation balloons above Pearl Harbor. . . . Also advise me whether or not the warships are provided with anti-mine nets." While with hindsight the purpose of this and the preceding requests regarding Pearl Harbor seems glaringly obvious, they were, at the time, not given immediate priority by American codebreakers.

The Japanese had unwitting evidence from Roosevelt himself that their duplicity was working. On the same day that Foreign Minister Togo was asking for more intelligence on Pearl Harbor, FDR received Nomura and Kurusu in the Oval Office. The President's demeanor was cool as he warned them that he possessed information revealing that their country was moving a large expeditionary force south from Shanghai toward Indochina. The Americans evidently still knew nothing of the task force steaming toward Hawaii.

On December 4, Lieutenant Commander Kramer had in hand an intercepted message that informed all recipients to execute the so-called winds message to destroy their ciphers and coding machines. The communication was strong evidence that Japan intended to sever diplomatic relations with the United States, but not a clear war signal, nor was it handled as such.

On December 5, Ensign Yoshikawa again flew a reconnaissance over Pearl Harbor in a Piper Cub enabling him to report to Consul General Kita that nine battleships, three light cruisers, and seventeen destroyers were in the harbor, plus four light cruisers and two destroyers in dry dock. His figures were off by only one light cruiser, two heavy cruisers, and ten destroyers. He could further report that the Americans were not using their new torpedo nets; nor did they have barrage balloons aloft.

The final Japanese diplomatic stall began on Saturday evening, December 6, after a preoccupied FDR left his dinner guests early, skipping the musicale. Grace Tully had thought a long day was finally over when the President unexpectedly summoned her back to his study. He wanted to make one last effort to head off war with Japan through an unprecedented channel, a direct appeal to Emperor Hirohito "to restore traditional amity and prevent further death and destruction in the world." As the President was dictating his message, the first thirteen parts of a fourteen-part Japanese message to the embassy in Washington were being intercepted by a U.S. Navy listening post near Seattle. Though the President had by now put an end to the pointless system of Magic deliveries by the Army in one month and the Navy in the next, codebreaking was still being done on alternate days by the two rival services. Though the Navy had intercepted the multi-part message, December 6 was an Army day to decrypt, and the Navy wasted time sending the intercept to the Army's Signal Intelligence Service. The delay was compounded by the fact that SIS cryptanalysts had already taken off for the weekend. Delivery of one of the most vital communications ever handled in American foreign relations was further delayed as the long message was returned for the Navy to break. An embarrassed SIS officer finally put together an emergency shift to help the Navy, not, however, before the two teams agreed on one final inanity: Any message parts broken by the Army were still to be typed up by the Navy.

While FDR was testing different phrases in his appeal to Hirohito, an overworked Lieutenant Commander Kramer carefully checked the translations of the first thirteen parts of the Japanese message. FDR's appeal to Hirohito was dispatched at 9 P.M. A half hour later Kramer arrived at the White House with his decrypt in a locked pouch. The moment marked the first time that Magic traffic had ever been delivered to the President outside regular office hours. Kramer turned the message over to a young lieutenant, Lester R. Schulz, a naval aide filling in on a Saturday night for Captain Beardall. It was only Schulz's second day on the job when the junior officer hesitantly tapped on the door of the President's study. There he found FDR in somber conversation with his principal confidant and White House boarder, the cadaverous Harry Hopkins, who slouched in an armchair opposite Roosevelt. As Schulz stood by, the President began to read the long dispatch. He read slowly. A good ten minutes passed. Finally, he turned to Hopkins and said, "This means war." Hopkins replied that it was a pity "we could not strike the first blow and prevent any sort of surprise." "No," the President said, "we can't do that. We are a democracy and a peaceful people." The jaw set belligerently as he added, "But we have a good record." Schulz later remembered of FDR and Hopkins's conversation, "The only geographical name I recall was Indo-China. The time at which the war might begin was not discussed . . . there was no indication that tomorrow was necessarily the day." There had been no mention, Schulz was positive, of Pearl Harbor.

In Hawaii, the Army commander, Lieutenant General Walter Short, and the Pearl Harbor fleet commander, Admiral Kimmel, had been in possession for the previous ten days of Admiral Stark's November 27 "war warning" that "an aggressive move by Japan is expected within the next few days." General Short had contingency plans for three conditions. Number 1 was for "a defense against sabotage, espionage and subversive activities without any threat from the outside." Number 2 was to defend against air, surface, and submarine attack. Number 3 required preparations for "a defense against all-out attack." Short chose number 1, thereby bunching up his aircraft wingtip to wingtip and locking up guns and ammunition to protect the planes and weapons from saboteurs. He chose this level of alert to avoid unnecessarily frightening civilians with scare stories about the Army preparing for attack. For the same reason, Admiral Kimmel, the naval commander, did not increase the state of readiness of his ships in the harbor. The two men cannot be blamed entirely for fearing local saboteurs over foreign attackers. The Navy chief, Admiral Stark, while warning the Pacific Fleet of "hostile action possible at any moment," had added that any measures taken "should be carried out so as not repeat not to alarm civil population. . . ." Stark was reflecting a by now embedded national conviction, fostered in no small measure by the President himself. For the previous two years, Americans had been indoctrinated that subversion from within was the prime threat to their country. Still, the November 27 message and a supplementing War Department message to General Short sent the same day warning of "hostile action possible at any moment," though not mentioning Pearl Harbor, would seem unmistakable calls to gird for an attack from within or without.

One last warning remained. On Sunday morning, December 7, Navy cryptographers were decrypting the last piece of the fourteen-part Japanese message, the so-called Final Memorandum, which declared that Tokyo was breaking off negotiations. At the same time, Army cryptographers were breaking a separate instruction to Ambassador Nomura to submit the long message to the State Department at 1 P.M. Washington time. Colonel Rufus Bratton, the astute head of the Far East section of Army intelligence, was struck by the preciseness of the hour and its unusual Sunday afternoon delivery. To Bratton, this timing signaled a Japanese attack at that hour, probably, he guessed, against the Philippines. Precious time was lost while Bratton tried desperately to locate General Marshall, who was off on his regular Sunday horseback ride. Two and a half hours later, Bratton was finally explaining his interpretation of the 1 P.M. delivery to Marshall. The Army Chief of Staff immediately fired off to commanders in the Pacific a warning that the Japanese had, in effect, presented an ultimatum and "to be on the alert accordingly." The message went first to Manila, next to the Panama Canal, and last to Hawaii. "Fired off" is perhaps not the right phrase regarding the Hawaii delivery since the signalmen could not get through on their military circuits, and Marshall's warning of imminent hostilities had to be sent by commercial cable. By the time the warning reached General Short's headquarters, the skies over Pearl Harbor were dotted with Japanese planes. The church bells announcing Sunday services were being drowned out by torpedoes exploding against Kimmel's clustered warships and by bombs destroying Short's bunched-up planes.

The Japanese diplomats had been instructed to deliver the Final Memorandum at 1 P.M., but it was not brought to Secretary of State Hull until 2:20 P.M., with the attack well under way. The delay would later enable Japanese officials, wanting to escape the dishonor of making a sneak attack, to blame the tardy delivery on administrative bungling and on time spent decoding garbles. Subsequent research in the Japanese foreign ministry archives, however, makes manifest that the Japanese never intended a proper declaration of war. An entry in the Japanese war diary dated December 7 reads: "[O]ur deceptive diplomacy is steadily proceeding toward success." On an idyllic Sunday morning, on an island demi-paradise, American blood was copiously spilled, the nation's pride wounded, and anger aroused until retribution became the only tenable response. "No matter how long it may take us to overcome this premeditated invasion," the President told Congress the next day in asking for a declaration of war, "the American people in their righteous might will win through to absolute victory."

That same day Britain declared war on Japan. On December 11, Hitler kept his word to the Japanese and declared war on the United States. Senator Wheeler's leak of Rainbow Five appears to have figured into his decisions since, Hitler said, ". . . there has now been revealed in America President Roosevelt's plan by which, at the latest in 1943, Germany and Italy are to be attacked in Europe. . . . Germany and Italy have been finally compelled in view of this and in loyalty to the Tripartite Pact, to carry on the struggle against the United States and England jointly and side by side with Japan for the defense, and thus for the maintenance, of liberty and independence of their nations and empires." A leak engineered by isolationists to keep America out of war had helped produce the opposite effect.

Hitler had detailed knowledge of what had been said in the White House on the day of Pearl Harbor. The chain was long, but effective, and the first link was located astonishingly close to the President. The Swiss minister to the United States, fifty-two-year-old Dr. Charles Bruggmann, had previously served in Washington eighteen years before, when he had met and married Mary Wallace, the sister of FDR's vice president. Through the years, Henry Wallace developed a deep affection for his brother-in-law. They met often, and talked on the phone almost daily. Wallace felt safe in confiding to Bruggmann the most intimate secrets to which his position made him privy. Months before Pearl Harbor, on August 17, 1941, Wallace told Bruggmann about the briefing the President had given the cabinet regarding FDR's meeting on the Atlantic with Churchill. Soon after Pearl Harbor, Wallace told Bruggmann what he had heard and seen on the day of the attack as he sat among those summoned by the President. Whatever his family ties to the Vice President, Bruggmann was first of all a professional diplomat. What Wallace confided to him he cabled back to the Swiss foreign ministry in Bern. What Bruggmann did not know was that a German agent, code-named Habakuk, had penetrated the Swiss foreign ministry and read all of his reports. Thus, soon after Pearl Harbor, Habakuk was able to send a message to Berlin of "precise and reliable information" that Bruggmann had heard "in strictest confidence" from Vice President Wallace. He told his superiors, almost word for word, how FDR had characterized the first gathering as: "The most serious Cabinet session since Lincoln met with the Cabinet at the outbreak of the Civil War." The spy was further able to report the President's revelations of the losses the Japanese had inflicted at Pearl Harbor.

The blame for Pearl Harbor has been the assiduous study of eight official investigations, the most thoroughgoing of which, conducted by Congress after the war, ran to fifteen thousand pages of testimony. With the mass of intelligence available to President Roosevelt, with his capacity to read Japan's most secret communications at almost the same time that Japanese diplomats read them, with the pointed Japanese inquiries about Pearl Harbor's layout, known to American cryptanalysts, with his own admission that the Japanese Final Memorandum "means war," how could the President not have known, almost down to the hour, that Pearl Harbor would be attacked?

His seeming ignorance of the strike must be examined against three possible explanations. One, FDR genuinely did not know that Pearl Harbor was targeted. Two, he knew and deliberately did not act in order, as revisionist historians have claimed, to force America into a war that he believed was just but that most Americans did not want. Three, Prime Minister Churchill possessed intelligence, as again has been argued by revisionists, revealing the Japanese attack, but deliberately withheld it in order to see the United States drawn into war on Britain's side.

Choosing the correct one of these three explanations must be prefaced by an overarching question: Why did Japan choose to attack Pearl Harbor in the first place? The strike was intended not to entangle Japan in a protracted war against the United States, but as a knockout punch. It was supposed to eliminate America's floating fortress, the Pacific Fleet, and thus force the United States to withdraw from Southeast Asia and leave Japan free there to work its will. The blow was analogous to having one member of a gang take out the guard so that the rest can then rob the bank unimpeded. The Japanese were well aware that the United States had its attention focused on the war in Europe and that its president wanted to join that fight. They could not imagine that the Americans would undertake two prolonged wars, one across the Atlantic *and* one in the Pacific.

Against this backdrop, the question arises again, given the wealth of intelligence available to him, how could President Roosevelt not have divined that Pearl Harbor was the target? In retrospect, the clues seem to lead to that conclusion like lights on a well-marked runway. The truth, however, is that not one of the 239 messages intercepted between Tokyo and the Japanese envoys in Washington in the six months before December 7 ever mentioned Pearl Harbor. So closely held was the secret that even Nomura and Kurusu were left in the dark that the American base was to be attacked. Though told to wrap up their negotiations by November 25, a deadline extended to the 29th, and though told, "After that things are automatically going to change," the two envoys were never informed precisely of what these "things" were. After the war, Nomura told an interviewer that he had been "the worst-informed ambassador in history."

Magic may actually have contributed to the failure of preparedness at Pearl Harbor. Analysis of Magic intercepts led American military leaders to anticipate a Japanese move, not to the east against Pearl Harbor, but against Southeast Asia. Admiral Stark's "Memorandum for the President," submitted just ten days before the attack, warned of possible Japanese attacks against the Burma Road, Thailand, Malaya, the Netherlands East Indies, the Philippines, and even to the north against the Russian Maritime Provinces, but said nothing about Pearl Harbor. The following day, corroborating intelligence came from the American assistant naval attaché in Shanghai, who reported, "Many transports sighted during the week 19–26 November between Hong Kong and Shanghai heading South. A number of these transports had troops on board." When, on December 2, Roosevelt received Nomura and Kurusu for the last time, he warned them that he had intelligence of this southerly expedition, but made no mention of Yamamoto's task force approaching Pearl Harbor, which would have been a far sharper rebuke of Japanese duplicity had he known of it.

Some Pearl Harbor researchers have made much of the "winds" messages, which were to be inserted into Japanese weather reports, the implication being that the signal "East Wind Rain" meant that Japan was about to attack the United States. This signal, however, meant only that the designated Japanese embassies were to destroy their codes and coding machines. But what of the decrypted messages from Foreign Minister Togo to Consul General Kita in Honolulu requesting information on facilities and ship movements in Pearl Harbor? The problem with viewing these intercepts as clear indications that the Japanese had targeted Pearl Harbor is that American codebreakers received them among a flood of requests for similar information on nearly a dozen other ports. Further, no evidence exists that any of the decrypts handled at this level were shown to FDR. If any American did have solid evidence in hand that the Japanese were preparing an attack on Pearl Harbor, it was J. Edgar Hoover. Yet, Hoover's visceral dislike of the double agent Dusko Popov and his superficial handling of the microdot questionnaire that Popov carried deprived anyone in the U.S. government, including FDR, of strong evidence that the Japanese had targeted Pearl Harbor.

"The Fog of War" is an apt description of the confusion that obscures what is actually happening in the heat of battle. A corollary phrase, the "Flood of Intelligence," might explain why outcomes look clearer after rather than before the fact. After the fact, the threads connecting A to B to C to Pearl Harbor appear to stand out unmistakably. But that clarity emerges only in retrospect, only after these strands have been teased from a dense bundle of other threads. At the time, the relevant strand stood out no more visibly than hundreds of competing threads—the true, the false, the misleading, the contradictory, the irrelevant.

Physically, what FDR received from his couriers was a decryption form indicating From, To, Date, Time of Transmission, Time of Interception, and Time of Translation. He rarely received any analysis connecting these bits and pieces. In effect, the President and other members of the War Council, including Hull, Stimson, Knox, and Marshall, were delivered raw decrypts and were left to evaluate them, acting as their own intelligence officer. This situation was best described by the Army's codebreaking genius, William Friedman, who later observed: "[T]here was *nobody* in either the Army or the Navy intelligence staffs in Washington whose most important, if not sole duty, was to study the whole story which the MAGIC messages were unfolding. . . . [N]obody whose responsibility it was to try and put the pieces of the jig-saw puzzle together."

Based on the information FDR had in hand on the eve of Pearl Harbor, if asked if Japan was going to attack the United States, he would certainly have answered "Yes." He made clear this conviction in the War Council meeting of November 25 where, according to Stimson's diary, FDR stated, "We were likely to be attacked perhaps next Monday. . . ." If asked if he knew with certainty where the Japanese would strike, he would have to have answered "No." Given the targets suggested in the Japanese intercepts, if asked if Pearl Harbor was in danger, he likely would have answered, "Probably not." Never in any report or intelligence, whether from agents or broken codes, did FDR ever receive a warning that said Pearl Harbor will be attacked. General Marshall told FDR that the harbor was invincible and a most unlikely target. It was, the general said, ". . . the strongest fortress in the world. . . . Enemy carriers, naval escorts and transports will begin to come under air attack at a distance of approximately 750 miles. This attack will increase in intensity until within 200 miles of the objective, the enemy forces will be subject to all types of bombardment closely supported by our most modern pursuit."

Undeniably, Roosevelt wanted to enter the war, but the war in Europe, which he had all but done in the Atlantic, lacking only a formal declaration. Yet, none of his speeches, warning of Nazi machinations in South America, threats to the Panama Canal, or the alleged unpremeditated U-boat attack against the destroyer *Greer,* had aroused sufficient public ire to lead the nation into that war. If then, a president wants war with Germany, why does he invite an attack on Japan? Put another way, if Tom is itching to fight Dick, why provoke a fight with Harry? Does the intelligence available to the President and his inner circle support the thesis that FDR invited the blow at Pearl Harbor to propel the country into the war?

One argument pressed by revisionists is that the President had prior knowledge of the impending attack through intercepted radio signals from the Japanese task force bound for Pearl Harbor. A corollary claim is that had the President alerted the Pearl Harbor defenders of the approaching

menace, the Japanese fleet would have turned back. A major source supposedly proving this thesis has been identified only as "Seaman Z" who
worked in the intelligence branch of the 12th Naval District in San Francisco. One of Z's duties was to plot communications intercepted anywhere
in the Pacific, commercial or military. The revisionist claim is that prior to
the attack, Z managed to get cross bearings on mysterious signals that
could be a missing Japanese carrier force.

Among the documents at the Roosevelt Library in Hyde Park is the
transcript of an interview of Robert D. Ogg conducted by I. G. Newman, a
historical consultant and former naval officer. Ogg, it turns out, was Seaman Z. Newman asked Ogg if his superior, Lieutenant Elsworth A. Hosmer, had ever been ordered to relocate a missing Japanese carrier force.
Ogg replied, "My comment on that is that in no way was he ordered to do
so. . . . I don't think he had any reason to feel from anything that was conveyed to me that they [the Japanese task force] went East, West, South or
where." Newman asked Ogg if his plotting of cross bearings led him to tell
Hosmer, "It could possibly be the missing task force." Ogg replied, "I
never made such mention to Hosmer whatsoever." Ogg further told his interviewer, ". . . [D]uring those four or five days [prior to Pearl Harbor] I
certainly had no feeling that an entire Jap fleet . . . was involved. . . ." The
airwaves across the Pacific were indeed filled with signals, many emanating from Japanese vessels. But the weight of evidence is that the Japanese
task force never broke radio silence, not even from one ship to another;
thus there would have been no signals to intercept. This position is supported by Minoru Genda, one of the key architects of the attack, who
claims that the Pearl Harbor task force "kept an absolute radio silence." A
member of the task force itself, Lieutenant Commander Chuichi Yoshioka,
has stated, "[R]adio silence *was* imposed even before the ships assembled
in a small bay in Intara Island on November 24th." A recent revisionist,
Robert B. Stinnett, claims to have found documentary proof that the
Japanese task force did break radio silence, that American monitors intercepted these transmissions, and that they were decrypted and sent to FDR.
Thus, Stinnett's word is pitted against those of Japanese who actually par-
ticipated in the Pearl Harbor attack and who had no motive to protect
Franklin Roosevelt's position in history. The revisionist premise is that ex-
posure of the Japanese task force would have forced its leader, Admiral
Chuichi Nagumo, to turn around and go home. Therefore, FDR said nothing because he wanted the attack to proceed. Yet, while the Japanese

sought the advantage of surprise, it was not indispensable. As Ronald Spector, a well-regarded historian of this period, writes, "Admiral Nagumo and his staff half expected to have to fight their way in." Indeed, encountering opposition was one of the alternatives practiced by the Japanese task force in war-gaming the strike.

The final conspiracy theory to be dealt with from the intelligence standpoint is whether or not Prime Minister Churchill had knowledge of the impending attack on Pearl Harbor from his own sources, and deliberately withheld this information from Roosevelt so that the Japanese would succeed in their attack and thus plunge the United States into the war. As James Rusbridger claims in *Betrayal at Pearl Harbor,* "Churchill was aware that a task force had sailed from northern Japan in late November 1941, and that one of its likely targets was Pearl Harbor." Rusbridger goes on to say that "Churchill deliberately kept this vital information from Roosevelt, because he realized an attack of this nature, whether on the U.S. Pacific Fleet or the Philippines, was a means of fulfilling his publicly proclaimed desire to get America into the war at any cost." It must be asked whether drawing the United States into a war with Japan was a logical way for Churchill to get FDR into the war in Europe. Churchill was certainly capable of manipulating intelligence to serve his country's ends. He had no qualms about Stephenson's BSC manufacturing stories to feed to Roosevelt that the Nazis were conspiring to invade South America and threaten the Panama Canal. He allowed Roosevelt to continue thinking that Hitler would invade Britain when his own Ultra interceptions made clear that this danger had passed. However, an attack that would have brought America into a war with the Japanese was a risky bet for Churchill. How he viewed his best interests is clear from a five-page report written on November 12, 1941, less than a month before Pearl Harbor, by the American ambassador to Britain, John Winant. Winant had spent three days with Churchill in the country. According to Winant's notes, forwarded to FDR, Churchill set out three positions in which Britain might find itself. The worst-case scenario, which Churchill considered unthinkable, was that Japan would come into the war against Britain and that America would stay out. The next best outcome would be for neither Japan nor America to enter the war. But Churchill's preference, the PM told Winant, was that "the United States enter the war without Japan." With this as his first choice, it hardly seems that Churchill would deliberately enable a Japanese attack on America by withholding intelligence from Roosevelt.

Finally, Churchill possessed no sources of signal intelligence in the Pacific that were not already available to FDR. What the Prime Minister concluded, as late as November 25, was that Japan was irrevocably committed to attack Thailand.

Ironically, in order to get America into the European conflict, Churchill had to depend on Adolf Hitler to declare war on the United States. As expressed by the diplomat and later presidential advisor George Ball, "If Hitler had not made this decision and if he had simply done nothing, there would have been an enormous sentiment in the United States . . . that the Pacific was now our war and the European war was for the Europeans, and we Americans should concentrate all our efforts on Japan." Churchill, with the Ultra secrets at his fingertips, nevertheless learned of the attack on Pearl Harbor just as millions of Britons did. As Captain Malcolm Kennedy, a Japanese linguist at Bletchley, wrote in his diary on December 7, ". . . [T]he news on the 9 P.M. wireless, that Japan had opened hostilities with an air raid on Pearl Harbor, more than 3000 miles out in the Pacific, came as a complete surprise." Winston Churchill had not learned of Pearl Harbor through advance intelligence that he withheld from FDR. He learned about it on the BBC.

The revisionist theory requires a certain path of logic. First, FDR had to know that Pearl Harbor was going to be bombed. His secretaries of state, war, and Navy either did not know or, if they did, they all lied and conspired in the deaths of twenty-four hundred Americans and the near-fatal destruction of the Pacific Fleet. Pearl Harbor is nowhere mentioned in Admiral Stark's November 27 war warning to the fleet, unless, again, we imagine the chief of the American Navy deliberately misleading the defenders of Pearl Harbor and conniving in the mass death of men under him and the destruction of his ships. If Nomura and Kurusu did not know what their government intended, it is difficult to argue that the American President or his chief aides knew. For FDR to fail to alert the defenders of an attack that he knew was coming, we must premise that the President had enlisted men of the stature of Stimson, Hull, Knox, and Marshall in a treasonous conspiracy, or that he had a unique source of information on Japanese fleet movements unknown to anyone else in the government.

The conspiracy theory fails most abysmally in that it would *not* achieve its supposed end. It would not have brought America into the European war. FDR's legendary "day that will live in infamy" speech declared war only on Japan, not Germany. For that war, FDR, too, had to depend on

Adolf Hitler. As he had told Churchill four months before aboard the *Augusta,* a fight with Japan would be "the wrong war in the wrong ocean at the wrong time."

Why, then, one may wonder, have authors and scholars, some of distinction, embraced the conspiratorial thesis that has led ordinary citizens to ask, "Is it true that FDR knew the Japanese were going to attack Pearl Harbor?" The best answer lies in the fact that dramatically scripted conspiracies provide high theater, while the truth is often messy, random, illogical, even dull. The thesis of a Roosevelt-engineered attack on Pearl Harbor joins the perennially recycled conspiracy theories about the assassinations of Abraham Lincoln and John F. Kennedy, which will go on and on and on. The inescapable, if prosaic, truth is that no evidence whatever exists that President Roosevelt wanted a war in the Pacific, and all the evidence demonstrates that he wanted to enter the war in Europe. A monumental distraction from that objective, a war with Japan, was the last thing he needed. All the secrets, the intelligence, the intercepted Japanese codes, the very stuff with which the historian works, support this conclusion: Pearl Harbor was a catastrophe, not a conspiracy.

Chapter XI

Secrets of the Map Room

O N THE evening of December 22, 1941, just two weeks after Pearl Harbor, a whirlwind struck the White House. Prime Minister Churchill arrived. The President's sometime speechwriter Robert Sherwood caught the Prime Minister's motive for the trip: "When Churchill and his staff came to Washington in December of 1941," Sherwood later wrote, "they were prepared for the possibility of an announcement by Roosevelt that due to the rage of the American people against Japan and the imperilled position of American forces in the Philippines and other islands, the war in the Pacific must be given precedence." This was a strategy that Churchill was determined to derail while at the White House and he expected to pursue his strategic objectives among the comforts to which he had become accustomed. He wanted no talking outside his room, no whistling in the corridors, and his libations were to be served on time. He instructed the White House usher, Alonzo Fields, "I must have a tumbler of sherry in my room before breakfast, a couple glasses of scotch and soda before lunch and French champagne and 90 year old brandy before I go to sleep at night."

A seventeen-year-old girl, Margaret Hambley, whom FDR regarded as his godchild, has left a vivid picture of Churchill at the White House. "He has," Hambley wrote, after attending a dinner for the PM, "a very pink face, whitish, red thin hair and very piercing pale blue eyes. His nose has a very strange shape. It looks as if it was chiseled. . . . He is not a conversationalist for formal dinners, he is much more apt to ask very deep, thought-provoking questions. He has a habit of asking a question and then when the person is nicely involved in a long oratory, the PM will suddenly turn away and join in another conversation just as if he were listening to both and found the other more interesting. He has a very keen mind much more so than the President but of course he has not that wonderful charm and personality. It is as if his round cherubic face had an entirely different mind behind it." Young Hambley found the powerful orator of the House of Commons an indifferent speaker over the roast beef and Yorkshire pudding: "He has a very poor voice. One can hardly understand him it is so indistinct and stammering, but he uses the most wonderful language imaginable." Churchill's humor surprised her: "He was looking very gloomily down at his plate but with a twinkle in his eye and said how perfectly dreadful the man [Hitler] was to bomb all the beautiful scotch whiskey and cigar warehouses. He said he didn't know what would happen to [his] country when its supplies of whiskey and cigars ran out."

The Rose Suite became the temporary seat of British government. White House staffers—shifting beds and other furniture to accommodate Churchill's retinue—found themselves weaving among a steady stream of uniformed couriers delivering the secrets of empire in the locked red dispatch cases bearing a warning, THIS BOX IS ONLY TO BE OPENED BY THE PRIME MINISTER IN PERSON. And Churchill kept the key. It soon became apparent that Churchill's and Roosevelt's living habits meshed like mismatched gears. The President, after reading in bed, ordinarily turned lights out by 10:40 P.M. Churchill liked to stay up talking, talking, talking into the small hours. FDR was generally awake by 8:30 A.M. The Prime Minister liked to stay in bed until noon.

Churchill's ceaseless prowling of the White House, steady drinking, and late hours appear to have caught up with him and produced one of the better-kept secrets of the war. On the fourth day of the Prime Minister's visit, he and Roosevelt had retired late after agreeing that the war in the Pacific would be run out of Washington and the war in the West out of London. Churchill found the heat in his bedroom stifling, and he struggled to open a jammed window. As he told his doctor, Charles Wilson (later Lord Moran), "I noticed all at once I was short of breath. I had a dull pain over my heart. It went down my left arm." Wilson instantly recognized the classic symptoms. Churchill had had a mild heart attack. As the physician wrote in his diary, the "textbook treatment is at least six weeks in bed. That would mean publishing to the world, and the American newspapers would see this, that the PM was an invalid with a crippled heart and a doubtful future." Wilson said nothing about a heart attack to Churchill and told him only, "Your circulation is a bit sluggish. It is nothing serious . . . but you mustn't do more than you can help in the way of exertion for a little while." Thus, not only Churchill, but his host, FDR, never knew exactly what befell the Prime Minister while he stayed in the Rose Suite.

During one of their nocturnal conversations, FDR and the PM discussed exchanging knowledge of their countries' codes. Churchill remained a hungry consumer of signal intelligence far more than Roosevelt, who still favored the cloak-and-dagger over keyboards and rotors. At home, the Prime Minister insisted on having Ultra decrypts brought by special courier from Bletchley Park to 10 Downing Street several times a day. The stolen secrets of other nations had long been a Churchill passion. Before coming to power he had written, "I attach more importance to [decrypts] as a means of forming a true judgment of public policy in these spheres, than to any other source of knowledge at the disposal of the state." His Bletchley codebreakers, in Churchill's phrase, were "the geese who laid the golden eggs and never cackled." An early Churchill name for the intercepted German codes had been Boniface, chosen to mislead the enemy into thinking that the source was an agent rather than a penetrated cipher system. The name, with its medieval ring, appealed to Churchill, who clung to it long after Ultra became used exclusively by everyone else in on the secret.

The Prime Minister accepted, in theory, that in codebreaking the Americans deserved to be Britain's partner. Since February 1941 the British had been in possession of the Japanese machine for encoding Purple, along with keys for breaking the code, courtesy of their American colleagues. Thus, in the months preceding Pearl Harbor, the British were able to read essentially the same Japanese diplomatic secrets as did FDR. The Americans, however, remained decidedly junior, even limited partners, since the British questioned their ability to guard secrets. Though the Americans had given a Purple machine to Bletchley, the British did not turn over an Enigma machine to Arlington Hall. The Americans saw of Ultra decrypts only what the British chose to share.

Churchill, however, did have a confession to make. "Some time ago," he cabled FDR after his return to London, "our experts claimed to have discovered the system and constructed some [code] tables used by your

Diplomatic Corps. From the moment we became Allies, I gave instructions that this work should cease." In fact, the British had been reading U.S. State Department codes for over two decades. The reason for Churchill's admission and promise to stop the practice was hardly an instance of English fair play. Rather, he was warning FDR that if an ally was breaking America's codes, the ". . . danger of our enemies having achieved a measure of success, cannot, I am advised, be dismissed. I shall be grateful if you will handle this matter entirely yourself, and if possible burn this letter when you have read it. The whole subject is secret in degree which affects the safety of both our countries. The fewest possible people should know." The cable, however, was not burned.

Churchill's preoccupation with code security was fully warranted. On February 1 the German navy had shifted to a new four-rotor enciphering combination for submarine traffic, replacing a system Bletchley had cracked. In intelligence parlance, British cryptanalysis had gone "blind," and in subsequent months ship sinkings soared. A despairing Churchill told Roosevelt, "When I reflect how I have longed and prayed for the entry of the United States into the war I find it difficult to realise how greatly our British affairs have deteriorated since December 7." His desperation was understandable. When U-boat torpedoes sank two average-size cargo vessels and one tanker loaded with American supplies bound for Britain, the loss amounted to approximately 42 tanks and 428 tons of tank parts and supplies, 236 artillery pieces, 24 armored cars, 5,210 tons of ammunition, 600 rifles, 2,000 tons of stores, and 1,000 tank loads of gasoline. To achieve similar destruction by bombing, it was estimated the enemy would have to conduct 3,000 sorties.

Part of the considerable baggage Churchill had brought during his White House stay included a portable version of his Map Room, the original located in a bombproof underground London headquarters at Storey's Gate. The traveling Map Room had been installed in the Monroe Room of the White House, and Churchill later described FDR's fascination with it: "He liked to come and study attentively the large maps of all the theatres of war which soon covered the walls, and on which the movement of fleets and armies was so swiftly and accurately recorded." After Churchill's departure, FDR had to have his own Map Room. Always more comfortable with Navy personnel, he turned the task over to his new naval aide, Captain John L. McCrea, who had replaced Captain Beardall. McCrea had been a reluctant recruit to the Roosevelt staff. The doughty sea dog had been slated for command of a cruiser when Admiral King, commander in chief of the U.S. Fleet, drafted him to serve FDR. McCrea had all the qualifications, one of his Navy pals kidded him; he was over six feet tall and had a strong back. McCrea protested the assignment to King and Navy secretary Knox. He had been raised a Republican, never voted, and was no fan of the New Deal, he complained. "Well, what do you think I am?" Knox replied.

From their first encounter in January 1942, Roosevelt blinded McCrea with his electric charm, nimble mind, and razor-sharp memory. FDR could recite the captain's naval career over the preceding twenty years. McCrea began to relish his place within FDR's inner circle. David Kahn, the preeminent American historian of cryptography, paints a vivid picture of the working arrangement between the President and his naval assistant: "When McCrea arrived in the morning, Roosevelt would usually be either in bed, in which case McCrea would hand him the papers, or in the bathroom shaving. If the latter, the naval officer would go in, close the toilet cover, sit down on it, and in that inglorious position read the leader of the most powerful nation in the world some of the most secret documents of the greatest war in history." As they reviewed the deployment of the fleet, Roosevelt would astonish McCrea with his mastery of geography, down to remote specks on the globe. The President explained his expertise as a by-product of his hobby. "[I]f a stamp collector really studies his stamps," the President told his aide, he would know the world. McCrea was amused by Roosevelt's continuing references to "when I was in the Navy," and the pleasure FDR took in reminding him that he had supervised all the current naval brass when they were junior officers—Stark, King, Leahy, Admiral Chester W. Nimitz, Halsey, and dozens of others whom he could recall by name, rank, and early assignments. What welded the anti–New Deal Navy officer most closely to his new chief was FDR's habitual geniality, the utter lack of self-pity. McCrea was filled, he said, with admiration at "the patience with which he bore his affliction . . . with never a reference to it."

McCrea attacked the President's order for a map room with zeal. He expropriated a ladies' room on the first floor of the White House ideally located across from the elevator the President used to reach the Oval Office and next to the room occupied by the President's physician, Admiral McIntire, whom FDR saw almost daily. Within days of Churchill's departure, the Map Room was functioning. Blowups of maps papered the walls from floor to ceiling. Lieutenant (Junior Grade) Robert Montgomery, the Hollywood actor now on active duty as McCrea's assistant, added creative touches that delighted FDR. Montgomery designed pins to indicate where the major chiefs of state were at a given moment. Roosevelt's pin was shaped like a cigarette holder, Churchill's like a cigar, Stalin's like a pipe. Other shapes and colors indicated the location of units of the U.S., Allied, and enemy fleets. One U.S. Navy vessel, the destroyer on which Franklin D. Roosevelt Jr. served, had its own pin. The maps were updated two and three times a day and hung at sitting level so that the President could study them from his wheelchair.

The Map Room gradually assumed a more sensitive function than merely presenting a pictorial plot of the war. The cables the President sent to other world leaders were encoded in the Map Room and their messages to him decoded there. War plans were filed in the onetime ladies' room, along with records of all military discussions and decisions. The President had his Magic intercepts kept there in what he called "The Magic Book." As Churchill had done in London, FDR made his Map Room America's wartime nerve center. He was wheeled in and out of the room at least twice a day. He had a sign posted on the door, NO ADMITTANCE, and approved a list of only six others allowed to pass in and out without permission. The former ambassador to Vichy France, the stolid, reliable Admiral William D. Leahy, whom FDR had brought back to serve as Chief of Staff to the commander in chief, headed the list. The other five were Captain McCrea, Admiral McIntire, Harry Hopkins, and William Rigdon, a former ship's clerk who had risen to become an invaluable factotum to the President and whose duties ran from supervising the Filipino stewards on the presidential yacht to monitoring secret messages coming into the Map Room. The admissions policy was strictly enforced. Frank Knox complained bitterly to FDR when he was barred entrance. Mrs. Roosevelt casually walked in, past dumbfounded guards, to find Captain McCrea with his pants down in the one place he thought it safe to change uniforms. Grace Tully, whom the President often sent to the Map Room to pick up and deliver dispatches, remained unimpressed. She found the room a "hodge podge of varicolored pins, arrowhead lines, and generally confusing symbols." But it was right up FDR's alley. The President, she said, "took to that sort of thing like a duck to water."

A young Navy watch officer, Robert Myers, received his initiation into the Roosevelt style when he had to deliver an urgent message from the Map Room to FDR after the President had gone to bed. Uneasy at disturbing him, Myers asked Roosevelt for future guidance when messages arrived at irregular hours. "Well, if they aren't important and you come up and wake me," the President answered, "you're in trouble. And if they are important and you don't come up and wake me, you're in trouble. So you take it from there."

The President set up communication procedures to serve another end. He sent all his outgoing messages through the Army Signal Corps. He received messages to him only through Navy personnel. Consequently, the Army knew some of what he knew. The Navy knew some. But only FDR knew it all.

★

One name not appearing on the list of those granted admittance to the most secure depository of secrets in America was that of the President's chief of secret warfare, William J. Donovan, director of the COI. Still, other than that exclusion, Donovan appeared to enjoy the President's favor. In his first six months in the post, Donovan had flooded the President with over 260 phone calls and written memoranda. Nine hand-delivered reports arrived at Grace Tully's desk on December 15, 1941, alone and eleven more the next day. They rained down on the Oval Office so profusely that Donovan's messages were identified by time as well as date—11 A.M., 1 P.M., 5 P.M., etc. The chief courier was twenty-nine-year-old Navy Lieutenant (Junior Grade) Edwin J. "Ned" Putzell, another lawyer out of Donovan's New York law firm. As Putzell described his duties: "I'd be standing by while General Donovan dictated his messages to the President. Usually he classified them 'Secret' or 'Top Secret.' I put the memoranda, as many as five or six a day, into a zipped leather briefcase with a strap that I wound around my wrist. Freeman, the General's black driver, then took me to the White House in an Army sedan where I was so familiar that the guards waved me through. I took the dispatches directly to Grace Tully. If the President was tied up, I left them with her. If he was free, she sent me right in. The President always greeted me like a long lost friend. On one occasion, I pulled out a pocket watch with my Phi Beta Kappa key attached. He said, 'Lieutenant, that's something I always aspired to.' I'd wait while he read the memoranda. He'd 'Mmmm' over certain passages, or nod his head. Occasionally he might scribble something in the margin." Of his countless deliveries, however, Putzell recalled, "I don't remember him ever giving me specific instructions to take back to Donovan."

Just days after Pearl Harbor, the President had received from Donovan a transcript of a radio talk made by E. D. Ward, described as "one of the two Americans broadcasting in the Nazi pay from Berlin." Ward's message expressed sorrow that his nation had been suckered into war against Germany. He repeated what an American professor in Berlin had told him: "Whatever happens, America will lose. Meaningless slogans about salvaging democracy and civilization are shibboleths which will lead to shambles. It is a war for control of European politics. The blessings of democracy will vanish in the war. The fusing of oligarchic England and Bolshevistic Russia cannot produce an American way of life." Ward's broadcast concluded: "The United States should, for its own good, remain aloof and mind its own business. However, more powerful influences and interested groups have decreed otherwise." It seemed routine claptrap from a Nazi sympathizer and paid lackey. But in the post–Pearl Harbor climate, FDR took Ward's behavior seriously. He directed Donovan, on the very day that he received the transcript, to have the State and Justice Departments investigate Americans working for the enemy. "I think they still come under some old law and can have their property in the United States confiscated," he said, and "whether they automatically lose their citizenship should be looked into."

Donovan forwarded to the President a five-page handwritten letter penned by Hollywood's quintessential swashbuckler, Errol Flynn, suggesting an appropriately dashing adventure to be produced by the COI and starring Flynn himself. Noting that his father, T. Thomson-Flynn, dean of the faculty of science at Queen's University, was esteemed in all of Ireland, Flynn wrote, ". . . [P]erhaps you know that the Irish, both North and South, are great movie goers. When last there, it was a constant source of astonishment to me that while Bridget O'Toole had only the foggiest notion whether the Panama Canal divides America or Africa, she did know without a shadow of a doubt that Clark Gable cherishes a marked antipathy for striped underwear and that Hedy Lamarr wears a false bust. . . . Now in view both of this well disposed attitude toward me personally as a Hollywood figure plus my father's position there . . . it seems to me that if Uncle Sam were to put me in American Army uniform and send me over there I could be of value to your department. One presumes America needs the Irish bases in the South . . . I could work well perhaps better than most to this end. . . ." Flynn saw himself ideally cast as a spy because of ". . . the excellent opportunities which seem to come, almost without effort on my part, to a man in my peculiar position in life, to acquire a certain sort of intimate information that would be of use to your department. . . . If I were to go there openly as a Hollywood figure in an American Army uniform, I would be far less suspected of gathering information than the usual sort of agent."

FDR knew that Flynn was a friend of his son Franklin Jr. and that the actor knew Eleanor Roosevelt because of his work helping polio victims through the March of Dimes. But Franklin Jr.'s opinion did not advance Flynn's cause. "Errol used to join me and the Whitneys in fox hunting in Virginia," young Roosevelt said. "Knowing how he hated Jews, we used to call him 'Flynnberg' to annoy him." More damaging, the year before Flynn had exploited his acquaintance with the President's wife to try to stop a citizenship revocation proceeding against Dr. Hermann Erben, a physician suspected by the FBI of being a Nazi spy. Much of the Irish hatred for England translated into sympathy for Germany. Exactly who Flynn might be working for in the Emerald Isle was thus questionable. FDR did not accept Flynn's offer to take on a new role as a spy.

Bill Donovan did not limit himself merely to reporting intelligence and passing along agent candidates to the President. He showered Roosevelt with strategies bred in his hothouse mind. Less than a month after Pearl Harbor, he urged that the President use what was left of the Pacific Fleet to transport fifteen thousand American commandos—which the United States did not have—for an "out of the blue strike" against the Japanese home island of Hokkaido. That same January, Donovan had another brainstorm. He suggested to the President that the United States should announce that Japan intended to attack Singapore or the Panama Canal. Then, when the Japanese failed to do so, which Donovan assured FDR was the case, the United States could trumpet this "failure" as the turning point of the war. Alas, Japan did attack Singapore and capture it on February 15. Two days later, Wild Bill rushed the President a warning from an agent who "has previously given correct information regarding moves of the Axis in Europe and the Orient." This informant reported, "Next move of the Nazis will be frontal attack on New York, synchronized with general Nazi organized revolution in all South American countries, timed to follow closely the fall of Singapore." Donovan also passed along information that leading Nazis—Göring, Rudolf Hess, von Ribbentrop, and Goebbels— had made large secret bank deposits in Latin America, Holland, Switzerland, and even the United States. He proposed that this information be broadcast over his own COI shortwave radio service to demonstrate the top Nazis' lack of faith in their own regime.

The man who pressed these ideas is perhaps best understood in the way he went about recruiting a New England chemist and businessman, Stanley Lovell, to run COI's Research and Development branch. Lovell, then age fifty-two, was heading his own Lovell Chemical Company when he was persuaded to go to Washington early in 1942 to talk to Colonel Donovan. Upon their meeting, Donovan told Lovell, "Professor Moriarty is the man I want. . . . I think you're it." What Donovan had in mind, he said, was a laboratory of dirty tricks. Lovell left to think over whether or not he wanted to pattern his life after the evil genius of the Sherlock Holmes stories. A few days later, he returned to Donovan's home and pointed out: "Dirty tricks are simply not tolerated in the American code of ethics." "Don't be so goddamn naive, Lovell," Donovan responded. "If you think America won't rise in applause to what is so easily called 'un-American' you're not my man." Lovell signed on and caught on. He was soon exploring schemes, including one to inject Hitler's vegetarian diet with female hormones that would cause his mustache to fall out and his voice to turn soprano.

That FDR tolerated what in retrospect seems such patent nonsense requires an understanding of the President's own occasionally overheated imagination. In January, FDR received a letter from Lytle S. Adams of Irwin, Pennsylvania. Mr. Adams, of unspecified credentials, claimed that the Japanese had a phobic fear of bats. He urged the President to launch a surprise attack, dropping large numbers of bats over Japan, thus "frightening, demoralizing and exciting the prejudices of the people of the Japanese Empire." The President sent Adams's letter to Donovan with a note reading, "This man is not a *nut*. It sounds like a perfectly wild idea but is worth looking into." Donovan seized upon the scheme, enlisting the participation of the curator of mammals at the American Museum of Natural History as well as the Army Air Corps. The bat mission was seriously pursued and given up only after the bats, in test flights, froze to death in the high altitudes required.

John Ford, the movie director Donovan had recruited, described his new chief as "the sort of guy who thought nothing of parachuting into France, blowing up a bridge, pissing in *Luftwaffe* gas tanks, then dancing on the roof of the St. Regis hotel with a German spy." The description would have tickled FDR. Chairbound himself, he loved vicarious flights of derring-do, stories of missions potent with danger and mystery. There was in Bill Donovan something of himself. If you are knocked down, if your schemes fall flat, if you are dead wrong, you get up, dust yourself off, and storm the next barricade.

FDR's initial admiration for Donovan and the adulation of the colonel by his subordinates did not extend to intelligence competitors, MID and ONI. Ever on guard against the man's naked ambition, they managed to freeze Donovan out of the best intelligence. Wild Bill was not permitted to see Magic or Ultra.

In the post–Pearl Harbor fear of fifth column subversion, Donovan reported to FDR that German saboteurs were about to descend on America's shores, supported by U.S. bands of Nazi-style storm troopers. The President received a further warning from Donovan that Japanese soldiers disguised as civilians were mobilizing to move against San Diego. Both reports were taken seriously at a time when an underground shelter with a thick bombproof roof was being dug under the White House's East Wing with room enough to accommodate a hundred officials, a time when the White House roof bristled with guns. Donovan next warned of an imminent Japanese air strike against Los Angeles. To strengthen the report's credibility, he pointed out that the intelligence had come through the President's son Jimmy, Donovan's liaison with the Marine Corps. Jimmy had informed Donovan of a warning received from a COI agent traveling aboard a ship from Havana to Germany. On Pearl Harbor day, the agent had radioed a message, to his wife, reading, "Get out of Los Angeles and go back home." "I interpreted this to mean," Donovan told FDR, "that there would be an air attack on Los Angeles." He had shared this information with General John L. DeWitt, chief of the Army's West Coast command, and "General DeWitt placed the same interpretation on it."

Donovan also contributed to the mixed messages FDR was receiving about what to do with Japanese living on the West Coast, both the Nisei, American-born citizens of Japanese parentage, and the Issei, immigrants from Japan. On December 15, Donovan advised the President, "[T]here was no reason so far to suspect the loyalty of Japanese-American citizens." The President received the same advice from John Franklin Carter. Months before Pearl Harbor, Carter's man, Curtis B. Munson, had concluded that the Japanese in America "are more in danger from the whites than the other way around." Munson, however, gave himself some cover. As for Hawaiians of Japanese descent, he reported, if the enemy fleet appeared off Hawaii, "doubtless great numbers of them would forget their American loyalties and shout 'Banzai!' "

After Pearl Harbor, the perception of disloyalty among Japanese Americans, if not the reality, grew rapidly. While Donovan and Carter were essentially reporting the loyalty of this group, Navy secretary Knox made a statement on December 15, carried by the major news services, that offered his version of the disaster of December 7: "I think the most effective fifth column work of the entire war was done in Hawaii. . . ." Pressure on

FDR to do something to eliminate the perceived danger of the Japanese living on the West Coast and in Hawaii began to mount. California's governor, Culbert Olson, the state's attorney general, Earl Warren, later to be a liberal chief justice of the United States, and the West Coast Army chief, General DeWitt, urged the President to intern the Japanese. Supposed proof of Japanese sabotage included reports "that ground glass had been found in shrimp canned by Japanese workers and that Japanese saboteurs had sprayed overdoses of arsenic poison on vegetables . . . a beautiful field of flowers on the property of a Jap farmer near Ventura, California, had been plowed up because it seems the Jap was a fifth columnist and had grown his flowers in a way that when viewed from a plane formed an arrow pointing in the direction of the airport." Where no evidence of sabotage surfaced, a perverse logic provided it anyway. General DeWitt concluded, "The very fact that no sabotage has taken place to date is a disturbing and confirming indication that such action will be taken."

Yet even FBI director J. Edgar Hoover, no civil libertarian or lover of minorities, saw through the calls for rounding up the Japanese. "The necessity for mass evacuation is based primarily upon public and political pressure rather than on factual data." Hoover concluded, "Public hysteria and, in some instances, the comments of the press and radio announcers have resulted in a tremendous amount of pressure being brought to bear on Governor Olson and Earl Warren." As late as February, Donovan forwarded to the President the opinion of General Ralph Van Deman, respected chief of military intelligence during World War I, that mass evacuation of the Japanese was unnecessary and "about the craziest proposition that I have heard of yet."

However, continuing bleak news from the Pacific did nothing to elevate tolerance for the Japanese in America. Before the first month of the war ended, Manila had surrendered to the enemy, American and Filipino troops were being driven down the Bataan peninsula, and the American garrison on Wake Island had been overcome. The President, with intelligence from his three major sources, Donovan, Hoover, and Carter, telling him that Japanese residents posed no credible threat, nevertheless ordered their internment. Reaching back to the Alien Enemies Act of 1798, he issued Executive Order 9066 on February 19, 1942, "to apprehend, restrain, secure and remove" presumably dangerous persons. As a consequence, over 114,000 men, women, and children of Japanese ancestry were uprooted and kept under armed guard in remote, barren locations that FDR himself described as "concentration camps."

Why? Partly, the answer lay in the President's sincere and ingrained fear of internal subversion, however unfounded. Eleanor Roosevelt once observed to the writer John Gunther: "The President never 'thinks'! He *decides.*" Francis Biddle, the attorney general, uncomfortable himself about internment, sensed how the President had made his decision. The two men had first known each other at Groton when Biddle had been a new boy and Roosevelt a sixth-former. The younger student had looked upon the older as a "magnificent but distant deity, whose splendor added to my shyness." Over the years, Biddle had gained some insight into FDR's singular thought processes. "I do not think he was much concerned with the gravity or implications of this step," Biddle observed of the internment. "He was never theoretical about things. What must be done to defend the country must be done." FDR was a politician before he was a statesman, who recognized that survival in the former role had to precede elevation to the latter. The near-irresistible public pressure on him, in a bruised and uncertain post–Pearl Harbor America, was to round up the Japanese, however unstatesman-like future historians might judge that act.

The indiscriminate imprisonment of thousands of Japanese Americans was not lost on the enemy. A message intercepted from General Oshima, the Japanese ambassador in Berlin, to Foreign Minister Togo laid out a propaganda line to exploit the internment issue. "In the present great war," Oshima noted, "the United States has maltreated Japanese citizens, including American citizens of Japanese ancestry. . . . It is indeed evident that this war [for America] is not merely to annihilate Hitlerism but it is for the purpose of maintaining superiority of the white race. . . . In other words, it is a vast struggle between the white and colored races."

Only recently recognized, after more than half a century, is the treatment of two other ethnic targets of the Alien Enemies Act. Over 11,000 American residents of German ancestry were held in custody or moved inland during the war. Over 11,600 alien Italian and Italian Americans spent part of the war interned or relocated. However, a sharp difference distinguished the Germans and Italians from the Japanese. In the case of the former, some basis in law, however flimsy, was employed to declare an individual potentially dangerous. But the Japanese, including American citizens, were relocated en masse for a reason having nothing to do with their loyalty, but only for the color of their skin.

The paranoia reached beyond U.S. borders. In one well-suppressed episode the President allowed the American military, abetted by the State and Justice Departments, to pressure sixteen Central and South American countries to round up Germans, Japanese, and Italians residing in their lands. The rationale was to "preserve the integrity and solidarity of the American continent" from "subversive activities." Many of these people had lived in their adopted homelands for decades, often settling in the hinterlands. One German farmer, upon being arrested, inquired about the kaiser, who had been in power when he emigrated thirty years before. If the host countries were reluctant to hold these people in custody themselves, the United States intended to do the job for them. Some 2,800 Germans and 1,000 Japanese from Peru alone were among over 5,000 men, women, and children living in Latin America who were deported to two dozen camps in the United States.

While catching any dangerous aliens or spies in these dragnets was purely accidental, the people detained did serve one purpose. As an Army directive put it, "These interned nationals are to be used for exchange with interned American civilian nationals," tourists and businesspeople who had been trapped on enemy soil when the war broke out. Hundreds of interned Germans and Japanese were taken aboard ships, like the SS *Gripsholm,* to be, in effect, bartered for stranded Americans. Six such exchanges were conducted with Germany and two with Japan. Most of the internees were exchanged against their will. Among the Germans apprehended in Latin America, some bore names like Rosenbaum, Feldmann, Rothenthal, Stein, Goldmann, and Isenberg, Jews who were deported to Germany to an unknown fate.

Chapter XII

Intramural Spy Wars

O N FEBRUARY 19, the day that FDR signed the executive order to
intern Japanese on the West Coast, events on the East Coast
seemed to justify his preoccupation with fifth column subversion.
The French luxury liner *Normandie,* being refitted as a troop carrier,
caught fire and capsized at a pier in New York Harbor. Robert Sherwood
observed at the time, "[T]he long arm of the German saboteur had reached
West 49th Street." If the *Normandie* was, in fact, sabotaged, the disaster
fell into Vincent Astor's province. At the news that the ship was afire, the
friend FDR had made his intelligence controller for the New York area
sped to the *Normandie.* As Astor later reported to Roosevelt, "I do know
the facts for I arrived aboard within ten minutes of the outbreak of the fire
and remained there or in the immediate vicinity for most of the period up
to the time she capsized twelve hours later." Astor maintained that he had
the solution to the *Normandie's* destruction. Not saboteurs, but careless
workmen cutting metal with acetylene torches had set the ship afire.

The *Normandie* would prove to be Astor's last assignment for FDR. A
week later his cover was blown. Grace Tully told the President, "Vincent
Astor telephoned me yesterday to say that the *Journal American* carried a
story about his duties. He has no idea where they got their information but
he said it had enough truth in it to be dangerous or harmful. He got hold of

someone and had the story killed in the next editions." That Astor could kill a story in a major New York daily with a phone call demonstrated his influence, but he was not immune to the machinations of rivals in the intelligence game. Who had leaked the damaging story to the *Journal American*? John Franklin Carter was a prime suspect. Four days after Pearl Harbor, Carter had complained to FDR that Astor failed to cooperate with him since "he does not know what I am supposed to be doing." Further, Carter charged that Astor was wasting money and manpower by duplicating his work. Carter was a smart competitor. And while no proof exists that he leaked the story to the newspaper, whoever did so commenced the decline and fall of Vincent Astor. The grueling pressure, the constant conflict with the FBI, jealous Navy officers, and Carter began to tell. Astor was hospitalized and came out an exhausted man. He accepted his defeat in the intelligence realm, noting, "[T]he President gave his approval to my discontinuing this activity." The gentleman-yachtsman amateur had been knocked out of the ring by tougher, shrewder players. Astor's duties shifted to chartering fishing vessels for the Navy.

By now, FDR was using Carter to pry into everything from the loyalty of high-ranking federal officials to the feasibility of jet engines. But Carter's cover as a Washington columnist had created a dilemma for him. His desire for secrecy conflicted with his need to be recognized by government agencies with which he expected to deal. An encounter with Vannevar Bush, director of the Office of Scientific Research and Development and FDR's chief science advisor, illustrated Carter's quandary. In one of his casually tossed-off ideas, the President had asked Carter to evaluate a secret internal combustion engine being considered for the Navy. Carter had gone to Bush, whom he knew was heavily involved in the project. Instead of enlightening Carter, Bush had stiffed him. He told Carter, "I have no corresponding instruction from the President to enter into this matter now being considered by other organizations than my own. Will you kindly let me have a copy of your direction from the President?" Carter thereafter asked FDR to provide him with proof of his legitimacy. He drafted a "Dear Jack" letter to himself and asked Roosevelt to sign it. The letter read: "In order to facilitate the execution of your assigned duties and to assure you and your representatives the friendly cooperation of the other government services, you should establish contact with the heads of the Federal Bureaus, Departments and Agencies and with other intelligence services." Carter told FDR that he needed this proof of his bona fides to "avoid embarrassment" in carrying out his intelligence role.

The President told Grace Tully to inform Carter that the answer was no. "I think it is better for him to give his men credentials," FDR advised. The rejection did not mean that Roosevelt was unhappy with the Carter operation, and the following January he agreed to raise Carter's secret budget. But the President's visceral resistance to committing anything to paper had again come into play. By refusing to sign the letter allowing Carter to snoop at will, FDR was merely saying, let someone else leave the fingerprints.

★

Early in 1942, Congress began debating H.R. 6296, a bill sponsored originally in the Senate by Kenneth McKellar, Democrat from Tennessee, which upon a casual reading seemed innocuous enough. Agents of foreign governments working in the United States were henceforth to register with the Justice Department rather than the State Department. However, the fine print in this legislation contained a requirement that was to ignite the hottest fight thus far in America's secret warfare, not with an enemy but with an ally. Along with registering, foreign agents had to disclose the activities they were conducting in the United States, who was carrying them out, and how much was being spent for these purposes. The bill drew no distinction between friendly and unfriendly foreign powers. Bill Stephenson, as head of the New York–based intelligence front British Security Coordination, was aghast. As soon as he read the bill's requirement that "all records, accounts, and propaganda material used by foreign agents would be liable to inspection by U.S. government authorities at any time," he sped to Bill Donovan's office. If the McKellar bill became law, he said, he was out of business and Donovan would be too, so close was their dependence on each other.

Adolf Berle, given by FDR the job of coordinating the actions of all federal agencies with intelligence duties, took the opposite tack. He vigorously urged the President to approve the bill. Berle particularly resented the freewheeling Stephenson and his BSC operations in America. Knowing the President's desire for close cooperation between U.S. and British intelligence operations, Berle had warily gone along with the deal allowing Stephenson's people to use the FBI's shortwave radio facilities for transmitting messages between the United States and London. In one month, August 1941, nearly seven hundred such messages had been sent. What galled Berle was that the British refused to give the FBI either the code or decoded versions of what they sent over an American circuit. To the FBI's repeated requests for this information, Stephenson had replied piously that this circuit was also used for communications between the President, Churchill, and other high officials in England. Consequently, he could not possibly give "the code to anyone without first being sure it would meet with the approval of the President."

Berle suspected that Stephenson had Donovan in his back pocket. On one occasion he noted, "Though it is not possible to say so, Bill Donovan gets a good many of his ideas from the British." He told his boss, Sumner Welles, "[T]he really active head of the intelligence section in Donovan's group is Mr. Elliot, who was assistant to Mr. Stevenson [sic], the head of British intelligence here. In other words, Stevenson's assistant in the British Intelligence is running Donovan's Intelligence Service."

Berle not only supported the McKellar bill, he had helped write it. In urging the President to sign this act, he told FDR, "I do not see that any of us can safely take the position that we should grant blanket immunity for any spy system, no matter whose it is. Logically, why have it? If our interests diverge, it is adverse; if they are the same, our own people ought to be able to do the job. . . ." In his diary, Berle was more blunt. "No one has given us any effective reason why there should be a British espionage system in the United States. I believe now they [the British] have gone to Colonel Donovan and that Colonel Donovan is secretly trying to get the bill stopped. . . ."

As the McKellar bill was coming up for a vote, Donovan called Grace Tully, to whom he always paid courtly attention, and asked to see the President. He was invited for dinner with the President on January 27, along with Jimmy Roosevelt's wife, Betsey, and the socialite businessman Cornelius Vanderbilt "Jock" Whitney, now serving in the Army Air Corps. Tully was filling in as hostess to cover one of Mrs. Roosevelt's frequent absences. Given a few minutes to speak in confidence with the President, Donovan was at his persuasive best. Yes, the McKellar bill had a laudable intent. It had grown out of a congressional investigation into enemy subversion and was designed to flush out fifth columnists operating in the United States. But in Congress's rush to catch enemies, its net had snared a friend, the BSC, Donovan argued. He repeated to FDR Stephenson's fears. "If our reading of the bill is correct," Stephenson had told Donovan, "the future working in the United States of our office will become impossible. Our files would become a matter of 'public record.' " BSC was not spying on the United States, Donovan told the President, "but simply supplies this government with information about other countries. Thus, their service is of direct benefit to us." The bill did not have to be scrapped, Donovan suggested; it only had to make certain exceptions.

He carried the day. Congress did pass the McKellar bill on January 28, but FDR vetoed it. The measure resurfaced with an exemption: It did not apply to foreign governments "the defense of which the President deems vital to the United States." FDR signed the amended version early in February. BSC was saved, and, in Berle's jaundiced view, so was its subsidiary, Donovan's COI.

To Stephenson, the McKellar battle had been a close call. The quietly combative Canadian was determined to make sure that Berle, clearly his enemy, could not threaten him again. The McKellar law had barely been on the books a week when, on February 13, Berle received an unsettling call from J. Edgar Hoover's deputy Ed Tamm. The FBI had learned that a BSC agent, Denis Paine, was poking into Berle's personal life to "get the dirt" on him. The purpose, Tamm reported, was to leak this information to American newspapers and thus drive Berle out of the State Department. Tamm reported that the FBI, consequently, had ordered Stephenson to get Paine out of the country by six o'clock that day or see him arrested. Stephenson, according to Berle's diary, lamely expressed "surprise and horror that any of his men should do such a thing." Nevertheless, Paine was on the next plane to Montreal. "It developed," Berle noted, "that the only dirt they had dug up so far was a column about having twin bath tubs in our house."

———═══★═══———

Chapter XIII

Premier Secret of the War

ON THE day before Pearl Harbor, FDR made a decision that would ultimately decide Japan's fate. He held a secret meeting, unrecorded even in the White House log, with Dr. Vannevar Bush, his science advisor, and four other men: Dr. Lyman J. Briggs, Dr. Ernest O. Lawrence, Dr. James B. Conant, the president of Harvard, and Dr. Arthur Compton, a Nobel laureate in physics for his discovery of the "Compton effect." All were linked by a common interest in nuclear physics. They had come to persuade FDR that a bomb produced through atomic fission was a theoretical possibility. The clinching argument, made by Compton, was: "If atomic bombs could be made, only one plan was possible. We must get them first." Compton, who had never met or voted for Roosevelt, remembered being impressed by the President's instant grasp of the strategic significance of what the scientists were telling him. Before they left the White House, FDR asked them to explore every possible path to determine if such a weapon was feasible and to report back in six months. If their answer was yes, he assured them, they could count on the nation's every resource to produce the bomb.

This meeting took place almost two years after FDR was introduced to the atom. In the summer of 1939, a Hungarian Jewish refugee physicist, Leo Szilard, one of the first to conceive of a nuclear chain reaction used as a bomb, had driven out to Nassau Point on Long Island to meet the world's preeminent physicist, Albert Einstein. Szilard was chauffeured by another young physicist, Edward Teller. Szilard had been persuaded by a Russian-born American financier, Alexander Sachs, that the way to get things done in America was to go directly to the President, whom Sachs claimed to know intimately. Consequently, Szilard had drafted a letter to President Roosevelt which he hoped to persuade Einstein to sign that described the workability of an atomic weapon. Einstein did sign the letter, and Sachs promised to deliver it to the White House personally.

Alexander Sachs, forty-six at the time, was a self-important figure who, with his thick semicircle of curly hair and receding chin, resembled an intellectual Harpo Marx. He was given to tortured locutions, saying, for example, that he was "a member of the cognate older faith," by which he meant that he was a Jew. He casually tossed off words such as "beblinkered," referring to people who wore glasses. Nevertheless, Sachs's boast that he knew Roosevelt was true. He had worked in FDR's 1932 presidential campaign, contributing economic ideas to speeches, and his advice had been sought out from time to time by Roosevelt throughout the thirties.

The letter that Einstein signed on August 2, 1939, read in part: ". . . [I]t may be possible to set up a nuclear chain reaction in a large mass of uranium, by which vast amounts of power . . . would be generated. . . . This new phenomenon would lead to the construction of bombs. . . . A single bomb of this type, carried by a boat and exploded in a port, might well destroy the whole port, together with some of the surrounding territory." Einstein urged the President "to have some permanent contact maintained between the Administration and the group of physicists working on chain reactions." The letter pointed out how scarce uranium was in America, while Czechoslovakia, now swallowed up by Germany, was rich in this ore. The letter closed on an ominous note: "I understand that Germany has stopped the sale of uranium from the Czechoslovakia mines which she has taken over."

Though Einstein had signed the letter in August, it was not until October 11 that Sachs managed to see Roosevelt. That Wednesday afternoon he waited outside the Oval Office, while the President's aide Pa Watson thumbed through the papers Sachs had brought with him—the Einstein letter, an amplification of it by Szilard, and Sachs's own digests of two pertinent scientific articles. Finally, Watson ushered Sachs in to see the President, where he was greeted with arms flung up and a grinning welcome,

"Alex, what are you up to?" Despite the impression that Roosevelt was thrilled to see him, Sachs had trouble getting the President's attention as FDR's verbal fireworks dominated the visit and threatened to exhaust the time Pa Watson had allotted. Sachs, however, was a formidable adversary at repartee. He saucily reminded the President that he had paid for this trip to Washington himself, could not deduct it from his income tax, and expected to get his money's worth. He caught the President's attention with a parable about a young American inventor who had once written to Napoleon. He could build the emperor a fleet, the inventor claimed, that could move without sails, be powered without wind, and invade England in a few hours in any weather. Napoleon supposedly scoffed at Robert Fulton's steamboat and dismissed the inventor with, "Bah! Away with your visionists." The President must not now play Napoleon to his Fulton, Sachs explained, since he carried an idea that could revolutionize warfare. FDR sent, appropriately, for a bottle of Napoleon brandy, poured Sachs and himself a glass, and prepared to listen.

Sachs proceeded to read, not Einstein's letter or Szilard's memorandum, but his own eight-hundred-word summary of the articles on atomic fission. After reading his report, word for word, Sachs next pulled from his papers a lecture delivered by another scientist, Francis Aston, and read FDR its concluding paragraph: ". . . [T]here is no doubt that sub-atomic energy is available all around us, and that one day man will release its almost infinite power. We cannot prevent him from doing so and can only hope that he will not use it exclusively in blowing up his next door neighbor." The President paused long and thoughtfully, and then said, "Alex, what you are after is to see that the Nazis don't blow us up."

"Precisely," Sachs answered.

The President called Pa Watson in. "This requires action," he said, handing him Sachs's papers.

FDR sent Einstein a thank-you note a week after Sachs's visit. And, as a result of his instruction to Watson, expert committees were formed and studies conducted, culminating in the meeting that FDR held the day before Pearl Harbor with the scientists to whom he had given six months to decide if a bomb could work. Their answer came back an emphatic yes. Thereafter, the President moved with dispatch. He was motivated most by the likelihood that Germany could beat America to the bomb. Among the physicist cognoscenti, no doubt existed that Germany held the lead. Nuclear fission had been conceived in Germany. The Einstein letter had warned of uranium mines in Czechoslovakia, now in the Nazi grip. The world's only heavy-water plant, crucial to atomic development, was in Nazi-occupied Norway. Above all, Germany possessed the expertise of a half-dozen major world physicists, among them Werner Heisenberg, considered by one British scientist as "the most dangerous possible German in the field because of his brain power." When asked by a deputy of Albert Speer, Germany's arms czar, how big an atom bomb would be required to destroy a city, Heisenberg cupped his hands and said, "As large as a pineapple." Speer thereafter ordered the physicist to let him know "the measures, the sums of money and the materials they would need to further nuclear research." Heisenberg indicated that, given maximum support, it would take at least two years to build a bomb. Speer immediately reported to Hitler the stupefying power of an atomic weapon, but, as he later stated, "the idea quite obviously strained his intellectual capacity." Nevertheless, Heisenberg was to proceed and the effort to produce a German atomic bomb rested substantially with him.

In America, Roosevelt assigned the bomb's development to Secretary of War Henry Stimson. He also took Harry Hopkins and Vice President Henry Wallace into his confidence. This appears to be one occasion where Wallace did not confide to his Swiss diplomat brother-in-law a secret he learned of in the Oval Office. As Stimson passed along FDR's orders, some military leaders balked. What was this thing? What would it cost? Wouldn't it swallow up resources needed elsewhere? Pa Watson told the doubters, "The boss wants it, boys. Get it done."

By May, Stimson told a mystified Treasury secretary, Henry Morgenthau, to loan 40,000 of his department's 47,000 tons of silver to something called the Defense Plant Corporation. Next Stimson wanted 6,000 tons of silver for electromagnets released to a secret plant somewhere in the South. When Stimson subsequently asked Morgenthau to put $12 million into a Federal Reserve Bank account in New York, without explaining why, the Treasury secretary angrily insisted on knowing the reason. Stimson held his ground. The matter was "so much more secret than anything else that I've ever had that I don't feel able to do that," he answered. In August the President approved the creation of a new division within the Army Corps of Engineers, "The Manhattan Engineering District," to carry out the mysterious project.

Grace Tully had no idea what the Manhattan Project was about, though she worked at the President's side every day. When FDR finished reading a progress report on what he referred to as "atomistics," he told her, "Grace, this is red hot. Put it in a sealed envelope and deliver it to Admiral

Brown. Tell him to lock it in his safe. It is for nobody's eyes." On another occasion, Roosevelt told her to put a similar document in a sealed envelope and to lock it up, adding, "I can't tell you what this is, Grace, but if it works, and pray God it does, it will save many American lives."

The cerebral, left-leaning physicist J. Robert Oppenheimer had been chosen as the Manhattan Project's scientific leader. As Oppenheimer began building his team, the President sent him a warning. He reminded Oppenheimer that he was engaged in "a hazardous matter under unusual circumstances . . . of such great significance to the nation." The President assured Oppenheimer that he would allot the project whatever budget it needed. He wanted it "pushed not only in regard to the development, but also with due regard to time." He reiterated his conviction that American science was in a race with Nazi science. "Whatever the enemy may be planning, American science will be equal to the challenge," he assured the physicist. Oppenheimer replied that the secret would be safe and the progress swift. "[W]e as a group are profoundly aware of our responsibility, for the security of our project as well as its rapid completion," he assured the President, with more confidence than future events would warrant.

———═══★═══———

Chapter XIV

Enter the OSS

THE PRESIDENT had appointed Bill Donovan head of COI to co-ordinate intelligence within the bureaucracy and to conduct espi-onage. Donovan acted with particular energy on the latter. Within six months, his payroll already topped over a thousand and was still swelling. But Donovan was hemmed in by peculiar boundaries set in Franklin Roosevelt's mind. Robert Sherwood well captured this enigmatic terrain. "Being a writer by trade," Sherwood wrote, "I tried to look beyond his charming and amusing and warmly affectionate surface into his heav-ily forested interior. But I could never really understand what was going on in there. His character was not only multiplex, it was contradictory to a be-wildering degree." One decision that emerged from that heavily forested interior was that the whole world was not to be Bill Donovan's intelligence province.

Young Nelson Rockefeller, age thirty-two, Roosevelt's coordinator of inter-American affairs, had already elbowed Donovan out of radio propa-ganda in Latin America. Rockefeller was no silver spoon idler. Ruggedly handsome, bounding with energy, and aggressive, he saw the lands from the Rio Grande to Tierra del Fuego as his territory. He did not want Bill Donovan there in any role. Otherwise, he told the President, he would have to resign. Granted, J. Edgar Hoover had his Special Intelligence Service operating in Latin America, but Hoover was not a rampart that Rockefeller was about to storm. Instead, he became Hoover's ally in excluding Donovan from the region. Hoover refused even to share with the nation's supposed intelligence coordinator what his spies learned south of the border. Hoover and Rockefeller had another ally. Adolf Berle warned the President, "Bill Donovan wants to take over the FBI work in South America. At least he does not say so, but he wants to put his own man in. He does not even say that, but you can never pin him down to saying what he really wants to do."

To FDR, Nelson Rockefeller was like family, a scion from his own social station. Hoover was useful and too cunning to rebuff. In the contest for Latin America, Donovan was sacrificed to these two. On January 16, 1942, the President issued a directive that the COI was to stay out of the region. Further, Donovan was not to carry out any intelligence operations within the United States; this remained strictly Hoover's bailiwick. For Donovan, being excluded from Latin America amounted to an amputation. But this was not enough for his military rivals, who went beyond Rockefeller and Hoover. They sensed an opportune moment for total dismemberment. The Joint Chiefs of Staff assigned Navy Captain Francis C. Denebrink to investigate the COI and make recommendations for its future. While Denebrink was studying Donovan's fate, Wild Bill counterattacked. He went to the President with a proposal not to retrench, but to expand. "In order to give privacy and security to both our Special Intelligence service [SI] and our Special Operations group [SO], we have to have a separate building," Donovan argued. "It has occurred to me that if the State Department passes upon the legality and wisdom of seizure, we would, with your permission, like to obtain the use of the Japanese Embassy." Donovan had about as many friends at State as he did in the armed services and the FBI. They all united to thwart his latest ambition, and FDR left the Japanese embassy empty.

Captain Denebrink's report, submitted on March 8, went for the jugular. He recommended scrapping the COI. The Joint Chiefs happily endorsed the captain's proposals, which were about to go to FDR, when General Walter Bedell Smith, the politically astute JCS secretary, had second thoughts. Donovan, Smith knew, had standing in the Oval Office. A plan simply to boot Wild Bill out would never win FDR's approval. It might be wiser to bring the COI, currently a civilian body flowing freely between the JCS and the White House, firmly under military control. That way the military could benefit from COI's virtues while controlling Donovan's ambitions.

When Donovan got wind of General Smith's intention, he was not unhappy. He recognized that his dependence on a president with a thousand other cares was thin protection against his enemies. The strength of that enmity is reflected in what Assistant Secretary of State Breckinridge Long penned in his diary that April: "Donovan has been a thorn in the side of a number of the regular agencies of the government—including the Department of State. He is into everybody's business—knows no bounds or jurisdiction—tries to fill the shoes of each agency charged with responsibility for a war activity." Long then added, reflecting the mythology growing around Donovan, "He has almost unlimited money and a regular army at work and agents all over the world." While the Bedell Smith suggestion to absorb the COI under the JCS was still before the President, a new adversary emerged in the very military Donovan hoped would adopt him. General George Veazey Strong was a lean, leathery West Pointer who began his career as a cavalryman fighting Ute Indians. Strong earned a law degree, taught law at West Point, and now in his mid-fifties, still smooth-faced and fit, had been picked personally by General Marshall to head the Army's Military Intelligence Division. Strong veritably glowed hot with ambition, and was known around Washington as King George for his authoritarian manner. His distrust, dislike, and disdain for Donovan had been instantaneous. In Strong's eyes, the honorary colonel was still a civilian poking into military matters; Donovan employed a bunch of socially connected amateurs; he had a secret cache of funds; he used Communists. Though Donovan did hire Communists with the President's permission, this fact did not assuage Strong. He rejected Donovan's rationale for employing Reds, which ran roughly: Roosevelt and Churchill consort with top Communists, beginning with Joe Stalin, in order to defeat Hitler. Why not use lesser fry to the same end? But most sinful to Strong, Donovan was a rival. The Army intelligence chief set about to destroy the COI and its director with a malevolence better applied to the enemy.

Among Strong's powers was control of the distribution of Magic and Ultra within the United States. The enemy intentions that these decrypts revealed were as priceless to the Allies as divisions or fleets. Donovan may have been impetuous, but he was no fool. He knew that no spy, however crafty, could surpass the value of signal intelligence. Denied access to these decrypts, Donovan could never be the player in secret warfare that he hungered to be. Yet, the keeper of these jewels was his visceral foe, George Strong, who continued to keep him off the distribution list. Strong's given reason was that the COI was too careless to handle classified material. This charge was not wholly without merit, at least at the top. Donovan was always hectoring his subordinates about security—"Stanley, not a word to anyone for twenty years!" he once warned his science chief, Stanley Lovell. Yet, he drove his security officers to despair, blabbing about the most sanctified secrets for the titillation of guests at cocktail parties. Donovan's carelessness gave Strong a good reason to deprive the colonel of Ultra and Magic; but his real reason remained to starve the COI of vital intelligence and drive it from the field. Paper missiles began winging across this bureaucratic no-man's-land. Donovan sent a protest to the JCS arguing, "To exclude this agency from the processed intercepts can imply only that the material is not considered pertinent to the work of [COI] or that there is a question as to the loyalty, the intelligence or discretion of [COI] or the manner in which it would guard its security." The fight was bucked up to the President, to whom Donovan complained that his espionage wing, SI, could barely function without access to the intercepts. General Strong responded by trying to tighten the noose further around Wild Bill's neck. He drafted a memorandum for Marshall to send to FDR not only excluding the COI from Magic and Ultra, but specifically prohibiting Donovan's agency from engaging in its own codebreaking.

For the President, resolving the rivalry meant a juggling act. Donovan was useful and FDR liked him. But Marshall's staff, including Strong, was indispensable. Roosevelt ruled Donovan out of codebreaking. But he also directed that the COI could receive Magic and Ultra under one condition, a restriction that put Donovan back to square one. Strong's special branch, which handled the intercepts, would decide what the COI could see.

★

The intelligence that Hitler and his military commanders sought most eagerly in the spring of 1942 was to know whether or not the Western allies intended to invade Europe that year, launching the second front that Stalin kept demanding. The President had swung back and forth, but essentially favored going ahead "to draw off pressure on the Russians." As he reminded Churchill, ". . . [T]he Russians are today killing more Germans and destroying more equipment than you and I put together." Churchill believed the Allies were wholly unprepared to invade the Continent before 1943 at the earliest. Whose view would prevail was vital intelligence to the Nazis, since it would determine how many divisions and what armor and aircraft Hitler dared pull out of occupied Western Europe for use in his 1942 summer offensive against the Soviet Union.

On May 24, Germany seemed to have its answer. On that date, Major Hermann Baun, chief of the Eastern Desk of the Abwehr, sent a secret dispatch to German commanders in Poland and Russia and to General Reinhard Gehlen, the Army's intelligence chief on the eastern front. "From reliable sources, the views of American government circles, expressed in a conversation between a foreign diplomat and the American Colonel Donovan can be ascertained," Baun's message began. What this conversation revealed, he said, was, "The American government expects with certainty that Russia will hold out until the arms production of the U.S.A., which is now well underway, performs up to the requirements of the present war." Colonel Donovan further allegedly revealed, ". . . [T]he Russian Army should have over 360 divisions at its disposal for the coming summer offensive." Most astonishing, Baun reported, "Regarding Allied invasion plans in Europe during the coming summer, Donovan declared that efforts of great magnitude are out of the question. British and American diplomatic representatives in Europe, however, would spread reports of ostensibly planned large scale operations in order to mislead Germany." The intelligence was essentially correct, confirmed by other sources. The German army was relatively safe in resuming the offensive in Russia. It would not be facing a second front that season.

It is all but certain that this critical intelligence indeed came into German hands through Bill Donovan's indiscretion. A report in the files of the German foreign ministry found after the war traces the Donovan disclosures to a conversation between Wild Bill and a Polish intelligence officer, Count Mohl, which took place in Washington. Baun's information is also repeated in reports prepared by the German embassy in Lisbon. Thus, two possibilities open. Mohl may have unwittingly or deliberately passed revelations made by Donovan to a German agent in America, who relayed the information to the Abwehr. Or Donovan may have had a similar conversation with a Portuguese diplomat in Washington, who reported it to his foreign office in Lisbon, where the Germans had informants. However it happened, the journey of this vital secret, likely from Donovan's lips ultimately to German intelligence agents, was a breach of security of staggering proportions and priceless to enemy strategists. Nothing General Strong concocted could have more surely destroyed Donovan. But neither Strong, nor the President, nor anyone on the Allied side ever knew during the war of this loose-tongued blunder.

Donovan stayed on, though his road continued rocky. He tried to get into the South Pacific, but General Douglas MacArthur, then commanding the Southeast Pacific area, did not want him. Admiral Chester W. Nimitz, the Pacific Fleet commander, also turned him down. Wild Bill remained undeterred. He continued to lobby the President to transfer the COI to the Joint Chiefs of Staff. At one meeting FDR warned him, "They'll absorb you." "You leave that to me," Donovan replied. In the meantime, FDR quietly canvassed Sumner Welles, General Marshall, Sam Rosenman, and Robert Sherwood as to whether he should scuttle the COI. But he kept his own counsel.

Early in May, Adolf Berle met with Roosevelt. Over a lunch of trout and eggs Benedict, Berle patiently provided an audience for FDR's engaging ramble. The best trout, the President said, came from Germany, caught fresh in the brooks running alongside country inns. His mind leaped from frying trout to firewood. He had his birch sprout at Hyde Park cut and stacked and sold it for six dollars a cord, he boasted. Berle finally managed to turn the conversation to business. "I asked whether he had finally come to an arrangement on the Donovan outfit," Berle later wrote in his diary. "He said that, as I perhaps knew, that he had been trying to get a brigadier-generalship for the colonel; after which he was thinking of putting him on some nice, quiet, isolated island, where he could have a scrap with some Japs every morning, before breakfast. Then he thought the Colonel would be out of trouble and be entirely happy." The jest reaffirmed what Berle already knew. FDR was a canny judge of people, their strengths and flaws. Donovan possessed imagination, but too much zeal. The President began to think out loud about how he might reorganize the COI. Berle held his tongue. He was no Donovan fan and later wrote in the diary, "I had some ideas on that subject, but decided to keep them to myself."

A month later, and typically out of the blue, FDR decided. Donovan had left the country at the time, having gone to London on June 10 to meet with officials of Britain's Special Operations Executive, the SOE, a clandestine outfit organized to infiltrate agents into occupied Europe. The President had determined to dissolve COI, but he was going to reorganize it as something new, the Office of Strategic Services. The shake-up included taking away COI's radio arm, the Foreign Information Service, which would cost Donovan roughly half of his staff, now up to 1,630 persons. Roosevelt told Sherwood, who had gone to head the propaganda operation, "You are aware of course of what I am doing. . . . I strongly feel that your work is essentially information and not espionage or subversive activity . . . I know Bill Donovan does not agree with this."

Donovan uttered the cries of protest expected of an empire builder shorn of 50 percent of his empire. But FDR's decision presented him with a strategic retreat. The Joint Chiefs did not want Donovan's propaganda machinery in the military. But with it jettisoned, they might agree to take over the proposed OSS. Snooping, sneaking about, and sabotage did not rank high among the martial arts, and the generals and admirals were only too eager to avoid the dirty work. The JCS thus agreed to absorb the OSS without its propaganda branch and to give it two functions, to collect and analyze intelligence and to carry out special operations. Wild Bill saw in this new job description the opportunity to carry out both espionage and sabotage, functions in Britain requiring both MI6 and SOE. On June 13, 1942, the President made it official. He issued an executive order creating the Office of Strategic Services. On the same day he issued another order creating the Office of War Information, sliced off from Donovan's propaganda operation. Though now part of the military, Wild Bill did not immediately press for rank. He wrote to a British friend, General Sir Archibald Wavell, "[T]hese admirals and generals might be willing to sit down with citizen Donovan, but not with General Donovan."

If he believed his new status would keep his enemies at bay, Donovan was almost immediately disabused of that hope. That summer, FDR received an urgent request for a meeting with his upgraded spymaster. Mrs. Ruth Shipley ran the State Department's Passport Office like an absolutist monarch. Donovan came complaining to FDR that Mrs. Shipley insisted on stamping "OSS" on the passports of agents he was sending abroad. The grim joke around his headquarters was that they might as well wear a sign on their backs reading I'M A SPY. Roosevelt managed to reverse the redoubtable Mrs. Shipley, and Donovan's operatives went abroad under protective cover.

★

By the summer of 1942, most of the absurdities of delivering Magic to the President had been eliminated. The system by which the Army decrypted Japanese diplomatic traffic on one day and the Navy on the next was finally discarded by the secretary of war. Henceforth, the Army was to do all the Magic decrypting. But Navy pride had to be assuaged. The codes the Army broke continued to be delivered to the President by his naval aide. The

Navy also managed to maintain control over another cryptanalytic triumph. Its codebreakers had begun to crack the latest version of JN25, the Japanese navy cipher. Purple had bared the secrets of the enemy's diplomatic communication. JN25 now began to bare the movements of Japan's fleet.

On May 24 an untidy Navy commander, Joseph J. Rochefort Jr., left his equally messy, windowless basement office in the Naval Administration Building in Pearl Harbor and trotted up to the headquarters of Admiral Nimitz, the Pacific Fleet commander. Only Rochefort's genius as a codebreaker, exemplified by what he was about to deliver, excused his unmilitary appearance. Penetration of JN25 had parted the curtain on the most ambitious Japanese naval offensive since Pearl Harbor. Admiral Isoroku Yamamoto, chief of the Japanese fleet, the enemy's ablest strategist, had conjured a plan to cap Japan's string of victories in the Pacific and finally drive America out of the war. At the far end of the Hawaiian island chain stood the lonely American outpost of Midway. Yamamoto planned to capture Midway, thus achieving two objectives. The island would serve as his central Pacific base, blocking the American way to Japan. Further, an attack on Midway could be expected to lure what was left of the U.S. Pacific fleet to a place where Yamamoto's far larger force, the very carriers and their aircraft that had struck Pearl Harbor, would polish off the American Navy. The defeat would drive the United States to the negotiating table and out of the Pacific war. American codebreakers knew that a major Japanese strategy was brewing, but not where, only that the location was designated by the enemy as "AF." Commander W. J. Holmes, a Navy cryptologist, suspecting the site might be Midway, had an inspiration. Have Midway report to Pearl Harbor, in an easily decrypted U.S. code, that the islands' water-distilling plant had broken down. Soon afterward, Navy codebreakers intercepted a Japanese message that "AF" was short of water. This intelligence formed part of the mosaic that enabled Commander Rochefort to report to Admiral Nimitz that Midway was Yamamoto's objective. Subsequent intercepts showed Japanese army units confidently giving the islands as their next mailing address.

In Washington, the precision of the intelligence seemed too good to be true. Could the intercepts be trusted? Could Yamamoto's plan be merely a feint to draw the weakened American fleet away from a more important Japanese target, the Hawaiian Islands? Chester Nimitz decided to gamble on Rochefort's intercepts and to deploy his remaining three carriers 350 miles northeast of Midway. There they would wait. On the morning of June

4, an unsuspecting enemy came within range of Nimitz's carrier-borne dive bombers. The planes inflicted horrific destruction on the Japanese. All four of Yamamoto's irreplaceable aircraft carriers were sunk, along with one cruiser. Over 330 Japanese planes were lost. American casualties amounted to one carrier and 150 planes.

For the Japanese, far more than ships and planes lay at the bottom of the Pacific after the Battle of Midway. The whole Japanese strategy lay in ruins. After an unbroken round of victories—the conquest of the Philippines, Singapore, Hong Kong, Malaya, and the Dutch East Indies—the chain was snapped. Invasions planned for New Zealand, New Caledonia, and Fiji had to be scrapped. The threat to the Hawaiian Islands had been lifted. Midway marked the turning point in the Pacific war. From now on, the Japanese would be on the defensive. American sailors, crowded into cramped office corners amid the clatter of Teletypes, key punchers, collaters, and tabulators, laboring over seemingly meaningless jumbles of random letters, had enabled a surprise strike by the American Navy amounting practically to a Japanese Pearl Harbor, and, in the long run, more decisive. Admiral Nimitz had no doubt about the key to his epic triumph. Midway was, he said, "essentially a victory of intelligence."

The Japanese were handed an unusual opportunity to end this disastrous leakage of their secrets. The opportunity was presented by the *Chicago Tribune,* published by the arch Roosevelt-hater Colonel Robert McCormick. Stanley Johnston, a *Tribune* war correspondent, had been sailing the cruiser *New Orleans,* en route to Pearl Harbor. While in the captain's cabin, Johnston stole a look at a JN25 decrypt left on the desk, one revealing what the Navy knew about Yamamoto's Midway strategy and fleet deployment. The story Johnston wrote three days after the battle carried the headline NAVY HAD WORD OF JAP PLAN TO STRIKE AT SEA. The same account appeared in McCormick's New York *Daily News* and Washington *Times-Herald.*

Any reasonably alert reader would conclude that the United States had broken Japan's naval code. So flagrant was the *Tribune*'s breach of security that a Chicago grand jury was convened to consider possible violations of the Espionage Act. But rather than reveal anything about its cryptographic coup, the Navy chose not to participate, and the probe had to be dropped. Had the Navy cooperated in the grand jury proceeding, the President might have tasted delicious revenge against his most virulent critic. Stanley Johnston, as the correspondent, and Colonel McCormick, as the publisher, might well have been convicted of treason. But FDR was far too shrewd a player to trade fleeting vengeance for loss of a priceless secret weapon. Still, anger at the newspaper persisted. A congressman denounced the *Tribune* on the floor of the House, charging, rightly, that the *Tribune* story could lead the Japanese to change their code.

With all this public uproar in the United States—the news stories, the grand jury, the speech in the Congress—the Japanese, still believing JN25 impenetrable, did not change the code and continued to use it to the war's end. The Japanese may have spied brilliantly before Pearl Harbor, but afterward they had virtually no apparatus for espionage in the United States. Prior to hostilities, they had depended entirely on their American embassy and consulates. Once the war shut these down, the Japanese, in gauging their enemy's moves, had lost their eyes and ears. As to the secret of the Midway victory, Japan could not believe what millions of American newspaper readers knew.

★

While at the level of grand strategy the President was learning to appreciate the value of intercepted enemy ciphers, he retained his weakness for the gossipy products of agents like John Franklin Carter reporting to him personally. One can only wonder at some of the notions Carter relayed to the President from his nebulous sources. His "Secret Memorandum on U.S.S.R." advised Roosevelt that three Americans served on Stalin's secret strategy board, and one of them was helping the Russians to plan an air strike of eighty-three hundred planes hidden underground at Vladivostok that would burn "Japan and the islands from one end to the other." On another occasion Carter informed the President that the Free French leader, General Charles de Gaulle, and the U.S. mine workers leader, John Lewis, were plotting to seize control of the U.S. government. Late in May 1942, Carter had lunch at New York's Century Club with Harvey Davis, director of the Stevens Institute. Immediately afterward, Carter informed the President, "There has been a suggestion that our airmen spare a few bombs to drop down the craters of some of Japan's nine hundred semi-active volcanoes. Davis said that seismologists and volcanologists were of the opinion that a hearty explosion of a semi-active volcano will start the lava flowing and might burst out of the sides." To this bright idea, Carter added his own psychological warfare twist: ". . . [W]e could convince the mass of Japanese that their gods were angry with them, by dropping bombs down the craters and starting some nice local eruptions." FDR did not dismiss the idea. He sent it to the Army Air Forces chief, Lieutenant General H. H.

"Hap" Arnold. Arnold responded to FDR with admirable tact. "I do not feel that his [Carter's] suggestion can be dismissed without serious consideration," Arnold said. But, he cautioned, planes could not be spared until "our bombardment effort against Japan warrants directing our efforts toward anything but the most critical military objectives." FDR never asked again about bombing volcanoes.

And then Carter would come up with something useful. Early in June 1942 he alerted FDR to a glaring failure in U.S. security. "Gerald Haxton, Somerset Maugham's secretary [and lover], who has been a source of some value to this unit," he told the President, "reports that it is possible to pick up a telephone in New York and put a call through to Switzerland (and, it turned out, to Sweden, Spain, Portugal and Vichy France as well)." The significance was immediately evident to FDR. Allied shipping losses in the Atlantic were soaring, 108 ships sunk in March alone. The transatlantic telephone offered a deceptively simple way for an enemy agent in the United States to phone an Abwehr colleague in Bern with intelligence on convoy sailings and sightings. This information could then be relayed to the German navy to guide its U-boat wolf packs to these targets. FDR told Carter, "I see no reason why all trans-Atlantic conversations should not be completely severed with Sweden, Switzerland, Vichy, Spain and Portugal. I see no reason why foreign diplomats of these nations should not also be forbidden telephone communication. This should be a proper exercise of war power." Sumner Welles, much trusted by the President, suggested he go slow. Yes, shut off personal phone calls to these countries, but allow foreign ambassadors in Washington to call their governments, but have the United States monitor the calls. FDR wanted simply to cut off all foreign calls to neutrals, but went along with Welles. John Franklin Carter had earned his keep for another day.

The transatlantic phone severance was a small triumph for Carter, who believed that he was now about to pull off a more stunning triumph. That summer, he informed the President that he could produce a man who had been as close to Hitler as Hermann Göring, Heinrich Himmler, or Josef Goebbels, an ex-Nazi who had held a sensitive post in the Third Reich, a figure who could be exploited for Allied propaganda and provide a deep well of insider intelligence on the Nazi regime. The President was instantly interested in this singular person who, along with all his other credentials, had been a Harvard man, graduating six years after FDR.

Carter's potential catch was Ernst Franz Sedgwick Hanfstaengl, born in Munich to a wealthy father in the art reproduction business and an American mother, Catherine Sedgwick, of an old New England family. Though he grew to a portly six feet four, Hanfstaengl had been tagged by a governess with the nickname Putzi, from which he never escaped. By upbringing, Hanfstaengl was almost as American as German. He had been sent off to Harvard in 1905, where he mingled socially with T. S. Eliot, Walter Lippmann, Theodore Roosevelt Jr., and the budding Communist John Reed. Putzi was a gifted pianist, and young Teddy invited him to the White House, where he performed for President Theodore Roosevelt's family. After Harvard, Hanfstaengl remained in the United States, marrying an American woman and managing his father's branch art shop on Fifth Avenue in New York. There, he sat out World War I while one of his brothers was killed fighting for the kaiser.

By 1921, Putzi had returned to Munich. One day, a U.S. military attaché told him that he had met an impressive political newcomer who was going to be speaking at a beer hall that night. The two men went together to hear the speaker, who looked to Putzi like "a waiter in a railroad restaurant." Then the man began to talk, and Hanfstaengl was smitten on the spot by Adolf Hitler. He introduced himself to the fledging leader of the National-sozialistische Deutsche Arbeiterpartei, the National Socialist German Workers Party, and they soon became fast friends, especially since the wealthy Hanfstaengl helped bankroll Hitler's party newspaper, the *Völkischer Beobachter.* When Hitler fled Munich after his beer hall putsch failed in 1923, he took refuge in Putzi's country estate at Uffing, thirty-five miles from the city. While there, Hitler fell into a suicidal depression. Only the comforting of Hanfstaengl's wife, to whom the sexually ambivalent Hitler was attracted, stopped him from taking his life, surely a turning point in world history. Hitler was subsequently caught and arrested at the Hanfstaengl estate. But after his release from Landsberg prison, Putzi was there with his touring car waiting to pick him up.

After coming to power in 1933, Hitler made Hanfstaengl, with his flair for languages and cosmopolitan suavity, the Reich's foreign press chief. In the evening, Putzi entertained the Führer and his coterie with renditions of Wagner, and Harvard football marches and pep songs. But Putzi apparently had too much flair for the political henchmen around Hitler. He sensed their jealousy and feared they were plotting to kill him. He fled Germany for Britain, taking with him his young son, Egon. Hanfstaengl was interned when the war broke out and subsequently sent to a Canadian POW camp in Kingston, Ontario.

John Franklin Carter had known Putzi in the latter's Nazi heyday. Carter had been in Germany working as a freelance journalist in the mid-thirties, trying to get a line on the Hitler regime. A friend told him that the man to see was Putzi Hanfstaengl. Carter looked up Hanfstaengl in Munich and the chemistry was instantaneous. They came from the same crowd. Putzi's mother was the daughter of Ellery Sedgwick, a close friend of Carter's father. Putzi tried to get Carter an interview with Hitler, who, at the time, was seeing no one. But he did arrange for Carter to see Hitler's anointed successor, Hermann Göring.

Just after Pearl Harbor, while Winston Churchill was staying at the White House, Carter received disturbing news from Henry Field, the member of his ring whom Bill Donovan had tried unsuccessfully to recruit. Carter's operatives were keeping an eye on a woman named Viola Ilma, suspected of being a German spy. "She's staying at the White House!" Field had informed a stunned Carter. Ilma had run into Mrs. Roosevelt and said she was having a hard time finding a hotel room in war-crowded Washington. Eleanor Roosevelt, always tenderhearted toward strays, had said, "Well why don't you come and stay at the White House? There's nobody there but Franklin and the Prime Minister."

Distressed to discover that a possible Nazi spy had penetrated America's innermost sanctum, Carter began to track down Putzi Hanfstaengl, who had known Viola Ilma in Berlin. He learned, through the FBI, about Putzi's internment in Canada and managed to visit him there. He concluded from what Hanfstaengl told him that Ilma was not a Nazi, but more likely a British agent. More important, Carter discovered that Hanfstaengl was eager to work for the Allies against his old Nazi pals.

Carter went to see the President about bringing Hanfstaengl to America. Roosevelt airily claimed that he had known Hanfstaengl at college, though it is doubtful since he had left Harvard six years before the German. "What do you think on earth he could do?" FDR asked Carter. Carter pointed out that Hanfstaengl "actually knows all these people in the Nazi government; he might be able to tell you what makes them tick." "Yes. Go ahead," the President said, and then added something that impressed Carter with his sense of the enemy's culture. "You can tell [Hanfstaengl] that there's no reason on God's earth why the Germans shouldn't again become the kind of nation they were under Bismarck. Not militaristic. They were productive; they were peaceful, they were a great part of Europe. And that's the kind of Germany I would like to see. If he would like to work on that basis, fine."

Carter left the White House, fired by FDR's support and determined to find a way to bring Putzi under his wing. The task did not prove easy. Churchill, the Foreign Office, and the British embassy in Washington all balked. As one English diplomat put it, they were not inclined toward "confusing anybody's mind . . . into the belief that there are good and bad ex-Nazis." Carter realized that he would need Roosevelt's personal intervention to spring Hanfstaengl from captivity in Canada. On June 24, FDR, with Churchill's reluctant acquiescence, authorized an Army plane secretly to fly Hanfstaengl to Washington. His presence in the country was not to be known. He was to be quartered at Fort Belvoir near the capital under twenty-four-hour guard. Putzi was to be treated as a paroled captured officer and known as Ernst Sedgwick.

Though admitted to the country, Putzi had one more test to pass. As Carter put it, the British "warned me that Hanfstaengl was a homosexual," a compromising condition particularly for someone engaged in intelligence work. After all, the huge German had sung falsetto soprano in a Hasty Pudding show at Harvard. Carter went to New York to seek the advice of Clare Boothe Luce, the playwright and wife of *Time* magazine's publisher, Henry Luce. The beautiful Mrs. Luce suggested using Gerald Haxton, Somerset Maugham's beau, as bait. Haxton, then in America, could speak good German to the lonely Putzi, since he had spent two years as a POW in Germany in World War I. Carter arranged for Haxton to visit Hanfstaengl at Fort Belvoir. As Maugham's wife once said of Haxton, "If he thought it would be of the faintest advantage, he'd jump into bed with a hyena." The day after Haxton's visit, Carter went to see Putzi. The German's first remark was, "I wish you'd get rid of this man. One of the things I couldn't stand about Hitler was all the fairies he had around him. I don't like fairies." Putzi's sexual orthodoxy was confirmed.

Putzi soon appeared to demonstrate his use to his new keepers. During a visit to an Army base, he and Carter were studying a wall map when Hanfstaengl suddenly put his finger on Casablanca. "Of course, there's where you ought to land," he said. Army officials were stunned. He had pinpointed a major target of Operation Torch, the pending invasion of North Africa, which was to be America's first campaign on the Atlantic side of the war. Army officials feared there had to have been a leak. An investigation was ordered. The investigators concluded that the closely guarded German could not have learned of Torch. "It was just Hanfstaengl using his brain," Carter assured the Army. All the effort and trust the President had invested in bringing Hanfstaengl to America, Carter was now convinced, had been justified. This man would earn his way.

Chapter XV

———— ═ ★ ═ ————

"We Are Striking Back"

W HAT JAPAN would do that summer of 1942 became a burning quandary. If the Japanese chose to attack Russia, as Hitler wanted, the move might relieve pressure against America and Britain in the Pacific. More directly, it would mean that the Russians would have to divert troops engaging the Nazis on their western front and send them east to battle the Japanese. To both FDR and Churchill, the primary objective of the war remained to destroy Hitler first. A Japanese attack on Russia would delay that end. In his private musings, the President revealed to Adolf Berle how far he was willing to go to appease the Russians and keep them fighting. In a May diary entry, after lunching with FDR, Berle wrote, "He said that he would not particularly mind about the Russians taking quite a chunk of territory; they might have the Baltic republics, and Eastern Poland and perhaps the Bukovina, as well as Bessarabia." Such concessions, giving away half of Poland and rubber-stamping Russia's grab of Latvia, Lithuania, and Estonia, if known outside FDR's circle, would have represented a contradiction of the President's publicly pro-fessed support of self-determination for nations. Berle tried to steer FDR away from overly accommodating Stalin, arguing, "The Atlantic Charter might have something to say about this." He added, only half joking, that he hoped Roosevelt "would not be getting generous with Scandinavia" as well. FDR laughed off the gibe. But Berle was sure the President was over-feeding the Russian bear.

On July 27 disturbing word reached Roosevelt from the American minister in Bern, Leland Harrison. Since the German conquest of Russia had not gone according to schedule, Hitler had reportedly put out a peace feeler to Stalin through the Japanese. Worse still, the Russians had proved receptive. Such a peace would release the full might of the Wehrmacht against the West. Fortunately for the Western Allies, a suspicious Hitler came to distrust his Japanese intermediaries and decided instead to go ahead with his summer offensive against the Soviet Union.

As to whether the Japanese intended to attack Russia, FDR had intelligence coming directly out of Tokyo. On June 17, without identifying Magic as his source, he advised Stalin he had hard evidence that "the Japanese may be preparing to conduct operations against the maritime provinces of the Soviet Union." However, Russia would not be left in the lurch, FDR assured Stalin. "In the event of such an attack, we are prepared to come to your assistance with our air power. . . ." In July, Roosevelt informed the Soviet leader that the threat had hardened. The Japanese would definitely attack the Soviet Union in the first ten days of August, he warned. The Russians must have been mystified when, less than a month later, the President sent another secret cable, addressed to "Mr. Stalin," again based on an unrevealed Magic intercept, claiming, "I have information which I believe to be definitely authentic that the Japanese government has decided not to undertake military operations against the Soviet Union at this time." A decrypt dated November 29, from the foreign minister in Tokyo to his ambassadors abroad, further confirmed the safety of the Soviet Union's eastern flank. Classified "strictly secret," it read: "I believe that we must, at the earliest possible moment, devise some concrete means of contributing our influence to turning the tide in Europe. Nevertheless, we are now involved in trying to swing the situation in the Pacific and in sober truth, to suddenly divert our own reserve strength in sufficient quantity to be of material aid to Germany and Italy in their operations would be impossibly foolish." Possessed of this intelligence, FDR could tell Stalin to relax. He had it from the horse's mouth: The Japanese had their hands full in the Pacific and would not be attacking him from the rear. Stalin could keep the bulk of his forces west of Moscow fighting the Germans.

★

That summer of 1942, the President half won his argument with Churchill about the time and place to commit American forces in the European war. He accepted Churchill's and his own service chiefs' judgment that invading the Continent itself was impractical that year. The Allies were not yet ready. But he did win Churchill's acceptance of an invasion of North Africa. In pursuing this strategy, Spain would hold a key card. Would the Spanish caudillo, Generalissimo Francisco Franco, allow Hitler to reinforce his armies in North Africa by allowing German troops to land in Spanish Morocco? Would Franco remain neutral and lock out all belligerents? Or, in the worst outcome, would he enter the war on the side of the Axis? One way to plumb the Spaniards' intentions was to read their codes. This objective had been achieved by Bill Stephenson's BSC agents, who repeatedly burglarized the Spanish embassy in Washington to obtain keys to the ciphers Spain used. Since the keys were changed monthly, the BSC break-ins became a recurring affair, until passage of the McKellar Act. Thereafter, Stephenson was afraid to continue anything so blatant as burglary, which might cause the BSC to be booted out of the United States. Consequently, Bletchley Park went temporarily blind in penetrating Spain's intentions. Stephenson sought help from Bill Donovan. Another break-in of the embassy was critical since the Spanish had again changed their code in July. Stephenson's plea to Donovan to take over the break-ins might have put off a more prudent man. FDR had specifically banned the OSS from carrying on espionage inside the United States. Internal intelligence and counterintelligence, the President had ruled, belonged to Hoover's FBI. But Donovan spotted a fine crack in the wall excluding him. Technically, he would not be engaged in domestic spying. He would be penetrating what traditionally was considered foreign territory, a nation's embassy abroad. Donovan thus agreed to Stephenson's appeal. The assignment to burglarize the Spanish embassy fell to an agent who fulfilled the profile that led critics to characterize the OSS as standing for "Oh, So, Social." Donald Downes was a forty-year-old product of Exeter and Yale, an intellectual liberal who had previously taught in a private school on Cape Cod. He failed the ideal OSS image only by being unstylishly overweight. Shortly after 11 P.M. on July 29, Downes led a team into the Spanish embassy. They left at dawn the next morning with enough photographs of the ciphers to enable Ultra to resume breaking Spanish documents. Since, however, the Spaniards continued to change the keys every month, Downes and his cohorts continued to break in.

In October, in the course of their fourth burglary, Downes's team was startled by sirens audible for blocks. Two squad cars disgorged FBI agents outside the embassy who sealed off any escape. The OSS burglars were arrested. Downes was allowed to make a jailhouse call to Bill Donovan, who woke up a chief aide, James R. Murphy, and told him to spring his men. While in custody, Downes tried to explain to the FBI that he worked for the OSS. Hoover's agents were only too aware that they were dealing with Donovan's poachers on their turf. The bureau already had three agents of its own inside the Spanish embassy.

Bill Donovan was furious over the FBI raid. Donald Downes recalled, "I don't believe any single event in his career ever enraged him more." Wild Bill, for once matching his nickname, protested vigorously to the President, "The Abwehr gets better treatment from the FBI than we do." But FDR stuck by the boundaries he had drawn. Donovan had stepped over the line. Internal spying belonged to Hoover. After his release, Downes wondered aloud to a colleague if Congress might not punish Hoover for what seemed to him treasonous behavior. His friend answered, "No President dare touch John Edgar Hoover. Let alone congressmen. They are all scared pink of him." Indeed, Hoover had informants inside the OSS and was building a dossier on the foibles of Donovan's organization and the director himself. Wild Bill, however, was not intimidated. He started keeping his own file of FBI blunders and initiated a covert investigation into one of Washington's most persistent rumors, that Hoover and his chief aide, Clyde Tolson, were engaged in a homosexual liaison.

★

German espionage in the United States had largely become a shambles after Hoover's July 1941 dragnet in which thirty-three Nazi agents were arrested. Among the few shards of intelligence Germany now received from America were reports from an agent, Count Friedrich Saverma, who had refashioned himself, using his wife's maiden name, as a Scotsman named Douglas. The handsome couple were welcome adornments to New York and Washington society. Drawing on these connections, Saverma sent a "Top Priority" message to the Abwehr: "Reliable source confirms that Roosevelt is suffering from a uraemic condition causing serious disturbances of consciousness as a result of constant application of catheter in urinary tract. Recurrent announcements indicating mild soreness of throat and similar instances are made merely to camouflage his true condition." If true that Roosevelt's consciousness was afflicted, this represented valuable intelligence for the Abwehr, which concerned itself with the President's health almost as much as did FDR's own physician. In this case, however, Saverma/Douglas had the wrong end of the Roosevelt anatomy. The President did go almost daily to Dr. McIntire's office next to the Map Room, but to have his sinuses packed while Captain McCrea, his naval aide, read him the latest Magic decrypts.

An unhappy Hitler leaned on the Abwehr's chief, Admiral Wilhelm Franz Canaris, to penetrate the United States. Canaris, sallow-skinned, sad-eyed, his face deeply furrowed, and called the Old Man by his subordinates, though still in his forties, was no Hitler toady. His unprepossessing appearance concealed a tough old sailor. While held in an Italian prison during World War I, Canaris lured a prison chaplain into his cell, killed him, and then passed out of the prison in the priest's cassock. Though originally a Hitler disciple, the onetime U-boat skipper had gradually become disenchanted. The crude Nazi vilification of General Freiherr Werner von Fritsch, the Army commander and a model Prussian, had disgusted Canaris. Fritsch despised the Nazis, particularly the SS. Hitler therefore forced Fritsch into retirement on trumped-up evidence, provided by a professional blackmailer, that the lifelong bachelor was homosexual. Canaris had been further sickened by the persecution of the Jews. Though he came to detest Hitler and all he represented, Canaris still loved Germany. He did what was expected of a German officer, which meant obeying orders.

What Hitler wanted from him now was an Abwehr operation to disrupt American armaments production. Thus, in April 1942, Canaris approved Operation Pastorius, named for Franz Pastorius, the first German immigrant to America, who had arrived in 1683. That spring, eight Germans, all of whom had lived in the United States and two of whom were American citizens, reported to the Abwehr espionage academy at Quentz Lake, forty miles west of Berlin. The eight were Georg Dasch, an itinerant waiter when he had resided in America; Ernest Burger, a naturalized American citizen who had worked as a machinist in Milwaukee and Detroit; Herbert Haupt, an optical worker raised in Chicago, also an American citizen; Edward Kerling, a onetime chauffeur for the American bridge expert Ely Culbertson; Richard Quirin, who had been a mechanic in New York City; Heinrich Heinck, who had worked in New York as a machinist; Hermann Neubauer, a former cook in Chicago; and Werner Thiel, a onetime toolmaker in Philadelphia, Detroit, and Los Angeles. All were in their thirties, and all had willingly returned to Germany, inspired by the glowing promise of the Third Reich.

The fledgling saboteurs began a crash course in blowing up vital installations. They were provided with drawings of key bridges and railroad centers, locks on the Ohio River, the layout of the Aluminum Company of America, the New York City water supply system, and the Niagara Falls hydroelectric plant. They were to carry high explosives, disguised as lumps of coal, and incendiary devices looking like pen and pencil sets. The Pastorius plan was to divide the eight men into two teams, one to be led by Dasch, the other by Kerling, and infiltrate them into America. They were provided with smuggled American newspapers and magazines to acquaint them with hit songs, the latest movies and slang—in short, to become familiar with daily life in the United States. The teams split the formidable sum of $174,588 in American bills and coins to cover expenses and bribes. By the end of May, Operation Pastorius was ready for launching. Admiral Canaris, however, had scant confidence in the mission. On signing their final orders he remarked, "This will cost these poor men their lives."

On the night of June 13, in pitch darkness, Dasch's team clambered out of the conning tower of U-boat 202, the *Innsbruck,* and lowered themselves into a heaving rubber dinghy. Crewmen from the sub began paddling the boat toward the shore, where the four saboteurs were landed on a fog-shrouded beach near Amagansett, Long Island, 105 miles east of New York City. Dasch's group were still burying some of their gear when out of the mist appeared a twenty-one-year-old rookie Coast Guardsman, John C. Cullen, armed only with a flashlight. On spotting Dasch, Cullen shouted, "Who are you?" Standard procedure would have dictated killing the Coast Guardsman and hiding the body. Instead, Dasch, a garrulous loudmouth, but no tough guy, pulled a gun and shoved $260 into Cullen's hand, warning him, "Forget about this." Cullen hightailed it back to the Coast Guard station and immediately reported the improbable encounter to his superiors, who, in turn, called the FBI.

In the meantime, the Dasch team made its way to New York, where the men split and checked into two hotels, Dasch and Burger into the Governor Clinton and Heinck and Quirin into the Martinique. They began their mission in America by whooping it up, spending their unimaginable wealth on expensive clothes and fancy restaurants where Dasch, the onetime waiter, now played the free-spending patron and big tipper. Though a blowhard and not a leader—a psychiatrist would later describe him as suffering from an "obsessive, compulsive, neurotic, hysterical personality disorder"—Dasch was no fool. The close call on the Amagansett beach had opened his eyes to the perils of Pastorius. After a night on the town, back in their hotel room, Dasch probed his partner's commitment to the mission in a cautious conversation. He managed to persuade a receptive Burger that Pastorius was doomed. If they turned themselves in now, he argued, instead of being treated as enemies, they would be welcomed as heroes, feted by America, and might even get to meet the President. A few years before, Burger had run afoul of the Gestapo and had spent seventeen months in a concentration camp. He had been tortured and his pregnant wife had been so harshly interrogated that she suffered a miscarriage. He was only too willing to be talked out of the mission. On a Sunday evening, less than two days after their landing, Dasch telephoned the FBI and demanded to see J. Edgar Hoover personally. By the following Friday, he was at FBI headquarters in Washington, speaking not to Hoover, but to incredulous FBI agents. Dasch divulged everything, including the information that another four-man team, under Kerling, was to land at Ponte Vedra Beach south of Jacksonville, Florida.

On June 19 the President received an excited call from Francis Biddle, his attorney general. Six days before, Biddle told the President, "at 1:30 A.M. an unarmed Coast Guard patrolman near Amagansett, Montauk Point, Long Island, discovered two men placing material in a hole they had dug; one of them covered the patrolman with a gun, gave him $260 and told him to keep his mouth shut. I shall, of course, keep you informed." As J. Edgar Hoover's nominal boss, Biddle later recalled the FBI chief's demeanor while describing the plan to track down the rest of the saboteurs: "His eyes were bright, his jaw set, excitement flickering around the edge of his nostrils," Biddle remembered. The question now was how much to tell the public. Hoover wanted no announcement that might alert the men still at large. The President agreed, and the press was, for the moment, frozen out of the story.

FDR's longstanding preoccupation with sabotage now seemed validated. Biddle admitted, "I had a bad week trying to sleep as I thought of the possibilities. The saboteurs might have other caches hidden, and at any moment an explosion was possible." Dasch had, in fact, revealed that, along with their transportation and industrial targets, the Pastorius mission was supposed to spread terror by placing firebombs in department stores and delayed-action explosives in hotels and in crowded railroad stations.

On June 27, ten days after the Kerling team landed in Florida, the President, then at Hyde Park, took another call from Biddle. Hoover's G-men had seven of the saboteurs in custody and were about to arrest the last one. Nearly $174,000 of their Abwehr stake had been seized. FDR responded with the habitual geniality that Biddle, a stiff Philadelphia Main Liner, envied. "Not enough, Francis," Roosevelt said. "Let's make real money out of them. Sell the rights to Barnum and Bailey for a million and a half—the rights to take them around the country in lion cages at so much a head." Now the tale could be told, and in the ensuing publicity, Coast Guardsman Cullen became a national hero. Hoover played the capture of the ring as a case solved by the FBI, making no public mention of the fact that Dasch had turned himself in and squealed on his comrades.

Three days after all eight saboteurs were in custody, FDR sent Biddle a memo making clear his expectations. "The two Americans are guilty of treason," he told the attorney general. "I do not see how they can offer any adequate defense . . . it seems to me that the death penalty is almost obligatory." As for the six German citizens, "They were apprehended in civilian clothes. This is an absolute parallel of the Case of Major [John] André in the Revolution and of Nathan Hale. Both of these men were hanged." The President hammered home his point once more: "The death penalty is called for by usage and by the extreme gravity of the war aim and the very existence of our American government."

Biddle had never quite overcome his awe in dealing with FDR. Still, the nation's chief law enforcement official was troubled, finding himself trapped between the President's questionable pressure and his own reverence for the law. The Germans had been apprehended so quickly, Biddle recognized, that "they had not committed any act of sabotage. Probably an indictment for attempted sabotage would not have been sustained in a civil court on the grounds that the preparations and landings were not close enough to the planned acts of sabotage to constitute attempt. If a man buys a pistol, intending murder, that is not an attempt at murder." In a civilian court the Germans might at best be convicted of conspiracy, which Biddle estimated would carry a maximum sentence of three years. This outcome, he knew, would never satisfy Roosevelt.

FDR essentially took charge of the case. He told Biddle that he wanted the eight agents tried, not in a civilian court, but by a military tribunal, which he himself would appoint. They had forfeited any right to a civilian trial, as Roosevelt put it, because "[t]hese men had penetrated battlelines strung on land along our two coasts and guarded on the sea by our destroyers, and were waging battle within our country." They fell under the Law of War. A military tribunal would be quick, not subject to the protracted appeals procedures of civilian courts. It would not be hog-tied by the criminal courts' exacting rules of evidence. It could impose the death sentence, not as the civil courts required, by a unanimous verdict, but by a two-thirds vote. A military tribunal offered the advantages and the assured outcome that the President wanted. A civilian court was out of the question. FDR told Biddle, "I want one thing clearly understood, Francis: I won't give them up . . . I won't hand them over to any United States Marshall armed with a writ of habeas corpus. Understand!" Averell Harriman, FDR's special envoy to Moscow, had once described Roosevelt's "Dutch jaw—and when that Dutch jaw was set you couldn't move him." Biddle practically felt the jaw's thrust, and dutifully followed the President's instructions. Conviction should be simple, Biddle promised FDR, since "[t]he major violation of the Law of War is crossing behind the lines of a belligerent to commit hostile acts without being in uniform."

The British, early in the war, had imposed the traditional penalty on captured spies and saboteurs, execution. Seven arrested German agents were hanged with numerous others awaiting the gallows within months of the war's outbreak. Then, in 1940, a thirty-year-old Scottish major, energetic, articulate, imaginative Thomas A. "Tar" Robertson, assigned to MI5, proposed a new approach. What use to Britain were German spies moldering in anonymous graves? he asked his superiors. Instead, make an offer to them, turn or die. Thus was born the Double Cross, or XX, operation whereby most captured spies chose turning to dying. Some became double agents and sent false information back to Germany under British control. In other cases, British radiomen mastered "the fist," the distinctive sending style of these agents, and convincingly transmitted Double Cross fabrications to Germany. Double Cross was a rousing success. Only one German spy is believed to have reached Britain during the war without being caught. The alternative of turning the eight captured Germans never entered FDR's head. Their deaths were to serve notice to the Nazis of the certain fate of any other spies and saboteurs sent to America.

On July 2 the President announced that the eight accused would stand trial before a military commission composed of seven generals, and they would be charged with violating the eighty-first and eighty-second Articles of War dealing with espionage, sabotage, and conspiracy. Court-appointed lawyers for the defendants made a game effort to move the trial to a civilian court, taking the constitutional issue all the way to the Supreme Court, but the justices backed the legality of a military tribunal. Biddle himself was to prosecute, an unusual move, having a civilian serve as prosecutor in a military proceeding. But FDR was taking no chances. The Army's Judge Advocate General was rusty and had not tried a case for over twenty years. FDR wanted his own man before the bar.

On June 8 the prisoners, held in the District of Columbia jail, were shaved by prison barbers, lest they put the razor to their own wrists or throats, and hustled into two armored vans guarded by gun-toting military police. Nine Washington motorcycle patrolmen roared alongside, escorting the vans to the Department of Justice. Enterprising vendors soon were doing a thriving business selling ice cream and hot dogs to the crowds that gathered outside the department's iron gate every day to gawk at the enemy. The trial was held in Assembly Hall #1 on the fifth floor of the Justice Department, the windows shrouded by black curtains. As the trial opened, Hoover, sitting next to Biddle, fed pages of evidence to the attorney general. During a recess, one of the defendants asked the presiding general for a cigarette. The general responded stuffily that Army regulations made no provision for such a request. A disgusted Hoover took out a pack of cigarettes and handed it to the German.

In twenty-six days it was over. All eight were sentenced to death. The generals sent their verdict to the President. Roosevelt, acting, in effect, as the court of last resort, confirmed six of the death sentences, but commuted Burger's sentence to life and Dasch's to thirty years for their willingness to betray their comrades. August 8 was set for the executions, which would take place in the electric chair on the third floor of the District of Columbia jail. Eight weeks had elapsed from the night the first saboteurs had landed on Long Island.

On execution day, FDR was at Shangri-la, the presidential hideaway in western Maryland's Catoctin Mountains. The President liked to sit in the small screened porch playing solitaire or gazing by the hour out at the Catoctin Valley, lost in his private thoughts. This evening, he gathered his guests around him in the living room—Sam Rosenman and his wife, Dorothy, Daisy Suckley, Grace Tully, poet Archibald MacLeish and his wife, Ada. The First Lady was tied up in New York. The President settled into an easy chair and seemed in unusually fine fettle. He commenced his ceremonial role, mixing the cocktails. He was conceded to make a fine martini and an old-fashioned, though lately he had become enamored of a drink made of gin and grapefruit juice, which most guests found vile. As he mixed, he swapped jests with Rosenman and MacLeish while Daisy snapped photos. Once more Rosenman was impressed by FDR's gift for shedding the cares of office after hours, as if flipping a switch somewhere inside himself.

The President began reminiscing about his days in the governor's office in Albany where Rosenman had served as his legal counsel, recalling stories of appeals for clemency on the eve of executions. Sam marveled at FDR's memory, down to dates, places, offenses, and names of the condemned in a dozen New York capital cases. The President then segued into an Alexandre Dumas story about a barber who, during the 1870 siege of Paris, supplied delicious beef while thousands were starving. Gleefully, FDR related how a number of the barber's clients had turned up missing, and the "veal" was suspected of originating in the barber's chair.

What prompted FDR's black humor this evening went unspoken until Dorothy Rosenman raised the subject. The six condemned Nazi saboteurs had been electrocuted beginning at one minute past noon. By 1:04 P.M., the work was completed, an average of ten and a half minutes per man. One witness reported that they had gone to their deaths stunned, as if in a trance. Where, Mrs. Rosenman asked the President, would the bodies be buried? He had not yet decided, FDR answered. His only regret was that they had not been hanged. He then launched into a story about an elderly American woman who died while visiting Moscow and had accidentally been switched in a casket meant for a deceased Russian general who was shipped back to the States. When her family complained, the Russian government cabled back, "Suggest you close the casket and proceed with the funeral. Your grandmother was buried in the Kremlin with full military honors." The saboteurs were subsequently buried in a potter's field near Washington.

Was the evening of gallows humor Roosevelt's true mood or intended to mask the hard decisions he had had to make about six human lives? Mrs. Rosenman's firsthand account describes nothing but Roosevelt's humor and relaxed manner, but then, he was a consummate actor. In any case, the country was with him. Telegrams poured into the White House mail room. One read, "It's high time that we wake up here in this country and show the world we are not a bunch of mush hounds." It was signed, "Mother who has three loyal sons in the Army." The Victory Committee of German American Trade Unionists telegraphed the President, "We endorse the imposition of the death penalty on any saboteur or traitor. We know that no loyal German American need have the slightest fear providing he obeys the laws of the country." On Ellis Island, the execution of the six Germans was observed differently. Adolph G. Schickert and Erich Fittkau, Germans interned there, held a meeting of other internees. They announced the death of their countrymen, called for two minutes of silence, and then led the singing of the rousing Nazi anthem, the "Horst Wessel Lied."

★

The capture of the German saboteurs had stoked a national wave of suspicion. Thousands of Americans began performing as self-appointed spy catchers. The FBI was deluged with reports of suspect behavior, almost invariably false alarms. At one point, FDR asked J. Edgar Hoover, "Have you pretty well cleaned out the alien waiters in the principal Washington hotels? Altogether too much conversation in the dining rooms." Late in October, the President summoned Hoover to his private study. He revealed confidentially to the FBI director that he had received a report of suspicious goings-on in New Jersey. He did not tell Hoover that the source was a woman who was supposed to have left his life long ago.

Franklin had given Eleanor his solemn word twenty-four years before that he would never again see Lucy Mercer. The beautiful, stately young woman with the melting smile had first come into the Roosevelt household as Eleanor's social secretary while Franklin served as assistant Navy secretary. According to Jimmy Roosevelt, Lucy, to please Eleanor's husband, had enlisted as a Navy volunteer, whereupon Franklin had her assigned to his office as a yeoman. Again, according to young Roosevelt, Lucy had made at least two cruises with the assistant secretary. In 1918, as Franklin returned from his trip to the European front, his wife discovered a packet of love letters revealing his affair with Lucy Mercer. To preserve the marriage, Franklin promised to erase Lucy from his life. Subsequently, she had married wealthy Winthrop Rutherfurd.

Following the end of the affair, Eleanor had withdrawn from the marriage bed and began her slow transformation from dutiful wife and mother to world figure in her own right. One observer characterized Eleanor as "a woman of lofty liberal principles and a harpy." The more she constructed her individual identity, the greater became the separation between the Roosevelts as man and wife. The President of the United States, in his private hours, was a lonely man, hungry for the warmth and intimacy of a woman's companionship. By 1941, with her husband invalided by a stroke, Lucy reentered Franklin's life. The White House usher's log shows seven visits to the President over a fifteen-month period by "Mrs. Paul Johnson," whom the Secret Service knew to be Mrs. Rutherfurd. All the visits occurred while Eleanor was away.

The President was vague in his conversation with Hoover, saying that the tip he had heard concerning unusual activity in New Jersey had come to him from a friend in New York who had heard it from the original source. As FDR explained, this person had been driving along a road in New Jersey from Andover to Sparta and had turned down a dirt lane for a better view of Lake Perona. Partway down the road, the car was stopped by an "Italian-appearing individual," who rudely told the driver to stop and go back to the main road. Before leaving, however, the informant made other observations. Standing by a parked car was a "very German looking" man who kept staring. Some odd construction was also under way and, coincidentally, a German-American Bund camp, called Nordlund, was located nearby. As Hoover left, the President handed him a rough pencil-drawn map of the area.

Hoover immediately dispatched a senior FBI agent to investigate the situation. The agent made some curious discoveries, the most curious being that FDR's unnamed party who had stumbled onto the suspicious scene turned out to be a Mrs. Winthrop Rutherfurd, who owned an estate at nearby Allamuchy. As the agent continued investigating, the story began to unfold. Lucy Rutherfurd, driven by her chauffeur and accompanied by her son, daughter, invalid husband, and his nurse, had indeed gone down a dirt road to catch a better glimpse of Lake Perona situated on farmland owned by John Perona, whose family was described by neighbors as "loyal Americans." The construction Mrs. Rutherfurd reported seeing turned out to be an excavation for a culvert to pass under the road to drain adjoining fields. The Italian-appearing individual was indeed an Italian-born gardener who could barely speak English and who had tried to warn the Rutherfurd party to turn back because the culvert construction blocked the road ahead. It was his inarticulate speech and clumsy gestures that had struck Lucy as suspiciously un-American. As for the Nordlund Bund Camp, it had been abandoned long ago.

Hoover reported all this, not directly to FDR, but, tactfully, to the President's aide Pa Watson. His report made clear that his agent had gathered the evidence through third parties. "No contact," he told Watson, "was made with Mrs. Rutherfurd because her name was not given to me by the President and I gathered that it was not desired that it become known who may have been the original informant in this matter." Watson passed Hoover's report along to the President, who showed it to Lucy on her next visit. She complained of inaccuracies. Since no reason now existed to pretend to Hoover that the Perona informant was anyone but Lucy, FDR told the FBI director about the alleged discrepancies. The President insisted that Lucy be interviewed personally to get the facts straight. Hoover again dispatched his agent. But nothing Mrs. Rutherfurd said materially altered the facts of the case. Hoover, however, that unsurpassed collector of dossiers, now had proof that FDR had resumed contact with his long ago mistress.

★

One of the more ironic utterances of General Marshall, not noted for irony, was made after the war, concerning the American-led invasion of North Africa in the fall of 1942. Marshall had opposed the landing as had every U.S. military chief, including General Dwight D. Eisenhower, who was chosen to lead it. "We failed to see," Marshall later confessed, in grasping why FDR had pushed for a military campaign that his generals did not favor, "that the leader in a democracy has to keep the people entertained. That may sound like the wrong word, but it conveys the thought." The war in the Pacific was, at best, the stemming of reverses. Marshall came around to understand why Roosevelt was pressing for the North African offensive: The people had to be fixed on something positive, on American forces carrying the fight to the enemy, on action rather than reaction. The North African operation, code-named Torch, which Putzi Hanfstaengl had intuitively guessed at, demonstrated a marriage of FDR's political and strategic shrewdness. As historian James MacGregor Burns puts it: "TORCH was a project bound to activate and test Roosevelt's skill at deception and surprise and to gratify his flair for the complex and the indirect." On one point, however, Roosevelt was anything but indirect. "I feel very strongly that the initial attacks must be made by an exclusively American ground force," he told Churchill. He offered a political rationale: ". . . [T]he assumption [is] that the French will offer less resistance to us than they will to the British."

The President wanted the spearpoint of Torch hurled first against Casablanca, a target that posed problems both of deception and politics. The French defeat of 1940 had not been total. Under the armistice with Germany, the French had managed to hold on to a south-central band of their country, with Vichy as its capital and the aged World War I hero Marshal Henri Pétain as chief of state. This rump nation was also allowed to keep France's colonial possessions and the French Mediterranean fleet. Thus, Vichy ruled in Casablanca and other colonies stretching across French North Africa. Dealing with the Vichy government left Roosevelt perched on a precarious high wire. Liberals, tugging from one side, wanted a total break with a regime that had knuckled under and now collaborated with Hitler. The President's own instincts pulled in the opposite direction. By dealing with the Vichy government, he hoped the French fleet or Pétain would not be driven totally into the arms of the Nazis.

Early in 1941, even before the United States had entered the war, the President had kept one eye cocked on North Africa. He sent Robert D. Murphy, a State Department career official, to Algiers bearing the formal title consul general but actually to work out a deal with General Maxime Weygand, Vichy's high commissioner for French North Africa. Under a secret arrangement, the United States would free up frozen French funds, enabling Vichy to purchase food, cotton, and oil, and would also arrange with the British to allow these shipments to pass through their blockade of North Africa. In turn, the United States would be allowed to set up twelve vice consuls in the French African colonies, ostensibly to make sure none of these items were transshipped to Germany or Italy. While "vice consul" had a diplomatic sound, the twelve men, to be selected by the War and Navy Departments and foisted on a reluctant State Department, were to form FDR's North African intelligence ring. They were a mixed bag, including a winemaker, an anthropologist, and a Harvard librarian. The pact was sealed on March 10, 1941, and FDR's "twelve disciples," as they came to be called, were operating by June, before either the COI or OSS had been created.

Months after launching the ring under Murphy, FDR brought Bill Donovan into his plans for North Africa. On a brisk winter morning, six weeks after Pearl Harbor, the President called Donovan to the White House and handed his then COI director his most substantive assignment so far. The twelve disciples were to serve, with Rooseveltian imprecision, under both Donovan and Robert Murphy. Donovan was to find out which way French colonials would jump if invaded—to the Allied side, to the Nazis, or would they hang on the fence. Further, his agents were to determine if Generalissimo Franco intended to block Gibraltar and allow German troops to land from Spain into Spanish Morocco. If that happened, an invasion of North Africa would likely be doomed. It was in trying to plumb Franco's intentions by breaking his codes that the OSS had made the ill-fated break-in of the Spanish embassy. Donovan's agents had another North African assignment that further tested the nascent OSS's capacity for the clandestine. The organization was to invent diversions to mislead the Germans into thinking that, should an African invasion take place, it would occur at Dakar, on the continent's western bulge, fifteen hundred miles from the intended landing site.

Though American generals regarded Torch with skepticism, Donovan became a staunch supporter. He saw, at last, the opportunity to make his organization a serious player within the military. Many of Bill Donovan's ideas had misfired, even backfired. But in one arena, his charismatic character had worked. Donovan attracted superb people to the OSS. He chose as his chief North Africa agent, William Eddy, age fifty-three, who had been born to American missionary parents in Syria, spoke fluent Arabic, was a former president of Hobart College, a much-decorated World War I intelligence officer, and now a Marine Corps colonel under cover as the American naval attaché at Tangiers. When a friend offered to introduce General George S. Patton to Eddy at an earlier London party, Patton glanced at Eddy's five rows of campaign ribbons and observed, "I've never met him, but the son-of-a-bitch has sure been shot at enough!" With the arrival of Colonel Eddy in North Africa, the twelve disciples fell under his control. Their tasks ranged from mundane detail—measuring the height of the surf on Casablanca's beaches—to assessing which French leaders were pro-Allied and persuading the French military not to oppose an invasion.

Abwehr agents in North Africa had easily penetrated the guise of the twelve American "vice consuls" and dismissed them as feckless amateurs. "All their thoughts are centered on their social, sexual or culinary interests," one report to Berlin read. ". . . [P]etty quarrels and jealousies are daily incidents with them. We can only congratulate ourselves on the selection of this group of enemy agents who will give us no trouble."

Robert Murphy, FDR's chief North African representative, reported to the President that what the French colonials wanted most was to be "complacently neutral. Far from wanting to be liberated, they just wanted to be left alone." But the wishes of the French were not Roosevelt's priority. On September 4 he secretly brought Murphy back to Hyde Park. The diplomat sensed the President's almost childlike delight in what he was about to divulge. Nearly 100,000 troops, the vast bulk of them American, he told Murphy, would land at twelve points stretching over a thousand miles from French Morocco to Algeria. The President admonished him not to breathe a word at the State Department. "That place is a sieve!" FDR warned. Murphy felt uneasy at learning of a major wartime decision that his superior, Secretary of State Cordell Hull, did not know about. "Don't worry about Cordell," FDR said. "I will take care of him. I'll tell him our plans a day or so before the landings." Murphy left Roosevelt and returned to North Africa to persuade the French against resisting an attack.

FDR handled secrecy as great sport. Just days after seeing Murphy, he embarked on a nine-thousand-mile tour of U.S. war plants and training facilities. His wartime movements were supposed to be handled with utmost security, and the traveling press was honor-bound not to reveal his itinerary. At a shipyard stop where his daughter, Anna Boettiger, launched a vessel, FDR spoke to a cheering crowd of twenty thousand and said, impishly, "You know I am not supposed to be here today." As the audience joined in his laughter, he could not resist tweaking the press corps. He told his listeners, "You are the possessors of a secret which even the newspapers of the United States don't know. I hope you will keep the secret because I am under military and naval orders . . . and my motions and movements are supposed to be secret." The crowd loved it. The reporters were not amused.

The President returned to Washington to find an OSS analysis that reinforced his intuition: North Africa made both political and military sense as America's debut into the European war. According to anti-Nazi colonial officers with whom Colonel Eddy met secretly, the French army would put up only token resistance against the invasion.

The President had taken out one more insurance policy. He had asked the respected Princeton pollster Hadley Cantril to do some discreet sampling. The challenge was formidable even for a pulse taker of Cantril's stature. His people were to evaluate how North Africans, particularly the French, would react to an American invasion—and do so without arousing suspicion that an invasion was in the offing. Cantril's staff managed to conduct only 142 usable interviews across North Africa. Statistically, the sampling was small to the point of near invalidity. But the responses were agreeable to the President's ear. Those polled were far less opposed to an American than a British invasion. FDR also had devised a cover story. The moment the troops landed, Marshal Pétain in Vichy was to be handed a personal message from Roosevelt explaining why Americans were attacking French territory. The President had it on good authority, his message would explain, that the Germans were planning to seize all of French North Africa, a potential disaster for both France and the Allies. No evidence, however, supported his rationale.

One last clandestine scheme had to be fitted into Torch. In mid-October, General Marshall brought to the President a bold plan to defuse French resistance to the operation. Robert Murphy, after returning to North Africa, had rendezvoused secretly in Algeria with Major General Charles Mast, Chief of Staff of the French XIX Corps, and five other French colonial leaders. On this occasion, Murphy practiced his own deceit. He revealed that the Allies, spearheaded by the Americans, were going to invade

French North Africa. In order to discourage French resistance, he described the power being massed for the offensive: two thousand planes, seven aircraft carriers, eight battleships, a hundred destroyers, and, most astonishing to General Mast, a half million men. The ship count for Torch was close; the number of planes exaggerated; but the manpower figure had been inflated by 400 percent. Murphy then posed the question Roosevelt most wanted answered: Would the French cooperate to avoid spilling blood between two old allies? When the Americans landed, would the French hold their fire?

Mast raised the greatest French fear, that a landing in North Africa would provoke the Germans to occupy all of France. The general wanted a fuller picture of the invasion than the diplomat could provide. He wanted Allied military commanders to be spirited into Algeria to describe for him exactly what the colonials could expect. Murphy communicated Mast's wishes back to the White House. The reward for neutralizing French forces without bloodshed was so desirable that Mast's request was immediately forwarded to Torch's commander in chief, General Eisenhower, then in London. On October 17, a Saturday, Eisenhower dared interrupt Prime Minister Churchill's weekend at Chequers to ask for an emergency cabinet meeting, to which Churchill grumpily agreed.

Attending the meeting with Churchill and Eisenhower was Ike's deputy, Major General Mark Clark, tall, confident in speech, manner, and bearing, and with a hawkish face that suggested the American eagle. Of course, General Mast should be courted into their camp by his military peers from the Allied side, all agreed. But insinuating a military mission into a French North Africa torn between pro-Nazi Vichyites, pro-Allied leaders, and fence straddlers was going to be risky. Suppose this contact exposed the imminence of Torch, thus destroying the critical element of surprise. And who should undertake this risk? The officer most familiar with the strategy of Torch, down to the nuts and bolts, was Mark Clark. Clark's immediate reaction was, "When do I go?" Eisenhower and Churchill agreed on one point that would immeasurably complicate Clark's task. Both leaders considered French security a sieve. Clark was to try to enlist Mast's support for Torch without revealing its time or place.

Five days later, on a moon-bright night and a smooth sea, the British submarine P-219, the *Seraph,* surfaced in the Mediterranean and glided within two miles of an isolated beach seventy-five miles west of Algiers. High above a steep bluff, a light shone in one window of an otherwise darkened house. General Clark and four high-ranking officers slid down the side of the *Seraph* into bobbing foldboats, collapsible wood and canvas craft. Before leaving London, Clark had written a letter to his wife, Renie, in which he said, "I am leaving in twenty minutes on a mission which is extremely hazardous but one . . . I have volunteered to do." He had scrawled across the envelope, to "Mrs. M. W. Clark. Deliver only in the event that I do not return." He and the men boarding the foldboats carried five- and ten-dollar gold pieces and the equivalent of $10,000 in French francs should they have to bribe their way back to safety.

By 6 A.M. Clark's party, greeted by Robert Murphy, was conferring with General Mast in the remote house which belonged to the father of Lieutenant Jacques Teissier, a Mast aide, who had dismissed the Arab servants for the day. Clark repeated Murphy's exaggeration that the invasion force would total a half million men. Mast asked if so powerful a force might also land in the south of France to stave off a German takeover of the unoccupied territory. That, Clark replied, was logistically impossible. Mast then asked for two thousand rifles, ammunition, and grenades for his troops, and five days' advance notice of the invasion. Clark agreed to the weapons but still hedged on D-Day. Four and a half hours later, having made clear his willingness to side with the Americans, General Mast left.

For Clark, extricating himself proved the most hazardous part of the mission. French police had been tipped off by suspicious Arabs that something was going on at the Teissier house. As the policemen approached, Clark and his group snatched up the papers strewn around the living room and hid themselves in a sour-smelling wine cellar. The police arrived but did not search the cellar. After they left, Clark's party made it back to the beach only to encounter a raging surf. Clark's foldboat capsized. Down to the bottom went the gold he was carrying. Not until the middle of the following night did the general, by now semi-naked, soaked, and trembling with cold, make it back aboard the *Seraph* and ultimately to London. There, Eisenhower decided to risk alerting General Mast four days before the invasion. If Clark had succeeded, a major French force would not be cutting down GIs on the Algerian beaches.

On Saturday, November 7, FDR gathered Harry Hopkins and a handful of other trusted friends at Shangri-la. That evening, as the guests gathered for drinks and dinner, Roosevelt's habitual geniality was absent, supplanted by a palpable unease. Earlier, the President had marked a passage from the Thirty-ninth Psalm of the Book of Psalms that read, "O spare me, that I may recover strength, before I go hence, and be no more."

The unflappable composure that FDR ordinarily exhibited was purchased at a high price. The fears that roiled beneath the aplomb can be glimpsed in a diary entry by Roosevelt's frequent companion, the devoted and undemanding cousin Daisy Suckley. "The P. had an awful nightmare last night," Suckley wrote during a visit to the White House. "I woke out of a sound sleep to hear him calling out for help in blood curdling sounds!" The next morning at breakfast the President told Daisy, "I thought a man was coming through the transom and was going to kill me." Suckley ended the entry, "I wondered why the SS [Secret Service] didn't rush in, but he says they are quite accustomed to such nightmares."

That November evening at Shangri-la the sudden ring of a telephone shattered the muted conversation. The President took the receiver from Grace Tully with a visibly shaking hand. The War Department was calling. The President listened, nodding vigorously, and hung up. He surveyed his guests, suddenly beaming, the anguish banished from his face. "We have landed in North Africa," he announced, and early casualty reports were low. "We are striking back." He grinned.

Ironically, America's first offensive in the European war was not against the declared enemy, Nazi Germany, but against the nation's oldest friend, France. Nor was it the cakewalk predicted by the President's intelligence sources, including Donovan's OSS. Yes, the invasion had achieved total surprise. The first warning had been the throb of landing craft engines approaching the beaches. The deceptions succeeded too. As the forces landed, seven squadrons of German planes circled Cap Bon, three hundred miles from the nearest fighting, searching for a fictitious convoy, bound supposedly for Malta. But in answering the crucial question, would French forces resist the invasion? the Americans had been blinded by optimism. General Mast managed only to slow the French response to the landings in Algeria. But Allied troops had to fight their way ashore against fierce resistance, particularly in the port cities. Almost fifteen hundred Americans were killed, wounded, or missing in a stiff three-day engagement that cost the French triple that number of casualties. While the losses had not been catastrophic, Torch was hardly a dustup.

A week after the invasion, on November 15, a self-satisfied President called his cabinet together. At times it seemed that FDR had been the only believer in Torch. Now, in victory, he was not averse to taking the lion's share of the credit. The successful operation had combined strength with cunning. Torch confirmed another of the President's gambles. He had created the COI/OSS against the resistance of every military and civilian organization with a hand in intelligence. He had sensed in Bill

Donovan—despite the latter's bent for stepping on toes, or because of it—
the qualities of boldness and enterprise he wanted in a spymaster. He had
stuck by Donovan when rivals wanted his head on a platter. And the OSS
had played a respectable role in Torch. Colonel Eddy's team had amassed
an Everest of logistical data on tides, currents, depth of ports, locations of
bridges, tunnels, and airfields, placement of coastal guns, the strength and
deployment of French forces, and the most favorable landing sites. On certain beaches, OSS agents, waiting to greet the troops, handed them French
military maps and guided them inland. The enemy was where these agents
said it would be, armed as predicted and in the numbers estimated. Bill
Donovan's organization was now part of the military force, if still a decidedly junior partner.

★

The saboteurs' landing in the United States had confirmed FDR's nagging
worry over subversion and fifth column infiltrators. That enemies could
penetrate America's shores seemed to validate J. Edgar Hoover's repeated
warnings to the President, echoed since 1938, that the Nazis had planted
secret agents among the tens of thousands of Jews seeking to flee Germany. This possibility had shaped the President's priority, which was not
so much to help refugees enter America, but to keep spies out, a posture
questionable in hindsight, but reflective of FDR's state of mind at the time.

Still, his behavior had to be measured against startling intelligence the
President was receiving on the plight of the Jews, even before the war in
Europe had begun. Bill Bullitt, his former ambassador to France, had
come into possession of a document smuggled out of Germany, which he
sent to the White House marked "Secret and Personal for the President."
On March 12, 1939, over five months before the war had started, Bullitt
managed to obtain the transcript of remarks made by Hitler at a secret
meeting of German officers, government officials, and Nazi Party leaders.
In the privacy of his inner circle, Hitler had revealed his timetable. Germany had already acquired the Czech Sudetenland through the 1938 Munich Pact. Within the week, the remaining rump of Czechoslovakia was to
be seized. "Poland will follow," Hitler announced. "German domination is
necessary in order to assure for Germany Polish supplies of agricultural
products and coal. As far as Hungary and Romania are concerned, they be-
long without question to Germany's vital space." In 1940, certainly no
later than 1941, Hitler assured his staff, "Germany will settle accounts

once and for all with her hereditary enemy, France. That country will be obliterated from the map of Europe." In his most brutal prediction, Hitler declared: ". . . [E]nemies of the German people must be exterminated radically: Jews, democracies and international powers." Near hysteria marked his closing threat: ". . . We will settle accounts with the 'dollar Jews' in the United States. We will exterminate this Jewish democracy and Jewish blood will mix with the dollars."

Since it was impossible for FDR not to know what was happening to the Jews of Europe, the pertinent question is how he and his circle dealt with this knowledge. Supreme Court Justice Felix Frankfurter, a Jew, was as close to the President as any figure in the administration, and had been something of a one-man recruiting agency for the New Deal. Frankfurter was all too familiar with the historic odyssey of the Jews. His parents had left Austria when Felix was twelve and settled on the Lower East Side of New York. Reared in poverty, the boy nevertheless displayed his brilliance, graduating from City College at age nineteen and going on to Harvard Law School, where he subsequently joined the faculty. His devotion to FDR was total. He had even braved the disfavor of his colleagues to support the President's high-handed 1937 attempt to pack the Supreme Court. The Frankfurters still had relatives in Austria. In 1938, the year before Roosevelt elevated him to the Court, Frankfurter received word that his eighty-two-year-old uncle, Solomon Frankfurter, a distinguished Viennese scholar, had been hauled from his bed at 3 A.M. and jailed by the Nazis. Frankfurter's first impulse had been to reach for the phone and call the President. But on second thought, he held back. Suppose the press got wind of the story and blew it out of proportion? Roosevelt was already attacked by his enemies as a tool of the Jews, even a Jew himself. Bigots parodied his New Deal as the "Jew Deal." Frankfurter decided instead to turn to the State Department to help win his uncle's release. He had chosen a poor ally. State's visa division was notoriously unsympathetic toward Jews. Frankfurter was advised that intervention was impossible. In desperation, he appealed to the American-born Lady Nancy Astor in London. In that period, before war broke out, her Cliveden set favored appeasing Hitler, and this stance gave her some influence with the German ambassador to England, who did arrange for Solomon Frankfurter's release. Roosevelt was never involved.

Even closer to FDR, Sam Rosenman also hesitated to go directly to the President with his family's problem. Rosenman had a refugee cousin living in America who came to him pleading for help in finding out what had happened to his wife and three children trapped in German-occupied Warsaw. Instead of going to Roosevelt, Rosenman chose to see Adolf Berle, a rare sympathetic listener at State, who tried to help.

It is fair to ask if the President could have done more to save Jews seeking refuge in the United States. The transcript Bullitt had sent him exposed Hitler's intentions. The Nuremberg laws were stripping Jews of their humanity. And the whole world knew of the anti-Semitic outrage of Kristallnacht. The answer to Roosevelt's conduct in the face of these facts lies in part in his earliest formation. He had been shaped in some degree by the genteel prejudices of his class. His wife, Eleanor, who grew in character to become a paragon of liberal virtues, had herself exhibited a fashionable bigotry when she was younger. After an evening with Bernard Baruch, when she was thirty-three, she wrote her mother-in-law: "The Jew party [was] appalling. I never wish to hear money, jewels or labels mentioned again." FDR had named Jews, an ethnic group that then represented only 3 percent of the U.S. population, to 15 percent of his top administration posts. But as his son Jimmy once observed, FDR took his social companionship almost wholly from his own class. "I now think he travelled with that group as an escape, back to the world of Groton, Harvard and Hyde Park. These people had everything, so they didn't want anything from father," Jimmy concluded. "He was more comfortable with them than he was with his political associates, who constantly pestered him with their problems." Whatever his social preferences, Roosevelt remained foremost a politician who dared not get too far ahead of his constituents. Barely out of the Depression, still haunted by unemployment, most Americans were not eager to open the floodgates to job competition from immigrants, including oppressed Jews. A 1938 Roper poll posed the question, "What kinds of people do you object to?" The people most cited were Jews, singled out by 35 percent of the respondents.

The tight immigration laws in place since the twenties allowed for only 153,774 immigrants annually, of which Germany's quota was 25,957, a trickle compared to the flood of German Jews trying to reach America. At the State Department, these laws were applied not so much strictly as mean-spiritedly. Even unfilled quotas were bottled up and withheld from Jews seeking to flee Europe. Congress could be equally insensitive. A bill introduced in the House to make it easier for European Jews under age sixteen to get at least a tourist visitor's visa to America never made it out of committee.

The saga of the SS *St. Louis* illustrates the atmosphere of the era. The

Hamburg-Amerika liner, carrying 930 Jewish refugees, left Germany for Cuba on May 13, 1939, before the war in Europe began. At Havana, however, Cuban officials refused to allow more than a handful to disembark. The captain then circled the Florida coast for days, close enough for the passengers to glimpse the lights of Miami, while negotiators sought permission to land the refugees. State and immigration authorities applied laws prohibiting the landing with chilling exactitude. The refugees dispatched a telegram to President Roosevelt pleading for help. It went unanswered. The *St. Louis* returned to Europe, where its passengers were resettled in Britain, France, the Netherlands, and Belgium. Many who landed in countries soon to be occupied by Hitler ultimately perished in the Holocaust.

The President believed that the answer to the Jews' dilemma lay outside the United States. "The whole trouble is in England," he told Henry Morgenthau. Palestine was the obvious place to resettle Jewish refugees, FDR suggested. But the British would do nothing that might antagonize Middle East Arabs. Unable to overcome the resistance within the country and within himself to deal with the plight of European Jewry, Roosevelt thrashed about in futile speculation. As the situation worsened, Morgenthau came again to the President to see if something might be done. FDR offered that maybe the Jews could be settled in the Cameroons, on Africa's western coast, where they would find "some very wonderful high land, table land, wonderful grass and . . . all of that country has been explored and it's ready." FDR mentioned that he had tried to talk the president of Paraguay into taking in more Jews. He also suggested to Morgenthau an idea that demonstrated a certain bleak clairvoyance: "I actually would put a barbed wire around Palestine, and I would begin to move the Arabs out of Palestine. . . . There are lots of places to which you could move the Arabs. All you have to do is drill a well because there is this large underground water supply."

As for early reports of Nazi barbarism, a seed of doubt existed in Roosevelt's mind sown by memories of alleged German atrocities during World War I. The kaiser's armies, depicted in the Allied press as bull-necked Huns, were accused of torturing the wounded, slaughtering innocent civilians, and impaling Belgian babies on the points of their bayonets for sheer sport. All had turned out to be British-inspired fabrications.

Well into the war, on May 27, 1942, Donovan was feeding the President information confirming FDR's early judgment that the British had been the impediment to rescuing the Jews. A movement was afoot to form a Jewish army in Palestine that would fight with the Allies. Unwise, Donovan's experts cautioned. The State Department went further and drafted a release for the President to issue that read: "The post-war settlement cannot be prejudiced by commitments at the present time in respect of an army for Palestine which would be exclusively Jewish." With Operation Torch in the planning stage at the time, how could the interest of hapless Jews compare to the need not to rile millions of Arabs living from North Africa to the Middle East? the opponents of a Jewish army argued.

In England, the war, instead of increasing sympathy for the Jews, was having a contrary effect, according to further intelligence that Donovan supplied to the President. "From Midland and London areas and from police duty room reports," Donovan noted, "an increase in anti-semitism, said to be due principally to the frequent occurrence of Jewish names in news of black market cases. Other reasons cited for the increase or prevalence of anti-semitism are the many current stories of Jewish evasion of duties and regulations."

On July 10, 1942, John Franklin Carter delivered to the White House reports written by eyewitnesses to the horrors of daily life in concentration camps in Poland and Lithuania. One account described the mass electrocution of Jews in a place called Belzec. Bill Donovan's people contributed further to the catalogue of horrors. His agents interrogated steamship passengers landing in New York, one of whom, a banker who had fled Berlin in November 1941, gave a harrowing account of how the Nazi regime went about rounding up Jews and transporting them to the camps.

Solid intelligence of what was happening to the Jews mounted as Ultra intercepted Nazi dispatches. Decrypts forwarded to Churchill included a report from Erich von dem Bach-Zelewski, an SS general operating in occupied Russia, sent to his superior in Berlin. Dated July 18, 1941, it read: "Yesterday's cleansing action in Slonim, carried out by Police Regiment Centre, 1,153 Jewish plunderers were shot." Three weeks later Bach-Zelewski informed Berlin, again in code: "Up to today, midday, a further 3,600 have been executed. . . . Thus the figure of executions in my area now exceeds 30,000." No records exist indicating whether or not these decrypts reached FDR as well as Churchill. Curiously, in the stream of secret messages passed directly between them throughout the war, no substantive mention was ever made of the atrocities against the Jews.

After the North African landings succeeded, the President went to Casablanca and, in a meeting with the French resident general at Rabat, delivered an astonishing opinion. "The number of Jews engaged in the practice of the professions—law, medicine etc.—should be limited to the percentage that the Jewish population in North Africa bears to the whole of the North African population," he urged. "This plan would further eliminate the specific and understandable complaints which the Germans bore towards the Jews in Germany, namely, that while they represented a small part of the population, over fifty percent of the lawyers, doctors, school teachers, college professors, etc. in Germany were Jews." He had echoed the rationale that the Nazis had carried to barbaric limits.

After the war, after images had been burned into the world's consciousness of skeletal, hollow-eyed concentration camp survivors and heaps of pallid corpses bulldozed into mass graves, it is difficult to accept that Roosevelt could not have done more for the Jews. But these images were yet to come. And, late in the day, he did do more. At the time Hitler took power, 525,000 Jews lived in Germany. Of these, nearly three quarters managed to get out before the war. The largest number, nearly 105,000, were allowed into the United States. By late 1941, in contrast to the dismal fate of the *St. Louis*'s passengers, ships were permitted to debark Jewish refugees in the United States. One, the Portuguese *Serpa Pinta,* arrived in New York one week after Pearl Harbor, and was allowed to land all its passengers, almost entirely Jewish refugees. The harsh truth is that, after 1940, once Hitler had conquered much of Europe, it was as if a massive gate had clanged shut imprisoning millions of Jews and other victims of the Third Reich. Once that gate closed, little could be done to rescue them. Ideas were put forth. One stratagem, still widely cited, was that Allied bombers could have struck the rail lines leading to major death camps, such as Auschwitz. This seemingly simple solution ignored certain realities. Throughout the war, the Germans were to display a dismaying swiftness in restoring rail lines just hours after a bombing. And when lines were ruptured, the Jews and other Nazi victims were marched to their deaths.

On December 8, 1942, FDR finally and publicly condemned the Nazi extermination of the Jews and declared America's policy—those perpetuating mass murder would be dealt with as criminals when the fighting ended. In the meantime, Roosevelt's principal response to ending the mass murder of the Jews was to win the war.

Chapter XVI

———═★═———

An Exchange: An Invasion for a Bomb

THE BETRAYAL of the greatest secret of the war, the development
of the atomic bomb, follows a sinuous path leading to Winston
Churchill.

On June 19, 1942, FDR sat waiting in his Ford Phaeton convertible
alongside a rudimentary landing strip near Hyde Park. He watched a small
aircraft drop from a cloud-dappled sky and come to a bumpy halt practically next to the car. Out stepped a short figure of comfortable bulk waving an outsized cigar. Winston Churchill was making his second wartime
visit to the United States. He entered the passenger side of the car, and the
President, with a bucking takeoff, started to demonstrate how the manual
controls worked, as he whipped the car around the family estate. They
spurted past Springwood, the Roosevelt home, and came to a halt on a
grassy bluff behind the house affording a stunning panorama of the Hudson River Valley. FDR backed out and darted into the thick woods carpeting the decline between the house and the river. He took sudden twists and
turns through familiar terrain, trying to give the Secret Service the slip.
Noticing Churchill's uneasiness at his extravagant whipping of the steering
wheel, FDR told him not to worry. He had biceps that a boxing champion
had once envied, he said, and asked Churchill to feel his muscle while he
steered with the other hand.

After the drive and lunch, they retired to a small, stuffy room off the portico, FDR's "snuggery." The President pointed out a recent installation, an RCA television set with a twelve-inch screen and magnifying mirror to enlarge the picture, a model introduced at the 1939 World's Fair. After an initial look at the flickering images beamed from New York City, the President had quickly lost interest in the set. The Prime Minister seated himself alongside the President in the small room which was almost filled by FDR's desk, and which he described as "dark and shaded from the sun." After reviewing the current military situation, Churchill edged the discussion toward something troubling him. Research on the atomic bomb was now well under way. Churchill asked where they ought to construct the large-scale uranium-processing plants vital to the bomb's development. Britain had already been battered from the sky by the Luftwaffe, and "vast and conspicuous factories" there, as Churchill put it, would offer irresistible targets. Canada might do, he suggested. But, as he later recorded of their talk, he was relieved "when the President said he thought the United States would have to do it." That matter settled, Churchill brought up Britain's right to full partnership in the pursuit of atomic weapons.

The Prime Minister had every reason to expect parity. Separate operations would amount to wasteful duplication that neither Britain nor America could afford. Besides, the British considered themselves leading the United States in nuclear physics, and in a position to help, rather than be helped by their American colleagues. Two American physicists, Harold Urey and G. B. Pegram, had gone to England in the fall of 1941 and been given free run of British laboratories. What the British had shared with their American colleagues had been decisive in persuading FDR that a bomb was feasible. And it was FDR who had first written Churchill urging that they develop the bomb together, a joint project code-named Tube Alloys.

After the two leaders met at Hyde Park, the partnership seemed to be sailing smoothly until storm warnings arose early in 1943. The Manhattan Project was now under the direction of a security-obsessed Brigadier General Leslie Groves, who wanted the rules changed in mid-game. His intermediary was the eminent Dr. James Conant, chairman of the National Defense Research Committee. Conant presented the new U.S. position to Wallace Akers, director of the British Tube Alloys project, at the very moment that Akers had come to America expecting to share atomic secrets. On January 7, Conant handed the Briton a memorandum that read: "[I]nterchange on design and construction of new weapons and equipment is to be carried out only to the extent that the recipient of the information is in a position to take advantage of this information in this war." The British might still be carrying out theoretical physics, but under the present arrangement they would not actually be building the bomb. That part of the enterprise belonged to the Americans. Therefore, there was no need to tell British physicists how a bomb might be constructed. Toughness in wartime, with allies or enemies, came easily to Conant. Serving with the Army Chemical Warfare Service in World War I, he had been in charge of manufacturing the deadly gas lewisite. Conant expressed General Groves's position that bringing in the British simply increased the risk that the secrets of the Manhattan Project might be compromised. Besides, the project's guardians believed that the United States had a proprietary interest in the bomb since millions upon millions of American taxpayer dollars, not British pounds, were underwriting the project.

Upon learning that FDR approved the restrictive new policy, Churchill objected vociferously. On February 16, 1943, he rose from his sickbed to fire off a complaint through Roosevelt's confidant Harry Hopkins, a straight shooter whom Churchill knew would relay his displeasure to the President. "The War Department is asking us to keep them informed of our experiments," Churchill wrote Hopkins, "while refusing altogether any information about theirs." The message was signed "Prime" and classified "Secret." Churchill evidently felt that he had been too gentle, and followed up the next day with another message to Hopkins marked "Personal, Immediate and Most Secret." The Prime Minister now charged FDR with bad faith. "There is no question of breach of agreement," he said. He cabled Hopkins yet a third time, complaining that the change ". . . entirely destroys the original conception of a coordinated or even jointly conducted effort between the two countries." The Americans had chucked the British concept of fair play and reneged on a deal.

The issue was batted back and forth over the next several months. Late in May 1943, Churchill again came to America, sailing the *Queen Mary,* whose lower decks carried proof of rising Allied fortunes, thousands of German and Italian prisoners of war captured in North Africa. The Prime Minister bypassed the British embassy and chose to stay again at the White House, where he could work his will directly on FDR. The imperiled Tube Alloys partnership was still much on his mind. Vannevar Bush had become the President's shield in deflecting British ire. On May 25, Bush and Harry Hopkins met with Lord Cherwell, Churchill's friend and chief science advisor, who had accompanied the Prime Minister. Cherwell told the Americans that it was the PM's intention to build his own weapon, a profligate duplication of resources, if the Americans continued to balk at sharing the bomb-manufacturing process. Further, should lack of cooperation slow the program, Churchill feared that the Germans could win the atomic race and threaten Britain and America into submission. He was only slightly less appalled by the prospect that the Russians might get the bomb first. Cherwell frankly confessed another British motive. His government wanted to share in all atomic secrets so that Britain would also emerge as an atomic power after the war.

Churchill thus far had stubbornly resisted Roosevelt's pressure for a second front to be spearheaded by a massive assault across the English Channel. The issue might appear unrelated to the PM's insistence on full British partnership in the quest for an atomic weapon, but the two became intertwined. Privately, Churchill disparaged the cross-Channel strategy, now code-named Overlord, as "impossible [and] dangerous." At one point, he told General Eisenhower, with tears in his eyes, of his nightmarish visions of an English Channel choked with Allied corpses. So obvious was British foot-dragging that the American general, Albert Wedemeyer, concluded the British "never had any intention of executing a cross channel operation if they could avoid it." On the evening after Hopkins, Bush, and Lord Cherwell met, Churchill unexpectedly began tempering his objections to Overlord. And a conciliatory FDR began brushing aside the dire warnings of Vannevar Bush and the others opposed to sharing atomic research.

A month later, on June 24, FDR summoned Bush to the White House where, over one of Mrs. Nesbitt's uninspired lunches, they again discussed Tube Alloys. Where did they now stand? the President wanted to know. Bush stuck by his earlier position, telling a nodding FDR that the British still need not be told anything, "since our program is not suffering for lack of interchange . . . and the British had practically quit their efforts." Henry Stimson buttressed Bush's argument. The secretary of war advised Roosevelt that since Americans were doing nine tenths of the work, why give away ten ninths of the secrets? But Harry Hopkins appealed to the President's conscience. "I think you made a firm commitment to Churchill," he reminded FDR, on July 20, ". . . and there is nothing to do but go through with it."

Vannevar Bush, unaware that the influential Hopkins had reached FDR, had gone to England still thinking his mission was to see how little the United States could give away to the British. While in London, he received a coded message from the President, sent immediately after Hopkins had spoken to Roosevelt, containing fresh instructions. "Dear Van, while I am mindful of the vital necessity for security in regard to this," FDR began, "I wish . . . that you renew, in an inclusive manner, the full exchange of information with the British government regarding Tube Alloys."

On August 17 the President and Prime Minister met again, this time in Quebec. There, Churchill withdrew completely his objections to Overlord. Stimson described the Prime Minister as "magnificent in reconciliation as he was stubborn and eloquent in opposition." But was it all one-sided? A dividend that Churchill extracted for ending his opposition to Overlord was formal affirmation that Britain and America were full atomic partners. On the same night that he withdrew his objection to the cross-Channel strategy, the PM and President closeted themselves in their quarters in Quebec's Citadel. When they emerged, Churchill had in hand that rarity, a written agreement between himself and FDR "to bring the Tube Alloys project to fruition at the earliest moment. . . . This may be more speedily achieved if all available British and American brains and resources are pooled."

Churchill's bulldog tenacity had paid off, but Bush, Conant, and other U.S. atomic policy advisors were still unhappy at sharing America's expensively gained secrets. Conant suggested a compromise: "It would be in the best interests of the total war effort to have professor [James] Chadwick and perhaps one or two other British subjects come to the United States and join Dr. Oppenheimer's work." This concession would mean that instead of America exporting the Manhattan Project, British brains would be imported to strengthen it in the United States. Churchill snatched at the opportunity and immediately had British Tube Alloys officials assemble a small team of physicists to travel to that compound of drab buildings sprouting at Los Alamos in the New Mexico desert, the heart of the Manhattan Project. Among them was a slight, high-domed, bespectacled and reclusive thirty-two-year-old bachelor selected for his expertise in resolving a tough obstacle to atomic fission, the separation of uranium 235. The man was Emil Julius Klaus Fuchs, a German-born alien living and working in England and a dedicated Communist. As a result of Churchill's pressuring Roosevelt to make Britain a full partner in building the bomb, Klaus Fuchs would eventually gain entry into General Groves's atomic fortress of Los Alamos.

★

The most persuasive argument propelling FDR into the exorbitant and uncertain quest for an atomic bomb was his fear that Germany would get there first. As he had told Alexander Sachs three years before, "[W]hat you are after is to see that the Nazis don't blow us up." Nazi persecution had driven distinguished Jewish physicists into exile and ultimately to the Manhattan Project. Still, plenty of brainpower remained in Germany, where the uranium atom had first been split in experiments at the Kaiser Wilhelm Institute in Berlin in 1938. Otto Hahn, Carl von Weizsäcker, Max von Laue, and, above all, Werner Heisenberg, who had won the Nobel Prize in 1932 for his work in quantum theory and nuclear physics, were all in Germany conducting atomic research. Though, as Albert Speer had said, Hitler had a slim grasp of the fundamentals of physics, the Führer counted an atomic bomb among the *Wunderwaffen,* the wonder weapons, he expected to hurl against Germany's enemies. Hitler told Field Marshal Erwin Rommel in September 1942 that Germany was developing a secret explosive so powerful that it "would throw a man off his horse at a distance of over two miles."

On April 4, 1943, Vannevar Bush was horrified by a story appearing in *The New York Times.* Under a headline reading, NAZI HEAVY WATER LOOMS AS WEAPON, the *Times* reported that Allied saboteurs had blown up the huge electrochemical Norsk-Hydro plant at Rjukan in Nazi-occupied Norway. The plant produced a "queer chemical known as 'heavy water' . . . and it can be used in the manufacture of terrifically high explosives" by splitting the atom, the article read. Bush sent the story, along with a hastily scribbled note, to Harry Hopkins, chiding him for urging FDR to share atomic secrets. "The attached clipping shows what can happen when control is loose and security insufficient," Bush wrote. In an I-told-you-so tone he reiterated his position: "Knowledge be given only to those who really need it."

The *Times* article indicated how far along the Germans were in atomic science. But what was the likelihood that Germany might win the atomic race? Hitler and his arms czar, Speer, essentially had to depend on the Nobel laureate Heisenberg to advise them on the probability of readying an atom bomb in time for the war. Heisenberg was a loyal German but no Nazi and had refused to join the party. According to Thomas Powers, chronicler of Heisenberg and the German atomic program, "At every point during the argument where his voice can be heard, he is saying two things—yes, a bomb is theoretically possible; no, it can never be built in time to affect the outcome of the war." Speer claimed after the war, no doubt self-servingly, that he feared, even if the energy of the atom could be released, it might not be contained. "Professor Heisenberg had not given any final answer to my question whether a successful nuclear fission could be kept under control with absolute certainty or might continue as a chain reaction," he noted. Hitler, too, he maintained, feared releasing the genie of the atom. "Hitler was plainly not delighted with the possibility that the earth under his rule might be transformed into a glowing star," Speer recalled. Thus, at the very time in the summer of 1942 that FDR was ordering full speed ahead on the Manhattan Project, Speer recalled, ". . . [W]e scuttled the project to develop an atom bomb." Henceforth, Heisenberg and his colleagues were scaled back to investigating the potential of atomic energy rather than atomic weaponry. Consequently, when two hundred B-17 Flying Fortresses took off from England to bomb the already sabotaged Norsk-Hydro plant, they were flogging a dead horse. With Germany out of the game, the rush to produce an atomic bomb had turned out to be a race with only one entry. The raid may have been most notable for exploding the myth of surgical pinpoint bombing. Of 1,006 bombs dropped, only twelve damaged the target, but twenty-two Norwegian civilians were killed.

Ironically, the nuclear research that the Reich did continue to conduct contributed unintentionally to the Manhattan Project. While Bill Donovan was raining down memoranda on FDR on every subject from Austrian clothing stocks to a scheme for bombing enemy water supplies with human feces, his staff occasionally produced an idea of simple brilliance. Possibly the least flamboyant was the creation of an entity with a ho-hum title, the Interdepartmental Committee for the Acquisition of Foreign Publications. The committee's job was to smuggle scientific journals out of Germany and occupied Europe. The President, a voracious consumer of every form of information, instantly recognized the potential of the OSS scheme and approved it. Running the scientific smuggling operation fell to an energetic Harvard chemistry professor recruited into the OSS, twenty-nine-year-old Frederick Kilgour. Kilgour recruited private citizens in neutral Switzerland, Sweden, and Portugal to subscribe to German technical publications. Since, unknown to the Allies, the Germans had given up on the atomic bomb, its scientists were allowed to publish papers on nuclear fission previously kept secret. Between 1942 and 1943, eleven major papers were published in the German *Zeitschrift für Physik* and *Die Naturwissenschaften* alone. Kilgour's subscribers slipped the articles to OSS agents in the neutral countries, who microfilmed them and rushed the film back to the United States. So eagerly awaited by Manhattan Project scientists were the microfilms that upon their arrival in New York a Kilgour aide placed a call from a safe house to an anonymous phone number, saying only, "I have received a package." Within minutes, a mysterious "Dr. Cohen" would arrive in a taxi and disappear with the microfilm, bound either for Los Alamos or the Manhattan Project's laboratory at Columbia University.

★

The eclectic talents that Donovan attracted hatched another operation far removed from the popular conception of spying. Cornelius V. Starr was a California-born insurance magnate who headed what would eventually become one of the world's insurance giants, American International Group. Searching for a way his industry could contribute to the war effort, Starr helped the OSS put together a small Insurance Intelligence Unit, rarely numbering more than half a dozen members. The unit based its work on one of the fundamentals of the insurance business, that insurers require a detailed description of the properties they insure—their size, location, a complete physical profile. This condition included policies written on the plants of German and Japanese arms makers, the details of which would provide priceless intelligence for Allied bombers. However, the enemy could ferret out the same facts about U.S. plants—including plane makers, tank factories, and shipyards—through information traded in the international insurance market. Thus the Insurance Intelligence Unit carried out a two-pronged mission, to acquire by covert means target information disclosed in the insurance policies of enemy enterprises and to plug similar leaks from the Allied side. The unit's harvest was far ranging, from the layout of rail lines and marshaling yards run by the Japanese in Asia to the location of a German chemical plant producing the poison to gas Jews. FDR, whose early law practice and business ventures had acquainted him with insurance customs, appreciated the sophistication of this mundane but productive Donovan initiative.

★

In early April 1943, Eleanor Roosevelt returned hopping mad from a speaking engagement in Seattle. On the way west, on the night of March 27, she had stopped over in Chicago at the Hotel Blackstone with her secretary, Malvina "Tommy" Thompson. On checking out, a hotel employee astonished Mrs. Roosevelt by telling her that her room had been bugged. The eavesdropping had been carried out by the CIC, the Army's Counter-Intelligence Corps, motivated by interest in a guest whom Mrs. Roosevelt had entertained at the Blackstone. Joseph Lash, age thirty-three at the time, had first come to Eleanor's notice in 1939 when he was serving as national secretary of the American Student Union. Lash, by his own admission, "practically became a member yet was not a member of the [Communist] party." His youthful ultra-liberalism appealed to Mrs. Roosevelt from their first encounter. The young man was soon a frequent visitor to the White House and Hyde Park, where FDR mixed the drinks and Lash served them to the President's guests. In April 1942, Lash had been drafted and was stationed at the Army's school for weather observers at Chanute Field, Illinois. It was from this post that the First Lady had invited him, on a weekend pass, to come up to the Blackstone in Chicago and occupy an adjoining room, for which Mrs. Roosevelt paid.

Because of the soldier's radical politics Lash's every move was being tracked by the CIC. The man could be a dangerous subversive, a Communist fifth columnist, the Army feared. Thus investigators opened his mail, tailed him, and bugged Mrs. Roosevelt's room during Lash's visit to the hotel. Eleanor vented her outrage to Harry Hopkins, who took the matter up with General Marshall. The general reviewed the CIC record, a thick dossier on the First Lady consisting of surveillance reports, photocopies of letters she had sent to Lash, and the transcripts of other bugged hotel conversations, a file totaling over a hundred pages. A recording of what had gone on at the Blackstone, the CIC agents wrote, "indicated quite clearly that Mrs. Roosevelt and Lash engaged in sexual intercourse during their stay in the hotel room." The affection that Eleanor bore young Lash was undeniable. After an earlier visit she had written him, "I'm so happy to have been with you. . . . You forget how much you love certain movements of the hands or the glance in the person's eyes or how nice it is to sit in the same room & look at their back!"

The bugging of the Blackstone had been the second CIC surveillance of the First Lady and Lash. Earlier, on March 5, Army investigators had followed them to the Hotel Lincoln in Urbana, Illinois, near Chanute Field, where Lash also occupied a room adjoining Mrs. Roosevelt's. The following week, Lash was again at the same hotel in a room bugged by the CIC, but this time with Trude Pratt, a married but separated woman with whom he was having an affair and whom he later married. On this occasion, the

CIC agents reported, "Subject and Mrs. Pratt appeared to be greatly endeared to each other and engaged in sexual intercourse a number of times." In the CIC report submitted to General Marshall, the Lash-Pratt sexual involvement had inexplicably become a Lash-Roosevelt tryst. There had been no sex in the Blackstone between the fifty-nine-year-old Eleanor and Joe Lash, twenty-six years her junior. Actually, they had played gin rummy with Tommy Thompson until Lash grew tired and fell asleep on a twin bed.

Was the confusion in the CIC recordings an honest mistake? General Marshall did not find this explanation credible. At the prompting of a furious FDR, Marshall ordered the CIC's domestic spying operations disbanded and its surveillance files destroyed. The CIC was supposed to hunt foreign agents, not harass American citizens. But not every file copy was destroyed.

Long before the Hotel Blackstone incident, Eleanor Roosevelt had made a lifelong enemy of J. Edgar Hoover, not only by daring to stand up to him, but also by exposing him to ridicule. Edith B. Helm, after a dozen years as Eleanor's social secretary, had been appointed by FDR to an advisory committee of the Council of National Defense. The appointment required a routine FBI background check. Eleanor went to her husband and to the attorney general complaining of what she regarded as a slight against a loyal White House staff member whose husband and father were both Navy admirals. Hoover, learning of the First Lady's displeasure, sent her an apology. Subsequently, Eleanor discovered that the FBI was investigating her personal secretary, Tommy Thompson. She wrote Hoover: "This type of investigation seems to me to smack too much of the Gestapo methods. . . . [I]f you have done this type of investigation of other people, I do not wonder that we are beginning to get an extremely jittery population." Word went round the Washington gossip circuit that Eleanor had walked where others feared to tread. At a meeting at Treasury, Secretary Morgenthau gleefully told his staff, "[O]h gosh, Hoover has apologized to Mrs. Roosevelt and to General Watson and to Mrs. Helm and everybody else. . . . They will never live it down. Have you ever heard of anything more stupid?"

J. Edgar Hoover was proud, sensitive to every slight, and hardly pleased to be thought a fool. His liaison officer with Army intelligence, George Burton, was slipped a copy of the Lash-Roosevelt file before the CIC destroyed its surveillance records. At the FBI, the hundred-page report went into the Do Not File category. The designation was misleading. It meant that material so classified was not to be placed in the regular FBI archives but kept in the director's office and handled exclusively by his personal secretary, Helen Gandy. The Do Not File file was filled with so-called intelligence of the flimsiest substance. One example was a report claiming that after learning of his wife's supposed misconduct, FDR, late one night, ordered the Army intelligence chief, General George Veazey Strong, and Colonel Leslie Forney, head of G-2, to report immediately to the White House. There, allegedly, a recording of Mrs. Roosevelt's sexual encounter with Lash was played before FDR, Harry Hopkins, and General Watson. Roosevelt was then said to have summoned his wife, confronted her with the evidence of her infidelity, and a frightful row ensued between them in front of the others. Finally, the President is supposed to have called the Army Air Corps chief, General Hap Arnold, and ordered him to have Lash shipped out to a combat zone within ten hours with a warning by FDR that "anybody who knew anything about this case should be immediately re-leaved [sic] of his duties and sent to the South Pacific for action against the Japanese until they were killed." It was all undiluted trash, as Hoover well knew. But he did not relegate the file to the trash bin. He was to keep the scurrilous and false account of Mrs. Roosevelt's behavior in his Do Not File cabinet long after FDR's death.

★

The President's yachtsman pal Vincent Astor had faded from the White House espionage constellation. John Franklin Carter, however, still served as odd job man. On February 23, 1943, Carter sat quietly at the back of the Oval Office as the President held a press conference. After the senior correspondent dismissed the reporters with, "Thank you Mr. President," Carter caught FDR's eye signaling him to stay behind. As Carter took a seat across from him, Roosevelt began one of his uncharted monologues, joking that all the "bosses want me to speak about is motherhood and God," and so he was going to preach from Corinthians and the Sermon on the Mount at his Washington Day speech. He shifted randomly to his working with the Navy Bureau of Medicine on an antisubmarine ray while he had been assistant secretary twenty-five years before. "Doctors know more about these rays," he said, "than engineers." The latter point briefly enabled Carter to bring up a confidential project he was pursuing, an anti-shark device to save seamen who had to abandon ship. Oh yes, FDR interrupted, he knew that asafoetida had a smell that would keep sharks away. He began spouting, almost verbatim, information on dead shark decomposition that Carter had briefed him on five months before.

Roosevelt suddenly switched his verbal wandering to the fortune to be made by the first person who learned how to desalinate seawater. Then, for no apparent reason, he began a critique of student societies at Harvard. This subject gave Carter a chance to bring into the conversation Putzi Hanfstaengl, FDR's fellow Harvard alumnus. He explained that Putzi's son, Egon, now in the U.S. Army, was writing a book exposing the corrupting influences on boys of the Hitler Youth movement, to which young Hanfstaengl had belonged. The President broke in, telling Carter to take out his reporter's notebook. Chin lifted, he began dictating a suggested preface to Egon's book, punctuating his thoughts with his cigarette.

At this time, Egon's father was being held in a filthy, mosquito-ridden house at Fort Belvoir. The two guards assigned to Putzi Hanfstaengl, Sergeant Ledunn, a white, and Sergeant Lee, a black, did not consider housekeeping among their duties. Nor did Putzi, a man of breeding, expect to serve as his own housemaid. Consequently, dirty dishes piled up in the sink, floors went unswept, and the insects multiplied. Twice a day, Sergeant Lee ventured out and returned with plates of cold, greasy beans and slices of beet root. Hanfstaengl found it particularly offensive that Lee drew these rations from the Negro mess hall. During the night he listened to shortwave German broadcasts, slapping mosquitoes and taking notes on which he based reports for Carter. He believed himself utterly unappreciated. He complained bitterly that he should not be treated as some sort of convict stool pigeon when he had chosen to help America of his own will. His son, Egon, he liked to point out, had dropped out of Harvard to enlist in the Army ten months *before* Pearl Harbor.

FDR did occasionally seek out Hanfstaengl's inside knowledge of the enemy psyche. At one point, he asked Carter what Putzi would suggest to assure the German people that the Allies did not intend to massacre them en masse and that the fight was against the Nazi regime. Putzi, recognizing that the marriage between Hitler and the German army had never been ardent, proposed a dividing wedge. A top-ranking American military leader, Marshall or Eisenhower, who could speak to the Junkers on an equal footing, should broadcast to Germany a message pitched to its armed forces. "When the Hitler regime begins to crumble," Hanfstaengl claimed, "the Army will be the only remaining group in Germany with the will, and above all, the weapons with which to remove the Nazis." Carter relayed Hanfstaengl's advice to the President, adding, "The Army could really be turned against the Party, instead of nursing a 'stabbed-in-the-back' alibi as after Versailles." Putzi's idea had a surface appeal. Possibly the German generals could be awakened to their latent power. But FDR was already secretly mulling over his own formula for Germany's defeat, and it had no place for Junker militarists.

Putzi continued to dredge his memory of Hitler's inner circle for tidbits that might earn him better treatment and keep him from being shipped back to the POW camp in Canada. The President enjoyed Hanfstaengl's tittle-tattle as much as the man's strategic concepts. One of Putzi's more prurient reports described the extracurricular services that Heinrich Hoffmann, the Führer's personal photographer, provided for Hitler. After coming to power, Hitler had gone to great cost to have Hoffmann recover pornographic drawings he had made as a starving artist in Vienna, Hanfstaengl said. Hoffmann also served as Hitler's *maître de plaisirs,* his chief procurer. Among his deliveries was the daughter of a Munich professor, a slender, shapely, blue-eyed blonde who worked in Hoffmann's photography shop. Her name was Eva Braun, known as Effi, and, according to Hanfstaengl, Hitler had bought Effi a house on the Chiemsee, halfway between Munich and Berchtesgaden, where he trysted with her in assured secrecy.

Of more substance was a report that Carter relayed to FDR from Hanfstaengl entitled "Probable Mode of Exit of Adolph Hitler from the Stage of History." The statement began: "Hitler is familiar enough with ancient history to know that especially the Romans, affected by the Stoic doctrine, recognized many legitimate reasons for suicide . . . in the course of 1923 [the year of Hitler's failed putsch] Hitler told [me] that he would not hesitate to commit suicide if, having lost his freedom of action, he felt that his opponents were exploiting that fact. . . . In such a case, he said, 'I would not hesitate a moment to make an end of it.' "

★

In January 1943 another FDR chum was about to enter the President's espionage orbit. George Howard Earle 3d was the scion of a rich, rock-ribbed Republican Philadelphia Main Line family that had made its bundle in the sugar trade. The adventure-loving Earle had dropped out of Harvard and in 1916 joined General Pershing's army trying to hunt down Pancho Villa in Mexico, where the Philadelphian won a second lieutenant's commission. When America entered World War I, Earle joined the Navy, skippered a submarine chaser, and was awarded the Navy

Cross. After the war he amused himself playing polo, flying his own plane, and chasing women.

He startled his family by supporting Roosevelt for president in 1932, and surprised FDR by being elected governor of Pennsylvania as a Democrat in 1934, launching his "Little New Deal." Roosevelt was drawn to men of Earle's stripe, adventurers of the kind that he himself could no longer be. In 1940, before the United States entered the war, FDR had sent this gruff charmer to Bulgaria as American minister because he knew Earle was a vocal anti-Nazi. Earle quickly confirmed the President's appraisal. On one occasion, the burly envoy beat a confession out of a suspected Nazi spy caught in the embassy. Earle became a familiar figure on the Sofia nightclub circuit. At one dance hall, he listened impatiently as the band played a request for the "Horst Wessel Lied," the Nazi anthem honoring a Berlin pimp. As soon as the last note ended, Earle jumped up and demanded that the orchestra play the British World War I favorite, "Tipperary." An empty whiskey bottle flew through the crowded club from a table of Germans and crashed among Earle and three pals. A Pier Six brawl ensued, with the club's furniture the chief loser. Earle's escapade got back to the President, who delighted in regaling visitors with the story of what he called "The Battle of the Bottles in the Balkans." State Department careerists were less amused by the unorthodox minister the White House had foisted on them. After Bulgaria joined the Axis powers and Earle returned to America, State blackballed him for any further diplomatic posting. Secretary Hull made clear he wanted this loose cannon spiked. Earle, however, pestered the President endlessly to send him abroad again. FDR, still fond of his rambunctious friend, found a solution to satisfy Earle without angering State. Neutral Turkey was a hive of espionage and a haven for anti-Nazi Germans. Roosevelt had Earle commissioned a lieutenant commander in the Naval Reserve and sent him off to Istanbul as assistant naval attaché. FDR told him to report to him personally, short-circuiting formal channels. Earle set off for his new post with his tarnished star replated. The old capital of the Ottoman Empire, where the exotic and the clandestine intertwined, would mesh perfectly with his character.

When the President went to Casablanca in January 1943 to meet with Churchill after the success of Operation Torch, he included Earle, then en route to Istanbul, in his entourage. Earle was thus privy to most of the secrets exchanged between the two Allied leaders, including a decision to invade Sicily that summer. During this summit FDR also divulged the surprise he had been secretly mulling over. On January 24, the final day of the Casablanca meeting, Roosevelt and Churchill held a press conference. FDR spoke first. After saluting American and British unity, he began, in his storytelling fashion, "[W]e had a General called U. S. Grant. His name was Ulysses Simpson Grant, but in my, and the Prime Minister's, early days he was called 'Unconditional Surrender' Grant. The elimination of German, Japanese, and Italian war power means the unconditional surrender by Germany, Italy, or Japan." Churchill was aghast. He later complained to Robert E. Sherwood, "I heard the words 'Unconditional Surrender' for the first time from the President's lips at the Conference. . . . I would not myself have used these words, but I immediately stood by the President." Churchill's statement was not literally true. Unconditional surrender had been tossed about between the two leaders before, along with other alternatives for ending the war, but never agreed upon. Nor had the State Department been informed of what FDR intended. Secretary of State Hull, on hearing FDR call for unconditional surrender, was dumbstruck.

Churchill further confided his dismay in a secret message to Anthony Eden: "We certainly do not want, if we can help it, to get [the enemy] fused together in a solid desperate block," he said. Any crack in Axis unity was all to the good. "A gradual break-up in Germany must mean a weakening of their resistance and consequently the saving of hundreds of thousands of British and American lives." General Eisenhower put "unconditional surrender" in blunt terms that any soldier could understand: "If you were given two choices—one to mount the scaffold and the other to charge twenty bayonets—you might as well charge twenty bayonets."

Roosevelt's later explanation for his solitary decision seemed almost flippant. "[S]uddenly the press conference was on, and Winston and I had had no time to prepare for it, and the thought popped into my mind that they had called Grant 'Old Unconditional Surrender' and the next thing I knew I had said it." Franklin Roosevelt rarely made an uncalculated utterance in his life. The most plausible explanation for his raising unconditional surrender, since he never left a fuller explanation, lay with Joseph Stalin. Ever in the forepart of the President's mind was the awareness that the Russians were suffering and inflicting the highest casualties. At their recent February 1943 victory at Stalingrad, the Red Army had dealt the Wehrmacht over 237,000 casualties, including twenty-four generals captured, but had lost over a million men killed, wounded, or missing, punishment dwarfing American and British losses. FDR had two fears: first, that Stalin might sign a separate peace with Hitler, and then it would be American and British boys taking the fearful casualties; second, that the ever-suspicious Stalin might fear that the Western Allies were considering a separate peace with Hitler and lose his incentive to fight on. A policy of uncompromising total surrender should put both fears to rest. One intimate was aware that FDR had known exactly what he meant to say at Casablanca. The night before, Roosevelt had confided to Harry Hopkins, "Of course, it's just the thing for the Russians. They couldn't want anything better. Unconditional surrender. Uncle Joe [Stalin] might have made it up himself." But if FDR expected gratitude from Stalin, he had misread the Soviet dictator. Stalin believed that leaving the Germans no hope could serve only to weld them into a desperate unity. As for U.S. domestic consumption, the President still liked "unconditional surrender." It had a crusading ring. The President was not risking American lives to achieve a brokered deal with the devil, but to destroy him.

★

George Earle had left Casablanca the day before FDR delivered his press conference shocker. Upon checking into Istanbul's luxurious Park Hotel on January 23, he sent a telegram to an old flame in Budapest, Adrienne Molnar, described in Gestapo files as "a Jewish cabaret dancer." Apparently feeling lonely with his wife, Huberta, and their four sons, far off in America, he wanted the beautiful Hungarian to join him in Istanbul. He signed the telegram with Adrienne's pet name for him, Hefty.

Louis Matzhold, an Austrian journalist and his wife, Asta, also living in Budapest, were good friends of Adrienne's. The former chorus girl went to Asta for sisterly advice on how to respond to Earle's invitation, since the Matzholds had known the man in Washington. Journalism now served as a cover for Louis Matzhold's true function, spying for the Abwehr, the Sicherheitsdinst, and Foreign Minister Joachim von Ribbentrop's intelligence service. Matzhold was well aware of Earle's personal connection to the American President, and Earle was now asking Adrienne Molnar to join him. Here was an espionage bonanza waiting to be mined. Ten days after Earle checked into the Park Hotel, Matzhold boarded a German courier plane bound for Istanbul and was in Earle's suite that evening. He was acting, he explained, as Adrienne's guardian, looking out for her interests in case she should take up Earle's offer. Given the woman's past, chaperoning hardly seemed necessary. Matzhold also claimed to be a covert anti-Nazi who had managed to penetrate the German intelligence services.

He was privy, he said, to the Reich's innermost secrets, which he was willing to reveal to Earle. Sensing their use to each other, the two men began to talk more freely. Earle ordered wine sent up to his suite. He boasted to Matzhold that he had been with Roosevelt at Casablanca and then, incredibly, revealed that, when the Germans were driven from North Africa, the Allies would make their first incursion into Europe by invading Sicily.

Earle let the Matzhold encounter percolate in his mind for a few days, then fired off a coded message for the President, sent through Harry Hopkins. Its content made clear that Earle was hardly the naïve, loose-tongued womanizer that he had played for Matzhold's benefit. He described Matzhold as "unquestionably a Nazi agent [who] flew directly from Budapest to Istanbul to see me . . . on a plane used only by German officials." Matzhold had told him, Earle reported, that "Russian communism was a hundred fold greater menace to the democracies than National Socialism . . . that Germany was sick of bloodshed and would like peace on fair terms . . ." and they would go down in history as the men who set in motion the talks to end this horrible carnage. His cable went on: "I told Matzhold that if I had anything to do with negotiating any peace except unconditional surrender, I would go down in German history but I would hate to see what American history would say about me." Still, Matzhold was coming back to see him in a few days, and Earle asked for instructions in exploiting the contact: "What shall I say, if anything, when he returns?" Hopkins answered Earle regarding Matzhold's offer to mediate: "There is no comment on his request here and believe you should also have no comment." At the same time Hopkins sent a wire for the eyes only of the latest U.S. ambassador to Turkey, Laurence Steinhardt, asking his opinion of the President's pleasure-loving pal. To Hopkins's relief Steinhardt cabled back, "Earle is cooperating and relations are excellent."

Each time Earle met Matzhold, he fed him new intelligence as to where the Allies intended to return to the Continent. In the course of these confidences, he divulged thirty-four places where the Allies were going to invade, including Spain and the Balkans, with Sicily lost in this fog of disinformation. When the Allied troops did invade the island, it was with surprise equal to that of their invasion of North Africa eight months before.

One day FDR received a large envelope from Earle stamped "Abwehr." Handwritten across the front it read, "Property of Louis A. Matzhold, for the Mister President of the United States." FDR emptied the contents with unconcealed delight. Out slid stamps recently issued by countries now under German occupation, editions largely unattainable outside Hitler's Europe. Earle knew of the President's love of stamps and thought that by forwarding Matzhold's gift to the White House, the Austrian could be made to believe that he really had entrée to the President.

For his part, Matzhold felt jubilant that what had started as a long shot had produced a triumph. His reports to Joachim von Ribbentrop convinced the foreign minister that through the Matzhold-Earle connection Germany had a line into the Oval Office. Ribbentrop instructed Matzhold to use this link to persuade the President that assisting the Soviets was like providing rope to one's hangman. America's aid would only help the Communists rule the world—a world, as the foreign minister put it, where "there would be no place left for millionaires like Roosevelt and Earle."

Adrienne Molnar did come to Istanbul, but by the time she arrived George Earle's roving eye had fixed on a Belgian beauty. Still, the ex-lovers had use for each other. Adrienne, believed to be the mistress of President Roosevelt's man in Istanbul, found herself showered with attention from practically every espionage service in the city, each thinking that, through a Hungarian chorus girl, it had a pipeline into the White House. Among the gifts pressed on her was a six-carat diamond ring. Whatever she heard she relayed to Earle, enabling him to establish the identities of scores of Axis agents operating in Turkey.

Chapter XVII

———— ★ ————

Leakage from the Top

GENERAL MARSHALL, bred in the cool, methodical school of warfare, well recognized the superiority of intercepted enemy transmissions over the more romantic intrigues of spies. Yet, he had trouble persuading his commander in chief, who was still drawn to the adventures of secret agents like George Earle, and from the ever-burgeoning Donovan organization and John Franklin Carter's ring. At one point, Marshall reproached the President, "I have learned that you seldom see the Army summaries of 'Magic' material." But one decrypt coming into the President's hands had to make clear the pricelessness of broken enemy codes. On April 14, 1943, Navy listening posts snatched from the air and Army cryptographers broke a Japanese message reading "C in C [Commander in Chief] combined fleet will visit RYZ and RXP in accordance with the following schedule. . . ." The officer would depart Rabaul on New Britain Island, the chief Japanese naval base in the South Pacific. He would fly in a medium bomber escorted by six fighters scheduled to arrive at the islands of Ballale and Buin in the northern Solomons. There he would make a tour of inspection and "will visit the sick and wounded. . . ." The commander in chief in question was the highest-ranking figure in the Japanese navy, Admiral Isoroku Yamamoto, Harvard-educated and a principal architect of early Japanese Pacific victories, beginning with Pearl

Harbor. Yamamoto's trip was intended to encourage high morale by awarding medals and personally congratulating the men who had achieved these triumphs.

But from the moment the admiral began his journey, American fighter pilots, in effect, had him in their crosshairs. The messages broken by Magic revealing Yamamoto's schedule, route, and mode of travel were relayed to the U.S. naval commander in the Pacific, Admiral Chester Nimitz. Nimitz's operations officers immediately began to construct a trap to ambush the Japanese leader. In the early morning hours of April 18, eighteen Army Air Corps P-38 Lightning fighters equipped with special long-range fuel tanks took off from Henderson Field on Guadalcanal, flying low to evade enemy radar. At the tip of southern Bougainville, five hundred miles later, Yamamoto's plane appeared, like clockwork, and the Lightnings shot it out of the sky. The Americans had taken a gamble, weighing the possible revelation of their codebreaking success by the pinpoint reception given Yamamoto against robbing Japan of likely its greatest military thinker. So regarded was Yamamoto by Japan's Axis partner, that after his death, the Germans struck a posthumous medal honoring him.

The American codebreakers' luck held. While the Battle of Midway had been noisily trumpeted in American newspapers as a victory for cryptanalysis and while scuttlebutt swirled around U.S. Pacific bases that the same codebreaking had done in Yamamoto, the Japanese still failed to change their codes. Yamamoto was a figure of such stature that his assassination might have had political repercussions. It has been speculated that Nimitz sought FDR's permission before ordering the lethal strike. No documents exist, however, establishing that Roosevelt's approval was sought, though the decision did go up to Navy secretary Frank Knox. Whether FDR blessed the mission or learned of it after the fact, the demise of the mastermind of Pearl Harbor at last stimulated in the President, as General Marshall had hoped, a keener appreciation for Magic.

The intercepted Japanese communiqués provided an advantage extending beyond the strategic edge they offered in the Pacific. The messages encoded in Purple, the enemy's diplomatic cipher, and broken at Arlington Hall, opened a window of astonishing breadth, revealing what was being said, done, and planned not only by Japan, but by its Nazi ally on the other side of the world. The principal and unwitting betrayer of the Reich's topmost secrets was Hiroshi Oshima, an army general in his mid-fifties, from a prominent Japanese family, and since 1938 Japan's ambassador to Berlin. Oshima, short, stocky, strong-jawed, strutting, something of an oriental Prussian, had become a familiar figure around the Reich's Chancellery. The ambassador loved Germany, spoke its language fluently, and was enamored of Hitler. The American journalist-historian William L. Shirer wrote: "Oshima often impressed this observer as more Nazi than the Nazis."

The ambassador was practically a member of Hitler's inner circle. He became a social companion and confidant of Foreign Minister Joachim von Ribbentrop, who supplied him daily with the foreign office's intelligence summary. The Führer himself comfortably discussed with the Japanese his most closely guarded war plans and arranged guided tours for Oshima of the Russian front and the Atlantic Wall, the coastal defenses in France erected to block an invasion. After each such confidence, Oshima radioed what the Nazis shared with him to his superiors in Tokyo, his reports encoded in Purple. His relaying of Germany's secrets to the home office was only marginally different from transmitting them directly to the White House, since Purple had long become captive to Magic, and the choicest intercepts were delivered to the Map Room for the President's reading.

A sampling of intercepted traffic suggests the value of Magic. In the summer of 1943, British aircraft, equipped with radar, and ships using "Huff Duff"—high frequency direction finders—began targeting German U-boats to deadly effect. Oshima met with Admiral Karl Doenitz, architect of the U-boat wolf pack strategy that had previously proved devastatingly successful in sinking Allied shipping. Oshima later cabled Tokyo: "I took occasion to ask him with regard to this matter, to which the Admiral replied that because the enemy has begun to use a new direction finder and because they have attached auxiliary aircraft carriers to their convoys, the losses in German submarines have become very great, so that we have to stop the use of submarine wolfpacks." FDR, leafing through Magic decrypts as Dr. McIntire massaged his shrunken legs in the dispensary next to the Map Room, knew that the Battle of the Atlantic was essentially over. He had it from Admiral Doenitz's lips.

On July 25, Shinrokuro Hidaka, the Japanese ambassador in Rome, had a private audience with Italian dictator Benito Mussolini, who berated Hitler for the stalled, costly Russian campaign. Mussolini lamented to the ambassador, "Why does Germany have to take areas where no Germans live? My God! She has been able to do practically nothing since she took those areas. . . . I don't see any reason why Germany can't use sense and retire to the 1939 line." During this discussion Mussolini divulged an intelligence gem. "Enemy bombers have played hell with our industries," Il Duce told Hidaka. "Our synthetic petroleum plant at Livorno was bombed and it will take four months to get it back in shape. We have one single synthetic rubber factory at Bologna. It is working overtime and if they hit that, it will be a terrific blow."

Decoded by Magic cryptanalysts, Mussolini's observations both exposed a crack in Axis unity and provided more precise target intelligence than photo reconnaissance by air. Coincidentally, on the very day of Mussolini's revelations to Hidaka, his own sun set. Before the day was out, Italy's King Victor Emmanuel announced that Mussolini's long reign as Italy's strongman was over.

That July, with Sicily almost conquered and with Mussolini fallen, Hitler revealed to Ambassador Oshima his fallback strategy. "Before long, as things now look, they are going to be on the Italian mainland. When they land I certainly am not going to be fool enough to fight them down at the tip of the boot. There are plenty of fine encampments north of Rome. There, in natural fortifications, I shall form three lines over the Apennines, along the River Po and the Alps." FDR now had in hand the plan that Hitler essentially would follow; except that the fighting in Italy continued harsh and bloody all the way up the Italian boot to the Führer's designated lines.

Oshima's communiqués to Tokyo enabled FDR, sitting in his study, to know what only a handful of Germans knew of the Reich's military output. On August 17, 1943, 315 American bombers struck aircraft plants in Schweinfurt and Regensburg, both inflicting and suffering heavy damage, with sixty U.S. planes shot down. That day, Field Marshal Erhard Milch, Hermann Göring's chief Luftwaffe deputy, admitted to Oshima, "Well, it is quite true that these bombings are fierce. . . . Speaking man to man, the German air force has its back to the wall." Milch then cautioned Oshima, "Please keep this number absolutely secret," and revealed to him, "Our present output is a monthly number of about 2,700 first line planes, but in about 15 months, we plan to double this figure. . . . So if we keep up with our plans, we will leave [the Allies] behind."

Tokyo received intimations of what Japan could expect from American air raids through Oshima's reports of the experience of Japanese diplomats living in Berlin. In one summary, the ambassador reported that the Berlin homes of seventy-nine of his staff members had been "burned and utterly destroyed." Sounding gamely optimistic, Oshima closed noting that light and heat had been restored to his embassy, and that he expected telephone service to resume soon. A Magic decrypt provided a firsthand account of the effect of Allied raids on another key German city. After massive British and American strikes on Hamburg, the Japanese envoy there, Doctor Kuroda, reported to Tokyo, "Local municipal authorities told me that up to August 12th, 22,000 bodies had been recovered. In addition to this, there are no doubt from thirty thousand to forty thousand bodies in the shelters. . . . It is very difficult and dangerous to recover the bodies from underground shelters. . . . The authorities are using prisoners in this work. Public utilities, including gas, electricity and water, have been completely destroyed. . . . In a word, Germany's proud second city received a fatal blow. . . . The restoration of the city will take fifty years."

The day and night pounding of German cities by Allied bombers was driving the Luftwaffe to consider suicide missions. A decrypted directive from the inspector general of the German air force bemoaned the failure of anti-aircraft batteries and fighters to shoot down more Allied planes. "The main reason is failure to close to shortest ranges," the inspector general noted. "There has been set up therefore a Pursuit Assault Force whose task will be to break up enemy formations using more heavily armored pursuit planes in all-out attacks in close formation from the closest range and pushing the attack home even to the extent of ramming without regard to losses. . . . Volunteers for these storm units are being obtained on a secret basis." The Luftwaffe, it appeared, had anticipated Japanese kamikazes by well over a year, though the scheme for employing German suicide pilots never went beyond the planning stage.

Forever searching for a silver lining in the rubble of Berlin, Ambassador Oshima, in an intercept dated September 14, 1943, reported sagging morale among Allied fliers: ". . . [T]he prisoners tell us . . . for example, it is a fact the orders have been issued to pilots setting off from a given base that they shall land at different bases so that they will not know which of their comrades have been killed." In this dispatch, Oshima also revealed the effect of Allied raids on the progress of German secret weapons development. After a conversation with Hitler, the ambassador quoted the Führer telling him of the V-1 and V-2 programs, ". . . [W]e have not been able to get ready because the enemy has been bombing us too effectively, for example, at Peenemünde and Friedrichshafen." Hitler cautioned Oshima, "Please keep the names of these places utterly and absolutely secret," and concluded, "So we are having to postpone [use of the secret weapons] more or less. But my guess is that by winter we may be able to start." Because of the continued bombing, Hitler's projection proved premature by nearly eight crucial months.

In another broken Purple message, classified "Absolutely and Strictly Secret," yet available to Roosevelt within days, Oshima revealed the cold-blooded calculus that ruled Hitler's thinking on the war in Russia. On September 25, Oshima cabled Tokyo: "When I talked with Chancellor Hitler not so long ago, he said that if there are five liters of blood and it is all spilled, death ensues immediately; and that if a liter and a half or two liters are spilled, as long as the enemy cannot restore it, in time, exhaustion sets in of itself; and that this is the kind of strategy Germany has adopted."

On October 4, Oshima cabled the foreign ministry on the progress of Hitler's bloodletting strategy but also reported an admission by the Führer that likely sent a chill through Tokyo. After inventorying the staggering losses the Germans had inflicted on the Russians—Hitler claimed 3.5 million Red Army men lost, 7,500 planes and 18,500 tanks destroyed—he told the Japanese envoy, "Well, this is the very first time since the war began that we Germans had to take the defensive . . . we are going to have many difficulties as a consequence." Hitler, however, did not want Oshima to leave the Chancellery with the wrong impression. "I want you to know that I am not worried at all about the way the war is going," he told the departing Japanese ambassador.

Another Magic decrypt illustrated the growing brutality on all sides as the war ground on. On December 15 the Japanese foreign office sent a circular message, Number 467, to its major embassies abroad. It reported, "Japanese hospital ship *Buenos Aires Maru* was attacked by a United States aircraft, Consolidated B24. Vessel was hit by a bomb on port side and sunk in about forty minutes." Survivors—wounded soldiers, doctors, and a large contingent of nurses going home on leave—then crowded into eighteen lifeboats. The message went on to report that though red sheets forming a red cross had been held aloft, an American plane, coming in at an altitude of only about three hundred feet, machine-gunned the lifeboats. The attack on the *Buenos Aires Maru* was not an isolated incident. The communiqué reported that ten other clearly marked hospital ships had been attacked by American aircraft. Message Number 467 was not among those delivered to FDR.

The cooperation of the Spanish regime with the Axis powers emerged in a decrypted message from Japanese ambassador Suma, in Madrid to the foreign ministry in Tokyo. A Spaniard, spying for Japan in the United States, an official of Generalissimo Francisco Franco's Falangist Party, had been arrested on a charge unrelated to espionage. Ambassador Suma's greatest concern was "that there may be raids on other Spaniards as well," further reducing Japan's few intelligence sources in the United States. Among those on the distribution list for this dispatch, besides the President, was the country's chief spy catcher, J. Edgar Hoover.

A late 1943 decrypt offered an eerie premonition of the future of U.S.-Soviet relations once the war ended. The message from the Japanese foreign office to its envoy in Kuibyshev, to which elements of the Russian government had retreated began: ". . . [L]ooking at it from the American point of view, the Soviet denies the right of private ownership of property and for more than ten years the American people have been suspecting that Russia's policy is to Bolshevize the whole world. Nevertheless, America does intend to continue to use the Soviet against Japan and Germany, going, I suppose, on the theory that you have to fight fire with fire. After the war, however, we may well surmise that the United States will be faced with the fear that Russia will endeavor to communize the United States. What then . . . ?"

In 1943 over four hundred messages from Ambassador Oshima alone were intercepted. Reading these and the rest of the Magic decrypts was, for the President, better than a peek at the other fellow's hand. It was closer to holding his cards. General Marshall paid Oshima a tribute that would have doubtless devastated Germany's fervent champion. Oshima, Marshall was later to state, "was our main basis of information regarding Hitler's intentions in Europe."

This incomparable source was almost lost in the summer of 1943 if General Strong, the Army's intelligence chief and Bill Donovan's nemesis, is to be believed. That July 7, Strong sent General Marshall a report charging that Donovan's bunglers had probably compromised Magic. Through a roundabout Magic intercept out of Rome, Strong claimed that the Italian General Staff had tipped off the Japanese that "[a]n American espionage agency in Lisbon not only knows to the minutest detail all the activities of the Japanese ministry in Lisbon, but is also getting Japanese code books, too." The agency making this penetration was the OSS. Obviously, if the Japanese believed their codes had been stolen, they were going to change to a new system, an outcome that Strong told Marshall "would be nothing less than a catastrophe." All this had been risked, Strong claimed, by "the folly of letting loose a group of amateur spies in neutral countries . . . with unlimited money to squander operating under no proper definition and subject to no proper control." Strong recommended to Marshall ". . . that steps be taken immediately to recall from Spain and Portugal all OSS personnel who are engaged in espionage in those countries in open violation of the directive of the Joint Chiefs of Staff which excludes them from such activities in neutral countries."

OSS agents had, in fact, penetrated the office of the military attaché in Japan's Lisbon embassy. In Strong's telling, Donovan's men had stolen the most secret cipher and left the office in such a shambles that "the ill advised and amateurish efforts of [Donovan's] representatives in Lisbon have so alarmed the Japanese that it is an even money bet that the codes employed by the Japanese are in imminent danger of being changed." The President was advised of Strong's accusation, and the Joint Chiefs ordered the burglary investigated.

Finally, it seemed that Donovan had been pinioned. Still, Strong had not reckoned with his opponent's counterpunching. Yes, he had recruited two Portuguese agents inside the Japanese embassy in Lisbon, one who worked there as a messenger and the other as an interpreter-stenographer, Donovan admitted. But he was able to prove to JCS investigators that General Strong had been informed in advance of this penetration. The general had been shown the very papers lifted from the wastebaskets of the Japanese military attaché which U.S. Army cryptanalysts found were encoded in a cipher "used by the Japanese for material of low intelligence value," certainly not the Purple diplomatic code. Most telling, Donovan was able to prove that the Japanese were still using the high-level cipher that Strong claimed had probably been compromised. Indeed, continuing intercepts encoded in Purple made that point for him. In another decrypt, the Japanese ambassador in Lisbon, Morishima, defended his embassy's security practices. He described all the safeguards taken in the code room, including sealing all doors and windows with wax to tell if they had been broken into. He concluded, "Nothing has happened to the code books in safekeeping here." The Japanese foreign minister replied, "I am inclined to believe that this is a planted report to throw us off balance." Donovan had not yet run out of lives. The Joint Chiefs investigation cleared him, and the Japanese continued using Purple.

★

High-level eavesdropping did not occur only in one direction. Roosevelt and Churchill had mistakenly come to believe that their transatlantic telephone conversations were inviolable. Bell Telephone System scientists had developed A-3, a technology for scrambling radio-telephone conversations so that an outsider listening in would hear nothing but gibberish. The transmitting frequencies were changed often, further frustrating enemy monitors. Scrambled calls offered other advantages. They did not have to be encoded or decoded and thus saved time. They were, in effect, person-to-person communication, bypassing layers of diplomatic and military bureaucrats and affording the President and Prime Minister near-total privacy.

Democracies, however, are porous institutions. In the fall of 1939, *The New York Times* had carried a story headlined ROOSEVELT PROTECTED IN TALKS TO ENVOYS BY RADIO SCRAMBLING TO FOIL SPIES ABROAD. The article went on to describe how the scrambling device had been installed in a soundproof room in the White House basement and that it had been used for the first time when FDR received the September 1939 call from his ambassador to France, William C. Bullitt, informing him that the Germans had invaded Poland. A German spy in New York, Simon Emil Koedel, clipped the story from the *Times* and sent it to an Abwehr officer in Bremen. Thereafter, the information made a slow journey through the German bureaucracy. The Abwehr forwarded the story to Wilhelm Ohnesorge, chief of the Deutsche Reichspost, Germany's state telephone and telegraph system. Ohnesorge, an elderly, grandfatherly Nazi Party member, wondered if these transatlantic conversations might not be unscrambled. Not until the summer of 1941 did he assign his chief engineer, Kurt E. Vetterlein, to investigate the possibility. Vetterlein, with essentially nothing to go on as a model, managed to replicate Bell's A-3 system. By March 1, 1942, German signalmen, operating from a secluded former youth hostel near Eindhoven in occupied Holland, began rotating a giant antenna across the Atlantic. Within a week, a proud Ohnesorge sent a message to Hitler reporting that his staff had "completed . . . an installation for the interception of the telephone traffic between the USA and England." His agency, he added, had "succeeded in rendering conversations, that had been made unintelligible, intelligible again at the instant of reception." Soon the signalmen at Eindhoven were intercepting up to sixty phone calls a day between Allied leaders using the A-3. What they said across the ocean became available to Hitler within hours.

At 11 A.M. on the morning of July 29, 1943, General Alfred Jodl, the military operations chief who briefed Hitler daily, showed the Führer the transcript of a telephone conversation that had been picked up earlier that day between Churchill and Roosevelt. They had talked just days after Mussolini had been deposed, and Hitler was eager to know which way Italy, his faltering ally, would jump now. The two leaders had discussed a proclamation that Eisenhower might issue should Italy surrender. Churchill said, "We do not want to propose armistice conditions before we are definitely asked about them." Roosevelt answered, "That's right." Churchill then added, "We could even wait one or two days." That was all Hitler needed to hear. The entry in the official German War Diary for that day concerning the intercepted phone call reads: "This is incontrovertible evidence that secret negotiations between the Anglo-Americans and the Italians are already in progress." Hitler had decided three days before to pour his own troops into Italy before the peninsula fell to the Allies. He now knew that his decision had been correct. He accelerated the occupation to a total of twenty divisions.

After the Allies did invade Italy, Roosevelt and Churchill made another damaging admission over the scrambled transatlantic line. According to a postwar interview of Vetterlein by David Kahn, the writer on cryptanalysis, the German scientist claimed that the two Allied chiefs discussed an amphibious attack on central Italy, presumably the Anzio invasion. As a result, the German High Command in Italy was alerted in time to regroup its forces and bottle up the invaders, thwarting their role of spearheading a breakthrough to Rome.

At times, the intercepted discussions of the two leaders took on comic overtones. In one conversation, Churchill was puzzled to hear FDR giggling at the other end of the line. The Prime Minister subsequently learned that the A-3 equipment made his voice, when unscrambled, sound like Donald Duck. Churchill threatened that he would never use the infernal machine again. The Bell system engineers went back to work and managed to make Churchill sound more Churchillian. Roosevelt and Churchill were not the only voices that the Germans intercepted on the scrambler phone. The list reads like an Allied Who's Who: Harry Hopkins, Anthony Eden, W. Averell Harriman, Lord Keynes, the economist, and a dozen more officials possessed of the most coveted Allied secrets. By late 1943, however, the Bell engineers had redesigned A-3 to make it almost impenetrable.

★

Bill Donovan's fortunes continued to gyrate. In December 1943 he had reason to feel confident. The OSS was elevated to co-equal status with the Military Intelligence Division and the Office of Naval Intelligence. Further, Wild Bill received a star. The JCS had even been amenable to two stars, but for the time being FDR found brigadier general sufficient. His bureaucratic rivals, however, ignored Donovan's new standing, refused to accept him into the club of intelligence, and waged unceasing guerrilla warfare against the OSS. His situation became so untenable that on February 20 he drafted a letter to the President reading, ". . . in view of the position which you have taken, I feel that there is no longer any useful purpose for me to serve, and I hope you will accept my resignation." The intolerable position the President had taken was to seek an end to the squabbling by transferring control of the OSS to General Strong. The situation was analogous to asking the cannibals to look after the missionaries and would certainly have spelled the end of Donovan's organization. Then, in another Rooseveltian turnabout, the President decided not to deliver Donovan to the mercies of George Strong. Instead, he signaled that Wild Bill had been given a reprieve by inviting him and his wife, Ruth, to join the Roosevelts for a special church service at St. John's across from the White House on Lafayette Square, an occasion, FDR said, that he shared only "with certain friends."

It was the bureaucratic infighting and not Donovan's often madcap schemes that explained the swings in his standing. One OSS proposal called for pouring mustard gas into a water-filled flower vase at an estate where Hitler and Mussolini were to meet at the Brenner Pass. The fumes thus released would blind the Axis dictators. In another ploy, female hormones would somehow be introduced into Hitler's diet, raising his voice, swelling his breasts, and causing his mustache to fall out. These cockeyed capers did not offend, but seemed to excite the President's own imagination. A banker from Buffalo, New York, wrote FDR suggesting that American bombers drop counterfeit currency and ration books over enemy cities to confound their economies. The banker pleaded that his idea be spared the presidential wastebasket. Rather than the wastebasket, FDR sent the letter to Donovan for action. Donovan pointed out that the OSS already had similar plans in the pipeline, awaiting only the President's blessing. Britain's Lord Louis Mountbatten pleaded with Robert Sherwood for FDR's support of a British proposal, an unsinkable ship to be made from blocks of ice. In Roosevelt's mind, Donovan's or Mountbatten's or any stranger's idea not patently crackpot merited a hearing. Nor was the President apparently put off by the avalanche of Donovan messages hand-delivered to Grace Tully at the White House almost daily, typically accompanied by a note reading, "Dear Grace, I think the attached memorandum will be of interest to the President. Will you please see that it gets to his desk." Most went unanswered and possibly unread. If Donovan had merely whetted FDR's appetite with a few judicious items, the President might have given him more attention. Instead, Wild Bill stuffed the man to a point where much of what he served was left on the plate.

The half-baked quality of many of Donovan's ideas and the distracting turf battles tended to obscure the OSS's areas of solid performances. Switzerland, a neutral island in the heart of Europe, was a nest of intrigue that every foreign intelligence service sought to exploit. Donovan informed the President that he had an ideal chief posted to Switzerland. Oddly, while describing the man's eminent suitability, he never mentioned his name, possibly for reasons of security but more likely because he chose not to emphasize that his agent was a Brahmin who had run unsuccessfully as a Republican candidate for Congress in 1938 and who had worked against Roosevelt's reelection in 1940. The OSS had already taken on the patina of an exclusive Republican preserve that Donovan was not eager to reinforce. OSS staffers with lesser social credentials referred to their well-born colleagues as "white shoe boys." The chief agent whom Donovan had sent to Bern, of white shoe pedigree but strong fiber, was Allen Welsh Dulles. His older brother, John Foster Dulles, of equally firm will, would one day emerge as President Eisenhower's secretary of state. Allen Dulles at the time was forty-nine years old, gray-haired, scholarly-looking, pipe-puffing, wearing rimless glasses and bow ties and looking as if he might have been raised in the home of a Presbyterian parson, which he had. His genial, avuncular air provided good cover. Beneath the tweedy charm was a tough, cunning, and ruthless man. "Espionage is not a game for arch-bishops," the parson's son liked to say.

That he had arrived in Switzerland at all had been sheer luck. The day after Allied forces invaded North Africa, the Germans immediately seized unoccupied France, thus shutting off Switzerland from the outside world and completing its encirclement by Nazi-controlled territory. Dulles arrived only hours before the Nazis sealed the French border. He came to Bern officially as "special legal assistant" to the American minister, Leland Harrison. The Swiss newspapers described him as the "personal representative of President Roosevelt." Though the description was exaggerated, Dulles did nothing to rebut it. The conjecture could only increase his influence. He brought with him letters of introduction to prominent Swiss at every level and soon came to know anti-Nazi German politicians, labor leaders, religious figures, scientists, professors, diplomats, and businessmen exiled in Switzerland. Dulles was also a ladies' man who found innumerable amorous opportunities in the intrigue-ridden Swiss capital, particularly with his wife, Clover, still back in America.

In Bern, Dulles had taken up residence at Herrengasse 23, a solid bourgeois home on a hilly side street in an old residential neighborhood. He had the lightbulbs removed from the lamp outside the door so that visitors could arrive and depart in darkness. Some nine months after Dulles's arrival, a man knocked at the Herrengasse address, begging to speak to an American. The caller was a gnomelike, fidgety figure who hardly inspired confidence. During a diplomatic assignment to Bern during the First World War, Dulles had turned down an opportunity to meet an obscure Russian revolutionary, possibly a crackpot, named Vladimir Ilich Lenin. This time around, he intended to keep his pores open. He agreed to see his uninvited visitor. The man's name was Fritz Kolbe, and he explained that he worked in the German foreign office in Berlin for Karl Ritter, Joachim von Ribbentrop's liaison to the military high command. The forty-three-year-old Kolbe, speaking in nervous bursts, told Dulles that his job was to arrive early at the office and read the overnight dispatches from German embassies and military commands all over the world, selecting those worthy of Ritter's attention. Unsuspected by his superiors, this inconspicuous drone was a devout Catholic with a deep hatred for the regime he served and eager to work against it. Kolbe had engineered a courier run to get himself to Bern. His first attempt to help the Allies had been rebuffed at the British embassy in Switzerland. A tall British attaché looked down on the little German's pate of sparse blond hairs and announced, "I don't believe you. And if you are telling the truth, you are a cad."

A devastated Kolbe had next tried Allen Dulles. Aware of the skepticism he aroused, he reached into his overcoat and extracted a thick bundle, 186 messages stamped *Geheime Reichssache,* secret state document, which he proceeded to strew over the living room floor. Dulles was still not about to accept this apparent windfall as genuine. Kolbe might be an agent provocateur. Upon the German's departure, Dulles forwarded the pilfered reports to Washington to be checked by the OSS and military intelligence against German documents from other sources. The experts dragged their heels for seven months before pronouncing Kolbe's papers authentic.

Dulles took another precaution. He sent copies of Kolbe's messages to Claude Dansey, assistant chief of MI6, no fan of the OSS or Dulles. Dansey was described by his own people as a "curmudgeon" and a "cantankerous son of a bitch." He pronounced Kolbe "obviously a plant" whom "Dulles had fallen for . . . like a ton of bricks." However, when Kolbe's purloined messages were compared with German traffic intercepted by Ultra, his take was again pronounced authentic. Dulles now assigned Kolbe a code name, George Wood, and dubbed material from him Boston.

Among the documents that Kolbe had spread on Allen Dulles's floor, one message revealed that Madrid had promised Germany, "[S]hipments of oranges will continue to arrive on schedule." This, Kolbe explained, meant that Generalissimo Franco, violating his pledge to the Allies, was continuing to ship to Germany in orange crates the tungsten critical for tempering steel. From a cable sent by the German embassy in Buenos Aires, Dulles learned how the departures of Allied convoys from the United States were signaled to Admiral Doenitz's U-boats. Another foreign office communiqué to Dublin revealed that the Germans were being allowed to operate a shortwave radio station in Ireland, well situated to report on Allied ship movements.

After reading agent Wood's documents for months, Bill Donovan felt confident enough to inform FDR, "We have secured through secret intelligence channels a series of what purport to be authentic reports, transmitted by various German diplomatic, consular, military and intelligence sources to their headquarters." The first fourteen messages from Kolbe/Wood's Boston series were delivered to FDR in January 1944. The President now had a source in Berlin reporting on what passed between Ribbentrop's foreign office, Nazi embassies worldwide, and the German military. And this prize had simply walked in off the street.

★

Bill Donovan might move on the margins of FDR's galaxy. But Sumner Welles was a glowing star near its center, one whose luster was about to be dimmed. In 1937 the President had appointed Welles undersecretary of state, the number two man in the department. A special closeness knit the Roosevelt and Welles families. The first Delano, the ancestor of FDR's mother, had arrived a year after the *Mayflower*, the first Roosevelt in the 1650s, and the first Welles even earlier, in 1635. Thirteen-year-old Sumner had served as a page at Eleanor and Franklin's 1905 wedding, where the boy carried the bride's wedding train as she walked alongside her uncle President Theodore Roosevelt, who gave her away. Sumner Welles later roomed with Eleanor's brother Hall at prep school.

Welles married an heiress and then embarked upon a seemingly unstoppable State Department career, becoming the expert on Latin America. It was capped by FDR's appointment of him as deputy to Secretary of State Cordell Hull. Hull's appointment in January 1933 had been strictly a political payoff for a supportive senator, since the man had not a shred of foreign policy qualification. His chief attributes were an unbending honesty and his appearance. Tall, lean, white-haired, and dignified, Cordell Hull looked like a secretary of state. But for all practical purposes, Welles performed that job for FDR, since the President found Hull narrow-minded, unimaginative, and a hopeless administrator. Welles, consequently, became privy to most state secrets in the Roosevelt administration. Furthermore, Cordell Hull was suffering from diabetes and tuberculosis; and as he became increasingly debilitated, the President turned ever more to Welles, which bred a seething hatred in the secretary for his undersecretary.

In September 1940, Welles had gone to Alabama with Vice President Henry Wallace to represent Roosevelt at the funeral of William Bankhead, late Speaker of the House of Representatives. Four months after the funeral, the President summoned Harry Hopkins from his quarters in the Lincoln study. FDR's habitual geniality was missing as Hopkins entered the President's bedroom. Sumner Welles, reserved, soft-spoken, immaculately attired, and the very soul of the patrician, Roosevelt explained, was suspected of gross indecency. FDR had heard rumors that during the return train ride from Alabama a drunken Welles had rung his bell, summoning a porter to his compartment. Upon the porter's arrival, Welles exposed himself and made a lewd proposition. When the porter declined his advances, Welles kept ringing the bell for other porters, with the same lack of acceptance. After the trip, the first porter he propositioned filed a complaint with his employer, the Southern Railway Company.

The President handed off to Hopkins the unpleasant task of bringing in J. Edgar Hoover to find out just what had happened on the train. What Hoover's deputy Ed Tamm subsequently discovered, after questioning the porters, was not reassuring. Welles's behavior turned out to be much as suspected, and this occasion had not been his first delinquency. He had made homosexual passes on an earlier presidential train en route to Chicago and had cruised Washington restrooms and parks seeking homosexual partners, preferably blacks. Hoover, aware that he himself was rumored to be homosexual, was not about to be thought soft on perversion, and had his agents relentlessly track down every accusation against Welles. Though the acts Welles had allegedly committed were felonies, Hoover's investigation was not conducted as a prelude to a criminal indictment. The results were kept in the FBI's "OC" (Official/Confidential) file, reserved for reports of homosexuality, alcoholism, and infidelities among Washington's high and mighty. On January 29, a little over three weeks after completing his investigation, Hoover went to see the President personally and delivered his unwelcome findings. Roosevelt reacted noncommittally in the face of news that had to be upsetting. He had already heard Welles's explanation, a claim that Bill Bullitt had bribed the porter to incriminate him. According to FDR's son Jimmy, despite the overwhelming evidence against Welles, the President was half inclined to believe the worst of the ambitious Bullitt. Bullitt's friendship with the President contrasted diametrically with the former ambassador's relationship to Welles, which was a compound of hatred and envy. To Bullitt, waiting since the fall of France for a new assignment, Welles held the job he ought to have. Bullitt had somehow managed to get his hands on the porter's written complaint against Welles, and FDR had been told that he was retailing the Welles story all over Washington and that he had even leaked it to the President's arch foe, Senator Burton K. Wheeler. Bullitt was further suspected of peddling the story to Cissy Patterson, Joseph Medill Patterson, and Colonel Robert R. McCormick, publishers of the Roosevelt-hating Washington *Times-Herald,* New York *Daily News,* and *Chicago Tribune,* respectively.

In April 1941 the egocentric Bullitt had gone to see FDR to derail a civil defense assignment Roosevelt had in mind for him. Then he steered the subject around to Sumner Welles. He handed the President a document summarizing the homosexual charges against Welles. FDR glanced at the first page, flipped through the rest, and answered dryly, "I know all about this already. I have had a full report on it already. There is truth in the allegations." Roosevelt went on to say that he believed the story too scandalous for any newspaper to print. Besides, he pointed out, Welles had promised never to misbehave again. FDR had arranged for a guardian, under the guise of a bodyguard, he explained, to watch the man day and night. Bullitt continued to press the case against Welles, playing his last card. Having a man of Welles's character in charge of their careers was ruining morale among State Department officials, he claimed. The President, unnoticed, pressed a button under his desk that summoned Pa Watson. As the general stepped in, FDR said, "Pa, I don't feel well. Please cancel my appointments for the rest of the day." Bullitt left, but went on to take the smarmy tale to Welles's superior, Secretary Hull, who somehow had been excluded from the knowing circle.

On July 16, 1943, nearly three years after the train incident, Hull believed the scandal could no longer be contained. He met with the President, telling FDR that he feared foreign governments would learn of Welles's perversion and try to blackmail him. After all, the man knew everything. Hull pleaded with the President to fire his undersecretary and end the threat to security. Eleanor Roosevelt, who overheard the conversation, expressed horror. Sumner was like family. He might commit suicide if the President dismissed and disgraced him. FDR struggled to make light of the matter. "Well, he's not doing it on government time," he said with a wan smile.

Long ago FDR had had his own brush with blackmailers, an experience he confided to Daisy Suckley. As a twenty-one-year-old he had been touring Switzerland with a friend named Bradley. The two young sports, each carrying a then substantial thousand dollars, cultivated the acquaintance of two beautiful women at the next table in their Geneva hotel. The women turned out to be "the baroness so and so and the countess so and so, aunt and niece." The foursome hit if off famously, subsequently traveling together the tourist circuit around Lake Geneva, Bradley paired with the niece and Franklin with the older woman. After two days of this delightful companionship, the maître d'hôtel asked to see Franklin in his office. There he explained, "Monsieur, I am an old man. I have known your uncle and aunt for a great many years [Mr. and Mrs. Franklin Delano], and I have known you since you were a child. You will forgive me if I speak frankly." The maître d' proceeded to explain that the lovely ladies were neither baroness nor countess, and "were not ladies at all, but the best known pair of international blackmailers in Europe." Their modus operandi was to maneuver well-to-do young gentlemen into compromising situations and then have them send home for ten thousand dollars to hush up the affair. FDR admitted to Daisy that he had been genuinely frightened, offered the two women a lame excuse about bad news from home, and then fled with Bradley on the next train to Paris, leaving no forwarding address.

FDR's forbearance in the matter of Sumner Welles was both personal and partisan. He could take a quite different stance against a foe. When New York police and ONI officials raided a homosexual brothel looking for Nazi agents, they thought they had found an isolationist senator, David I. Walsh, of Massachusetts, among the clientele. Though Walsh was later cleared as a victim of mistaken identity, FDR had no doubts as to how such matters were handled by men of honor. He told Senator Alben Barkley that in the Army fellow officers would leave a loaded gun with the miscreant, and it was expected that he would have the decency to use it on himself.

As for Welles, Roosevelt could no longer resist the pressures enveloping him from Hull, Congress, and looming newspaper exposure. The undersecretary recognized the hopelessness of his situation, and FDR accepted his resignation to take effect September 30, 1943. He, however, managed to bring his arch antagonist down with him. Shortly after Welles's resignation, Bill Bullitt, still seeking a major diplomatic post, secured another meeting with the President. As Bullitt stepped through the door, FDR intoned biblically, "William Bullitt, stand where you are. Saint Peter is at the gate. Along comes Sumner Welles, who admits to human error. Saint Peter grants him entrance. Then comes William Bullitt. Saint Peter says: 'William Bullitt, you have betrayed a fellow human being. *You-can-go-down-there!'* " he said, pointing hellward. He never wanted to see Bullitt again, he said. Bullitt had fulfilled the description of him painted by Washington columnist Marquis Childs, "an Iago of Iagos."

The President had an idea that would continue Welles's usefulness while easing his exit from public life honorably and gradually. He offered his old friend a temporary assignment as his special representative in meetings in Russia between Foreign Minister Vyacheslav Molotov and the British counterpart, Anthony Eden. If Welles was prey to blackmail in the United States, where even railroad porters turned him in, one can only speculate how vulnerable he would have been in Moscow, where the NKVD would have been far more imaginative at enticing him into homoerotic traps. Welles thanked the President for the offer, but decided, "If I go to Moscow, I'll not have support and I can't do an effective job." Instead, he withdrew to private life.

Chapter XVIII

─══ ★ ══─

Distrusting Allies

I
T WAS the premier secret of the war. The President had personally
cautioned physicist Robert Oppenheimer to guard zealously what was
happening in the barren wastes of New Mexico. Still, the Germans,
imagined rivals in the race for an atomic bomb, appeared to be evidently on
to something. The intelligence chief of the Luftwaffe, Josef Schmid, had
written a colleague eight months before the Manhattan Project was formally launched: "As far as it is known, work in the field of nuclear physics
is already so far advanced, especially in the United States, that if the war
were prolonged it could become of considerable significance." Schmid
added, "It is therefore desirable to acquire through the Abwehr additional
information about American plans and the progress made in the United
States in the field of nuclear research." The Abwehr agreed to a plan to infiltrate a spy into the United States, "preferably a physicist." The candidate
settled on was Walter Koehler, a man of mixed strengths and weaknesses.
As for shortcomings, Koehler was no physicist, but rather a jeweler by profession, with a rusty degree in engineering. His knowledge of nuclear science barely exceeded that obtainable in a course in Physics 101. Nor was
Koehler's past unblemished. He had once served six months in prison for
stealing a friend's briefcase containing six thousand guilders. But Koehler
did have strengths. He was a Dutch citizen and a Catholic, two good covers

for a person fleeing Europe as a presumed refugee from Nazism. He had relevant experience, having spied for Germany in the First World War. And Koehler, who had lived in New York until June 1941, knew America well. Just as helpful, he did not remotely resemble anyone's image of a spy. He was fifty-seven years old, squat, overweight, and shy, with watery blue-gray eyes squinting behind glasses as thick as a bottle. When he smiled he exposed rotting teeth with the front two missing. Koehler was briefed by the Abwehr on his assignment—to find out the processes used in the production of uranium, any raw materials used in related processes, and where American nuclear scientists conducted their research. His first stop en route to the United States was Madrid, where, posing as an anti-Nazi refugee, Koehler was to apply for an entrance visa from the American consulate. Instead of hearing still another story of fear and oppression, the young consular official who handled this servile and inconspicuous applicant gasped at what Koehler told him. He said nothing at all about being a refugee. Instead, Koehler told the official that he was supposed to be going to America to spy for the Abwehr. To validate his story, he opened a battered suitcase and dumped onto the astonished American's desk a kit for assembling a wireless radio, a codebook, and a camera for microfilming documents. He had accepted the Abwehr assignment, he explained, only to get out of Germany. He was ready to work, not for the Nazis, but against them. His offer was radioed ahead to the FBI, which took an instant interest in Walter Koehler. Thus, as soon as a neutral Portuguese steamer out of Lisbon deposited him in the United States, Hoover's men took Koehler in hand. They set him up at the phony German radio station on Long Island from which he transmitted to Germany a mixture of harmless truths and outright fabrications about the American nuclear effort.

Koehler's defection proved a boost to the Manhattan Project. J. Edgar Hoover sent to FDR the questions Koehler had been assigned by the Abwehr, adding, "This information is being made available to you as possibly indicating the degree to which the Germans have progressed in the development of atomic explosives." The answer, unknown to the Allies, was that Germany was going nowhere. But simply knowing what the Germans were trying to find out suggested that the race was still on and reinforced White House backing for whatever the Los Alamos scientists wanted.

Keeping the secret of the bomb from the enemy was child's play compared to protecting it from an ally. Thirty British scientists had been chosen to go to America as a result of Churchill's insistence to FDR that the United States and Britain must share nuclear secrets equally. Among them was the German-born Klaus Fuchs. Fuchs's salient characteristics were professional brilliance and personal reserve. As a young Communist in Germany hunted by the Gestapo, this minister's son had fled to England in 1933. The sophistication of his published papers in mathematics caught the eye of British scientists, who recruited Fuchs in 1941 for their embryonic atomic weapons program. While engaged in this work, Fuchs continued to believe the party line that the British and Americans were hoping the Germans and the Russians would bleed each other to death, thus destroying Nazism and communism while saving capitalism. Before the year was out, Fuchs had passed his first secrets to a London agent of the GRU, Soviet military intelligence.

Fuchs was admirably suited for the role of spy. He was inconspicuous in appearance. More important, he possessed imagination and self-reliance, had no need for the approval of others, and exhibited the rare ability to live a split life. When he learned in 1943 that he was going to America, he informed his Soviet controller, whom he knew only as Sonya. She was, in fact, Ruth Kuczynski, a German refugee Communist herself, dark-haired and sultry, who shared her sexual favors with other party faithful but apparently not with the monastic Fuchs. Sonya explained to Fuchs how to establish contact on his arrival in New York with an American controller, known only as Raymond. Thus, Fuchs, in a scene out of pulp fiction, found himself on a crisp Saturday afternoon early in 1944 strolling down Manhattan's Lower East Side clutching a tennis ball in his left hand. A pudgy, pasty-faced, bespectacled man in his mid-thirties, wearing one pair of gloves and carrying another, came up to Fuchs and asked, "Can you tell me the way to Grand Central Station?" Fuchs had connected with Raymond. His new controller was actually Harry Gold, also the contact for two other Americans enlisted in Soviet espionage, Julius and Ethel Rosenberg. Gold, a chemist by profession, had been passing industrial secrets to the Russians since 1936.

★

Several years before, on September 1, 1939, President Roosevelt's appointments secretary, Marvin H. McIntyre, had received a visitor in his White House office. McIntyre was a former newspaperman who had impressed FDR while working in the Navy Department's press office during the First World War. He was an outgoing soul whom reporters enjoyed dropping in on for a chat and a bit of White House gossip. His visitor this

day was Isaac Don Levine, a forty-seven-year-old Russian-born naturalized American, now a magazine writer and editor. Levine confided to
McIntyre that he had a source who knew a great deal about Soviet penetration of the American government and that the man was prepared to talk.
But his source insisted on immunity from prosecution and would speak
only to the President. World peace at that moment hung suspended by a
badly frayed thread, with Germany having just invaded Poland and Britain
pledging to go to war if the Germans did not withdraw. McIntyre explained
that this might not be the best time for the President to be distracted, but
that he would happily arrange for Levine's informant to speak confidentially to Adolf Berle of the State Department.

On Saturday night, September 2, Berle and his wife received Levine
and another dumpy, furtive figure at their luxurious Woodley Place home,
formerly owned by Henry Stimson. Levine introduced his visibly uncomfortable companion only as "Karl." They were meeting at Berle's because
the stranger had said that if he could not talk directly to the President, he
did not want to be seen in any government office. Berle, working fourteen-
hour days on the world crisis, was exhausted and had only reluctantly
agreed to see these visitors. After a desultory conversation about the Polish situation, Mrs. Berle withdrew, and the three men moved onto the lawn
to catch a cooling breeze. Karl, Levine explained, was an ex-Soviet spy
who was willing to tell Berle his story. The man, tense and uneasy, began
to talk, barely opening his mouth in order to conceal his bad teeth. He had
been part of a Communist underground cell from 1934 to the end of 1937,
he said. He had broken with the party after growing disillusionment with
Marxism capped by his disgust over Stalin's show trials of the late thirties.
He was, as a result of his former role for the Soviets, aware of several
American government officials spying for Russia. Levine urged the man to
provide names, and Karl proceeded to do so, identifying several highly
placed officials. These people, he claimed, removed classified documents
from their files, photographed them, and turned the copies over to their Soviet underground contacts. Karl stressed that the whole point of this conversation was that he expected Berle to place this information before the
President. Berle promised he would do so.

After his guests left, Berle, more tired than ever after the bizarre three-
hour visit, did not go directly to bed. He remained in his study and began
to jot down Karl's charges. He headed his notes "Underground Espionage
Agent." Among the names Karl had mentioned were Alger Hiss, then with
the State Department and described as "Member of the Underground

Com.—Active," Hiss's wife, Priscilla, and brother, Donald. Also mentioned by Chambers were Laurence Duggan, another official at State, a "Mr. White," and, most surprising to Berle, Lauchlin Currie, a valued member of FDR's personal White House staff alongside whose name he added Karl's description, "Fellow Traveler—helped various Communists—never went the whole way."

Did Berle keep his promise and lay Karl's allegations before FDR? Isaac Don Levine later claimed that Berle did so, as did the radio gossip columnist Walter Winchell, who also heard Karl's recital and claimed to have informed FDR himself. The President was reported to have scoffed at the idea of Soviet spies penetrating his administration. After all, Berle had checked with respected figures such as Supreme Court Justice Felix Frankfurter and Dean Acheson, then assistant secretary of state, about the Hiss brothers. According to Berle, Acheson claimed he had known them since they were boys "and he could vouch for them absolutely." Felix Frankfurter gave the Hisses an equally clean bill of health. Oddly, however, Berle, the President's chief advisor on internal security, did not make these inquiries until 1941, almost two years after Karl's disclosures to him. And Berle's otherwise detailed diaries make no mention of briefing FDR on the Karl matter. Whether informed or not, Roosevelt would have had trouble accepting the accusations of an obscure, unappealing, and anonymous informant. The people Karl had denounced were FDR's kind of people, and vouched for by FDR's kind.

Berle's foot-dragging may have two explanations. First, like the President, he was bound to wonder about charges brought by so seedy a figure as Karl against solid members of the New Deal establishment. Further, by the time Berle got around, in 1943, to answering the FBI's request for the notes he had taken that odd September night four years before, the Soviet Union was America's ally and few in FDR's circle were looking to make waves that might swamp this fragile alliance.

Karl, it turned out, was Whittaker Chambers, indeed an ex-Communist who, six months after the meeting with Berle, went to work for *Time* magazine as a writer and who in the 1950s was to emerge as the right-hand icon to Alger Hiss's left in the heavily symbolic trial of Hiss for perjury.

★

The lengths to which Roosevelt and Churchill would go not to imperil the alliance with Stalin emerge in their secret correspondence regarding the

Katyn affair. On April 12, 1943, when German radio first announced the discovery in the Katyn forest near Smolensk of the bodies of an initial 4,143 Polish officers, the Nazis and Russians blamed each other, claiming the mass murders had occurred when the other side occupied the territory. The world at the time had scant reason to doubt that the massacre of Poles was merely another in the mounting catalogue of Nazi atrocities. Yet, through secret sources, FDR and Churchill knew otherwise.

Stalin, nevertheless, acted quickly to blunt the charge that his regime was responsible for the deaths of the Poles. FDR was in Monterrey, Mexico, on a goodwill visit when Cordell Hull forwarded to him a blistering "Confidential" message from the Soviet leader dated April 21. In it, Stalin told Roosevelt, "The campaign of calumny against the Soviet Union, initiated by the German Fascists regarding the Polish officers they themselves slaughtered in the Smolensk area on German occupied territory, was immediately taken up by the [Polish General Wladyslaw] Sikorski government [in exile] and inflated in every possible way. . . . In view of these circumstances, the Soviet government has come to the conclusion of the necessity for breaking relations with the present Polish government." The alliance between the Western Allies and the Soviet Union was like a tightrope. Stretched just taut enough, it provided a link over which help could pass. Pulled too hard by suspicions, recriminations, or mistrust, it would surely snap. This was an outcome that FDR was determined to avoid. From Monterrey, he drafted a message to "Mr. Stalin, Moscow" all but begging the Soviet leader not to end relations with the Polish government-in-exile and exhibiting a willingness to gloss over the deaths of thousands of Poles in a Russian forest. If anyone was to blame for the ugly issue, it was, in FDR's view, General Sikorski, who "has made a stupid mistake in taking up this particular matter with the international Red Cross." Secretary of State Hull managed to persuade the President to drop only the word "stupid" from the cable. On April 29 the Soviet ambassador in Washington, Maxim Litvinov, came to the White House with Stalin's reply, marked "Private and Confidential." Stalin was unmoved. It was too late, he said. He had already broken off relations with the Poles. "Since the Polish Government, throughout nearly two weeks, not only did not discontinue, but actually intensified, in its press and radio, a campaign which was hostile to the Soviet Union and advantageous only to Hitler. . . ." In Stalin's telling, Sikorski was a dupe who "allowed himself to be led by certain pro-Hitler elements within the Polish government or in its entourage, and as a result the Polish government . . . became a tool in Hitler's hands."

The truth was that Lavrenti Beria, the NKVD chief, had laid out for Stalin the case for eliminating the Polish prisoners while they had been in Russian hands: "The military and police officers in the camps," Beria wrote on March 5, 1940, "are attempting to continue their counterrevolutionary activities and are carrying out anti-Soviet agitation. Each of them is waiting only for his release in order to enter actively into the struggle against Soviet authority." The obvious solution was to hold "[s]pecial tribunals . . . without summoning those detained and without bringing charges." The equally obvious denouement was to apply "the supreme penalty, shooting." Documents released following the collapse of the Soviet Union reveal that between nine thousand and fifteen thousand Polish military officers, government officials, intellectuals, and landowners were murdered in the Katyn forest on Stalin's orders in April 1940 as "hardened and uncompromising enemies of Soviet authority."

The hypocrisy of the Soviet government during the Katyn affair was egregious even by Stalin's standards. But Churchill and Roosevelt were prepared to swallow it. That they knew all along the cynical game Stalin was playing is obvious in a long dispatch the Prime Minister sent to FDR on August 13, 1943. More than two months before, Owen O'Malley, British representative to the Polish government-in-exile, had provided to Churchill's foreign secretary, Anthony Eden, twenty-four detailed points describing where and when the murdered Poles had been found, the climate and clothing worn at the time of their execution, the past use of the Katyn forest by the Reds to execute its czarist enemies, and the contradicting explanations the Soviets had given for the disappearance of the Poles. Most damning, letters the prisoners had been sending to their families ceased after April 1940, while the Katyn forest was still in Russian hands. O'Malley made clear his own conclusion that "in light of all the evidence" the Soviets had murdered the Poles. The Briton, torn between the case for pragmatism and his humane impulses, accepted the necessity of the former. He told Eden, "[I]n view of the immense importance of an appearance of Allied unity and of the heroic resistance of Russia to Germany, few will think that any other course would have been wise or right." But O'Malley could not resist adding the price of turning a blind eye to evil. "If," his message ended, "we, for however valid reasons, have been obliged to behave as if the deed was not theirs, may it not be that we now stand in danger . . . of falling under St. Paul's curse on those who can see cruelty 'and not burn.' " Churchill was prepared to risk Saint Paul's curse. In his note forwarding O'Malley's report to FDR, he concluded that it was too convincing to suit their policy of not antagonizing Stalin. What O'Malley had revealed "is a grim, well written story, but perhaps a little too well written," the Prime Minister wrote. "Nevertheless, should you have time to read it, it would repay the trouble. I should like to have it back when you have finished with it as we are not circulating it officially in any way."

FDR, too, was willing to respect the Faustian bargain: Keep the Soviets at our side killing Germans, and say nothing of Stalin's crimes and hypocrisies. The President never made a public statement accusing the Russians of Katyn. Nor did Hitler, after his initial propaganda barrage attempting to bring the Soviets to his moral level. With the stunning defeat at Stalingrad, with the Russian steppes littered with German corpses and the burnt-out hulks of Wehrmacht tanks, and with no major offensive feasible for 1943, Hitler began considering a way out of the Soviet morass. A Magic decrypt picked up between a Japanese diplomat and Tokyo noted, on June 7: "All the fierce anti-Soviet propaganda that Germany started about Soviet soldiers mass murdering a group of Polish officers at Katyn has calmed down and is now scarcely a whisper. This is regarded as being done on Hitler's own secret orders and that the Chancellor in his own heart is trying to figure out a way to negotiate for peace with the Kremlin." This decrypt was routed to President Roosevelt, who, determined not to embarrass the Soviets, found himself engaged in this conspiracy of silence.

One of the people whom Whittaker Chambers had fingered as a "fellow traveler" in his meeting with Adolf Berle was the State Department official Laurence Duggan, a studious, quiet man married to a wife described in a Soviet cable to Moscow as an "extraordinarily beautiful woman: a typical American, tall, blonde, reserved, well-read, goes in for sports, independent," and also of leftist sympathies. Duggan, according to Soviet wartime documents unearthed in the mid-1990s by Allen Weinstein and Alexander Vassiliev and described in *The Haunted Wood,* had been passing documents to Soviet agents since 1936. By 1939, Duggan had begun to pull away from direct involvement with the NKVD, although he was still intermittently passing along State Department information as late as 1943. In March of that year, Vice President Henry Wallace received a letter from a Mrs. Ann M. Dziadulskato containing a list of Polish officers, including her husband, held by the Russians and asking the Vice President's help in obtaining information on the men who had disappeared. Wallace bucked the letter to the State Department, asking, "Is it possible and advisable to do some discreet work on the problem which this woman presents?" The answer that came back on June 9 read: "Mr. Duggan feels that no reply

As a Harvard student, FDR developed a code to mask
his diary entries, particularly those about his relations
with a young Boston lady. (FDR Library)

FDR as assistant secretary of the Navy. His favorite component of the Navy
Department was the Office of Naval Intelligence, which he expanded and
staffed with trusted socialite friends. (FDR Library)

FDR with his friend Vincent Astor (left), who carried out espionage from his ocean-going yacht and who fed the President intelligence before World War II through The Club, a secret society of highly placed Americans. (FDR Library)

John Franklin Carter, a Washington columnist who ran a spy ring for FDR directly from the Oval Office. (Sonia C. Greenbaum)

British Prime Minister Winston Churchill and FDR along a stream at the President's retreat, Shangri-la. Their partnership began with secret correspondence predating America's entry into the war. (FDR Library)

General Claire Chennault (center), the American aviation advisor to China, who became involved in FDR's scheme to firebomb Tokyo—before Pearl Harbor. The plan fell through but led to Chennault's formation of the legendary Flying Tigers. (FDR Library)

The Japanese attack on Pearl Harbor on December 7, 1941, was the result of the greatest intelligence failure in American or perhaps all military history. Responsibility for the incident is still hotly debated. (FDR Library)

FDR with Vice President Henry Wallace, who unwittingly provided Germany with some of its highest-level intelligence through leaks to his brother-in-law, a Swiss diplomat. (FDR Library)

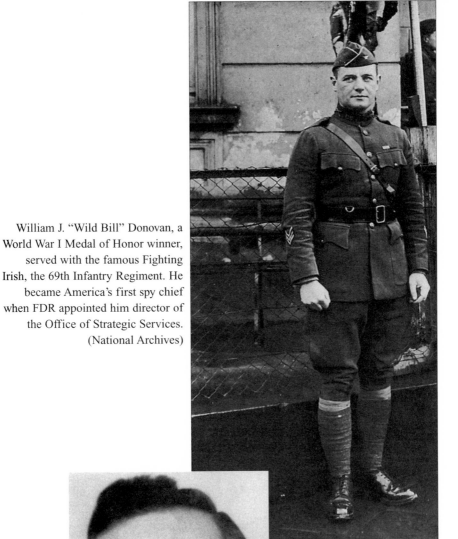

William J. "Wild Bill" Donovan, a World War I Medal of Honor winner, served with the famous Fighting Irish, the 69th Infantry Regiment. He became America's first spy chief when FDR appointed him director of the Office of Strategic Services. (National Archives)

Passport photo of Sir William S. Stephenson, the head of British intelligence in the United States, who fed FDR fabricated evidence of alleged hostile Nazi intentions in the Americas in order to draw the United States into the war. (Thomas Troy)

LUFTVERKEHRSNETZ
DER
VEREINIGTEN STAATEN
SÜD-AMERIKAS
HAUPTLINIEN

The map of South America that British intelligence
sent to FDR supposedly revealed how Hitler proposed to divide the continent into five Nazi duchies.
(FDR Library)

FDR gave Adolf Berle the thankless task of coordinating
rival U.S. intelligence services. Berle learned early on of
possible penetration of the Roosevelt administration by
Soviet spies. (FDR Library)

The Duke of Windsor, formerly King Edward VIII, aboard the USS *Tuscaloosa* shortly before he sought to suggest to FDR a near-treasonous peace plan between Britain and Germany. (FDR Library)

Frank B. Rowlett, leader of the cryptanalytic team that broke Japan's Purple diplomatic code and thus provided the best U.S. intelligence of the war. FDR, with his preference for spies over ciphers, did not initially appreciate these decrypts, which were designated Magic. (National Security Agency)

General Hiroshi Oshima, Japan's ambassador to Germany and FDR's best source of intelligence from Hitler, thanks to the breaking of the Purple code by American cryptanalysts. (National Archives)

In this decoded message from Ambassador Oshima to Tokyo, Hitler speculates on where the Allies are likely to launch the "second front."
(National Archives)

From: Berlin (OSHIMA)
To: Tokyo
2? January 1944
JAE

#82   (Parts 1, 2, 4, and 5 of a 6 Part message)

OSHIMA: "Does Your Excellency have any idea where they may land?"

HITLER: "Honestly, I can say no more than that I do not know. For a second front, beyond any doubt, the most effective area would be the Straits of Dover, but to land there would require great readiness and its difficulty would be great. Consequently, I don't think that the enemy would run such a risk. On the other hand, along the Bordeaux coast and in Portugal, the defenses are relatively weak, so this zone might be a possibility."

OSHIMA: "When you say Portugal, do you have any basis for suspecting something there?"

HITLER: "No, only I consider it a theoretical possibility and we Germans are preparing for any event, with air bases and submarines. We Germans have plenty of plans, and listen, I don't want you to say anything about them to a living soul."

Japanese
SECRET

Bletchley Park in England, site of Ultra, which broke the cipher of Germany's Enigma coding machine. This achievement was a secret so zealously guarded that Churchill and Roosevelt concealed an American blunder that cost hundreds of British lives rather than reveal that the tragedy was discovered through a decoded German message. (National Security Agency)

Inmates at the Buchenwald concentration camp. FDR had early access to information on the fate of the Jews and other victims of the Nazis through smuggled eyewitness accounts and German messages intercepted by British codebreakers. (FDR Library)

Two of eight captured German saboteurs, Herbert Haupt (left) and Georg Dasch (right), flank an Army officer during their trial. Dasch and another defendant escaped execution by betraying the other members of Operation Pastorius, including Haupt. (Federal Bureau of Investigation)

Ernst "Putzi" Hanfstaengl, a former member of Hitler's inner circle, was smuggled into the Washington area, where he reported to FDR on everything from rivalries among Nazis to the possibility that the Führer would commit suicide. (National Archives)

It was universally assumed that FDR would want General George C. Marshall to lead the invasion of Europe. But General Eisenhower, seen here with FDR in Sicily in 1943, had a sense that the President was secretly auditioning him. (National Archives)

Hollywood's leading swashbuckler, Errol Flynn, volunteered to spy for FDR, claiming that no one would suspect a movie star. FDR declined the offer. (National Archives)

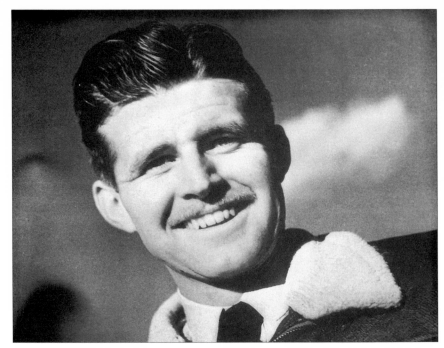

Navy Lieutenant Joseph P. Kennedy Jr., eldest brother of the future President, volunteered for a controversial secret mission proposed by FDR, which ultimately led to the young flier's death. (National Archives)

Myron Taylor, FDR's personal representative to the Vatican, with Pope Pius XII. Taylor exposed the biggest intelligence hoax committed against the White House in World War II. (FDR Library)

FDR with Joseph Stalin at the Big Three summit in Tehran, where a plot to assassinate the President was uncovered. (FDR Library)

Russian maids prepare a room in the American quarters during FDR's meeting at Yalta with Stalin and Churchill. The Soviets had planted dozens of hidden listening devices in all the rooms. (FDR Library)

An American sailor trains a Russian sailor during Operation Hula, in which the United States secretly turned warships over to the Soviet Union as part of FDR's strategy to draw Stalin into the war against Japan. (Naval Historical Center)

Churchill's pressure on FDR to make Britain a full partner in the development of the atom bomb led to the assignment of British scientists to Los Alamos, among them Klaus Fuchs, who stole secrets about the bomb for the Soviet Union. (UPI/Bettmann Archive).

FDR with his 1944 running mate, Senator Harry S. Truman. Truman later claimed he knew nothing of the atomic bomb before becoming President, but Roosevelt may have told him of the weapon during this lunch on the White House lawn. (FDR Library)

Lauchlin Currie, a close FDR aide. Was he consciously providing White House secrets to the Soviet Union, or was he merely an ingenuous dupe? (FDR Library)

Elizabeth Bentley, a former courier for the Soviet Union, who went to the FBI and then before Congress to denounce alleged spies in the Roosevelt administration. (National Archives)

FDR aboard the presidential yacht *Potomac* with his distant cousin and confidant, Margaret "Daisy" Suckley (center), with whom he shared wartime secrets. She was with him at the time of his death. (FDR Library)

should be made to it." Laurence Duggan was now a personal advisor to Secretary of State Cordell Hull. The advice to ignore the distraught woman's cry for help may have revealed Duggan's lingering protective sympathies for the Soviet Union. If so, he was in good company with the President and the Prime Minister of Great Britain. The dead Poles were buried not only physically but metaphorically, their memory subservient to a colder calculus in the mathematics of war.

★

Soviet practice was not to engage American Communists as spies since they were usually known to the FBI. Earl Browder, general secretary of the Communist Party of America, told an interviewer postwar, "There's been an awful lot of silly talk about the Communists in those days infiltrating the Roosevelt Administration. As a matter of fact, the Communists weren't interested in anything of the kind. . . . And we influenced everyone that came under our ideas to get active in mass work and not get into some governmental department." *The New Yorker* magazine profiled Browder as "a haggard little man with grizzling hair and a stubby moustache who looks as though he had eaten something that didn't agree with him . . . [and] moved about briskly, somewhat in the low-slung manner affected by Groucho Marx." Browder preferred to portray himself as a corn-fed son of Kansas, a midwestern American who just happened to have chosen communism as his politics over that of the Democrats or Republicans. In actuality, Browder was a conduit who led American Communists beyond street-corner pamphleteering into spying for the Soviet Union.

In 1940 the old Bolshevik had been railroaded into a four-year prison sentence for a minor passport irregularity: he failed to mention that he had obtained passports previously, a violation at its worst incurring a sentence of months, not years. The sentence had been handed down after the 1939 Russo-German peace pact, placing Browder, at that point, on the wrong side of American popular sentiment. His conviction, however, did not deter Browder from running for president in 1940 before entering the federal penitentiary in Atlanta. By 1942, with the international lineup reversed, and Russia now America's ally, President Roosevelt came under left-wing pressure to release Browder from prison as a gesture of Soviet-American amity. FDR looked for a graceful exit. According to Browder's account, Roosevelt found it in New York's mayor, Fiorello La Guardia. The feisty La Guardia came to the White House to urge the President to free Browder. FDR asked the mayor, "Tell me one good reason why I should act in this at this time." La Guardia answered, "Because Browder's sons are being kept off the baseball teams in school because their father's in prison." "That's the best reason I've been given so far," the President responded with relief. "Let's release him!" Whether for this explanation or less colorful reasons, Browder was, in fact, sprung from the penitentiary by presidential order.

Early in the next year, a dumpy, washed-out figure, Elizabeth Bentley, an underground courier between American spies and their Soviet controllers, recalled meeting with Browder. He directed Bentley to extend her courier runs to a new ring serving the Soviets. As she later put it, "They had been engaged in some sort of espionage for Earl Browder" for a considerable time. By freeing Browder to placate the Russians, the President had unwittingly restored a key link in Russia's spy chain in America.

★

That fall of 1943, FDR's desire was not merely to back the Soviets but to woo Stalin personally, to subject the Soviet dictator to the fatal Roosevelt charm that so rarely failed to conquer. He had finally persuaded Stalin to meet with him and Churchill outside the Soviet Union. Stalin had previously refused to do so, arguing that his country could not risk his absence, as if FDR and Churchill were less essential to their countries' survival. More likely, Stalin feared turning his back on rivals, real or imagined, should he leave Russia. Indeed, the strongest proponent for Stalin's staying home was his secret police chief, Beria. Finally, Stalin agreed to travel as far as neighboring Iran to meet his allies in the capital, Tehran, in November 1943. Roosevelt was so eager for an opportunity to deal with Stalin face-to-face that he would probably have agreed to a meeting in the Gobi Desert. At Tehran, Stalin could be expected to accelerate his steady drumbeat for a second front. But what FDR wanted went beyond the war in Europe; it was to realize a dream that he might go down in history as the man who brought democracy and communism together in peace. Nothing could shatter that dream more swiftly than the slightest suspicion on the part of the paranoid Stalin that Roosevelt and Churchill might cut a separate deal with Germany. It was precisely this worst fear, at the worst possible time, that a Bill Donovan alumnus nearly triggered.

Of all the individuals engaged in espionage on the American side in World War II, few could match Theodore Morde for sheer gall. Morde, at age thirty-two, had gone to Cairo in March 1942 with Donovan's COI. When the Office of War Information split off from COI, Morde stayed with the former organization. At some point in 1943, for reasons best known to himself, Morde resigned and went to work in the Cairo office of the *Reader's Digest* international organization. To Robert Sherwood, now with the OWI, it was good riddance since Morde "had been making a certain amount of trouble." Morde next showed up in Istanbul posing as a war correspondent with no more credentials than an American passport. The smooth talker dropped names and spoke of his high-level experiences with a confidence that lent weight to otherwise invisible qualifications. The correspondent guise enabled Morde to win the trust of an anti-Nazi German professor in Turkey, who in turn led him to the German ambassador, Franz von Papen. During a meeting on October 5, 1943, Morde told the ambassador that he "had come on a highly secret and important mission from the United States for the sole purpose of seeing Von Papen." His mission was so delicate, he explained, that he "carried no other credential than my passport." The passport carried a notation that the bearer was "the assistant to the American minister" in Cairo, an out-of-date position left over from Morde's OWI days. This identification, however, satisfied Papen. During a long conversation Morde proposed that the ambassador lead a plot to overthrow Hitler. If carried off, he could promise nothing for sure, Morde added modestly, but doubtless, the removal of Hitler would lead to peace and save Germany. Papen, a canny diplomatic survivor, and a former chancellor of Germany, took the opportunity to protest the indiscriminate Allied bombing of German cities, noting that only one bomb in ten struck a military target. He also warned Morde that Roosevelt's policy of unconditional surrender was driving the German people in a direction the Western Allies could not possibly have intended. Because the bombing was destroying their material comforts, the German people, Papen claimed, were turning to communism. That concern vented, the ambassador then listened to the young American read from a formula for peace terms between Germany and the Western Allies, a twenty-six-page document born of the pen of Theodore Morde.

A week later, Morde was back in Cairo, where he managed to see Lieutenant Colonel Paul West, OSS operations chief for the Middle East. He confidently explained that he was engaged in a highly secret mission and was under orders to get back to Washington at once to report directly to President Roosevelt. So urgent a mission, Morde said, rated nothing less than a number one passenger priority on the next flight to the United States at a time when civilian airspace was next to unobtainable. OSS obligingly arranged the flight and Colonel West alerted General Donovan of the imminent arrival of this important figure. On his arrival in the United States in mid-October, Morde almost made it into the Oval Office. He did manage to see Pa Watson, who turned him over to Morde's old OWI superior, Robert Sherwood. Morde told Sherwood that his mission to Papen had been sponsored by Brigadier General Patrick Hurley, FDR's personal representative in Cairo. After Morde's departure, Sherwood sent the President a report of his encounter with Morde. "The story he brought back was an amazing one," Sherwood told FDR. "He said that under the sponsorship of General Pat Hurley he had been to Istanbul and had two interviews with Papen, in which he discussed a possible deal for the overthrow of Hitler and the Nazi Party." But no more enamored of Morde than he had been earlier, Sherwood went on to say that he had checked out the self-anointed negotiator and his peace plan with the general. Hurley, he told FDR, "disclaims all responsibility for it and denounces Morde." What infuriated Sherwood, apart from Morde's brazen manipulation, was the anti-Roosevelt posture of the man's present employer, *Reader's Digest*. At this time, the magazine was printing huge editions for distribution to American troops abroad. Sherwood told Roosevelt that while supporting the war in general, "the *Reader's Digest* has become more and more bitter and partisan in its attacks on this Administration. In its world-wide circulation it is, in effect, undoing the work that my outfit [OWI] is constantly trying to do overseas." FDR, too, was incensed by the editorial direction of the *Digest*. But he was enraged most by the rashness of Morde's talk of a separate peace with Germany on the eve of the Tehran conference with Stalin.

Just three days after Sherwood's scuttling of Morde, FDR received a communication from Bill Donovan of stunning naïveté. Morde, as arranged by Lieutenant Colonel West, had indeed gone to see Donovan in Washington and had briefed him on his conversation with Papen and his peace proposal. Donovan then sent the twenty-six-page document to FDR with the following notation: "I beg you to read this carefully. It contains an idea that your skill and imagination could develop." Donovan went on to repeat Morde's fabrication that General Hurley knew of the plan and had even agreed to carry it out. It is difficult to understand how a spymaster could have been so far behind the curve of events and support a scheme so inimical to what the President hoped to achieve at Tehran, particularly the risk of dealing behind the Soviet Union's back. West, in writing to his OSS chief about Morde, had added a postscript in longhand that read: "It is my understanding that Morde has orders to report to the President through General Strong." Donovan may possibly have been ensnared by his own competitive impulses. The idea that Morde's plan might reach the President through his mortal enemy may have led Wild Bill to elbow his way in, paying less attention to the validity of Morde's intrigues than to beating Strong into the Oval Office.

On November 10, the day before he was to leave for Tehran, FDR rode out to National Airport to meet Cordell Hull, who was returning from a mission to Moscow. With the President were Mrs. Hull, and the acting secretary of state, Edward R. Stettinius. The trip out was cold and sunless as the heavy limousine lumbered through Washington's gray streets. Previously, FDR had traveled in a car seized by the Treasury Department from Al Capone. But Mike Reilly, chief of the President's Secret Service detail, concluded that while the automobile may have carried enough armor for a gangster, it was insecure for a president. Reilly had persuaded friends in the Ford Motor Company to build Roosevelt an 8,000-pound bullet- and bombproof vehicle. As they rode along, FDR fed Stettinius, page by page, Bob Sherwood's denunciation of the Morde report, followed by Bill Donovan's simplistic endorsement of it. The President wanted Theodore Morde's passport yanked. People like him had no business causing mischief outside the country in the middle of a war, he told Stettinius. For anyone else, support of the discredited Morde would have marked a humiliating defeat. But not for the unsinkable Donovan. The President kept him on, and Wild Bill proceeded blithely on to the next rampart.

★

What the high-spirited, high-living George Earle was telling the President from Istanbul in the fall of 1943 seemed farfetched, but nevertheless alarming. On October 14, Earle sent the White House a coded cable reading: "Turkish source of my last four telegrams gives me following just received. Devastating robot land torpedo plane attack on England will surely take place this month from Northern France and Belgium." Earle, as an intelligence operative, had compiled a spotty record thus far. A few months before, in August, he had reported to the President that the U.S. raid launched from Libya by 178 B-24 bombers against Romania's Ploeşti oil fields had been "a marvel of precision," which it had not. The raid had caused substantial damage to fuel storage tanks and refineries; but Earle's estimate that a year to eighteen months would be required to rebuild the refineries and that "one half of Rumanian production [was] lost for a year" proved highly inaccurate. Furthermore, the raid had been carried out at a horrific cost. Of 1,733 airmen, 446 were killed, and only 33 of the aircraft flew home intact. The rest of the planes were shot down or shot up beyond repair.

Still, Earle had tapped some valuable sources, including the assistant air attaché at the German embassy in Turkey, a covert Austrian anti-Nazi. And his prediction of "robot" aerial strikes on London was not hollow. Eleven days after Earle's message, FDR received a confirming cable from Churchill, reading: "I ought to let you know that during the last six months evidence has continued to accumulate from many sources that the Germans are preparing an attack on England, particularly London, by means of very long-range rockets which may conceivably weigh 60 tons and carry an explosive charge of 10 to 20 tons." Churchill further reported German experiments under way on a pilotless bomb-laden aircraft, Earle's "robot land torpedo plane." Earle's intelligence had been essentially correct, but he was off in citing the year in which this weapon, the V-1, would strike Britain.

Churchill's science advisors were split as to whether the Germans could actually produce a workable rocket or robot. The Prime Minister, however, was less sanguine. He told FDR, "I am personally as yet unconvinced that they cannot be made." His fear, shared by the President, was that flying bombs and rockets would disrupt the military buildup under way in Britain, "rupturing the Anglo-American plans for a major cross-channel return to the Continent." So concerned was Churchill that he wanted the V-weapons branded as an unlawful form of warfare, and if Roosevelt and Stalin concurred, he wanted to retaliate by using poison gas against the Germans. He was dissuaded only by the argument of his advisors, not that using gas was immoral, but that a better countermeasure existed. "For this reason," Churchill continued in his message to FDR, "we raided Peenemünde, which was their main experimental station."

What was happening at Peenemünde, a thumb of land extending into the Baltic Sea, was indeed a high Hitler priority. He personally inspected the installations in 1943. Churchill, in his memoirs, describes the Führer's commitment to the work: "About June 10, he told his assembled military leaders that the Germans had only to hold out. By the end of 1943, London would be levelled to the ground and Britain forced to capitulate. October 20 was fixed as zero day for rocket attacks to begin." But in the months between the Führer's visit and the scheduled unleashing of the secret weapons, the Peenemünde raid took place. On the night of August 17–18, 600 RAF heavy bombers dropped high explosives and incendiary bombs on the supposedly secret installations. Over 120 scientists and 600 foreign workers perished, including several laborers from Luxembourg who had been spying for British intelligence. The strike had set Hitler's timetable back; the question was by how long. On November 5, Roosevelt received an assessment from George Earle. "Austrian officer gives me following from his conversation yesterday with Dr. Zever Kuehn, Chief German war organization [in] Turkey," Earle reported. The President quickly relayed verbatim to Churchill what Earle had told him, including misspellings. "We too have received many reports of the German rocket activity. Production is said to have been delayed due to death in bombing the experimental station at Peenemünde of Lieutenant General Shemiergembeinski. The only information recently coming to me, which might be of value to you, is a statement that factories manufacturing the rocket bomb are situated in Kania Friedrichshafen, Mixtgennerth Berlin, Kugellawerke Schweinfurt, Wiener Neustadt." Earle had presented to FDR a typical spy's report, a mélange of fact, rumor, and misinformation. No one, for example, with the near-unpronounceable name of the reportedly dead general was ever identified as involved in German rocket building. Despite the raid, Hitler's confidence in and dependence on the super weapons did not waver. After Peenemünde was struck, he ordered that work be continued in an underground plant hollowed out of the Harz Mountains near Wordhausen in central Germany.

More alarming to FDR was what Earle further reported, that after the predicted aerial "torpedo" strike against England, "Stratospheric attack on America will follow." Were Earle's sources alarmist or merely premature? Did Germany possess weapons capable of reaching the United States? Magic decrypts available to the President in September and October 1943 from Ambassador Oshima's embassy in Berlin to Tokyo seemed to confirm the possibility. Oshima described a high-performance, long-distance aircraft that Luftwaffe aeronautical engineers were working on, the Me-264. The objective, he revealed, was a bomber that could reach New York.

Chapter XIX

———=★=———

Deceivers and the Deceived

O N THE raw, drizzly night of November 11, 1943, the President left the White House to begin a multi-legged journey that would eventually bring him to Tehran to join Churchill and meet Stalin for the first time. He chose to spend the nine-day Atlantic crossing aboard the battleship *Iowa,* a floating fortress bristling with nine 16-inch guns and manned by a crew the size of a small city, twenty-six hundred officers and men, and commanded by his former naval aide Captain John McCrea. As the presidential party made its way up the gangway to furled banners and the boatswain's pipe, Mike Reilly, the White House security chief, went over his checkoff list for presidential sea voyages. As Reilly once described this list, it included: "A supply of money to bank the President, he never carried any in his own pockets. A supply of special foods. FDR's tastes were easily satisfied. Give him corned beef hash for breakfast, and coffee in his big cup, four and a half inches in diameter, and the day was well started." Other presidential necessities included cases of Saratoga Springs mineral water, long wooden matches, the only kind FDR would use to light his cigarettes, deep-sea fishing gear, and enough movies to show one a night, particularly slapstick comedies, leggy musicals, and films starring Walter Huston, FDR's favorite actor. For bedtime, Reilly laid by a well-stocked library of whodunits.

After the *Iowa* deposited him at Oran, Algeria, the President flew to Cairo, where he met briefly with Chiang Kai-shek. On Saturday, November 27, Roosevelt, an uneasy flier, boarded the presidential Douglas DC-4, the *Sacred Cow,* and long hours later touched down beneath the massif of the Elburz Mountains at a Soviet-controlled airfield outside Tehran. With him were Harry Hopkins, Averell Harriman, Pa Watson, Admiral William Leahy, General Marshall, FDR's daughter, Anna, and her husband, Major John Boettiger. Hopkins saw his role regarding Roosevelt and Churchill as "a catalytic agent between two prima donnas."

The Tehran script was largely foreordained. Stalin would press for an Anglo-American invasion of Europe at the earliest possible date. Churchill, though largely resigned to the landings in France, would continue to argue for a run up through the Balkans, and FDR would seek to please both. Further, the Big Three would try to design a strategy to draw Turkey into the conflict on their side. And they would toss back and forth the hand grenade of Poland's postwar fate. FDR's personal priority remained the political seduction of Joseph Stalin. As he once told a disbelieving Bill Bullitt, who thoroughly distrusted the Soviet dictator, "I think if I give [Stalin] everything I possibly can and ask for nothing from him in return . . . noblesse oblige, he won't try to annex anything and will work with me for a world of democracy and peace." The Stalin whom Roosevelt hoped to win over with sweet reason had, during the purges of the thirties, murdered all of Lenin's Politburo, the exiled Leon Trotsky, the chief of the General Staff, and 25 percent of senior Soviet military officers, 1,108 of the 1,966 delegates to the Seventeenth Party Congress, 98 of 139 members of the 1934 Central Committee, 90 percent of Soviet ambassadors, and two secret police chiefs, Genrikh Yagoda and Nikolai Yezhov, who had produced the trumped-up evidence against the other victims. It was as if an American president upon coming to power would have had most of the House and Senate shot, along with opposition leaders and potential rivals within his own party, most of the generals, and the American ambassadors to nine out of ten countries.

Mike Reilly was wrestling with a more immediate problem than the strategic decisions before the three Allied partners. The burly Irishman who lifted the President, as he would a child, in and out of limousines, on and off trains, and up stairwells had come to the Iranian capital in advance of the presidential party to work out security arrangements. Upon his arrival, his Soviet counterpart, General Artikov of the NKVD, told Reilly that thirty-eight German agents had recently parachuted near Tehran. They had two missions, Artikov claimed: One was to sabotage the railroad connecting Basra and Tehran, thus cutting the lifeline for shipping American lend-lease armaments and supplies through Iran to the Soviet Union. The second mission was to assassinate the Allied leaders.

Hitler was fatalistic about his own life. In 1942 he told his staff: "There can never be absolute security against fanatics and idealists. . . . If some fanatic wishes to shoot me or kill me with a bomb, I am no safer sitting down than standing up." However, he had shown no taste for killing enemy heads of state, at least in the early part of the war. But as the crimes of his regime became known, Hitler's position shifted. He recognized that should Germany lose, he could expect no mercy from the victors. Thus, there was no point in exempting their leaders from assassination.

By the fall of 1943, the SD, the intelligence wing of Heinrich Himmler's SS, had discovered that the Allied leaders planned to meet in Tehran sometime toward the end of November. With this intelligence in hand, an assassination plot had hatched in the fertile imagination of SS officer Otto Skorzeny, the daredevil Hitler favorite who had recently snatched the deposed Mussolini from his Allied captors off a stoutly guarded Italian mountaintop. Under Skorzeny's tutelage, a hit team began training near Vinnitsa in German-occupied Ukraine. Its members practiced assassination by explosives, firearms, knives, and poison. By September 10, SS chief Himmler had secured Hitler's approval of the plot. The mission to murder the Allied leaders was code-named Long Pounce.

Even before his arrival in Tehran, FDR had found himself at the center of a hospitality tug-of-war. Churchill wanted him to stay at the British embassy, and Stalin wanted him at the Soviet diplomatic compound. FDR declined both. As he told his staff, "I like to be more independent than a guest can hope to be." He and Churchill had shared quarters at the August 1943 Quebec conference, and FDR had found the Prime Minister's drop-ins at all hours, however stimulating, crowding his freedom to maneuver. The President chose to stay in Tehran at the American legation as the guest of the minister, Louis G. Dreyfus.

At nine-thirty the following morning, a Sunday, Averell Harriman found the President breakfasting on corned beef hash served on his own White House china and silver flown in on the *Sacred Cow* and sipping coffee from his giant mug. Harriman explained that he had an urgent message from Stalin. The Soviet and British embassies in Tehran were practically next-door neighbors, but the American legation was almost two miles away. Stalin feared, Harriman said, that the three Allied leaders, in traveling back and forth through Tehran, could face an "unhappy incident." What sort of incident? FDR asked. "Assassination," Harriman replied. The pro-Allied shah, Reza Pahlavi, had many enemies, Harriman added, and Tehran teemed with Nazi agents and sympathizers. Therefore, Stalin wanted Roosevelt to be safe at the Soviet compound.

FDR declined, still resisting becoming a prisoner of either British or Soviet hosts. Until now, Mike Reilly had hesitated to alarm the President. But upon hearing Harriman, he was emboldened to make a rare intrusion into a Roosevelt conversation. He told the President about General Artikov's report of German agents parachuted into the area. All the more reason for the President to move, Harriman urged. Suppose Stalin was attacked by these assassins en route to the American embassy to see Roosevelt? The responsibility would be on the President's head, Harriman noted. The argument carried the day. Roosevelt decided to move.

The legation became a whirlwind of motion as Reilly's Secret Service agents, military attachés, and embassy staff swung into action. By 3 P.M., a motorcade had been assembled—jeeps armed with machine guns, military police revving their motorcycles, three automobiles full of Secret Service agents cradling tommy guns, and in the middle the gleaming black limousine of the President. The caravan rolled out of the legation grounds onto Ferdousi Avenue, the main route to the Soviet compound. Russian and American troops lined the thoroughfare shoulder to shoulder, a human wall sealing off the presidential party from the Iranian masses. The Red Army alone, under security chief Beria's orders, had brought in three thousand men to protect the Allied leaders.

Few of the enemy parachutists trained by Skorzeny in Ukraine were German; most were anti-Communist Russians recruited from Wehrmacht prisoner-of-war camps. They had been outfitted with Russian army uniforms to blend into the Soviet security force in Tehran, where they would reassemble to carry out their mission. However, in a conspiracy within a conspiracy, several of the presumed collaborators were actually loyal Communists who, upon arriving in Tehran, immediately betrayed the plot to the Soviet army command. All but six of the hit men were quickly rounded up. But the six remaining, led by a German SS Sturmbannführer, Rudolf von Holten-Pflug, who hoped to become the next Skorzeny, remained determined to fulfill their mission.

Any soldier, Russian or American, in that human cordon on Ferdousi Avenue who hoped to catch a glimpse of Franklin Roosevelt was doomed to be deceived. The figure in the limousine wearing the familiar Roosevelt fedora was Robert Holmes, a Secret Service agent, posing as FDR, on only the second known occasion during which the President used a double, the first being during the 1941 Atlantic conference. As the motorcade left the American legation, the President, Harry Hopkins, Major Boettiger, and Admiral Leahy, slipped out of a back entrance. The President was lifted into a nondescript Army staff car and the others piled in after him. Reilly instructed the driver to get the President to the Soviet embassy as swiftly and inconspicuously as possible, stopping for nothing. No escort accompanied the lone car as it plunged into narrow back streets, alleyways, and at one point bumped along a dirt path. FDR grinned the entire way, reveling in the excitement, while the others tried to share his enthusiasm. For a man condemned to a wheelchair, it was a rare treat to experience physical adventure. The car slid through the gates of the Russian compound just ahead of the official entourage.

Stalin gave up the main residence, the only steam-heated building in the city, to Roosevelt and moved his party into a smaller villa. "The servants who made the President's bed and cleaned his room," Harry Hopkins later noted, "were all members of the highly efficient OGPU [secret police] and expressive bulges were plainly discernible in the hip pockets under their white coats." Along with the comfortable accommodations and attentive servants, every room in the villa was bugged by hidden microphones.

The President had barely settled in when Stalin came calling. FDR was wheeled into a commodious sitting room to meet the source of all power in the Soviet Union. Approaching him was a compact figure, two hundred solid pounds packed onto a five-foot six-inch frame. Stalin wore a plain but well-tailored brown uniform adorned with a single medal, a gold star suspended from a red and gold ribbon. However lacking in stature, the man projected a palpable presence. As he extended his hand to FDR, the President smiled eagerly and said, "I have tried for a long time to bring this about." Harry Hopkins has left a sharply etched sketch of the marshal. "There was no waste of word, gesture, nor mannerism. It was like talking to a perfectly co-ordinated machine, an intelligent machine. . . . No man could forget the picture of the dictator of Russia . . . an austere, rugged, determined figure in boots that shone like mirrors, [and] stout baggy trousers. . . . He laughs often enough, but it's a short laugh, somewhat sardonic, perhaps. There is no small talk in him." They made an odd pair: the revolutionary who had robbed banks to topple the czar and who had the blood of millions of his countrymen on his hands, and the Hudson River patrician, governed by humane, idealistic impulses. It was as if little Lord

Fauntleroy in his velvet suit was determined to show fairness and fraternity toward a streetwise urchin.

That night, the President hosted a dinner for Stalin and Churchill. The Filipino mess stewards, having managed to prepare the meal in a strange kitchen on short notice, were clearing away the plates when all eyes turned toward the President. "Roosevelt was about to say something," one guest recalled, "when suddenly, in the flick of an eye, he turned green and great drops of sweat began to bead off his face; he put a shaky hand to his forehead," and complained of severe stomach cramps. Had the assassins succeeded? Had the President been poisoned? Harry Hopkins had FDR quickly wheeled to his bedroom and summoned Admiral McIntire. The President's physician examined his patient, and minutes later a smiling Hopkins returned to the dining room to report that the President had suffered only from acute indigestion.

The Tehran conference ended on December 1. Stalin won assurance that Overlord, the invasion of France, would occur in May 1944, six months off. Poland's postwar borders were not agreed upon, and the Turks were not lured into the war. At one point the President had thrown out a suggestion that must have appealed to Stalin. Maybe the way to spike Germany's aggressive impulses in the future, he said, would be to break the country into the five separate states existing before Bismarck had forged them into modern Germany.

Back home, holding a press conference after the Tehran meeting, the President gleefully took a reporter's question allowing him to segue into the assassination plot. He was asked, "Is there anything you can tell us about the method of your travels?" He could not give a direct answer, FDR replied, because the enemy "would know that you were leaving, and you are always, the whole distance—you are under—practically under the range of German planes. And it's like—like shooting a duck sitting on the water for a German pursuit plane to go after a transport plane without any guns on it." He then described how Stalin had persuaded him to leave the American embassy for the Soviet compound. "And that night," he added, "I got word from Marshal Stalin that they had got word of a German plot. Well, no use going into details," he ended with a mysterious smile.

When news of the alleged assassination plot hit the newspapers, the Iranians were outraged. The foreign minister cabled his ambassador in Washington, in a message stamped "Secret," but broken by Arlington Hall cryptanalysts: "Do you realize what a bad impression this statement will make in the circumstances in Iran and the whole world? Also the truth is that there was no plot against these three persons in Iran." But as for publicly repudiating the charge, the Iranians felt stymied. As the ambassador put it, "The author of the statement was the American President and the originator of the report the Russian Premier." He feared that "denying of statements made by the heads of the two states" could prove rash for a small country squeezed between American power and the Soviet border. The closest to an apology that Iran could eke out was Cordell Hull's private assurance to the Iranian envoy that "whatever was said was concerning each of the three persons, and was not at all intended to reflect upon the Iranians."

The six surviving Skorzeny parachutists managed to elude capture for three months by hiding among mountain Bedouins. Eventually, they were tracked down by Russian troops and executed.

★

One of the war's most speculated-upon secrets was sealed inside a single mind, that of the President. As Henry Wallace had said, the only certainty in dealing with Roosevelt was uncertainty. At Tehran, Churchill had presented Stalin with a magnificent sword forged by English craftsmen to honor "the steel-hearted citizens of Stalingrad." Stalin had appeared deeply touched, tears clouding his eyes upon gripping the splendid weapon. But sentimentality in the Soviet dictator was short-lived. At a subsequent meeting, Stalin had asked bluntly, "Who will command Overlord?" Roosevelt answered, "It has not been decided." "Then nothing will come out of these operations," Stalin replied.

His impatience over the Allied failure yet to launch a second front was understandable. As far back as 1942, FDR had pressed General Marshall and Admiral Ernest King to prepare Sledgehammer, the code name for a limited landing in northwestern Europe. "I do not believe we can wait until 1943 to strike at Germany," FDR told the two chiefs. In an aide-mémoire shared with Roosevelt, Churchill seemed to agree, saying, "We are making preparations for a landing on the Continent in August or September 1942." Then Churchill had backed off. "No responsible British general, admiral or air marshal," he subsequently wrote FDR, "is prepared to recommend Sledgehammer."

In August 1942, Churchill had gone to Moscow for his first encounter with Stalin, a mission he described as "like carrying a large lump of ice to the North Pole." His chilling message for the Soviet leader was: no second front that year. Churchill later described this visit in a secret cable to FDR.

Stalin, the Prime Minister reported, had been insulting, "especially about our being too much afraid of fighting the Germans, and if we tried it like the Russians, we would find it not so bad. . . ." Stalin had also reminded Churchill "that we had broken our promise about Sledgehammer." It was true, and thereafter, Roosevelt had insisted at least on the invasion of North Africa, which served Britain well in keeping its Mediterranean lifeline open, but hardly satisfied the Soviet Union.

Though Churchill had finally agreed at Quebec to the cross-Channel invasion, after extracting from FDR a full partnership on Tube Alloys, the PM still remained unenthusiastic. Two factors explained his continuing resistance. Still fresh in his mind were the World War I slaughterhouses, Passchendaele and the Somme. He feared a frontal attack on Europe would turn the English Channel into a "river of blood." At one point, he stood in the House of Commons and looked about "at the faces that are not there," the generation that perished between 1914 and 1918. In the summer of 1943, FDR had sent Henry Stimson to England to press the argument for a second front. Stimson reported back that Churchill and his military advisors believed "Germany can be beaten by a series of attritions in northern Italy, in the eastern Mediterranean, in Greece, in the Balkans, in Rumania and other satellite countries and that the only fighting that needs to be done will be done by Russia." Stimson saw clearly the flaw in the British argument. "None of these methods of pinprick warfare," he counseled the President, "can be counted by us to fool Stalin into the belief that we have kept [our] pledge."

Churchill may well have preferred nibbling Hitler to death in southeastern Europe, believing the job could be accomplished with far fewer lives lost, but his fierce anti-communism suggests the real reason. Ernest Cuneo was a member of FDR's outer circle, a stocky, onetime all–Ivy League football star, an aide to New York's Mayor La Guardia, and, during the war, a liaison man for Bill Donovan. On one errand for the OSS director, Cuneo went to London to meet with Sir Desmond Morton, who prepared Churchill's daily intelligence digest. Late of an evening, Cuneo and Sir Desmond were descending the Duke of York steps, discussing where the Allies should strike next. "Why is the Prime Minister so anxious to go up through the Balkans?" Cuneo asked. Sir Desmond stopped abruptly, grabbed Cuneo by the shoulders, and said, "Because the Prime Minister says that if we send ten divisions up the Vardan Valley, we can crush the retreating right flank of German armies and save middle Europe from the Russians!"

As for Stalin's query, "Who will command Overlord?" though Roosevelt had not yet declared himself publicly, his choice was no secret. Everybody knew. Churchill had agreed, as U.S. transports poured GIs, tanks, artillery, and ammunition into England in quantities vastly outweighing British resources, that the leader had to be an American. FDR set forth his preference in a long message to Churchill. "The importance of the command of Overlord cannot be disclosed to the American people without grave, perhaps disastrous violations of security," he began. Nevertheless, he went on, "I believe General Marshall is the man who can do the job, and should at once assume operational control of our forces in the war against Germany." The choice of Marshall had appeared confirmed when FDR met with Churchill at Quebec at the same time that the Prime Minister had finally agreed to Overlord. As Henry Stimson remembered the moment, the Prime Minister also wanted Marshall to command Overlord, and the matter appeared settled.

Roosevelt's preference, however, was not universally applauded. Retired General John J. Pershing, who had led the American Expeditionary Force to victory in World War I, learned of the President's leaning, and on September 16 wrote FDR "to transfer [Marshall] to a tactical command in a limited area, no matter how seemingly important, is to deprive ourselves of his outstanding strategical ability and experience. I know of no one at all comparable to replace him as Chief of Staff." FDR handled the old soldier with customary suavity. "You are absolutely right about George Marshall—and yet I think you are wrong too," Roosevelt replied. "As you know, the operations for which we are considering him are the biggest that we will conduct in this war. . . . More than that, I think it is only a fair thing to give George a chance in the field. . . . The best way I can express it is to tell you that I want George to be the Pershing of the second World War—and he cannot be that if we keep him here."

Roosevelt supported his choice even more emphatically to General Eisenhower. In November 1943, during a stopover in North Africa on his way to the Tehran conference, he had asked Eisenhower to give him a tour of the Tunisian battlefield. As they drove past the burnt-out detritus of war vanishing under the desert sands, FDR said casually, "Ike, you and I know who was the Chief of Staff during the last years of the Civil War but practically no one else knows, although the names of the field generals— Grant, of course, and Lee, and Jackson, Sherman, Sheridan and the others—every schoolboy knows them. I hate to think that 50 years from now practically nobody will know who George Marshall was. That is one of the reasons why I want George to have the big command—he is entitled to establish his place in history as a great General." Roosevelt confided to Eisenhower that he had big plans for him too. Ike would be coming back to Washington to replace Marshall as acting Chief of Staff.

The men whose judgment Roosevelt most prized agreed with his choice. "I believe that Marshall's command of Overlord is imperative for its success," Henry Stimson said. Harry Hopkins saw an even broader role for the general. "Marshall should have command of all the Allied forces, other than the Russians, attacking the Fortress of Germany," he urged Roosevelt. What precisely the President told Marshall about the Overlord command is lost in FDR's penchant for committing as little as possible to paper. The diffident Marshall never uttered a word himself suggesting that his appointment was in the bag. But Mrs. Marshall began to move the couple's personal belongings from the Army Chief of Staff's residence at Fort Myer and store them in their home in Leesburg, Virginia, in preparation for a likely move to England.

And then it began to unravel. General Pershing's position that no one else possessed Marshall's global grasp of strategy was seconded by Admirals Leahy and King and the Army Air Corps commander, Hap Arnold. They argued further that the Overlord command amounted to a demotion, since Eisenhower would now be issuing orders to Marshall, his former superior. Even the enemy entered the speculation. A Nazi broadcast out of Paris reported that Marshall had been dismissed and that "President Roosevelt has taken over his command."

Though Marshall continued to keep his counsel, the command of Overlord would mark the logical capstone to his career. Still, the only certainty in the Roosevelt universe was indeed what went on inside FDR's head, and a major shift had occurred between his departure for and return from Tehran. On December 3, on his way back to Washington, the President flew into Cairo, where he stayed at the luxurious Villa Mena, a hotel on the outskirts of town. On Sunday morning, FDR summoned Marshall to join him for a private lunch. The general later described this pivotal moment in his life as he and the President gazed out the window at the eternal pyramids of Giza. "I was determined that I should not embarrass the President one way or the other," Marshall recalled. "I was utterly sincere in the desire to avoid what had happened in other wars—the consideration of the feelings of the individual rather than the good of the country. After a good deal of beating around the bush, he asked me just what I wanted to do. Evidently it was left up to me." The command he longed for was Marshall's for the asking. However, this reserved and selfless paragon was a longtime student of the President and well understood the man's zigzag style in moving toward his ultimate goals. By leaving the decision in Marshall's hands, Roosevelt had signaled the subtlest shift in his past thinking that the general was his choice. FDR, for his part, knew that Marshall would never promote his personal interests. Whatever he yearned for in his heart, Marshall did not ask for Overlord that morning. When he failed to ask, the President's supple mind allowed him to convince himself that the old soldier had chosen to stay put. "The [President] evidently assumed that concluded the affair," Marshall recalled of the end of the meeting, "and I would not command in Europe." FDR threw the departing general a well-aimed consolation: "Well, I didn't feel I could sleep at ease if you were out of Washington."

As word of the President's change of heart spread throughout the staff, so did the shock. "I said frankly that I was staggered when I heard the change," Henry Stimson noted, "for I thought that the other arrangement was thoroughly settled at Quebec." FDR later shared with Stimson his version of the conversation with Marshall: "The President said he got the impression that Marshall was not only impartial between the two but perhaps really preferred to remain as Chief of Staff," a rationalization of the first magnitude, Stimson recognized. The secretary of war tried to arouse a twinge of guilt in the President, telling him, "I knew in the bottom of his heart it was Marshall's secret desire above all things to command this invasion force into Europe; that I had had very hard work to wring out of Marshall that this was so, but I had done so finally beyond the possibility of misunderstanding."

The President had one more party to bring into his confidence. He invited Churchill, also in Cairo, to join him for a ride past the pyramids. "He then said, almost casually, that he could not spare General Marshall," Churchill recalled of their conversation. "He therefore proposed to nominate Eisenhower to Overlord and asked me for my opinion. I said it was for him to decide but that we had also the warmest regard for General Eisenhower." What everyone had known, what was common knowledge, what Churchill, Stimson, Hopkins, Stalin, and even Marshall himself knew, that the general was to command Overlord, had somehow been derailed in the curves of the Roosevelt mind. No confidant, however close, had been consulted by FDR. The secret had been uncontaminated by sharing until the President popped it.

Roosevelt's next stop after Cairo was to return to Tunis, where he communicated ahead to have General Eisenhower standing by to meet him. His first words on his arrival were: "Ike, you'd better start packing." Eisenhower assumed that Roosevelt was referring to his return to Washington to replace Marshall. Not until they were aboard the President's plane, headed for an inspection tour of Malta and Sicily, did FDR enlighten the general. He cautioned Eisenhower that, once settled in his new job, he would be surrounded by strong, often prickly Britishers, the strongest and prickliest being Winston Churchill. These were people, Roosevelt warned, who believed that a frontal attack across the Channel into France was destined to fail. These were the doubters whom Ike had to convert.

The near-saintly Marshall was given the task of drafting a statement announcing Eisenhower's appointment to the command he had so desperately wanted for himself. At the bottom of the note, Marshall penned, "Dear Eisenhower you might like to have this as a memento. It was written very hurriedly by me as the final meeting broke up yesterday, the President signing it immediately." Something in Eisenhower's manner, his bearing, his thinking, had resonated with FDR during that earlier visit back in November as Ike guided him through the Tunisian battlefield. Eisenhower later claimed that, at the time, he had had a sense that he was being studied, almost auditioned.

The President gave the most convincing explanation for his unexpected switch during a conversation with his Marine captain son, Jimmy. FDR answered when Jimmy asked why he had, in the end, picked Ike for Overlord: "Eisenhower is the best politician of the military men. He is a natural leader who can convince men to follow him and that was what we need in this position more than any other quality." His own juggling of competing forces in governing the country had taught FDR a priceless lesson. Unless the Overlord leader also possessed a talent to reconcile rival politicians, generals, and admirals from opposite sides of the ocean, military genius alone would not suffice. Marshall could provide the latter. But Eisenhower could best supply the indispensable ingredient, the capacity to guide strong antagonists finally to say yes.

Soon after Eisenhower's appointment, Churchill received encouragement from an unwitting source that he had not acted unwisely in agreeing to support Overlord. Roosevelt made sure that the Prime Minister saw a December 1943 Magic decrypt addressed to Tokyo from Hiroshi Oshima, the Japanese ambassador in Berlin. Oshima had taken up Hitler's invitation to tour the German defenses forming the West Wall in France. In his report, Oshima described fortifications and troop deployments in terms that finally led Churchill to conclude that, while formidable, Hitler's Fortress Europa was not impregnable.

★

By 1943, Russia had dealt Germany its most telling loss thus far in the war, the defeat at Stalingrad. Further, Italy had broken with Germany, surrendered, and been invaded by the Allies. New air and sea anti-submarine tactics, aided by deciphered German codes, had broken the backs of Nazi wolf packs in the North Atlantic. What if, before Overlord could be launched, the Germans bowed to the inevitable and offered to surrender? FDR wanted to be prepared for this possibility, lest the Red Army find clear sailing all the way from the Oder River to the Atlantic Ocean. Thus he endorsed a hyper-secret, three-phased plan code-named Rankin, to which he won Churchill's agreement. Should Germany appear to be collapsing in the west, Rankin A would put an Allied force ashore well in advance of Overlord to take the Cotentin Peninsula and the port of Cherbourg. In the event of a complete Nazi pullout from occupied France and Norway, Rankin B would provide for seizing these territories. Rankin C was predicated on a total German surrender before Overlord. Roosevelt confided to his aides, as part of Rankin C, that if Germany did suddenly collapse, he was prepared to parachute American troops into the heart of Berlin to block the Red Army. "Every regulation, every restriction must go by the board if necessary," the Rankin plan decreed. International niceties were not to stand in the way. The objective was "to transport the Army to Europe rather than obey Board of Trade regulations."

However, despite major setbacks, German defenses stiffened rather than softened. In Italy the enemy held fast at the Cassino line, despite the Allied flanking operation at Anzio. The Germans were retreating in Russia, but not in a rout, rather with good order and discipline. The closer the May 1944 invasion date approached, the more irrelevant Rankin became, until, by the spring, it was shut down and its staff transferred to the main show.

★

Karl von Clausewitz, over a century before, had identified the element crucial to the success of Overlord. ". . . [T]here is an indirect way of gaining superiority of numbers," he wrote. "It does this through surprise—attacking at an unexpected place. Surprise achieves superiority almost as strongly as direct concentration of forces." During the Big Three meeting at Tehran, Churchill had made his famous remark, "Truth is so precious that she should always be attended by a bodyguard of lies." The plotting of Overlord must not only proceed, its progress must also be concealed. Churchill wrote in his memoirs, "Stalin and his comrades greatly appreciated this remark . . . and upon this formal note, our formal conference ended gaily." Before leaving Tehran, FDR and Churchill had settled on a passage in "The Military Conclusions" that read, "In particular it was agreed that a cover plan to mystify and mislead the enemy as regards these operations should be concerted between the Staffs concerned."

Beneath the pavements of Westminster, under four feet of concrete reinforced by old London tramway rails, stood Churchill's wartime command post. Here the British began putting Clausewitz into practice. In December 1943, less than a month after Tehran, two Allied operations were launched, Bodyguard and Fortitude, their planning almost as elaborate as that for Overlord itself. Bodyguard was designed to confuse the Germans as to where the Allies would land. Fortitude was to steer them to the wrong landing site, specifically, to persuade Hitler that a successful invasion across the English Channel had to occur at its narrowest point, the Pas de Calais. London Controlling Section, the deliberately gray-faced organization that oversaw Bodyguard and Fortitude, was led by Colonel John Henry Bevan, sandy-haired, mild-looking, a grandson of the founder of Barclay's Bank, a winner of the Military Cross in the First World War, a stockbroker by trade, and an unlikely professional deceiver.

"I cannot prophesy. I cannot tell you when or where the United Nations are going to strike next in Europe," FDR said during his 1943 State of the Union address. "I cannot tell you whether we are going to hit them in Norway, through the low countries, or in France, or through Sardinia or Sicily or through the Balkans or through Poland—or at several points simultaneously—yes, the Nazis and the Fascists have asked for it—and they are going to get it." Roosevelt was as much anticipating the necessary deceptions of Bodyguard as he was stoking Allied morale.

Hitler's erratic intuition, sometimes brilliant, sometimes mystifying, sometimes dead wrong, played into Allied hands, at least initially. A decrypt brought to FDR as far back as October 9, 1943, enabled the President to read Hitler's thinking about the invasion site. The Führer invited General Oshima to the Wolfsschanze (Wolf's Lair), his headquarters in Rastenburg, East Prussia, located in a mosquito-infested marshland chosen,

Hitler complained, because, "No doubt some government department found the land was cheapest there." Whatever the discomforts of the dank bunkers at the Wolfsschanze, Ambassador Oshima still prized his private moments with Hitler and the confidences entrusted to him. Oshima's latest intercepted cable reported that Hitler had told him, "I am inclined to believe that the Allies would land in the Balkans. . . ."

Still, a landing in France could never be omitted from Hitler's calculations. By entering the minds of Allied strategists, the Germans could narrow the options considerably. The attack would likely have to get under way by moonlight to help the invading fleet stay in formation. Troops would probably be put ashore just as day was breaking in order to give them some visibility without subjecting them to enemy fire in broad daylight. The attack must occur during a season when the waters were not too rough. The troops would likely come ashore, not at high tide when the landing craft would be impaled on the upright steel girders spiking the West Wall beaches, nor at low tide, when the troops would have to traverse too much open beach under heavy fire. They would probably land midway between high and low tide. All these conditions, as the Germans could calculate as well as the Allies, coalesced on the French coast in a few days in late May or the fifth, sixth, and seventh of June.

★

Early in January 1944, German intelligence services obtained a copy of a British telegram to General Eisenhower classified "Most Secret." "Our object is to get Turkey into the war as early as possible," the message read, "and in any case to maintain a threat to the Germans from the eastern end of the Mediterranean until Overlord is launched." This most zealously guarded code word, Overlord, had found its way into German hands by a convoluted route. Since the message concerned Turkey, a copy had been sent to the British ambassador in Ankara, Sir Hughe Knatchbull-Hugessen. The ambassador had a valet, a swarthy, compact Albanian in his forties, heavily browed and black mustachioed, named Elyesa Bazna. His credentials included petty thief, locksmith, fireman, and chauffeur. Bazna had used his locksmith skills to copy a key to the ambassador's bedroom safe. While the ambassador was in his office or entertaining guests, Bazna was photographing documents from the safe and selling them to the Germans, including the above telegram. He was to become a legend, known to every intelligence buff, moviegoer, and reader of espionage thrillers as Cicero.

The Allies learned of the alarming leak of the invasion code word through OSS Bern's well-placed agent in Berlin, the inconspicuous Fritz Kolbe. While going over incoming traffic in the foreign office, Kolbe spotted the intercepted British message mentioning Overlord which Cicero had sold to the Germans. Kolbe, on his next phony courier run to Bern, strapped the message to his leg along with other Reich secrets and delivered them to Allen Dulles. The Bern OSS chief, upon learning that the Nazis had a source directly inside the British embassy in Turkey, immediately phoned his British counterpart, the MI6 man in Switzerland, and suggested a quiet rendezvous at an inn outside of town. There he explained that an unidentified person somehow had gained access to the most sensitive documents in the British embassy in Turkey and was passing them to the Germans. The Britisher alerted his government, and soon counterespionage agents were swarming over the Ankara embassy and interrogating the staff, except those employed in the ambassador's residence. Cicero, feeling the approaching breath of exposure, smashed his camera, threw it into a river, never photographed another document, and resigned his post on April 20, 1944.

The crafty German ambassador to Turkey, Franz von Papen, meanwhile, had cabled Berlin his guess as to what "Overlord" meant: "Apparently attack out of England." Still, it was only a single word, submerged in the torrent of communications the Germans intercepted, just as strong signals of a Japanese attack on Pearl Harbor had been lost in the effluvia of unrelated and irrelevant data. The word "Overlord," by itself, did not betray the crucial where or when. These were the truths that Bodyguard and Fortitude had been created to befog.

British intelligence operatives would later claim that they had known about Cicero all along and had manipulated him as a conduit for supplying disinformation to Berlin. It was a plausible defense from an espionage service caught with its pants down. Years after the war, however, in 1951, the British foreign secretary, Ernest Bevin, admitted in the House of Commons that "the ambassador's valet succeeded in photographing a number of highly secret documents in the Embassy and selling the films to the Germans." Bevin offered no defense that Cicero had been under British control. The man was never caught.

——— ══ ★ ══ ———

Chapter XX

The White House Is Penetrated

THE WORLD War II myth that Prime Minister Churchill, through Ultra, knew that Coventry was about to be bombed but failed to alert the city in order to protect the codebreaking secret has proved a durable tale. However, there has remained untold for well over a half century an actual tragedy that was indeed concealed in order to protect Ultra.

Since 1943 clouds of British bombers by night and American aircraft by day had been leveling Germany's cities. President Roosevelt, through Magic and the now-sprawling OSS spy chain, received eyewitness accounts of the depth of this destruction. In one instance, Iran's minister to Sweden had been permitted to stop in Berlin to visit his wife's grave while en route from Stockholm to Tehran. Continuing his journey, the diplomat provided an OSS agent in Turkey with his firsthand account of daily life in the battered German capital. Bill Donovan had the report of the Iranian's debriefing hand-delivered to the White House. From this account, FDR learned that, except for one, "all the major railroad stations in Berlin have been completely demolished . . . 50 percent of the buildings on Unter den Linden are intact and the other 50 percent destroyed. . . . not a wall is standing at the airport which is a shambles. . . . Informant claims he drove in a cab through central and west Berlin for a distance of six miles without observing a single house standing. . . . For the most part, the population of Berlin is living underground." During a single raid in March, the report went on, forty thousand Polish and Russian conscript workers, barred from shelters, were killed. The Berliners' best hope, the Iranian believed, was "that England and America may, in self interest, turn against Russia once they see that the Soviet is about to assume complete control." Yet, for all this punishment, the President must have been surprised by the informant's conclusion: "The essential business of Berlin proceeds to function doggedly."

At one point raids became so devastating that General Marshall warned the President that the Germans were threatening to try downed American and British airmen as war criminals. Marshall recommended that Roosevelt and Churchill issue a joint warning "that immediate retaliatory action will be taken if such threats are carried out." FDR craftily told Marshall, "It seems to me that such action need not be announced before hand but that it should be put into effect the minute the Germans start anything. I think the American public would back this up. . . . I think I am right in saying that we and the British hold more German prisoners than they hold of ours."

The Bletchley Park codebreakers contributed to the success of Allied raids. American bomber pilots, gathered in makeshift briefing rooms throughout southern England, heard their meteorological officer describe weather conditions all the way to the target and back. The airmen were unaware that the source of this data was not anemometers, barometers, or balloons, but Ultra decrypts of German weather reports.

On February 15, 1944, General Marshall sent FDR a memorandum concerning a German message out of Rome that Bletchley Hall had broken. The Wehrmacht commander had reported that thirty American bombers attacked a train while it was crossing a bridge near Orvieto, Italy. "Entire train on bridge when first bombs, including heaviest calibre, dropped on it," the broken report read. Sixteen cars had been completely destroyed. The German commander described a hellish scene: "Half of these [cars] fell into the riverbed and other half burnt or shattered on the bridge. About five hundred prisoners, mainly English, killed. Salvage and rescue hampered or even prevented by considerable number of delayed action bombs so that some of the severely wounded, who would otherwise have been saved, also died." Churchill, upon learning through this Ultra decrypt of the grisly, unwitting American assault on his own troops, instructed Sir Stewart Menzies, chief of the British secret service, "[T]his information should be given to President with assurance that no feeling of complaint whatsoever is implied." The "Most Secret" message was to be seen by only General Marshall and the President, "and information should not (repeat not) be made available to any other person." The British also made clear that knowledge of this catastrophe would be tightly circumscribed at their end. Beyond the Prime Minister, the secret was known to only a handful of top officials "and will not (repeat not) be passed down to lower levels." Before passing Churchill's message along to FDR, Marshall added a note: "The reason the British authorities are so insistent that no other eyes than yours, mine and [General Clayton] Bissell's [Army G-2] see this, as a leak would point directly to British control of German code."

The story of Churchill's refusal to warn Coventry that it was to be bombed proved apocryphal. The hushed-up account of American bombers killing hundreds of British POWs, however, provided an actual instance of the Prime Minister's determination to protect Ultra.

★

Two types of bodies circled the Roosevelt heavens—planets, such as General Marshall, Admiral Leahy, and Secretary Stimson, steady in their orbits, unspectacular, dependable; and shooting stars, fiery, unpredictable, occasionally burning out—a Bill Bullitt, a George Earle, a Wild Bill Donovan. The latter group exhibited a pattern. They were all mold breakers, channel jumpers, charmers, and high-wire artists, mirroring sides of FDR's character. Late in 1943, Donovan embarked on one of his boldest gambits. With the President's approval he flew to Russia to attempt to arrange a swap of American and Soviet intelligence missions—an OSS station in Moscow for an NKVD station in Washington. Donovan arrived in the snow-blanketed Soviet capital two days before Christmas, where he was taken in tow by FDR's troubleshooting ambassador, Averell Harriman, and greeted warmly by the ordinarily dour Soviet foreign minister, Vyacheslav Molotov. Two days after Christmas, through Molotov's intercession, Donovan and Harriman found themselves inside the NKVD headquarters, a grim, czarist structure at 2 Dzerzhinsky Street. There they met with the Soviet foreign intelligence chief, General Pavel Fitin, and a man introduced only as General Alexander Ossipov. The latter, unknown to the Americans, was Gaik Ovakimyan, the NKVD official in charge of subversion in foreign countries, including the United States. The two Soviets formed a classic good-cop bad-cop duo. Fitin, blond, blue-eyed, and soft-spoken, appeared an unlikely spymaster. Ossipov/Ovakimyan, however, was described by another American present as easily passing for "the boon companion of Boris Karloff." Donovan proceeded to lay out his espionage exchange scheme, arguing that it would enable two allies fighting the same enemy to trade useful intelligence, to avoid operations that stepped on each other's toes, and to swap methods for carrying out sabotage inside the Reich. As a sweetener, he immediately offered to share with the NKVD the OSS's spy-training curriculum. By the end of the day, Fitin had agreed to the exchange and to allowing Donovan to set up an OSS mission in Moscow under Colonel John Haskell, a close Donovan associate, also present. The proposal was placed before Stalin, who approved with an alacrity that might have aroused suspicion. The Soviets soon announced that their candidate to head a seven-man NKVD office in Washington would be Colonel A. G. Grauer.

On January 6, 1944, in a raging snowstorm, Donovan flew out of Moscow. All that now remained for him was to win approval of his scheme from the Joint Chiefs of Staff and the President. But J. Edgar Hoover beat him to the punch. The FBI chief had quickly ferreted out what Donovan had been up to in Russia, likely tipped off by Army G-2, his ally in the turf battles against Donovan. He dictated a letter to his secretary, Helen Gandy, headed "Personal and Confidential" to "Dear Harry," and had it hand-delivered to his tested conduit, Harry Hopkins. Hopkins read Hoover's letter and told Grace Tully to make sure the President saw it "at once." Hoover's warning was dire. Donovan's U.S.-Soviet intelligence swap was a Russian ruse, the FBI chief charged, "a highly dangerous and most undesirable procedure" that would "establish in the United States a unit of the Russian Secret Service which has admittedly for its purpose the penetration into the official secrets of various government agencies."

Donovan did not get to the President until five days later, and was now on the defensive. He had not yet won approval for the exchange from the Joint Chiefs of Staff, but he gamely assured the President that his prospects looked good. The move was wise, he insisted, offering "[m]ilitary advantages accruing to the United States in the field of intelligence both in so far as Germany and Japan were concerned." As for Hoover's alarm over Soviet penetration of the United States, in Donovan's judgment, the FBI chief displayed surprising naïveté. "I don't need to suggest to you that the OGPU [predecessor of the NKVD] came here," Donovan pointed out, "with the coming of Amtorg and is already here under the protection of the embassy. . . . I was not unmindful of someone's trying to make capital of the OGPU's coming here," he added, "but I think the complete answer is 1. They are already here and 2. The military people who come here are in the open and under such rules as are imposed by us and here solely and only for military reasons and joint operations against our common enemy." The President, Donovan thought, appeared to agree.

Hoover, however, was leaving nothing to chance. He began squeezing Donovan from another direction. He went to his nominal boss, Attorney General Francis Biddle, warning that the NKVD was already "engaged in attempting to obtain highly confidential information concerning War Department secrets." Biddle sent Hoover's letter to FDR, alerting the President to another danger. "Under the statutes, these Russian agents would probably have to register," Biddle pointed out. "Public knowledge of such an arrangement might have serious consequences. I have been informed that you have approved the plan generally, but I do not know whether you have considered its implications." The implication Biddle so delicately raised was that 1944 was a presidential election year, and Roosevelt must know that Hoover, if thwarted, was not above making damaging leaks to the press.

The President threw up his hands. He sent Biddle's letter to Admiral William Leahy, his military chief of staff, asking, "What do we do next?" Three weeks of infighting ensued among the War Department, the OSS, and the FBI, but Donovan never had a chance. Hoover, in that era, was a national hero, the director whose G-men had triumphed over John Dillinger, "Pretty Boy" Floyd, "Baby Face" Nelson, and other arch criminals who had terrorized the country. Hoover's capture of dozens of Nazi agents and saboteurs had been front-page stories. Donovan's plan may have been good for intelligence but it was risky politics. Going into a possible fourth term campaign with the albatross around his neck that he had allowed Soviet spies to settle on the banks of the Potomac was not something Roosevelt relished. Leaving the delivery of the coup de grâce to Leahy, who also opposed Donovan's scheme, FDR directed the admiral to inform the service chiefs and Bill Donovan that "an exchange of O.S.S. and N.K.V.D. missions between Moscow and Washington is not appropriate at the present time. . . ."

The irrepressible Donovan was not through. His plan to exchange missions had been torpedoed, but he went ahead, on his own hook, swapping intelligence with the NKVD. He provided the Russians with American special weapons manuals, miniature cameras, and microfilming equipment. The Russians, in turn, revealed their techniques for sabotaging German installations. Donovan also assured the Soviets that once the election was out of the way, he could get the mission exchange back on track.

★

One man who knew immediately of the President's decision to kill off the spy swap was Duncan Lee, another lawyer protégé of Bill Donovan's who had become the director's executive assistant. Almost immediately upon formation of the OSS, Moscow had made the fledgling espionage service a priority target. The Soviet intelligence strategy for 1942 specifically stated: "[O]ur task is to insert there our people and carry out cultivation with their help." The NKVD found a wedge in Lee, who epitomized the establishment figures inhabiting the upper reaches of the OSS. Thirty years old in 1944, he had been born to missionary parents in Nanking, China. He had returned home and graduated from the Woodbury Forest School in Virginia, took a B.A. from Yale, became a Rhodes scholar at Oxford, then received a law degree from Yale. A Communist intermediary described Lee as "[a]verage height, medium brown hair and light eyes, glasses, rather studious looking." Though Lee was not a Communist, he would prove a profitably placed NKVD source. Immediately after graduating from law school, Lee had been snapped up by Wild Bill's Manhattan law firm, Donovan & Leisure, and subsequently followed his boss to Washington. By the time the COI became the OSS, Lee had received a direct Army commission, risen to the rank of captain, and worked in the Donovan front office secretariat. Essentially, whatever happened in the OSS was known to Duncan Lee.

Early in 1943, Lee opened his fourth-floor apartment door at 3014 Dent Place in Washington to a plain-looking thirty-five-year-old who introduced herself as Helen Grant. "I am the gal who is going to be your contact," she explained. The woman was Elizabeth Bentley, the Soviet courier. She would one day turn against communism, but at this point she was a steadfast party apparatchik. An FBI agent later described Bentley as "buxom, blue-eyed, had big feet, short, brown curly hair, poor taste in clothes and was neither attractive nor unattractive." Her background was not dissimilar to Lee's. She claimed ancestry from *Mayflower* forebears and was a bookish 1930 graduate of Vassar. During the Depression, Bentley had become disillusioned with capitalism and was drawn to the Communist Party. This product of a stern New England upbringing became a welcome recruit to the Soviets, one of whom described her as "a genuine American Aryan." Her principal duty was to collect intelligence from a circle of sources in the American government and pass it on to her NKVD controllers.

Bentley and Lee began meeting in a drugstore on Wisconsin Avenue and once in a German beer hall on Fifteenth Street. Lee, according to the courier, passed to her ". . . highly secret information on what the OSS was doing, such as, for example, that they were trying to make secret negotiations in the Balkans . . . parachuting people into Hungary, that they were sending OSS people into Turkey. . . ." The Soviets were delighted with Lee. Bentley's superior and lover, Jacob Golos, notified Moscow concerning Lee: "Cables coming to the State Department go through his hands. He collects them and shows them to Donovan at his discretion. All the agent information from Europe and the rest of the world also comes through his hands."

Bentley, however, found Lee a difficult source. "He was one of the most nervous people with whom I had to deal," she observed. Lee forbade Bentley to phone him, refused to turn over actual documents, and permitted her no note-taking in his presence. As Bentley described their routine to Moscow, "A long time ago, I had to promise him that I would not write down data communicated by him. Therefore, I have to remember his data, until I am elsewhere and can write it down. . . . [H]e is one of 'the weakest of the weak sisters,' nervous and fearing his own shadow."

Still, Lee's take proved worth her pains. On the delicate matter of Poland's future, Lee described an OSS report crossing his desk that revealed Churchill was willing to cede Eastern Prussia to Poland. When Bentley asked Lee about activities at Oak Ridge, Tennessee, ". . . he told me," she later claimed, "that he had word that something very secret was going on at that location. He did not know what, but he said it must be something supersecret because it was shrouded in such mystery and so heavily guarded." Oak Ridge was the site of the Manhattan Project's operation to separate U235 from U238 in sufficient quantity to make an atomic bomb. At one of their drugstore rendezvous, according to Bentley, Lee gave her a detailed account of a White House meeting over Donovan's proposed OSS-NKVD exchange, including Admiral Leahy's opposition. At the prospect of NKVD agents coming to Washington, Lee told her, "I'm finished. They'll come to call on me, and when I let them in, they'll shake my hand and say, 'Well done, comrade.' "

Though fearing exposure, Lee continued to cooperate with Bentley. He told her that the OSS security staff had compiled a list entitled "Persons Suspected of Being Communists on the Agency's Payroll." A message from the NKVD New York station to General Fitin in Moscow read, "According to Kokh [Lee's apparent code name] advice a list of 'reds' has been compiled by IZBA," the code name for the OSS. Four of the names on the list of suspects, Lee revealed, were indeed providing intelligence to the Russians.

By 1944, Lee's personal life was becoming messy and his paranoia mounting. His wife discovered that he was having an affair with another Communist courier, Mary Price. He feared Donovan had begun to suspect him. He distrusted Elizabeth Bentley. Another NKVD contact, code-named X, reported, after dealing with Lee, that he "came so scared to both meetings that he could not hold a cup of coffee since his hands trembled." Lee eventually broke off with the NKVD and spied no more. The Soviets were just as happy to see this emotional wreck go away. Through him, however, for a period of over two years, whatever the OSS shared with the White House, and vice versa, was often available to the Soviet Union. While representing the prize Soviet catch in the OSS, Duncan Lee was hardly alone. Post–Cold War examination of NKVD documents suggests that the number of Soviet agents planted in the OSS ran into the double digits.

Elizabeth Bentley provides interesting glimpses into how the NKVD taught her to deal with contacts on her courier route. In order to avoid being followed, she was instructed to locate "drug stores with two exits, if possible, and movie theatres and other places that would be suitable for dodging in and out rather quickly, and thereby eluding any surveillance." Another technique was to have a partner wait behind at a suitable distance to see if she was being followed. If a suspicious car appeared outside a building that she was exiting, Bentley was told to "memorize the last two numbers of the license plate, and then attempt to determine if this particular car was following you." A way to shake a car tail was "to go down one or several one-way streets in the opposite direction to the regular vehicle traffic." Bentley was advised to cross and recross the street to determine if anyone was following her erratic movements. She was never to turn around, indicating that she was aware of being followed. As a last resort, if a tail could not be shaken, she was "to turn around and start following the person who was following you." If she was meeting a fellow agent and suspected she was being followed, she should wait until her contact was in sight and then light a cigarette to warn her accomplice away.

If she had incriminating material in her apartment her instructions were to "place a book behind my front door. . . . In the event that anyone had entered my apartment in the meantime, this book, of course, would not be in the same place I left it." If she kept sensitive papers or equipment in a trunk, "a thin black thread should be placed around the lock . . . in such a manner that if it were opened in my absence, I would be able to tell upon my return." For her travels between New York and Washington, "I was to remove all identification marks from my clothing, and was also instructed not to carry anything that would indicate to anyone my real identity." No conversation of substance was ever to be carried out over the telephone, and she was cautioned to listen for "any unusual buzzing or clicks" suggesting the line was tapped. When using a pay phone, she "should either use a phone booth in between two booths already occupied or else should select a booth which would allow observation of persons going in to occupy adjacent booths." Either Bentley's training was sound or she was a natural, since this nondescript woman, code-named Good Girl by her controllers, was never caught in the six years during which she carried microfilm and classified documents in her knitting bag between American spies in Washington and her NKVD handlers in New York.

Soviet agents like Elizabeth Bentley were cogs in a spy apparatus dating back to 1933, when Roosevelt granted diplomatic recognition to the Soviet Union. The image the President had of a Russian spy was of a wild-haired, hot-eyed labor agitator. The truth was startlingly different. Among those serving the Soviet cause, many, like Lee, were impeccable members of the American establishment, some known socially to the Roosevelts. Martha Dodd was the beautiful, flamboyant, reckless daughter of William E. Dodd, a historian from the University of Chicago who served as FDR's ambassador to Germany from 1933 to 1938. Miss Dodd openly confessed, "I have a weakness for the Russians." She displayed this penchant by plunging into a love affair with a Russian diplomat, Boris Vinogradov, a romance stage-managed by the NKVD. About her parent whom she was all too willing to betray, she proudly announced to her Soviet controllers, "[M]y father has great influence on Hull and Roosevelt. . . . I have access mainly to the personal, confidential correspondence of my father with the U.S. State Department and the U.S. President," she boasted. As an NKVD officer put it, Martha "checks Ambassador Dodd's reports to Roosevelt in the archive and communicates to us short summaries of the contents." She did not hesitate to use her charms to seduce Nazis as well for whatever intelligence of use to the Soviets she could acquire in bed, numbering among her conquests General Ernst Udet, chief of Luftwaffe plane production.

When her father's tenure as ambassador ended, Martha Dodd returned to America, where the Russians still found use for her. A 1942 cable instructed the New York NKVD station: "She should . . . be guided to approach and deepen her relationship with the President's wife, Eleanor. . . ." Dodd would remain unwavering in her attachment to Marxism, fleeing after the war from FBI investigators to the USSR and Czechoslovakia during which time she and the wealthy Communist she had married, Alfred Stern, were convicted in absentia of spying for the Soviet Union.

Like Martha Dodd, another young socialite who shared her political sympathies had a close connection to the White House. Michael Straight was the son of wealthy parents who were founders of *The New Republic* magazine, and early friends of Franklin and Eleanor. Young Michael had gone to England to study at Cambridge in the thirties. There he joined the Communist Party and was drawn into the web of Soviet spies that included Donald Maclean, Guy Burgess, Harold "Kim" Philby, and Anthony Blunt, later curator of the queen's art collection. The Roosevelt archives show at least five visits to the White House by Michael Straight, invitations to tea, dinner, and, on one occasion, a lone session with FDR. The usher's log for October 21, 1941, lists Straight and his wife as houseguests along with "Mrs. Douglas Fairbanks, Jr." According to *The Haunted Wood* by Weinstein and Vassiliev, who in 1994 were given access to NKVD wartime archives, Straight had discussed with the Roosevelts his interest in finding a job. The First Lady suggested that he take an agricultural credit post in the administration, which Straight found useless for his purposes. Thereafter, he wrote to Theodore Mally, chief of the London NKVD station, that he preferred Treasury or the Federal Reserve Board. "In those places," he said, "possibilities are great because of the influence on Roosevelt. . . . Treasury has great significance. Its head is Henry Morgenthau, who knows my parents well." Straight eventually managed a State Department post, but his deliveries to his Soviet contacts were disappointing. The Nazi-Soviet pact of August 23, 1939, disillusioned the idealistic Straight. By 1942, at age thirty-one, he broke completely with Soviet espionage. As the current chief of the NKVD New York station advised Moscow, Straight believed, "[O]ne should render assistance to the Soviet Union only as long as the war which the USSR wages is advantageous for England and the U.S."

Next door to the White House, in the Treasury building, the NKVD had made another penetration. Well before Pearl Harbor, on July 2, 1941, Treasury secretary Henry Morgenthau, FDR's garrulous Hyde Park neighbor, received a disquieting anonymous phone call. The next day, Morgenthau contacted Harry Dexter White, his advisor on international monetary policy, lend-lease, foreign funds, and later to become assistant Treasury secretary. "I got a very mysterious call last night," Morgenthau explained to White. The caller had said that he had found some of White's papers and "this fellow wanted a reward." The papers contained highly confidential information, and the secretary had been particularly disturbed because the anonymous caller had a "strong German accent." White, valued by Morgenthau as the man "in charge of all foreign affairs for me," had an explanation. He had forgotten the classified papers in his government car on the ride home. The Secret Service investigated, but no German-accented caller was ever traced and the search petered out.

Morgenthau's concern about a leak from his office was understandable, but in the wrong direction. Germany was not the threat in this case. Harry White was one of the American officials whom Whittaker Chambers had fingered as Communist agents at the home of Adolf Berle that long ago September night. No evidence exists that Berle ever alerted Morgenthau to this accusation. The Treasury secretary continued to have implicit faith in the man variously code-named by his Soviet controllers Lawyer, Richard, Jurist, and Reed.

Harry Dexter White, heavyset, full-faced, bespectacled, and mustachioed, was apparently a willing but timorous resource for the NKVD. After meeting with him, a Russian agent cabled Moscow that the Treasury official was "ready for any self-sacrifice; he does not think about his personal security, but a compromise would lead to a scandal. . . . Therefore he would have to be very cautious." Rather than having a Soviet contact come to his apartment, White proposed "infrequent conversations lasting up to half an hour while driving in his automobile." However gingerly handled, the Soviets knew what they wanted from the Treasury official. Pavel Fitin, after receiving a three-page draft memorandum written by White for Morgenthau, noted, "Timely receipt by us of these materials could turn out to be very useful. . . . [A] secret document of the [U.S.] Foreign Economic Administration about the future of Germany . . . would be of major interest to our leading government organizations. . . ."

Ironically, it was not a spy's misstep but an ugly divorce and custody suit that almost blew the lid off Soviet espionage operations in the United States. Katherine Wills Perlo, wife of Victor Perlo, an American supplying secrets to the Soviets from the War Production Board, became so vengeful after the couple divorced and he won custody of their daughter that she warned Perlo she had written to President Roosevelt exposing his spy cell. No record of this letter has surfaced at the Roosevelt archives, though an NKVD source in the Justice Department, Judith Coplon, later claimed that it had indeed been sent. Coplon's knowledge of the letter suggests that the White House bucked Mrs. Perlo's denunciation to the Justice Department for disposal. If so, no action against the Perlo ring took place as a result.

What prompted privileged and sophisticated Americans, a Lee, a Hiss, a Dodd, a Straight, a White, to become servants of communism? The answer lies in an amalgam of their beliefs—capitalism, as demonstrated by the Great Depression, had failed; an American democracy that accommodated racism displayed rank hypocrisy; and a brighter future for mankind could be glimpsed in the example of the Soviet Union. They found little to forgive in their own country and everything to admire in a romanticized vision of Russia. And, doubtless, they savored the adrenaline rush of playing spy, of living double lives and taking risks in a presumably noble cause. If, as has been said, religion was the opiate of the masses, communism was the opiate of these intellectuals.

Their betrayal of their nation's secrets seems malevolent after forty years of Cold War conditioning. But during the war years, their political godhead, the USSR, was America's ally in the struggle against Nazism and fascism. They judged their actions not as treasonous, but simply as a way of making sure that the ally was not shortchanged. Roosevelt was highly sensitive to the fact that the Red Army was losing eight Ivans for every Allied soldier killed in battle. He told Donovan, "Bill, you must treat the Russians with the same trust you do the British. They're killing Germans every day, you know." As a gesture of solidarity, the President asked John Franklin Carter to get for him a recording of a Red Army marching song he liked. "Pappy thought American words could be put to the one he had heard about," Carter noted in his diary. How much different were their meetings with and deliveries to Soviet agents, the American spies could argue, than Roosevelt and Churchill's conferences with Stalin and military aid sent to the Soviet Union? Did they not all serve the same end?

What FDR felt about the nature of communism was best revealed in a note he sent to his Navy secretary, Frank Knox. They had been discussing hiring radio operators who were known Communists. Roosevelt was not opposed. "The Soviet people in Moscow," he told Knox, "are said to have little liking for the American Communists and their methods—especially because it seems increasingly true that the communism of twenty years ago has practically ceased to exist in Russia. At the present time their system is much more like a form of the older Socialism, conducted, however, through a complete dictatorship combined with an overwhelming loyalty to the cause of throwing every German out of Russia."

Not everyone in the administration was as sanguine about the USSR as Roosevelt. Adolf Berle described himself as "[h]aving had my fingers burned in Russian affairs several times in my life." Berle felt no hesitation at blocking the Soviets. When they asked to send engineers into American war plants, he warned: "The list of the military secrets requested itself shows very efficient espionage." He noted in his diary: ". . . [T]he engineers they have wished to let in the plants are the same ones who were doing espionage for Russia and Germany" until the Nazis attacked the USSR. As far as Berle was concerned, "The Russian denouement is unpredictable. There might be a Peace of Brest-Litovsk," he warned the White House, referring to Russia's dropping out of the fight against Germany in World War I.

The Army, Navy, and FBI, guided by Berle, allowed Soviet engineers into the United States to inspect only lend-lease equipment destined for the Soviet Union, and not another gun. It was not until the spring of 1944 that the United States shared the Norden bombsight with the Red Air Force. At one point, Russian navy officials asked the Soviet foreign office to pressure the U.S. embassy in Moscow not only to deliver "specifications of the latest [American] battleship, cruiser, destroyer, and submarine," but to provide the American Navy's secret coding devices. The U.S. naval attaché in Moscow, a Captain Duncan, upon learning of the request, warned Washington that only misplaced "sentiment or plain stupidity" could favor the Russians' request.

How close the Soviets came to penetrating the American government at the highest level is suggested in Vice President Henry Wallace's alleged intentions should he ever become president. Wallace is said to have planned to appoint Laurence Duggan as his secretary of state and Harry Dexter White as his secretary of the Treasury. Given that FDR did not live out his final term, only Harry Truman's displacement of Wallace as vice president in 1944 derailed this possibility.

Chapter XXI

———═★═———

If Overlord Fails

A S 1944 opened, the fifth year of the war for Britain, the third for the United States, the great guessing game was on: Where and when would the Western Allies strike the inevitable blow against the Nazi-held continent, the second front? In the meantime, the offensive from the air continued to deliver fearsome punishment to Germany. City after city lay in ruin. In four consecutive raids on Hamburg, 50,000 civilians were killed and 800,000 left homeless. German towns were being incinerated at a rate of two per month. Given this relentless leveling, strategists pondered whether the enemy might be defeated more cheaply from the air than by a massive bloodletting on the ground. Early in the year, President Roosevelt received an imaginative assessment commissioned by General Hap Arnold. Arnold had asked several of the country's leading historians to review "all secret and confidential intelligence in our possession." The scholars, including Carl Becker of Cornell, Henry S. Commager of Columbia, and Dumas Malone of Harvard, concluded, ". . . [T]here is no substantial evidence that Germany can be bombed out of the war. . . . Surrender will come when, through lack of adequate air defense, Germany finds herself unable to maintain ground operations. . . ." In short, the war had to be won by the foot soldier; airmen could only speed the day.

Bill Donovan forwarded to FDR an Allen Dulles appraisal drawn from Fritz Kolbe and other anti-Nazi Germans traveling between their homeland and Switzerland. "The OSS representative in Bern sees no evidence that the German morale has been greatly affected by recent bombings. . . . There is no longer any such thing as morale in Germany, as we normally use the term," Dulles reported. "There are in Germany millions of tired, discouraged, disillusioned, bewildered, but stubbornly obedient people who see no alternative other than to continue their struggle."

Hitler's detachment from reality was evident in a Magic decrypt of a cable Ambassador Oshima sent to Tokyo at the height of the Allied bombings. While thousand-plane armadas were turning Germany's cities into rubble and ash, Oshima reported that Hitler had ordered his armaments minister, Albert Speer, to proceed at once with a plan for rebuilding Germany as soon as the war was won. Speer, a realist, put together a team of urban planners and went through the motions in order to indulge his Führer's fantasy, while continuing to build tanks, guns, and planes.

The code word Overlord, thanks to Cicero, was now known to the enemy, but it existed in a vacuum, revealing neither time nor place. FDR's military staff advised him that, if the Allies were to achieve tactical surprise, the invasion site and the moment had to be concealed from the enemy until four hours before the troops hit the beaches. Should the Germans divine the plan as little as forty-eight hours in advance, Overlord was doomed. The feints, twists, and deceptions of Bodyguard and Fortitude remained crucial.

An unhappy, though talented actor in the Fortitude charade was one of FDR's favorite generals. The President had known George S. Patton Jr. since the latter's days as a dashing cavalry officer at Washington's Fort Myer. Patton was widely quoted around the capital for his response after spending the night in the company of a beautiful woman not his wife. "A man who does not screw will not fight," was the general's defense. Two weeks before the North African invasion, FDR had invited Patton to join him at the White House to hear what a soldier whose intelligence and bluntness he admired thought about Operation Torch. Soon after the desert victory, Patton regaled the President with a cabled account of a tea given by the sultan of Morocco. "During the tea some screams were heard followed by two shots," Patton wrote the President. "The Sultan excused himself and walked out with great dignity and after a while returned. . . . He said that one of the panthers in the museum had made a very beautiful leap . . . and started to eat up one of the ladies of the harem, but some of the guards had shot it." Patton closed, "The lady was only cut on the throat, and it made little difference as she was not a wife but a concubine. With this slight interruption the tea went on." Finishing Patton's account, FDR told his secretary, "This report must be kept secret until after the close of the war. . . . Patton is a joy and this report of his first days in French Morocco is a classic."

But by 1944, Patton's armor was badly tarnished. His brilliant generalship in North Africa and Sicily had been overshadowed by his slapping of two GIs hospitalized for combat fatigue. Eisenhower, consequently, sidelined him. On D-Day, Patton would not be storming the beaches of France with his onetime subordinate General Omar Bradley or with his detested rival Field Marshal Bernard Montgomery. Instead, the proud, haughty, theatrical soldier would serve as a decoy, a star in the Fortitude deceptions.

Two massive army groups, Montgomery's 21st and what would later become General Omar Bradley's 12th, began assembling in southern and southwestern England for the cross-Channel strike. A third force, the First United States Army Group, FUSAG, supposedly massing in southeastern England opposite the Pas de Calais, was commanded by Patton. One hitch spoiled the FUSAG command for this ambitious soldier. Its genuine units were not under his command but actually under his rivals, Bradley and Montgomery; and the armies he did command were fictitious, except for the Third Army, which was still in the States. To foster the impression that he commanded real troops, Patton moved around England with conspicuous secrecy. He made fire and brimstone speeches to authentic units, cautioning the GIs, on one occasion, "A man must be alert all the time if he expects to stay alive. If not, some German son of a bitch will sneak up behind him and beat him to death with a sock full of shit!" And after they had beaten the Germans, he told the GIs, they were going to lick those "purple-pissin' Japs!"

Stalin, at Tehran, had agreed to perform as an accomplice in Bodyguard. Russia's assignment was to leak intelligence suggesting that the Red Army could not possibly launch a major offensive on the eastern front until at least July; and the Western Allies added clues that D-Day could not take place until the landings could be coordinated with a Russian campaign. The Russians even agreed to make actual diversionary raids at misleading sites. For all the cooperation the Soviets offered, however, the Western Allies dragged their feet in confiding the D-Day secret to their partner. The initial policy had been to say nothing. As late as November 1943, the Joint Chiefs of Staff instructed General John R. Deane, heading

the American military mission in Moscow, ". . . [D]etails for the preparation for the operation Overlord should not be disclosed to the Russians."
But this exclusion proved impractical after the deal made at Tehran to co-
ordinate D-Day with a Soviet offensive in the East. Stalin demanded to be
told the precise details and date of the invasion. On April 14, 1944,
Churchill sent a cable asking FDR, "Would it not be well for you and me
to send a notice to Uncle Joe [Stalin] about the date of Overlord?" Roosevelt cabled back that a message had already been sent to General Deane
and to British General Brocas Burrows in Moscow instructing them to inform the Russians, ". . . [I]t is our firm intention to launch Overlord on the
agreed date" May 31, which might be pushed back or forward a day or two
depending on first light, the tides, the moon, and the weather. The President added that Burrows and Deane should "pay a handsome tribute to the
magnificent progress of the Soviet armies" to encourage Stalin to begin
carrying out the simultaneous attack.

The Russians, though reluctantly let into the secret, did make one extraordinary contribution to Overlord. Over a year before, the Red Army
had mauled Germany's 320th Infantry Division, capturing its codes and
classified documents. The 320th was the force that had smashed Allied
troops at Dieppe on August 19, 1942, during a small-scale landing
launched to test German coastal defenses in France. After bloodily beating
off the landing force, the 320th's officers prepared a critique of all the mis-
takes the Allies had made, a virtual how-not-to manual. The Russians
turned over this analysis to the British, who shared it with the Americans.
An Army G-2 officer described the critique of Dieppe as "probably the
most important document exploited in preparation for D-Day."

Kept from the D-Day secret was another presumed ally. General
Charles de Gaulle, leader of the French Committee of National Liberation,
was now operating out of Algiers. The proud, sensitive De Gaulle had, by
the spring of 1944, managed to alienate both Roosevelt and Churchill by
styling himself the head of the French government-in-exile. The two leaders were willing to accept De Gaulle as commander of Free French forces
and of the French resistance, but they resented his presumption that he led
France. So annoyed was Roosevelt with De Gaulle's arrogance that at one
point he suggested the imperious general be arrested and kept under guard.
Churchill declared, "We call him Joan of Arc, and we're looking for some
bishops to burn him."

FDR cabled Churchill about the Free French, "Personally, I do not think
that we can give military information to a source which has a bad record of

secrecy." The Prime Minister agreed, telling FDR that De Gaulle should not be allowed to leave Algiers for London until "D-Day at dawn." Still, keeping De Gaulle in the dark proved ticklish. As Churchill advised FDR, "The resistance army numbers 175,000 men." These underground fighters were counted on, once Overlord was launched, to blow up bridges and rail lines, to harass German troops from the rear, to do everything possible to slow the shift of enemy reinforcements to the invasion beaches. At an opportune moment, Roosevelt and Churchill wanted De Gaulle to go on the air to appeal to the French people to support the invasion. But, kept in the dark as Overlord's stepchild, the Frenchman was not eager to cooperate. Making De Gaulle privy to the operation too soon, however, risked having the crucial date leaked to the French underground, which the Germans had penetrated. Telling him too late would negate the value of his appeal to his countrymen. In the end, FDR and Churchill agreed that De Gaulle should be brought to England, but not until twenty-four hours before D-Day, to be briefed by Eisenhower. Ike was to lead him to believe that the assault on the Normandy beaches was only a diversion. The misled De Gaulle grudgingly agreed to make the broadcast to his people.

FDR worried about another soft spot in security. Obeying the old adage that the enemy of my enemy is my friend, many Irish, in their hatred for the British, behaved sympathetically toward Germany. Early in the war, FDR had been angered by Irish prime minister Eamon de Valera's refusal to grant the United States anti-submarine bases on Ireland's west coast. Now, with Overlord approaching, Bill Donovan reported to Roosevelt, "[A] great deal of information pertaining to Allied activities in England and Ulster comes from the German embassy in Dublin." Fritz Kolbe, in scanning the Nazi foreign office correspondence which he passed to Allen Dulles in Bern, reported that German diplomats in Dublin had managed to identify six hundred air installations in England involved in Overlord.

When FDR learned that agents of the German intelligence service, the Sicherheitsdienst (SD), equipped with wireless radios, were parachuting outside Galway, he decided that Irish neutrality had been stretched far enough. He found particularly disconcerting that every move of the U.S. XV Corps, stationed in Ulster and preparing to transfer to England for Overlord, was reported to the German General Staff by Abwehr agents in Ireland. FDR instructed the American ambassador, David Gray, to deliver a note to President De Valera charging that Irish neutrality "continues to operate in favor of the Axis powers." The note ended with Roosevelt's demand that the Irish shut down the German and Japanese embassies in

Dublin, seize their radios, and sever diplomatic relations with Tokyo and Berlin. De Valera, as much the politician as FDR, knew how far he dared push his countrymen in a tilt toward Britain. Consequently, Roosevelt's pressure only partially succeeded. Police from the Irish Special Branch did raid the Axis missions in Dublin and seize their radios. But the Irish government did not end its relations with Germany or Japan.

That unimpeachable source, Ambassador Oshima, continued as Roosevelt's unwitting eyes and ears, revealing the prized secret of the enemy's strength. Early in 1944, Oshima saw Hitler and, as usual, faithfully reported to Tokyo the Führer's words. In this conversation, Hitler confided to him, "Now as for the question of the second front in the west; no matter when or at what point it comes I have made adequate preparations for meeting it. In Finland we have seven divisions; in Norway, twelve; in Denmark, six; in France, including Belgium and the low countries, sixty-two. . . . I have got together as many armored divisions as possible; among them are four SS Divisions and the Hermann Goering Divisions, so you see what I have been able to do in the way of preparing. But how vast is that sea coast! It would be utterly impossible for me to prevent some sort of landing somewhere or other. But all they can do is establish a bridgehead. I will stop, absolutely, any second front in the real sense of the word." Hitler described his trump card. "Then too, there is that revenge against England. We are going to do it principally with rocket-guns. Everything is now ready. Practice shows that they are extremely effective. . . . I cannot tell you just when we will begin, but we are going to really do something to the British Isles." Oshima pressed for more detail on the second front and asked, "Does Your Excellency have any idea where they may land?" "Honestly, I can say no more than that I do not know," Hitler answered. "For a second front, beyond any doubt, the most effective area would be the Straits of Dover, but to land there would require great readiness and its difficulty would be great. Consequently, I don't think that the enemy would run such a risk. On the other hand, along the Bordeaux coast and in Portugal the defenses are relatively weak, so this zone might be a possibility." Wherever the blow was struck, Hitler assured his ally, "We Germans have plenty of plans, and listen, I don't want you to say anything about them to a living soul."

Early in May, German radio monitors on the Dutch coast believed they had scored what Walter Schellenberg, their SD chief, rated a bull's-eye. By then, German engineers had succeeded in unscrambling the more complex device developed by the Bell Telephone System for protecting the highest-level Allied phone conversations. Barely a month before the invasion was to take place, monitors at Eindhoven listened in on a five-minute transatlantic talk between Roosevelt and Churchill. The breakthrough, however, proved more impressive in technique than in substance. The two leaders discussed the massive invasion buildup in southern England, but were mute on where and when. The transcript, delivered to Hitler, contained a curious good-bye from Roosevelt which the enemy searched for hidden meaning: "Well, we will do our best—now I will go fishing."

As the date for Overlord neared, Hitler abandoned earlier guesses that the Allies might strike through the Balkans, Scandinavia, Portugal, or the French Atlantic coast. He issued Directive 51, pinpointing the Pas de Calais: "For it is there that the enemy must and will attack," even though "diversionary attacks," as at Normandy, "are to be expected." He was now telling Ambassador Oshima, whose report was again snatched by Magic, "They would establish a bridgehead at Normandy or Brittany, and that after seeing how things went, they would embark on establishing a real second front in the Straits." Hitler also predicted with alarming closeness that "the Cotentin [Peninsula] would be the first target of the enemy." Consequently, two seasoned German armored divisions and two infantry divisions were added to the Normandy defenses. Still, Hitler kept his strongest forces facing Dover, across the Pas de Calais.

Three weeks before D-Day, FDR sent a proposal classified "Top Secret" to Churchill and Stalin. As soon as the invasion was under way, he suggested that he broadcast the following message to the Continent: "What I want to impress upon the people of Germany and their sympathizers is the inevitability of their defeat. . . . Every German life that is lost from now on is an unnecessary loss. From a cold-blooded point of view, it is true that the Allies will suffer losses as well; but the Allies so greatly outnumber the Germans in population and resources that on a relative basis the Germans will be far harder hit. . . . The government of the United States—with nearly twice the population of Germany—send word to the people of Germany that this is the time to abandon the teachings of evil." Churchill did not like the idea. "I brought your No. 341 before the Cabinet," he cabled back. "Considerable concern was expressed at the tone of friendship shown to the Germans at this moment when the troops are about to engage. . . . The message might conceivably be taken as a peace feeler." Stalin was equally negative. "I have received your message regarding the appeal to the German people. . . . Taking into consideration the whole experience of war with the Germans and the character of the Germans, I think that the proposal by you cannot bring positive effect. . . ."

At the same time that FDR was proposing this appeal to the Germans, his private operative John Franklin Carter suggested to him something more devilish, born in the imagination of Putzi Hanfstaengl. "I assume that somewhere here or in England we already have a man who can imitate Hitler's voice and style in speechmaking," Carter told the President. "On the eve of the invasion, let the fake Hitler broadcast over all of our black radio stations along these lines: Instruct the German troops, German civilians and citizens of occupied countries to put up only a token resistance to the invasion and to cooperate with Anglo-American forces." Carter went on to suggest that the phony Führer declare "that he has reached an understanding with the leaders of England and America for Anglo-American forces to cooperate with Germany in holding back the Jewish hordes of Asiatic Bolshevists from Europe. Let him state that U.S. bombers will soon establish air-bases in Germany to enable the forces of civilization to reconquer Moscow, Leningrad, Stalingrad etc."

Oddly, FDR, always so cautious not to provoke Stalin, did not reject Carter's scheme out of hand, but sent it to the country's propaganda chief, Elmer Davis, head of the Office of War Information, with a note asking, "What do you think of this idea?" Davis displayed a healthy skepticism, advising the President, "For a matter of two or three hours it might cause considerable confusion in Germany." But, Davis warned, "the success of the invasion is not likely to depend on two or three hours." Putzi's brainstorm ended up in FDR's wastebasket.

Though the Germans were still in the dark about Overlord, Churchill was haunted by the operation's potentially exorbitant cost in bloodshed. At one point the Prime Minister told Eisenhower, "When I think of the beaches of Normandy choked with the flower of American and British youth, and when in my mind's eye I see the tides running red with their blood, I have my doubts. I have my doubts." British commanders reported that 90 percent of their junior officers did not expect to survive D-Day. General Omar Bradley discovered that 90 percent of the men of the 29th Infantry Division, destined to hit Omaha Beach, also expected to die. An alarmed Bradley gave the division a pep talk dismissing the likelihood of casualties so high. But driving back to London with his aide, he confessed, "I doubt if I did much good."

On May 7, with the invasion date less than a month off, Churchill lamented to FDR the number of innocent French lives that would be lost when Allied bombers began blasting rail centers. "I am personally by no means convinced that this is the best way to use our air forces in the preliminary period, and still think that the GAF [German air force] should be the main target." Early estimates by his war cabinet were that French civilian casualties could reach 20,000 dead and 60,000 injured. Subsequently, the estimate was revised downward to 10,000 dead. Still, Churchill found the price appalling, and he told Roosevelt, ". . . [T]he war cabinet shares my apprehension of the bad effect which will be produced upon the French civilian population by these slaughters, all taking place so long before D-Day. They may easily bring out a great revulsion in French feeling towards their approaching United States and British liberators." But General Eisenhower wanted rail lines that were capable of moving German troops to the beaches to be interdicted. And FDR, unlike Churchill, was disinclined to overrule the judgments of his military chiefs.

Less than a week before D-Day, the President received precise knowledge of how the Germans were bracing for the attack. On May 28, Oshima again met with Hitler and asked, "I wonder what ideas you have on how the Second Front will be carried out?" According to the ambassador's dispatch to Tokyo, the Führer, sticking by his earlier hunch, answered, "Well, as for me, judging from relatively ominous portents, I think that *Ablenkungsoperazionen* (diversionary action) will take place against Norway, Denmark, the southern part of Western France and the coasts of the French Mediterranean—various places. After that, after they have established bridgeheads on the Norman and Brittany Peninsulas and seen how the prospect appears, they will come forward with the establishment of an all out Second Front in the area of the Straits of Dover." Both Bodyguard and Fortitude were evidently working. Roosevelt had it from Hitler's mouth, courtesy of the codebreakers at Arlington Hall. The timing of the invasion, however, was beginning to pierce the fog of disinformation. Oshima spoke to the chief of German intelligence in Bern, who told him, ". . . [M]ost indications point toward this action sometime around the last of May." It was harrowingly close. As for the where of Overlord, the same officer told Oshima, "[I]n my judgment they will strike with might against the Netherlands, Belgium, and west coast of France. . . ." The other predicted sites were too garbled for the Magic codebreakers to decipher.

Every night, members of the French resistance huddled around their clandestine shortwave radios listening to the recital of short, seemingly meaningless "personal" messages broadcast by the BBC from London. They had been alerted that when they heard the line by the French poet Paul Verlaine, "Les sanglots longs des violons de l'automne" (The long sobs of the violins of autumn), the invasion would occur within fifteen days. When a second Verlaine line, "Blessant mon coeur d'une langueur monotone" (Wounding my heart with a dull languor), was broadcast, the invasion was about to begin. Abwehr agents, too, knew the two-part code. They had beaten it out of a captured resistance leader. The first signal was heard on June 1. On June 5, at 9:15 P.M., a German monitoring station under a concrete bunker at Tourcoing in northern France picked up the second Verlaine line. Though distributed throughout Wehrmacht commands, this warning did not provoke a heightened state of readiness beyond what already existed.

The hour had arrived. All was risked on this cross-Channel throw of the dice. No contingency plan existed. If Overlord failed, it could not be re-mounted.

Chapter XXII

———===★===———

Cracks in the Reich

D URING THE war years, not all the President's tightly held secrets were military. For the world's greatest power, immersed sinew and spirit in a global war, the appearance of strength in its leader was symbolically as important as the strength of the nation itself. Franklin Roosevelt, tethered to a wheelchair for the past twenty-three years, his legs shrunken from disuse, had nevertheless for eleven years of his presidency displayed astonishing strength and vitality. But in the year of greatest stress, as the war's outcome hinged on the gamble of Overlord, the man began to slip into visible decline. The first to express concern was his daughter, Anna. She had been with her father the previous fall at Tehran, where she noticed that his weight had dropped alarmingly, his appetite was poor, and his hands trembled constantly as he scattered cigarette ashes over his clothes and papers. Purple half-moons developed under his eyes. His fingernails displayed a blue-gray cast. His breathing was shallow, and the timbre of that sonorous voice had thinned. Occasionally, his mouth hung open, and he left sentences dangling.

In March 1944, Anna left her home in Seattle to stay for a time at the White House. Alarmed at her father's continuing deterioration, she begged his physician, Vice Admiral McIntire, to arrange a thorough physical examination. The admiral, a nose and throat specialist, recognized the likely cause of his patient's waning health and accepted his limitations in that sphere. On March 27 he called the Bethesda Naval Hospital and arranged for Lieutenant Commander Howard Bruenn, Bethesda's best cardiologist, to see the President. Before Bruenn saw his patient, McIntire warned him that no matter what he found he was not to tell Roosevelt anything. He was to report only to the admiral. McIntire described the appointment to curious reporters as the President's "annual check up." For years, part of the physician's job had been to assure the world that, in spite of his paralysis, Franklin Roosevelt enjoyed splendid health. He saw no reason now to change that portrayal.

After exhaustively examining FDR at Bethesda, Doctor Bruenn came the next day to McIntire's office next to the White House Map Room. The report he submitted was dismal. The President was suffering from hypertension, hypertensive heart disease, and failure of the heart's left ventricle. His blood pressure was a stratospheric 218 over 120. The years of forced inactivity and limited exercise had taken their toll. Roosevelt was an old sixty-two. Bruenn estimated the life left to him at somewhere between months and, at the outside, two years. After the examination FDR had simply shaken his hand and said only, "Thanks, Doc." He had not asked a single question. The admiral next arranged for the young physician to be transferred to the White House as FDR's physician-in-attendance. Though the doctor examined his patient daily, Roosevelt still never asked why he had been assigned a full-time cardiologist. The only persons fully cognizant of the President's condition were McIntire, Bruenn, and Anna, but not the First Lady.

The mid-forties were not a favorable era for victims of heart disease. The first diagnosis that a patient had suffered a heart attack had not been made until 1910. Cardiology had not become a medical specialty until the early 1920s. And once cardiovascular disease was diagnosed, even a specialist such as Bruenn could do little. The drugs and surgical procedures that could prevent death from heart attacks and forestall strokes were a generation in the future.

FDR's decline remained a sometime thing. He still displayed flashes of the old exuberance. He continued to amaze Admiral Leahy with his near-photographic memory. Leahy was another recruit from FDR's days as assistant Navy secretary. He had then been in command of Secretary Daniels's dispatch boat, the *Dolphin,* which Roosevelt frequently commandeered. A strong favorable impression had stayed with FDR, and, after he became president, he appointed Leahy ambassador to France's Vichy government and then brought him to the White House as chief of staff to the commander in chief. Leahy served as the President's link to the armed forces. Of this duty, he once remarked, "He would ask my opinion. Sometimes my recollection was not functioning as fast as his own, but I always gave him some kind of answer. . . . He would look at me quizzically and say, 'Bill, that's not what you told me a year ago.' I frequently wondered if he was doing it on purpose."

FDR sought to husband his depleting resources through his gift for turning instantly from work to play. He continued watching movies and reading the light novels that distracted him, though in this most burdensome year of the war he had less and less free time. When an aide asked if he had read Kathleen Winsor's racy best-seller of the 1944 season, *Forever Amber,* he answered with a twinkling eye, "Only the dirty parts." Still, much of the old élan was fading, as if he had rounded the track too many times. What was sapping his vitality was simple enough to describe, though difficult to treat. The hardening arteries of this essentially immobile man were delivering insufficient blood to the brain. Still, he continued with the routines of his life, yielding to Dr. Bruenn's probing, poking, and thumping. And the charade went on. The President asked nothing about his condition, and Bruenn offered nothing. The rest of the staff remained in the dark as to what lay behind their chief's shaking hands, the ashen pallor, the grape-colored cast of his sagging lips, the occasional lapses of mental acuity.

FDR only appeared to be burying his head in the sand. He could level with one person as confidentially as if he were talking to himself—the discreet and devoted Daisy Suckley, as her diary was about to reveal. Early in May, Roosevelt was staying at Hobcaw, Bernard Baruch's lavish South Carolina estate. At lunch with Baruch, Dr. Bruenn, and Daisy, FDR picked listlessly at a dish of minced chicken on toast. After the doctor and Baruch left the room, he asked Daisy to stay. She later recorded their conversation: "I had a good talk with the P. about himself. He said he discovered that the doctors had not agreed together about what to tell him, so that he found out that they were not telling him the whole truth and that he was evidently more sick than they said! It is foolish of them to attempt to put anything over on *him.*" The conspiracy of silence went on. Roosevelt, leading the nation into the crucial hour of the war, intended to keep the state of his fitness a part of the web of secrecy along with Overlord itself.

★

On Monday afternoon, June 5, the President seemed outwardly relaxed as he played with his Scottie, Fala, and watched his grandson Johnny Boettiger perform somersaults on the sofa. Still the tension in his study was palpable. Grace Tully noted that the President's hands shook constantly, and his skin had taken on the color of cement.

At eight-twenty, after dinner, his valet, Arthur Prettyman, wheeled FDR into the Diplomatic Reception Room and positioned him behind a clutch of microphones. The President glanced over his script and then began to deliver a fireside chat to the American people, the voice solemn, the pace deliberate, his principal subject being the fall of Rome to the Allies that day. Left unsaid, but consuming his thoughts, was what was about to happen the following morning some eight hundred miles northwest of the Italian capital.

After the broadcast, Eleanor, Anna and her husband, Major John Boettiger, and Daisy Suckley joined FDR for a movie in the makeshift projection room set up in the colonnade leading to the White House East Wing. The fare this evening was not the comedies or musicals the President favored, but newsreels dealing with the war. At five minutes past 11 P.M. FDR retired to his study, followed by Eleanor and Daisy. As he sipped at a glass of orange juice, he told them he had a secret he wanted to share. Within hours, American GIs would be storming the beaches of Normandy. Eleanor responded that now she would not be able to sleep and almost wished he had not confided in them. Sensing the pall that his words had cast, FDR shifted his mood and began making jokes about what he was going to do to Hitler the moment the Führer surrendered.

As he spoke, the mightiest armada ever assembled was already crossing the English Channel—6,500 vessels, ranging from a half dozen battleships to 4,250 landing craft carrying 57,500 American troops and 75,215 British and Canadians, accompanied by 20,000 vehicles and 1,500 tanks, a flotilla one hundred miles wide and five miles deep. Overhead, 10,000 planes blackened the sky. FDR, usually so quick to nod off, did not sleep that night. He kept picking up his bedside phone, asking, "Hackie," Louise Hackmeister, the chief White House telephone operator, to put him through to the Pentagon for whatever scrap of information on the progress of the invasion force he could glean.

On the other side of the Atlantic, as troops waded ashore at Omaha, Utah, Sword, Gold, and Juno Beaches, all had not gone without mishap. Paratrooper units missed their drop zones; gliders crashed on landing, spilling troops from fragile wooden hulls; at Omaha Beach, German guns began cutting down American infantrymen the instant the Higgins boats dropped their ramps and until the GIs found scant shelter under the cliffs of Pointe du Hoc. Still, the major objective of the enterprise was stunningly achieved. Surprise had been total. A fleet covering approximately 500 square miles had crossed the Channel undetected. Allied casualties— a substantial 10,300 killed, wounded, and missing on that longest day— were one seventh of the worst estimates.

For all the elaborate machinations of Bodyguard and Fortitude, the greatest deception had been a gift of nature. June 5, Eisenhower's original invasion date, had proved so stormy, the winds so strong, the rains so heavy, the skies so overcast, that his meteorologists persuaded him to postpone the landing, even though part of the fleet had already set sail and would have to be recalled. June 7 was predicted to be equally inhospitable. So certain was Field Marshal Erwin Rommel that the Channel was too rough to permit an invasion that he had left France on June 4 to celebrate his wife's birthday at their hillside home in the fairy-tale town of Herrlingen. There Rommel presented Lucie-Maria with a pair of Parisian shoes, and then went to Berchtesgaden to discuss the Atlantic defenses with Hitler. But on June 5, at Suffolk House in Portsmouth, Ike's senior meteorologist, Captain J. M. Stagg of the Royal Air Force, spotted a narrow window of milder weather the next day. The rain should stop, the seas should calm slightly and remain so, at least throughout the morning before they rose again. The opening was fleeting, hardly ideal. Still Eisenhower wondered aloud to his staff, ". . . [J]ust how long you can hang this operation on the end of a limb and let it hang there." "OK, let's go," he said. Overlord began the following morning.

That night, Roosevelt made a fifteen-minute radio broadcast, leading the nation in a prayer for the young Americans committed to the battle. "They will need thy blessings," he said. "Their road will be long and hard. For the enemy is strong." And then he made his final contribution to the Bodyguard deception. "The Germans appear to expect landings elsewhere," he said. "Let them speculate. We are content to wait on events." Indeed, the enemy was still waiting for the real blow after the presumed feint at Normandy. The Wehrmacht's Foreign Armies West intelligence chief, Baron Von Roenne, reported: "Not a single unit of the 1st United States Army Group [FUSAG], which comprises around 25 large formations . . . has so far been committed." Much of the German strength remained rooted at the Pas de Calais, waiting for Patton's ghost army. Three days after the invasion, Hitler still rejected the plea of his commander in France,

Field Marshal Gerd von Rundstedt, to engage the 1st SS Panzer Division in Normandy. Instead, Hitler ordered the division to back up the Fifteenth Army for an expected main assault across the Dover Straits.

Through an OSS source in Bern rated "fairly dependable," Bill Donovan was able to inform the President that Hitler had called Rommel and Rundstedt on the carpet, demanding that they mend their destructive rivalry. "Rommel had insisted on bringing up the full German reserves," the informant reported, "while Rundstedt wanted to retain sizeable concentrations of troops in the Black Forest and to the North and East of Paris, where he feared paratroop landings. . . ." After Hitler issued an order to hold the key port of Cherbourg to the last man, Rundstedt tried to explain to the Führer's chief toady, Field Marshal Wilhelm Keitel, that the order meant lives wasted. "What shall we do?" moaned Keitel. "Make peace, you fools," Rundstedt replied. The next day, Hitler removed the old soldier from his command.

Fortitude continued to enjoy a remarkable shelf life. Not until nearly two months after the Normandy assault, after Field Marshal Guenther von Kluge had replaced Rundstedt, did Hitler accept the hard truth. He had been duped. The tens of thousands of troops who might have thrown the D-Day invaders back into the sea had waited futilely for the "real" strike at the Pas de Calais. On August 3, Hitler allowed Kluge to shift forces from the strait to face the steadily swelling Allied armies in Normandy. On August 7, Kluge conceded that a second major landing was "improbable." By then, the Allies had well over a million troops in France, including George Patton, now commanding an authentic force, his Third Army.

★

The capacity of Germany to fight on so stubbornly on two fronts—to keep its armies well equipped, supplied, and refurbished—opens one of the great moral quandaries of the war, the behavior of neutral countries in supporting, even prolonging, the ability of the Nazi war machine to fight on. In light of revelations over half a century later, particularly pointed at Switzerland, the question arises: through the intelligence available to President Roosevelt, what did he know of the decidedly unneutral behavior of certain nonbelligerents, and what did he do about it?

Over two years before D-Day, an unhappy Charles Bruggmann, the Swiss minister to Washington and recipient of the confidences of his brother-in-law, Vice President Henry Wallace, came to see Adolf Berle.

The *New York Post,* Bruggmann complained, had published an article defaming Switzerland and questioning its neutrality. The *Post* story charged that the Swiss National Bank and the Swiss government were providing U.S. dollars to Germany to purchase the matériel of war. Bruggmann claimed to know the source of this report, FDR's Jewish Treasury secretary, Henry Morgenthau Jr., who had tried to freeze Swiss bank accounts in the United States from the moment America entered the war, believing that Switzerland was already collaborating with the Nazis. "I said that in a country which had a free press, there was not a great deal that could be done," Berle later wrote of his response to Bruggmann. What FDR's intelligence representative at State was too tactful to say was that the *Post's* story was essentially accurate.

As the war progressed, FDR learned, through the OSS, that Allied attempts to block neutral countries from aiding Germany were having all the effectiveness of a sieve. On July 10, 1944, Bill Donovan sent the President a report, one of nine that day, obtained from "a high German official in Switzerland." Donovan's source revealed that while the Allies had been negotiating with its officials urging "that the Swiss should halt gold transactions between the Swiss and Reichsbank," the president of the country's National Bank, a man named Weber, was simultaneously making secret deals to accept German gold for over forty million Swiss francs per month. In effect, the deal amounted to money laundering. Certain suppliers of war matériel to Germany refused to accept gold in payment, rightly suspecting the Nazis had stolen it. But they would accept Swiss francs. The Germans had, in fact, looted gold from the central banks of France, Belgium, the Netherlands, other occupied countries, and Italy. Their rapacity surfaced in a message sent from the Irish minister in Rome to the foreign office in Dublin, a cable intercepted by Magic. "Roman Jews were obliged to furnish 50 kilogrammes of gold within 24 hours," it read. "Otherwise 200 of their young men would be sent as hostages to Germany." The communication sheds further light on the checkered record of the Catholic Church regarding the plight of the Jews. If the Roman Jews could not raise that much gold, the Irish diplomat reported, the Vatican offered to help them pay. A cryptic intercept from Tokyo to Berlin suggested a surprising additional source of gold for the Third Reich. "At our last meeting," Japan's foreign minister informed Ambassador Oshima in Berlin, "it was decided informally to send about 2 tons of gold at the next opportunity. The Navy has no doubt already studied this and made provision for transportation."

The President and his informants did not then know the most unspeakable source of Germany's bullion, gold stripped from the Jews in concentration camps, from their jewelry, from gold teeth and fillings pulled from the mouths of the murdered. The Swiss would later deny knowledge of this source, and likely told the truth, since the Germans did not trumpet their barbarism. However, that the gold ingots traded for Swiss francs and other currencies were stolen had to be known by Europe's bankers. The Germans had entered 1940 with approximately $200 million in monetary gold, yet during the war somehow acquired $909 million worth.

Five days after Donovan's July 10 report, FDR had another message from the general. "We would like to warn you especially about using this material," Wild Bill cautioned, "for it could be easily traced back to the source." Allen Dulles had been tipped off that the Germans were using a loophole in Swiss customs regulations to buy an additional three million Swiss francs' worth of ball bearings for their combat aircraft. Twice in 1943, the U.S. Eighth Air Force had conducted raids targeted at German ball bearing production in Schweinfurt. The cost had been frightful, over 120 bombers lost, which meant 1,200 American fliers dead, captured, or missing. And here were the Swiss, taking up the slack, trading ball bearings for Nazi gold.

The Swiss had a rationale for their conduct. Switzerland occupied a geopolitical position as precarious as the peaks of its Alps. The country was completely surrounded by Nazi-controlled territory. A Wehrmacht that had subdued most of Europe could surely have overrun tiny Switzerland. The Swiss saw themselves as a small creature in the embrace of a great beast that could devour it at will. Their objective was to comply with the beast's wishes and do nothing to goad it to rashness. Furthermore, war or no war, the Swiss were tied economically to the Germans. Switzerland sold electrical power to Germany, and in return received the coal and fuel that the Swiss lacked. Actually Switzerland had a foot in both camps. While it was selling Germany weapons, ammunition, aluminum for aircraft and locomotives, and even allowing bombed-out German plants to rebuild on Swiss soil, it also traded with the Allies. Switzerland exchanged more gold with Germany's enemies than with the Reich, the distinction being that the Allied gold was not stolen or yanked from people's mouths. The Swiss had also been evenhanded in allowing their nation to become an espionage hotbed for all sides, including the OSS operation under Allen Dulles. They had allowed American fliers who crash-landed in Switzerland to stay in Dulles's compound, where they were put to work radioing to Washington the bundles of intelligence that Fritz Kolbe smuggled out of the foreign office in Berlin. The unspoken Swiss attitude was, spy if you must, but do so discreetly. Don't let us catch you and have to intern you.

On April 11, 1944, the American Eighth Air Force accidentally bombed the Swiss city of Schaffhausen in a raid on southwest Germany, damaging the railroad station, factories, a museum, and homes, and killing numerous civilians. Rumors whispered in the Bern diplomatic circle had it that the raid had been deliberate, to knock out Swiss ball bearing production going to Germany. Yet, so determined was the United States to respect Swiss neutrality, that FDR secretly paid $1 million out of the President's emergency fund to mollify the Swiss and downplay the blunder.

"Safehaven" was a Roosevelt strategy to block German leaders from smuggling their stolen riches into comfortable exile, as well as to deny Germany the wealth to start another war, and to keep its plunder in Europe for the Allies to use to rebuild a shattered continent. The approach was simple: Gain control of gold and currency transactions conducted by the neutrals. Donovan's OSS was assigned to track down the flow of gold from Germany to Switzerland and through it to other nonbelligerents. As FDR put it to Wild Bill, "We ought to block the Swiss participation in saving the skins of rich or prominent Germans." Few enterprises expose the moral contradictions of war more nakedly than Safehaven's fate. While the OSS did succeed in preventing some ill-gotten German wealth from leaving Europe, it hardly succeeded in blocking all of it. One story had it that a gold-laden U-boat made its way to Nazi-friendly Argentina. The most gaping holes in Safehaven, however, were punched, not by the Germans, but by an ally, even by rival U.S. agencies working at cross-purposes. Britain, already looking toward postwar commerce, wanted to expand trade with the neutrals, not punish them. Henry Morgenthau Jr., on the other hand, wanted his Treasury Department to deal harshly with any neutral nation helping Germany, particularly Switzerland. But the State Department, respecting Switzerland's rights as a neutral, valuing the country as an intelligence bonanza, and appreciating Swiss leniency toward American fliers crash-landing there, opposed forcing Safehaven strictures down Swiss throats. Safehaven's leverage was not even used to end the Swiss trade in munitions with Germany. And while most Swiss loved democracy and favored an Allied victory, the bankers of Zurich paid lip service to Safehaven while profiting from trade and gold exchanges with the Nazis to the very end of the war.

In dealing with Nazi Germany, Switzerland could point a we're-not-the-only-one finger at other neutrals, most notably Sweden. After the American raids on Schweinfurt, Swedish technicians came to the city to rebuild the damaged ball bearing plants, since 60 percent of all ball bearings produced there were made by a subsidiary of Svenska Kullager Fabriken (SKF), a Swedish firm. FDR's Board of Economic Warfare estimated that without the export of high-grade Swedish iron ore for steelmaking, the Nazi war machine would grind to a halt. British war economists branded Swedish iron exports to Germany "the most valuable of all of the contributions of neutral countries to the German war effort." While Sweden's aid to Germany angered the Allies, it at least produced one espionage dividend. According to an OSS report, ". . . [R]ush orders given to SKF by the Germans [made] it possible for bomb damage experts to gauge the harm done to German ball bearing factories by Allied attacks from the air."

Sweden's flouting of neutrality went beyond economic profiting. The Swedish navy escorted German troopships crossing the Baltic Sea to embarkation points in the East. Over 250,000 of Hitler's forces sent to occupy Norway were transported on the Swedish railway system. More egregiously, the Swedes had allowed German troops to cross their territory as part of the buildup for the invasion of Russia. Swedes fell back on the same rationale as the Swiss. Theirs was a small country with a population less than that of New Jersey trapped in a triangle, with Germany on the south, Nazi-occupied Norway on the west, and Finland, Germany's ally, on the east. Cut off by the Allied blockade from other sources of oil and rubber, the country depended on Germany for these essentials. Thus Roosevelt's representatives made a secret deal with the Swedes. The Allies would permit oil and rubber destined for Sweden to pass through the blockade; in return, the Swedes must stop enemy forces from using their country as a German highway and start reducing their shipments to the Reich. Before 1944 was out, Swedish trade with Germany had halted completely.

Besides Switzerland and Sweden, Generalissimo Franco's Spain, its heart with the Nazis, stretched neutrality almost to bursting. Spain's Blue Division, forty thousand strong, fought alongside the Wehrmacht in Russia. Spain at one point was providing 30 percent of Germany's wolfram, indispensable for making the tungsten used in producing hard metals. Portuguese businessmen were getting rich, supplying twice as much wolfram as Spain through a secret deal with the Reich. All told, 90 percent of Germany's reliance on this material was supplied by neutrals. By the spring of 1944, Allied trade negotiators thought they had a deal. They would allow Spain to receive gasoline through the blockade; in exchange, the Spanish would stop all wolfram exports, both to the Allies and Germany, by the end of the year. But the Japanese ambassador in Madrid unwittingly revealed Spain's continuing duplicity. In a message decrypted at Arlington Hall, the ambassador repeated a conversation he had had with a Spanish official regarding wolfram shipments during which he was told, ". . . [W]e Spaniards and Portuguese are, to tell you the truth, going to cooperate and keep sending more of it to Germany. For that purpose the Portuguese Finance Minister came here and has concluded with Spain a secret understanding to that effect."

Turkey, which the Allies had long been trying to enlist in the war on their side, was Germany's prime supplier of chromite ore, which was converted into chromium. Albert Speer, the German armaments minister, feared that without chromite supplied to the Reich by Turkey, German arms production would be shut down in ten months.

With the successful invasion of France and the Nazis retreating from Russia, the hovering shadow of a once omnipotent Germany should no longer be so fearsome to European neutrals, FDR believed. He was determined that their aid to Germany not prolong the war by a day. But the course of wisdom was not always clear. The American ambassador in Madrid, Carlton Hayes, sent FDR a confidential communication urging him not to be too harsh with the Spanish. Hayes pointed out that "65 percent of Allied intelligence—and 90 percent of American—concerning German military dispositions in France are derived from our intelligence services in Spain while the Spanish looked away." The Spaniards had allowed over nine hundred downed American airmen coming out of France to pass through their country to rejoin the fight. Hayes added a sentimental argument to the case for leniency. He told the President how Spanish authorities had allowed full military honors at the burial of an American flier whose body washed ashore on a Spanish beach. As for wolfram exports to Germany, Hayes pointed out, "We certainly want to cut down. . . . But the means of doing this must be realistic also."

Ultimately, the shipments of Portugal's wolfram and Turkey's chromite ore to Germany were ended through pragmatic capitalism. The United States simply bought up these strategic commodities to keep them out of the Nazis' hands.

★

Field Marshal von Rundstedt was just one of a growing number of Germans who saw perpetuation of a lost cause as a policy of nihilism. In late

January 1944, Allen Dulles sent Donovan a message from Bern using a new code word, Breakers, to refer to a "German oppositional group . . . composed of various intellectuals from certain military and government circles." Dulles's chief source of information on anti-Hitler movements within the Reich was Hans Bernd Gisevius, a hulking forty-year-old Prussian and agent of the Abwehr working undercover as a vice consul in the German consulate in Zurich. The six-foot four-inch Gisevius, whom Dulles referred to behind his back as "Tiny," presented an anomaly of strength and vulnerability. His vision was so poor that he could not drive a car or use a typewriter. He had joined the Gestapo almost at its creation, thinking it a legitimate police force. He quickly became disillusioned, and asked a colleague, "Tell me, please, am I in a police office, or in a robbers' cave?" By 1943, Gisevius had become active in anti-Nazi circles. In one of his clandestine meetings with Dulles, Gisevius dropped a bombshell. He told the Bern OSS chief that a plot was under way in Germany to assassinate Hitler and overthrow the Nazi regime. He cited a date for the coup, March 13, 1943. But when that day came and passed, Dulles's doubts deepened that conspiracies could escape the all-seeing eye of the Gestapo. Still, he continued to send messages to Washington bearing the Breakers code name to report dissent inside the Reich, some 146 such dispatches by May 1944.

Several weeks before D-Day, Dulles had informed Donovan that Rundstedt, at the time still commanding German forces in the West, would, if given certain assurances, allow the Allies to land in France unopposed, thus avoiding carnage on both sides. The plan envisioned an orderly retreat from the West, and the transfer of crack divisions to face the Russians on the eastern front. Three weeks before D-Day, the conspirators informed Dulles of what they would expect in exchange from the Allies—three divisions to be parachuted into the Berlin area and amphibious landings near Bremen and Hamburg. The principal fear of the anti-Nazis was echoed in another communication that Dulles relayed to Washington after D-Day: "The Breakers group wishes [to] keep as much as possible of the Reich from falling into the hands of the Russians." Still another dispatch out of Bern reported that the leadership of the conspiracy ". . . is especially concerned that they should not have to negotiate with Moscow. . . . The chief reason for such a request on their part is their ardent wish to keep Central Europe from coming under the sway of the Soviets. . . . They feel certain that in the latter case democracy and Christian culture . . . would vanish in Europe."

Gisevius informed Dulles that another date, not far off, had been set for Hitler's assassination. On July 12, Gisevius left Switzerland for Germany, and on the same day Dulles sent a cryptic telegram, relayed to FDR, reading, "There is a possibility that a dramatic event may take place up north, if Breakers courier is to be trusted."

Astonishingly, knowing and sharing the President's taste for strategic rumors, Donovan never sent FDR any of the specific Gisevius intelligence that conspirators were plotting to assassinate Hitler and that the Nazi regime might be overthrown and replaced by a government ready to make peace. What was set before the President from Donovan seemed to point in the opposite direction. On the day that Gisevius departed for Berlin, Donovan relayed another report from Dulles, obtained from a "neutral observer," that read: "A revolution is not to be expected; the people are too apathetic and too closely supervised by the police. A collapse can only come as the Allied troops arrive. . . . The opposition are not in any position to take such a step."

Three days later, FDR had another appraisal from Bern, this one gingerly questioning FDR's policy of unconditional surrender. Inside Germany, Dulles reported, "Goebbels has taken and twisted the slogan of unconditional surrender and made the people feel that the slogan means unconditional annihilation." He went on to predict that "any opposition to the Nazi regime involves the gravest risk of immediate execution."

The closest Donovan ever came to advising the President that he had knowledge of a plot brewing was to share the following: "Those opposed to the Nazis realize . . . that the next few weeks may be their last chance to show that they are willing to take some risks in making the first move to clean up their own house." Donovan advised, "We must judge whether the encouragement of any effort towards a revolution in Germany will, at this juncture, help to save thousands of lives of Allied soldiers. . . ." He believed it would. Churchill had already pointed out to FDR "the desirability that the German people themselves should take steps to overthrow the Nazi government. I believe that it would be helpful if a similar and somewhat expanded statement could be authoritatively made on our side at this time." But FDR remained obdurate in his opposition: no negotiated peace, only unconditional surrender. He wanted the Germany of Adolf Hitler driven to its knees. Only then could a better nation be reborn.

That summer, Eleanor Roosevelt came across a memorandum that Churchill had written in 1919 during the Russian civil war, describing how the Allies had tried to strangle the Red revolution in its cradle. "Large sums of money and considerable forces have been employed by the Allies against the Bolsheviks during the year," Churchill wrote. He noted that over eight thousand American troops in Siberia were fighting the Red Army. Further, Japan and Finland stood ready to commit substantial forces to the anti-revolutionary side, and Britain and France were prepared to commit millions in aid lest "the Bolshevik armies are supreme over the whole vast territories of the Russian Empire." In a cramped scrawl across the top of the memorandum, the First Lady had written, "It is not surprising if Mr. Stalin is slow to forget!" She then passed Churchill's long ago sentiments on to the President. Here was the seed of East-West distrust that Roosevelt was determined to overcome.

On the very eve that the anti-Nazis planned their coup, the President received from Donovan another report from Bern stating flatly that "Hitler is still functioning as the Supreme Commander of the Army." The only hint of restive generals in this communication dealt with the V-1 rockets the Germans had begun dropping on England. The generals opposed the weapon, "not on any grounds of principle. . . . They felt that the employment of this bomb had little strategic value."

Yet Donovan also had the dozens of Breaker messages anticipating a plot against Hitler, and given the boost in his standing if these reports proved accurate, his failure to inform the President is mystifying. In the ten days prior to July 20, Donovan's memoranda to the President dealt with the possibility of Bulgaria entering the war, profiles of several Chinese generals, a draft Chinese Constitution, and information on the Timor islands, but nothing about an attempt on Hitler's life. On July 20 the conspirators did strike. Colonel Klaus Schenk Graf von Stauffenberg, missing an eye, one hand, and three fingers on the other hand, planted a briefcase bomb in the Wolfsschanze, Hitler's East Prussian headquarters. Four of the men in the room with Hitler were killed outright or suffered fatal wounds. Hitler was only slightly injured. The coup had failed.

A memorandum delivered to the White House two days after the plot suggested that Donovan did not want it to appear that his organization had been caught flat-footed. He sent FDR a transcript of a radio telephone conversation he had had with Allen Dulles which read: "The developments did not come as a great surprise except to the extent that there were reasons to doubt whether any high officers of the German Army, who had remained in positions of power after the successive purges, would have the courage to act. . . . We had ample advance warning that a plot was in the wind," the transcript concluded, "if this attempt has failed, the Germans will probably have to wait for the complete military collapse of Germany to rid themselves of the Nazis. . . ."

Details of the failed coup came dribbling in, but little more than could be gleaned from monitored German broadcasts and newspapers reaching neutral Switzerland. "Photographs appearing in the German press of Hitler bidding farewell to Mussolini, after his visit to headquarters," Donovan reported to FDR, "may indicate that Hitler's right hand is wounded, since he is giving Mussolini the left hand." Donovan included one more detail passed along by Dulles to tantalize the President: "I have just heard tonight from a good source that Berger, Hitler's co-worker, who was the only one who was immediately killed at the time of the attack on Hitler, was Hitler's double. Possibly Stauffenberg, who probably did not know Hitler well, made a mistake." Donovan also reported that the assassination attempt had occurred not in East Prussia, but in Hitler's Alpine retreat at Berchtesgaden in Bavaria. The report was inaccurate as to the site, the number killed, and the supposition that Stauffenberg had been misled by a double. The one accurate disclosure Wild Bill reported was that the blast at Rastenburg marked the fourth failed attempt by these conspirators on Hitler's life. One OSS prediction proved dead on. "The blood purge will be ruthless," Dulles cabled Washington. The Gestapo had immediately embarked on a remorseless manhunt, arresting thousands, however remotely traceable to the plot.

Actually, FDR had little need for the tardy and speculative intelligence on the plot from Donovan's spies. He had a much swifter, more accurate source, the unwittingly obliging Ambassador Oshima. Days after the failed coup, the ambassador had a long conversation with Joachim von Ribbentrop in which the Reich's foreign minister revealed the leaders of the plot, their intentions, the collapse of their enterprise, and their fate. Ribbentrop told Oshima, according to the ambassador's report to Tokyo, "Colonel Stauffenberg entered a meeting which was in progress in order to make a report to Chancellor Hitler. After he had placed a bag in which the bomb had been put upon the floor about two meters from where Chancellor Hitler was, he said that he had some other business and left the room." Ribbentrop next told Oshima, ". . . [T]he bomb exploded with tremendous force after the lapse of about five minutes. . . . What was really mysterious was the fact that the Chancellor, who was nearest to the bomb when it exploded, was unhurt with the exception that his clothes were torn to pieces by the blast and he sustained a few burns." Oshima gave Ribbentrop's view of the genesis of the coup. "I think that this was a plan for attempting a

compromise with England and America after the people involved had secured in this way the real power for themselves. However, while there is
some suspicion that the bomb which Colonel Stauffenberg used was of
British make, we have not yet secured any proof that Beck [General Ludwig Beck, a plot leader] was communicating with England and America."
Through Magic, this account from the lips of the German foreign minister
was available to the President just five days after the coup. Oshima sought
credit for warning the Führer. "I as well as others had advised Chancellor
Hitler that resolute steps should be taken against this attitude, but the
Chancellor is a man who prefers to deal with problems of this kind with
forbearing and gentle measures, and therefore, so long as there was no
clear proof, he did not consent to the taking of measures such as we suggested."

★

FDR's resolve not to provoke Soviet suspicions about a separate peace was
matched only by Stalin's hypocrisy. An OSS agent in Sweden, Abram Hewitt, had managed to penetrate the Nazi SS, through the personal physician
of Heinrich Himmler, head of the terror apparatus. Dr. Felix Kersten, a
Finn, had developed a promising nerve therapy with which he treated leading Europeans, including Benito Mussolini, Il Duce's son-in-law, Count
Galeazzo Ciano, Prince Henry of the Netherlands, and Himmler, who by
now monopolized the doctor's time. Hewitt had met Kersten on one of the
doctor's frequent visits to Stockholm and found him willing to cooperate
with the Allies. Between them, they concocted an imaginary back ailment
for the American which Kersten would pretend to treat while briefing Hewitt. Most alarming was what the Finn revealed about peace maneuvering
between the Soviet Union and Germany. "The doctor reported," Hewitt cabled Washington, "that Prince Wied, the German Minister to Stockholm,
had come with a peace proposal from the Russians to SS Headquarters
about the time of Stalingrad, and that Papen had come with another one
from Ankara in May 1943. The outlines of the proposals were that Germany should take about one-half the Baltic countries to the north of East
Prussia; and that Poland should be divided along the 1939 lines; that Russia should demand the whole coast to the Black Sea, including the mouth
of the Danube, and should go as far as Constantinople and Salonika, and
should also have a port on the Adriatic." Kersten told Hewitt during a sub-

sequent back treatment of the fate of the Russian scheme: "Ribbentrop and Goebbels had been in favor of accepting these proposals, while Himmler and Hitler were against them. Even with the defeat at Stalingrad, Hitler had convinced himself that Russian reserves would be exhausted and the Eastern front would stalemate." He needed to concede nothing to Stalin.

Donovan forwarded Hewitt's entire seventeen-page report to the President on March 20, at the same time that the numerous Breakers communications were revealing the German conspirators' hopes for a separate peace with the West. If FDR regarded separate peace talks with the Germans as betrayal of the Soviet Union, Hewitt's report provided indisputable evidence that Stalin was only too willing to betray his Western Allies. Ever since Tehran, however, FDR had persuaded himself that he could not only work with Stalin, but could trust him. Furthermore, the remorseless retreat of Germany from east to west convinced him that the Russians, at this point, must prefer to destroy rather than deal with their enemy.

★

The performance of the OSS continued to seesaw. Donovan's great strength remained his ability to attract talent. By the third year of the war, his forces in the field had penetrated all the occupied countries, providing arms, communications, and heart to resistance movements. An esprit de corps sprang up, tinged with self-mocking irony. One favorite ditty, sung to the tune of the "Battle Hymn of the Republic," described the fate of an OSS agent parachuted into occupied territory:

> He hit the ground, the sound was splot,
> His blood went spurting high.
> His comrades then were heard to say,
>   "a helluva way to die."
> He lay there rollin' around in the welter of his gore,
> And he ain't gonna jump no more.

The products of Donovan's Research and Analysis branch, under William Langer, noted Harvard professor of European history, won grudging respect even from the military. Langer's staff engaged Dr. Henry A. Murray of the Harvard Psychological Clinic to prepare an "Analysis of the

Personality of Adolf Hitler: With Predictions of His Future Behavior and Suggestions for Dealing with Him Now and After Germany's Surrender." Copy number one of thirty copies of the two-hundred-page profile went to the White House and confirmed Putzi Hanfstaengl's earlier reading of his erstwhile Führer. "Hitler has often vowed that he would commit suicide if his plans miscarried," Murray reported, "but if he chooses this course, he will do it at the last moment and in the most dramatic possible manner. He will retreat, let us say, to the impregnable little fortress he has built for himself on the top of the mountain beyond the Berghof [at Berchtesgaden]. There alone he will wait until troops come to take him prisoner. As a climax he will blow up the mountain and himself with dynamite."

Along with the gems, the OSS continued to submit clinkers. While American and Allied armies were hopping across the islands of Guadalcanal, New Guinea, Tarawa, Bougainville, Kwajalein, and Saipan, Donovan's Morale Operations branch offered its contribution to victory in the Pacific. The Japanese were reportedly circulating pornographic pictures of American women throughout India and other Asian countries to demonstrate the enemy's depravity. Morale Operations mounted a counterattack. The FBI reported, "Mr. Towell of OSS has requested that permission be granted to a representative of OSS to come to the Bureau and select copies of obscene materials [of oriental women]. . . . The laboratory has a collection of 25 or 30 photographs of this nature. It is suggested that OSS be permitted to obtain copies of a representative group of these photographs for their project," to demonstrate the low morals of the Japanese. "O.K.," Hoover scrawled across the bottom of the OSS request. Finally, an endeavor had been found in which the rivalrous Donovan and Hoover could cooperate.

In the fall of 1944, Wild Bill met with Vice Admiral Lord Louis Mountbatten, Supreme Allied Commander of the Southeast Asia Command, to try to inveigle himself into the Pacific war from which General MacArthur had thus far excluded him. Donovan told Mountbatten that if he had a job requiring two or three thousand men whom the admiral could not spare, he would happily provide twenty or thirty OSS operatives who could do it. It was, of course, hyperbole, but tinged with the Donovan hubris. The man managed to retain FDR's confidence, not in spite of his excesses, but because of them. Roosevelt had dealt with enough people to recognize the dearth of original thinking. Maybe only five of a hundred of Donovan's ideas had any merit; but most people never had five good ideas in a lifetime. Further, Donovan knew how to play to the President's pleasures. In one note FDR wrote to him, "Dear Bill, Ever so many thanks for the Himmler and Hitler stamps. I had heard that there was such a stamp as the Himmler one and it will be an interesting addition to my stamp collection."

Donovan was both the beneficiary and victim of his zeal. What Wild Bill did possess was a powerful amalgam of Irish charm, courage, and contagious optimism. In these qualities FDR could see himself reflected. Still, Wild Bill never cracked the Roosevelt inner circle. He was never an architect of strategy, never invited into FDR's war councils along with Marshall, Leahy, Admiral King, and other shapers of the battle. One colleague described Bill Donovan as "a Cortez who . . . never found his Mexico."

Chapter XXIII

A Secret Unshared

L IKELY THE loneliest and least contented of the President's intelligence sources sat for hours every night before a powerful Hallicrafter shortwave radio in a shabby redbrick Virginia farmhouse some twenty miles south of Washington. Putzi Hanfstaengl, now dubbed the "Dr. S Project," had been transferred to Bush Hill, one hundred ragged acres alongside a railroad track, after the Army wanted him out of Fort Belvoir. However unhappy Hanfstaengl might be, he still represented to John Franklin Carter the thoroughbred in his agent stable, a man who provided a rare window into the world of the Third Reich. The outsized, shaggy, jut-jawed German proved a prickly asset, however. His fixed pose was to gaze disdainfully down a long patrician nose at the plebeian American soldiers assigned to tend him. His daylight hours were spent demanding more from Carter—more money, more freedom, more care for his bad teeth. Then, while others slept, Hanfstaengl monitored German news broadcasts, summarizing their content and analyzing their meaning for the White House. He self-pityingly styled himself "America's first prisoner of State."

In 1943 he wrote directly to the President complaining that as long as he was treated by the British as a prisoner of war and by the Americans as an enemy alien, his work carried no weight. He wanted to be freed. FDR broke the bad news to Carter. "I talked with the Prime Minister about this and the answer is 'no.' I think that too many difficult questions are present." For all the grief Putzi caused him, Carter still believed that the man provided dollar value. He eagerly delivered to FDR another sixty-nine-page portrait of Hitler's psyche prepared by Hanfstaengl. In it, the President read of Hitler's mother fixation, his spotty education, his professed spiritual kinship to Frederick the Great and Napoleon, his vegetarianism, his ecstasy over the music of Richard Wagner, his surprising physical courage and ambiguous sexuality. Putzi recalled how in 1923, when Hitler was still a political upstart, he advised him that his patch of a mustache was unattractive and that he should grow it wider; to which Hitler replied, "If it is not the fashion now, it will be later because I wear it." None of Putzi's revelations influenced the conduct of the war, but they fed the President's appetite for high-level tittle-tattle. FDR called Hanfstaengl's reports his "Hitler bedtime stories."

Carter sought to use Putzi's contributions to leverage his budget. He had started out with $10,000 from the President's emergency fund, buried in the State Department for "foreign reporting." By fiscal 1943–1944, he was asking for $10,000 a month, including money to have Putzi's tonsils removed and to repair botched dental work on his prize catch. Carter defended the request with the explanation that while Hanfstaengl was in a British POW camp, his captors "allowed their embryo doctors and dentists to practice on prisoners of war."

Early in 1944, Carter brought to FDR another scheme concocted by Hanfstaengl. Rudolf Hess, once number three in the Nazi Party hierarchy, had, in 1941, made his quixotic solo flight to Britain to try to persuade Churchill to make a separate peace with Germany. Hess had never gotten near the Prime Minister, and for his pains had been locked up as a war prisoner. Carter urged the President to ask the British to allow Hanfstaengl to fly to England and meet with Hess, whom Putzi knew from the old days, in order to extract more recent intelligence from inside Hitler's realm. FDR vetoed the scheme. The British, he explained, were not going to let anyone question the possibly insane Nazi, who had recently hurled himself head-first down a flight of stairs.

Carter did manage to have Hanfstaengl's son, Egon, now a U.S. Army sergeant, reassigned from the South Pacific to serve as his father's secretary at Bush Hill. Egon presented Carter with his own scheme to place before the President, one worthy of his father's panache. On his next visit to the White House, Carter explained that Egon, as a result of boyhood hikes, was well acquainted with Hitler's mountain retreat at Berchtesgaden. Armed with forged papers, Egon believed that he could slip over the Swiss border into the area. By affecting disgust over his father's defection to the Allies, and having once been a paragon of the Hitler Youth, he believed he could bluff his way into the Führer's headquarters. "If I can get close enough to shake his hand, I can kill him," Egon had assured Carter. The President dismissed young Hanfstaengl's scheme with "a curt and clear negative," Carter later recorded in his diary. FDR's reaction was of a piece with his other positions—his unwillingness to bomb concentration camps ostensibly to save Jews, or to support the anti-Nazi generals, or to back off from unconditional surrender. To Roosevelt, there was no alternative to victory on the battlefield.

By mid-1944, Putzi's star, always in tenuous orbit, began to fall and Carter's momentarily wobbled. Undersecretary of State Edward Stettinius called Grace Tully to tell her, "very confidentially, that the State Department did not know what [Carter's people] were doing for their $10,000 a month and that the State Department does not feel this work is of enough value to warrant spending that amount of money." She relayed Stettinius's qualms about the Carter operation to FDR, and soon Hanfstaengl was being dismissed around the White House as "Hitler's piano player." Within a week, FDR made his decision. The rest of Carter's work could continue, but he "did not feel it was worthwhile to continue the Dr. S. [Hanfstaengl] project and therefore it will be terminated as of July 1." On September 25, Carter returned from a trip to New York to find a curt note from Lieutenant Colonel B. W. Davenport, his Army liaison officer with Hanfstaengl. Without consulting Carter, the Army had flown Putzi to England, where he became again an ordinary POW. Davenport's note said only, "I thought you would want this information for the completion of your files." Furious, Carter could only rage impotently in a message he sent to the President. "My own opinion on the subject," he said, "is that it was officious in the extreme for the Army to take this matter into their own hands and above all to take this action without notifying me. . . ." The President responded as he usually did to the unpleasant and unchangeable, with silence.

The last had not yet been heard from Putzi. Late in the fall, he wrote from a POW camp in Liverpool asking Carter to sell the Steinway piano installed for him at Bush Hill "and send the money to me." However, Colonel Davenport informed the White House that the piano had been bought "with government money allocated to Mr. Carter." At this final rejection, Putzi wrote Carter that in light of the "two years and three months during which I worked loyally and unremittingly in aid of the cause my son is fighting for, my reinternment seems a rather mediocre finale to a noble beginning."

Despite the fall of Hanfstaengl, Carter's standing with FDR rebounded. Espionage need not be limited to foreign countries, and Carter found other ways to earn his keep. He had infiltrated an informant into the arms industry who was providing him with inside reports of failures in Army ordnance. He brought these critiques to the President cautioning, "The source of this information is a responsible Army officer who would certainly be subject to Pentagon reprisals if his connection with these reports should be established." The President then sent the reports to General Marshall, adding his own layer of deception. "Dear George," he wrote, "An occasional correspondent who sometimes makes sense, sends me the enclosed. He is an engineer of some experience. I thought I ought to pass his remarks on to you. . . ."

★

Early in the war, Hitler had made a serious blunder. His intention all along, despite the 1939 peace pact with Stalin, had been to attack Russia in mid-1941. In launching the invasion, he faced a deadline that even the then invincible Wehrmacht could not move, the element that had defeated Charles XII and Napoleon before him, the Russian winter. Hitler had six months to subjugate the vast Soviet landmass before winter set in. However, he had allowed himself to be diverted by what amounted essentially to a fit of personal pique. In March 1941, Yugoslavia had signed a treaty that made the small Balkan state practically a German puppet. Then, to Hitler's outraged astonishment, this pliant Yugoslav government was overthrown by nationalists of stiffer spine. During delirious celebrations in Belgrade's streets, the crowds jeered at Nazis and spat on the car of the German minister. "The beginning of the Barbarossa operation [to attack Russia] will have to be postponed up to four weeks," Hitler said. First his generals must complete "Operation Punishment." On April 6, German bombers pulverized Belgrade, killing seventeen thousand people and creating the nightmarish spectacle of crazed animals from the zoo dashing through the smoke and fire of the shattered city. The punitive diversion set Barbarossa back six crucial weeks; and three years later, Yugoslav resistance fighters were still tying down twenty-five divisions of the Wehrmacht.

The first Yugoslav resistance fighter known to FDR was Colonel Draza

Mihailovic, heading a force called the Chetniks. One might have expected the President's ally Prime Minister Churchill to support Mihailovic since the Serb was an avid monarchist bent on restoring King Peter to the throne. Initially Churchill did support him, but the Chetnik leader seemed more interested in destroying political opponents than Germans to the point of making deals through which Chetnik and Wehrmacht forces agreed to leave each other alone. Mihailovic's chief rival was Josip Broz, the tough, barrel-chested, Moscow-trained general secretary of the Yugoslav Communist Party, who headed the Partisans and styled himself "Tito." While Tito was the antithesis of a monarchist, Churchill concluded that he was making a real fight against the Nazis, and thus the Prime Minister threw Britain's support to the Communist and away from the royalist. When one of his staff asked him about the wisdom of backing a Communist army, Churchill replied, "Do you intend to make Yugoslavia your home after the war?" "No," the subordinate answered. "Neither do I," Churchill replied.

This split over Chetniks and Partisans was to lead to the sharpest intelligence rivalry thus far between the President and the Prime Minister. Roosevelt's objective was to heal the fractures in Yugoslav politics. In the fall of 1943, he had cabled Churchill, ". . . [T]he guerrilla forces appear to be engaged largely in fighting each other and not the Germans. . . . In the present confused condition the only hope I see for immediate favorable action is the presence of an aggressive . . . officer." He had just the man for the job, Wild Bill Donovan. "I do not believe he can do much harm and being a fearless and aggressive character he might do much good." Churchill shuddered at the name of this nominee, whom he had come to regard as a loose cannon. "I have great admiration for Donovan," Churchill replied to Roosevelt. "But I do not see any centre in the Balkans from which he could grip the situation." Besides, the Prime Minister observed, over eighty British intelligence teams inside Yugoslavia had the situation well in hand. To an aide, Churchill complained that Donovan "is shoving his nose in everywhere. We are hardly allowed to breathe."

After Churchill dumped Mihailovic in favor of Tito, Donovan suggested to the President that the United States at least ought to maintain a nonpolitical and not necessarily supportive contact with the Chetnik leader just to know what he was up to. FDR concurred, noting, "We have no sources of intelligence whatever in a part of the Balkans which may become an important area. . . ." It was not simply a matter of collecting information, Donovan told FDR, but of not caving in to the British, who blithely assumed the senior partnership in any joint espionage. To Donovan's proposal to have the OSS parachute a mission and thus maintain contact with Mihailovic, Roosevelt replied, "I completely approve of the plan. . . . We intend to exercise this freedom of action for obtaining independent American secret intelligence." But even a modest American listening post inside the Chetnik camp was too much for Churchill. On April 6 he cabled FDR, "We are now in the process of withdrawing all our missions from Mihailovic and are pressing [exiled] King Peter to clear himself of this millstone. . . . If at this very time, an American mission arrives at Mihailovic's headquarters, it will show throughout the Balkans a complete contrariety of action between Britain and the United States." Forced to choose between Wild Bill and Winston Churchill, the decision of the President was inevitable. To Donovan's bitter disappointment, Roosevelt answered Churchill two days later, "In view of your expressed opinion that there might be misunderstanding by our Allies and others, I have directed that the contemplated mission be not *repeat* not sent."

An OSS agent already in Yugoslavia, Lieutenant Colonel Lynn M. Farish, managed to get out an eleven-page report that Donovan sent to the President in July 1944. Farish described a scene with an eerie contemporaneous ring. "The situation," he wrote, "has from the beginning been terribly confusing, and almost beyond the comprehension of an impartial outside observer. The deep-rooted causes of the internecine strife are contained in racial, religious, and political disputation which are so long standing that the people themselves do not understand them." Each side, he reported, believed that "their first enemy is the other, with the Germans second. . . . It is useless now to endeavor to decide which side first did wrong." Farish closed, dismayed that "the combined strength and influence of the Soviet Union, Great Britain and the United States could not put an abrupt end to the civil wars in Yugoslavia. . . . That it has not been done is, in the eyes of many, not a good portent for the future."

The President directed Admiral Leahy to "[p]lease ask General Marshall, Admiral King, and General Arnold to read this amazing report and to let me know what they think we should do about it." Farish's observations confirmed what FDR had long since concluded. He told the British foreign secretary, Anthony Eden, that these Yugoslavs had little in common, particularly the Serbs and Croats, and that the only practical solution was to separate them.

★

The President ran into resistance from Churchill on another secret operation. He cabled the Prime Minister in March 1944, reminding him that the U.S. and British military had been cooperating on a pilotless, remote-controlled bomber "to be launched against large industrial targets in Germany, each bomber to be loaded with some 20,000 pounds of high explosives and set on course to target. . . ." But the British chiefs of staff reneged and persuaded Churchill to back off from the deal. As Air Chief Marshal Sir Charles Portal put it, "[T]he possibility of retaliation against the unique target of London had been felt to outweigh the advantages of the employment of this weapon." To FDR, such reasoning was naïve. He reminded Churchill that the Allies already knew Germany was building new weapons to strike England, their development slowed but not stopped by Allied air raids. ". . . [I]f the enemy were to take effective measures against the cities of England with this type of weapon," Roosevelt argued, "he would have done so regardless of any use by us of pilotless aircraft." One week after D-Day, FDR was proved right when the Germans launched the first of eight thousand pilotless V-1 buzz bombs against London. In the meantime, the Americans continued to develop their flying bomb, and Roosevelt advised Churchill that its use would not end in Europe: "Combat experience with this weapon on the continent will make possible the most effective use of this type of weapon in the battle against the highly concentrated areas of the Japanese homeland." The President urged "that you ask your Chiefs of Staff to consider their withdrawal of concurrence on this project." Churchill gave his lukewarm consent.

A handsome, dark-haired twenty-nine-year-old American Navy pilot, with two combat tours of duty already completed and with orders to return home, volunteered instead to train for the flying bomb project. The pilot was Lieutenant Joseph Kennedy Jr., the son of FDR's former ambassador to Great Britain. Kennedy had already been recommended for a Navy medal for valor and the President had graciously agreed to pin it on him in a White House ceremony. The event did not come off because, in the end, Joe Sr. decided that it would be unwise to show his son special attention. Nevertheless, the President's willingness marked an upward tick in the ever fluctuating relations between FDR and his former ambassador. The low point had been reached three years before, after Kennedy had returned home from London and before the United States entered the war. Kennedy had addressed the graduating class at Notre Dame in the spring of 1941, after which the White House received a letter from someone who claimed to have heard Kennedy's off-the-record remarks. According to this informant, Kennedy had said, ". . . Hitler was the greatest genius of the century. . . . [His] diplomatic ability was superior to anything the British could hope to muster. . . . Britain is hopelessly licked and there will be a negotiated peace within sixty days." It was hearsay. Still, the reported comments rang true to the Joe Kennedy of 1941.

Not to be outdone, Bill Donovan was also exploring a remote-controlled weapon that would employ even newer technology. Rudimentary television broadcasting had been carried out by the BBC in England as early as 1937; and FDR had watched faint, flickering images on the embryonic receiver in the snuggery at Hyde Park. But television had not yet been enlisted in the war. Stanley Lovell, Donovan's science chief, saw an opportunity. In a joint OSS/Army Air Corps report, Lovell noted, "Harbors sheltering naval and merchant vessels . . . are highly protected. Against attack from the air there will be concentrations of anti-aircraft and machine gun fire. Barrage balloons over docks and ships prevent low-level attack. . . . To make successful attacks against specific targets in defended harbors without prohibitive losses in men and equipment requires a different mode of attack." Lovell and Air Corps engineers believed they had the answer in a project ultimately called Javaman. The man Donovan chose as project officer to ride herd on the mission was an OSS Navy lieutenant commander, John Shaheen, a twenty-nine-year-old coil of energy born on a farm in Illinois but who, with his small, dark appearance, reflecting Middle Eastern antecedents, could more easily have passed unnoticed in Cairo than in a cornfield. Shaheen and the Javaman team set to work developing a thirty-four-foot light, high-powered motorboat capable of speeds up to forty-five miles per hour that would have a television camera mounted on its forward deck affording a twenty-six-degree field of vision. The boat was to have a rusty, seaworn aspect, allowing it to pass as a fishing craft or other innocuous vessel. The hold was to be crammed with eight thousand pounds of high explosives. The boat would be launched from a mother ship some twenty miles from an enemy port. From then on, it would be radio-controlled by a plane flying up to fifty miles distant. A television receiver installed aboard the plane would display whatever the camera on the boat deck saw. Once a warship or large merchantman was spotted, the remote controller in the plane would bring the boat to top speed and use the television image to guide it to explode against its target.

By June 17, 1944, eleven days after D-Day, Shaheen reported to Donovan that test runs conducted at the Navy's Little Creek Mine Command in Virginia had succeeded and that the Army had provided sixteen expendable Hacker boats for Project Javaman. Only a few final glitches remained to be worked out.

In the meantime, the Air Force's flying bomb project had graduated from experimental to operational. The first six missions failed, with loss of life and aircraft. On August 12 the first mission organized by the Navy, called Aphrodite, was launched. A PB4Y-1 Liberator lifted off from a concrete runway at Fersfield aerodrome in southern England, destined for a V-1 launching site near the French coast. The crew consisted of the pilot, Lieutenant Kennedy, and the co-pilot, a thirty-five-year-old regular Navy officer and father of three, Lieutenant Wilford J. Willy of Fort Worth, Texas. Tightly packed behind them were ten tons of explosives. With them flew several escort aircraft. Once under way, Kennedy and Willy would bail out and an escort plane would then use remote-control radio to guide the explosives-laden Liberator to crash into the launching site. Flying among the escorts was Colonel Elliott Roosevelt, the President's son. Just twenty-eight minutes after takeoff, while still over the English coast, Colonel Roosevelt saw a blinding flash. The Kennedy Liberator burst into a fireball and fell to earth near the village of Newdelight Woods. Why the plane exploded prematurely was never determined and the bodies of Kennedy and Willy were never recovered. For years, the cause of Kennedy's and Willy's deaths was veiled in mystery because British military officials did not want their people to know that planes packed with explosives, under shaky radio control, were flying over the country.

The President sent Joe Kennedy Sr. his condolences, and, later, a destroyer was named for Joe Jr. But the elder Kennedy remained grief-stricken and embittered by the loss of his first son, in whom he had invested great dreams, including, someday, possibly the presidency of the United States. That fall of 1944, Senator Harry Truman, in Boston campaigning as FDR's vice presidential running mate, invited Joe Kennedy to join him at the Ritz-Carlton Hotel for a chat and to put the arm on the wealthy ex-ambassador for a campaign contribution. Kennedy, wearing a tam-o'-shanter, marched into Truman's suite and immediately began to berate Roosevelt. "Harry," he snarled, "what the hell are you doing campaigning for that crippled son-of-a-bitch that killed my son Joe?"

★

Flying bombs and floating missiles were as firecrackers alongside the hopes for the Manhattan Project. The atom bomb was supposed to be the most tightly guarded secret of the war. Yet, the President was disconcerted to discover that someone as uninvolved as Supreme Court Justice Felix Frankfurter knew what was happening at Los Alamos. Frankfurter had first learned of the Manhattan Project through a young physicist working on it named Irving Lowen. Lowen had earlier talked himself into Eleanor Roosevelt's Washington Square apartment in New York where he urged the First Lady to warn the President that Germany was ahead in the race for an atomic bomb. Lowen later took his fears to the justice. Even then, the field of physics was not entirely foreign to Frankfurter. During a year at Oxford in the early thirties, he had become friends with the Danish physicist Niels Bohr, a 1922 Nobel Prize winner now trapped in Nazi-occupied Denmark.

Eager to exploit Bohr's expertise, British atomic scientists plotted to spirit him out of his homeland to work on Tube Alloys. The physicist initially resisted. But when Hitler ordered the roundup of Danish Jews, Bohr's conscience was stirred. His mother was a Jew. The British secret service arranged for Bohr to slip into neutral Sweden by boat, and then bundled him into the bomb bay of a British Mosquito bomber. He arrived in England on October 6, 1943. Bohr subsequently went to America at the urging of Sir John Anderson, then heading Tube Alloys research in England. Bohr's mission was twofold, to lend his knowledge of nuclear physics to the Manhattan Project and to uphold Britain's full partnership in development of the bomb. On his arrival, Bohr was astounded at the speed with which Robert Oppenheimer's team was proceeding toward its goal. He told the Americans, incorrectly, that he was certain the Germans were building a bomb, which further spurred the Manhattan Project. By now, Bohr had also developed a political position on the bomb. He believed that the United States and Britain should bring Russia into the secret. Soviet scientists, too, he knew, were involved in atomic research. Should Russia learn that its Western allies were hogging the secret, attempting, in effect, to achieve a monopoly, the result would be, Bohr predicted, a nuclear arms race. The swift pace of work at Los Alamos only convinced him further of the need to bring the Russians in on the project.

After leaving Los Alamos, Bohr went to Washington to meet his friend Felix Frankfurter, who invited him to lunch in his Supreme Court chambers. The justice, a short, sharp-witted, agnostic Zionist, explained that he had been approached by scientists seeking advice on some of the political problems raised by a certain project involving atomic energy. Frankfurter and Bohr pussyfooted around the forbidden subject until the jurist made a reference to Project X, another code name for the Manhattan Project. They now knew that each shared the secret. Bohr, aware of Frankfurter's closeness to Roosevelt, took the opportunity to reiterate his concern that the Allies' most covert operation had to be shared with a Communist regime for the sake of postwar peace.

Bohr returned to England, where on May 16, 1944, he managed to obtain a meeting with Churchill. According to an eyewitness account by Sir Alexander Cadogan, the Foreign Office advisor to the Prime Minister, they met a ponderous old gentleman who presented his argument in incomprehensible physics jargon, and then looked up hopefully for understanding. "He talked inaudibly for three-quarters of an hour—about what, I haven't the faintest idea," Cadogan later wrote. Churchill's thoughts, at the time, were entirely consumed with last-minute plans for the invasion of Normandy, and here was a rambling old Dane pressing the mad idea of giving away the secrets of the atom bomb to the Soviet Union. The Prime Minister, through his own intelligence channels, had learned that a leading Soviet scientist, Peter Kapitsa, had invited Bohr to come to work on the Russians' own atomic project, under way since 1942. Anything Bohr required, Kapitsa had promised, would be his. The Dane declined, but knowledge of the offer did little to assuage Churchill. After the meeting, he carped at Lord Cherwell, his scientific advisor, "I did not like the man when you showed him to me, with his hair all over his head, at Downing Street."

By June the peripatetic Bohr was back in the United States. Felix Frankfurter, in a "Dear Frank" letter dated July 10, pleaded with FDR to see the physicist. His strongest case was that Bohr possessed information "pointing to a feverish German activity on nuclear problems." The Nazis' progress, Bohr feared, would soon be known to the Russians. Better Stalin should learn of the possibilities of the bomb from his ally, America, than from the enemy, Frankfurter argued. He included along with his handwritten letter to FDR a long memorandum that Bohr had sweated over in a humid Washington hotel room, a document as impenetrable as his speech.

On August 26, FDR met with Bohr and his physicist son, Aage. After the gruff reception the Dane had received at the hands of Churchill, he was apprehensive about Roosevelt's reaction to him. But FDR displayed his patented charm, regaling his visitors with stories about his dealings with Churchill and Stalin at Tehran. He also gave the two men all the time they needed to present their case. Bohr and his son left FDR's office after an hour and a half full of optimism. As Aage Bohr later recorded the encounter, "Roosevelt agreed that an approach to the Soviet Union of the kind suggested must be tried, and said that he had the best hopes that such a step would achieve a favourable result. In his opinion Stalin was enough of a realist to understand the revolutionary importance of this scientific and technical advance. . . ." As for the pounding Bohr had taken at Churchill's hands, Aage Bohr added, "Roosevelt said he and Churchill always managed to reach agreement and he thought that Churchill would eventually come around to sharing his point of view in this matter." Niels Bohr had even been led to believe that Roosevelt, if Churchill concurred, might ask him "to undertake an exploratory mission to the Soviet Union." The physicist had experienced the facet of the Roosevelt persona that desired to be all things to all people.

Shortly after this encounter, Roosevelt and Churchill held their second meeting at Quebec in September 1944. Afterward, the Prime Minister traveled down to Hyde Park along with Mrs. Churchill and their daughter Mary. He looked forward to both the serenity of Roosevelt's riverside estate and the chance to resolve privately a dangling concern. Lunch was served immediately upon the Churchill's arrival, and another Roosevelt guest turned out to be the Duke of Windsor. Whatever doubts Churchill had about the loyalty or good sense of his former monarch, he nevertheless behaved toward the duke with deference and cordiality. Amid the sparkling conversation, however, the current governor of the Bahamas was not to be made privy to anything of significance.

The next day, Churchill closeted himself with the President in the snuggery to describe his twin frustrations. First, he reiterated his conviction that Britain was still not being treated as a full atomic partner. Next, the interfering Niels Bohr rankled him. Churchill raised the matter of Bohr's contact with the Soviet scientist Kapitsa. The only reason the Russians wanted the Dane in Moscow, Churchill warned, was to spy on Tube Alloys. To make his position absolutely clear, Churchill drafted and persuaded Roosevelt to sign an aide-mémoire with all the subtlety of a sledgehammer. Its first paragraph read: "The suggestion that the world should be informed regarding Tube Alloys, with a view to an international agreement regarding its control and use, is not accepted. The matter should continue to be regarded as of the utmost secrecy, but when a 'bomb' is finally available, it might perhaps, after mature consideration, be used against the Japanese, who should be warned that this bombardment will be repeated until they surrender." The statement ended even more harshly: "Enquiries should be made regarding the activities of Professor Bohr and steps taken to ensure that he is responsible for no leakage of information, particularly to the Russians." That day Churchill left Hyde Park by train to board the *Queen Mary* and return to England, content that he had slain the dragon of ill-advised cooperation on the atom with Russia. While aboard ship, he wrote Lord Cherwell: "He [Bohr] is a great advocate of [atomic] publicity. He made unauthorized disclosure to Justice Frankfurter. . . . The professor [Kapitsa] urged him to go to Russia to discuss matters. What is this all about? It seems to me that Bohr ought to be confined or at any rate made to see that he is very near the edge of mortal crime."

Roosevelt, typically, left no explanation for what appears to be a complete flip-flop on sharing atomic secrets with Russia. For all his determination to keep the Russian war machine grinding on through lend-lease and total fealty to Stalin, FDR, like Churchill, was aware that if this thing worked, this atomic bomb, its possessor would wield the dominant power in the postwar world. The secrets of Los Alamos were not to be donated to the Soviets.

In guarding the secret of the atom bomb, the loyalty of Niels Bohr was the least of Roosevelt's and Churchill's worries. The Russians had other resources. And they understood perfectly the global ramifications of an atomic monopoly. The NKVD code name revealed the rank given to the Manhattan Project: ". . . [W]e call it 'ENORMOZ.' " The month before Churchill convinced FDR to reject the Danish physicist, a slight, inconspicuous figure with a retreating hairline, a veined forehead, receding chin, and turkey neck reported to the bomb design and assembly laboratory at Los Alamos, New Mexico. The mild-mannered Klaus Fuchs instantly impressed Robert Oppenheimer, the project's scientific leader, when he half apologetically pointed out a flaw in a key equation. Thereafter, Oppenheimer invited Fuchs to the weekly meeting of division and group leaders.

Despite his retiring manner, perhaps because of it, the bachelor physicist enjoyed a full after-hours social life at Los Alamos. The shy Fuchs aroused the maternal instincts of Manhattan Project wives, who saw to it that he was invited to their picnics, dinner parties, and dances, where he proved surprisingly light on his feet. The job, nevertheless, remained Fuchs's obsession. As his immediate superior, Hans Bethe, put it, "He worked days and nights. He was a bachelor and had nothing better to do, and he contributed very greatly to the success of the Los Alamos project." As Fuchs later described his dual existence, in "one compartment I allowed myself to make friendships, to have personal relationships . . . I knew that the other compartment would step in if I approached the danger point." He had an expression for his mind-set, "controlled schizophrenia."

Even before coming to Los Alamos, Fuchs had already begun slipping atomic secrets to his Soviet contact in New York, Harry Gold, code-named Raymond. Now he was positioned deep within the atomic sanctum, able not merely to provide to his Soviet superiors the marginalia of nuclear physics, but the very heart of the bomb's construction.

Fuchs was not alone at Los Alamos in his hidden loyalties. Theodore Alvin Hall, son of an immigrant New York furrier, was a physics prodigy who skipped whole grades in secondary school. He was initially accepted by Columbia University but turned away when it was discovered he was only fourteen. He next attended Queens College and in 1942, at age sixteen, entered Harvard as a junior. There he demonstrated a genius for quantum mechanics. When Manhattan Project recruiters discreetly inquired at Harvard about promising physicists, Ted Hall, now an eighteen-year-old senior, was suggested.

From early youth the precocious Hall had been drawn to radical politics, joining the left-wing American Student Union when he was thirteen. At Los Alamos, the boy physicist, with the slender, handsome looks, soon adopted the moral conviction of several of his colleagues that knowledge of the bomb should be shared with the Soviet Union. As he later described his state of mind, "I was worried about the dangers of an American monopoly of atomic weapons if there should be a post-war depression." In October 1944, while visiting his family in Forest Hills, he went to the Amtorg purchasing office at 238 West Twenty-eighth Street and boldly offered to give atomic secrets to the Soviet Union. Two months later, now assigned a Russian controller, he made his first delivery, pages of handwritten notes jotted down in the privacy of his room at Los Alamos. Some scholars would later rate the notes that Hall handed to the Soviets as superior even to Fuchs's disclosures in that the young physicist was the first to reveal to Russia the implosion method for detonating the bomb. Hall was nineteen when he provided the Soviet Union with possibly its most priceless atomic secret thus far.

★

Nineteen forty-four was a presidential election year, and espionage intruded into the campaign. Once Roosevelt had cleared the third-term barrier, and with the country in the midst of war, a fourth-term bid seemed unremarkable. FDR initially remained coy about his intentions. One person, however, privy to his thoughts was Daisy Suckley. Over the past twelve years, he had exhausted the nation's appetite for liberal politics, he told her. As she recorded in her diary after she and Roosevelt had finished a lone lunch, ". . . [H]e remembers Woodrow Wilson telling him that the public is willing to be 'Liberal' about a third of the time, gets tired of new things and reverts to conservatism the other two-thirds of the time." On May 22, 1944, FDR made another admission to his spinster confidant, something he had first raised at Bernard Baruch's South Carolina estate. He knew he was sicker than his doctors had let on. But on this subsequent occasion, discussing a fourth term, he told Daisy, "What will decide me will be the way I feel in a couple of months. If I know I am not going to be able to carry on for another four years, it wouldn't be fair to the American people to run for another term." Should that be his decision, he claimed, "I have a candidate—but don't breathe it to a soul." FDR paused conspiratorially, then said, "Henry J. Kaiser."

Suckley was astonished. No one, she thought, could be more unlike the President. True, the sixty-two-year-old Kaiser was an eighteen-hour-a-day dynamo, a bottleneck breaker, who was on his way to turning out over a thousand Liberty ships, some in just days, a man so hyperactive that he wore two watches, one set to East Coast time and the other to West Coast time. He was known as the New Deal's favorite tycoon. But Kaiser's knowledge and experience of politics were nil and his personality less than magnetic. Suckley could not tell if the President was sincere or merely fishing for encouragement to run again by comparing himself to so unlikely a successor. Nor could she know how sincere this byzantine personality was when FDR told her, "[I]f the election were held tomorrow, he would be beaten by almost any Republican." That July, however, Roosevelt did accept a fourth-term nomination as naturally as breathing. He chose Senator Harry S Truman as his running mate, shedding Henry Wallace, whose ultra-liberal politics and eccentricities had become anathema to Democrat bosses. FDR's Republican opponent was to be New York's governor and former racket-busting prosecutor, Thomas E. Dewey.

The choice of Truman would eventually plug a flagrant security leak. In January 1944, Fritz Kolbe was shocked by a document that came across his Berlin foreign office desk. Vice President Wallace had continued to confide the most delicate secrets to his trusted brother-in-law, Charles Bruggmann, and the Swiss diplomat had continued to cable these conversations to his superiors in the Swiss foreign ministry. What Kolbe came across was Wallace's account of what had happened in the innermost councils of a Moscow conference of foreign ministers in October 1943. This information had found its way to Berlin through Habakuk, the German plant in the Swiss foreign office. Kolbe delivered the incriminating document to Allen Dulles on his next trip to Bern. Upon receiving it, Dulles alerted Donovan, who in turn took the report to the President's military chief of staff, Admiral Leahy. The admiral, stunned by the enormity of Wallace's indiscretion, immediately showed the message to the President. Leahy was equally amazed by FDR's reaction. "The OSS report did not seem to surprise Roosevelt," Leahy noted. "I do not recall that he commented on it at all except to say that it was quite interesting." Two possible answers explain the President's bland reaction. Either FDR's powers of concentration were flagging or he knew, come July, that Wallace would not be on the ticket with him.

Arlington Hall's work was not limited to decrypting Japanese ciphers. In April 1944 a broken message sent by the Swiss ambassador in Tokyo to Bern painted a gloomy portrait of Japan's capital in the third year of war with America. The decrypt, sent to FDR, read: "Stores are closing one by one and Tokyo presents a pitiful spectacle. The Japanese are more and more dependent on the black market, and the distress of the people is great. . . . Thousands of families are leaving the capital, driven out by hunger." The President could only hope that the picture of Tokyo was more accurate than the one the Japanese were receiving about the American home front. A German who had been interned in the United States returned home in early March 1944 aboard an exchange ship and gave this description to Ambassador Oshima: "Living conditions of the people in general in the United States are growing steadily worse. Prices are soaring and quality declining. Distribution of articles, particularly necessary for daily use, is poor. Foods, particularly meats, vegetables, sugar and fresh fish, are scarce. It is the same with goods of secondary necessity. Such things as shoes are almost unobtainable."

The collision of presidential politics and espionage occurred less than two months before the 1944 election. James V. Forrestal, the Navy secretary, who had succeeded Frank Knox after the latter's death that year, first sounded the alarm. "My Dear Mr. President," Forrestal wrote in his neat longhand on September 14, "Information has come to me that Dewey's first speech will deal with Pearl Harbor." An unidentified anti-Roosevelt Army officer, it turned out, had informed Dewey that FDR had access to broken Japanese codes long before December 7, 1941. Therefore, the President had to have known of the impending attack and had done nothing to prevent it. Consequently, the Dewey camp reasoned, FDR was guilty of criminal negligence at best and treason at worst. General Marshall, aware of the leak, and given his visceral loathing of politics, dreaded entering into this political sinkhole, but saw no choice. Without saying anything to Roosevelt, he proceeded with his own counterattack.

On September 25, Dewey, then campaigning in Tulsa, Oklahoma, received a visitor, Colonel Carter Clarke, dressed for the day in a recently reactivated civilian suit. Ushered into the candidate's hotel suite, Clarke handed Dewey an envelope stamped in red "Top Secret." As the former prosecutor eyed the envelope warily, Clarke explained that he had come directly from General Marshall. Dewey, with the trademark black mustache and a cold-eyed gaze, a shorter man than the officer had expected, extracted a letter from the envelope. "Well," Dewey said, after reading it with a lawyer's scrutiny, "Top Secret—that's really top, isn't it?" Clarke could not tell if the candidate was genuinely impressed or being sarcastic.

Marshall's letter began, "I am writing to you without the knowledge of any other person except Admiral King. . . . The conduct of General Eisenhower's campaign and of all operations in the Pacific are closely related in conception and timing to the information we secretly obtain through . . . intercepted codes. They contribute greatly to the victory and tremendously to the saving in American lives. . . . Our main basis of information regarding Hitler's intentions in Europe is obtained from Baron Oshima's messages from Berlin reporting his interviews with Hitler and other officials. . . . These are still the codes involved in the Pearl Harbor events." He went on to explain that Magic had provided the edge in the naval battles of the Coral Sea and Midway. The heavy shipping losses inflicted on the emperor's fleet, he explained, ". . . largely result from the fact that we know the sailing dates and routes of their convoys and can notify our submarines to lie in wait at these points." He warned of the disastrous impact of compromising the secret of the broken codes with an unadmiring reference to the OSS: ". . . Some of Donovan's people, without telling us, instituted a secret search of the Japanese embassy offices in Portugal. As a result, the entire military attaché code all over the world was changed, and though this occurred over a year ago, we have not yet been able to break the new code. . . ." The last point, while persuasive, was not quite true; and given Marshall's reputation for probity, it had probably been fed to him by Donovan's enemies in Army intelligence. The Japanese had not changed their codes after the OSS black bag job inside the Lisbon embassy.

Dewey knew that he faced a cunning opponent in FDR and feared a trap. He found it hard to dismiss a suspicion that Marshall was doing the

President's dirty work in order to rob him of a powerful campaign issue. A Dewey aide pointed out to Clarke that tens of thousands of people knew that the United States had broken the Japanese codes. Hadn't the *Chicago Tribune* carried that story after Midway? To which Dewey added, "Well, I'll be damned if I believe the Japs are still using those two codes." As unlikely as it seemed, Colonel Clarke insisted, they were. For all his toughness and his own cunning, Tom Dewey was, at bottom, a patriot. After another meeting with Colonel Clarke at the governor's office in Albany, he accepted Marshall's plea. He did not raise Magic as a campaign issue, and the Japanese continued to use their compromised codes.

General Marshall, despite Dewey's suspicions, had been honest in claiming that the President knew nothing of his approach to the Republican candidate. Not until days before the election did Harry Hopkins go to FDR with the story, after Marshall had confided it to Roosevelt's closest aide. "The President was surprised at the action Marshall had taken but expressed no criticism of that action," Hopkins later recalled. "He merely stated that he felt confident that Governor Dewey would not, for political purposes, give secret and vital information to the enemy." FDR also revealed a surer grasp of popular sentiment than Dewey. He told Hopkins, "My opponent must be pretty desperate if he is even thinking of using material like this which would be bound to react against him."

If he had lost a campaign issue, Dewey had won an unwanted fan. The Nazi RSHA, which included the Gestapo and the SD intelligence operations, received a dispatch from "an entirely trustworthy informant in Spain," claiming, "Dewey hereby showed an instinctive antipathy to the Jews. . . . Many Jewish elements were to be found among the gangsters he had fought [as a district attorney]. This attitude is, according to the informant's view, traceable to Dewey's Irish ancestry as well as to his defeat in the 1938 campaign against the Jewish-Democratic candidate [for governor, Herbert] Lehman. . . . And the informant mentioned the possibility of an understanding between Germany and the U.S.A. under Dewey's presidency." It was rubbish passing for intelligence and demonstrated the uselessness of information tailored to fit prejudices, in this case, the anti-Semitism of Adolf Hitler.

That fall, FDR found occasion to lecture Churchill about security. *The New York Times* had carried a story headlined INVENTION GIVES U-BOATS NEW LIFE, BRITON ASSERTS. A Royal Air Force senior officer was quoted saying that "the Germans were fitting an extendible air intake to their U-boats so that they could recharge batteries and ventilate the submarines without surfacing." FDR cabled the text of the *Times* story to Churchill, adding, ". . . [O]ur own submarine campaign in the Pacific is playing such an important role that the Barbarian will seize desperately upon any information that will help him in anti-submarine measures. I do hope, therefore, that we may continue to keep anyone from talking too much. I have no doubt that indiscretions are committed in our press but the enclosed has recently appeared under a London dateline. I will do what I can to keep the lid on here and I know I may count on you for similar measures."

★

The war eventually was going to be won. Normandy had settled the outcome on the western front; Stalingrad had settled it in the East. The questions remaining were how much longer the victory would require and how to deal with the enemy afterward. Germany's postwar treatment had been the subject of heated debate at Tehran in the fall of 1943. Roosevelt and Stalin favored a peace as simple as it was harsh; they wanted Germany broken up. Churchill was opposed. Keeping secret the dissension among the Allies became critical, for how hard the Germans continued to fight depended in part on how they expected to be treated in defeat.

On August 19, 1944, Henry Morgenthau, who had long concerned himself with the fate of European Jewry at the hands of the Nazis, went to the White House to discuss with FDR his ideas for dealing with postwar Germany. The President's thinking happily coincided with his own. "We have got to be tough with Germany," FDR told his Treasury secretary, "and I mean the German people not just the Nazis. We either have to castrate the German people or you have got to treat them in such manner so they can't just go on reproducing people who want to continue the way they have in the past." Morgenthau liked the punitive ring of the President's comments. "Nobody is considering the question along those lines," he responded to FDR. "In England they want to build up Germany so she can pay reparations!" After leaving the White House, he wrote in his diary that the President "left no doubt whatsoever in my mind that he personally wants to be tough with the Germans."

It was outside his domain, but Morgenthau sensed a vacuum in postwar policy waiting to be filled. He went to a necessary ally, Henry Stimson, to test some fresh approaches. "I . . . gave him my idea of the possibility of removing all industry from Germany and simply reducing them to an agricultural population of small land-owners," he later wrote of this conversation. Morgenthau had then described a plan for reshaping the German character. He told Stimson, ". . . [I]f you let the young children of today be brought up by SS Troopers who are indoctrinated with Hitlerism, aren't you simply going to raise another generation of Germans who will want to wage war? . . . Don't you think the thing to do is to take a leaf from Hitler's book and completely remove these children from their parents and make them wards of the state . . . ?" Ex-Army officers from the United States, Britain, and Russia could run schools, he suggested, "and have these children learn the true spirit of democracy." Stimson expressed horror at Morgenthau's draconian ideas. The Treasury secretary responded, "[T]hat is not nearly as bad as sending them to gas chambers."

To Stimson, Morgenthau was not seeking a viable policy, but wanted Jewish vengeance. He immediately sent to the White House a "Handbook" prepared in his department describing a more moderate approach to a defeated Germany. Roosevelt's response, the most stinging that Stimson ever received, left no doubt that FDR preferred Morgenthau's divide, disarm, and denazify approach. "This so-called 'Handbook,' " Roosevelt began, "is pretty bad. . . . [A]ll copies should be withdrawn. . . . It gives me the impression that Germany is to be restored just as much as the Netherlands or Belgium. . . . [E]very person in Germany should realize that this time Germany is a defeated nation. . . . [I]f they need food to keep body and soul together beyond what they have, they should be fed three times a day with soup from Army soup kitchens. . . . [T]hey will remember that experience all their lives. . . . There exists a school of thought both in London and here which would, in effect, do for Germany what this Government did for its own citizens in 1933 when they were flat on their backs." FDR told Stimson, "I see no reason for starting a WPA, PWA or a CCC for Germany when we go in with our Army of Occupation." The Third Reich was not to be replaced by the New Deal.

Thus was born, out of the Treasury secretary's drive and FDR's concurrence, the Morgenthau plan to subdivide Germany into small states to be peopled by farmers. "All Junker estates," the draft read, "should be broken up and divided among the peasants and the system of primogeniture and entail should be abolished." All German aircraft were to be confiscated; a nation of farmers did not need planes. The plan incorporated the President's own ideas for taming the Teutonic martial streak: "No German shall be permitted to wear . . . any military uniform or any uniform of any quasi-military organization." Further, there were to be no military parades, no military bands. The word went out from the White House that the plan "must not be shown to anyone." Stimson remained adamantly opposed and predicted that Morgenthau's proposal "will tend through bitterness and suffering to breed another war. . . ."

On September 10, Roosevelt and Churchill met again at Quebec. At first it appeared that the President had sold a reluctant Prime Minister on the Morgenthau plan through a quid pro quo, a substantial expansion of lend-lease to Britain. He and Churchill then signed a memorandum describing their intention to convert Germany "into a country primarily agricultural and pastoral in its character."

The veil of secrecy surrounding the Morgenthau plan, however, was soon pierced. *The Washington Post* reaching the President's desk on September 21 carried columnist Drew Pearson's uncomfortably accurate account of the disagreements inside the administration over Germany's postwar fate. The next day, *The New York Times* had a story by Arthur Krock on the Morgenthau proposal, and the following day *The Wall Street Journal* printed details of both the closely guarded plan and the secret Quebec codicil. News stories began flooding the country raising the spectacle of a divided administration. Once the bare-knuckled approach to Germany leaked out, the enemy's ingenious propaganda minister, Josef Goebbels, leaped upon the Morgenthau plan to instill a fight-to-the-death mentality in Germany. Defiance, he preached, was preferable to serfdom.

The election was less than six weeks off when Dewey, deprived of the Magic issue, saw another opening. By mid-September, Allied troops stood on German soil for the first time since the war began. But the Wehrmacht gave ground grudgingly. Dewey charged that German resistance had stiffened because of the leaked Morgenthau scheme. American GIs, he predicted, were going to die unnecessarily because the Roosevelt administration intended to impose a brutal peace on the enemy. FDR, politically sensitized to his fingertips, began to back off. On September 29, Morgenthau, clutching a batch of newspaper clippings dealing with his now endangered proposal, planted himself in the entryway to Roosevelt's private study. He told FDR's daughter, Anna, "I will stay here outside the President's door in case he should want to see me." Anna went into the office and emerged a few minutes later. "She said that the President didn't want to see me," a crestfallen Morgenthau confided to his diary, "and she kept moving me toward the elevator."

That same day, FDR quietly assigned the task of deciding Germany's postwar fate to a Morgenthau adversary, the State Department. The Treasury secretary was to stick to finance. Barely three weeks after he and

Churchill had signed the Quebec memorandum to dismember Germany, FDR had made a 180-degree turn. "No one," he told Cordell Hull, "wants complete eradication of German industrial production capacity. . . ." Four days after Morgenthau had been rebuffed, the secretary of war talked to Roosevelt and later recorded their conversation. FDR, Stimson wrote, "grinned and looked naughty and said, 'Henry Morgenthau pulled a boner. . . .' He had no intention of turning Germany into an agrarian state. . . ." Though Stimson had seen his own position vindicated, he wanted to make sure that FDR did not trip over his own contradictions. He read to the President from the Quebec memorandum language unmistakably proposing to convert Germany into a nation of farmers. Roosevelt managed to appear stunned. He could not believe, he said, that he could have agreed to such a statement.

The Morgenthau plan was dead, though Tom Dewey kept flogging it. In his last speech of the 1944 campaign, he charged that disclosure of the plan had indeed cost the needless deaths of American GIs. Its advantage to the enemy had been, he said, the equivalent of "ten fresh German divisions."

★

A lack of grounding in the political culture of the enemy could produce intelligence of astonishing naïveté. After Lieutenant Colonel Otto Skorzeny had succeeded in his daring rescue of the deposed Mussolini, Magic intercepted a message from the Japanese ambassador in Turkey to Tokyo that read: "According to what American officials here say, President Roosevelt had a little scheme for sending Mussolini to the United States and using him there for propaganda purposes in his move for re-election. Consequently Mussolini's escape, it is thought, was a . . . severe blow to Roosevelt."

FDR hardly needed a fallen fascist dictator to win the presidency for the fourth time. On November 7 he carried out his election day ritual at Hyde Park. Eleanor, other family members, and the immediate staff sat around a small dining room table, tally sheets and sharpened pencils at hand, while the President nibbled on his wife's one culinary accomplishment, scrambled eggs. A clattering Teletype machine in the corner brought in early returns. Seventeen days before, Roosevelt had told Daisy Suckley that he thought Dewey had waged an effective campaign. FDR ". . . feels there is an excellent chance of his being defeated in the election," she wrote in her diary. "The President is planning his life after he leaves the White House. . . . He will write and can make a lot of money that way." If he genuinely feared Dewey, no sign appeared in Roosevelt's cool and unconcerned demeanor. By 1:30 A.M., surrounded by crumpled papers, spilling ashtrays, and cold, half-finished cups of coffee, he was still scribbling on his tally sheets, out of habit, although it was already clear that he had won. Not until 3:16 A.M., however, did Dewey read a concession statement to a near-empty ballroom at his campaign headquarters. He did not congratulate the victor. As the President was wheeled to his bedroom, he remarked to his aide William Rigdon, "I still think he is a son of a bitch."

Chapter XXIV

———— ═ ★ ═ ————

"Take a Look at the OSS"

B Y THE fall of 1944, the OSS payroll numbered over eleven thousand. Professors, scientists, philosophers, writers, journalists, lawyers, doctors, engineers, public relations experts, and actors crowded the cubicles on E Street. Secret agents had been spirited into every Nazi-occupied country. Supporting the Normandy invasion, the OSS infiltrated 523 agents into France to arm the resistance, radio back intelligence, and wreak havoc behind the lines. The London OSS staff forged papers and concocted cover stories for its spies and saboteurs that held up even against the Gestapo. Donovan had followed Overlord with his premier coup to date, espionage easing the way for Operation Anvil, the invasion of southern France. On August 15, 1944, General Alexander Patch's Seventh Army swarmed ashore at the chic Riviera beaches between Toulon and Cannes, suffering light casualties in no small measure because of OSS's advance work. Donovan's agents, teamed with the French resistance, provided Patch's forces with a virtual X ray of German defenses, coastal gun emplacements, minefields, roadblocks, airfields, even distinguishing real fortifications from false redoubts. One OSS dispatch reported the sand content of a concrete wall that the Seventh Army needed to blow. The Army's evaluation was glowing: ". . . [T]he results achieved by OSS in respect of Southern France before [Anvil] were so outstanding that they should be brought to the attention of interested authorities." Donovan's outfit had achieved the "best briefed invasion in history."

By September, the OSS embarked on its boldest enterprise, infiltrating agents directly into Germany. British intelligence had dismissed the possibility. Successful penetration of Nazi-controlled countries, MI6 warned, had depended on resistance fighters to provide safe houses, clandestine communications, food, clothing, and knowledge of the local landscape. No such support would be available in the enemy homeland with its populace in the grip of the Gestapo, with informers planted on every block and in every apartment building. Still, Donovan's increasingly sophisticated organization was eager to declare its independence, and how better than by succeeding in a mission that British intelligence considered foolhardy. On September 2 the OSS parachuted its first agent into the industrial Ruhr, Jupp Kappius, a German anti-Nazi socialist whose mission was to foment sabotage. Kappius became the forerunner of an eventual two hundred OSS agents who penetrated nearly every major German city before the war ended.

Donovan, though a rock-ribbed Republican of conservative social bent, had shown himself to be flexibly pragmatic in recruiting agents. German Communists were among the most ardent anti-Nazis who had fled the Gestapo dragnet, many finding refuge in Britain. In seeking to recruit Germans who could pass unnoticed inside the Reich, the OSS's Joseph Gould, a former movie publicist, hung around a left-wing London bookshop where he correctly guessed he would encounter Communist refugees. Through his bookshop contacts, Gould recruited German Reds, some under Gestapo death warrants, who were willing to parachute back into their homeland and spy against the Nazi regime. Aaron Bank, a forty-two-year-old OSS Army captain, trained a company of phony German infantry to be parachuted into the National Redoubt, the rumored stronghold where die-hard Nazis were expected to prolong the war indefinitely. Bank's mission, Iron Cross, was to attempt to seize Hitler and other top Nazis seeking sanctuary in the Redoubt. His recruits were Communists almost to a man.

Donovan, however willing to enlist Communists and Germans during wartime, knew he would face a contentious situation once the fighting ended. He took his quandary to FDR. On December 1, 1944, he sent the President a memorandum asking guidance on "a question which will rise with increasing frequency in connection with those of German nationality who work for us behind German lines." Donovan wanted to know "what we are prepared to do in their behalf in regard to offering firm guarantees of protection and post-armistice privileges to Germans whom we recruit and who work loyally for our organization." He asked the President to grant "permission for entry into the United States after the war, the placing of their earnings on deposit in an American bank and the like for these German nationals working for us within Germany at great risk." The President appreciated the courage displayed by these agents and their value. He had personally approved the employment of known Communists as radio operators on merchant ships. But bringing Germans, particularly Communists, to the United States after the war presented risks for a Democratic president long under attack by the American right wing for being soft on communism. FDR bucked Donovan's request to Edward Stettinius Jr., who by now had replaced the ailing Cordell Hull as secretary of state. "What do you think?" Roosevelt asked Stettinius. The secretary drafted a suggested reply for the President to send to Donovan. "I do not believe that we should offer any guarantees of protection in the post-hostilities period to Germans who are working for your organization," it read. "Such guarantees would be difficult and probably widely misunderstood both in this country and abroad. We may expect that the number of Germans who are anxious to save their skins and property by coming over to the side of the United Nations at the last moment will rapidly increase. Among them may be some who should properly be tried for war crimes." State's objections carried the day. No American safe harbor was to be provided after the war to anti-Nazi Germans, however usefully they had served the Allied cause or at what personal risk. The President's decision, however, did not deter OSS operatives from continuing to recruit German Communists or entering POW cages looking for soldiers willing to spy against the Nazi regime. And fulfillable or not, the OSS continued to dangle inducements before these prospects—U.S. citizenship, jobs, an automobile dealership in some American city—if they would spy against their country.

★

As the war progressed, Donovan began an offensive to ensure that his hard-won gains did not evaporate with the arrival of peace. A lifelong student of power, he began by reconnoitering the surest allies in the White House. Judge Samuel Rosenman, FDR's longtime confidant and potent phrasemaker of so many Roosevelt speeches, became a target. Donovan sent a rough outline for a permanent postwar intelligence service to Rosenman, hoping he would endorse it and forward it to FDR. Nothing came of this approach. A more unlikely but eventually more productive channel turned out to be a small, bald, bespectacled labor economist and statistician, Isadore Lubin, whom the President had put in the Map Room to work on wartime statistics. On October 12, Donovan dispatched Major J. H. Rosenbaum to the White House to enlist Lubin in support of his post-war dream. Rosenbaum happily reported back to Donovan, "Dr. Lubin was definitely impressed by the idea." Lubin advised only that Donovan amend his proposal to assure the Army and Navy that their intelligence branches would not be eclipsed by his scheme. "If we will get this changed plan back to [Lubin] right away," Rosenbaum reported, "he will present it to the President at once. This reaction is very satisfactory, as Dr. Lubin is usually successful in getting adopted what he has recommended." Donovan sent a response to Dr. Lubin expressing gratitude for his support of a permanent "central intelligence agency." It was the first time, outside of the OSS, that he had employed this phrase. Lubin took the revised proposal to the President on October 25, telling him, "Bill Donovan's Office of Strategic Services has been doing some swell work. It occurred to me that there will be room after the war for a service in the United States Government which would carry on some of the work now being done under Donovan's auspices."

Donovan's plan was bound to leak, and his rivals remained implacable. The first to strike back without having read the proposal was John Franklin Carter. Days after Lubin had taken Donovan's idea to the President, Carter warned FDR, "In my opinion, consideration should be given to the probability that British Intelligence has already penetrated the Donovan organization and is thoroughly familiar with its methods, plans and personnel." As for the future, Carter suggested an insulting role for the OSS: ". . . [I]ts greatest usefulness might be as a means of letting the British think they know what information is reaching us." He had a much more sensible idea, Carter advised the President, and cheaper too. It "involves a small and in-formal central office, adequately camouflaged, utilizing chiefly foreign contacts of American business, with the dispatch of occasional 'look-see' agents in special circumstances. If you should wish," he added, "I would like to organize and direct it." Carter was, in effect, proposing to make his own tight little ring permanent. His proposal was obviously not intended for Donovan to see, though that is exactly to whom FDR gave it with a cover note reading, "I am sending the enclosed to you for your eyes only. Will you be thinking about this in connection with the post-war period?" Donovan read Carter's dismissive critique, and four days later FDR had

Wild Bill's counterblast. "I am afraid that the author is in the 'horse and buggy' stage of intelligence thinking," Donovan observed. "Under your authority and with your support, there has been established for the first time in our history an independent American Intelligence Service which has already won the respect of similar services in other countries." Donovan rejected Carter's charge that the British had penetrated his OSS. "In point of fact," he told the President, "you would be interested to know that both our Allies and our enemies know less about our inner workings than we do about theirs."

Beating off Carter's attack was only a secondary skirmish. What mattered more to Donovan was that the President had actually asked him to start thinking about postwar intelligence. While FDR waged the final week of his presidential campaign, Donovan's top staff was huddled at his E Street headquarters into the small hours designing a permanent espionage apparatus. One week after the election, the general delivered to Grace Tully a suggested executive order with his customary plea that she place it before FDR immediately. Under his proposal, the new service would be freed from control of the military and placed directly under the President. The plan made a polite bow to the continuing necessity of military intelligence, MID and the ONI; but their connection to the new entity would be strictly advisory. Finally, Donovan's brainchild was not to be barred from practicing any reasonable form of espionage. It would have the authority to spy on foreign governments and carry out "subversive operations abroad."

If the President concurred, he had only to sign the executive order, and Donovan would have planted in the United States government its first permanent central intelligence agency. The general added a cryptic rationale as to why the President should make a quick decision. "Though in the midst of war, we are also in a period of transition," he noted. "There are commonsense reasons why you may desire to lay the keel of the ship at once." Donovan's appeal for quick action had been influenced by Robert B. Joyce, a sharp-minded political advisor on his staff who had studied the Soviet Union at first hand. By now, the Red Army had driven the Germans out of large tracts of Eastern Europe, and Joyce advised Donovan, "The Russians do not desire OSS activities in areas controlled by them or under their influence." What Donovan was saying to FDR, however obliquely, was that after the war, Europe would be weak, and Russia's behavior in it could not be presumed to be benign. A continuing American espionage capability would be vital to decode Stalin's intentions.

The postwar proposal Donovan set before the President was framed in the bloodless prose of the bureaucracy. But within the OSS, a document circulated that made the true intent clear. This secret internal paper was entitled "Interpretive Notes of Memorandum for the President." It envisioned a recasting of American intelligence on a breathtaking scale. Intelligence collected by other government offices, the document read, "must be furnished promptly and unreservedly to the central agency." Furthermore, no longer would Donovan's people be excluded from the Magics and the Ultras of the future. Other federal agencies were to act, in effect, as parts manufacturers while Donovan's apparatus would become the "assembly line," delivering the finished product to the Oval Office. The spy service was to have the pick of the litter: "In the armed services those officers who have demonstrated their superior aptitude for intelligence should be chosen for key positions in the intelligence agency." Further, this central service would be allowed to hire any talents it required, and "civil service regulations should be made inapplicable to such specialists." The document brashly styled the proposed agency "a national intelligence cartel."

Four days after receiving Donovan's suggested executive order creating a central intelligence agency, FDR told Admiral Leahy to take it to the Joint Chiefs of Staff for a recommendation. By now, Wild Bill's arch enemy, General George Veazey Strong, had been replaced as head of Army G-2 by General Clayton Bissell, who proved equally belligerent. Bissell argued, before the Joint Chiefs, that Donovan's super spy agency would have the authority to decide what intelligence the President did or did not see. "Such power in one man is not in the best interests of a democratic government," Bissell charged. "I think it is in the best interests of a dictatorship. I think it would be excellent for Germany. . . ."

While the military struck from one flank, J. Edgar Hoover attacked Donovan from another. The FBI director had made himself nearly indispensable to the White House. At the President's behest, his FBI had placed Vice President Wallace under surveillance ever since his loose-tongued indiscretions to his brother-in-law had been exposed. While Allen Dulles spied for the OSS in Switzerland, FBI agents spied on his sister, Eleanor, at home, reporting that her affair with a Russian translator had been consummated every Tuesday, Saturday, and Sunday for the previous five years. Even the private life of the President's trusted Harry Hopkins was not out of bounds. The President was furious over leaks of near-verbatim White House conversations that appeared in the antagonistic Washington *Times-Herald*. The shadow of suspicion fell upon Hopkins's third wife, Louise, a former Paris editor of *Harper's Bazaar,* a great beauty, and a woman with a past. She reportedly numbered among several wealthy lovers Bernard Baruch and Jock Whitney. After she married Hopkins, Louise moved into her husband's quarters in the White House. In the beginning, the President was smitten by her. Eleanor, however, was less enthralled at having another permanent houseguest, and a charmer to boot. Still, FDR wanted the couple to stay, particularly to keep Hopkins at hand day or night. In December 1944, with his frustration over the newspaper leaks mounting, Roosevelt had the FBI start watching Louise Hopkins. Hoover placed her under "physical and technical surveillance," which meant that she was followed and her phone tapped. Revealing his closeness to FDR, or his distrust of his wife, Hopkins himself made the arrangements for the FBI to spy on her. The investigation came up dry. Louise was neither spilling White House secrets nor betraying her husband.

Hoover used his closeness to Hopkins to point out the superiority of his organization in the espionage field. He sent a "Dear Harry" message that he knew Hopkins would forward to FDR and in which he described how a truly professional espionage organization performed. He cited as an example the FBI's control of the Abwehr's Long Island shortwave radio station. "The Germans believe that this station is operated by one of the agents whom they dispatched to the United States," Hoover noted, "but the Bureau has controlled this circuit and operated it for several years." He added "a rather amusing sidelight on the Bureau's operations," quoting a message the Abwehr control post in Hamburg had radioed to the compromised station: "Best wishes for 1945 and many thanks for your very valuable cooperation." Next, Hoover began pouring poison directly into Donovan's well. "As of possible interest to you and the President," he wrote to Hopkins, he had received word from an informant inside the OSS that Donovan was plotting a propaganda blitz. "The well known American writer, John Steinbeck, author of *The Moon is Down, Of Mice and Men,*" he claimed, "even has been charged with keeping abreast of OSS accomplishments so that he will be in a position to write a book exploiting these experiences when the proper time comes." Not only was Donovan a publicity hound, Hoover charged, but he was dishonest as well. "OSS intends, according to this source, to represent to the American people that it sends its own members across the lines into enemy territory, although this is not actually the case since, because of many blunders committed by that service, Allied Supreme Headquarters about May of 1944 instructed the OSS Espionage Section to refrain from dispatching any more agents into enemy territory." The last charge was not true. But Hoover was not too scrupulous about the venom employed.

On November 27, FDR led his retinue to Warm Springs for his longest rest since Pearl Harbor and to enjoy Thanksgiving dinner with polio patients. The Secret Service first delivered him in his armored car via backstreets to an obscure railroad siding in the basement of the Bureau of Engraving and Printing Annex on Fourteenth Street. Reporters making the trip had been directed at the last minute to street corners where they would be picked up. They were not told their destination. At the siding, the President boarded his private car, the armored *Ferdinand Magellan* with three-inch-thick windows and weighing nearly twice as much as an ordinary Pullman. The *Ferdinand Magellan* was preceded by a pilot train running one mile ahead to scout any danger to the presidential party along the route. At FDR's request, the engineer rarely exceeded thirty miles an hour. The President said he liked to be able to watch the towns and farms pass by. The truth was that he could not brace his feet, and at faster speeds the swaying of the train pained his thin buttocks.

Back at the White House, running the Map Room was Colonel Richard Park Jr., thirty-three, a politically astute second-generation Army officer who had previously served as an assistant military attaché in Moscow and as Pa Watson's White House assistant. Park owed his appointment as Map Room chief to the maneuvering of his sponsor, General George Strong. Park's duties put him in almost daily contact with Roosevelt, and the colonel would later claim that on December 18, "the day the late President departed for Warm Springs, he authorized me to make an informal investigation of the Office of Strategic Services and report on my findings and conclusions." Something rings tinny in Park's claim since on that date the President was not leaving for Warm Springs, but en route back to Washington. Park may at some point have received one of FDR's offhand oral assignments to "take a look at the OSS," though nothing to that effect exists in writing. This opening, nevertheless, was seized upon by Strong and the anti-Donovan cabal in military intelligence as a heaven-sent opportunity finally to polish off the OSS. But FDR's behavior hardly suggests a leader unhappy with his spy chief. At roughly the same time that Park claims to have received this assignment, the President approved a second star for Wild Bill, elevating him to the rank of major general and boosting the salary finally approved for him by $2,200. However seriously, or specifically, or if at all, FDR had directed Park to poke into the OSS, the colonel began to catalogue the agency's sins with relish.

Donovan, optimistic as ever, kept skating along like a man who does not hear the ice cracking. He felt buoyed these days, not threatened. In a note to a government procurement office he wrote, "Cadillac automobile is essential for use in official capacity." While Colonel Park was indicting his organization, Donovan was amassing proof of its indispensability. Those who rejected the OSS, he maintained, did so at their peril. He could cite Lieutenant General Courtney Hodges's First Army, where his agents had been treated like stepchildren. When the First needed more space on Normandy invasion ships, the OSS team was bumped. When OSS personnel did land, they found themselves without rations, quarters, or transportation, and banned from First Army headquarters. Over the next several months, the OSS was essentially kicked out of that Army. And then, on December 16, the Germans had stunned the Allies, striking through the Ardennes in operation *Wacht am Rhein,* Watch on the Rhine, an offensive that history would record as the Battle of the Bulge. Several factors contributed to the complete surprise the Wehrmacht achieved against First Army positions. Among them, Donovan believed, was the removal of the eyes and ears that the banned OSS detachment could have provided. Ultra, ironically, also contributed to the First's being caught flat-footed. British codebreakers had proved so predictive of German actions for so long that when they intercepted nothing foretelling a drive through the Ardennes, it was assumed nothing would happen. Bletchley Hall had not detected the buildup because German communications, in effect, went off the air. Prior to the offensive, Wehrmacht orders were issued over telephone land lines or hand-delivered by motorcycle. Nature, at this hour, favored the Wehrmacht as thick fog hid the massive German buildup from Allied reconnaissance planes.

On the very day the Germans burst through the Ardennes, Allen Dulles reported from Bern that Hitler was so ill that Himmler, Goebbels, and Martin Bormann, the Führer's secretary, had usurped his powers. "Himmler proposes to keep him in the upper background as a sort of [President Paul] von Hindenburg," Dulles cabled Washington. But Hitler was still in charge of his destiny, and Dulles could not have been more wrong.

On December 19, President Roosevelt, accompanied by his cousin Daisy Suckley, was back in the White House after three weeks at Warm Springs. For the previous two days he had been receiving depressing reports from the Map Room describing the Ardennes breakthrough. Germany was supposed to be beaten, driven backward onto its own soil and incapable of conducting an offensive. That fall, GIs strung along a front running from Belgium to the Swiss border had talked of returning home by Christmas. And then the panzers had exploded out of the forest. In its stealth and sweep, Hitler's bold stroke was something of a European Pearl Harbor. Roosevelt now stayed glued to the charts covering the Map Room's walls, following grim-faced officers who moved red pins forward, representing German forces, and green pins back, representing the American army. Casualties were steep. The initial ferocity of the assault practically annihilated the American 28th and 106th Divisions. FDR did not question his commanders as to why they had been so completely caught off guard. He did not meddle in military maneuvering. He was somber, but remained calm. "In great stress, Roosevelt was a strong man," observed General Marshall, another model of self-control.

★

Late in December, with the Battle of the Bulge still raging, the President summoned Henry Stimson to the White House. The secretary of war brought with him a six-foot Army officer with cold blue eyes, heavy jowls, and a swelling waist. General Leslie Groves gave an overall impression of heaviness—heavy of features, of girth, of purpose. He was a West Pointer and a get-it-done Army engineer who had overseen construction of the Pentagon, the largest office building in the world, in a record sixteen months. He now ran the Manhattan Project. Groves, whose only vice appears to have been fueling his boundless energy with frequent candy bars, was sketched neatly by a fellow engineer, Lieutenant Colonel Kenneth D. Nichols, as "the biggest sonovabitch I've ever met in my life, but also one of the most capable individuals. He had an ego second to none. . . . He had absolute confidence in his decisions and he was absolutely ruthless in how he approached a problem to get it done."

The President studied this bulldog figure as he and Stimson discussed the disaster in the Ardennes. The bloodshed was appalling, and before the battle ended, over twenty-one thousand American GIs would die. Obviously, the Wehrmacht retained a sharp sting. As soon as an atom bomb could be ready, FDR said he wanted it dropped on Germany. Groves, for once, seemed nonplussed. But he quickly recovered and said that bombing Germany posed a serious risk. What risk? the President wanted to know. If the bomb turned out to be a dud, Groves warned, the Germans would then have a model to build one of their own, including unspent fissionable material. A failure would be the next thing to handing the Germans an atomic bomb. Furthermore, the discussion was academic, Groves pointed out, since a workable bomb was still months away. Were Groves's arguments sincere or a rationale to conceal a veiled racism? Oddly, while worrying about a dud falling into the hands of the Germans, he expressed no such concern about the Japanese.

Japan, all along, had been targeted to feel the fury of the first atom bomb. When FDR and Churchill had met in the President's snuggery at Hyde Park the previous September to discuss the weapon and to disparage Niels Bohr, they signed an aide-mémoire that read: ". . . [W]hen a 'bomb' is finally available, it might perhaps, after mature consideration, be used against the Japanese, who should be warned that this bombardment will be repeated until they surrender."

The exponential destructiveness of an atomic weapon began to raise moral issues beyond those posed by conventional modes of killing. Just before the shock of the Bulge, Alexander Sachs, who had first brought the possibility of an atomic bomb to Roosevelt's attention in 1939, came again to the White House. Between the two compulsive talkers, Sachs managed to keep FDR quiet long enough to read from a memorandum he had prepared. "Following a successful test," he noted, "there should be arranged (a) a rehearsal demonstration before a body including internationally recognized scientists from all Allied countries and, in addition, neutral countries supplemented by representatives of the major faiths; (b) that a report on the nature and the portent of the atomic weapon be prepared by the scientists and other representative figures; (c) that, thereafter, a warning be issued by the United States and its allies in the Project to our major enemies in the war, Germany and Japan, that atomic bombing would be applied to a selected area within a designated time limit for the evacuation of human and animal life, and finally (d) in the wake of such realization of the efficacy of atomic bombing, an ultimatum demand for immediate surrender by the enemies be issued, in the certainty that failure to comply would subject their countries and peoples to atomic annihilation." As Sachs finished reading, FDR raised a few points he wanted clarified, all the while nodding in seeming agreement. As Sachs later described the end of their conversation, he urged the President, "For God's sake tell someone" about conducting a nonlethal test, to which Roosevelt answered that he would have Pa Watson look into the matter. Sachs left the White House believing that when the bomb became operational it would be demonstrated first against an unpopulated target, giving the enemy fair warning to surrender and save its people from mass slaughter. Sachs also left that day aware of something he had not observed before, long pauses in the President's speech in which FDR "was there, yet in a sense not there."

No evidence exists that Roosevelt ever did anything about Sachs's plea for a nonlethal demonstration. To the contrary, Jimmy, his son and frequent aide-de-camp, recalled, "Only I know that my father was prepared to drop an atom bomb on Japan." No reason existed for FDR to expect a swift end to the war in the Pacific. The Japanese had yielded every beach, jungle, and cave on Pacific atolls grudgingly, producing horrendous casualties on both sides. FDR was shown an interview that an Argentine diplomat who had served in Tokyo later gave to an American colleague. The Argentine reported, "Regarding the morale of the Japanese people . . . there was complete confidence in victory—indeed of victory's having been achieved. . . . The Ministry of Information has launched a slogan of a 'hundred-years war' and this has been accepted without criticism by the rank and file." The Argentine provided another curious insight into the effect of the war on Japanese culture: "Since 1943 the government has increasingly applied puritanical measures with the result that both the prostitutes and the geishas have enormously diminished in number; the geishas have diminished by ninety percent from about 40,000 to 4,000."

Germany's capacity and intention to develop nuclear weapons remained unknown to the Allies. By 1943, the thorough Leslie Groves had created his own intelligence operation to find out where the enemy stood. Either intentionally or unthinkingly, he called the operation Alsos, the Greek word for "grove," and put it in charge of Boris T. Pash, a former high school teacher, now in Army G-2, a trim, tough, balding, and flamboyant Slav who had previously earned a reputation for hunting down Communists. Pash took his Alsos team to Europe close behind the advancing troops. While Paris was still being liberated, Pash raced under German gunfire to the Radium Institute on the rue Pierre Curie to seize whatever nuclear material or research he could find. He ransacked a German physics lab on the grounds of the Strasbourg Hospital. He and his team pored over reams of captured documents. "We studied the papers by candlelight for two days and nights until our eyes began to hurt," Pash later wrote. "The conclusions were unmistakable. The evidence at hand proved definitely that Germany had no atom bomb and was not likely to have one in any reasonable form." The British concurred. A report issued in January 1944 by the Directorate of Tube Alloys found, "The Germans are not in fact carrying out large scale work on any aspect of T.A. [atomic weapons]. . . . [T]he German work is now confined to academic and small scale research."

FDR, however, remained unpersuaded. "If we do not keep ahead of our enemies in the development of new weapons," he noted, "we pay for our backwardness with the life blood of our sons." Germany in December 1944 was not yet beaten. Japan remained to be beaten. With his concurrence, the work at Los Alamos intensified.

Chapter XXV

———— ═══★═══ ————

Sympathizers and Spies

I N 1939, SIS, the Army's Signal Intelligence Service, at Arlington Hall, began intercepting messages sent between the United States and the Soviet Union by agents of the NKVD and the GRU, the Soviet military espionage arm. Interception proved simple enough since the messages were filed over ordinary commercial circuits. But the ciphers in which they were encased proved impenetrable. The Soviets were employing the one near-perfect coding system, the one-time pad. It consisted of pages of random numbers which were added to a message already encoded in another cipher. The sender and receiver each had a copy of an identical one-time pad, and if each page was used only once, the system remained foolproof. In effect, each message sent via a one-time pad was a new cipher, never used again.

Then, in 1942, Magic cryptanalysts learned that the Finns had made minor inroads into the Soviet codes, proving they were not invulnerable. Colonel Carter Clarke of SIS was inspired to create a special team to attack the Soviet ciphers. The operation, initially called Bride, eventually became known as Venona, the origins of the name as elusive as the secrets it sought to reveal. However, apart from whatever small success the Finns may have had, Arlington Hall seemed stymied. And then Soviet cryptologists blundered. For a few months in 1942, probably because of the de-

mand placed on Russian intelligence by the German invasion, some duplicated pads were printed and spotted by the Americans. Here was an opening, since the heart of cryptanalysis lies in finding repeated patterns. In
October 1943, given this wedge, Lieutenant Richard Hallock, a former archaeologist at the University of Chicago, now at Arlington Hall, made a
small break into coded traffic between Moscow and Amtorg, the Soviet
trade mission and espionage front in New York. Still, the traffic of the
NKVD and GRU remained essentially inviolate as an eventual 200,000
unbroken messages accumulated at Arlington Hall. The next major breakthrough, beyond Hallock's work, would not come for almost three more
years. By then, the war would be over.

If the Americans had been as successful in breaking Soviet codes as
they had been in cracking Japanese ciphers, the President would have
known that the Manhattan Project had been penetrated by Russia. Had the
Soviet codes been decrypted, Whittaker Chambers's 1938 allegations that
key government officials—among them Alger Hiss, Donald Hiss, Laurence Duggan, and Harry Dexter White—were aiding the Soviet Union
could have been verified. Had the codes been broken contemporaneously,
their contents would have proved particularly startling to the security-
obsessed General Leslie Groves at Los Alamos. A December 1944 message from the NKVD station in New York to Moscow, entitled "List of
Scientists Engaged on the Problem of Atomic Energy," identified most of
the major figures associated with the Manhattan Project, Hans Bethe,
Arthur Compton, Enrico Fermi, George Kistiakowsky, Ernest Lawrence,
Edward Teller, and Harold Urey among them. Robert Oppenheimer's name
was doubtless included but part of the message was garbled. A September
1944 message from New York to Viktor, a code name for Lieutenant Gen-
eral Pavel Fitin, the youthfully handsome and bemedaled director of the
NKVD's foreign intelligence branch, reported that "Kokh" knew about
four OSS personnel "who are supplying information to the Russians."
Years later, the Venona codebreakers tentatively identified Kokh as Bill
Donovan's executive assistant, Duncan Lee. Another message that September advised Moscow "of the new cover names," among them Liberal,
Prince, and Richard, referring, respectively, to Julius Rosenberg, Laurence
Duggan, and Harry Dexter White. In a cable, the contents of which, if
known at the time, would have staggered Henry Morgenthau, an agent
identified as Koltsov described problems in meeting with Jurist, another
code name for White, the Treasury secretary's indispensable aide:
"... [H]e himself did not think about his personal security, but a compro-

mise would lead to a scandal," Koltsov informed Moscow. "Therefore he would have to be very cautious. . . . Jurist has no suitable apartment for a permanent meeting place, all his friends are family people. Meetings could be held at their houses. . . ." On another occasion, the New York station cabled that White, this time referred to as Richard, "would have refused a regular payment but might accept gifts as a mark of our gratitude. . . ."

Roosevelt and Churchill popped up frequently in NKVD traffic, the President code-named Kapitan and the Prime Minister, Kaban, or Boar. Vice President Henry Wallace was Lotsman, and the French leader Charles de Gaulle, Ras. A cable from New York to Viktor reveals how close the Russians came to losing their prize informant on the Enormoz project, Klaus Fuchs, referred to as R. On June 15, 1944, while Fuchs was still working in New York, an NKVD agent reported, "R expressed doubt about the possibility of remaining in the COUNTRY. . . . R assumes that he will have to leave in a month or six weeks." Fuchs not only managed to stay on, but went to work inside Los Alamos two months later.

The gift that had dropped into the Soviets' lap, the boy physicist Theodore Hall, code-named Mlad, Russian for "youth," was proudly announced to Moscow on November 12, 1944. A Soviet agent, Sergei Kurnakov, described Hall as having "an exceptionally keen mind and a broad outlook, and is politically developed. At the present time H. is in charge of a group at CAMP-2 [Los Alamos]. H. handed over to Beck [Kurnakov], a report about the CAMP and named the key personnel employed on ENORMOZ."

In a cable from the Washington station to Moscow, the sender referred to "ALES," subsequently identified by the Venona codebreakers as Alger Hiss. "ALES has been working with the neighbors [GRU] continuously since 1935," the NKVD reported, "the group and ALES himself work on obtaining military information only."

Doubtless, FDR would have been amused by the Communist assessment of his chances in the 1944 election. Again, it was the New York NKVD post reporting to Moscow "transmitting information written down by RULEVOI." *Rulevoi,* the Russian word for "helmsman," referred to Earl Browder, the American Communist leader whom FDR had pardoned from prison as a sop to the Soviet Union. Six months before Election Day, Browder advised, "If the election were to take place at the present time, ROOSEVELT would probably receive an insignificant majority of the popular vote, but he would lose the election since the votes in his favor are strongly concentrated in the South. . . ." FDR not only took the popular vote handily but also the electoral college vote by 432 to 99. Oddly, Roosevelt's pardon proved politically disastrous to Browder. The fact that he had secured an early release from prison through the intercession of the President of the United States made his loyalty to their cause suspect to Red leaders. In 1944, Moscow engineered his expulsion from the American Communist Party.

The deepest Soviet penetration was into the White House itself. Lauchlin Currie, sharp of nose, chin, and mind, a slight man in his early forties with thinning gray hair and a pencil line mustache, had come out of Nova Scotia, Canada, taken a doctorate in economics at Harvard, fallen in love with the New Deal, and become an American citizen. In the summer of 1939, he was working for the Federal Reserve Board chairman, Marriner Eccles, when Eccles got a call from the White House.

"Marriner," FDR began, "I guess you are going to give me hell."

"Mr. President," Eccles replied, "I do not know what good it would do me to give you hell, even if I wanted to."

"Well," Roosevelt went on, "I am going to steal 'Lauch' Currie from you." FDR put the Roosevelt gloss on the raid. "You, of course, see the advantage at once of having a friend in court who can represent and speak for your point of view," he told Eccles. The President had been watching Currie over the previous two years and liked what he saw. Ordinarily, FDR regarded economists with less than awe, especially those preaching academic theories in incomprehensible jargon. Currie spoke economics in plain English. FDR also admired the man's ability to disagree without putting his ego on the line in every policy contest. Currie came to the White House as one of six all-purpose administrative assistants who displayed that passion for anonymity which became the staff ethic in the Roosevelt administration.

Currie's willingness to labor anonymously was, however, broken in January 1941. Working the Washington power circuit at the time was T. V. Soong, brother-in-law of the Chinese leader, Generalissimo Chiang Kai-shek. Soong's mission was to convince the Roosevelt administration that Chiang's regime could stand up against the Japanese if only the United States would provide enough military aid, especially airpower. Soong arranged for Currie to be invited by Chiang to China to advise the government on raging inflation and tumbling foreign exchange rates. Currie consulted with FDR, who readily endorsed the trip. Roosevelt knew that Chiang's armies were rife with corruption and were putting up a feckless fight against the Japanese. A fresh assessment by a smart, no-nonsense observer could prove invaluable in guiding U.S.-China policy. Thus, in January 1941, well before Pearl Harbor, an uneasy Currie had boarded a plane for the first time in his life and headed for the Orient. Once in Chungking, he quickly grasped that his advice on inflation and foreign exchange rates was a pretext for what Chiang really wanted from him, American arms. Currie also deduced that the generalissimo would turn U.S. military aid against his Communist rivals as happily as against the Japanese. He met often with the taciturn, stubborn Chiang and his forty-three-year-old wife, the American-educated Mei-ling, the sister of T. V. Soong, and a steel lotus blossom of manipulative charm. A British general who dealt with Madame Chiang described her as "a queer character in which sex and politics seemed to predominate, both being used to achieve her ends." If he really wanted to undercut the Communists, Currie advised Chiang and his wife to borrow a page from Roosevelt's New Deal by making liberal economic reforms that would help the Chinese masses and by cleaning up China's squalid government.

In light of what subsequently befell Currie, it is worth noting his recommendations to FDR when he returned to Washington in March 1941. The President asked him if Chiang was a reliable ally, and whether the United States should provide aircraft to China, the sale of which would, incidentally, make T. V. Soong a rich man. Currie had no illusions about Chiang. "I alerted FDR to the inefficiency, corruption and completely authoritarian character of the Chiang regime," he later wrote, "but Chiang was the head of the government just as Stalin was." With a pragmatism that FDR shared, Currie reported, "It appears to me to be profoundly in our national interests to give full support to the Generalissimo, both military and diplomatic."

Back in 1940, FDR had favored the incendiary bombing of Japan by Chinese pilots covertly flying American aircraft. That scheme had not come to pass, but Claire Chennault's American Volunteer Group, the Flying Tigers, had grown out of it. And even though Currie was not enamored of the jagged-edged Chennault character, the Flying Tigers would never have gotten off the ground without Currie's backing at the White House. More significantly, it was Currie who pressed for tacking Chinese military aid onto the lend-lease bill under debate at the time in Congress. With the bill's approval, Currie became the administrator of Chinese lend-lease along with his other ragbag of duties. At the time of his China mission, he exhibited no detectable affinity for Chinese or any other Communists.

★

As America entered its fourth year of the war, with Hitler's Ardennes offensive blunted, with Allied troops now on German soil, with the border between France and Switzerland cleared of enemy forces, the President moved to end a condition that still rankled him, the continuing trade between Switzerland and Germany. On January 19, 1945, he wrote a confidential letter to the Swiss president of the Confederation, Eduard von Steiger, tactful in style but unmistakable in intent. "We have respected the traditional neutrality of your country and have sympathized with the past difficulties of your position," FDR wrote. "We forbore pressing our demands when you were isolated by our enemy and were in no position to do other than carry on a large trade with him. Now, however, the fortunes of war have changed. . . . I know in these circumstances that you will be eager to deprive the Nazis of any further assistance. It would indeed be a trial for any freedom-loving Swiss to feel that he had in any way impeded the efforts of other freedom-loving countries to rid the world of a ruthless tyrant. I speak strongly as every day the war is prolonged costs the lives of my countrymen." Should there be the slightest doubt as to his meaning, FDR further informed the Swiss leader that he was sending a delegation, to be headed by Lauchlin Currie, to renegotiate any prior American deals with Switzerland now that the country was no longer landlocked by Nazis.

A month later, Currie was in Bern. Through a skillful application of strength and tact, he managed to cut the flow of strategic exports that the Swiss had been selling to Germany. With the border between France and Switzerland now open, he made clear that the Swiss no longer needed to trade electricity for German coal. The Allies could supply them with this fuel. Currie pressed the Swiss to abide by Safehaven, the American strategy to stop Nazis from using Swiss banks to funnel gold and other assets to hiding places where they might seek refuge after Germany was defeated. Currie thought he had a deal. When he got back to Washington, Treasury secretary Morgenthau told him, "You have not only thwarted the Nazis' plan for using Switzerland as a financial hideout, but have also laid the basis for the Allied Military Government in Germany to take control of German assets in Switzerland." But the head of the Swiss banking system, Herr Doktor Weber, was a longtime collaborator with the Reichsbank vice president, Emil Puhl. And only weeks after the Currie agreement, Allen Dulles learned from his agent in Berlin, Fritz Kolbe, that Puhl had gone to

Switzerland to meet with Weber and other friends in Swiss banking. Puhl, according to Kolbe, "has made careful plans to go underground and that every essential figure had been given a specific assignment." "Nazism," Puhl boasted, "would not end with Germany's political defeat because it is like a religion rather than a mere political regime." Unknown to Currie, Swiss bankers reneged on their promises to stop gold transfers or to freeze German assets, a betrayal that would reverberate down through the decades.

Alongside this invaluable aide to the President walked another Lauchlin Currie. In 1940 he had become involved with two men with names close enough to create confusion. One was Abraham George Silverman and the other Nathan Gregory Silvermaster. Currie had been a graduate student at Harvard when he met Silverman, who was then teaching economics at the Massachusetts Institute of Technology. When Silverman came to the capital to work for the Railroad Retirement Board, the two men renewed their acquaintance, and Currie now considered Silverman "one of the top ranking statisticians of Washington." He met Gregory Silvermaster in 1940 when FDR asked Currie to look into an alleged shipboard mutiny, actually only a one-day in-port work stoppage. Silvermaster had become involved in the dispute as an employee of the Maritime Labor Board. Thereafter, Currie continued to see both Silverman and Silvermaster, whom he described as strictly social acquaintances.

Silvermaster was born in Odessa, Ukraine, and raised in China, where he attended a school run by an English religious order. He came to the United States at age sixteen, eventually earning a doctorate in economics and philosophy from the University of California at Berkeley. When Currie met him, he was in his early forties, a trim man with steel gray hair, horn-rimmed glasses, a neatly trimmed mustache, and the manner of an English headmaster. In mid-1942 the Board of Economic Warfare, the mobilization planning organization, thought it could use Silvermaster more profitably than could the Farm Security Administration to which he had transferred. Silvermaster then went to work for the BEW on loan. His new employment provided access to sensitive intelligence—America's production schedule for tanks, planes, other armaments, and the raw materials they required. His very presence at the BEW alarmed agencies involved in wartime security. The Civil Service Commission, MID, and ONI all sent warnings to the board claiming that Gregory Silvermaster was an out-and-out Communist with a long record of Communist associations, and certainly not a man to be trusted with military secrets. A Civil Service

Commission investigation concluded: "Mr. Silvermaster is one of the really important operatives of the undercover Communist Party in the United States." The military agreed and wanted BEW to fire him.

Among the undecipherable cables piling up at Arlington Hall, one from New York to Moscow dated September 2, 1943, demonstrated the NKVD's close interest in Silvermaster. "A few days ago," it read, "two representatives of the Khata visited Pazh and began to [garbled] about Pel, in particular, is he a Fellow countryman." Pel was Silvermaster and Khata the FBI. Pazh, meaning "page," was "possibly Lauchlin Currie," according to Venona's later decryption. The FBI had indeed questioned Currie as to whether he considered his friend Silvermaster a Communist. Currie drew a fine distinction. He told Hoover's men that for him the dividing line was June 22, 1941, the date Germany invaded the Soviet Union. Until then, the German-Soviet peace pact applied and a Communist would have opposed the United States going to war against Germany. But Silvermaster, during that time, had favored war. Therefore Currie did not regard him as a Communist, but simply a liberal New Dealer like himself.

Elizabeth Bentley served as the courier between Silvermaster and the New York NKVD station. She later gave an account of what happened after the security agencies began going after Silvermaster. She had gone to his home to pick up purloined secret documents and found him slumped in an armchair. "What's the matter?" she asked. Silvermaster handed her a letter to the BEW from then Army G-2 chief, George Strong, stating that the military intelligence agencies had proof that Silvermaster was a Communist disloyal to the United States and demanding that he be removed from his sensitive post. Bentley recalled Silvermaster saying, "It's no use fighting this thing. They've probably got enough to hang me. I'd better resign now before they kick me out." This potential loss to the spy ring alarmed Bentley. She had started out collecting three or four rolls of microfilm per trip to Washington gathered by Silvermaster from fellow spies inside the government to turn over to her controller/lover, Jacob Golos, in New York. Silvermaster's productivity had grown so swiftly that the knitting bag Bentley carried on the New York train now bulged with some forty rolls every two weeks. She pleaded with him not to give up so easily and urged that he "pull every string you can to get this business quashed. Use Currie, White [Harry Dexter White], anybody else you know and trust."

Silvermaster then went to Currie for help. By now the two men had become close socially, having dinner in each other's homes with some frequency. Currie called the undersecretary of war, Robert P. Patterson, and asked that Silvermaster's case be reviewed. He was later to claim that his intercession was neutral, and that he made no recommendation for or against Silvermaster. Nevertheless, on July 3, 1942, Patterson wrote to the BEW saying, "I have personally made an examination of the case and . . . I am fully satisfied that the facts do not show anything derogatory to Mr. Silvermaster's character or loyalty." While Silvermaster's fate was being decided, Moscow took the precaution of ordering a two-month break between him and his ring. The final resolution of the case was described by Bentley: "Greg [Silvermaster] was permitted to resign from the Board of Economic Warfare and return to the Department of Agriculture—and with a clean slate! After a sigh of relief that must have echoed throughout the entire Russian secret police apparatus, we went back to our normal routine." Vasili Zarubin, code-named Maksim, the NKVD *rezident,* or espionage chief, in New York and later in Washington, happily informed Moscow in October 1943: "Recently [Silvermaster] told us that [Currie] made every effort to liquidate his case."

During this period, Currie was also becoming more interested in the Chinese Communists. That spring he had sent FDR "a letter from a friend in China. We get so little about conditions in Communist China that I thought this might interest you." Currie's correspondent spoke admiringly of the Red Chinese enclaves, reporting that he "could find no evidence of graft or scandal, either financial or sexual. . . . The people in the Communist area are much more alive intellectually and are filled with an ideal. . . . They teach the Army how to read and have newspapers circulating pretty widely." Currie, in forwarding this report to FDR, could be seen as proselytizing for the Chinese Communists. Still, he had promoted, even administered lend-lease for the Nationalist regime of Chiang Kai-shek, however graft-ridden and ineffectual it was in fighting the Japanese. And his correspondent's views on the Chinese Communists were no doubt accurate and worth reporting to the President. Currie was always careful that his contacts with Communists not be misconstrued. On one occasion, after lunch with the Russian ambassador, Konstantin Oumansky, he immediately sent the President a memorandum. "I accepted, thinking that I might be able to pick up something interesting or significant which I could pass along to you," he assured FDR.

Currie, though possessing the President's implicit trust, nevertheless had his critics within the administration. In 1943, Henry Morgenthau, Jr., discussed with the President possible candidates for a key international economic post in London. "Who do you want?" FDR asked. Morgenthau replied that either Currie or James Landis would suit him fine. Roosevelt said, "I think Lauch Currie would be good. He is doing lots of odds and ends and this will give him a lot to do." But when Morgenthau floated the name to Henry Stimson, the secretary of war answered that he "did not want Currie and would not take him unless the President so ordered." The Army, Stimson explained, had no confidence in Currie's loyalty. John Franklin Carter noted in his diary for April 14, 1943, that the Nationalist envoy, "T.V. Soong, had opposed Laughlin [*sic*] Currie's nomination as ambassador to China. Must tell Pappy."

Currie informed Harry Hopkins in August 1943 that he had recently talked to "Mr. Zubilin" of the Soviet embassy about an immigration case. Zubilin was a cover name for Vasili Zarubin, now operating out of the embassy at 1125 Sixteenth Street. The building, an eighteenth-century-style Italianate marble mansion built by Mrs. George Pullman, wife of the sleeping car tycoon, seemed an odd outpost for the anti-capitalist champions of the proletariat. The beneficiary of Currie's intercession was Paul Hagen, known as Karl Frank before he came to America, an Austrian refugee and an admitted former Communist whom the FBI suspected of being "a secret agent of the Soviet government." What Currie had done for Hagen was to appear as a character witness when he applied for a reentry visa allowing him to visit Canada and then return to the United States. On August 7, J. Edgar Hoover received an anonymous but astonishingly accurate letter, sent apparently by a disgruntled NKVD official, disclosing the names of the Soviet Union's top eleven agents in America and two of their American associates. Zarubin was one of those exposed, and the last line of the letter noted that he had some "high-level agent in the office of the White House."

Another New York to Moscow cable dealt with Currie's old MIT associate and Washington friend, Abraham George Silverman, a member of the Silvermaster ring described by a fellow agent as a whiner always complaining about the heavy party dues he had to pay. Silverman evidently was attracted to at least one facet of capitalism. He worried constantly about his financial straits and had turned to Currie for advice on playing the stock market. Currie was apparently a better government economist than a market seer, since Silverman lost money on his investments. Elizabeth Bentley later stated that upon taking a civilian job with the Air Corps in the Pentagon, Silverman "began to bring documents to the Silvermaster home." According to an August 1944 NKVD cable, when it appeared that

Silverman was to be transferred, he tried to use Currie's influence to find a job that would keep him in Washington, even though "Pazh [Currie] . . . is in strained relations with Aileron [Silverman]."

Among his miscellany of White House assignments, Currie was also tracking the development of RDX, a secret plastic explosive. He prepared a "Memorandum for the President" in which he reported, "I have been reliably informed that this explosive gives an effect 40% greater than TNT." At this time, Bentley somehow managed to acquire information on RDX which she delivered to her controller. Currie further reported progress on the B-29 bomber to the President. Bentley delivered plans for the B-29 to the NKVD while the development of the plane was still under wraps. Others may have supplied Bentley with the RDX and B-29 secrets; but Currie was privy to this information, and was in touch with Silvermaster, whose job was to pass intelligence on to "Good Girl."

Possibly the most incriminating charge against Currie also came from Bentley, though at second hand. She claimed that in 1944 "Mr. Silverman told me that Mr. Currie came dashing into Mr. Silverman's house sort of out of breath and told him that the Americans were on the verge of breaking the Soviet code." Bentley's charge against Currie was hearsay. It achieves some credibility, however, in that Currie did have access to decrypts coming out of the Map Room where he could have learned that Arlington Hall was trying to break the Soviet ciphers.

A case against Currie as a Soviet spy working next to the President cannot be rejected out of hand. The evidence, however circumstantial, is considerable—his vouching for Gregory Silvermaster's placement in a sensitive wartime job; his testimony in favor of Paul Hagen, a suspected Soviet agent; that he reportedly gave classified documents to Abraham George Silverman, an agent of the Soviet Union; that he was approached to keep Silverman in a Washington job; that he had insider knowledge of RDX and the B-29 which the Russians learned about; that he had alerted the Soviets about American progress in cracking Soviet codes; and that at least eight NKVD cables between New York and Moscow refer to Pazh, most plausibly Currie. In *The Haunted Wood,* Currie is referred to unequivocally by authors Allen Weinstein and Alexander Vassiliev as one of several "Soviet agents," a "fellow-agent," and "the only presidential aide then also working for Soviet intelligence."

Several NKVD cables between the United States and Moscow, however, indicate that the Soviets did not regard Currie as an agent in their back pocket, but rather as a longtime target for recruitment. One cable sent in

1942 bemoaned the lack of agents "surrounding Roosevelt or such persons as Hopkins." An NKVD message dated April 6 of that year stated bluntly, "[P]enetrating the surroundings of Roosevelt himself is the goal that we seek in our everyday work." A later message urged Silvermaster to continue to try to recruit "Pazh." Three years later, Moscow still appeared to be trying to enlist Currie. "Find out from Albert [an NKVD officer] and Robert [Silvermaster] whether it would be possible for us to approach Pazh direct." A message filed a month later suggested Pazh's close cooperation, but not outright control by the NKVD. "P. [for Pazh] trusts R [Silvermaster], informs him not only orally but also by handing over documents. . . . Up to now, Pazh relations with Robert were expressed, from our point of view, only in common feelings and personal sympathies." Obviously, Moscow considered Pazh highly worth recruiting but yet to be recruited.

Elizabeth Bentley later admitted that she had never met Currie, that he never turned over any information or documents directly to her. She even stated, "The man was not a Communist." She was not sure that Currie knew that intelligence from him eventually found its way into Soviet hands. An NKVD correspondent cabled his superiors that "Pazh" still did not yet understand that Silvermaster was a spy for the Soviet Union.

In the literal sense of the word, did the Soviet Union have a "spy" in the Roosevelt White House? It clearly had a manipulable sympathizer so useful that it may be a quibble as to whether or not the man was consciously involved in espionage for a foreign power. However, a line exists that one crosses in moving from being used to knowingly spying for another country. While Lauchlin Currie provided aid and comfort to a rival if not an enemy power, it does not appear that he consciously crossed that moral divide. Currie was a New Deal liberal and, in associating with a Silvermaster and a Silverman, imagined himself in the company of like-minded souls. He appears to have given the information he provided as an act of solidarity, looking upon these associates as legitimate comrades in the struggle against fascism. His behavior was hardly singular. Harry Hopkins, before the Tehran conference, tipped off the Soviet embassy in Washington that the FBI had bugged a secret meeting in which Vasili Zarubin passed money to Steve Nelson, a Yugoslav immigrant, an alumnus of Moscow's Lenin Institute, and the San Francisco organizer for the American Communist Party. Hopkins, reflecting FDR's determination to do nothing to upset the Soviets, had acted while unaware that Zarubin was the Soviet *rezident*.

Even after the war the FBI continued to poke into lingering suspicions against Currie, but nothing ever came of it. As Harvey Klehr, a scholar of the period, writes, "No one who talked to the Bureau believed that Currie was a Party member, secret or otherwise. . . . Over all the FBI file suggests that Currie was hardly a controlled agent but an eccentric, rather self aggrandizing individual who enjoyed the sensation of manipulating events from behind the scenes." He may have described his level of complicity best himself. In a letter to a friend, Richard H. Wels, written six years after the war, Currie said, "I was probably too accessible and not sufficiently circumspect. However, I certainly had no idea what the world would be like today. As you remember, in the early days the New Deal was in the nature of a crusade and New Dealers felt a strong sense of camaraderie. . . . We were all united in pushing along with the War. The atmosphere of suspicion and caution only arose after I left the government [in 1945]."

Lauchlin Currie's behavior runs like a thread through the lives of numerous well-placed Americans who proved useful to the Soviet Union. Their rationale can be roughly synthesized as follows: We and Russia are Allies in the war against fascism. Therefore, our ally is entitled to know what we know. In its extreme form, this mentality motivated the men who were stealing the secrets of Los Alamos for the Soviet Union. Currie's involvement was of a lesser order. In him, the Soviet Union did not have a spy in the White House; it had a friend.

Chapter XXVI

———═══★═══———

A Leaky Vessel

L AUCHLIN CURRIE'S reportedly breathless alert to the Silvermaster ring that U.S. cryptanalysts were on to Russian codes was, it turned out, a false alarm, at least in part. The United States was indeed in possession of certain Soviet codebooks, but not those used by the NKVD for traffic passing between Washington, New York, and Moscow which Arlington Hall was attempting to break, thus far with scant success. What Currie had learned, probably through Map Room scuttlebutt, was about an unrelated spy escapade born halfway around the world.

In November 1944, Wilho Tikander, the OSS chief in another espionage haven, neutral Sweden, dangled a beguiling proposition before his boss, Bill Donovan. Finland had dropped out of the war as Germany's ally the month before, and Finnish officers approached Tikander in Stockholm offering to sell codebooks seized from the Soviet consulate in Petsamo. Ordinarily, Donovan would have leaped at the opportunity, but he was in a rare prudent mood, trying to win allies, not adversaries, in his campaign to propel the OSS into the postwar world. He was supposed to inform the State Department of any OSS contacts with foreign governments, and for once he chose the path of discretion, relaying the Finns' offer to the new secretary of state, Edward Stettinius. Stettinius well understood FDR's supersensitivity to any act that might arouse Soviet suspicions. Consequently, he recommended to Donovan that buying Russian codes from the Finns "would be inadvisable and improper." Donovan chafed at the secretary's caution. His impetuous side surged to the fore. He instructed Tikander to proceed with the purchase, for an undisclosed sum, through which over fifteen hundred pages of Russian cryptographic material, including a charred codebook, passed into OSS hands. On December 11, Donovan proudly sent the President a letter trumpeting his acquisition. "I wanted you to know," he told FDR, "that our chief representative in Stockholm was able to obtain three diplomatic codes and one military through special sources . . . We have made the necessary payments. . . . You are the only one to whom I have disclosed these facts."

Edward Stettinius had a reputation as a suave, handsome courtier, possibly in over his head. But Donovan's rejection of his recommendation gave him an opportunity to show some spine and at the same time play to FDR's prejudices. Though Donovan had tried to limit knowledge of what he had done, Stettinius learned of it, doubtless from Roosevelt. Two days before Christmas, the secretary of state went to the White House and made an easy convert. He persuaded the President that the codes should be returned to the Soviets. He and FDR then concocted an explanation as to how this material had come into America's hands. Donovan was to inform his counterpart in Moscow, General Fitin, that an unspecified U.S. agency, in the course of its work, had happened to run across certain documents that apparently related to Russian-encoded communications. Specifically, he was to tell the Russians, ". . . [W]e had taken advantage of the opportunity to prevent this material from falling into the hands of the enemy and that we would immediately make it available to the Soviet government if they so desired."

Of course, Fitin replied, the Russians would like to have their ciphers back. All that remained was to arrange a method of delivery. On February 15, 1945, a wary Andrei Gromyko, the Soviet ambassador, greeted Donovan at the Sixteenth Street embassy. Donovan's aide Ned Putzell followed behind carrying the thick sheaf of codes and keys, some burned around the edges. Gromyko in Washington and Fitin in Moscow felt more bafflement than gratitude at the return of the documents. Such behavior by the NKVD would have been unthinkable. What were the Americans up to? In the minds of the Soviets, only one explanation made sense. By making it appear that the codes were still secure, the Russians would continue using them while the Americans could continue breaking them.

For their part, American cryptanalysts heard in disbelief that the White

House had ordered the ciphers returned. Colonel Carter W. Clarke, head of G-2's Special Branch, remembered going to Arlington Hall to report this decision to the staff. Clarke told them that the First Lady had learned of their attacks on Soviet codes and said that it had to stop. The colonel was indulging in hyperbole. Eleanor Roosevelt had no authority to issue orders in this realm. But she did share her husband's impatience with schemes that could menace the fragile East-West alliance and was not reticent about expressing her feelings. The Russian codes sold by the Finns had had to be returned, but Clarke, with a wink and a nod, told the codebreakers to keep working on the ciphers that were still being intercepted between NKVD agents in the United States and the USSR.

Did Donovan copy the Soviet codes obtained from the Finns before returning them? It would seem instinctive behavior for a spy chief. However, Putzell, who carried the documents to the Soviet embassy for his chief, insists that Donovan played it straight and that no copy was made. Neither the archives of the OSS, currently maintained by the CIA, nor the codebreaking National Security Agency, nor President Roosevelt's papers yield any trace of the codes or any reference to their being duplicated.

Contemporary observers, with opinions colored by forty years of Cold War distrust, may be forgiven for finding Franklin Roosevelt the naïf in this drama, with his oversolicitous concern not to upset Stalin. But the President's actions must be judged against the political backdrop of 1945. Finland had just left the war as a Nazi ally. How would it appear to the Soviets if FDR acquiesced in buying the codes of a presumed partner from a recent enemy? The President was then trying to engineer another three-power summit meeting among Churchill, Stalin, and himself, at which his chief objective was to draw the Soviet Union into the war against Japan. For Stalin to suspect, on the eve of such a meeting, that his capitalist partner was dealing behind his back could well have poisoned the atmosphere. All the performers in this ring behaved according to their natures: Donovan as a spymaster, Stalin as a distrustful ally, and Roosevelt as a leader trying to see beyond short-term advantage.

★

The President had sent the rambunctious George Earle, former Pennsylvania governor, former ambassador, and permanent playboy, to Istanbul in 1943 as his eyes and ears. Earle's reports from that den of intrigue had proved a mixed but respectable bag. He had provided FDR with solid, if unwelcome intelligence on what the Russians had done to the Poles in the Katyn forest. He had correctly predicted German rockets falling on England. But he had overestimated the destruction and underestimated the time for the Germans to rebuild the bombed Ploeşti oil fields.

Earle was not above exploiting his closeness to the President for personal advantage. In the summer of 1944, he wrote FDR, "[W]ith all the tremendous burdens now upon you, I am terribly sorry to bother you with a comparatively unimportant personal matter." Earle had become eligible for promotion, and since he reported directly to the White House, though he operated undercover in Turkey as assistant naval attaché, he sent FDR a blank Navy fitness report to complete. Roosevelt handed the task over to his current naval aide, Rear Admiral Wilson Brown, telling the admiral, "From all I hear, he [Earle] has been doing useful work and doing it well." Brown completed the form and the President happily signed it. In due course, Earle rose from lieutenant commander to full commander. That fall, the restless agent wrote again: "My dear Mr. President, Turkey has for the most part lost her value as a listening post and my position here as a personal observer for you is rapidly becoming valueless." He wanted FDR to send him to Germany as soon as that enemy was defeated, again as the President's personal observer. Of course, he made clear, he had always hated Nazism, but a Red menace would replace the Nazis as soon as Germany surrendered. "Eighty million Germans after their capitulation must not be left entirely without hope," Earle warned. Again, FDR bucked the request to Admiral Brown. The admiral wrote back to Earle, "There is no vacancy on the very small naval mission earmarked for Germany and your age makes it difficult to find a good sea billet for you that you would find satisfactory." Instead, Brown arranged for Earle to be brought back to Washington while the Navy decided what to do with the President's over-age friend.

Late in 1944, just before he was due to come home, Earle came upon intelligence that seemed to dispel his opinion of Turkey as a valueless listening post. He fired off a warning to the President on December 5 that the Germans, already using V-1 buzz bombs and V-2 rockets against England, were about to launch another secret weapon, the V-3, against the American East Coast. The pilotless, sputtering V-1s, the "buzz bombs," had been raining hell on London since the week after D-Day. FDR's ambassador in London, John G. Winant, the Lincolnesque former Republican governor of New Hampshire, had described to him the psychological impact of the weapon: "The fact that this raiding is continuous, with warning sirens still operating, has disturbed people more than the heavy bombing of earlier periods. Fatigue seems to be the worse general result." Casualties from the V-1s were building toward an eventual six thousand British civilians killed. Three months after the Normandy landings, on September 8, 1944, the first V-2 rocket had struck London. Its supersonic double crack soon played a fearful tympany over London since the V-2, unlike the buzz bombs, arrived without warning and thus could not be shot down.

Earle had made an unfulfilled prediction of a "stratospheric attack" on America well over a year before. This time, the President told Admiral Leahy that Earle was again probably retailing a rumor, "but every precaution should be taken." On December 7, Leahy carried out the President's order and placed the entire East Coast on alert. The leader who had been caught flat-footed at Pearl Harbor three years before was not about to be caught again. Leahy, still skeptical, nevertheless notified coastal land, sea, and air commanders to be prepared for the possibility of an attack within the next thirty days. The following night at dinner with his cousin Daisy, FDR poured out his concerns over the V-3. He told her he had received a secret report from a source who had proved reliable in the past that the Germans had a weapon capable of killing by concussion everyone within a mile. They were planning to use it on New York. The President said that he was particularly worried over the growing laxity in U.S. defenses. As Daisy recorded in her diary, "The entire Atlantic Seaboard has relaxed all its dim-outs and air raid precausions [sic] etc. . . . He feared that in the next war, the side which first uses these new explosives will undoubtedly win."

The threat of secret weapons targeted against the United States was not all that farfetched. Even before Earle's warning, the President had learned from J. Edgar Hoover that a German agent in the United States, under FBI control, had received instructions from Berlin to determine "the extent of offshore coastal protection of the United States and particularly as to any areas where this protection may have been curtailed." The Germans, obviously, were probing for a soft spot.

To the creators of the V-1 and V-2 the possibility of striking the American mainland was not simply theoretical. The director of the Peenemünde Rocket Research Institute, Major General Walter Dornberger, admitted: "This development of the [V-2] did not satisfy our ambitions. . . . We wanted to cover thousands of miles." Thus German rocket scientists had been conducting exploratory research since 1937 on a missile referred to variously as the "New York bomber," or the "American Rocket." Dornberger and Wernher von Braun, his brilliant thirty-two-year-old partner, building on their success with the V-2, had a new design on the drawing board. They would place a winged V-2 atop an even more powerful missile, the A-10, an eighty-seven-ton behemoth. The A-10, within a minute of blastoff, would propel the V-2 to a speed of 2,700 miles per hour. The A-10 would then fall away, sprout a parachute, and be retrievable for reuse. The winged V-2 would continue on, achieving a speed on its own of 6,300 miles per hour at an altitude of 35 miles. "Very fast stratos-high supersonic speed had reached design stage," Dornberger claimed. "They would be able to cross from Europe to America in forty minutes." Indeed, a rocket launch site angled along the great circle route to New York was found when Allied troops liberated Wizernes, France.

If the A-10 booster could not be readied in time, German engineers were also exploring the possibility of a rocket launched from a submarine. Allied photo reconnaissance over the coast of Nazi-occupied Norway had, in fact, spotted a U-boat of the 740-ton class fitted with rails running from the conning tower to the ship's bow. "The purpose of this," the report concluded warily, "is unknown." Besides experimenting on launching missiles from a heaving deck the Germans were working on more stable launching rafts to be towed by U-boats. The German navy's chief, Admiral Karl Doenitz, pleaded with Hitler to allow him to construct these platforms, assuring him that his wolf packs could surface off New York City in the dark of night, launch rockets, and turn the city into flame and rubble. In one test, a rocket launched from a submarine platform had traveled 250 miles, a range that would put dozens of major U.S. coastal cities within the arc of destruction.

The photo of the U-boat with rails had been taken on September 19, 1944, a date disturbingly close to the October warning that J. Edgar Hoover made to the President that German spies had been instructed to probe weak points along the Atlantic coast. That same month, a Nazi agent arrested by the FBI reported that while in Europe he had watched U-boat crews practicing rocket launches from their decks. Confirming Admiral Doenitz's strategy, crew members told the agent that they were practicing to proceed to within two hundred miles of the United States, where they would fire their rockets. Leahy, in his alert to the East Coast defense commands, had warned, "The capability exists . . . for small scale attacks by flying bombs or by rockets, smaller than the V-2, launched from specially fitted submarines."

While Doenitz's submariners were experimenting with floating launch pads, the Luftwaffe was testing the Junker Ju 390. This six-engine bomber had supposedly test-flown a 6,000-mile round trip for thirty-two hours and skirted, without detection, within twelve miles of New York. And well over a year had passed since intercepted cables from Oshima's embassy in Berlin had reported work on the Me-264, a bomber also intended to reach New York.

But the Germans' bedevilment was time. Little doubt existed about their technological prowess, as the V-1s and V-2s shattering London made clear. In another engineering triumph, Me-262s, the first operational jet fighters, capable of flying 540 miles per hour, had come on-line in the summer of 1944 and were shooting Allied bombers out of the sky before conventional fighters could catch them. But were enough resources and will left in a country whose ultimate defeat seemed inevitable? The President chose to err on the side of caution. George Earle's rocket warning coincided with the December Ardennes offensive, a shock that made Germany appear a still formidable foe. The reality, however, was that secret weapons destined for American cities would never get beyond blueprints, drawing boards, and experiments. For Nazi Germany, time was running out.

The rocket scare passed, and on February 15, Commander Earle came home from Turkey, resuming his turbulent life without missing a beat. The very next day his wife, Huberta, mother of his four sons, filed for divorce, charging that Earle had absented himself from her "without cause" since January 1942. Earle's last battle took place soon afterward. He left his bachelor digs in the Philadelphia Racquet Club and, in spite of a fever of 103 degrees, boarded a train for Washington to see FDR. On his arrival, still trembling with illness, he was greeted by the President's correspondence secretary, William D. Hassett. Hassett, known around the White House as "the bishop" for his magisterial manner, informed Earle that the President was too busy to see him. Earle returned to his Philadelphia club and sulked. He then wrote a letter to FDR's daughter, Anna, pointing out that though he had started out as a Republican, he had been among the first to rally to Roosevelt's candidacy in 1932. "Imagine my shock," he told her, "when I arrived to find myself about to be brushed off to the inactive list . . . for what Admiral Brown has been frank enough to say on several occasions was because of my anti-Russian attitude. In other words, because I told your father the truth about conditions in Russia and countries occupied by Russia, that near-Bolshevist group of advisers around the President had persuaded him to force me out of the picture." Earle was not about to go quietly into the night. Unless the President objected, he told Anna, "I want to present the following to the members of Congress and to the American people. . . . I shall point out why Russia today is a far greater menace than Germany ever was, because of its manpower, natural resources, prospect of Bolshevizing Europe, including Germany, and because of its millions of fifth columnists. I shall show how Russia twenty-five years after its Revolution is exactly the same Red Terror it was then, of its 15 million people in concentration camps, of its treatment of the Jews and of Labor. I shall prove how Stalin deliberately started this war with his pact of friendship with Hitler so that the capitalistic nations would destroy each other. . . . If I do not hear from you in a week, I shall understand the President has no objection to me sending this letter to members of Congress and the press."

Three days later, Earle had the President's response. For all his intimacy with FDR, he had gauged the man badly. "I have read your letter of March 21st to my daughter Anna," Roosevelt wrote, "and I have noted with concern your plan to publicize your unfavorable opinion of one of our allies at the very time when such a publication from a former emissary of mine might do irreparable harm to our war effort. . . . You say you will publish unless you are told before March 28th that I do not wish you to do so. I not only do not wish it but I specifically forbid you to publish any information or opinion about an ally that you may have acquired while in office or in the service of the United States Navy." FDR then called in Admiral Brown and instructed him to send a message to Navy secretary James Forrestal with a copy to the Bureau of Personnel. He wanted it understood "that Commander Earle no longer has any special instructions or responsibility to the President." Earle backed down. He promised FDR, "I shall issue no public statement of any kind again so long as you are the President." All he asked for now was "that I be transferred to inactive duty." He was not to get off so lightly. "Your orders to the Pacific have already been issued," FDR wrote back. "I think you had better go ahead and carry them out." For all the President cared, George Earle could spend the rest of the war aboard a rust bucket off Guam.

★

In the first week of January 1945, J. Edgar Hoover sent a young agent to the White House to hand-deliver a report that the FBI chief believed the President must see. The message offered proof either of the obstinacy or the vitality of the enemy. Three years had passed since the President had pressed for the execution of six out of the eight German saboteurs who had landed on the East Coast. Now Hoover was telling him that he had caught two more spies delivered by submarine, one supposedly related to the President.

William Colepaugh had never fit in. He was a bony, six-foot-two twenty-six-year-old from a good Connecticut family, but a social outcast and a loner. Attorney General Francis Biddle remembered the teenage Willy Colepaugh. The Biddles had been vacationing at Black Point, Connecticut, where Willy's father frequently fixed their windmill-powered water pump. "Willy, I suppose about sixteen at the time," Biddle later recalled, "must have been something of a problem even then, for I can remember our neighbors saying when the boy got into some small scrape, 'I wonder what will happen to Willy Colepaugh.' " His parents managed to get the boy into Admiral Farragut Academy in New Jersey, and Willy then went on to study marine engineering at Massachusetts Institute of Technology. But he flunked out of MIT, studying too little and drinking too much. Only one thing appeared to engage Colepaugh's imagination. His mother's parents had emigrated from Germany, and Willy swelled with borrowed pride at the Reich's early victories. He went into the Navy, but his vocal Nazi sympathies led to his discharge in 1943, "for the good of the service." By January 1944, though Germany's military fortunes had begun to wane, Colepaugh's faith remained unshaken and he took a fateful step. He earned a berth on the Swedish liner *Gripsholm,* jumped ship in Lisbon, and made his way to Germany. There he was recruited into the SD by the legendary Major Otto Skorzeny, rescuer of Benito Mussolini.

During spy training at The Hague, the SD teamed Colepaugh with Erich Gimpel, eight years his senior and an expert in high-frequency radio. The two men, with Colepaugh in command, formed *Unternehman Elster,* Operation Magpie. They were to be infiltrated into the United States by submarine to spy on shipyards, airplane factories, and rocket-testing sites. Colepaugh managed to persuade his SD superiors that a single man in America needed $15,000 per year to live on, at a time when the average U.S. annual family income was $2,378. Thus two men embarked on a mission estimated to last two years would need $60,000, according to Colepaugh. Not only did the SD unquestioningly provide this sum in cash, but also added ninety-nine diamond chips, in case the two agents were somehow parted from their dollars.

On November 29, 1944, U-1230, after passing an unnerving eight days avoiding American patrols by resting on the sea bottom off the coast of

Maine, slipped into Frenchman Bay and put Colepaugh and Gimpel ashore. The two spies subsequently made their way to New York City, where Colepaugh showed little appetite for espionage, but keen interest in drinking and womanizing from his seemingly bottomless finances. The carousing was partly a mask to conceal Colepaugh's mounting anxiety. On Christmas Day he went to the home in Queens of an old Farragut school chum, Edward Mulcahy, where he bared his soul. The two spent most of the holiday holed up in Mulcahy's bedroom wrestling over what Willy should do. The next day, he turned himself in to the FBI and readily volunteered where the agents would find Gimpel.

What Hoover, in reporting the arrests to the President, conveniently omitted was that, as in the case of the eight earlier saboteurs, the Magpie mission had been undone not by brilliant FBI detective work but because Colepaugh gave himself up. In a subsequent report to the President, Hoover revealed that Havel Lina Colepaugh, Willy's mother, upon being questioned by the FBI, claimed that her son was FDR's third cousin. Willy bore the same relationship to the Theodore Roosevelt branch of the family, she claimed. Consequently, he was also related to the First Lady. During the 1927 funeral of her husband, Mrs. Colepaugh told her interrogators, "the Colepaugh family Bible disappeared" and later popped up in the Franklin Roosevelt family's possession. "She stated that at the President's Inauguration in Washington, it was discovered that the Bible purported to be the Roosevelt family Bible was in reality the Colepaugh family Bible." FDR was unmoved. He told Hoover, "[H]e [Willy] is no relation of mine. Finally, the family Bible on which I take the oath of office happens to be a Roosevelt one with manuscript notations of births and deaths as far back as the 17th Century. Enuf said!" On Valentine's Day 1945, Colepaugh and Gimpel were convicted by a military tribunal of espionage and were sentenced to death. A week later, Bill Donovan, in the very sort of interference that infuriated Hoover, sent the President a wrap-up of espionage and sabotage cases in the United States since the war's outbreak. Twenty cases, including Colepaugh's and Gimpel's, had been brought to trial, with sixteen completed, one under way, and three pending. Donovan's unsubtle point was that the tip-off in sixteen of these cases had been provided by British intelligence, and it was he who was thickest with the British, not J. Edgar Hoover.

★

FDR believed that another meeting with Stalin and Churchill was imperative. The controversial postwar frontiers of Poland had to be settled. The occupation zones of conquered Germany, roughed out at Tehran, had to be fixed. Most critical, the President intended to marshal his powers of persuasion toward drawing Stalin into the war in the Pacific. The Russians had agreed in principle at Tehran to join the battle, but where and how soon? What Henry Stimson and the Joint Chiefs of Staff were telling Roosevelt in 1945 was chilling. No assurance yet existed that the hushed activities at Los Alamos would succeed. The atomic bomb could well prove to be a $2 billion dud. Planning for Operation Olympic, the invasion of Japan, was therefore proceeding on the assumption that conventional forces would have to defeat the enemy. The assault against the Japanese home islands, FDR was told, would engage five million American troops. D-Day was set for November 1, 1945, and the war could not be won, the Joint Chiefs projected, before the end of 1946. Churchill was even less sanguine. He feared that the Pacific war would drag on into 1948. Roosevelt's objective was to diminish the bloody American casualties predicted by enlisting the Red Army against Japan.

A physically failing FDR had hoped to achieve his ends without making another exhausting journey abroad. Months before, he had confided to Daisy Suckley that he thought this time he could persuade Stalin to come to him. "When I first got to Tehran," he told her, "Stalin came to call on me. Of course I did not get up when he came into the room. We shook hands and he sat down, and I caught him looking curiously at my legs and ankles." Later at dinner, "when Stalin was seated on my right, he turned to the interpreter and said, 'Tell the President that I now understand what it has meant for him to make the effort to come on such a long journey. Tell him that the next time I will come to him.' " It was not to be. As plans for the three-power summit advanced, Roosevelt cabled Churchill, "I have received a reply from U.J. [Uncle Joe] which is not very helpful in the selection of a place for our next meeting. He stated that if our next meeting on the Black Sea is acceptable, he considers it an extremely desirable plan. His doctors to whose opinion he must give consideration do not wish him to make any big trips." Thus the paraplegic with the failing heart agreed to travel over seven thousand miles to accommodate the Soviet leader who still had eight years to live.

On January 23, 1945, FDR boarded the cruiser USS *Quincy* for the first leg of his journey. He sailed the *Quincy* to Malta and from there flew the presidential plane, the *Sacred Cow,* for seven hours to an airfield at Saki in the Crimea. The field was crusted with snow and the Soviets had marked off its perimeter with soldiers placed shoulder to shoulder. FDR was lowered by a makeshift elevator from the plane to a waiting automobile. The worst was yet to come. The President, to whom the swaying of a train was agonizing, began a jolting eighty-mile odyssey mostly over dirt roads across the steppes and through the Yalta Mountains. As Admiral Leahy described the journey, "That mountain road had been built in the era of the horse when long base cars had never been dreamed of. The curves were short and sharp without retaining walls, and jutted out to the very edge of the continuous precipice."

The route was littered with the waste of war, burnt-out houses, charred tanks, upended railroad cars, and rotting animal carcasses, resulting from fierce fighting to drive the Germans out of the Crimea. The visible suffering of the people, the ruination of their farms and villages, and the massive casualties reconfirmed FDR's long-held conviction that the Russians still bore the brunt of the war. On reaching Yalta, he was put up at the Livadia Palace, the three-storied marble summer retreat of the last czar, Nicholas II, one of a handful of buildings still standing in the city. Churchill, on his arrival, observed, ". . . [I]f we had spent ten years on research, we could not have found a worse place than Magneto [code name for Yalta]." He told his aides that he could survive only "by bringing an adequate supply of whiskey."

The three powers each brought its priority to Yalta: the British to maintain their empire, the Soviets to solidify their conquests in Europe and seize land in the Far East, and the Americans to bring Russia into the Pacific war. The last goal represented a serious miscalculation by FDR. He believed that he had to persuade Stalin to join the fight against Japan and was prepared to grant concessions, hold out enticements, and otherwise bait the hook. Consequently, Roosevelt supported and Churchill reluctantly agreed to Stalin's demand that Russia be allowed to take back all the territory it had lost in the 1904–1905 war with Japan, plus the Kuril Islands and the southern half of Sakhalin Island. The truth, so clear in retrospect, is that nothing could have kept the Soviet Union out of the Asian war once Germany was beaten. The Russians were keen to assuage the humiliation of their long ago defeat by Japan. They wanted back the lost territories and more. They wanted access to the warm water harbor of Port Arthur. Spoils were to be won in the Pacific, and Stalin expected his share. Churchill's foreign minister, Anthony Eden, observed that the Western Allies needed to concede nothing to get Russia into the Pacific. But Roosevelt was operating not on the premise of Japanese cities soon to be reduced to ash by atomic bombs, but by the projection of tens of thousands of American bodies carpeting the beaches of Kyushu and Honshu. He was ready to meet Stalin's price.

FDR was performing under enormous physical and mental stress. Both his regular physician, Admiral Ross McIntire, and his full-time cardiologist, Lieutenant Commander Howard Bruenn, accompanied him to Yalta. The President also brought along his daughter, Anna, who wrote to her husband, back in Washington, about the most zealously guarded secret in the Roosevelt White House. "Ross and Bruenn are both worried because of the old 'ticker' trouble—which, of course, no one knows about but those two and me. . . . I have found out thru Bruenn (who won't let me tell Ross that I know) that this 'ticker' situation is far more serious than I ever knew. And the biggest difficulty in handling the situation here is that we can, of course, tell no one of the 'ticker' trouble. It's truly worrisome—and there's not a heluva [sic] lot anyone can do about it." She closed with a warning to her husband, "(Better tear off and destroy this paragraph.)"

The secret was far less hidden from a professional eye. Lord Moran, Churchill's personal physician, wrote after seeing FDR at Yalta, ". . . [T]he President appears a very sick man. He has all the symptoms of hardening of the arteries of the brain in an advanced stage, so that I give him only a few months to live. But men shut their eyes when they do not want to see, and the Americans here cannot bring themselves to believe that he is finished." One intimate, however, had fooled Moran. "His daughter thinks he is not really ill," the doctor added to his diagnosis.

The Yalta conference ended on February 12. FDR left frail in body but buoyant in spirit. The Russians had promised to break their nonaggression pact with Japan and come into the war within two or three months of the defeat of Germany. Occupation zones for the vanquished Reich were confirmed and unconditional surrender remained the demand for ending the fighting.

The tall, patrician Alger Hiss, onetime law clerk for Supreme Court Justice Oliver Wendell Holmes and now a rising star in the State Department, had been among the President's advisors at Yalta. After the conference, Hiss traveled to Moscow to confer with Andrei Vyshinsky, Soviet commissar for foreign affairs. Hiss was one of the men whom Whittaker Chambers had denounced to Adolf Berle before the war as a Soviet agent. At the time, Berle had done nothing to investigate this accusation. Hiss's impeccable credentials and blue ribbon sponsors, in Berle's judgment, lifted the man above suspicion. Among the stacks of intercepted but still undecipherable Soviet messages gathering at Arlington Hall was one from Vasili Zarubin, the NKVD *rezident* in Washington, sent to Moscow and dealing with someone code-named Ales. Had the American cryptanalysts been able to crack the code, they would have read: "After the Yalta conference a Soviet personage in a very responsible position (Ales gave us to understand that it was Comrade Vyshinsky) allegedly got in touch with Ales and at the behest of the military NEIGHBORS [GRU, Soviet military intelligence] passed on to him their gratitude and so on." The telegram noted further, "Ales has been working with the Neighbors continuously since 1935," and "Recently Ales and his whole group were awarded Soviet decorations." Years later, when the Venona project had succeeded in breaking the Soviet ciphers, this message was decrypted, with the notation, "Ales: probably Alger Hiss."

★

Opening the *Chicago Tribune* was a chore the President approached with loathing and trepidation. He had still been out of the country at Yalta when on February 9 the *Tribune* carried a lead story that seemed calculated to drive up FDR's blood pressure, already at a level that troubled his physicians. The newspaper had obtained Bill Donovan's secret draft proposal for a postwar intelligence service. Emblazoned across the front page, the headline read, NEW DEAL PLANS SUPER SPY SYSTEM. The subhead went on, SLEUTHS WOULD SNOOP ON U.S. AND THE WORLD. The jump to an inside page proclaimed, SUPER GESTAPO AGENCY IS UNDER CONSIDERATION. The exclusive, carried in the *Tribune* and its sister papers, The Washington *Times-Herald* and the New York *Daily News,* had been written by Walter Trohan, a resourceful, well-connected Washington correspondent. "Creation of an all-powerful intelligence service to spy on the postwar world and to pry into the lives of citizens at home is under consideration by the New Deal," the article began. So sweeping were the powers of the proposed spy organization that its "director might employ the FBI on some task and charge the G-men not to report to J. Edgar Hoover, their chief. . . ." The agency would "presumably have secret funds for spy work along the lines of bribing and luxury living described in the novels of E. Phillips Oppenheim." Among those in the know, the article went on, "the proposed unit is known as 'Frankfurter's Gestapo' because the sister of Supreme Court Justice

Frankfurter is said to hold a confidential personnel post in OSS. It is assumed she would pick key personnel, at the suggestion of her brother." Most startling, along with the Trohan article, the paper printed Donovan's plan, classified "Top Secret," verbatim.

Indiana's Republican senator, Homer Capehart, deplored "any new superduper Gestapo." Senate Democrat Edwin Johnson of Colorado declared that the country did not want "any Democratic Gestapo." Clare Hoffman, a House Republican, branded the Donovan plan "another New Deal move right along the Hitler line." London's *Economist* positively gloated at American bumbling. "[T]his document, emanating from an office wrapped in secrecy, and dealing with a matter retailed only in whispers, has been published in full on the front pages of the McCormick-Patterson newspapers," proving that American innocents were incapable of keeping a confidence, a columnist for *The Economist* wrote. "Once upon a time," the writer went on, "President Cleveland was asked if he thought a certain secret well kept. 'I find the White House cat knew all about it,' Cleveland said." The writer had parting advice for Britain's American cousins: ". . . how many more water mains are to be pierced before the United States Congress passes an Official Secrets Act to protect itself and its Allies. Is freedom to blab essential to democracy?"

Even the German news service, DNB, pounced on the Trohan story. A commentator asked, "What is happening here? Despite the bitter frost and snowstorm the people are stopping in front of the *Daily News* building. Similar crowds are gathering in Washington in front of the *Times-Herald* and in Chicago in front of the *Tribune*. All of these people are gazing at the neon letters and can hardly believe their own eyes. One of [the organization's] functions is to act as a police instrument, which is to suppress and eliminate in good time all criticism of the Roosevelt dictatorship."

Two days later, Trohan fired a second salvo, carried on the front page of the Sunday editions of the McCormick-Patterson papers. "The joint chiefs of staff," Trohan wrote, "have declared war on Brigadier General William J. Donovan OSS Director, who advanced a scheme, at the behest of President Roosevelt, for unification of intelligence activities abroad and superseding existing intelligence agencies at home." The Joint Chiefs, the article went on, had submitted "a highly secret letter from the generals and admirals to the President urging rejection of the plan." The reporter had again secured a copy of this classified letter, and, as in the case of Donovan's proposal, the papers printed it word for word.

Donovan had been out of the country when both torpedoes struck, but his top aides immediately launched a damage-control operation. On February 13, *The New York Times* carried a story that read, "Comparing the proposal of Major General William J. Donovan to coordinate United States intelligence services to the organizing of an 'American Gestapo' was received with surprise and not a little disapprobation in informed circles today." The report went on to reject the idea that "such an organization could be turned into an agency for intimidation or inquisition over the American public. . . ." It was an unusual story, sourced only by the anonymous "informed circles," and read more like an editorial than news. OSS's upper echelon was staffed with well-connected people to whom gaining the ear of *The New York Times* did not pose insuperable problems. Similar spadework preceded an editorial in *The Washington Post*. "Donovan is one of the trail blazers in our war organization," the *Post* declared. His OSS is "a kind of brain trust for the men charged with making decisions based upon exact knowledge of all the detailed elements in hitherto unknown situations."

Donovan was soon back in Washington to fight his own battles. He confronted the Joint Chiefs of Staff and charged that the Trohan exposé "was not the result of an accident or a 'leak,' but a deliberate plan of sabotage. . . ." The accusation that Frankfurter, a Jew on the Supreme Court, intended to run an American "Gestapo" was particularly enraging. Odder still was the story's presumption that the ambitious Donovan would allow the judge, through his sister, to pick key staff for an organization that Wild Bill expected to run. He continued his counterattack: "The falsehood concerning the Frankfurter appointment, the characterization of the proposal as a 'Gestapo' and 'Superspy' scheme of the President, the immediate canvassing of Congress based on misstatements and distortions of fact, all make clear, a design and intent, through the incitement of suspicion and antagonism to prevent adoption of my proposal." He found the affair treasonable and demanded an investigation "by a judicial or quasi-judicial body armed with the power of subpoena and to compel testimony under oath." The chiefs agreed to act.

Still fuming, Donovan did not wait until the President was back from Yalta before taking his case to FDR via airborne pouch. But first he conducted a little detective work. He had sent an assistant to the Joint Chiefs of Staff to compare the postwar plan that he had submitted with the version appearing in the Trohan story. The JCS staff had made changes to Donovan's proposal, then redesignated it "JCS 1181," classified it "Top Secret," and distributed only fifteen numbered copies among State, the FBI, the Se-

cret Service, and military branches involved in intelligence. Wild Bill's assistant, dispatched to the JCS, found that the version printed in the newspapers contained changes made *after* Donovan had submitted his plan to
the chiefs, making clear that the leak had come from within the JCS or
from a recipient of the classified document. Donovan was thus able to
write the President: "A reading of these articles makes clear that the disclosure was no mere leak but a deliberate plan to sabotage any attempt at
reorganization of this government's intelligence services. . . . The entire
situation is most disturbing because it looks like 'an inside job' or at least
it was abetted by someone on the inside."

How had the *Chicago Tribune* correspondent obtained copies of a top-
secret proposal? Since Donovan's arch rival, J. Edgar Hoover, was on the
distribution list for JCS 1181, the shadow of suspicion fell not surprisingly on him. Hoover "goes to the White House," Henry Stimson had earlier noted in his diary, "and poisons the mind of the President." Yet, no
evidence was ever turned up connecting the FBI director to the leak. Walter Trohan always maintained that he had obtained the documents from an
astonishing source, the White House itself. He and Steve Early, the President's press secretary, were longstanding friends who had traded journalistic favors in the past. Trohan explained their friendship, noting that in
the "New Deal environment, we were both anti-Socialist." As the reporter
described the affair, Early had given him the classified papers because
"Roosevelt thought Donovan was getting too big for his britches." By deliberately leaking the documents FDR would also, Trohan claimed, have a
chance to see how Donovan's postwar intelligence agency played before
the American public. The explanation rings hollow, particularly since the
President and Early were in Yalta when the Trohan stories were being prepared.

Technically, the leaks may well have come out of the White House since
the Map Room appears the specific source. Colonel Park, running that
nerve center, had access to JCS 1181. He was also at the time conducting
his investigation of the OSS, which was dispatching the fox to clean up the
henhouse. Park's report was already in draft form at the time of the Trohan
stories. A close reading of it seems to solve the question of where Walter
Trohan managed to obtain Donovan's postwar plan. Park's draft read in
part, "[T]he British were believed to know almost without exception, the
name, location, cover, and assignment of OSS agents throughout the
world." Trohan's story read: "The British knew almost without exception
the name, location, cover and assignment of every OSS man in the world."

Trohan's article was peppered with similar nearly identical passages from Park's "Top Secret" document. Park, as the likely leaker, had performed his role in the covert campaign of Army intelligence to kill off Wild Bill Donovan and his offspring. Trohan's stories were not the first time that someone in the military had leaked sensitive secrets to the President's journalistic nemesis. The same thing had happened nearly three years before when the *Chicago Tribune* recklessly revealed that the victory at Midway had been made possible by Magic.

Once the Donovan plan had been leaked, FDR did have an unintended opportunity to gauge public reaction to a permanent espionage agency, and he could sense a split decision. During this period, while Donovan was taking the heaviest pounding of his tempestuous career, the President never uttered a word in his defense. As for Wild Bill's demand that the JCS investigate the incident, a halfhearted inquiry was made, then allowed to wither, with no perpetrator ever identified.

★

The President's reversal of Donovan on the purchase of the Soviet codes followed by the *Chicago Tribune* debacle might have been staggering blows to anyone lacking the general's resilience. Instead he believed he was about to deliver an espionage triumph that must overcome any misgivings the President may have had about the OSS, one ranking with Magic's piercing of Japanese ciphers and Fritz Kolbe's spying from inside the Nazi foreign office. The key lay in Rome.

Virgilio Scattolini was a short, fat Roman with an oily, confident air and a damp handshake. As a young man, he had enjoyed success in the back alleys of literature with his first pornographic work, *Such Women,* about Roman whores. His next, *Amazons of the Bidet,* became a best-seller. One would be hard-pressed to imagine that anything produced by Virgilio Scattolini would find its way onto the desk of the President of the United States. Yet, a sharp turnabout in Scattolini's destiny put him on that path. He married a beautiful and pious woman and turned his back on his unsavory past. He and his wife attended Mass every morning. He became a tertiary, a minor layman's rank in the Franciscan order. He wrote "The Poem of Holy Rome," a work praising the papacy. The poem caught the eye of the editor of *L'Osservatore Romano,* the Vatican newspaper, who hired Scattolini to write film reviews. In this position he was privy to much that happened within the Vatican. Unfortunately, someone unearthed Scattolini's earlier career as a pornographer and he was fired. Scattolini, now a dutiful husband and a doting father, took up freelance reporting to support his family. When the Allies marched into Rome on June 5, 1944, he saw a chance to augment his slender living.

Soon after the liberation of the Eternal City, the OSS set up a headquarters run by Victor Scamporini, a former State Department official. In mid-1944 a windfall dropped into Scamporini's lap. Through an intermediary named Filippo Settacioli, he began receiving tantalizing intelligence from within the supposedly impenetrable Vatican. In the midst of war, the Holy See had continued to maintain embassies throughout the world in belligerent and neutral capitals alike. The first delivery to Scamporini was a copy of a cable from the pope's apostolic delegate in Tokyo, reporting on events inside the Japanese capital. Soon the Vatican reports began to flow so heavily that one OSS radio operator was occupied solely with translating and transmitting them to Washington. Donovan's front office was overjoyed with both the volume and quality. In January 1945 these reports were assigned a special code word, "Vessel," and classified "Top Secret/Control," which meant that only those on a restricted list could see this intelligence.

The OSS was not blind to the potential dangers of an unverified source, however promising. Vessel could be a double agent, an enemy plant, a fabricator of intelligence for profit. "This series offers great promise," Washington cabled Scamporini, but warned, "For its full usefulness a careful evaluation of the sources is essential." Scamporini knew only that Settacioli received the intelligence from an unidentified source with access to the pope's Department of Extraordinary Affairs, the latter serving as the papal foreign office. The informant also had access to Bishop Giovanni Battista Montini, the pope's undersecretary of state, who would later become Pope Paul VI. Scamporini found Vessel's intelligence well worth the $500 a month paid to the informant through Settacioli, a trifling sum to the OSS, but munificent in defeated and impoverished Italy. What he did not know was that the source of these prized secrets was Settacioli's brother-in-law, Virgilio Scattolini.

The OSS's counterintelligence branch, X-2, was assigned to vet Vessel. The task was delegated to a recent arrival in the Rome X-2 office, Lieutenant James Jesus Angleton, young, brilliant, armored with the skepticism of the counterintelligence professional, but hugely overworked. His office was handling over a thousand counterespionage cases with just thirty agents, only one of whom, a green lieutenant, could be spared to check out Vessel.

X-2 had not yet completed its clearance of Vessel, but an impatient Wild Bill found the intelligence so valuable and the source sufficiently credible that he chose not to wait any longer. On January 11, while still out of the country, he authorized his acting director, Charles S. Cheston, to send the first Vessel message to the White House with a cover note, "I think [this] will be of interest to the President." The content was extraordinary. Vessel message 7a, as it was designated, reported a private conversation between Pope Pius XII and Pietro Cardinal Fumasoni-Biondi, prefect of the Propaganda Fides, the church's missionary arm. In it, the cardinal said: "I think that the Russian government has already decided to renounce the neutrality pact with Japan and that in the coming conference between Stalin, Roosevelt and Churchill the three leaders will fix the method and time for the renunciation." To which the pope responded: ". . . [I]t will be necessary to ascertain the peace conditions which would be offered by Great Britain and America, in order that we may be able to see whether the difference between the two stands could be resolved by mediation." The cardinal was pessimistic: "This will be very difficult, probably impossible, for the Allies want unconditional surrender." The pope was still hopeful and concluded: "At any rate, we must try. . . . Please inform your man in Tokyo that it is necessary to know the attitude of the Tokyo government before determining whether our intervention is opportune." For Roosevelt, knowing the massive casualties the JCS predicted to conquer Japan, the possible intercession of the Vatican in hastening the end of the Pacific war would be heaven-sent.

OSS Washington received twelve more Vessel messages before 20a was considered vital enough to send to the President. In it Cardinal Fumasoni-Biondi responded to Pius XII's request to find out the Japanese conditions for peace. The cardinal's subordinate in Tokyo, the apostolic delegate to Japan, reported: "The Japanese minimum demands for a negotiated peace are the following: Japan will renounce all occupied territories except Hainan and Hong Kong. . . . The Philippines are to be independent and sovereign, free from all United States ties. India is to be elevated to dominion status in the British Commonwealth of Nations. . . . Australia is to be opened to Japanese immigration." The papal envoy showed a sensitivity to the importance of saving face in the Orient, noting that the Anglo-Americans must remember "the form rather than the substance of their demands should be tempered and that the psychology of the Orientals should be protected." Choice Vessel intelligence continued to go to the President. Vessel 24b was especially impressive since it relayed a report directly from within the Imperial Palace. The Vatican's apostolic delegate reported: "On 10 January the Japanese Emperor attended a secret council meeting during which someone dared to speak about peace feelers. . . . The Emperor did not express any disapproval of these efforts."

Along with the White House, Donovan began sharing Vessel's reports with State and the military intelligence branches, both for strategic use and to boost his own standing. Relevant Vessel messages also went to Admiral Nimitz at U.S. Pacific Fleet headquarters in Hawaii. This intelligence enabled OSS Washington to alert the Nimitz staff: "The Japanese have recently put into service a new battleship with nine of the largest guns in the world. This warship is commanded by Rear Admiral Yanuchi, a Catholic." Using Vessel to cultivate the Navy especially appealed to Donovan since he was eager for Nimitz's permission to let him operate in the Pacific, from which the OSS was still shut out.

Even while the President had been at Yalta he continued to receive Vessel traffic through a special Navy radio circuit. One such message reported: ". . . [T]he Japanese Government is confident that Stalin will categorically refuse to abrogate the non-aggression pact with Japan. . . . The Japanese Government feels that Japan can continue the Pacific war indefinitely in view of Russia's certain refusal to enter the war"; grim news for FDR if true. Roosevelt's secretary, Grace Tully, informed Wild Bill of the Vessel traffic: "The President finds this material most interesting and reads every one carefully." It was indeed an extraordinary penetration. Vessel's revelations could influence the President's strategy in bringing Russia into the Pacific war; they could help him gauge the seriousness of the peace movement inside Japan, and even influence his decision regarding the necessity of using the atom bomb against the Japanese.

At the same time that Donovan was feeding the Vessel disclosures to the White House he presented the President with another coup. In 1943, Mussolini's foreign minister, Count Galeazzo Ciano, hoping to spare Italy further suffering, had voted with the Fascist Grand Council to remove Mussolini from power. Thereafter, with Mussolini's acquiescence, the Germans arrested Ciano, kept him in jail in Verona, and then shot him. Il Duce had, in effect, condemned the husband of his daughter, Edda, to death. The widow then fled to Switzerland disguised as a peasant, concealing in her underwear twelve hundred pages of the diaries Ciano had kept since 1939. Allen Dulles, in Bern, managed to buy the diaries from the sick, financially strapped Countess Ciano, while she was recuperating in a Swiss hospital. Donovan considered acquisition of the diary, which had been sought by several other intelligence services, proof of OSS's growing stature.

As for Vessel, an unexpected opportunity presented itself to test the source's authenticity. A Vessel message forwarded to the President on January 27 reported a meeting between the pope and Myron Taylor, FDR's personal envoy to the Vatican. The pope had reportedly asked Taylor if he would be willing to meet with the Japanese ambassador to the Holy See, referred to as Harada Ken, to discuss the prospects of papal intervention in ending the Pacific war. Taylor was said to have told the pope that he was not precisely an official of the United States government and thus could speak only as a private individual. But he did promise to present the pope's request to the President. Here was a perfect opportunity to ask Taylor about his meeting with the pontiff and see if it squared with Vessel's account. Lieutenant Angleton sent a man to Taylor's office at the Holy See to inquire about the papal encounter. Taylor was not pleased. What passed between him and the pontiff, he maintained, was privileged. The OSS base in Italy thereafter sent a message to Washington concluding, ". . . Vessel report was undoubtedly authentic or Taylor would have said so if it were not."

On February 3 a small cloud rose over the Vessel horizon. OSS Rome had sent a copy of a Vessel report to Allen Dulles as an information addressee. Dulles read it and replied that he questioned Vessel's veracity, and "was investigating further." Rome's reaction was to cut Dulles from the distribution list. No future Vessel cables were to be sent "to any place other than Washington." Rome further cautioned OSS headquarters to "warn all people handling Vessel material of necessity of extreme caution in view ever constant risk killing source completely."

On February 16, Vessel 67a provided another opportunity to verify the agent's bona fides. This message described the meeting the pope had asked for between Myron Taylor and Harada Ken. "Harada," Vessel reported, "declared that Japanese elements desirous of peace are not responsible for the Pacific War, and that those elements might make their will felt if the Anglo-Americans would offer acceptable terms. Taylor reminded Harada that American public opinion still remembers the unprovoked attack on Pearl Harbor." Both men feared that their respective countries' positions were too far apart for fruitful negotiations.

On March 7, OSS Rome sent Washington a muted alarm. "We have very good reason to believe that VESSEL SERVICE is not exclusive OSS source. It is virtually certain that several other governments have access to this source." Rome was aware of ten other recipients. What this discovery meant was that if Vessel's other clients included neutral nations with representatives in Rome, through them his information could reach the enemy. For that reason the message ended, ". . . suggest you also consider appropriately advising the White House and State Department that all activities, reports, and discussions of U.S. officials near the VESSEL source are most probably subject to leakage."

The possibility of a leak to foreign intelligence services proved to be the least of OSS's problems. A copy of 67a, reporting the Taylor/Harada Ken conversation, had been sent to Assistant Secretary of State James Dunn, the department's liaison with the OSS. On March 2, Dunn advised Donovan's office, "We immediately sent a telegram to Myron Taylor asking him if he had a conversation with the Japanese Ambassador as reported." Dunn now had Taylor's reply, which he shared with Donovan. "I have not seen or talked with Ken Harada. I do not even know Ken Harada," Taylor had answered. Taylor's reversal of the Japanese name only served to underscore his lack of familiarity with the man. OSS Washington immediately warned the Italy office, "Conversation as reported . . . known to be pure fabrication." A sharp crack ran through the tower of intelligence erected by Vessel. Bill Donovan immediately put himself on the side of the angels. He wrote Dunn, "Dear Jimmie . . . your statement confirmed us in our suspicion of the source of this material. For some time we have been inquiring into information coming from a certain source coming from that institution [the Vatican]." Cautious skepticism, however, was hardly the spirit in which Donovan had sent numerous unverified Vessel reports to the White House.

Jim Angleton had never been comfortable with Vessel. He found it hard to swallow that an institution as tightly shrouded in secrecy as the papacy, whose intelligence activities reached back for a millennium, could be so easily breached. Angleton, a Catholic of near-mystical vision, had his own pipeline into the Vatican, the same Bishop Giovanni Battista Montini who was Vessel's supposed entrée. Still, Angleton faced a classic intelligence dilemma. To inquire about a source in the Vatican would be to reveal that the OSS was spying on the Vatican. Angleton managed to walk the tightrope. He learned that one of Bishop Montini's duties was to maintain the Holy See's archives. Vessel had informed the OSS: "The procedure of the Papal audiences is the following: After each audience, Monsignor Pio Rossignani, private secretary to the Pope, heard personally from the Pope what was said. He often writes a rough copy that the Pope corrects so that it may be registered in the archives." Access to these archives was presumably what had enabled Scattolini to provide his controllers with near-verbatim reports of what passed between the pope and his inner circle. Scattolini had, in fact, provided detailed accounts of twenty such private papal audiences. All told, his reports had generated over seventeen hundred OSS documents. But, as Angleton learned through Bishop Montini, no transcripts of papal audiences were ever made. None existed in the Vatican archives.

All that Virgilio Scattolini did have access to was a fertile imagination. His earlier work at *L'Osservatore Romano,* his ear as a playwright for convincing dialogue, and a spongelike memory had combined to produce plausible fabrications swallowed at the highest levels. The Rome station chief had been fooled. OSS Washington had been fooled. Donovan himself had been fooled. At times, State, the War Department, the Joint Chiefs of Staff, and the military services appear to have been taken in. But was the object of Donovan's keenest attentions, the President, duped as well?

Inexplicably, and inexcusably, not only did Donovan fail to notify the President that the communications he had rushed to the White House were suspect, but he also continued to send FDR Vessel reports even as his counterintelligence officers in Rome were exposing the pornographer/playwright/con artist. More than a month after Donovan wrote James Dunn of his suspicions of Vessel, number 84a went to the White House, in which the "Apostolic Delegate in Yokohama" tells the Vatican that a prince of the Japanese royal family is preparing "a set of conditions which they judge acceptable to the Anglo-Americans" to achieve peace.

Scattolini, never imagining how high his fictions would reach, could not know that some of what he fabricated could be checked for authenticity by the President himself. While FDR was en route to Yalta, a Vessel report relayed to him told of a "White House spokesman" forwarding a message for the Vatican regarding Poland's future. The President had to know that no such message ever existed. Most telling, the President received Magic, the direct interception of Japanese diplomatic traffic coming out of Rome, Berlin, and other capitals, intelligence that did not square with what Vessel was reporting. FDR had no need to depend on hearsay from an anonymous spy in Rome. If the OSS had not been shut out of Magic, Donovan would likely have been spared the humiliation of having his proudly trumpeted source exposed as a swindle.

It was FDR's habit, upon receiving any communication of consequence to the war, to forward it to Leahy, Stimson, Stettinius, or whomever he wanted to deal with the matter, usually with an appended note reading, "Please take care of this," "What do you make of this?" or "What are we doing about this?" No record exists among the voluminous Roosevelt archives that FDR ever forwarded a single Vessel message to anyone, no matter how seemingly urgent, as in the case of supposed Japanese peace feelers. No evidence establishes that FDR took any action as a result of a Vessel report. The question then arises, if he must have known the spuriousness of this source, why did FDR never say so to Donovan or anyone else? Roosevelt may have chosen not to embarrass a man whose boldness and energy, if not his reliability, he genuinely admired. However, the likeliest explanation, given the President's crushing burdens coupled with his steady physical decline, is that FDR lacked the time or energy to focus on a misbegotten Donovan venture. Whatever the reasons, leaving the matter in limbo was not odd, but typical of FDR's impenetrable motives.

As for Virgilio Scattolini, he never knew that he had been unmasked. Indeed, at Angleton's insistence, the Italian kept receiving his monthly $500 stipend, not for his worthless product, but because Angleton, of a conspiratorial bent that would persist throughout his long subsequent CIA career, could not believe that one lone figure could have produced the torrent of Vessel intelligence. He wanted to uncover the chain that, he was convinced, would lead from Scattolini to a wider ring of deceit.

The Vessel fiasco came at a bad time for the OSS, exploding within weeks after the *Chicago Tribune* debacle. Donovan would now have to survive the twin batterings of Walter Trohan and Virgilio Scattolini.

————═ ★ ═————

Chapter XXVII

Who Knew—and When?

T HE SOVIET Union was still at peace with Japan, outwardly respecting the nonaggression pact between the two countries. Stalin had told FDR at Tehran in 1943, "We Soviets welcome your successes in the Pacific," but as for Russian participation, his forces in the East were, he claimed, sufficient only for defense. If the United States wanted the Soviet Union fighting Japan, Stalin estimated, "Our forces . . . must be increased about three-fold." Out of this demand was born a secret collaboration between the United States and USSR beginning in October 1944 to bring the Soviet Union to offensive strength in the Pacific. The operation was code-named Hula. Under Hula, the United States would covertly turn over to the Soviet Union a flotilla of thirty U.S. frigates, sixty minesweepers, fifty-six submarine chasers, and thirty large landing vessels. Chosen to head the project was one of the least likely officers in the U.S. Navy, a newly minted forty-five-year-old captain named William S. Maxwell. Maxwell had been born in Warsaw and his surname at birth was Dzwoniecki. The boy went to sea at age thirteen and, penniless and not speaking a word of English, jumped ship in New York City. He was subsequently adopted by a U.S. Navy recruiter, George Maxwell, joined the Navy, and rose from seaman apprentice to his present rank, forging along the way a reputation as a hard-driving but fair commander. Besides his get-things-done record, Maxwell was chosen for Hula because he spoke a bastard Russian. This Polish American, his thick Slavic features set in permanent resolution, was to complete his mission at one of the most inhospitable spots on earth, Cold Bay, on the southwestern tip of the Alaskan peninsula, where the average annual rainfall was forty inches and the port was shrouded in fog half the time. Here, Maxwell began receiving fifteen thousand Soviet naval officers and enlisted men, housing them, feeding them, and training them to take over the American ships, all without Japan's knowledge.

★

Roosevelt had decided at Yalta not to tell Stalin about the Manhattan Project. It did not matter. Klaus Fuchs, Theodore Hall, and other covert servants of the Soviet Union had filled the void. Other major figures who did or did not know about the war's most precious secret formed a crazy quilt pattern. In mid-1943, FDR had written Robert Oppenheimer to warn the project's scientific leader of the absolute necessity of protecting the secrecy of the enterprise. Yet, to the President's dismay, Supreme Court Justice Felix Frankfurter had learned of the bomb. General Douglas MacArthur, despite his towering role in the Pacific war, knew nothing of the weapon until the eve of its use. General Eisenhower had only a sketchy understanding. He knew more about what the Germans were up to in the realm of the atom than what was happening in Los Alamos. "From time to time," he wrote in his wartime memoirs, ". . . staff officers from Washington arrived at my headquarters to give me the latest calculations concerning German progress in the development of new weapons, including as possibilities bacteriological and atomic weapons. . . . I was told that American scientists were making progress in these two important types. . . ." Still, FDR never directly revealed the secret to Ike, who later admitted, "I did not then know, of course, that an army of scientists had been engaged in the production of the weapon." That army, by now, had grown to 150,000 persons, most of whom had no idea of the end point of their efforts.

Though Eisenhower was not directly informed, one of his subordinates heard the secret from the President's mouth. General Omar Bradley, fresh from victory in Sicily as commander of II Corps, had been recalled to Washington in September 1943 to brief General Marshall and the President. As Bradley told the story, "I reported as requested. I had seen Roo-

sevelt at aforementioned White House receptions when I was a lowly lieutenant colonel, but I did not really know him." Marshall, Bradley believed,
set up the White House appointment to give FDR a chance to judge a
promising American commander. If so, Bradley appeared to pass the test
since, he recollected, "When I finished, Roosevelt astounded me with a
fairly detailed briefing on our Manhattan Project, the effort to build an
atomic bomb, then one of our most secret projects and one I had never
heard of." The President also confided to Bradley, "[T]he Germans might
be leading us in the race to build this revolutionary weapon. . . ." Bradley
felt burdened by the confidence. As he later wrote, "I decided that the President, however well intentioned, had spoken out of turn. Not once during
the war did I question Marshall or Ike about the atomic bomb, nor did they
mention it to me."

Eisenhower did not learn definitely about the bomb until Henry Stimson
informed him at the Potsdam conference in July 1945. By then, FDR was
dead and use of the bomb less than three weeks off. Soon afterward, Ike
shared the secret with his son and aide, John. Though troubled by the
morality of using so annihilating a weapon, he wondered aloud, "What if
the Germans had had this bomb on D-Day?" The military men in almost
daily contact with FDR, General Marshall and Admiral Leahy, were privy
to the secret, the latter convinced that an atomic weapon "is the biggest
fool thing we have ever done. The bomb will never go off, and I speak as
an expert in explosives."

Edward Stettinius was summoned to the White House one day in January 1945. The secretary of state arrived just as the steward was clearing
away the tray from which the President and Grace Tully had shared sand-
wiches. FDR waited until the door closed behind his secretary, directed
Stettinius to sit down, and then swore him to secrecy. He proceeded to
brief his goggle-eyed visitor about the bomb. "I am not sure how long it
will take to perfect," he told Stettinius, but its potential was awesome. If
dropped on the intersection of Broadway and Forty-second Street, it
"would lay New York low." While trusting in Stettinius, Roosevelt had
withheld the knowledge for years from the less compliant Cordell Hull,
who had been his secretary of state when the Manhattan Project was
launched. Hull's independent streak may have explained FDR's choice in
whom to confide. But no discernible reason existed to share the secret
with the prickly, aggressive Jimmy Byrnes, formally director of the War
Mobilization Board, whom FDR had installed in a White House office as
"my assistant President." Byrnes had accompanied Roosevelt to Yalta,

and after FDR told him of the atomic bomb, became a vigorous advocate for its use.

Congressional leaders had been brought in on the secret at the narrowest level. Until 1944 the administration had been able to hide the cost of building the bomb in obscure pockets of the War Department's budget. But the costs had soon outgrown these concealments. The President directed his three associates most respected for their integrity, Stimson, Marshall, and Vannevar Bush, to meet with Sam Rayburn, Speaker of the House, John W. McCormack, the majority leader, and Joseph W. Martin, the minority leader, to tell them only that the financing of a weapon of unimaginable power was at stake. The leaders accepted the word of the President's emissaries and shepherded through Congress, without debate, massive appropriations to continue the work at Los Alamos.

Henry Morgenthau Jr., as Treasury secretary, had played an early and unwitting role in juggling funds and providing silver to build the bomb. Still, that proud and garrulous confidant of the President was not admitted to the knowing circle. He wrote in his diary why he believed he had been instructed to shift the money and metal: "I got the impression it's some secret weapon." Roosevelt knew of the secretary's vehement opposition to the use of poison gas, and Morgenthau later reasoned that this was why he had not been told about the atom bomb.

Two other members of the President's immediate circle learned about the bomb, not from FDR, but indirectly through his wife, who herself first heard the secret from the unlikely 1943 encounter with Irving Lowen, the young physicist who had managed to talk his way into the First Lady's apartment in New York. Nearly a year later, on June 25, as she returned from grocery shopping, Lowen again showed up at her place. As she later rashly wrote her friend Joe Lash, still in the Army, "We now have the discovery I'm told which he [Lowen] feared Germany would have first but I gather no one wants to use it for its destructive power is so great that no one knows where it might stop." Sensing that this was one arena where she could not influence her husband, she asked two of his trusted associates, Steve Early, the White House press secretary, and Sam Rosenman, to see Lowen. The two men met thereafter in Early's office with the furtive, jumpy scientist, who ran his hands over the walls and demanded to know if the room was bugged. He opened the door and peered in both directions to see if anyone was eavesdropping. He insisted that no secretaries be allowed in. He then told his two astonished listeners in detail about the Manhattan Project, of which they had previously known nothing. He had gone to see Mrs. Roosevelt, Lowen said, because big corporations, particularly Du Pont, were taking over the project so that they could monopolize the production of atomic energy after the war. On Lowen's departure, Early promptly reported him to the War Department. He was subsequently removed from the atomic program.

Two more Manhattan Project physicists chose to spill out their fears about the bomb to the First Lady, Leo Szilard and Enrico Fermi. It was Szilard who had originally drafted the letter Albert Einstein signed alerting FDR, "A single bomb of this type, carried by a boat and exploded in a port, might well destroy the whole port together with surrounding territory." Now, in the spring of 1945, as success neared, Szilard and Fermi were having second thoughts. They met with Mrs. Roosevelt and urged her to warn her husband of its unimaginable destructive force. Though she had already learned of the Manhattan Project from Lowen, there is no indication that the First Lady was ever told by her husband about the bomb or that she ever discussed its use with him.

One of her sons almost knew the secret. Jimmy Roosevelt had been granted leave to come home from the South Pacific to attend FDR's muted fourth inauguration. On finding his father in his study, the young Marine embraced him, tears welling in his eyes. He later recalled the moment. "When he asked about my emotion, I said simply that although we were winning, we still had a lot of fighting to face and I could not know I would be coming back; that the invasion of Japan, for example, was bound to be bloody." The President answered, "James, there will be no invasion of Japan. We have something that will end our war with Japan before any invasion ever takes place." Jimmy asked what it was. FDR replied, "I am sorry, even though you are my son, I cannot tell you. . . . But it is there, it is something we can use and will use if we have to, something we will certainly use before you or any of our sons die in an invasion of Japan."

J. Edgar Hoover learned of the bomb through a roundabout route. Steve Nelson, the Communist Party's West Coast organizer, had managed to penetrate the Manhattan Project by cultivating Joseph W. Weinberg, a physicist employed at the Berkeley laboratories, who passed secrets to him. Nelson, though unaware of it, was being tailed and wiretapped by the FBI. Thus, in the spring of 1943, Hoover learned of the bomb through Nelson's recorded conversations. Hoover's rival, Wild Bill Donovan, heading an agency employing thousands of persons engaged in intelligence, knew nothing of the atom bomb.

A quandary lingers as to when Harry Truman learned of the bomb. His predecessor as vice president, Henry Wallace, had been a member of the atomic energy policy group and had been present with Roosevelt, Churchill, and Harry Hopkins when bomb developments were discussed. Considering Wallace's other loose-lipped disclosures to his Swiss diplomat brother-in-law, leakage of the secret of Los Alamos to Germany seemed more than a remote possibility. But on this subject, Wallace kept his mouth closed. Truman denied ever being informed of the bomb before becoming president. He writes in his memoirs that the day after FDR died, "Stimson told me that he wanted me to know about an immense project that was under way—a project looking to the development of a new explosive of almost unbelievable destructive power. . . . It was the first bit of information that had come to me about the atomic bomb. . . ."

Yet, a respected historian and leading Truman scholar, Robert Ferrell, offers an alternative version. On August 18, 1944, FDR invited his daughter, Anna, and his then vice presidential running mate, Senator Truman, to join him for lunch. The staff set up a table under the shade of a magnolia tree on the rear lawn of the White House. The President behaved that day very much as the senator had come to know him. As Truman once told a reporter, "He does all the talking, and he talks about what he wants to talk about, and he never talks about anything you want to talk about, so there isn't much you can do." During the alfresco lunch, Truman mentioned that his wife, Bess, was out of town, which prompted a Roosevelt story about Eleanor. In a later letter to his wife the senator wrote, "[T]he president told me that Mrs. R. was a very timid woman and wouldn't go to political meetings or make any speeches when he first ran for governor of N.Y. Then he said, 'Now she talks all the time.' "

FDR suggested to Truman that they defeat the heat of the day by taking off their jackets. Photographers and newsreel cameramen, pleased to film the Democratic ticket in shirtsleeves, circled the table orchestrating their shots. At the end of the lunch, Anna left, and the President dismissed the press and asked to be left alone with his running mate. Later, Truman told his friend Harry Vaughan that he had been shocked by FDR's appearance. The President seemed feeble, and when he tried to pour cream into his tea more went into his saucer than the cup. ". . . [H]e's just going to pieces," Truman told Vaughan. "I'm very much concerned about him."

Later accounts of that lunch cast new light on when Truman might have originally learned of the bomb. Professor Ferrell was among the first to gain access to the oral history of Tom L. Evans, an early member of the Boss Tom Pendergast Kansas City Democratic political machine. Evans, a successful businessman who owned a chain of drugstores and a radio and television station, remained an unswerving friend of Truman for life and a frequent recipient of his confidences. Evans has claimed that he asked Truman when he had first learned about the atomic bomb. "You remember when we were together," Truman reportedly responded, referring to the lunch with Roosevelt on the White House lawn, "and the pictures appeared in our shirtsleeves?" "Yes," Evans answered. "That's what we were talking about," Truman replied. The Evans account is corroborated by what Admiral Leahy told Truman biographer Jonathan Daniels, son of the Navy secretary Josephus Daniels, under whom FDR had served as assistant secretary. "Truman told me that FDR had told him much about [the bomb] situation though not details," Leahy stated. Why Truman's account in his autobiography of when he learned of the bomb differs from that of Evans, a trusted friend, and Admiral Leahy remains cloaked in mystery. Prior to becoming president, Truman was not supposed to know. Therefore, even though FDR might have shared the secret with him, he might have felt obliged to behave as if he did not know.

He had known all along, however, that something extraordinary was in the wind. As a senator who chaired a watchdog committee investigating waste in military spending, Truman had once pressed Stimson for an explanation after a staffer, Fred Canfil, uncovered huge expenditures for housing and more mysterious outlays at plants in Oak Ridge, Tennessee, and Hanford, Washington, both sites involved in the Manhattan Project. "It may be necessary for the committee," Truman wrote Stimson, "to consider the appointment of a subcommittee to investigate the project." Stimson had needed to enlist his massive reputation for integrity to persuade Truman to back off. In his diary entry for March 13, 1944, Stimson wrote of Truman, he "is a nuisance and pretty untrustworthy man. He talks smoothly but acts meanly." But after Truman dropped the threatened investigation, Stimson found him as "mild as milk."

Sometime after Leo Szilard had his meeting with Mrs. Roosevelt, he found himself pacing up and down the Midway near the University of Chicago, wrestling with his conscience and debating with his colleagues "the wisdom of testing bombs and using bombs." Szilard became convinced that the President had to face up to the moral consequences of using a weapon introducing a new magnitude of horror. Once again, he went to Albert Einstein with some ideas he had drafted. In March 1945, FDR received a letter from Einstein, posted from the physicist's home in Princeton, New Jersey. The letter was strangely elliptical. In it Einstein spoke of

Szilard and his nuclear credentials and asked the President to see the Hungarian scientist. He added, however, "I do not know the substance of the considerations and recommendations which Dr. Szilard proposes to submit to you." Einstein did tell Roosevelt, "I understand that he [Szilard] now is greatly concerned about the lack of adequate contact between scientists who are doing this work and those members of your Cabinet who are responsible for formulating policy." In the time left to him, the President did not get around to answering Einstein.

Concurrently, FDR was being pressed by others to proceed apace. On March 15, Henry Stimson wrote in his diary, "The President . . . had suggested that I come over to lunch today. . . . First I took up with him a memorandum which he sent me from (name omitted) who had been alarmed at the rumors of extravagance in the Manhattan Project. (name omitted) suggested that it might become disastrous and he suggested that we get a body of 'outside' scientists to pass upon the project because rumors are going around that Vannevar Bush and Jim Conant have sold the President a lemon on the subject and ought to be checked up on." Stimson himself had no qualms about the bomb's perfectibility, and ended his entry, "I gave the President a list of the scientists who were actually engaged on it to show the very high standing of them and it comprised four Nobel Prize men, and also how practically every physicist of standing was engaged with us in the project."

FDR had confided to General Bradley that he had launched the Manhattan Project because he felt the hot breath of German science on his neck. Reinforcing this fear was a warning J. Edgar Hoover delivered to the White House on November 16, 1944. Hoover, by now cognizant of the project, wrote, "A German espionage agent presently in the United States under the control of this Bureau advised that he was instructed to obtain, among other subjects (1) the progress made by the United States since 1941 with respect to the development of atomic explosives, (2) whether 'heavy water' is used instead of helium in their manufacture, (3) the type of container in which the atom of uranium is, and (4) the probable reaction of the people of the United States if Germany used the explosive power obtained through the splitting of the uranium atom." Hoover closed saying, "This information is being made available to you as possibly indicating the degree to which the Germans have progressed in the development of atomic explosives." The report also indicated that the Germans had an inkling, if not certain knowledge, of what the United States was up to.

Despite Roosevelt's persisting concern, atomic developments in the

Third Reich posed no threat to the Allies, as Boris Pash was finding out in Europe. By the spring of 1945, this research was invested primarily in attempting to discover the atom's potential for generating power. The last time uranium had been considered for a military purpose had occurred nearly two years before, and had nothing to do with an atomic bomb. In the summer of 1943, Albert Speer approved an experiment by the Wehrmacht to test the effect of adding uranium to armor-piercing shells to make them penetrate more deeply. As Thomas Powers puts it in *Heisenberg's War,* ". . . [H]ope for a German bomb was so utterly extinct that the precious metal seized in Belgium in 1940—source of so much anxiety in Britain and America—was to be *thrown* at the enemy."

★

Franklin Roosevelt was a devout anti-imperialist. He believed in what he and Churchill had enunciated in the Atlantic Charter in 1941: ". . . [R]espect the right of all peoples to choose the form of government under which they will live." This sentiment hardly reflected what Churchill felt in his heart. But in those dark early days, the Prime Minister would have been willing to sign practically anything that linked America to Britain. A year later, with the United States in the war, Churchill made a speech at home expressing his true sentiments, including the oft-quoted, "Let me, however, make this clear, in case there should be any mistake about it in any quarter. We mean to hold our own. I have not become the King's First Minister in order to preside over the liquidation of the British Empire." He had been particularly irked when Roosevelt urged that he grant India independence on the principle that the Atlantic Charter extended to the Indian Ocean, to Asia, indeed throughout the globe. Churchill complained to his foreign minister, Anthony Eden, "I imagine it is one of his [Roosevelt's] principal war aims to liberate Indo-China from France," which was true. To Roosevelt, Churchill's imperialism was something he had to tolerate while the war went on and deal with when the war was over. He knew to be true, even if he could not publicly echo it, the sentiment of an OSS officer who wrote from India, ". . . [I]f we really believed our own propaganda, we would have to declare war on the British, for they have set themselves up as the master race in India. British rule in India is fascism; there is no dodging that." Of all the colonial masters, FDR found the French particularly reprehensible. He had confided to his son Elliott at the Casablanca conference that he considered French rule so exploitive that the Indochinese might prefer their Japanese occupiers. To Roosevelt the war was a crusade to free all oppressed peoples, including the colonies even of America's allies.

The President's anti-imperialist stand had its espionage dimension. Bill Donovan had long wanted to extend his reach into Asia, thus far with little success. One OSS strategy was actually designated "Project Penetrate MacArthur," but the general continued to rebuff Donovan. Even OSS intelligence that could have shortened battles and saved lives in the Pacific went unused. On February 19, 1945, two U.S. Marine divisions invaded Iwo Jima. They encountered beaches composed of volcanic ash rather than the anticipated sand. This ash, lacking any binding element, afforded poor traction to armored vehicles. The OSS, among its array of talents, included geologists in the Research and Analysis branch who had determined the composition of Iwo Jima's beaches *before* the invasion. But this intelligence never reached the invading Marines. An angered Bill Donovan shot off a query to his third in command, Charles Cheston, demanding to know, "Had we passed this along? If so—when, if not, why not?" The eagerness of the staff had doubtlessly been dulled by repeated rejections in the Pacific.

Donovan tried to win FDR's approval for limited OSS cooperation with the French resistance fighting the Japanese in Indochina. These remnants of colonial rule eagerly sought any opportunity to draw the Americans to their side. They offered to conduct joint sabotage missions and provide weather information to U.S. vessels operating in the Southwest Pacific. Roosevelt remained adamant. He viewed any such alliance as a wedge that the French would exploit to reinsert themselves into the region. He warned the State Department, "I do not want to get mixed up in any military effort toward the liberation of Indochina from the Japanese." Reflecting the President's wishes, General Marshall instructed General Daniel Sultan in India: "OSS personnel not to be employed in Indochina at present." FDR made one exception. He informed General John E. Hull, the War Department's chief of plans and operations, that he had no objection to espionage or sabotage in Indochina uncontaminated by colonialists. He told Hull that he favored "anything that was against the Japs provided that we do not align ourselves with the French." Much of the OSS leadership reflected the President's distaste for rejuvenated imperialism. They were appalled by the British attitude, so nakedly expressed by Colonel Sir Ronald Wingate of Churchill's staff: "We had been at war with Germany longer than any other power, we had suffered more, we had sacrificed more, and in the end we would lose more than any other power. Yet here were these God-awful American academics rushing about, talking about the four freedoms and the Atlantic Charter."

Churchill complained to FDR that OSS teams were working against the British Empire's interests in another quarter of the world. American clandestine operations in Greece, the Prime Minister charged, were designed to keep the Greek king from regaining his throne, while Churchill's aim was to reinstall him as a reliable ally along Britain's Mediterranean route of empire. FDR, however, was not about to chastise the OSS for practicing what he preached. The President found it an uninspiring battle cry to tell Americans that when all the sacrifice, hardship, and bloodshed had ended, the world would be much the same as before. He supported the sentiments expressed by another friend. The onetime OSS chief in London, William Phillips, wrote an appreciative FDR that the colonial peoples deserved "something better to look forward to than simply a return to their old masters."

In China, the OSS worked both the Nationalist and Communist sides of the street. With characteristic bravado, Donovan informed General Tai Li, director of Nationalist Chinese counterintelligence, "I want you to know that I am going to send my men into China whether you like it or not. I know that you can have them murdered one by one, but I want you to know that will not deter me." At the same time, Donovan's agents were providing FDR with a firsthand assessment of the Chinese Communists. An operative working with Mao Tse-tung's forces at Yenan in Shensi Province reported that Mao commanded an army totaling, between regular and militia forces, 2.5 million men. "Morale is very high," Donovan informed the President through his source. "The troops know what they are fighting for. . . . Discipline is essentially good, and orders are carried out even to death. Popular support of the Armed Forces is extremely good. . . . In the guerrilla areas the government is underground, sometimes literally so in caves and tunnels. . . ."

Bill Donovan did manage one penetration into Indochina. His agents began working with a figure determined not to have his people recolonized by the French, a Communist named Ho Chi Minh. In years to come, in a divided land called Vietnam, Ho's army and guerrilla forces would sound remarkably like the Chinese described to FDR.

Chapter XXVIII

———═★═———

"Stalin Has Been Deceiving
Me All Along"

I NITIALLY, THE only information available to the Allies on the failed
twentieth of July attempt on Adolf Hitler's life had been what the Nazi
propaganda minister, Josef Goebbels, chose to tell the German people
and the world, a story of almost divine salvation of the Führer. A narrow
window into the plot opened two months afterward. Otto John, a lawyer
with Lufthansa, the German passenger airline, who worked undercover for
the Abwehr and who was a member of the conspiracy, provided an eyewitness account. Previously, while moving between Berlin and Lisbon, John
had delivered intelligence to the Allies on German atomic research and on
rocket and missile testing conducted at Peenemünde. He had managed to
escape to Madrid four days after the coup collapsed. There he told his story
to the OSS chief in Spain, an account subsequently relayed to FDR.

John described how he had arrived in Berlin on July 19, 1944, to play
his part in the overthrow of the Nazis. The next day, at 6 P.M., he went to the
Bendlerstrasse, the German General Staff headquarters. There he saw
Lieutenant Colonel Count Klaus Schenk Graf von Stauffenberg, who, five
and a half hours before, had planted the bomb to kill Hitler at the Wolfsschanze, the Führer's military headquarters in East Prussia. After Stauffenberg had returned to the Bendlerstrasse, he announced confidently that
the Führer had been killed. "I myself saw Hitler being carried out dead," he

said, which was not true. But thereafter his authority was accepted unquestioningly by far senior officers. John was struck by Stauffenberg's cool self-possession as he reeled off orders and made phone calls to set in motion a strategy to seize the levers of government. John was especially surprised to hear Stauffenberg take a call from Albert Speer, the Reich's armaments czar and Hitler favorite. In an organization chart that the conspirators had drawn up for their new government, Speer's name appeared in a box marked "Armaments." If Speer was coming over to them, the plotters reasoned, that would spell success.

They had, however, already committed fatal blunders. Despite Stauffenberg's assurances, Hitler was not dead, not even seriously hurt. Secondly, the plotters failed to cut communications between the Wolfsschanze and Berlin. Consequently, Stauffenberg's orders were countermanded almost instantly by Hitler's chief military aide, Field Marshal Wilhelm Keitel. Sensing that the plot was unraveling, John slipped out of the Bendlerstrasse. Upon his arrival home, as he recounted, "I heard the radio announce a message by Hitler. I could not believe my ears and was convinced that the Nazis were using a double." They were not. The conspirators had also failed to seize control of Berlin's radio stations, and Goebbels quickly exploited the blunder by putting the Führer on the air.

Upon telling his story to the OSS in Madrid, John turned over a list of the plotters and their sympathizers, adding a fervent plea: "The following information must not be used as propaganda. It must be placed only at the disposal of such persons who will promise that the names followed by X will remain secret, as the fate of these persons is still uncertain, and they would run the risk of being exposed to reprisal action by the Nazi terror if their names were to be linked in a general way with the attempt against Hitler."

John's and Ambassador Oshima's were the only insider accounts available to Roosevelt until Allen Dulles obtained a report from Hans Bernd Gisevius. The hulking, half-blind Abwehr agent and conspirator assigned to the German consulate in Zurich had, without a word to Dulles, suddenly disappeared back into Germany on July 12. Three weeks after the failure, a German undercover courier arrived at Herrengasse 23 with a message for Dulles from Gisevius. The American was happily surprised. He had assumed that the man had perished in the massacre the Gestapo was conducting against the plotters. Yes, the coup had failed, Gisevius wrote, but conditions within Germany were still unstable. ". . . [I]t is only necessary for the Allies to strike hard and the entire German structure will collapse," he claimed. When five more months passed and nothing further was heard, Dulles again concluded that Gisevius had been caught and executed. Just days after the thwarted coup, Dulles had cabled Washington, "The blood purge will be ruthless." The Gestapo had indeed continued its remorseless manhunt, arresting anyone however distantly connectable to the plot while the Nazi People's Courts dispensed drumhead justice. The vendetta ultimately cost the lives of 4,980 officers and civilians, with Count von Stauffenberg and Otto John's brother among the earliest victims. In the end, all that the twentieth of July plot achieved was to enable the Gestapo to solidify its grip on the German populace.

The courier from Berlin returned again, and Dulles was amazed to learn that Gisevius was still alive, hiding in the apartment of his girlfriend, Gerda. The Bern spy chief notified the OSS mission in London, which set a rescue strategy in motion. The plan demonstrated how far OSS technical sophistication had advanced in just two and a half years. Since Gisevius had once been an early member of the Gestapo, the London station forged papers to cast him again as an agent of that organization. The first obstacle was to locate a photograph. Gisevius's face could be found only in a group shot. The London counterfeiting section managed to enlarge the image of his head to passport size. Stationery seized from Gestapo headquarters in liberated areas was rushed to London and used to produce phony orders. The thorniest challenge was to replicate the Gestapo's Silver Warrant Identity Disk, a gray medallion of unknown alloys, and serially numbered. Possession of the medallion provided the bearer with unlimited access anywhere and the power to arrest.

On January 20, 1945, the six-month anniversary of the failed plot, Gisevius heard the bell ring in Gerda's apartment. He opened the door a crack and spotted a package on the doorstep. In it he found the medallion, Gestapo ID, a German passport, and orders to proceed from Berlin to Switzerland as Dr. Hoffmann of the secret police. Thus armed, the huge and imperious Gisevius managed to bully his way through several checkpoints, and by January 22, he was at Herrengasse 23 giving Allen Dulles the fullest firsthand account yet of what had happened at the Bendlerstrasse. Five days later, the conspirator's report was on the President's desk. Gisevius explained that the July 20 attempt on Hitler's life had been the third that month. An earlier bomb had been set to go off during the Führer's visit to Munich on July 6, but an Allied air raid upset this plot. Ten days later, General Helmuth Stieff brought a concealed explosive into the Wolfsschanze, but at the last minute lost his nerve and left. Four days later,

Stauffenberg carried out the attempt that Hitler miraculously survived. Gisevius confirmed Otto John's identification of the fatal flaws in the coup, particularly the failure "to destroy Central Information office including all communications installations of East Prussian Headquarters to prevent any communication. So that even if Hitler was not killed, he would not be able to make this known until plotters had control of the situation."

Gisevius's most startling revelation was contained in another report Donovan relayed to FDR on January 27, five days after the German's escape. It dealt not with the mechanics of the plot, but with its politics. Until now, the assumption in the White House had been that anti-Nazi conspirators were interested only in making peace with the Western Allies in order to keep the Russians out of Germany. But Gisevius revealed that Count von Stauffenberg intended to conclude a peace with the Soviets if the putsch were successful, and proposed to announce the establishment of a "workers and peasants" regime in Germany. "The present situation on the Eastern Front and the general trend of the situation in Germany," Gisevius concluded, "indicate that an eastern solution of the war may be more attractive to Germany." He claimed further that Stauffenberg had been in secret contact with the Seydlitz Committee, led by General Walter von Seydlitz, who was captured at Stalingrad and had gone over to the Russians. Seydlitz had assured Stauffenberg that the Soviet Union would accept fair peace terms and not demand that the Wehrmacht disarm completely. The Seydlitz conditions could have been extended only with Moscow's approval and made one thing clear: for all of FDR's scrupulous determination never to give even the appearance of abandoning the Soviet Union, Stalin was evidently willing to consider a separate peace that would leave Britain and America to fight on alone.

Donovan urged the President to change course. FDR's insistence on unconditional surrender, the general argued, could drive Germany into the Russians' arms. He suggested "a subtle psychological approach" to turn anti-Nazi Germans toward the West while still sticking to unconditional surrender. Under Donovan's formula, if the German officer class would give up a hopeless struggle and end further bloodshed, "Wehrmacht officers who contribute to such a constructive policy . . . would be treated with the consideration due their rank and according to the services which they render in the liquidation of the Nazi regime. . . ." Roosevelt disregarded Donovan's recommendation to soften unconditional surrender by so much as a word, just as he had rejected every other suggestion that might conceivably trigger Stalin's distrust.

★

The fact that Hitler had utterly crushed his opponents after the conspiracy became manifest five months later when he was able to mobilize the Wehrmacht for its stunning offensive through the Ardennes. Even before the Battle of the Bulge, OSS Bern had produced troubling evidence of Hitler's intention to fight to the death. The Germans were reportedly building a "National Redoubt" centered in the Salzkammergut, rugged and inaccessible mountain terrain in western Austria and bordering southern Germany. There, according to Bern, "vast underground factories, invulnerable in their rocky depths," were being hewn from the mountainsides. Preparations were said to be under way to enable Nazi leaders to withdraw into this impenetrable fastness where elite troops, sustained by huge, buried stores of food, fuel, arms, and ammunition, would carry on the struggle. Bern predicted that subjugation of the Redoubt could extend the war from six months to two years and exact more casualties than all the previous fighting on the western front.

The superheated rhetoric of an Alpine rampart "defended by nature and by the most efficient secret weapons yet invented" had the ring of thriller fiction. General Eisenhower, however, did not dismiss the threat. "If the German was permitted to establish the Redoubt, he might possibly force us to engage in a long, drawn-out guerrilla type of warfare, or a costly siege," he wrote in his memoirs. "Thus, he could keep alive his desperate hope that through disagreement among the Allies, he might yet be able to secure terms more favorable than those of unconditional surrender." Eisenhower concluded: "The evidence was clear that the Nazi intended to make the attempt. . . ."

Oddly, the signals of a last-ditch Nazi stand were contradicted by intelligence also coming out of OSS Bern. "This whole project seems fantastic," Dulles cabled Washington. He had become more interested, not in a Nazi scheme to prolong the war, but with an opportunity presented to him to hasten its end. He had word that the commander of German forces in northern Italy, the former Luftwaffe star tactician, Field Marshal Albert Kesselring, might consider a secret surrender. The struggle up the Italian boot had been long and bloody with Kesselring conducting a brilliant withdrawal and giving up every mile grudgingly at a steep price to the Allies. If such a surrender could be arranged, it would remove one of the most stubborn German forces from the field, and, coincidentally, represent a major coup for the OSS.

The possibility of a secret surrender on the Italian front, so seemingly desirable at first blush, was to initiate a particularly acrimonious chapter in the long saga of East-West distrust. A split among the Allies remained the dying Nazi's last hope against obliteration. That objective became apparent in a long Ultra intercept picked up between Berlin and Dublin and relayed to the White House in February 1945. Hitler's foreign minister, Joachim von Ribbentrop, had prepared a policy directive to be transmitted in the Enigma code to all German embassies in neutral countries. Each chief of mission was to attempt a high-level contact from among enemy representatives. As Ribbentrop instructed, ". . . [R]estrict yourself to one particularly important English and American channel through a secret agent." This go-between was to leak Berlin's current thinking, which ran: "The new and greatest fact that this war has brought out is the military power of the Soviet Union. Stalin has subjected [*sic:* subjugated] all of Eastern Europe and the Balkans (Romania, Bulgaria, Macedonia, Greece, Serbia, Hungary). . . . Russia has no intention of ever releasing them again. . . . it intends to make these countries finally communistic states as part of the Soviet Union. . . . The offensive against Germany, however, shows that Stalin is pursuing a much greater objective even beyond that: he wishes to conquer and occupy Germany and thus complete the conquest of Europe." Ribbentrop further directed his ambassadors to tell their Allied targets that "Germany is today the only power still fighting the Soviet Union. . . . If Stalin should succeed in overcoming German resistance on the East Front, the BOLSHEVIZATION of Germany, and consequently of all Europe, would be once and for all an irrefutable fact." Lest the British and Americans think they would be spared, Ribbentrop told his emissaries to make clear that "Stalin hates England. After the conquest of Europe, therefore, the destruction of the English Island by the Soviets would only be a question of time. . . . The Bolshevization of the U.S.A. itself would then only be a question of time. The only political and spiritual counterpoise against the undoubtedly strong doctrine of Communism is National Socialism, therefore just the factor which the English and Americans want to exterminate. The English Crown, the English Conservative Party and the American governing class should therefore have only the wish that nothing should happen to Adolf Hitler." The Nazi foreign minister directed his representatives to express dismay at the pigheadedness of Western leaders. They were to say to their contacts, "One marvels in Berlin that in London and Washington no one is willing to see this and that the present policy of the English and American governments must lead not to securing a long period of peace, but quite to the contrary, to producing a state of perpetual war." Ribbentrop anticipated that any agent peddling this line would be asked about the fate of the Jews. "The question of the Jews," they were to answer, "is a German domestic affair which, if Germany doesn't want to fall to Communism, must be solved in Germany. The Jewish question in other countries does not interest Germany." He neatly sidestepped the fact that millions of non-German Jews from all over occupied Europe had already perished in Nazi extermination camps.

While the foreign minister's instructions were to make his arguments known through high-level Britons and Americans, his message reached the most prominent American of all within days. The Ultra cable delivered to FDR by the British comprised a remarkable stew of lies, truth, and prophecy. Ribbentrop's forecast of the postwar fate of the Balkans and Eastern Europe, then being overrun by the Red Army, and the emergence of "perpetual war" between East and West, at least a cold war, proved remarkably on target.

Roosevelt has left no indication of his reaction to Ribbentrop's intercepted stratagem. However, its existence made not a dent in his determination to stick by the Soviet Union, a resolve that was tested just days later by the latest news out of OSS Bern. Two months had gone by since the first hint that Field Marshal Kesselring might be receptive to a separate German surrender in Italy. Then, on February 25, Dulles learned through Baron Luigi Parilli, an Italian industrialist, that Karl Wolff, an SS general associated with Kesselring, wanted to meet with him secretly. According to Parilli, General Wolff claimed that the Germans in Italy were demoralized by their remorseless retreat up the Italian peninsula. They wanted to quit.

Dulles put Wolff to the test. The Germans had captured two leading Italian resistance fighters, Ferruccio Parri and Antonio Usmiani, the latter also an OSS spy in Milan. Dulles would talk to Wolff only if he released the two men. Three days later, he received word to present himself at a hospital in Zurich. On his arrival, he was taken to a room where he met the unshaven, unkempt, but beaming Parri and Usmiani. They had been blindfolded and driven over the Italian-Swiss border on Wolff's orders the very day that they were condemned to be shot. In giving up the two Italians, the SS officer believed he had proved his good faith. He next sent Dulles a message from Italy suggesting they meet in Switzerland to start discussing a surrender.

Within days, Dulles found himself in a country inn outside Zurich where a tall, thin man, with a knife-edge profile and self-important air, rose to greet him. Karl Wolff, dressed in civilian clothes, first engaged Dulles in small talk, boasting of how he had managed to relieve the Italian king, Victor Emmanuel, of his coin collection. Dulles, nevertheless, knew that he was dealing with no Nazi bon vivant. Ultra intercepts suggested that Wolff was a key participant in sending Italian Jews to their death at Auschwitz. Finally, the SS general got down to business. Germany had lost the war, he admitted to Dulles. He believed that his superior, Field Marshal Kesselring, an independent spirit and no Hitler sycophant, would not only be willing to take his forces out of the fight, but would do so unconditionally. After the two men parted, Dulles returned to Bern and informed Field Marshal Sir Harold Alexander, commander of Allied forces in Italy, of his conversation with Wolff.

And then Wolff's hopes seemed to be dashed. Hitler's personal plane unexpectedly arrived at Kesselring's headquarters and whisked the field marshal away to become the Wehrmacht commander on the western front. Kesselring's replacement was to be General Heinrich von Vietinghof, an unknown quantity as far as his attitude toward surrendering his troops. Wolff managed to get a message through to Dulles that he would need a couple of weeks to work on Vietinghof. There the matter hung while General Donovan briefed FDR on what could be the OSS's greatest triumph of the war.

The threat of a National Redoubt was tied closely to what happened on the Italian battlefront. If the Germans in Italy fought on, they would provide a shield behind which the reported fortress in the Alps could be built. If they surrendered, the Redoubt would be exposed on its southern flank. Churchill, ever the geopolitician, saw that determining the truth or falsity of the Redoubt was crucial. Diverting troops to conquer it could reduce the Western Allies' chances of taking Berlin and would leave the city to the Russians. Who occupied the German capital, Churchill believed, would decisively influence who dominated postwar Germany. But the reality of the Redoubt remained confused. Just as Churchill was preparing to leave London for a mid-March trip to the western front, the Americans provided him with a Magic decrypt in which the Japanese ambassador to Bern informed Tokyo that the Germans were indeed turning the Alps into an impregnable stronghold. Dulles's operation, however, continued to send mixed signals. On March 6, FDR received a dispatch radio-telephoned from Bern reporting the publication in Swiss newspapers of maps showing the borders of the Redoubt and descriptions of vast stores piling up in underground bunkers. Another OSS assessment reported, "It is believed that eventually the Redoubt will hold 15–25 divisions composed of SS Storm Troop detachments, Hitler Jugend [Youth], and the special OKW Führer Reserve created for service in the Redoubt." Yet the same Bern operation concluded, "Much of this is probably fiction. . . . Talk of building in the mountains great new underground factories is nonsense. It would take years." Allen Dulles cabled Washington, "I do not believe . . . that months of elaborate preparation have been devoted to fortifying, arming, and stocking a great German reduit."

Sharing this skepticism, Churchill showered Roosevelt and Eisenhower with pleas not to abandon Berlin to the Soviets. On April 1 he sent the President a "Most Secret" message questioning Eisenhower's shifting of armies southward. "I say quite frankly that Berlin remains of high strategic importance. Nothing will exert a psychological effect of despair upon all German forces of resistance equal to that of the fall of Berlin. It will be the supreme signal of defeat to the German people. . . . The Russian armies will no doubt overrun all Austria and enter Vienna," he told Roosevelt. "If they also take Berlin, will not their impression that they have been the overwhelming contribution to our common victory be unduly imprinted in their minds, and may this not lead them into a mood which will raise grave and formidable difficulties in the future?" He advised FDR, ". . . [F]rom a political standpoint we should march as far east as we can into Germany as possible and that should Berlin be in our grasp, we should certainly take it." But Eisenhower was nevertheless diverting forces southward should the Redoubt prove real.

★

Bill Donovan's fortunes continued to gyrate. The OSS might succeed in arranging the early surrender in Italy of a tough, stubborn foe. Yet Vessel had been blown the day before Donovan gave FDR his first report on General Wolff's overtures for an Italian surrender. And then, not long after the Trohan stories had painted him as a potential American Gestapo chief, another potential disaster arose.

The OSS's employment of Communists had proved a tangled affair. On a simplistic level, it seemed obvious that no one should be employed by the United States whose allegiance was to a party favoring the overthrow of the government. But a world at war created ambiguities. Donovan, staunch Catholic, Wall Street Republican, thoroughgoing establishment figure, was using Communists knowing that they were virulent anti-Nazis. He had once remarked, "I'd put Stalin on the OSS payroll if I thought it would help defeat Hitler." Since the fall of the previous year, Donovan, in his determination to penetrate the Reich itself, had allowed his officers to recruit refugee labor leaders, including Socialists and Communists. In a remote corner of liberated France, the OSS ersatz German infantry company, the Iron Cross mission under Captain Aaron Bank, was continuing to train to parachute into southern Germany and capture high-ranking Nazis expected to flee into the Redoubt.

Still, FDR's journalistic nemesis, the McCormick-Patterson chain, was not about to let any Roosevelt vulnerability go unexploited. That March, the *Chicago Tribune* and the Washington *Times-Herald* published the names of ten Army officers alleged to be Communists or to have close Communist ties. Four of the ten belonged to the OSS. A subcommittee of the House Military Affairs Committee summoned Donovan to explain the presence of Reds on his payroll. In preparation, Wild Bill had Otto Doering, another alumnus of his New York law firm, now an OSS aide, check federal law on the hiring of Communists. Doering briefed his boss the day before the general was to testify and told him that he stood on solid legal ground. The War Department had issued instructions saying, "[M]embership in the Communist Party will not affect the status of Army personnel if it is established that their loyalty to this country is greater than any other loyalty." Furthermore, Doering could point out that the Supreme Court had recently stated it had not yet decided whether or not the Communist Party actually advocated the overthrow of the government by force.

On March 13 an Army sedan flying the two-starred flag of a major general halted under the Capitol portico. For the first time since the creation of the OSS, Donovan faced congressional interrogation. He well knew the prejudices he confronted. The OSS had a reputation as the place where the well connected could play at war. With its personnel recruited from the old-boy network, prestigious law firms, old-line banks, the academic elite, those who had been educated abroad, and friends of friends of these people, the agency's image as an enclave of privilege was inevitable. Far preferable for a draft-age American with influence to wrangle an OSS commission and comment mysteriously at Georgetown dinner parties, "I'm simply not in a position to discuss what I do," than to crouch in a foxhole at Anzio. To its enemies, the OSS was a preposterous fraternity of tycoons, scholars, football stars, scientists, financiers, playboys, pickpockets, counterfeiters, and safecrackers. Rumor even had it that the OSS sprang useful criminals from jail. The truth was rather less colorful. As for imprisoned counterfeiters, the OSS chief of document forgery observed, "These people were a bunch of dilettantes, amateurs. If they were any good, they wouldn't have been caught. We wanted professionals." In a probably accurate assessment of Donovan's personnel, one OSS veteran concluded, "In half of my comrades, I knew the bravest, finest men I would ever meet. The rest were phonies."

Taking this elite organization down a peg or two appealed enormously to anti–New Deal Republicans on the House Military Affairs subcommittee. But once in the hearing room, Bill Donovan, fixing his interrogators with cool blue eyes, speaking with the quiet authority that had become his trademark, stood by his people. "These four men I've been in trenches with," he testified, "I've been in the muck with, and I'd measure them up with any men. I did not find that they were Communists. I found that they were not." The hearings ended without any action taken against the ten officers, including the four from the OSS. Still, the anti-Roosevelt members of the subcommittee achieved a marginal victory. They had fresh ammunition for their old accusation, however denied, that the Roosevelt administration was riddled with Reds.

The general's protégé Duncan Lee, placed initially in the OSS front office and by now chief of the Japanese section, was not among the four allegedly Communist OSS officers named in the original newspaper story. By the time Donovan appeared before Congress, Lee had broken off his contacts with Communists. While Donovan knew the four officers against whom the charges had been lodged, he doubtless would have been staggered to learn that a member of his law firm whom he personally had brought into the OSS was reported to have spied for the Soviets.

Though he had come out of the congressional investigation with only flesh wounds, Donovan thereafter became more cautious in the use of Reds. Parachuting 175 well-armed German Communists into the Reich just as the country teetered on the rim of collapse might prove difficult to justify. The Iron Cross mission was scrubbed. Far better to display OSS's mettle by achieving the surrender of whole German armies in northern Italy than snagging a few Nazis on the run in the Alps. The former possibility grew when Field Marshal Sir Harold Alexander, the Allied commander in the Mediterranean, agreed that the pursuit of a separate peace in the Italian theater could go forward. On March 12 he notified the Combined Chiefs of Staff in Washington, who represented all Allied forces, that he was prepared to negotiate. An encouraged Allen Dulles gave the enterprise a code name, Operation Sunrise. The Combined Chiefs, however, notified Alexander to hold off until the Russians could be informed. FDR thereafter instructed Averell Harriman, his ambassador in Moscow, to alert the Soviet foreign minister, Vyacheslav Molotov, that peace negotiations on the Italian front were imminent. Molotov replied that Russia would immediately dispatch three Red Army officers to join the talks. The Americans rejected this move out of hand, as did Field Marshal Alexander. The Combined Chiefs of Staff concurred, suggesting that with the Soviets involved, something that might take "four hours would take four months." Harriman was instructed to advise Moscow that, at this preliminary stage, no point would be served by direct Soviet participation. Russians could attend, but only as observers. Molotov shot back that, under those conditions, they chose not to send anyone.

Operation Sunrise began to provoke an extraordinary exchange between the leaders of two presumed allies. Molotov, besides rejecting Soviet officers as mere observers, was now demanding that the talks be called off completely if the Russians could not take part. On March 24, FDR sent a "Top Secret" cable to placate Stalin. In it, he was not above dissembling. He told Stalin, "The facts are as follows: some few days ago unconfirmed information was received in Switzerland that some German officers were considering the possibility of arranging for the surrender of German troops . . . in Italy." He reminded Stalin that the Soviet government had immediately been informed of this development. Ignored in this message was the fact that two of Field Marshal Alexander's high-level officers had already been dispatched incognito to Switzerland to meet with General Wolff. FDR also maintained that if an enemy facing American troops appeared willing to surrender, his generals were bound to pursue the opportunity. "It would be completely unreasonable for me to take any other attitude or to permit any delay which must cause additional and avoidable loss of life in the American forces." He appealed to Stalin "as a military man" to understand his reasoning. FDR reminded the Soviet leader that his position was no different than Stalin's upon the recent entrapment of German troops by the Red Army at Koenigsberg and Danzig, a Russian matter in which FDR had no reason to involve the United States. Secretary of War Stimson put it more bluntly to the President. The surrender of German armies in Italy was, he said, "a matter in which Russia has no more business than the United States would have at Stalingrad."

Stalin's response was swift and the harshness of tone shocking. "I agree to negotiations with the enemy," he cabled Roosevelt, "only in the case where these negotiations will not make the situation easier for the enemy, if there will be excluded a possibility of the Germans to maneuver and to use these negotiations . . . to the Soviet front. . . . I have to tell you," Stalin went on, "that the Germans have already used these negotiations . . . in shifting three divisions from Northern Italy to the Soviet front." As for Roosevelt's analogy of Koenigsberg and Danzig, Stalin curtly dismissed it. The Germans in these sectors were surrounded, he said, and "if they surrender, they will do it in order to avoid annihilation. They could not be shifted elsewhere." As for the Italian front, Stalin could not understand "why representatives of the Soviet command were refused participation in these negotiations and in what way could they cause inconvenience to the representatives of the Allied Command." Stalin's reaction was not entirely paranoid. The Soviet leader understood that if the German army did surrender in Italy, every soldier, gun, and tank not immediately penned in by the Allies could be expected to be thrown against the Russians.

The shrillness of Stalin's message alarmed Roosevelt. He fired back, "I must repeat that the meeting in Bern was for the single purpose of arranging contact with competent German military officers and not for negotiations of any kind." He intended to set Stalin straight on one further point: "I feel that your information about the time of the movements of German troops from Italy is in error." He acknowledged that three German divisions had indeed been shifted from Italy to the Russian front. But "the last division of the three started moving about February 25, more than two weeks before anybody heard any possibility of surrender" in Italy. Roosevelt was so taken aback by Stalin's hostility that he asked Harriman to find out if the words represented the Soviet leader's thinking or merely that Stalin had signed a draft originating in the Kremlin bureaucracy. Harriman reported back that both the words and the sentiments were Stalin's. The President, who believed he could woo and win anybody and who had invested so much capital in charm and persuasion to establish mutual trust with the Soviet dictator, now began having second thoughts. His fear, he confided to an associate, was that "Stalin has been deceiving me all along."

The Soviet leader was not yet finished. On April 3 he fired an even more brutal salvo. He cabled FDR regarding the peace maneuvering in Italy: "You insist there have been no negotiations yet. It may be assumed that you have not been fully informed." Not only had negotiations been held, Stalin insisted, but the German commander on the western front "has agreed to open the front and permit Anglo-American troops to advance to the East, and the Anglo-Americans have promised in return to ease for the Germans the peace terms." This was not the first time that Stalin's deep-dyed distrust had surfaced. In March the American 9th Armored Division had been astonished to find the Ludendorff railroad bridge across the Rhine near the town of Remagen intact and had poured troops across it. The Russians did not regard this breakthrough as an American military triumph. German thoroughness and efficiency were legendary. How was it possible, the Russians reasoned, that the enemy had not blown a bridge pointing straight into Germany's heartland, unless they *wanted* the Americans to cross it? Stalin regarded the bridge's capture as further proof, as he put it to FDR, that "the Germans on the Western front have in fact ceased the war against England and the United States. At the same time they continue the war against Russia." The fact that Hitler had had four officers responsible for the loss of the bridge shot and that the Luftwaffe had bombed it into the Rhine were merely inconvenient facts interfering with Stalin's preconceptions.

An angered FDR called in Admiral Leahy and General Marshall to help him draft his reply to Stalin's cable of April 3. "I have received with astonishment your message," the response began, "containing an allegation that arrangements which were made between Field Marshal Alexander and Kesselring, 'permitted the Anglo-American troops to advance to the East and the Anglo-Americans promised in return to ease for the Germans the peace terms!' " Roosevelt repeated his argument that thus far no actual negotiations had taken place. ". . . [Y]our information," FDR went on, "must have come from German sources which have made persistent efforts to create dissention between us. . . . If that was Wolff's purpose in Bern your message proves that he has had some success. Frankly," Roosevelt concluded, "I cannot avoid a feeling of bitter resentment toward your informers, whoever they are, for such vile misrepresentations of my actions or those of my trusted subordinates."

Stalin now held out a slim olive branch. Three days after the President's retort, he cabled back, "I have never doubted your honesty and dependability. . . ." But he was still not done pressing his major premise, that Russia was being abandoned to carry on alone. The Germans, he noted, "continue to fight savagely with the Russians for some unknown junction, Zemlianitsa in Czechoslovakia, which they need as much as a dead man needs poultices, but surrender without any resistance such important towns in central Germany as Osnabrück, Mannheim, Kassel. Don't you agree that such a behavior of the Germans is more than strange and incomprehensible." He had one more charge to unload. Back in February, he claimed, General Marshall had tipped off the Red Army staff to expect major German attacks at two points, in Pomerania and at Maravska Ostrava. Instead, the Germans struck in a completely different sector southwest of Budapest, "one of the most serious blows in the course of the war. . . ." Here Stalin was accusing the chief of the American Army not simply of bad faith but of treachery. These exchanges marked the nadir in the three and a half years of wary alliance and threatened to create the only outcome that could give Hitler any hope of salvation, a rupture between the East and the West.

FDR still faced the threat that Hitler would hole up in the Alps for a fanatic Armageddon. In the midst of the Roosevelt-Stalin countercharges over Operation Sunrise, General Marshall sent the President an estimate on April 2 that the "will to fight of these [German] troops will depend largely on whether Hitler and his subordinate Nazi leaders, or the German High Command will have transferred their headquarters into the 'redoubt' area. If Hitler does so, a fairly formidable military task requiring a considerable number of divisions may still confront the Allies. . . ." Now was hardly the time to risk the alliance, especially since the Russians had made their first installment on their promise at Yalta to enter the war against Japan. On April 5 they broke their peace pact with the Japanese. Through a Magic decrypt it was as if FDR were in the room in Moscow when the Soviet foreign minister, Molotov, delivered the blow to the Japanese ambassador, Naotake Sato. Sato answered, hopefully, "The Japanese government expects that even after the abrogation of the treaty by the Russian government there will be no change in the peace in the Far East from what it has been in the past." Molotov gave a chilling answer: "At the time when this treaty was concluded Russia was not yet at war with Germany. . . . After that Japan began war with England and America which are allies of Russia." And, as Molotov well knew, the Americans, pursuing Project Hula, were already well along in turning over ships and training Soviet seamen to enter the war in the Pacific.

Chapter XXIX

———— ═★═ ————

"The Following Are the Latest Casualties"

THE PRESIDENT was at Warm Springs when he learned that Russia had broken its peace treaty with Japan. He now believed the Soviets genuinely meant to enter the Pacific war. A few days before, on March 29, he had brought two willing conscripts to his Georgia retreat, Daisy Suckley and Laura Delano, a maiden lady, the youngest sister of FDR's mother, known in the family as Polly. Eleanor Roosevelt was booked solid with appointments in Washington and New York and had begged off on the Georgia trip. FDR had tried earlier to recover his flagging energy at his customary refuge, Hyde Park, but it had not worked. He slept poorly in the raw Hudson Valley spring weather and told his wife, "It's no good. I must go to Warm Springs." He then boarded the train at Highland Falls for an interim stop in Washington, his four hundredth trip as president, over half a million railway miles logged by a man who could not take a step unaided. As the train was pulling out of the station, he instructed his staff to have the engineer keep the train's speed even lower than usual, down to twenty-five miles per hour to minimize the rocking and swaying.

Traveling with the President from Washington to Warm Springs was Lieutenant Commander Bruenn, the Navy cardiologist who over the past year had become a fixture in the Roosevelt entourage. Bruenn had started his White House duties as a staunch Republican, but had fallen under the Roosevelt spell. By now, he both treated and idolized his patient. The doctor well understood the reason for the President's chronic fatigue, his lapses of memory, and episodes of mental confusion. His heart had become enlarged by the struggle to pump blood through hardening and ever narrowing arteries. These shrinking passageways delivered less sustenance to the brain, especially sugar, producing the consequent loss in ability to think, to concentrate, to absorb fresh information. The President exhibited a classic case of arteriosclerosis.

After a few days at Warm Springs, FDR felt and looked better. The company of Daisy, with her crocheting, and Polly, with her ceaseless prattle of Dutchess County gossip, created a comfortable aura familiar to him since boyhood. Being at Warm Springs among other paralytic patients at the thermal baths had another appeal. Here FDR was part of the majority, where to be crippled and to live with pain was the norm, not the exception. Daisy and Polly had accommodated themselves to the visible contradiction in Franklin's life, his failing health and his unfailing spirits. After Bruenn and an assistant put the President to bed at night, Daisy wrote in her diary, "The Drs. love this little time with F. [Franklin] for while he is getting ready for bed, he tells them stories. We can hear the laughter from the living room." When FDR was finally alone, she and Polly would enter his bedroom with a little nourishment before he turned out his light. She described this moment in an entry in her diary that she later crossed out: "I get the gruel and Polly and I take it to him. I sit on the edge of the bed and he 'puts on an act:' he is too weak to raise his head, his hands are weak, he must be fed! So I proceed to feed him with a teaspoon and he loves it."

The President also confided to Daisy his private plans once the war ended. As she recorded this moment, "He took half his evening gruel and then decided to smoke a cigarette—he talked seriously about the S. Francisco conference, and his part in World Peace, etc. He says again that he can probably resign some time next year when the peace organization— the United Nations—is well started."

On the day he received word of the broken Soviet-Japanese peace pact, the President settled into the cottage's small parlor and resumed working with Grace Tully on his overflowing in-basket. He withdrew from it a memorandum from Isadore Lubin. The energetic Izzy was supposedly an economic advisor to the President; but like Lauchlin Currie and others in the inner circle, Lubin performed as an administration handyman for a chief who was more comfortable with versatile New Dealers than with specialist bureaucrats. Lubin had gone to bat again for Bill Donovan in the latter's floundering campaign to create a postwar spy service. FDR read from Lubin's memo, "As you probably know, the idea of having a centralized intelligence service, as proposed by General Donovan, has stalled in one of the subdivisions of the Joint Chiefs of Staff." In a model of understatement, Lubin further observed, "The difficulty seems to lie in the fear of certain agencies of the government that they will not be permitted to play their part in the proposed set up." What had actually happened was that the Joint Chiefs of Staff had indeed studied Donovan's postwar proposal and wanted no part of it. As Admiral Leahy tactfully put it to the President, ". . . [T]he possible advantages to be gained by the reorganization of intelligence activities and the establishment of a central intelligence service at this time are outweighed by the known disadvantages."

Lubin's memo to the President suggested a solution to the intelligence impasse: Lock representatives of the relevant agencies in a room and, ". . . a frank, across-the-table discussion would eliminate some of the difficulties." Lubin had attached a memorandum for FDR to send to Donovan giving the general authority to convene this no-holds-barred session. Grace Tully thought that FDR seemed remote and distracted as he glanced over Lubin's draft. He initialed his approval with a hand shaking so badly that he almost dropped his pen.

Upon receiving FDR's okay, a revived Bill Donovan instantly sent out a call for the gathering of twelve federal agencies concerned with intelligence. In the meantime, he felt secure enough to take off for a brief inspection trip to the new OSS headquarters in Paris. While he was gone, Attorney General Francis Biddle returned the first fire. Biddle noted that the current intelligence arrangement among the Army, Navy, and FBI worked just fine. "I should think that system should be built on rather than developing a new organization . . . in the middle of the war," Biddle urged the President. He recoiled at Donovan's congenital brashness, commenting that an "intelligence agency should be organized quietly and not in the manner suggested." Biddle's response was only the first wave in a tide of rejection rising from the federal bureaucracy to swamp Donovan's call for a meeting.

At 7:30 P.M. on April 11, Henry Morgenthau Jr. arrived at the Warm Springs cottage and found the President mixing drinks, his withered legs tucked beneath a card table. Among the guests, along with Daisy and Polly, were the Russian artist Madame Elizabeth Shoumatoff, there to paint the President's portrait, and Lucy Mercer Rutherfurd. Morgenthau later described his reaction to FDR that night: "I was terribly shocked when I saw him, and I found that he had aged terrifically and looked very haggard. His hands shook so that he started to knock the glasses over, and I had to hold each glass as he poured out the cocktail. . . . I found his memory bad, and he was constantly confusing names." Nevertheless, the President recovered his spirits by the time he was wheeled to the dinner table. There he began a stream of amused gibes about the cottage's furniture, which had been manufactured in a burst of New Deal industry by a firm Eleanor had created at Hyde Park. Morgenthau raised his pet issue of the fate of postwar Germany. "A weak economy for Germany means that she will be weak politically," he told the President, "and she won't be able to make another war." The mention of Germany launched the President into a shaggy staple from his fund of anecdotes, one about the German minister of finance, Hjalmar Schacht. Schacht had come to see him in the thirties, the President said, "three or four times saying that the Germans were going broke and they never did!" He then began talking about his forthcoming trip to San Francisco for the creation of the United Nations. "I am going there on my train," he told his guests gaily, "and at three o'clock in the afternoon I will appear on the stage in my wheelchair, and I will make the speech." He clasped his hands in mock reverence. "And then they will applaud me, and I will leave and go back on my train, go down to Los Angeles and dump my daughter-in-law, and I will be back in Hyde Park on May first." As FDR spoke, Morgenthau noted, he went at his dinner of veal and noodles and a dessert of a waffle topped with ice cream and chocolate sauce with a gusto not seen for weeks.

The next day, the President was again occupied with Donovan's organization, this time the still-dangling Operation Sunrise pursued by Allen Dulles. He read a dispatch from Averell Harriman in Moscow in which the ambassador admitted that he had not yet delivered FDR's latest message to Stalin on the secret surrender. In it Roosevelt had adopted a conciliatory tone, thanking the Communist czar for explaining the Soviet viewpoint and stating that, as far as he was concerned, the recent unpleasantness had faded from memory. The President forgivingly characterized the acidic exchanges over the past days as a "minor misunderstanding." Harriman explained why he had held up the delivery: "I respectfully request that the word 'minor' as a qualification of 'misunderstanding' be eliminated. I must confess that the misunderstanding appeared to me to be of a major character and the use of the word 'minor' might well be misinterpreted here." Harriman had missed the point, Roosevelt said in dictating a brusque reply to the ambassador. "It is my desire," he cabled Harriman, "to consider the Bern misunderstanding a minor incident."

Also in his in-basket was another memorandum from Bill Donovan describing new peace feelers from Nazis prepared to abandon Hitler's sinking ship. This latest transmission, pouched to the President from Washington, relayed Allen Dulles's report that Franz Xaver Ritter von Epp, governor of Bavaria, and his clique were "prepared to do everything in their power to cut short warfare in Bavaria." Dulles had also obtained disquieting news from Epp. "The redoubt is becoming a reality," he reported. "Large quantities of supplies are accumulating in the Salzburg area, prominent personages are arriving, and the local population is being evacuated. There are indications that the OKW [the German High Command] is being transferred from the Bendlerstrasse, Berlin, to Bad Reichenhall. . . ." But if the OSS would deal with him and his cohorts, Epp had said, they were prepared to stop the buildup of the Redoubt. This message would be the last of seventy-five hundred pages that Donovan had showered upon the President, roughly five a day for every day since FDR had first brought Wild Bill into his administration.

The intelligence out of Bern lay in the in-basket still unread at noon on April 12 as FDR posed before Madame Shoumatoff's easel. For all his decline, he was still a striking man. The double-breasted gray suit and bright red tie she had suggested complemented his color and for the moment, he actually seemed to glow. Shortly after 1 P.M., Daisy Suckley put down her crocheting, rose, and positioned herself near the fireplace, where she could see in an oval mirror what Shoumatoff had painted so far. She sat back down smiling, knowing she had outfoxed the artist, who did not want anyone to see the portrait until it was finished.

As she later recorded the next moments in her diary, "I glanced up from my work. F seemed to be looking for something: his head forward, his hands fumbling. I went forward and looked into his face: 'Have you dropped your cigarette?' He looked at me with his forehead furrowed in pain. He put his left hand up to the back of his head and said: 'I have a terrific pain in the back of my head.' " Roosevelt had suffered a massive cerebral hemorrhage. He lingered, unconscious, for another two and a half hours and then died.

Eleanor Roosevelt, upon being informed at the White House, sent a message to her four sons in the military: "Darlings, Pa slept away this afternoon. He did his job to the end as he would want you to do. Bless you. All our love. Mother." The next afternoon, the *New York Post* ran its daily column, "Today's Army-Navy Casualty List." "The following are the latest casualties in the military services, including next of kin," it began. The first listing read:

Roosevelt, Franklin D. Commander-in-Chief. Wife, Mrs. Anna Eleanor Roosevelt. The White House.

All FDR's wars, overt and covert, were ended.

Chapter XXX

Aftermath

THERE WAS no Redoubt. It was a fiction hatched in the fertile imagination of Josef Goebbels, a last gasp attempt to dispirit the Allies and give a doomed Germany a bargaining chip to play against unconditional surrender. On April 30, eighteen days after FDR's death, Adolf Hitler shot himself in the *Führerbunker,* a dank catacomb twenty feet below the Berlin sewer system. At 2:30 A.M. on May 7, General Alfred Jodl, operations chief of the German High Command, sat down at a battered examination table in a boys school in Rheims, France, and signed the surrender of the Third Reich to take effect at one minute past midnight on May 9. Allen Dulles's maneuvers to secure an early peace in northern Italy, plagued by continued Russian obstructionism, shaved only five days off the conflict.

FDR's death might have seemed a momentary respite for the Japanese. They determined, however, that gloating was the wrong tone. An intercepted message from Tokyo to outposts throughout Southeast Asia read: ". . . [W]e are wiring various points you should be aware of in propagandizing the death of President Roosevelt." Japanese officials were instructed to "[a]void observations such as Roosevelt's death will have an immediate effect on the fighting spirit and war strength of the United States. Do not make personal attacks on Roosevelt. Do not convey any impression that we are exultant over the death of Roosevelt." The removal of FDR from the world stage could make no difference except to the most hopelessly optimistic Japanese. In the island-hopping strategy pursued in the Pacific by American forces, Guadalcanal, Saipan, Guam, Tinian, and Iwo Jima had fallen, ever tightening the noose around Japan's throat. General MacArthur returned triumphantly to the Philippine Islands. Eleven days before the President's death, Army and Marine divisions had swarmed ashore on Okinawa, considered part of Japan proper and only 350 miles south of the home islands. Magic decrypts revealed that those Japanese who were spared home front propaganda understood the implacability of their enemy. Arlington Hall broke a message to Tokyo from a Japanese diplomat posted to Moscow reporting remarks made by the then American ambassador, Admiral William H. Standley: ". . . [T]he Americans will not forget Pearl Harbor," Standley was quoted as saying, "and they will as sure as death give Japan the beating of her life. He says with great heat that the Americans will fight till they are dead to accomplish this." The cable concluded, "If all Americans are of this mind . . . I don't know what will become of all of us." The answer came with blinding finality on the morning of August 6, 1945, when the first atom bomb dropped on an enemy exploded over the Shima Surgical Hospital in Hiroshima and three days later, when a second bomb incinerated Nagasaki. On August 14, Japan surrendered unconditionally.

Three weeks before, after a contentious Big Three meeting in the Cecilienhof Palace in Potsdam, President Truman had approached Stalin, who was standing with his interpreter. "I casually mentioned to Stalin that we had a new weapon of unusual destructive force," Truman later wrote of the encounter. Truman was telling the Soviet leader nothing that he did not already know.

The month before the Potsdam conference, Klaus Fuchs, on his Saturday afternoon off, had parked a battered automobile with rationed gas and balding tires at the Castillo Street bridge in Santa Fe, New Mexico. A sweating, heavyset figure peering through thick glasses moved from the shade of a park bench and entered the car. Fuchs's passenger was Harry Gold, the Philadelphia chemist and NKVD courier. Fuchs drove on and parked again, this time in a cul-de-sac. On the seat beside him rested an envelope stuffed with statistical charts, mathematical calculations, and scale drawings relating to the atom bomb, including instructions for producing a critical implosion lens. Fuchs tipped off Gold that the bomb would be tested soon in the New Mexico desert. Gold left the car, taking the envelope. No cash changed hands. The last time his Soviet controllers had tried to pay Fuchs $1,500, the physicist, his idealism offended, refused to take the money. On July 16, just before dawn in the New Mexico desert near Alamogordo, scientists and military observers protected by dark glasses had crouched on Compania Hill, twenty miles from ground zero, and witnessed a flash of light that surpassed the sun. Fuchs was among those present at the first detonation of an atomic bomb.

The knowledge that this test had succeeded was what had led Truman to confide to the unimpressed Stalin that the United States had a weapon of unprecedented destructive force. Stalin had not received Truman's revelation as a gesture of Allied solidarity. Instead, he interpreted it to mean that the President was flaunting America's newfound power in order to intimidate the Soviet Union. After returning to his quarters on Kaiserstrasse, Stalin called his NKVD chief, Lavrenti Beria, who had been tracking the progress of the American A-bomb through Fuchs and other Soviet agents, and ordered him to get in touch with Igor Kurchatov, head of Russia's own atomic project. "Tell Comrade Kurchatov," Stalin instructed, "that he has to hurry with his 'parcel,' and ask him what our scientists need to accelerate the work." The nuclear arms race was on. It is estimated that Soviet agents managed to acquire some ten thousand pages of technical data related to the Manhattan Project. This stolen treasure enabled Stalin's scientists to save up to four years in developing their own atom bomb. The first nuclear weapon the Soviets exploded was virtually a twin of the one detonated at Alamogordo.

While German agents operating in the United States had been ordered to penetrate America's atomic secrets, the effort failed since most of these spies were caught by the FBI. The Nazi regime essentially remained ignorant to the end of what was happening at Los Alamos. As for the Japanese, in the most literal sense, they never knew what hit them. The enterprise that Roosevelt had first approved in 1939 had been an astonishingly well-kept secret, at least from enemies.

Controversy over the use of the bomb against Japan will persist as long as contemporary generations cannot re-create the climate—political, military, and emotional—prevailing at the time it was dropped. As for FDR's position, his son James claimed that his father had never expressed any hesitation over using the bomb. Secretary Stimson states in his memoirs: "At no time from 1941 to 1945, did I ever hear it suggested by the President, or by any other responsible member of the government, that atomic energy should not be used in the war." The moral debate turns on this question: Was dropping a single bomb on Hiroshima and then another on Nagasaki more reprehensible than other methods of mass destruction, notably, raining thousands of conventional bombs on German and Japanese cities. On the night of March 9–10, 1945, General Curtis LeMay sent 334 B-29s, flying unopposed over Tokyo for three hours, carpeting the city with incendiary bombs. Between 80,000 and 100,000 Japanese civilians perished in the flames, the deadliest day of the war. In the atomic bombing of Hiroshima approximately 80,000 were believed to have died, in addition to tens of thousands injured. It is difficult to imagine that the victims in either city would have detected a moral distinction at being incinerated by a conventional versus a nuclear weapon.

★

While the sneak attack on Pearl Harbor seems at first a stupendous American defeat and an intelligence failure of staggering magnitude, in the end it proved to be a Japanese catastrophe. The misery of Japan at war's end, its major cities reduced to charred waste, two of them rendered into atomic ash, and two million Japanese military and civilian dead demonstrate that the attack of December 7, 1941, was as much an infamy inflicted by the Japanese on themselves as against the United States.

A blunder of equal magnitude was Hitler's declaration of war on America four days after Pearl Harbor. A Gallup poll taken just a month and a half before the attack revealed that only 17 percent of Americans favored war with Germany. FDR would have been hard-pressed to engineer through Congress a declaration of war against an enemy in Europe when the country had just been plunged into war in the Pacific. Hitler saved him the trouble. Hitler's attack on Russia placed the lid on the coffin of the Third Reich. His declaration of war against the United States nailed it down.

One area of intelligence that the President chose to disregard out of political expedience also began with Pearl Harbor. FDR had convincing information from Donovan's COI, John Franklin Carter's ring, the FBI, and Army intelligence that Japanese Americans and Japanese aliens posed no threat to American security. Still he chose to appease public paranoia and signed Executive Order 9066, which uprooted these people and sent them to remote and inhospitable "relocation centers" in Arizona, California, Wyoming, Utah, and Idaho. By May 1944, Henry Stimson quietly admitted to FDR that no military necessity existed for keeping loyal Japanese in the camps. Nisei, first-generation Japanese Americans, exemplified that loyalty. The all-Japanese 442nd Regimental Combat team that fought in Italy and France gained fame as the "Christmas tree regiment," the most decorated unit in the Army. Over seventeen thousand Japanese Americans eventually served in the armed forces. But, as the cabinet debated the desirability of releasing the interned Japanese, Stimson warned that other Americans might riot against them, and Japan might retaliate by harming American prisoners of war. FDR bought Stimson's argument. He told Edward Stettinius in June, after the Japanese had been penned up for over two years, "The more I think of this problem of suddenly ending the orders excluding Japanese Americans from the West Coast, the more I think it would be a mistake to do anything drastic or sudden." The act, once implemented, however unnecessary, provided its own momentum.

Other voices argued against the injustice. The First Lady, former secretary of state Cordell Hull, even Harold Ickes, who ran the relocation program, all pressed the President to free the Japanese. Finally, FDR reversed himself, and by September 1944, twenty thousand internees were being released every month. Still, the deed had been done. The American Civil Liberties Union branded the internment of the Japanese "the worst single wholesale violation of civil rights of American citizens in our history."

★

While the internment of the Japanese has been referred to as the American Holocaust, the reality of what the Jews of Europe suffered renders the comparison offensive. Doubtless, Roosevelt could have exerted stronger moral leadership, expressed greater public outrage, and warned the Nazis more ominously of the fate of those who practiced the policy of extermination. If only for the psychological effect, a few bombers could have been spared to disrupt the rail lines to the extermination camps. But as Professor William Rubinstein, author of The Myth of Rescue, concludes, "[N]ot one plan or proposal, made anywhere in the democracies by either Jews or non-Jewish champions of the Jews after the Nazi conquest of Europe could have rescued one single Jew who perished in the Holocaust." Since the Nazis continued murdering Jews right to the end of the war, even diverting for that purpose manpower and transportation desperately needed by their armies, it is evident that every day by which the war was shortened meant thousands of Jewish lives saved. Anything else would have amounted to a symbolic gesture. That was the reality FDR accepted.

★

The President died believing that the mission led by Lauchlin Currie had ended Swiss transactions aiding the Nazi regime. Another half century would pass before the full story came to light. Not only had Swiss bankers continued to buy gold after the Currie agreement, thus helping Germany to fight on, but after the war, certain Swiss banks knowingly kept gold and deposits belonging to murdered Jews even when the families tried to recover their inheritance. Many Jewish accounts had been emptied or supposedly disappeared, though auditors in the mid-1990s unearthed forty-five thousand such accounts established in Switzerland during the era of Jewish persecution. By the mid-1990s, investigations by private Jewish organizations and the U.S. government forced the truth to the surface. Under worldwide pressure, the two major Swiss banks agreed to pay $1.25 billion to settle all outstanding claims against the country. Jewish groups had sought $30 billion. The compensation agreement was announced jointly on January 30, 1999, by American Vice President Al Gore and Ruth Dreifuss, the first woman and the first Jew to become president of Switzerland.

★

Seven months after FDR's death, a stoutish, unfashionable, thirty-seven-year-old woman entered FBI headquarters in New York. Elizabeth Bentley, the NKVD courier, had come to unburden her soul. Her disenchantment with communism had begun the year before, after the death of her controller and lover, Jacob Golos. Bentley had inherited the task from him of passing intelligence to NKVD agents in the United States and had become increasingly disillusioned. "They made no bones of the fact that they had contempt for American Communists with their vague idealism, no bones of the fact that they were using the American Communist Party as a recruitment for espionage and in general," she charged, ". . . they were about the cheapest type of person I have ever seen, the gangster type." On November 30, 1945, Bentley began pouring out her story to Special Agents Thomas G. Spencer and Joseph M. Kelly in a deposition running to 107 pages and studded with the names of those whom she claimed had aided the Soviet Union, among them Duncan Lee of the OSS, George Silverman, Nathan Gregory Silvermaster, and Lauchlin Currie.

In 1948, Bentley became the star witness before the House Committee on Un-American Activities (HUAC) and a subcommittee of the Senate Investigating Committee. She was shaken to find her name splashed across the tabloids as "The Red Spy Queen" and "blonde bombshell" despite her forgettable appearance and mouse brown tresses. Whittaker Chambers, who nine years before had gone to Adolf Berle with the names of persons he said he knew to be aiding the Soviets, also repeated his charges before HUAC. Between Bentley and Chambers, accusations of espionage performed for the Soviet Union were lodged against nearly forty Americans, almost all federal officials during the war.

Harry Dexter White, Alger Hiss, and Lauchlin Currie all volunteered to testify before the House subcommittee, where they stoutly denied Bentley's and Chambers's accusations. A HUAC power, Congressman Karl Mundt, and the committee's star freshman, Richard Nixon, were particularly impressed by Lauchlin Currie's vigorous denials. Further working in Currie's favor was Bentley's admission that she had never actually met the man. Elizabeth Bentley lived, vilified from left and right, for another fifteen years and died in 1963.

Currie had submitted his resignation to President Harry Truman four days after FDR's death. Truman found him valuable and asked him to stay on. Two months later, Currie resubmitted his resignation "because of urgent personal considerations." This time Truman accepted, telling Currie, "I seem to have no alternative but to comply." In 1950, Currie moved to Colombia, became an economic advisor to the government, bought a cattle ranch, shed his first wife, and married a Colombian woman. He continued to live there until his death in 1993 at the age of ninety-three.

Alger Hiss, who had traveled with FDR to Yalta, doggedly denied that he even knew his accuser, Whittaker Chambers, a claim that resulted ultimately in a perjury trial in which the protagonists became the polarities for two irreconcilable camps, those who believed the U.S. government was riddled with Communists and those who believed the country was being poisoned by fascism. Hiss was convicted in 1950 and served five years in the Lewisburg, Pennsylvania, federal penitentiary. He died in 1996 at the age of ninety-two protesting his innocence to the end.

In those years following the war, the codebreakers at Arlington Hall kept crunching away at the thousands of intercepted NKVD wartime ciphers passing between Moscow, New York, and Washington. Lieutenant Richard Hallock, the archaeologist turned codebreaker, had made a small incursion into these ciphers in 1943. Not until three years later, in December 1946, did another cryptographer, Meredith Gardner, make a major break into a message, the two-year-old cable in which the NKVD had provided Moscow with a list of the leading atomic scientists. In 1949 another of these "Venona" decrypts uncovered the code name ChARL'Z, whom the Soviets said had provided priceless information about "the electromagnetic method for separation of ENORMOZ." The FBI traced ChARL'Z to Klaus Fuchs and notified British intelligence. Fuchs confessed. He was convicted and sentenced to fourteen years in prison. Released after nine years, he returned to physics, working in East Germany, where he died in 1998 at the age of seventy-six.

The Venona decrypts also incriminated Harry Dexter White, variously code-named Lawyer, Richard, and Reed in Soviet cables. The FBI informed President Truman that White was suspected of spying. Truman, unwilling to be stampeded by mounting anti-Communist hysteria, named White U.S. director of the International Monetary Fund. The appointee died, however, three days after disputing the Bentley-Chambers accusations against him before the House Un-American Activities Committee, officially of a heart attack, though reports persisted that he had overdosed on sleeping pills.

A Venona decrypt handed over to the FBI in 1950 unveiled Theodore Hall, the boy physicist who had worked at Los Alamos unsuspected, as a Soviet source of crucial atomic secrets. Upon being questioned, Hall refused to admit guilt. The bureau then faced the predicament that would allow several spies to escape prosecution. To introduce evidence based on broken Soviet codes before a grand jury meant exposing Venona. In the end, maintaining the secret was deemed more important than prosecuting the suspects. Hall eventually went to live in England. Of his days as a Soviet spy he later said, "I recognize that I could easily have been wrong . . . about some things, in particular my view of the nature of the Soviet Union. . . . But in essence, from the perspective of my seventy-one years, I still think that brash youth had the right end of the stick. I am no longer that person; but I am by no means ashamed of him."

★

As for Nazi spies, FDR never relaxed his clenched fist, however feckless these agents proved. Throughout the war, Tyler Kent's mother waged an unsuccessful campaign, lobbying the President and Congress for her son's release, after a British court had convicted the American embassy code clerk of espionage in 1940. In December 1945, the British deported Kent to the United States. His former employer, the State Department, showed no interest in prosecuting him. As one department official put it, "We do not give a damn what happens to him." Kent ended his days in a Texas trailer park and died in 1988 at the age of seventy-seven.

Hermann Lang, the German immigrant who stole the plans for the Norden bombsight, served nine years of a fourteen-year sentence before being deported to his homeland in 1950. A defeated nation felt no obligation to someone who had spied in its service, and Lang suffered long stretches of unemployment. The highly skilled optics technician finally found a job as a factory hand. To the end, Lang maintained, "Believe me, I was never a German spy." He was, in his eyes, simply a German patriot.

Not until the war ended was it revealed that two of the German saboteurs from Operation Pastorius had saved their skins by betraying their six comrades to the FBI. Georg Johann Dasch was sentenced to thirty years and Ernest Burger to life. Both were deported to Germany in 1948. There they became double pariahs, convicted spies to the occupying Americans and traitors to their fellow Germans for sending the other members of the mission to the electric chair. William Colepaugh and Erich Gimpel, the two agents put ashore in Maine in 1944 in likely the Third Reich's last attempt to penetrate the American mainland, had their death sentences commuted to life. Gimpel was released for deportation in 1955. Colepaugh's freedom followed five years later.

★

Even before FDR's death, John Franklin Carter continued to arouse suspicion and resentment inside the administration. In January 1945, Secretary of State Stettinius resisted renewing Carter's contract for a reduced $24,000. He would sign, Stettinius said, only if the President ordered him to do so. Twelve days after FDR died, Carter sent a secret memo to President Truman. He wanted to acquaint him, he said, with the "small special intelligence and fact-finding unit" that he had run for FDR. "I simply wish at this occasion to spare you the possible embarrassment of being consulted on a matter concerning which only President Roosevelt and myself had full knowledge." Carter's approach failed to overcome Truman's visceral distrust of anything covert, and, after six months, the ring was shut down. The journalist's facile pen, however, proved useful to the new president. During Truman's 1948 upset campaign of Tom Dewey, Carter served in the candidate's speechwriting stable. He was dropped, however, for taking too much credit for Truman's successful "give 'em hell" strategy. Christopher Andrew, a British writer on espionage, has credited Carter with "the booby prize for providing, against stiff competition, the most absurd U.S. intelligence report of the war." This nadir, in Andrew's judgment, was reached in Carter's "Secret Memorandum on U.S.S.R." informing Roosevelt that Stalin was being advised on foreign policy by three Americans and that Russia planned a raid on Tokyo by more than eight thousand bombers. Andrew's dismissal of Carter is too harsh. His reports on the essential loyalty of Japanese Americans, if heeded, could have forestalled a dark chapter in American history. It was Carter who alerted FDR, early in the war, that enemy agents in the United States could merely pick up the phone and relay intelligence on Allied convoys to their counterparts in neutral Switzerland via commercial telephone lines. While the Putzi Hanfstaengl operation bordered at times on opéra bouffe, the man did offer a unique vision into the Third Reich, and he was instrumental in a joint Carter-OSS project that created a biographic register of hundreds of leading Nazis, a useful tool in the denazification effort after the war. And Carter's well-placed business and journalist contacts abroad provided interim intelligence antennae until a more professional service was put in place. Carter evidently viewed his service as a spy for the President as something of a lark. As he later described those days, "It was a picturesque and wildly funny affair at times. Very fantastically amusing things happened as they always do in an off-beat operation and I think we all had fun." Carter died in 1967 at the age of seventy.

★

A more formidable rival for FDR's favor in the aptly named game of the foxes, J. Edgar Hoover, outlasted them all. Hoover was still running the FBI twenty-seven years after Roosevelt's death. A mutual usefulness, friendship is perhaps not quite the word, marked the relationship between the President and the director to the end of FDR's life. But Hoover, an implacable scorekeeper, could never forgive slights against him by Eleanor Roosevelt. Until his death in 1972 at age seventy-seven, he kept in his personal file the lone copy of the scurrilous Army Counter-Intelligence Corps report supposedly proving that Mrs. Roosevelt had a tryst with her young protégé Joe Lash in Chicago's Hotel Blackstone.

★

What exactly FDR may have told Colonel Richard Park Jr., the Map Room chief, is not known, other than the officer's claim that Roosevelt "authorized me to make an informal investigation of the Office of Strategic Services." Park's report, not completed until after FDR's death, constituted a damning indictment of the OSS. Park's description of the agency's training confirmed every suspicion of playboys at play. A training camp, the colonel claimed, was maintained at a country club in nearby Virginia where "the main purpose of this school was to subject a man to liquor tests to see how he would react to drinking." Park reported that the OSS had a greater number of jobs paying $8,000 per year or more than any other government agency. "In Portugal," he stated, "business people had a joke to the effect that when one saw all the Portuguese people on the streets in a happy frame of mind, it was because it was payday for OSS informants." The agency's amateurism, Park charged, began at the top. "Before Pearl Harbor General Donovan made a trip to the Balkans and lost his briefcase containing important papers in Bucharest," Park reported. "The briefcase was turned over to the Gestapo by a Rumanian dancer who was invited to attend a party at which [Donovan] was present."

After detailing 136 failings, Park added one paragraph reading: ". . . [T]here are some examples of excellent sabotage and rescue work. . . . Also the Research and Analysis Branch of OSS has been of great value in supplying necessary background material and maps." Some of Park's findings were accurate, more were speculative, and many maliciously untrue. He stated, ". . . [O]nly a few, if any, OSS operatives were known to be in any occupied country in Europe." This statement was patently false. OSS missions into occupied France alone numbered in the hundreds, and as Park was drafting his report, the OSS was engaged in putting 102 secret missions into Germany itself.

Park's recommendation was unambiguous. "If the OSS is permitted to continue with its present organization," he warned, "it may do serious harm to citizens, business interests and national interests of the United States." As for the postwar plan that Donovan had submitted before FDR's death, "It has," Park charged, "all the earmarks of a Gestapo system. . . . It is therefore recommended that General Donovan be replaced at the earliest possible moment by a person who shall be recommended by the Joint Chiefs of Staff."

It is difficult to believe that Roosevelt—had he lived—would have taken Park's hatchet job at face value. However, FDR had not lived, and Park moved quickly to make his investigation known to the new administration.

The day after Roosevelt's death, the colonel left the Map Room for his first encounter with President Truman. He carried with him in a locked leather Army briefcase his investigation of the OSS which he had classified "Top Secret" and which he left with Truman after a brief explanation of his alleged mandate from Roosevelt. Truman had a plain-speaking midwesterner's dislike of anything that smacked of deception, subterfuge, and double-dealing. Further, he saw the OSS as a Republican preserve and harbored little love for its chief. After Donovan's only visit to the Truman White House, an encounter lasting just fifteen minutes, the President wrote in his appointments book under the general's name, "Came in to tell how important the Secret Service is and how much he could do to run the government."

Park's report doubtless influenced what Truman was about to do. Within three weeks of Japan's surrender, the President turned the OSS's fate over to a "Committee on Agency Liquidation." The power on the committee was the Budget director, Harold Smith, who had always held a jaundiced view of Donovan's unregulated expenditures. Despite Wild Bill's struggle to keep it alive, his agency lacked a constituency. Offering no pool of jobs, no pork barrel construction projects, delivering no bloc of voters, the OSS had few champions on Capitol Hill. It was the child of a deceased president and the unloved stepchild of the Joint Chiefs of Staff. The death of Roosevelt marked the death of the OSS. By September 10, Harold Smith's staff had prepared Executive Order 9621, which transferred the OSS's admired Research and Analysis branch to State and moved its foreign intelligence agents into the War Department as the Strategic Services Unit. The rest of the OSS was dissolved. The executive order followed Colonel Park's recommendations to the letter.

How wise had FDR's creation of the OSS been? How well, on balance, did it perform? Wild Bill can be faulted for egregious failings, but in one crucial measure of leadership he proved superb. He was a magnet in attracting first-rate people. Along with the society set, he recruited Arthur Goldberg, a future Supreme Court justice; Robert Sherwood, Pulitzer Prize–winning playwright and presidential speechwriter; Arthur Schlesinger Jr., Pulitzer Prize–winning historian; James P. Baxter, president of Williams College; Archibald MacLeish, Pulitzer Prize–winning poet; William Vanderbilt, former governor of Rhode Island; John Ford, Oscar-winning movie director; John W. Gardner, later founder of Common Cause; Sterling Hayden, actor; Dr. Henry A. Murray, distinguished Harvard psychologist; Gene Fodor, travel writer; James Warburg, investment banker; Julia Child, television chef; and leading authorities in every imaginable specialty. Three OSS alumni, Richard Helms, William Colby, and William J. Casey, would go on to become directors of Central Intelligence.

FDR, in his opaque style, has left little trace of what he thought of Donovan or the intelligence fed to him. The general undeniably served up a good deal of twaddle, the Vessel messages being the most egregious example. But so did Vincent Astor, John Franklin Carter, and George Earle. Nevertheless, FDR's habit was to keep all his pores open.

One point is fairly certain: Roosevelt would not have summarily lopped off the nation's intelligence arm as Harry Truman did. FDR had given a great deal of thought to postwar espionage, and discussed the matter with top aides on numerous occasions. Just a week before his death, he had issued the instruction for Donovan to pull together all the government's intelligence elements and start mapping a permanent service. These actions hardly suggest that either Donovan or espionage after the war was finished.

Only four months after Truman killed off the OSS, a whimsical ceremony took place in the White House. On January 24, 1946, the President presented Admiral Leahy and Rear Admiral Sidney Souers with black cloaks, black hats, and wooden daggers. He then read a mock directive to the "Cloak and Dagger Group of Snoopers." The horseplay masked the moment's serious purpose, the appointment of Souers as the nation's first director of central intelligence and creation of the Central Intelligence Group, which within twenty months would metamorphose into the Central Intelligence Agency. Truman had felt chill winds blowing from the East and accepted that in the emerging Cold War the United States had to rearm and reenter the clandestine battleground.

In 1952, Donovan, then sixty-nine, thought he saw an opportunity to become the next director of the CIA. But his old nemesis, J. Edgar Hoover, remained unappeased. Hoover told Clyde Tolson, "I stopped him from becoming AG [Attorney General] in 1929, and I'll stop him now." Whether through Hoover's machinations or composite reasons, Donovan was never again to become the nation's spy chief. He died on February 8, 1959, his Dominican priest brother administering the last rites. On learning of Wild Bill's death, President Eisenhower remarked, "What a man! We have lost the last hero."

★

Deep in the makeup of FDR something reveled in the whispered secret, the clandestine mission, the mysterious agent. He delighted in his midnight rides through back streets to the obscure railroad siding under the Bureau of Engraving and Printing for dead of night departures from Washington. Merriman Smith, the veteran White House reporter, observed, "Mr. Roosevelt made a fetish of his privacy during the war." It was FDR who chose the exotic Shangri-la as the name for his hideaway in Maryland's Catoctin Mountains. After Tehran, he gleefully embroidered on the alleged plot to assassinate him there. Psychohistorians may explain this penchant for the covert as providing the vicarious adventure that FDR's useless legs denied him. But the predilection was present long before his paralysis, in the enthusiasm with which he directed the Office of Naval Intelligence as assistant secretary of the Navy, in the wide-eyed wonder with which he swallowed Admiral Blinker Hall's fabrications in England. It was evident even earlier in his invention of a code for concealing intimate entries in his college diary.

By the time FDR entered the White House, his attraction to the circuitous and byzantine had evolved into a reflexive behavior. The bureaucratic fog that he laid down was deliberate. As the onetime Brain Truster Rexford Tugwell described FDR, "He had long ago learned to conceal from friend and enemy alike his thinking and deciding processes and even many of his convictions. . . ." He did not want anyone to know how he did it. A frustrated Raymond Moley, another early New Dealer, concluded, "[F]ewer friends would have been lost by bluntness than by the misunderstandings that arose from engaging ambiguity."

FDR's preference for talking and his reluctance to commit anything to paper have created a maddening situation for scholars. Roosevelt forbade any note-taking in his presence. When George Marshall instructed General John Deane to bring a notebook to a White House briefing, "The President," according to Marshall, "blew up." Roosevelt himself rarely recorded his discussions, no matter how significant the issue or elevated the participants, even during private sessions with the heads of nations, to the frustration of State Department historians. Of his confidential talks with Churchill at the White House or Hyde Park, the department's history notes dryly, "[T]here took place a number of informal and unscheduled conferences between [Churchill] and Roosevelt, and the President, as was his custom, prepared no minutes or memoranda of conversations on them." Tugwell has summed up the scholar's frustration. "There is hardly a dependable record of a conversation in Franklin Roosevelt's whole life." The choicest secrets remained locked inside his head.

The President's personal predilections also explain his greatest weakness as a participant in secret warfare, his preference for working with human sources over signals intelligence, for "humint" over "sigint" in the shorthand of the trade. Magic, through Ambassador Oshima, provided access to the most intimate councils of war, inside Germany. Arlington Hall also broke the codes of Brazil, Chile, Egypt, Finland, Greece, Iran, Ireland, Italy, Mexico, Portugal, and Turkey. FDR's attitude toward human intelligence versus signals intelligence mirrored his character. The broken enemy codes set before him were the product of a laborious alphanumeric science. But FDR's character was drawn to intuition over analysis, boldness over methodology, romance over technology. He could grasp the terrifying potential of atomic weaponry when it was described to him and set the Manhattan Project in motion; but, day to day, he preferred the liveliness of personal contact to the detachment of science.

What cannot be gainsaid, for better or worse, is that FDR built espionage into the structure of American government when he created the OSS. He was present at the creation, was indeed the creator. The OSS, only temporarily scuttled, was essentially refloated by Harry Truman. In a generation, the United States went from no intelligence service to a permanent service; from dilettante amateurs to careerist professionals; from no spending and no personnel to a CIA which at the peak of the Cold War had a budget approaching $3 billion and employed approximately seventeen thousand persons; from attaché chatter picked up at embassy parties to billion-dollar satellites spying from space to Earth; from the almost homey codebreaking club at Arlington Hall to the ultra-secret National Security Agency, referred to as "No Such Agency," whose intelligence collection and codebreaking enterprises far outstripped the budget even of the CIA. In short, America went from a nation innocent of espionage to one embracing its inevitability.

Wars are not won by spies pilfering documents or math professors cracking codes. They are won by forces engaged in bloodletting, by combatants bombing targets, sinking ships, and seizing ground. How long these forces are engaged and how much blood is spilled, however, can be shortened by the spy and the codebreaker. The advantage of Magic alone is proof. It revealed the Japanese fleet's movements that led to the pivotal Pacific victory at Midway. Magic tracked and doomed Admiral Yamamoto, whose loss to the Japanese has been equated with the Allies losing Eisenhower. In the final tally, both America's and Britain's intelligence operations far outstripped the performance of the enemy for political and psychological as much as technological reasons. Hitler's megalomania and the fear the Führer planted in his subordinates discouraged their delivering bad news. Hitler once pronounced accurate intelligence on Soviet troop concentrations "completely idiotic." Across a report on Russian agricultural output he scrawled, "This cannot be!" In time, his lieutenants spared themselves grief and merely omitted the bitter dishes of German espionage from the Führer's menu. Joseph Stalin was much the same throughout World War II and into the Cold War. NKVD officials watered down the unpalatable since by telling Stalin the truth one risked transfer to the Gulag. This denial of reality by despots rendered even the best intelligence valueless, a point worth remembering when democracies tend to ascribe the advantage in covert activity to authoritarian regimes. The truth, the welcome and the unwelcome, is more difficult to suppress in open societies. The ironic conclusion is that, like individual freedom, espionage ultimately fares best in free nations.

In Franklin Roosevelt's character, the elements of secret warfare blended felicitously. His pragmatic outlook was reflected by an OSS agent who had parachuted behind the lines. "I was," this spy observed, "a burglar with morals." FDR's approach was not all that different: the devious route to a desirable goal; inconstant behavior directed toward constant ends; the warship hiding behind a smoke screen but steered by a moral compass. His biographer James MacGregor Burns describes the kind of public man FDR admired: "opportunistic in meeting problems but principled in outlook; flexible in negotiations but right-minded in the final test. . . ." It is a description of Roosevelt himself. Whether shaped by a privileged childhood, the cruel education of polio, or a dizzyingly complex persona to begin with, Franklin Roosevelt confidently led America in a cataclysmic war in which secret warfare figured significantly and for which he possessed a talent that sprang spontaneously from his nature.

Bibliography

BOOKS

Ambrose, Stephen E., with Richard H. Immerman. *Ike's Spies: Eisenhower and the Espionage Establishment.* Garden City, N.Y.: Doubleday, 1981.

Andrew, Christopher. *For the President's Eyes Only: Secret Intelligence and the American Presidency from Washington to Bush.* New York: HarperCollins, 1995.

Andrew, Christopher, and David Dilks, eds. *The Missing Dimension.* Urbana: University of Illinois Press, 1984.

Andrew, Christopher, and Oleg Gordievsky. *KGB: The Inside Story of Its Foreign Operations from Lenin to Gorbachev.* New York: HarperCollins, 1990.

Andrew, Christopher, and Vasili Mitrokhin. *The Sword and the Shield: The Mitrokhin Archive and the Secret History of the KGB.* New York: Basic Books, 1999.

Baker, Liva. *Felix Frankfurter.* New York: Coward-McCann, 1969.

Bell, Ernest L. *An Initial View of Ultra as an American Weapon.* Keene, N.H.: TSU Press, 1977.

Benson, Robert Louis. *A History of U.S. Communications Intelligence During World War II: Policy and Administration.* Washington, D.C.: Center for Cryptologic History, National Security Agency, 1997.

Benson, Robert Louis, and Michael Warner, eds. *VENONA: Soviet Espionage and the American Response, 1939–1957.* Washington, D.C.: National Security Agency and Central Intelligence Agency, 1996.

Bentley, Elizabeth. *Out of Bondage.* New York: Devin-Adair, 1951.

————. *Out of Bondage: The Story of Elizabeth Bentley,* afterword by Hayden Peake. New York: Ivy, 1988.

Beschloss, Michael. *Kennedy and Roosevelt: The Uneasy Alliance.* New York: Norton, 1980.

Biddle, Francis. *In Brief Authority.* Garden City, N.Y.: Doubleday, 1962.

Bishop, Jim. *FDR's Last Year, April 1944–April 1945.* New York: Morrow, 1974.

Bloch, Michael. *Operation Willi: The Nazi Plot to Kidnap the Duke of Windsor.* London: Weidenfeld & Nicolson, 1940.

Blum, John Morton. *Years of Urgency, 1938–1941: From the Morgenthau Diaries.* Boston: Houghton Mifflin, 1965.

————. *Years of War, 1941–1945: From the Morgenthau Diaries.* Boston: Houghton Mifflin, 1967.

Blumenson, Martin. *Mark Clark.* New York: Congdon & Weed, 1984.

————. *Patton: The Man Behind the Legend, 1885–1945.* New York: Morrow, 1985.

Bradley, Omar N., and Clay Blair. *A General's Life.* New York: Simon & Schuster, 1974.

Breuer, William B. *Hoodwinking Hitler: The Normandy Deception.* Westport, Conn.: Praeger, 1993.

Brinkley, David. *Washington Goes to War.* New York: Knopf, 1988.

Brown, Anthony Cave. *Bodyguard of Lies.* New York: Harper & Row, 1975.

————. *The Last Hero: Wild Bill Donovan.* New York: Times Books, 1982.

Buell, Thomas B. *Master of Sea Power: A Biography of Fleet Admiral Ernest J. King.* Boston: Little, Brown, 1980.

Bullitt, Orville H., ed. *For the President, Personal and Secret: Correspondence Between Franklin D. Roosevelt and William C. Bullitt.* Boston: Houghton Mifflin, 1972.

Burns, James MacGregor. *Roosevelt: The Lion and the Fox.* New York: Harcourt, Brace, 1956.

————. *Roosevelt: The Soldier of Freedom.* New York: Harcourt Brace Jovanovich, 1970.

Butcher, Harry C. *My Three Years with Eisenhower.* New York: Simon & Schuster, 1946.

Chambers, Whittaker. *Witness.* New York: Random House, 1952.

Charmley, John. *Churchill: The End of Glory.* New York: Harcourt, Brace, 1993.

Churchill, Winston S. *Memoirs of the Second World War.* Boston: Houghton Mifflin, 1959.

————. *The Second World War,* Vol. 5, *Closing the Ring.* New York: Bantam, 1962.

Clausewitz, Carl von. *On War,* edited and translated by Michael Howard and Peter Paret. Princeton, N.J.: Princeton University Press, 1976.

Cline, Ray S. *Secrets, Spies and Scholars*. Washington, D.C.: Acropolis, 1976.

Cole, Wayne S. *Charles A. Lindbergh and the Battle Against American Intervention in World War II*. New York: Harcourt Brace Jovanovich, 1974.

Cook, Blanche Wiesen. *Eleanor Roosevelt*, Vol. 1, *1884–1933*. New York: Viking, 1992.

Costello, John. *Days of Infamy: MacArthur, Roosevelt, Churchill—The Shocking Truth Revealed, How Their Secret Deals and Strategic Blunders Caused Disasters at Pearl Harbor and the Philippines*. New York: Pocket Books, 1994.

———. *The Pacific War*. New York: Rawson, Wade, 1981.

Cruickshank, Charles. *Deception in World War II*. New York: Oxford University Press, 1980.

Dallek, Robert. *Franklin D. Roosevelt and American Foreign Policy, 1932–1945*. New York: Oxford University Press, 1979.

Dallin, David. *Soviet Espionage*. New Haven, Conn.: Yale University Press, 1955.

Dornberger, Walter. *V-2*. New York: Viking, 1954.

Dorwart, Jeffrey M. *Conflict of Duty: The U.S. Navy's Intelligence Dilemma, 1919–1945*. Annapolis, Md.: Naval Institute Press, 1983.

———. *The Office of Naval Intelligence*. Annapolis, Md.: Naval Institute Press, 1979.

Doyle, William. *Inside the Oval Office: The White House Tapes from FDR to Clinton*. New York: Kodansha, 1999.

Dulles, Allen Welsh. *Germany's Underground*. New York: Macmillan, 1947.

Eisenhower, David. *Eisenhower at War, 1943–1945*. New York: Random House, 1986.

Eisenhower, Dwight D. *Crusade in Europe*. Garden City, N.Y.: Doubleday, 1948.

Eisenhower, John. *Strictly Personal*. Garden City, N.Y.: Doubleday, 1974.

Fagen, M. D., ed. *History of Engineering and Science in the Bell System: National Service in War and Peace (1925–1975)*. New York: Bell Telephone Laboratories, 1978.

Farago, Ladislas. *The Game of the Foxes*. New York: McKay, 1971.

Ferrell, Robert H. *The Dying President: Franklin D. Roosevelt, 1944–1945*. Columbia: University of Missouri Press, 1998.

———. *Harry S. Truman: A Life*. Columbia: University of Missouri Press, 1994.

Ford, Corey. *Donovan of OSS*. Boston: Little, Brown, 1970.

Freidel, Frank. *Franklin D. Roosevelt: A Rendezvous with Destiny*. Boston: Little, Brown, 1990.

Gellman, Irwin F. *Secret Affairs: Franklin Roosevelt, Cordell Hull, and Sumner Welles*. Baltimore: Johns Hopkins University Press, 1995.

Gentry, Curt. *J. Edgar Hoover: The Man and the Secrets*. New York: Norton, 1991.

Gilbert, Martin. *Winston S. Churchill,* Vol. 6. Boston: Houghton Mifflin, 1983.

Goodwin, Doris Kearns. *No Ordinary Time: Franklin and Eleanor Roosevelt: The Home Front in World War II.* New York: Simon & Schuster, 1994.

Greenblatt, Miriam. *Franklin D. Roosevelt: 32nd President of the United States.* Ada, Okla.: Garrett Educational Series, 1989.

Grodzins, Morton. *Americans Betrayed: Politics and the Japanese Evacuation.* Chicago: University of Chicago Press, 1949.

Gunther, John. *Roosevelt in Retrospect, A Profile in History.* New York: Harper & Brothers, 1950.

Harriman, Averell, and Elie Abel. *Special Envoy to Churchill and Stalin, 1941–46.* New York: Random House, 1975.

Hassett, William D. *Off the Record with F.D.R., 1942–1945.* New Brunswick, N.J.: Rutgers University Press, 1958.

Havas, Laslo. *Hitler's Plot to Kill the Big 3.* New York: Cowles, 1967.

Heideking, Jürgen, and Christof Mauch, eds., with the assistance of Marc Frey. *American Intelligence and the German Resistance to Hitler: A Documentary History.* Boulder, Colo.: Westview, 1996.

Herzstein, Robert Edwin. *Roosevelt & Hitler: Prelude to War.* New York: Paragon, 1989.

Higham, Charles. *American Swastika.* Garden City, N.Y.: Doubleday, 1985.

———. *Errol Flynn: The Untold Story.* Garden City, N.Y.: Doubleday, 1980.

Hinsley, F. H. *British Intelligence in the Second World War.* New York: Cambridge University Press, 1988.

Hull, Cordell. *The Memoirs of Cordell Hull.* New York: Macmillan, 1948.

Hyde, H. Montgomery. *Room 3603: The Story of the British Intelligence Center in New York During World War II.* New York: Farrar, Straus, 1962.

Irving, David. *Hitler's War.* New York: Viking, 1977.

———. *The Mare's Nest.* Boston: Little, Brown, 1964.

John, Otto. *Twice Through the Lines.* New York: Harper & Row, 1972.

Kahn, David. *Code Breaking in World Wars I and II.* Urbana: University of Illinois Press, 1984.

———. *Hitler's Spies.* New York: Macmillan, 1978.

———. *Seizing the Enigma: The Race to Break the German U-Boat Codes, 1939–1943.* Boston: Houghton Mifflin, 1991.

Keegan, John. *The Second World War.* New York: Viking Penguin, 1990.

Keegan, John, ed. *Who Was Who in World War II.* New York: Crescent, 1984.

Kent, George O., ed. *Historians and Archivists.* Fairfax, Va.: George Mason University Press, 1991.

Ketchum, Richard M. *The Borrowed Years, 1938–1941: America on the Way to War.* New York: Random House, 1989.

Kimball, Warren F. *The Juggler: Franklin Roosevelt as Wartime Statesman.* Princeton, N.J.: Princeton University Press, 1991.

Kimball, Warren F., ed. *Churchill & Roosevelt: The Complete Correspondence.* Princeton, N.J.: Princeton University Press, 1984.

Kirkpatrick, Lyman B., Jr. *Captains Without Eyes: Intelligence Failures in World War II.* London: Collier-Macmillan, 1969.

Klehr, Harvey, and Ronald Radosh. *The Amerasia Spy Case: Prelude to McCarthyism.* Chapel Hill: University of North Carolina Press, 1996.

Knightley, Phillip. *The Second Oldest Profession: Spies and Spying in the Twentieth Century.* New York: Norton, 1986.

Koskoff, David E. *Joseph P. Kennedy: A Life and Times.* Englewood Cliffs, N.J.: Prentice-Hall, 1974.

Kurzman, Dan. *Day of the Bomb: Countdown to Hiroshima.* New York: McGraw-Hill, 1986.

Larrabee, Eric. *Commander in Chief: Franklin Delano Roosevelt, His Lieutenants, and Their War.* New York: Harper & Row, 1987.

Lash, Joseph P. *Roosevelt and Churchill, 1939–1941: The Partnership That Saved the West.* New York: Norton, 1976.

———. *A World of Love: Eleanor Roosevelt and Her Friends, 1943–1962.* Garden City, N.Y.: Doubleday, 1962.

Leahy, William D. *I Was There: The Personal Story of the Chief of Staff to Presidents Roosevelt and Truman Based on His Notes and Diaries Made at the Time.* New York: McGraw-Hill, 1950.

Loewenheim, Francis L., Harold D. Langley, and Manfred Jonas, eds. *Roosevelt and Churchill: Their Secret Wartime Correspondence.* New York: Saturday Review Press/Dutton, 1975.

Lovell, Stanley. *Of Spies and Stratagems.* Englewood Cliffs, N.J.: Prentice-Hall, 1963.

MacArthur, Douglas. *Reminiscences.* New York: McGraw-Hill, 1964.

McCullough, David G. *Truman.* New York: Touchstone, 1993.

McCullough, David G., ed. *The American Heritage Picture History of World War II.* New York: American Heritage, 1966.

The "Magic" Background of Pearl Harbor, vol. 1, *February 14, 1941–May 12, 1941.* Washington: Department of Defense, United States of America, 1978.

Matloff, Maurice. *United States Army in World War II: Strategic Planning for Coalition Warfare.* Washington, D.C.: Office of the Chief of Military History, Department of the Army, 1959.

Miller, Nathan. *Spying for America: The Hidden History of U.S. Intelligence.* New York: Paragon, 1989.

Moran, Lord. *Churchill: Taken from the Diaries of Lord Moran.* Boston: Houghton Mifflin, 1966.

Mosley, Leonard. *Marshall: Hero for Our Times.* New York: Hearst, 1982.

Moss, Norman. *Klaus Fuchs: The Man Who Stole the Atom Bomb.* New York: St. Martin's Press, 1987.

Moynihan, Daniel Patrick. *Secrecy: The American Experience*. New Haven, Conn.: Yale University Press, 1998.

Newton, Verne W. *The Cambridge Spies: The Untold Story of Maclean, Philby and Burgess in America*. Lanham, Md.: Madison Books, 1991.

Persico, Joseph E. *Casey: From the OSS to the CIA*. New York: Viking Penguin, 1991.

———. *Edward R. Murrow: An American Original*. New York: McGraw-Hill, 1988.

———. *Nuremberg: Infamy on Trial*. New York: Viking Penguin, 1994.

———. *Piercing the Reich*. New York: Viking, 1979.

Petersen, Neal, ed. *From Hitler's Doorstep: The Wartime Intelligence Reports of Allen Dulles, 1942–1945*. University Park, Pa.: Pennsylvania State University Press, 1996.

Piszkiewicz, Dennis. *The Nazi Rocketeers*. Westport, Conn.: Praeger, 1995.

Polmar, Norman, and Thomas B. Allen. *Spy Book: The Encyclopedia of Espionage*. New York: Random House, 1997.

———. *World War II: America at War, 1941–1945*. New York: Random House, 1991.

Powers, Richard Gid. *Secrecy and Power: The Life of J. Edgar Hoover*. New York: Free Press, 1987.

Powers, Thomas. *Heisenberg's War: The Secret History of the German Bomb*. New York: Knopf, 1993.

Prange, Gordon W. *At Dawn We Slept: The Untold Story of Pearl Harbor*. New York: McGraw-Hill, 1981.

Prange, Gordon W., with Donald M. Goldstein and Katherine V. Dillon. *December 7, 1941: The Day the Japanese Attacked Pearl Harbor*. New York: McGraw-Hill, 1988.

Reilly, Michael F., as told to William J. Slocum. *Reilly of the White House*. New York: Simon & Schuster, 1947.

Rhodes, Richard. *The Making of the Atomic Bomb*. New York: Simon & Schuster, 1986.

Rigdon, William M., with James Derieux. *White House Sailor*. Garden City, N.Y.: Doubleday, 1962.

Roetter, Charles. *The Art of Psychological Warfare, 1914–1945*. New York: Stein and Day, 1974.

Roosevelt, Eleanor. *The Autobiography of Eleanor Roosevelt*. New York: Harper & Brothers, 1961.

Roosevelt, Elliott, ed., assisted by James N. Rosenau. *FDR: His Personal Letters, 1905–1928*. New York: Duell, Sloan and Pearce, 1948.

Roosevelt, James, and Sidney Shalett. *Affectionately, F.D.R.: A Son's Story of a Lonely Man*. New York: Harcourt, Brace, 1959.

Roosevelt, James, with Bill Libby. *My Parents: A Differing View.* Chicago: Playboy Press, 1976.

Roosevelt, Kermit, intro. *The Overseas Targets: War Report of the OSS,* Vol. 2. Washington, D.C.: Walker; New York: Carrollton, 1976.

Root, Waverley. *The Secret History of the War.* New York: Scribner, 1945.

Rosenman, Samuel I. *Working with Roosevelt.* New York: Harper & Brothers, 1952.

Rosenman, Samuel I., ed. *The Public Papers and Addresses of Franklin D. Roosevelt, 1944–45, Victory and the Threshold of Peace.* New York: Harper & Brothers, 1950.

Rout, Leslie B., Jr., and John F. Bratzel. *The Shadow War: German Espionage and United States Counterespionage During World War II.* Frederick, Md.: University Publications of America, 1986.

Russell, Francis. *The Secret War.* Alexandria, Va.: Time-Life, 1981.

Russell, Richard A. *Project Hula: Secret Soviet-American Cooperation in the War Against Japan.* Washington, D.C.: Naval Historical Center, 1997.

Sandilands, Roger J. *The Life and Political Economy of Lauchlin Currie: New Dealer, Presidential Adviser, and Development Economist.* Durham, N.C.: Duke University Press, 1990.

Sherwin, Martin J. *A World Destroyed: Hiroshima and the Origins of the Cold War.* New York: Vintage, 1975.

Sherwood, Robert E. *Roosevelt and Hopkins: An Intimate History.* New York: Harper & Brothers, 1950.

Shirer, William L. *The Rise and Fall of the Third Reich: A History of Nazi Germany.* New York: Simon & Schuster, 1960.

Smith, Bradley F. *The Shadow Warriors: O.S.S. and the Origins of the C.I.A.* New York: Basic Books, 1983.

———. *Sharing Secrets with Stalin: How the Allies Traded Intelligence, 1941–1945.* Lawrence: University of Kansas Press, 1996.

Snow, C. P. *Variety of Men.* New York: Scribner's, 1966.

Spector, Ronald H. *Eagle Against the Sun: The American War with Japan.* New York: Free Press, 1985.

Stafford, David. *Churchill and Secret Service.* Toronto: Stoddart, 1997.

Stevenson, William. *A Man Called Intrepid: The Secret War.* New York: Harcourt Brace Jovanovich, 1976.

Stimson, Henry L., and McGeorge Bundy. *On Active Service in Peace and War.* New York: Harper & Brothers, 1947.

Stinnett, Robert B. *Day of Deceit: The Truth About FDR and Pearl Harbor.* New York: Free Press, 1999.

Strong, Kenneth. *Intelligence at the Top: The Recollections of an Intelligence Officer.* Garden City, N.Y.: Doubleday, 1969.

Sudoplatov, Pavel, and Anatoli Sudoplatov, with Jerrold L. and Leona P. Schecter. *Special Tasks.* New York: Back Bay Books/Little, Brown, 1994.

Sun Tzu. *The Art of War.* New York: Oxford University Press, 1984.

Theoharis, Athan, ed. *From the Secret Files of J. Edgar Hoover.* Chicago: Dee, 1991.

Thompson, Robert Smith. *A Time for War: Franklin Delano Roosevelt and the Path to Pearl Harbor.* New York: Prentice-Hall, 1991.

Toland, John. *Adolf Hitler.* Garden City, N.Y.: Doubleday, 1976.

————. *The Rising Sun: The Decline and Fall of the Japanese Empire, 1936–1945.* New York: Random House, 1970.

Troy, Thomas F. *The Coordinator of Information and British Intelligence.* Washington, D.C.: Central Intelligence Agency, 1978.

————. *Donovan and the CIA: A History of the Establishment of the Central Intelligence Agency.* Frederick, Md.: University Publications of America, 1981.

————. *Wild Bill and Intrepid: Donovan, Stephenson and the Origin of the CIA.* New Haven, Conn.: Yale University Press, 1996.

Truman, Harry S. *Memoirs,* Vol. 1, *Year of Decisions.* Garden City, N.Y.: Doubleday, 1955.

Tugwell, Rexford. *The Democratic Roosevelt.* Garden City, N.Y.: Doubleday, 1957.

Tully, Grace. *F.D.R., My Boss.* New York: Scribner's, 1949.

Volkman, Ernest. *Spies: The Secret Agents Who Changed the Course of History.* New York: Wiley, 1994.

Volkogonov, Dmitri. *Stalin: Triumph and Tragedy,* edited and translated by Harold Shukman. New York: Grove Weidenfeld, 1999.

Ward, Geoffrey C. *A First-Class Temperament: The Emergence of Franklin Roosevelt.* New York: Harper & Row, 1989.

Weinberg, Gerhard L. *A World at Arms: A Global History of World War II.* New York: Cambridge University Press, 1994.

Weinstein, Allen. *Perjury: The Hiss-Chambers Case.* New York: Vintage, 1979.

Weinstein, Allen, and Alexander Vassiliev. *The Haunted Wood: Soviet Espionage in America—the Stalin Era.* New York: Random House, 1999.

West, Nigel. *A Thread of Deceit: Espionage Myths of World War II.* New York: Random House, 1985.

Whalen, Richard J. *The Founding Father: The Story of Joseph P. Kennedy.* New York: New American Library, 1964.

Wighton, Charles, and Gunter Peis. *Hitler's Spies and Saboteurs.* New York: Award Books, 1958.

Williams, Mary H. *United States Army in World War II: Chronology, 1941–1945.* Washington, D.C.: Department of the Army, 1960.

Williams, Wythe, and Van Narvig. *Secret Sources: The Story Behind Some Famous Scoops.* Chicago and New York: Ziff-Davis, 1943.

Winks, Robin W. *Cloak and Gown: Scholars in the Secret War, 1939–1961.* New York: Morrow, 1987.

Winterbotham, F. W. *The Ultra Secret.* New York: Dell, 1974.

Wohlstetter, Roberta. *Pearl Harbor: Warning and Decision.* Stanford, Calif.: Stanford University Press, 1962.

Young, Peter, ed. *The World Almanac Book of World War II.* New York: World Almanac Publications, 1981.

Ziegler, Philip. *King Edward VIII: The Official Biography.* London: Collins, 1990.

Ziemke, Earl F. *Stalingrad to Berlin: The German Defeat in the East.* Washington, D.C.: Army Historical Series, Office of the Chief of Military History, United States Army, 1968.

———. *The U.S. Army in the Occupation of Germany, 1944–1946.* Washington, D.C.: Center of Military History, United States Army, Washington, D.C., 1975.

ARTICLES

Allen, Louis. "Japanese Intelligence Systems." *Journal of Contemporary History,* vol. 22 (June 1975).

Bernstein, Barton J. "The Uneasy Alliance: Roosevelt, Churchill and the Atomic Bomb: 1940–1945." *Western Political Quarterly,* vol. 29 (June 1976).

Bratzel, John F., and Leslie B. Rout Jr. "Pearl Harbor, Microdots, and J. Edgar Hoover." *The American Historical Review,* vol. 7, no. 5 (December 1982).

Bullitt, William. "How We Won the War and Lost the Peace." *Life,* August 30, 1948.

Dawidowicz, Lucy S. "Could the United States Have Rescued the European Jews from Hitler?" *This World,* Fall 1985.

Dorwart, Jeffrey M. "The Roosevelt-Astor Espionage Ring." *New York History,* vol. 62, no. 3 (July 1981).

Etzold, Thomas H. "The (F)utility Factor: German Information Gathering in the United States, 1933–1941." *Military Affairs,* vol. 39, no. 2 (1975).

Finney, Nat S. "How FDR Planned to Use the A-Bomb." *Look,* vol. 14, no. 6 (March 14, 1950).

Furgurson, Ernest B. "Back Channels." *Washingtonian,* vol. 31 (June 1996).

Heppenheimer, T. A. "But on the Other Hand. . . ." *American Heritage,* September 2000.

Leutze, James. "The Secret of the Churchill-Roosevelt Correspondence, September 1939–May 1940." *Journal of Contemporary History,* July 10, 1975.

Mulligan, Timothy P. "According to Colonel Donovan: A Document from the Records of German Intelligence." *The Historian,* vol. 46, no. 1 (November 1983).

Nichols, Sheridan. "The Light That Failed: Intelligence Gathering Activities in North Africa Prior to Operation Torch." *Maghreb Review* 4 (July/December 1979).

Oursler, Fulton, Jr. "Secret Treason." *American Heritage,* December 1991.

Prior, Leon O. "Nazi Invasion of Florida." *Florida History Quarterly,* vol. 49, no. 2 (October 1970).

Sherwin, Martin J. "The Atomic Bomb and the Origins of the Cold War: U.S. Atomic Energy Policy and Diplomacy, 1941–1945." *The American Historical Review,* vol. 78, no. 4 (October 1973).

Spiller, Roger J. "Assessing Ultra." *Military Review,* vol. 1 (August 1979).

Swanberg, W. A. "The Spies Who Came in from the Sea." *American Heritage,* April 1970.

Sweet, Paul R. "The Windsor File." *Historian,* Winter 1997.

vanden Heuvel, William J. "America, FDR and the Holocaust." *Society,* vol. 34, no. 6 (September/October 1997).

Villa, Brian Loring. "The Atomic Bomb and the Normandy Invasion." *Perspectives in American History* 2 (1977–78).

Walker, David A. "OSS and Operation Torch." *Journal of Contemporary History,* vol. 22 (1987).

Warner, Michael. "The Creation of the Central Intelligence Group." *Studies in Intelligence,* Central Intelligence Agency, Fall 1995.

Warner, Michael, and Robert Louis Benson. "Venona and Beyond." *Intelligence and National Security,* vol. 12, no. 3 (July 1997).

DOCUMENTS

Beck, Alfred M. "The Ambivalent Attaché: Friedrich von Boetticher in America, 1933–1941." Ph.D. diss., Georgetown University, 1977 (unpublished).

The Archives of Margaret L. Suckley. Wilderstein Preservation Inc.

Boston Series Reports and Related Records. Greg Bradsher, National Archives and Records Administration, College Park, Maryland, 2000.

Breitman, Richard, and Timothy Naftal. "Report to the Interagency Working Group on Previously Classified OSS Records." National Archives, College Park, Maryland, 2000.

The Complete Presidential Press Conferences of Franklin D. Roosevelt, 1933–1945. New York: Da Capo, 1972.

Foreign Relations of the United States, 1939–1945. Washington, D.C.: U.S. Government Printing Office, 1970.

Hearings on Proposed Legislation to Curb or Control the Communist Party of the United States. Washington, D.C.: United States Government Printing Office, 1948.

Memorandum from Colonel Richard Park Jr. to President Harry S Truman, April 13, 1945. Harry S Truman Library.

Memorandum of Establishment of Service of Strategic Information. William J. Donovan to President Franklin D. Roosevelt, June 10, 1941. FDR Library.

Oral History Interview with Robert D. Ogg. Commander I. G. Newman (ret.), Aug. 23, 1983, Naval Security Group, unpublished. FDR Library.

Romerstein, Herbert. "Ideological Recruitment of Agents by Soviet Intelligence, in the Light of Venona." Symposium on Cryptologic History, National Security Agency, Fort Meade, Maryland, Oct. 29–31, 1992.

Slany, William. "Preliminary Study on U.S. and Allied Efforts to Recover and Restore Gold and Other Assets Stolen or Hidden by Germany During World War II." The author is the historian of the U.S. Department of State.

Statement of Elizabeth Ferrill Bentley to the Federal Bureau of Investigation, Nov. 30, 1945, New York.

The Year of Crisis—1943, John Franklin Carter Diary. John Franklin Carter Papers, University of Wyoming, Laramie, Wyoming, undated.

Yearbook 1982. Washington, D.C.: Supreme Court Historical Society, 1982.

FILMS

"Blood Money: Switzerland's Nazi Gold." Investigative Reports, Crisman Films, Inc., New York, 1997.

"FDR." *The American Experience* (PBS), David Grubin Productions.

"Patton Museum of Cavalry and Armor." www.generalpatton.org/qtvr.html (Internet).

"Roundup." *Dateline,* NBC News, New York, Sept. 4, 1998.

"The Spies Among Us." *In Search of History,* The History Channel, 1998.

Source Notes

SOURCE notes are keyed to the page number and a quotation or phrase occurring on that page. Citations from books, periodicals, and other attributed sources begin with the author's name followed by the title and page numbers. The sources are fully identified in the bibliography. Where more than one work by the same author is cited, a distinguishing word from the appropriate title appears after the author's name. Frequently cited sources are abbreviated as follows:

Day-by-Day	FDR: Day-by-Day, The Pare Lorentz Chronology, FDRL
FDRL	Franklin D. Roosevelt Library
FRUS	*Foreign Relations of the United States*
HH	Harry Hopkins
M 1642	Microfilm, National Archives, OSS Director's Office
MR	Map Room Files, FDRL
NA	National Archives
NYT	*New York Times*
POF	President's Official File, FDRL
PPF	President's Personal File, Roosevelt Library
PSF	President's Secretary's File, Roosevelt Library
RG 457	Record Group 457, National Archives
Suckley	Diaries of Margaret Suckley

FOREWORD

xi "You know I am a juggler. . . .": Morgenthau Diary, May 15, 1942, p. 1093, FDRL.

xii "I had a conversation with father. . . .": James Roosevelt, *My Parents,* pp. 160–61.

xii "He deliberately concealed. . . .": John Gunther, *Roosevelt in Retrospect,* p. 53.

xii "Nothing would have pleased him. . . .": Brian Loring Villa, "The Atomic Bomb and the Normandy Invasion," *Perspectives in American History* 2 (1977–78), p. 465.

PROLOGUE

xxi He sat in bed: John Gunther, *Roosevelt in Retrospect,* p. 119.

xxi He dressed casually: James Roosevelt, *Affectionately, F.D.R.,* p. 327.

xxi To one guest: Richard M. Ketchum, *The Borrowed Years, 1938–1941,* p. 765.

xxi The President had excused himself: Day-by-Day, Dec. 6, 1941, FDRL.

xxi "looked very worn. . . .": Gordon Prange, *December 7, 1941,* p. 28; Ketchum, p. 765.

xxii Prettyman lifted a drained FDR: Day-by-Day, Dec. 6, 1941, FDRL; Christopher Andrew, *For the President's Eyes Only,* pp. 116–17.

xxii The weather, for December: *NYT,* Dec. 7, 1941.

xxii The President had invited Murrow: Joseph E. Persico, *Edward R. Murrow,* p. 193.

xxii "Wild Bill" Donovan, just six months: Thomas F. Troy, *Donovan and the CIA,* pp. 115–16.

xxii As Prettyman removed the debris: William Doyle, *Inside the Oval Office,* p. 22.

xxii His chronic sinusitis: Eleanor Roosevelt, *The Autobiography of Eleanor Roosevelt,* p. 226.

xxii Washington was a: David Brinkley, *Washington Goes to War,* p. xi.

xxii The silence was broken: Ketchum, p. 765.

xxiii The President and his doctor: Prange, p. 247.

xxiii Portraits of the President's mother: Gunther, pp. 361–62; Doyle, p. 26; Robert E. Sherwood, *Roosevelt and Hopkins,* pp. 204–205.

xxiii Hu Shih left: Prange, p. 248.

xxiii He asked his valet: Grace Tully, *F.D.R., My Boss,* p. 7.

xxiii "I was disappointed. . . .": Eleanor Roosevelt, p. 226.

xxiv FDR picked it up: John Toland, *The Rising Sun,* p. 223; John Costello, *The Pacific War,* p. 4.

xxiv "Mr. President," he said: Gunther, p. 319.

xxiv Knox said that he had no further details: Prange, p. 248.

xxiv   There must be some mistake: James MacGregor Burns, *Roosevelt: The Soldier of Freedom,* p. 162.

xxiv   "His reaction to any great event. . . .": Geoffrey C. Ward, *A First-Class Temperament,* p. 591.

xxiv   the President responded: Sherwood, p. 431; Burns, *Roosevelt: The Soldier of Freedom,* p. 162.

CHAPTER I: GENTLEMAN AMATEURS

3   As she came in: John Gunther, *Roosevelt in Retrospect,* p. 26; Jim Bishop, *Roosevelt's Last Year,* pp. 1–2.

3   By now, eighteen years: Robert E. Sherwood, *Roosevelt and Hopkins,* pp. 205–206.

3   The President took from a can: Bishop, p. 15; William Doyle, *Inside the Oval Office,* p. 22.

3   The letterhead read simply: PSF Box 92.

4   The president-elect then joined: Michael F. Reilly, *Reilly of the White House,* p. 92.

4   And always the appended note: PSF Box 92.

5   "the richest boy in the world": *The Poughkeepsie New Yorker,* Feb. 3, 1959; *The Poughkeepsie Journal,* Oct. 16, 1977; Vincent Astor to Missy LeHand, June 23, 1937, FDRL.

5   "we grew to be. . . .": Ernest B. Furgurson, "Back Channels," *Washingtonian,* vol. 31 (June 1996); Vincent Astor to Missy LeHand, June 23, 1937, FDRL; *Poughkeepsie Journal,* Oct. 16, 1977.

5   "In a day and age. . . .": Christopher Andrew, *For the President's Eyes Only,* pp. 75–76.

6   "learned to anticipate . . ."; "We took secret pride. . . .": Doris Kearns Goodwin, *No Ordinary Time,* p. 77.

6   "You keep your cards. . . .": Doyle, p. 30.

6   Roosevelt was a man: Eric Larrabee, *Commander in Chief,* pp. 28–29.

6   Four months later: Miriam Greenblatt, *Franklin D. Roosevelt,* pp. 26–27.

6   "Whenever a Roosevelt rides. . . .": Larrabee, pp. 29–30.

7   In its thirty-first year: Jeffrey M. Dorwart, *The Office of Naval Intelligence,* pp. ix, x, 96, 104, 105, 108; Norman Polmar and Thomas B. Allen, *Spy Book,* pp. x, 408.

7   FDR's amateurs: Dorwart, *Office of Naval Intelligence,* pp. 96, 104–105.

7   ONI's roster: Dorwart, *Conflict of Duty,* p. 163; Dorwart, *Office of Naval Intelligence,* pp. 108–109; Andrew, p. 77.

7   German saboteurs were suspected: W. A. Swanberg, "The Spies Who Came in from the Sea," *American Heritage,* April 1970, p. 67.

7   One ONI informant: Dorwart, *Office of Naval Intelligence,* p. 117.

7   FDR ordered another investigation: Assistant Secretary of the Navy, Box 2, FDRL.

7   "The employees. . . .": Andrew, p. 77.

8   With FDR's fervent support: Dorwart, *Office of Naval Intelligence,* p. 117.

8   He wore the gun: Andrew, pp. 77–78.

8   On July 9, 1918: Elliott Roosevelt, ed., *FDR: His Personal Letters,* p. 375.

8   Hall had leaked the telegram: Dorwart, *Office of Naval Intelligence,* p. 105.

8   "Neither in fiction or fact. . . .": Polmar and Allen, *Spy Book,* p. 251.

8   "I am going to ask. . . .": Andrew, p. 78.

9   "Their Intelligence Department. . . .": Franklin D. Roosevelt, "Account of 1918 Trip to England, France and the Front," p. 387, FDRL; Andrew, pp. 2, 78.

9   Indeed, by the end: Andrew, p. 117.

9   As Roosevelt began: Vincent Astor to Missy LeHand, June 23, 1937, FDRL.

9   While the political views: Furgurson.

9   It would be Astor's gift: Dorwart, "The Roosevelt-Astor Espionage Ring," *New York History,* vol. 62, no. 3 (July 1981), p. 311.

9   Otherwise, it was: Vincent Astor to Missy LeHand, June 23, 1937, FDRL.

10 Astor backed reform: Dorwart, "Roosevelt-Astor Espionage Ring," p. 308.

10 Astor's fellow members: *U.S. News & World Report,* Jan. 12, 1987; Dorwart, "Roosevelt-Astor Espionage Ring," pp. 309–10.

10 Distinguished figures were invited: Dorwart, "Roosevelt-Astor Espionage Ring," p. 310.

11 ". . . estimable, socially acceptable. . . .": Dwight D. Eisenhower, *Crusade in Europe,* p. 32.

11 "could not be more clear": PPF Box 40.

12 "keep a security watch on me": ibid.

12 He ended confidently: ibid.

12 "I don't want to make you jealous. . . .": Andrew, p. 84.

12 The President spoke quickly: Suckley, Binder 16, p. 258.

12 "I will not say more. . . .": PSF Box 92.

12 "a 100% probability. . . .": ibid.

13 "only beer and sherry. . . .": ibid.

13 A small but zealous Friedman: Andrew, p. 105; Polmar and Allen, *Spy Book,* p. 222.

13 This breakthrough meant: Roberta Wohlstetter, *Pearl Harbor,* p. 170.

13 At about the time: Andrew, p. 105.

14 "The German future. . . .": Joseph E. Persico, *Nuremberg,* p. 43.

14 U.S. industry was willingly: Phillip Knightley, *The Second Oldest Profession,* p. 102.

15 "I want to do something. . . .": Charles Wighton and Gunter Peis, *Hitler's Spies and Saboteurs,* p. 27.

15 Piece by piece: David Kahn, *Hitler's Spies,* pp. 328–31; Ladislas Farago, *The Game of the Foxes,* p. 40; Daniel Patrick Moynihan, *Secrecy: The American Experience,* p. 125.

15 The British were not: Thomas H. Etzold, "The (F)utility Factor," *Military Affairs,* vol. 39, no. 2 (1975).

15 "Then it's happened. . . .": Dorwart, *Conflict of Duty,* pp. 119–20; Gunther, p. 303.

16 "Tomorrow I am starting. . . .": Dorwart, *Conflict of Duty,* p. 165.

16 He informed Roosevelt: Andrew, p. 93.

16 "in accordance with your wishes. . . .": ibid., p. 92; Dorwart, "Roosevelt-Astor Espionage Ring," p. 15.

16 "constantly crossing each other's tracks.": Thomas F. Troy, *The Coordinator of Information and British Intelligence,* p. 149.

17 "His mind does not easily follow. . . .": Stimson Diaries, Dec. 18, 1940, FDRL; Andrew, p. 86.

17 But over the long term: Roger J. Sandilands, *The Life and Political Economy of Lauchlin Currie,* p. 98.

17 He handed responsibility: Troy, *The Coordinator,* pp. 147, 148; Andrew, p. 86.

17 He attended: Andrew, p. 91; Troy, *The Coordinator,* pp. 149–50.

CHAPTER II: SPIES, SABOTEURS, AND TRAITORS

19 "No, you can't come in": Richard J. Whalen, *The Founding Father,* p. 310.

19 What they revealed: Norman Polmar and Thomas B. Allen, *Spy Book,* p. 309.

20 "I have always disliked. . . .": Michael F. Reilly, *Reilly of the White House,* p. 200.

20 "widely and deeply disliked": James Leutze, "The Secret of the Churchill-Roosevelt Correspondence, September 1939–May 1940," *Journal of Contemporary History,* July 10, 1975, p. 478.

20 "Mr. Churchill was sitting. . . .": ibid., p. 480.

20 "was one of the most. . . .": ibid., p. 470.

20 ". . . [T]here is a strong possibility. . . .": Robert Thompson, *A Time for War,* p. 200.

20 "The decisive hour has come. . . .": Doris Kearns Goodwin, *No Ordinary Time,* p. 15.

21 "I should like to speak. . . .": William C. Bullitt to Roosevelt, May 16, 1940, PSF Box 2.

21 "the British fleet would base itself. . . .": ibid.

21 He had received: Whalen, pp. 311, 312.

21 He had come to London: Polmar and Allen, *Spy Book,* p. 309.

21 Kent's fellow clerks: Whalen, p. 310.

22 "The more American ships. . . .": Leutze, pp. 483–84.

22 He began signing: Ladislas Farago, *The Game of the Foxes,* p. 339.

22 ". . . [T]heir [U.S.] patrols. . . .": Leutze, p. 484.

22 "I gave orders last night. . . .": ibid., p. 475.

22 "Take no sides. . . .": Robert E. Sherwood, *Roosevelt and Hopkins,* p. 128.

22 "Our objective. . . .": Thomas F. Troy, *Wild Bill and Intrepid,* p. 63.

22 "We should be quite ready. . . .": Leutze, p. 472; Farago, p. 39.

23 Tyler Kent, as he brooded: Whalen, p. 310.

23 "secretly and unconstitutionally. . . .": Farago, pp. 338, 350.

23 "All wars are inspired. . . .": ibid., p. 338.

23 He had, he later admitted: Whalen, p. 316.

23 And so Kent began: Farago, p. 342; Whalen, p. 316.

23 Anna's mother: Polmar and Allen, *Spy Book,* p. 309.

23 Captain A.H.M. Ramsay was: Farago, p. 341.

23 Further, he was: Whalen, p. 316.

23 Ramsay had fought: Polmar and Allen, *Spy Book,* p. 309.

24 "Jew's War": Farago, p. 341; Whalen, pp. 316–17.

24 Wolkoff, of the aristocratic past: Farago, pp. 340–41.

24 ". . . a maudlin and monstrous pile. . . .": Robin W. Winks, *Cloak and Gown,* pp. 271–72.

24 There a clutch: Polmar and Allen, *Spy Book,* pp. 73–74.

24 One report demonstrated: Farago, p. 340.

25 Hitler's foreign office: ibid.

25 "It would be possible to hand over. . . .": ibid.

25 The measure was narrowly defeated: Whalen, p. 208.

25 Next he began threatening: Jeffrey M. Dorwart, *Conflict of Duty,* p. 114.

26 "He . . . says that. . . .": John Morton Blum, *Years of Urgency, 1938–1941: From the Morgenthau Diaries,* pp. 90–91.

26 "about which he is. . . .": Leutze, p. 482.

26 Henceforth, FDR said: Irwin F. Gellman, *Secret Affairs,* p. 67.

27 "People come in here. . . .": Goodwin, p. 107.

27 "When you are in the center. . . .": ibid., pp. 108–109.

27 THIS IS A JEW'S WAR: Farago, pp. 340–42.

28 ". . . I asked him. . . .": Whalen, pp. 310–11.

28 As Jimmy described a conversation: James Roosevelt, *My Parents,* pp. 208–209.

29 "I have made arrangements. . . .": David E. Koskoff, *Joseph P. Kennedy,* pp. 116–17.

29 The luck of the Irish: Whalen, pp. 209–10.

30 Learning of the ambassador's: Charles Higham, *American Swastika,* pp. 26–27.

30 "ruthless and scheming": Leutze, pp. 479–90.

30 During this Washington sojourn: *NYT,* Feb. 16, 1967.

30 "Before long he. . . .": Whalen, p. 286.

30 "[H]e would say what he Goddamned pleased. . . .": ibid.

31 In this matter, at least: ibid., p. 313,

31 Kennedy declared: Farago, p. 343.

31 "Appalling . . . it means. . . .": Tyler Kent Papers, Box 1, FDRL.

31 "entirely contrary. . . .": Whalen, pp. 314–18.

31 The British were convinced: Goodwin, p. 103.

32 "Today's threat. . . .": Thompson, p. 241.

32 Pieces of the corpse: Nathan Miller, *Spying for America,* p. 202.

32 "protect this country. . . .": Christopher Andrew, *For the President's Eyes Only,* p. 91.

32 He had appointed Woodring: Goodwin, p. 23.

33 Instead, he had had to settle: ibid., p. 71.

33 Afterward, they could watch: Day-by-Day, Dec. 10, 1939, FDRL.

33 "I don't think it is likely. . . .": Troy, *The Coordinator of Information and British Intelligence,* p. 12.

33 Henry Stimson was a product: Richard Rhodes, *The Making of the Atomic Bomb,* p. 618.

33 At seventy-three: Goodwin, p. 71; Rhodes, p. 618.

CHAPTER III: STRANGE BEDFELLOWS

34 In 1939, when the war: Norman Polmar and Thomas B. Allen, *Spy Book,* pp. 267–68.

35 "I do not wish. . . .": Curt Gentry, *J. Edgar Hoover,* p. 231.

35 "I spoke to J. Edgar Hoover. . . .": ibid.

35 The FBI, in the name: *NYT,* Sept. 15, 1991; Polmar and Allen, *Spy Book,* p. 203.

35 "working in Buffalo . . .": Gentry, p. 231.

35 "Tell Bob Jackson. . . .": ibid.

36 "I have agreed with. . . .": Athan Theoharis, ed., *From the Secret Files of J. Edgar Hoover,* p. 134.

36 Nevertheless, Hoover, who: Robert Thompson, *A Time for War,* pp. 240–41.

36 "[H]e could make. . . .": Doris Kearns Goodwin, *No Ordinary Time,* p. 78.

36 "got along very, very well. . . .": Gentry, p. 223.

36 "I was very close. . . .": ibid.

37 "Edgar, what are they trying . . . ?": ibid., p. 224.

37 "The two men liked. . . .": ibid., p. 223.

37 "the treacherous use . . .": Goodwin, p. 103.

38 "Here are some more. . . .": Gentry, p. 225.

38 "a little too suave. . . .": Wayne S. Cole, *Charles A. Lindbergh and the Battle Against American Intervention in World War II,* p. 68.

38 Lindbergh's defense: ibid., pp. 41–43.

38　"a defense hysteria. . . .": Goodwin, p. 47.

39　"When I read. . . .": Cole, pp. 128–29.

39　"Dear Edgar": Gentry, pp. 226–27.

39　"Within the last few days. . . .": Astor, PSF Box 92.

40　Vice President Henry Wallace: William Doyle, *Inside the Oval Office,* pp. 19–20.

40　A White House stenographer: ibid., pp. ix, x, 10.

41　"Ah, Lowell. . . .": ibid., pp. 19–20.

41　Willkie may have been: Theoharis, p. 201.

41　"the most formidable candidate. . . .": Goodwin, p. 142.

42　"a serious mistake": Gentry, p. 227.

42　"had no wish . . .": Goodwin, p. 125.

42　"Dear Caesar": PSF Box 72.

42　"this infernal counterespionage. . . .": Adolf Berle Papers, Box 211, FDRL.

43　This time the FBI: Theoharis, p. 200.

43　"a carefully measured appearance. . . .": Brian Loring Villa, "The Atomic Bomb and the Normandy Invasion," *Perspectives in American History* 2 (1977–78), p. 465.

43　The objective of German diplomacy: Bradley F. Smith, *The Shadow Warriors,* pp. 22–23; Robert Edwin Herzstein, *Roosevelt & Hitler,* p. 333.

43　"today relies far more. . . .": Herzstein, p. 337.

43　Boetticher had been in Washington: David Brinkley, *Washington Goes to War,* pp. 33–34.

44　Boetticher's deliberate revelation: Alfred M. Beck, "The Ambivalent Attaché: Friedrich von Boetticher in America, 1933–1941" (Ph.D. diss., Georgetown University, 1977), pp. 276–80.

45　"a careful record be had . . .": Ladislas Farago, *The Game of the Foxes,* p. 356.

45　"The Germans desire to make peace. . . .": ibid.

45　"Naturally, any information. . . .": ibid.

46　Yet, he did manage: ibid., pp. 369–71.

46　"no wish to be a candidate again. . . .": Goodwin, p. 125.

46　After Nazi storm troopers smashed: Thompson, p. 199.

47　"American mothers, wage-earners . . .": Farago, pp. 381–89.

47　Ostensibly, the ad: ibid.

47　"Willkie's nomination is unfortunate. . . .": ibid., p. 381.

47　"after lengthy negotiations. . . .": ibid., pp. 378–79; *NYT,* July 23, 1997.

47　These tracts: Farago, p. 385.

47　"[A]ny old-time politician. . . .": Goodwin, p. 186.

48　"The first number. . . .": ibid.

48　"If we're attacked. . . .": Thompson, p. 275.

48　"Now this Mitsunaga fella. . . .": Doyle, pp. 33–34.

48 "With all their technical imperfections. . . .": ibid., p. 11.

49 "The supreme law. . . .": *NYT,* July 23, 1997.

CHAPTER IV: SPYMASTER IN THE OVAL OFFICE

50 He enjoyed Roosevelt's trust: Jeffrey M. Dorwart, "The Roosevelt-Astor Espionage Ring," *New York History,* vol. 62, no. 3 (July 1981), p. 318.

50 "British intelligence in this area. . . .": PSF Box 12.

51 "his government was preparing. . . .": PSF Box 82.

51 "It seems to me. . . .": PSF Box 92.

51 He turned Astor down: Christopher Andrew, *For the President's Eyes Only,* p. 93.

51 Confidential correspondence: Curt Gentry, *J. Edgar Hoover,* p. 265.

51 "In regard to the opening. . . .": PSF Box 92.

52 "We will be making a great mistake. . . .": Andrew, p. 98.

52 "Knowing your affection. . . .": Mrs. Johnson to FDR, PSF Box 92.

52 The President told Missy LeHand: PSF Box 92.

52 "The story about the theft. . . .": Astor to FDR, PSF Box 92.

53 Could the President instruct Stark . . . ?: PSF Box 52.

53 "I simply wanted you to know. . . .": PSF Box 40; Thomas F. Troy, *The Coordinator of Information and British Intelligence,* p. 174.

53 "Astor must have a job. . . .": Troy, *The Coordinator,* p. 177.

53 His successor was: Andrew, p. 93.

54 He settled in Britain: Norman Polmar and Thomas B. Allen, *Spy Book,* pp. 535–36.

54 His mission was to protect: Bradley F. Smith, *The Shadow Warriors,* p. 22.

54 "very tough, very rich. . . .": *Toronto Globe and Mail,* Jan. 16, 1999.

54 "broken-down boarding house": Andrew, p. 94.

54 The truth is rather: Nigel West, *A Thread of Deceit,* p. 131.

55 Late in 1940: Dorwart, *Conflict of Duty,* p. 123.

55 During the years of peace: Phillip Knightley, *The Second Oldest Profession,* p. 212.

55 In this position: Troy, *Wild Bill and Intrepid,* pp. 102–103; Dorwart, *Conflict of Duty,* p. 123.

55 "As Area Controller. . . .": PPF Box 40.

55 His authority had been: Troy, *Donovan and the CIA,* p. 49.

55 "number one man": PSF Box 92.

55 "Dear Mr. President, One might suppose. . . .": ibid.

56 "I have reported. . . .": ibid.

56 "You're going to be elected. . . .": John Franklin Carter Oral History, p. 2, FDRL.

57 "brilliant, cynical, occasionally cockeyed. . . .": Ernest B. Furgurson, "Back Channels," *Washingtonian,* vol. 31 (June 1996).

57 "pretty well loused up. . . .": Carter Oral History, p. 8.

57 The President was aware: Nathan Miller, *Spying for America,* p. 236.

57 "Techniques for gathering information. . . .": ibid.

57 Its members worked: Furgurson.

58 And FDR grasped: Dorwart, *Conflict of Duty,* p. 168.

58 "The overall condition was attached. . . .": The Year of Crisis, John Franklin Carter Papers, April 14, 1945.

58 State was then to finance: Adolf Berle Papers, Box 57, FDRL.

58 "Jay Franklin (J.F. Carter) came in. . . .": ibid.

58 Besides collecting intelligence: PSF Box 97.

58 It would no doubt: ibid.

58 Carter's operatives: Berle Papers, Box 57.

59 Thus he wore: Robert Thompson, *A Time for War,* p. 202.

59 "If you will stop shipping. . . .": John Morton Blum, *Years of Urgency, 1938–1941: From the Morgenthau Diaries,* pp. 349–50.

59 "breath . . . taken away. . . .": ibid.

59 "[T]his thing might give us. . . .": ibid., p. 350.

60 "By all means, they are great guys.": ibid.

60 ". . . [H]e [FDR] has mentioned it. . . .": ibid., p. 366.

60 "burn out the industrial heart. . . .": Thompson, p. 287.

60 "Well, his asking for 500 planes. . . .": ibid.

60 "Is he still willing to fight?": Blum, *Years of Urgency,* p. 367.

61 "This would give us a chance. . . .": ibid., p. 366.

61 "The four of you. . . .": ibid., p. 367.

61 "As war administrator. . . .": William Doyle, *Inside the Oval Office,* p. 9; James MacGregor Burns, *Roosevelt: The Lion and the Fox,* pp. 83–84.

61 The U.S. Army Air Corps: Thompson, p. 289.

61 "to try to get. . . .": Blum, *Years of Urgency,* p. 368.

62 FDR unhesitatingly approved: Sykes Main Page, "The Flying Tigers," pp. 1–3 (Internet).

62 Magruder came back: Roger J. Sandilands, *The Life and Political Economy of Lauchlin Currie,* pp. 114–15.

CHAPTER V: THE DEFEATIST AND THE DEFIANT

63 When that effort failed: Robert Thompson, *A Time for War,* p. 264.

63 "[F]rankly, if your proposal. . . .": Thomas F. Troy, *Wild Bill and Intrepid,* p. 25.

64 "fiendish memory": Frank Friedl interview with Admiral William Leahy, May 24, 1948, FDRL.

64 His rejection: Nathan Miller, *Spying for America,* p. 240.

64 "I fear that to put. . . .": Troy, *Wild Bill,* p. 25.

64 "That you took the time. . . .": PPF Box 6558.

64 He named another Republican: Troy, *The Coordinator of Information and British Intelligence,* p. 16.

64 On July 9: Troy, *Wild Bill,* pp. 46–47.

64 Over a quarter-million: H. Montgomery Hyde, *Room 3603,* p. 72.

64 But on a single day: Bradley F. Smith, *The Shadow Warriors,* p. 21.

65 There was no point: ibid., p. 33.

65 "a wave of pessimism. . . .": Christopher Andrew, *For the President's Eyes Only,* p. 95.

65 "We would appreciate. . . .": Troy, *The Coordinator,* p. 57.

65 "the height of nonsense": Smith, *The Shadow Warriors,* p. 34.

65 "We are already making. . . .": Troy, *Wild Bill,* p. 49.

65 "Please take this up. . . .": Troy, *The Coordinator,* p. 58; Troy, *Wild Bill,* p. 49.

66 Donovan was a man: Smith, *The Shadow Warriors,* p. 34.

66 "Stay where you are. . . .": Troy, *The Coordinator,* p. 43.

66 When he learned: Anthony Cave Brown, *The Last Hero,* p. 148; Troy, *Wild Bill,* p. 41.

66 On the morning of July 15: Troy, *The Coordinator,* p. 155.

66 On reaching London: Thompson, p. 262.

66 "FRENCH SIGN PEACE TREATY. . . .": Smith, *The Shadow Warriors,* p. 14.

66 The American-born Lady Astor: Troy, *The Coordinator,* p. 64.

66 "There is at the present moment. . . .": ibid., p. 65.

67 "I am happy to tell you that Winston. . . .": ibid., p. 67.

67 Donovan's most prophetic: ibid., p. 68.

67 "hard as granite. . . .": Phillip Knightley, *The Second Oldest Profession,* p. 112.

67 Menzies had been alerted: F. W. Winterbotham, *The Ultra Secret,* p. 30.

67 That he received more than a cursory: Thompson, p. 263; Brown, *The Last Hero,* p. 150.

68 The Royal Air Force: Troy, *The Coordinator,* p. 72.

68 "was to discover. . . .": Thompson, p. 263.

68 "so he can tell me. . . .": Troy, *Wild Bill,* p. 57.

68 He painted a picture: ibid.

68 Donovan continued to tell the President: Brown, *The Last Hero,* p. 150.

68 He had a recommendation: Thompson, p. 263; Andrew, p. 95.

68 Through their own sources: Hyde, p. 40.

69 "President has sanctioned. . . .": ibid.

69 Churchill had begged: Brown, *The Last Hero,* p. 150.

69 Donovan began lobbying: Smith, *The Shadow Warriors,* pp. 37–38; Doris Kearns Goodwin, *No Ordinary Time,* p. 142.

69 "He couldn't keep his mouth shut. . . .": Irwin F. Gellman, *Secret Affairs,* pp. 102, 172.

69 Two years and nine months: Richard J. Whalen, *The Founding Father,* pp. 327–32.

69 "I wouldn't say no. . . .": Troy, *The Coordinator,* p. 85.

70 "I intend to go. . . .": ibid.

70 There the President cheerily: Fulton Oursler Jr., "Secret Treason," *American Heritage,* December 1991, p. 61.

70 Murray, the Outlaw: Grace Tully, *F.D.R., My Boss,* p. 128; Suckley, Binder 4, p. RB11.

70 Oursler had scored: Oursler, pp. 55–58.

71 The high point: Philip Ziegler, *King Edward VIII: The Official Biography,* pp. 391–92.

71 His presence in England: Michael Bloch, *Operation Willi: The Plot to Kidnap the Duke of Windsor,* p. 4.

71 "The position of the Duke. . . .": Warren F. Kimball, *Churchill & Roosevelt: The Complete Correspondence,* pp. 52, 53.

71 "out of Hitler's grasp": Bloch, p. 4.

72 Prior to leaving: Paul R. Sweet, "The Windsor File," *Historian,* Winter 1997, pp. 263–80.

72 Churchill, his patience stretched: Bloch, p. 4.

72 He once confided: James MacGregor Burns, *Roosevelt: The Soldier of Freedom,* p. 603.

72 He considered it: Goodwin, pp. 73, 191, 192.

72 "Windsor is completely insignificant looking. . . .": Suckley, Binder 8, p. 166.

72 "Mr. President," Oursler said: Oursler, p. 61.

73 "[I]t would be a tragic thing. . . .": ibid., p. 58.

73 "Do you suppose that . . . ?": ibid.

73 "Would you enter into . . . ?": ibid., p. 60.

74 "Fulton," he said: ibid., p. 61.

74 "He could barely listen. . . .": ibid., p. 62.

74 "Why don't you just be . . . ?": ibid.

75 "You know your father was. . . .": ibid.

75 "Everyday from the offices. . . .": ibid.

75 "Now I have nothing to prove. . . .": ibid., p. 64.

75 "You cannot kill eighty million. . . .": Ziegler, p. 460.

76 Nearly a year later: Tully, p. 325; Day-by-Day, Oct. 28, 1941.

76 "Britain has virtually lost the war. . . .": Sweet, p. 280.

CHAPTER VI: "THERE IS NO U.S. SECRET INTELLIGENCE SERVICE"

77 "asked me if I would go. . . .": Thomas F. Troy, *The Coordinator of Information and British Intelligence,* p. 119.

77 Supporting this explanation: ibid., p. 127.

78 In pursuit of his assignment: Bradley F. Smith, *The Shadow Warriors,* p. 41.

78 "[Colonel Stewart Menzies] tells me that Mr. Stephenson. . . .": Anthony Cave Brown, *The Last Hero,* p. 152.

78 On the night before: ibid.

78 "taken fully into our confidence": Christopher Andrew, *For the President's Eyes Only,* p. 96.

78 "great influence with the President": Brown, *The Last Hero,* p. 153.

78 As he settled in: Andrew, p. 97; Brown, *The Last Hero,* p. 155.

79 "It was Donovan who was. . . .": Troy, *The Coordinator,* p. 127.

79 "I must thank you. . . .": Brown, *The Last Hero,* p. 155.

79 Hopkins, the onetime social worker: Robert E. Sherwood, *Roosevelt and Hopkins,* p. 203.

79 Still, Donovan managed to report: Troy, *The Coordinator,* p. 183.

80 "Disputes were settled. . . .": Andrew, p. 97.

80 FDR had confused the code names: ibid.

80 "the toughest division. . . .": Brown, *The Last Hero,* p. 160.

80 "the British government gathers. . . .": Troy, *The Coordinator,* p. 191.

80 "some one appointed by the President. . . .": Brown, *The Last Hero,* p. 161.

80 "take over the home duties . . .": ibid.

80 "sole charge of intelligence. . . .": ibid.

80 During the cabinet meeting: Troy, *Wild Bill and Intrepid,* p. 115.

80 Miles's riposte was swift: Brown, *The Last Hero,* p. 159.

80 "In great confidence. . . .": Andrew, p. 97.

81 Along with Little Bill Stephenson: Brown, *The Last Hero,* p. 163.

81 In late May: Troy, *The Coordinator,* p. 215.

81 "Even the more senior U.S. Navy. . . .": Andrew, pp. 98–99.

81 "These three departments. . . .": ibid., p. 99.

81 "There is no U.S. Secret Intelligence Service. . . .": ibid.

82 Godrey agreed with those Americans.: Brown, *The Last Hero,* p. 160.

82 "On this tenth day. . . .": Doris Kearns Goodwin, *No Ordinary Time,* p. 68.

82 "I wondered about the Italian vote. . . .": ibid.

82 "With this speech. . . .": ibid., p. 69.

82 Its productive capacity: ibid., p. 23.

83 "Dear Mr. President (Cousin Franklin). . . .": PSF Box 38.

83 "The moment approaches. . . .": Goodwin, pp. 192–93.

83 "I began to get the idea. . . .": ibid., p. 193.

84 "could not keep. . . .": Smith, *The Shadow Warriors,* p. 58.

84 "a very long day at the White House": Henry L. Stimson and McGeorge Bundy, *On Active Service in Peace and War,* p. 368.

84 Roosevelt feared that: ibid., p. 369; Irwin F. Gellman, *Secret Affairs,* p. 253.

84 "He is trying to see. . . .": Stimson and Bundy, p. 369.

84 Soon after the meeting: Gellman, p. 251.

84 "When we were squidging. . . .": Small Collections, Lunny/Leahy, FDRL.

85 "principally a defensive measure": Stimson and Bundy, p. 368.

85 "But you are not going. . . .": ibid., p. 369.

85 "He seems to be trying. . . .": ibid.

85 "Now this is a patrol. . . .": Gellman, p. 254.

85 Indeed, when a month after: ibid., p. 255.

85 "Should he order . . . ?": Brown, *The Last Hero,* p. 162.

86 The Roosevelt voice: Sherwood, pp. 297–98; Eric Larrabee, *Commander in Chief,* p. 56.

86 "[W]hat started as a European war. . . .": Larrabee, pp. 56–57.

86 "seven hours distance. . . .": ibid., p. 56.

86 The President shared: David Stafford, *Churchill and Secret Service,* p. 228.

86 "The blunt truth is this. . . .": Samuel I. Rosenman, *Working with Roosevelt,* p. 285.

86 "Our patrols are helping. . . .": Sherwood, p. 298.

87 That stage was over.: ibid., p. 296.

87 "an unlimited national emergency. . . .": Brown, *The Last Hero,* p. 162.

87 "The President was able. . . .": Rosenman, p. 355.

87 "They're ninety-five per cent. . . .": Sherwood, p. 298.

87 To the admiral, whose association: Gellman, p. 255.

87 Nevertheless, FDR continued: Brown, *The Last Hero,* p. 162.

87 Thereafter, the admiral was invited: ibid., p. 163.

87 "Memorandum of Establishment . . .": Andrew, p. 99; Troy, *The Coordinator,* p. 215.

88 "Strategy, without information. . . .": William J. Donovan to President Franklin D. Roosevelt, "Memorandum of Establishment of Service of Strategic Information," June 10, 1941, pp. 1–6, FDRL.

88 "[T]here is another element. . . .": ibid., p. 5.

88 Donovan was later to claim: Smith, *The Shadow Warriors,* p. 66; Troy, *Wild Bill,* p. 122.

88 "I am getting to be. . . .": Troy, *Wild Bill,* p. 123.

88 In 1932, Donovan had been: Curt Gentry, *J. Edgar Hoover,* p. 266.

88 "would almost certainly pull my leg. . . .": Andrew, p. 99.

89 "Oh yes, those West Indies. . . .": ibid.

89 "mustered up the semblance of a laugh": ibid.

89 "Hall had a wonderful intelligence service. . . .": ibid., p. 100.

89 "one intelligence security boss. . . .": ibid.

89 "This would be a full time job. . . .": Troy, *The Coordinator,* p. 209.

89 "I want to have him give. . . .": ibid., p. 217.

90 After leaving the White House: ibid., p. 220.

90 "JBJr. Please set this up. . . .": Troy, *Wild Bill,* p. 130.

90 They compromised finally: POF Box 4485.

90 However, they said, he could use: Troy, *The Coordinator,* p. 221.

90　"undertake activities helpful. . . .": POF Box 4485.

91　"It is sufficient to say. . . .": Troy, *The Coordinator,* p. 219.

91　Donovan, unconvincingly, wanted: Troy, *Wild Bill,* p. 121.

91　"assembling and correlating. . . .": POF Box 4485.

91　Guesses by journalists: Brown, *The Last Hero,* pp. 165–66.

91　"power to visualize. . . .": Nathan Miller, *Spying for America,* p. 243.

91　The two men differed: Smith, *The Shadow Warriors,* p. 32.

91　"Donovan saw President today. . . .": Troy, *The Coordinator,* p. 220.

91　"[A] most secret fact. . . .": Andrew, p. 101; Troy, *Wild Bill,* p. 133; Brown, p. 166.

92　He had been born to first-generation: Corey Ford, *Donovan of OSS,* pp. 13–14.

92　"He had read the inscription. . . .": Brown, *The Last Hero,* p. 19.

92　At the end of his third year: Ford, pp. 18–19.

92　He did not cut much: Brown, *The Last Hero,* p. 21.

92　"The Awakening of Japan": Ford, p. 19; Brown, *The Last Hero,* pp. 19–20.

92　Franklin Roosevelt had indeed: Ford, p. 20.

92　The unit, christened: Brown, *The Last Hero,* p. 26.

92　He was a leader: Ford, p. 23; Brown, *The Last Hero,* pp. 28–29.

93　Less than a month later: Ford, p. 23; Brown, *The Last Hero,* pp. 37–78.

93　The 69th Regiment: Brown, *The Last Hero,* p. 52.

93　He was awarded: ibid., pp. 54–56.

93　"Wild Bill is. . . .": ibid., p. 56.

93　"Look at me. . . .": Ford, pp. 11–12.

93　On October 19: Brown, *The Last Hero,* p. 62.

93　"They can't get me. . . .": ibid., p. 63.

93　Wild Bill was awarded: ibid., pp. 63–70.

93　After the war Donovan: ibid., p. 70; Gentry, p. 134.

93　He was first drawn: Gentry, p. 134; Robin W. Winks, *Cloak and Gown,* p. 65.

93　"a common mick": Brown, *The Last Hero,* p. 86.

94　"The law is the law. . . .": ibid.

94　In 1924, Donovan was promoted: Miller, p. 240.

94　Donovan was pulled under: Brown, *The Last Hero,* p. 121.

94　Thus far, in their marriage: ibid., p. 78.

94　"He was soft-spoken. . . .": Joseph E. Persico, *Piercing the Reich,* p. 6.

94　"The spy is as old as history. . . .": Phillip Knightley, *The Second Oldest Profession,* p. 3.

95　"One good spy is worth. . . .": ibid.

95　"dos'd themselves. . . .": Andrew, p. 6.

95　"immediate and pressing Duties.": ibid., p. 7.

95　"to establish a secret correspondence. . . .": ibid.

95　President Abraham Lincoln: Knightley, p. 3.

95 The Confederates employed women: Norman Polmar and Thomas B. Allen, *Spy Book*, p. 566.

95 Sir Francis developed an organization: ibid., p. 589.

95 England's lead in entering: Knightley, pp. 3–4.

96 America's Office of Naval Intelligence: Polmar and Allen, *Spy Book*, p. 30.

96 "Gentlemen do not read. . . .": ibid., pp. 606–607.

96 By the 1930s: Andrew, p. 92.

96 "a real undercover. . . .": ibid.

96 "I could never really understand. . . .": Sherwood, p. 882.

96 Secretary of State Hull might not: Jim Bishop, *FDR's Last Year,* p. 90.

96 "You are one of the most difficult. . . .": Robert Dallek, *Franklin D. Roosevelt and American Foreign Policy, 1932–1945,* p. vii.

97 "cryptic giant": John Gunther, *Roosevelt in Retrospect,* p. 146.

97 "Later, as the psychologists. . . .": ibid.

97 "[H]e simply liked mystery. . . .": ibid., p. 50.

97 "Roosevelt had the courage of a lion. . . .": ibid.

97 "[A]lthough crippled physically. . . .": Sherwood, p. 882.

97 The President ate heartily: Goodwin, pp. 202–203.

CHAPTER VII: SPIES VERSUS CIPHERS

98 "seems to those of us. . . .": William L. Shirer, *The Rise and Fall of the Third Reich,* p. 843.

98 They had worked out a system: ibid.

98 In early August 1940: James MacGregor Burns, *Roosevelt: The Soldier of Freedom,* pp. 71–72.

99 "grasp of world politics. . . .": Shirer, p. 843.

99 Then his informant gave him: F. H. Hinsley, *British Intelligence in the Second World War,* vol. 1, p. 444.

99 They were, the bureau reported back: Shirer, p. 843.

99 FDR chose to be direct: ibid., p. 842.

99 "Mr. Ourmansky turned. . . .": ibid., p. 843.

100 He called Hans Thomsen: David Brinkley, *Washington Goes to War,* p. 38.

100 On April 3, Churchill asked Cripps: Shirer, p. 843; Phillip Knightley, *The Second Oldest Profession,* p. 195.

100 On May 15, Sorge cabled: Lyman B. Kirkpatrick Jr., *Captains Without Eyes,* p. 62.

100 The Soviets' best source in Switzerland: ibid., p. 61.

100 "who has a record. . . .": PSF, May 16, 1941, Carter to FDR.

100 "The Germans are reported confident. . . .": ibid.; Bradley F. Smith, *Sharing Secrets with Stalin,* p. 14.

100 "any statement Churchill might make. . . .": Joseph P. Lash, *Roosevelt and Churchill,* p. 356.

101 "Not at all. I have only. . . .": ibid., p. 357; Martin Gilbert, *Winston S. Churchill,* vol. 6, p. 1119.

101 "Nazi Germany as the dominant power. . . .": Burns, *Roosevelt: The Soldier of Freedom,* p. 95.

101 Therefore, Russia had to try: ibid.

101 Within three hours Stalin: Kirkpatrick, p. 66.

101 For several days: Dmitri Volkogonov, *Stalin,* p. 409.

102 Magic meant, once again: Christopher Andrew, *For the President's Eyes Only,* p. 105.

102 But who should deliver: Roberta Wohlstetter, *Pearl Harbor,* p. 176.

103 Intelligence that could determine: Andrew, p. 108.

103 The inanity increased in July 1941: Gordon Prange, *At Dawn We Slept,* p. 119.

103 He determined who got to see FDR.: Robert E. Sherwood, *Roosevelt and Hopkins,* p. 207.

103 When Colonel Bratton informed: Andrew, p. 109; Prange, p. 119.

103 Fearing to contradict: Andrew, p. 109.

104 "[F]ather summoned me. . . .": James Roosevelt, *My Parents,* p. 258.

104 "This must be completely confidential. . . .": ibid.

104 "would do everything he could . . .": ibid.

104 "Hang on until we get in": ibid.

104 "If you speak publicly of it. . . .": ibid.

105 "First, I told him. . . .": Andrew, pp. 104, 107, 108.

105 "the product of a mind. . . .": ibid., p. 108.

105 The Japanese had reason to believe: Ladislas Farago, *The Game of the Foxes,* p. 473.

105 "As communicated to me. . . .": ibid., pp. 473–74.

105 "I have discovered that the United States. . . .": Andrew, p. 109.

106 They continued to send: Farago, p. 474.

106 And because the Japanese: Doris Kearns Goodwin, *No Ordinary Time,* p. 265.

106 "There is more reason. . . .": Andrew, p. 110.

106 After hurried consultations: ibid., p. 111.

106 The Prime Minister grabbed: F. W. Winterbotham, *The Ultra Secret,* p. 46; Jeffrey M. Dorwart, *Conflict of Duty,* p. 16.

107 The Germans calculated: Norman Polmar and Thomas B. Allen, *Spy Book,* pp. 192–93; David Kahn, *Seizing the Enigma,* p. 68.

107 The British quickly took the lead: Winterbotham, p. 31.

107 Among Turing's associates were: Polmar and Allen, *Spy Book,* p. 74.

107 Ultra was the designation: Winterbotham, p. 46.

108 Eventually, over a thousand: Polmar and Allen, *Spy Book,* p. 80.

108 So paramount was secrecy: ibid., p. 74.

108   Churchill demanded to see: Winterbotham, p. 189.

108   What doomed Coventry was: Nigel West, *A Thread of Deceit,* pp. 10–17; David Stafford, *Churchill and Secret Service,* pp. 194, 195; Christopher Andrew and David Dilks, *The Missing Dimension,* p. 149.

109   In exchange, their Bletchley counterparts: Andrew, p. 107.

109   "were not as security minded. . . .": John Costello, *Days of Infamy,* p. 305.

109   "divulging to the President. . . .": ibid.

109   "devise any safe means. . . .": ibid.

109   Britain's eavesdropping on a friend: Andrew, p. 107.

CHAPTER VIII: DONOVAN ENTERS THE GAME

110   "collect and analyze all information and data": Norman Polmar and Thomas B. Allen, *Spy Book,* p. 135.

110   "to carry out when requested. . . .": ibid., p. 135*n*189.

111   Ignoring civil service. . . .: Ray S. Cline, *Secrets, Spies and Scholars,* p. 42.

111   Conyers Read: Stanley Lovell, *Of Spies and Stratagems,* p. 183.

111   "It is a curious fact. . . .": Cline, p. 41.

111   Gregg Toland: Ephraim Katz, *The Film Encyclopedia,* 3d ed., 1998, pp. 435–36.

111   "All who knew him and worked. . . .": Curt Gentry, *J. Edgar Hoover,* p. 135.

111   After only three weeks: Thomas F. Troy, *Donovan and the CIA,* p. 110.

111   The bureau initially earmarked: Nathan Miller, *Spying for America,* p. 243.

111   payroll of ninety-two employees: Polmar and Allen, *Spy Book,* p. 135.

111   Within months the staff: Anthony Cave Brown, *The Last Hero,* p. 174.

112   Most of his funds were: ibid.

112   His staff first occupied: Cline, p. 42.

112   It was equipped with air conditioning: ibid., p. 57.

112   "closely resembled a cat house. . . .": Brown, *The Last Hero,* p. 174.

112   As *Life* magazine put it: Troy, *Donovan and the CIA,* p. 94.

113   He pressured the Bureau of the Budget: Brown, *The Last Hero,* pp. 175–77.

113   He was further preparing to conduct: PSF Box 128; Bradley F. Smith, *The Shadow Warriors,* p. 93.

113   "This seems to be a matter. . . .": M 1642, Reel 22, Frame 425.

114   "making the American people ripe. . . .": PSF Box 128.

114   ". . . [S]ince the appearances of articles in. . . .": ibid.

114   "Roosevelt has named the Colonel. . . .": Brown, *The Last Hero,* p. 166.

114   "Mr. Donovan is now head of the Gestapo. . . .": ibid., p. 791.

114   When he took his complaints: Gentry, p. 135.

114   "I stopped him from becoming AG. . . .": ibid., p. 148.

115   A full year before: Leslie B. Rout Jr. and John F. Bratzel, *The Shadow War,* p. 37.

115   Well before Donovan signed up: Gentry, p. 264.

115 Running this worldwide network: ibid.

115 "[H]e goes to the White House. . . .": Brown, *The Last Hero,* p. 159.

115 "more of a spoiled child. . . .": ibid.

115 The FBI still controlled: Phillip Knightley, *The Second Oldest Profession,* pp. 32–35.

115 The penetration was so complete: Robert Louis Benson and Michael Warner, eds., *VENONA,* pp. 15–16.

115 These triumphs, which Hoover described: Charles Wighton and Gunter Peis, *Hitler's Spy and Saboteurs,* p. 17.

116 "[A] thing like that ought not be given. . . .": Athan Theoharis, ed., *From the Secret Files of J. Edgar Hoover,* p. 333.

116 "Anything that I said. . . .": ibid., pp. 331–34.

117 Astor's conversations with the director: ibid., p. 330.

117 "most dangerous file clerk": *NYT,* Sept. 15, 1991.

117 "Roosevelt's folly": Miller, p. 244.

117 "There was no indication. . . .": Adolf Berle Papers, Box 213, FDRL.

117 "into the entire motion picture industry. . . .": ibid.

118 "what you ought to do. . . .": Troy, *Donovan and the CIA,* p. 163.

118 "It appears that some question. . . .": POF Box 4485.

118 "Wild Bill's face got red . . .": Ernest B. Furgurson, "Back Channels," *Washingtonian,* vol. 31 (June 1996).

CHAPTER IX: "OUR OBJECTIVE IS TO GET AMERICA INTO THE WAR"

119 "The heat in Washington. . . .": Doris Kearns Goodwin, *No Ordinary Time,* p. 262.

119 Washington mythology had it: David Brinkley, *Washington Goes to War,* p. 23.

119 "There was nothing. . . .": Goodwin, p. 262.

119 "told me that he was going. . . .": ibid.

120 Getting a man confined to a wheelchair: Gordon Prange, *December 7, 1941,* p. 16.

120 "As Mr. Roosevelt made his first turn. . . .": Eric Larrabee, *Commander in Chief,* p. 32.

120 Steaming toward the *Augusta:* Goodwin, p. 264.

120 "To some of my very pointed questions. . . .": Irwin F. Gellman, *Secret Affairs,* p. 257.

121 "reasonably longer distances. . . .": PSF Box 59.

121 Elliott, the first Roosevelt son: *Current Biography* 1946 (New York: Wilson 1947), p. 516.

121 His metal leg braces: William Doyle, *Inside the Oval Office,* p. 7.

121 As Churchill strode up the gangway: Suckley, Binder 20, p. 61.

121 Starling's impersonation was the first time: John Gunther, *Roosevelt in Retrospect*, p. 45; Grace Tully, *F.D.R., My Boss*, p. 247.

121 "We have all been laughing. . . .": Suckley, Binder 20, p. 57c.

122 "magnificent presence in all his youth. . . .": Warren F. Kimball, *The Juggler: Franklin Roosevelt as Wartime Statesman*, p. 355.

122 He subsequently held: Goodwin, p. 33.

122 He took to soldiering: John Charmley, *Churchill*, p. 141.

122 "I am so devoured by egoism": ibid.

122 "I don't like standing near the edge. . . .": Lord Moran, *Churchill: Taken from the Diaries of Lord Moran*, p. 179.

122 She was genteel, prudish: Suckley Papers, Wilderstein.

122 "He is a tremendously vital person. . . .": Suckley, Binder 20, p. 61.

122 ". . . [A]ll that was romantic in [Churchill]. . . .": David Stafford, *Churchill and Secret Service*, p. 6.

123 "free exchange of intelligence": ibid., p. 200.

123 "Are we going to throw all our secrets . . . ?": ibid.

123 "I simply have not got enough Navy. . . .": Goodwin, p. 265.

123 "the wrong war. . . .": ibid.

123 Their first objective: Gellman, p. 258.

123 Roosevelt and Churchill had agreed: Frank Freidel, *Franklin D. Roosevelt*, p. 387.

123 These goals were to follow: Goodwin, p. 266.

123 Britain's sea losses: David Grubin Productions, "FDR," *The American Experience*, PBS.

124 "Our objective is to get the Americans. . . .": Thomas F. Troy, *Wild Bill and Intrepid*, pp. 63, 229; Troy, *The Coordinator of Information and British Intelligence*, p. 88.

124 "was obviously determined to come in. . . .": Freidel, p. 387.

124 Three weeks after the Atlantic conference: Gellman, p. 257.

124 The U-boat's captain: Jeffrey M. Dorwart, *The Office of Naval Intelligence*, p. 258.

124 The *Greer* then fired several depth charges: James MacGregor Burns, *Roosevelt: The Soldier of Freedom*, p. 139.

124 Since the U-boat had remained: Gellman, p. 259.

124 When her sister was stranded in Europe: Gunther, pp. 162–63.

124 The loss of his mother: Robert Thompson, *A Time for War*, p. 353.

124 Wearing a light gray seersucker suit: Burns, p. 140.

125 "The United States destroyer *Greer*. . . .": ibid.

125 "It is clear. . . .": Gellman, p. 354.

125 He meant that American warships: Burns, *Roosevelt: The Soldier of Freedom*, p. 141.

125 ". . . [W]hen you see a rattlesnake poised. . . .": ibid.

125 "to subvert the government . . .": Christopher Andrew, *For the President's Eyes Only*, p. 102.

125 "Hitler will have to choose. . . .": Thompson, p. 355.

125 "There is no longer any difference. . . .": ibid.

125 Six weeks later, on October 27: Tully, p. 33.

126 On the dais, the President: Thompson, pp. 356–57.

126 The President seized on the incident: Nathan Miller, *Spying for America*, p. 246.

126 "We have wished to avoid shooting. . . .": Burns, *Roosevelt: The Soldier of Freedom*, p. 147.

126 "Hitler has often protested. . . .": Thompson, p. 357.

126 "a principal agent for Germany. . . .": Leslie B. Rout Jr. and John F. Bratzel, *The Shadow War*, pp. 32–33.

127 An MI6 report: ibid., pp. 26–27.

127 The American military, at that point: Miller, p. 229.

127 "has on it certain manuscript notations. . . .": Thompson, pp. 357–58.

127 Wheeler's suspicions: William Stevenson, *A Man Called Intrepid*, p. 299.

127 "Where did it originate?": ibid., p. 298.

127 The map's provenance: Thompson, p. 359; Stevenson, p. 297.

127 Sandstede, however, was not murdered: Thompson, p. 358.

127 "Air Traffic Grid of the United States . . .": ibid., pp. 358–59; Troy, *The Co-ordinator*, p. 149.

128 The letter from the Bolivian attaché: Andrew, p. 102.

128 "manufacturing documents detailing. . . .": Thompson, p. 360.

128 The answer clearly lies: Goodwin, p. 282.

128 The truth was that since June 1941: F. H. Hinsley, *British Intelligence in the Second World War*, vol. 2, p. 174.

128 Further, Hitler had not: Thompson, p. 244.

128 On November 8, after a close House tally: Goodwin, p. 283.

128 That same month a Gallup poll: Gellman, p. 252.

128 "German *and* Russian militarism. . . .": Bradley F. Smith, *The Shadow Warriors*, p. 87.

129 FDR's least recognized agent: Jeffrey M. Dorwart, *Conflict of Duty*, p. 168.

129 Within days, he delivered: Wayne S. Cole, *Charles A. Lindbergh and the Battle Against American Intervention in World War II*, p. 131.

129 Lindbergh, the President explained: ibid.

130 "about the whole problem. . . .": Dorwart, *Conflict of Duty*, pp. 168–69.

130 "Conditions both within and without. . . .": *The "Magic" Background of Pearl Harbor*, vol. 1, *February 14, 1941–May 12, 1941*, p. A-12.

130 "There are still Japanese. . . .": PSF Box 84.

131 But American-born Japanese: ibid.

131 "Your reporter . . . is horrified. . . .": ibid.

131 "[I]mmediate arrests may be required.": PSF Box 97.

131 If negotiations between America: Hinsley, vol. 2, p. 76.

131 Within the War Department: Charles Higham, *American Swastika,* p. 135.

132 Officers who thought: FBI Report, Dec. 5, 1941.

132 "Aren't you afraid of delivering . . . ?": Higham, p. 140.

132 "a right to know. . . .": ibid.

132 "Wedemeyer spent two years in Germany. . . .": FBI Report, Dec. 5, 1941.

133 "the greatest mind. . . .": Higham, *American Swastika,* p. 141.

133 FDR'S WAR PLANS!: ibid.

133 ". . . President Roosevelt calls. . . .": ibid., pp. 141–42.

133 "What would you think . . . ?": ibid., pp. 144–45.

CHAPTER X: CATASTROPHE OR CONSPIRACY

134 "Mr. President, it looks as if. . . .": William Doyle, *Inside the Oval Office,* p. 35.

134 "My God, there's another wave. . . .": ibid.

134 "His chin stuck out. . . .": ibid.

134 ". . . [W]e received indications. . . .": ibid., p. 36.

135 ". . . [T]hey were to agree to cease. . . .": ibid.

135 "equalled only by the Japanese. . . .": ibid.

135 "It looks as if out of eight. . . .": ibid., p. 37.

135 "demonstrated that ultimate capacity. . . .": ibid., p. 38.

135 Senator Tom Connally of Texas: ibid., p. 39.

135 "They will never be able. . . .": Ronald H. Spector, *Eagle Against the Sun,* p. 93.

136 ". . . If there is anyone I. . . .": Jeffrey M. Dorwart, *Conflict of Duty,* p. 172.

136 He had summoned the COI chief: Day-by-Day, Dec. 8, 1941.

136 "Colonel William Donovan, come. . . .": Thomas F. Troy, *Donovan and the CIA,* p. 116.

136 Stacks of books: Doyle, p. 26; John Gunther, *Roosevelt in Retrospect,* p. 362.

136 Gathering dust in one corner: Robert E. Sherwood, *Roosevelt and Hopkins,* pp. 203–204.

136 Removed from the President's desk: Doris Kearns Goodwin, *No Ordinary Time,* p. 289; Sherwood, p. 430.

136 "Never have I seen one. . . .": Joseph E. Persico, *Edward R. Murrow,* p. 194.

136 "We're all in the same boat now": ibid.

136 "They caught our ships like lame ducks! . . .": Anthony Cave Brown, *The Last Hero,* p. 6.

137 Nearly 350 planes had been destroyed: Eric Larrabee, *Commander in Chief,* pp. 168–69.

137 "They caught our planes . . . !": Persico, *Edward R. Murrow,* p. 194.

137 "It's a good thing. . . .": Troy, *Donovan and the CIA,* p. 116.
137 "A member of my Embassy. . . .": *The "Magic" Background of Pearl Harbor,* vol. 1, *February 14, 1941–May 12, 1941,* p. 5.
137 "Indications seem to be. . . .": ibid.
138 "that adoption and application. . . .": Larrabee, p. 84.
138 But FDR had stuck to: ibid., p. 85.
138 "I fully realize the difficulty. . . .": Robert Thompson, *A Time for War,* pp. 372–73.
138 "It is absolutely necessary. . . .": *The "Magic" Background of Pearl Harbor,* vol. 1, p. 22.
138 Behind this message: James MacGregor Burns, *Roosevelt: The Soldier of Freedom,* p. 155; Roberta Wohlstetter, *Pearl Harbor,* p. 349.
138 Popov came from a wealthy family: John F. Bratzel and Leslie B. Rout Jr., "Pearl Harbor, Microdots, and J. Edgar Hoover," *The American Historical Review,* vol. 7, no. 5 (December 1982), p. 1343.
139 Abwehr officials were so pleased: ibid., pp. 1343–44.
139 It was then that Sam Foxworth: Curt Gentry, *J. Edgar Hoover,* p. 270.
139 The Japanese wanted to learn: Bratzel and Rout, p. 1345; Gentry, p. 269.
139 But his most specific instructions: Gentry, p. 269.
139 Popov was to travel to Hawaii: Bratzel and Rout, pp. 1349–50; Gentry, pp. 269–70.
139 ". . . [I]n the event of the United States. . . .": Gentry, p. 270; Phillip Knightley, *The Second Oldest Profession,* p. 149.
140 The entire questionnaire: Bratzel and Rout, p. 1343.
140 "Mr. Hoover is a very virtuous man": Gentry, p. 270.
140 He rented a penthouse: ibid.
140 Another FBI report had Popov: Bratzel and Rout, p. 1345.
140 "If I bend over to smell. . . .": John Toland, *Adolf Hitler,* p. 270.
140 And he certainly was not going to let: Knightley, p. 150.
140 "I can catch spies. . . .": Gentry, p. 270.
141 "I thought the President and you. . . .": Bratzel and Rout, p. 1346.
141 "in connection with a current investigation. . . .": ibid.
141 But, astonishingly, Hoover: ibid., p. 1348.
141 He was allowed to go to Rio: ibid., p. 1345.
141 Malcolm R. Lovell: Brown, *The Last Hero,* p. 191.
141 "If Japan goes to war. . . .": PSF Box 128.
141 On November 13, Donovan: ibid.
141 "The deadline absolutely cannot. . . .": *The "Magic" Background of Pearl Harbor,* vol. 1, p. A-89.
141 "A surprise aggressive movement. . . .": ibid., p. A-90.
142 "We were likely to be attacked. . . .": Wohlstetter, pp. 239–40.
142 "The question was how we should. . . .": ibid., p. 240.

142 Two days later, FDR obtained: Thompson, p. 382.

142 The same day the President: PSF Box 59.

142 "This dispatch is to be considered. . . .": The "Magic" Background of Pearl Harbor, vol. 1, p. A-117.

142 "Well, you two ambassadors. . . .": Warren F. Kimball, Churchill & Roosevelt, p. 166; The "Magic" Background of Pearl Harbor, p. A-118.

142 "However, I do not wish. . . .": ibid.

142 ". . . [W]e certainly do not want. . . .": Kimball, p. 166.

143 The President should return to Washington: Burns, Roosevelt: The Soldier of Freedom, p. 158.

143 A Japanese task force: Christopher Andrew, For the President's Eyes Only, p. 113; Burns, Roosevelt: The Soldier of Freedom, p. 159.

143 ". . . Say very secretly to [the Germans]. . . .": Andrew, p. 114.

143 "With regard to warships and aircraft. . . .": Wohlstetter, p. 212.

143 He had arrived in Honolulu: Norman Polmar and Thomas B. Allen, Spy Book, p. 297.

143 Yoshikawa's assignment was to provide: Louis Allen, "Japanese Intelligence Systems," Journal of Contemporary History, vol. 22 (June 1975), p. 551.

144 All the while, this apparently: ibid.

144 "one of the best brains . . .": Polmar and Allen, Spy Book, p. 595.

144 "the bomb-plot message": Wohlstetter, pp. 211, 213, 390.

144 The decrypt was not even forwarded: ibid., p. 390.

144 Yet, this particular decrypt: ibid.

144 Tokyo was demanding: ibid., p. 213.

144 "In case of emergency. . . .": The "Magic" Background of Pearl Harbor, vol. 1, p. A-81.

144 "When this is heard. . . .": ibid.

144 "[T]o prevent the United States. . . .": ibid., p. A-1200.

145 ". . . [T]he presence in port of warships. . . .": Brown, The Last Hero, p. 199.

145 While with hindsight the purpose: Wohlstetter, p. 214.

145 The President's demeanor: Andrew, p. 113.

145 The communication was strong evidence: Wohlstetter, p. 218.

145 His figures were off: Brown, The Last Hero, p. 199.

145 He could further report: Allen, p. 551.

145 "to restore traditional amity. . . .": Grace Tully, F.D.R., My Boss, p. 253.

146 An embarrassed SIS officer: Andrew, p. 116.

146 "This means war": ibid., pp. 116–17.

146 "we could not strike the first blow. . . .": Wohlstetter, p. 273.

146 "No," the President said: Burns, Roosevelt: The Soldier of Freedom, p. 161; Andrew, p. 117.

146 "The only geographical name. . . .": Andrew, p. 117.

147 "an aggressive move by Japan. . . .": *The "Magic" Background of Pearl Harbor,* vol. 1, p. A-117.

147 "a defense against sabotage. . . .": Gordon Prange, *At Dawn We Slept,* p. 403.

147 Short chose number 1: Richard Gid Powers, *Secrecy and Power,* p. 245.

147 "hostile action possible at any moment": *The "Magic" Background of Pearl Harbor,* vol. 1, p. A-119.

147 "should be carried out. . . .": ibid.

147 For the previous two years: Richard Gid Powers, p. 246.

147 Still, the November 27 message: Polmar and Allen, *Spy Book,* p. 425.

147 To Bratton, this timing signaled: Spector, p. 95.

147 The Army Chief of Staff: ibid.

148 The message went first: Goodwin, p. 288.

148 The church bells announcing: Larrabee, p. 168; Spector, p. 95.

148 "[O]ur deceptive diplomacy is. . . .": *NYT,* Dec. 9, 1999.

148 "No matter how long. . . .": 77th Congress, Document No. 453.

148 ". . . there has now been revealed. . . .": Charles Higham, *American Swastika,* p. 135.

149 Thus, soon after Pearl Harbor: Ladislas Farago, *The Game of the Foxes,* pp. 346–47.

149 "The most serious Cabinet session. . . .": ibid., p. 346.

149 The spy was further able: ibid., pp. 345–47.

149 The blame for Pearl Harbor: Gentry, p. 296.

150 The truth, however, is: Spector, p. 2.

150 "After that things are. . . .": *The "Magic" Background of Pearl Harbor,* vol. 1, p. A-89.

150 "the worst-informed ambassador. . . .": Richard M. Ketchum, *The Borrowed Years, 1938–1941,* p. 767.

150 Admiral Stark's "Memorandum": PSF Box 59.

150 "Many transports sighted. . . .": *The "Magic" Background of Pearl Harbor,* vol. 1, p. A-117.

151 When, on December 2, Roosevelt: Andrew, p. 113.

151 This signal, however, meant: Wohlstetter, p. 219.

151 Yet, Hoover's visceral dislike: Gentry, pp. 269–73; Bratzel and Rout, Document D.

151 In effect, the President: Lyman B. Kirkpatrick Jr., *Captains Without Eyes,* p. 89.

152 "[T]here was *nobody* in either. . . .": Brown, *The Last Hero,* p. 200.

152 "We were likely to be attacked. . . .": Wohlstetter, p. 239.

152 ". . . the strongest fortress in the world. . . .": Spector, p. 2.

153 A major source supposedly: Commander I. G. Newman (ret.) Oral History Interview with Robert D. Ogg, p. 53, FDRL.

153 Ogg, it turns out: ibid., p. ii.

153 Newman asked Ogg if his superior: ibid., p. 50.

153 "My comment on that. . . .": ibid.

153 "It could possibly be. . . .": ibid., p. 53.

153 "I never made such mention. . . .": ibid.

153 ". . . [D]uring those four or five days. . . .": ibid., p. 58.

153 "kept an absolute radio silence": ibid., p. 62.

153 "[R]adio silence *was* imposed. . . .": ibid.

154 "Admiral Nagumo. . . .": Spector, p. 99.

154 "Churchill was aware. . . .": John Costello, *Days of Infamy,* p. 324.

154 "Churchill deliberately kept. . . .": ibid.

154 He allowed Roosevelt: David Stafford, *Churchill and Secret Service,* p. 233.

154 Winant had spent three days: PSF Box 128.

154 "the United States enter the war. . . .": M 1642, Reel 123, Frame 511.

155 What the Prime Minister concluded: Costello, p. 325.

155 "If Hitler had not made. . . .": William Stevenson, *A Man Called Intrepid,* p. 301.

155 ". . . [T]he news on the 9 P.M. wireless. . . .": Andrew, p. 121.

156 "the wrong war. . . .": Goodwin, p. 265.

CHAPTER XI: SECRETS OF THE MAP ROOM

157 "When Churchill and his staff. . . .": Robert E. Sherwood, *Roosevelt and Hopkins,* p. 952.

157 "I must have a tumbler. . . .": Doris Kearns Goodwin, *No Ordinary Time,* p. 302.

157 "He has," Hambley wrote: Suckley, Binder 15.

159 "Your circulation is. . . .": Martin Gilbert, *Winston S. Churchill,* Vol. 6, p. 714.

159 "I attach more importance. . . .": Christopher Andrew, *For the President's Eyes Only,* p. 104.

159 "the geese who laid. . . .": ibid.

159 An early Churchill name for: Warren F. Kimball, *Churchill & Roosevelt,* p. 214.

159 The Prime Minister accepted: David Stafford, *Churchill and Secret Service,* pp. 199–200.

159 The Americans saw of Ultra: ibid., p. 201.

159 "Some time ago," he cabled: PSF Box 4.

160 ". . . danger of our enemies. . . .": ibid.

160 On February 1 the German Navy: Stafford, p. 236; Andrew and Dilks, *The Missing Dimension,* p. 149.

160 "When I reflect. . . .": Stafford, p. 236.

160 When U-boat torpedoes sank: Sherwood, p. 498.

160 "He liked to come and study. . . .": Eric Larrabee, *Commander in Chief,* p. 21.

161 "When McCrea arrived. . . .": David Kahn in George O. Kent, ed., *Historians and Archivists,* p. 307.

161 "[I]f a stamp collector . . .": Larrabee, p. 24.

161 "the patience with which he bore. . . .": ibid.

161 McCrea attacked the President's order: William D. Leahy, *I Was There,* p. 999; Larrabee, pp. 21–23; William M. Rigdon, *White House Sailor,* pp. 8–11; Goodwin, pp. 310, 311.

162 "The Magic Book": Larrabee, p. 22.

162 As Churchill had done in London: Rigdon, pp. 2, 3, 7.

162 Mrs. Roosevelt casually: ibid., p. 9.

162 "took to that sort of thing. . . .": Larrabee, p. 22.

162 "Well, if they aren't. . . .": Rigdon, pp. 10–11.

163 The President set up: Larrabee, p. 22.

163 In his first six months: Anthony Cave Brown, *The Last Hero,* p. 192.

163 They rained down: PSF Box 147.

163 "I'd be standing by. . . .": interview with Edwin J. "Ned" Putzell, Nov. 29, 1999.

163 "one of the two Americans. . . .": M 1642, Reel 48, Frame 1422.

164 "Whatever happens, America. . . .": ibid.

164 "I think they still come under. . . .": ibid., Frame 1423.

164 ". . . [P]erhaps you know. . . .": PSF Box 147.

165 "Errol used to join me. . . .": Charles Higham, *Errol Flynn,* p. 142.

165 More damaging, the year before: ibid., pp. 142–43.

165 Less than a month after: Bradley F. Smith, *The Shadow Warriors,* p. 100.

165 That same January: ibid., p. 104.

165 Two days later, Wild Bill: M 1642, Reel 48, Frame 1036.

166 "Dirty tricks are. . . .": Thomas Powers, *Heisenberg's War,* p. 226.

166 He was soon exploring schemes: Nathan Miller, *Spying for America,* p. 245.

166 "frightening, demoralizing and exciting. . . .": Andrew, p. 126.

166 The President sent Adams's letter: PSF Box 8.

166 Donovan seized upon the scheme: Smith, *The Shadow Warriors,* p. 102.

166 The bat mission: Andrew, p. 126.

166 "the sort of guy. . . .": Stafford, p. 204.

167 Wild Bill was not permitted to see: Phillip Knightley, *The Second Oldest Profession,* pp. 223–24.

167 On Pearl Harbor day: PSF Box 147.

167 "I interpreted this to mean. . . .": Andrew, p. 126.

167 "General DeWitt placed. . . .": PSF Box 147.

167 "[T]here was no reason so far. . . .": Smith, *The Shadow Warriors,* p. 99.

167 "are more in danger from the whites. . . .": PSF Box 97.

167   "doubtless great numbers of them. . . .": Ernest B. Furgurson, "Back Chan-nels," *Washingtonian,* vol. 31 (June 1996).

167   "I think the most effective fifth column work . . .": PSF Box 97.

168   "that ground glass had been found. . . .": Morton Grodzins, *Americans Be-trayed,* p. 402.

168   "The very fact that no sabotage. . . .": Andrew, p. 128.

168   "The necessity for mass evacuation. . . .": ibid., pp. 127–28.

168   "about the craziest proposition. . . .": Smith, *The Shadow Warriors,* p. 99.

168   As a consequence: James MacGregor Burns, *Roosevelt: The Soldier of Freedom,* p. 267.

169   "The President never 'thinks'. . . .": Larrabee, p. 644.

169   "magnificent but distant deity. . . .": W. A. Swanberg, "The Spies Who Came in from the Sea," *American Heritage,* April 1970.

169   "I do not think he was much. . . .": Goodwin, p. 322.

169   "In the present great war. . . .": MR Box 163.

169   Over 11,000 American residents: James Brooke, "After Silence, Italians Re-call the Internment," *New York Times,* Aug. 11, 1997.

170   "These interned nationals are. . . .": "Roundup," *Dateline,* NBC News, Sept. 4, 1998.

CHAPTER XII: INTRAMURAL SPY WARS

171   The French luxury liner: Robert E. Sherwood, *Roosevelt and Hopkins,* p. 501.

171   "[T]he long arm of. . . .": ibid.

171   "I do know the facts. . . .": ibid., p. 960.

171   Not saboteurs, but: PSF Box 59.

171   "Vincent Astor telephoned me yesterday. . . .": PSF Box 92.

172   "[T]he President gave his approval. . . .": ibid.

172   Astor's duties shifted: Ernest B. Furgurson, "Back Channels," *Washington-ian,* vol. 31 (June 1996); PSF Box 92.

172   By now, FDR was using Carter: Nathan Miller, *Spying for America,* p. 237.

172   "I have no corresponding. . . .": PSF Box 98.

172   Carter thereafter asked FDR: PSF Box 97.

172   "In order to facilitate the execution. . . .": ibid.

173   "I think it is better. . . .": ibid.

173   Early in 1942, Congress: Christopher Andrew, *For the President's Eyes Only,* p. 128.

173   Agents of foreign governments: H. Montgomery Hyde, *Room 3603,* p. 163.

173   The bill drew no distinction: ibid.

173   Bill Stephenson, as head of: ibid., p. 104.

173   Adolf Berle, given by FDR: Adolf Berle Papers, Box 67, FDRL.

174 "the code to anyone. . . .": Berle Papers, Box 213.

174 "Though it is not possible to say. . . .": Andrew, p. 128.

174 Berle not only supported: Hyde, p. 104.

174 "I do not see that any of us. . . .": Berle Papers, Box 67.

174 "No one has given us any. . . .": Berle Papers, Box 2B.

174 As the McKellar bill was coming: Hyde, p. 104.

174 Tully was filling in as hostess: Day-by-Day, Jan. 27, 1942.

174 "If our reading of the bill. . . .": M 1642; NA memo from William J. Donovan to FDR, Jan. 6, 1942.

175 FDR signed the amended version: Hyde, p. 165.

175 The FBI had learned that a BSC: Berle Papers, Box 28.

175 "It developed," Berle noted: Berle Papers, Box 213.

CHAPTER XIII: PREMIER SECRET OF THE WAR

176 "If atomic bombs could be made. . . .": Eric Larrabee, *Commander in Chief,* p. 646.

176 Before they left the White House: ibid., p. 645.

177 He was given to tortured locutions: Alexander Sachs Papers, Box 1, FDRL.

177 ". . . [I]t may be possible to set up. . . .": ibid.

177 That Wednesday afternoon he waited: James MacGregor Burns, *Roosevelt: The Soldier of Freedom,* pp. 249–50.

178 He saucily reminded the President: John Gunther, *Roosevelt in Retrospect,* p. 304.

178 He caught the President's attention: Richard Rhodes, *The Making of the Atomic Bomb,* p. 313.

178 ". . . [T]here is no doubt. . . .": ibid., p. 314.

178 "Alex, what you are after. . . .": ibid.

178 "This requires action": ibid.

178 FDR sent Einstein a thank-you note: PSF Box 5.

179 "the most dangerous possible German. . . .": Thomas Powers, *Heisenberg's War,* p. vii.

179 "As large as a pineapple": Rhodes, p. 404.

179 "the measures, the sums of money. . . .": ibid.

179 Heisenberg indicated: ibid.

179 "the idea quite obviously strained. . . .": ibid.

179 In America, Roosevelt assigned: Brian Loring Villa, "The Atomic Bomb and the Normandy Invasion," *Perspectives in American History* 2 (1977–1978), p. 467.

179 "The boss wants it. . . .": Gunther, p. 304.

179 "so much more secret. . . .": John Morton Blum, *Years of War, 1941–1945: From the Morgenthau Diaries,* p. 13.

179 In August the President approved: Rhodes, p. 251.

179　"Grace, this is red hot. . . .": Grace Tully, *F.D.R., My Boss,* pp. 265–66.

180　"I can't tell you what. . . .": ibid., p. 266.

180　"a hazardous matter. . . .": Villa, pp. 468–69.

180　"Whatever the enemy may be. . . .": Larrabee, p. 647.

180　"[W]e as a group are. . . .": ibid.

CHAPTER XIV: ENTER THE OSS

181　Within six months: Bradley F. Smith, *The Shadow Warriors,* p. 128.

181　"Being a writer by trade. . . .": Michael Warner and Robert Louis Benson, "Venona and Beyond," *Intelligence and National Security,* vol. 12, no. 3 (July 1997), p. 9.

182　"Bill Donovan wants to take over. . . .": PSF Box 147; Adolf Berle Papers, Box 213, FDRL.

182　On January 16, 1942, the President: PSF Box 147; Leslie B. Rout Jr. and John F. Bratzel, *The Shadow War,* p. 39.

182　"In order to give privacy. . . .": PSF Box 148.

182　Captain Denebrink's report: Smith, *The Shadow Warriors,* p. 118.

183　"Donovan has been a thorn. . . .": William B. Breuer, *Hoodwinking Hitler,* p. 68.

183　Strong veritably glowed hot: Anthony Cave Brown, *The Last Hero,* p. 304.

183　In Strong's eyes, the honorary colonel: PSF Box 149.

184　"Stanley, not a word . . . !": Stanley Lovell, *Of Spies and Stratagems,* pp. 182, 183.

184　Yet, he drove his security: ibid., p. 182.

184　"To exclude this agency. . . .": Brown, *The Last Hero,* p. 313.

184　". . . [T]he Russians are today. . . .": James MacGregor Burns, *Roosevelt: The Soldier of Freedom,* p. 230.

184　Churchill believed the Allies: ibid., p. 235.

185　"From reliable sources . . .": Timothy P. Mulligan, "According to Colonel Donovan: A Document from the Records of German Intelligence," *The Historian,* vol. 46, no. 1 (November 1983), p. 85.

186　He tried to get into the South Pacific: Smith, *The Shadow Warriors,* p. 195.

186　"They'll absorb you. . . .": Brown, *The Last Hero,* p. 236.

186　"I asked whether he had. . . .": Berle Papers, Box 214.

186　"I had some ideas on that subject. . . .": ibid.

186　Donovan had left the country: Brown, *The Last Hero,* p. 236.

186　The shake-up included: ibid., p. 235.

186　"You are aware of course. . . .": POF 4485.

187　But with it jettisoned: Brown, *The Last Hero,* p. 235.

187　The JCS thus agreed to absorb: Smith, *The Shadow Warriors,* p. 119. Brown, p. 237.

187　"[T]hese admirals and generals might. . . .": Brown, *The Last Hero,* p. 238.

187 Roosevelt managed to reverse: Breuer, pp. 68–69; Curt Gentry, *J. Edgar Hoover,* p. 267.

188 Its codebreakers had begun to crack: Norman Polmar and Thomas B. Allen, *Spy Book,* p. 299; Christopher Andrew and David Dilks, eds., *The Missing Dimension,* p. 246.

188 This intelligence formed part: Polmar and Allen, *Spy Book,* p. 368.

188 Subsequent intercepts showed: Christopher Andrew, *For the President's Eyes Only,* p. 125.

188 On the morning of June 4: Warren F. Kimball, *Churchill & Roosevelt,* p. 507.

189 "essentially a victory. . . .": Andrew and Dilks, p. 147.

189 The Japanese were handed: Eric Larrabee, *Commander in Chief,* p. 386.

189 But FDR was far too shrewd: ibid.

190 With all this public uproar: ibid.

190 As to the secret: H. Montgomery Hyde, *Room 3603,* p. 214.

190 "Japan and the islands. . . .": Andrew, pp. 132–33.

190 On another occasion Carter: ibid., p. 133.

190 "There has been a suggestion. . . .": PSF Box 98.

190 ". . . [W]e could convince the mass. . . .": ibid.

191 "I do not feel. . . .": ibid.

191 "Gerald Haxton. . . .": ibid.

191 This information could then: ibid.

191 "I see no reason. . . .": ibid.

191 FDR wanted simply to cut off: ibid.

192 Hanfstaengl was interned: Ernest B. Furgurson, "Back Channels," *Washingtonian,* vol. 31 (June 1996); Brown, pp. 210–11.

193 But he did arrange for Carter: Carter Collection, Oral History, pp. 4–5, FDRL.

193 "Well why don't you come . . . ?": ibid., p. 10.

193 "What do you think on earth . . . ?": ibid., p. 12.

193 "actually knows all these people. . . .": ibid.

193 "You can tell. . . .": ibid.

194 "confusing anybody's mind. . . .": Furgurson.

194 On June 24, FDR: PSF Box 98.

194 Putzi was to be treated: Brown, p. 211.

194 "warned me that Hanfstaengl . . .": Furgurson.

194 "Of course, there's where you. . . .": Carter Oral History, p. 14.

194 "It was just Hanfstaengl. . . .": ibid., p. 15.

CHAPTER XV: "WE ARE STRIKING BACK"

195 "He said that he would not. . . .": Adolf Berle Papers, Box 214, FDRL.

196 FDR laughed off the gibe: ibid.

196   Fortunately for the Western Allies: PSF Box 3.

196   "the Japanese may be preparing to conduct. . . .": MR Box 8.

196   The Japanese would definitely attack: ibid.

196   "I have information which I believe. . . .": MR Box 48.

196   "I believe that we must. . . .": RG 457 #74682.

197   The assignment to burglarize: Anthony Cave Brown, *The Last Hero,* pp. 227–28.

198   The bureau already had three agents: ibid., pp. 229–30; William B. Breuer, *Hoodwinking Hitler,* p. 68.

198   "I don't believe any single event. . . .": Brown, *The Last Hero,* p. 229.

198   "The Abwehr gets better treatment. . . .": Curt Gentry, *J. Edgar Hoover,* p. 295.

198   Donovan had stepped over: ibid.

198   "No President dare touch. . . .": Brown, *The Last Hero,* p. 229.

198   "Reliable source confirms. . . .": Ladislas Farago, *The Game of the Foxes,* p. 330.

198   If true that Roosevelt's consciousness: ibid., pp. 298–330.

199   While held in an Italian prison: Farago, p. 6.

199   What Hitler wanted from him now: W. A. Swanberg, "The Spies Who Came in from the Sea," *American Heritage,* April 1970, p. 67.

199   Thus, in April 1942: ibid., p. 69.

200   They were provided with drawings: Francis Biddle, *In Brief Authority,* p. 325.

200   They were to carry high explosives: Swanberg, p. 67.

200   The teams split: ibid., pp. 67–68.

200   "This will cost. . . .": Leon O. Prior, "Nazi Invasion of Florida," *Florida History Quarterly,* vol. 49, no. 2 (October 1970), p. 132.

200   "Who are you?": Swanberg, p. 66.

200   Instead, Dasch, a garrulous loudmouth: ibid.

200   In the meantime, the Dasch team: ibid., p. 69.

200   "obsessive, compulsive, neurotic . . .": Biddle, p. 326.

201   A few years before, Burger: Swanberg, p. 68.

201   Dasch divulged everything: ibid., p. 87.

201   "at 1:30 a.m. an unarmed Coast Guard. . . .": PSF Box 57.

201   "His eyes were bright. . . .": Biddle, p. 327.

201   The President agreed, and the press: ibid.

201   "I had a bad week. . . .": ibid.

201   Dasch had, in fact, revealed: Swanberg, p. 87.

202   "Not enough, Francis. . . .": Biddle, pp. 327–28.

202   "The two Americans are guilty. . . .": PSF Box 56.

202   "they had not committed any act. . . .": Biddle, p. 328.

202   He told Biddle that he wanted: ibid., p. 330.

202   "[t]hese men had penetrated battlelines. . . .": POF Box 5036.

203 "I want one thing. . . .": Biddle, p. 330.

203 "Dutch jaw—and when. . . .": W. Averell Harriman and Elie Abel, *Special Envoy to Churchill and Stalin,* p. 389.

203 Biddle practically felt: Biddle, p. 330.

203 "[t]he major violation of the Law of War. . . .": POF Box 5036.

203 Thus was born the Double Cross: Farago, p. 176; Breuer, p. 49.

203 Only one German spy is believed: Norman Polmar and Thomas B. Allen, *Spy Book,* p. 190.

203 On July 2 the President: Prior, p. 137.

204 FDR wanted his own man: Biddle, p. 331.

204 On June 8 the prisoners: Swanberg, p. 89.

204 Enterprising vendors soon were doing: Biddle, p. 333.

204 The trial was held: Swanberg, p. 88.

204 A disgusted Hoover: Biddle, p. 333.

204 August 8 was set: Swanberg, p. 91.

204 He commenced his ceremonial role: Robert E. Sherwood, *Roosevelt and Hopkins,* p. 115.

205 By 1:04 p.m., the work was completed: Swanberg, p. 91.

205 Where, Mrs. Rosenman asked: Samuel I. Rosenman, *Working with Roosevelt,* pp. 352–53.

205 "Suggest you close the casket. . . .": ibid., p. 354.

205 The saboteurs were subsequently: Swanberg, p. 91.

205 "It's high time that we wake up here. . . .": POF Box 5036.

205 "We endorse the imposition. . . .": ibid.

205 They announced the death: Hoover to Hopkins, Aug. 26, 1942, FDRL.

206 "Have you pretty well cleaned . . . ?": PSF Box 57.

206 Again, according to young Roosevelt: James Roosevelt, *My Parents,* p. 100.

206 In 1918, as Franklin returned: Doris Kearns Goodwin, *No Ordinary Time,* pp. 19–20.

206 "a woman of lofty liberal principles. . . .": Jim Bishop, *FDR's Last Year,* p. xi.

206 By 1941, with her husband invalided: Goodwin, pp. 434–35.

207 His report made clear: PSF Box 57.

208 "We failed to see. . . .": Eric Larrabee, *Commander in Chief,* p. 9.

208 "TORCH was a project. . . .": James MacGregor Burns, *Roosevelt: The Soldier of Freedom,* p. 286.

208 "I feel very strongly. . . .": ibid., p. 289.

208 ". . . [T]he assumption [is]. . . .": ibid.

209 Under a secret arrangement: Sheridan Nichols, "The Light That Failed: Intelligence Gathering Activities in North Africa Prior to Operation Torch," *Maghreb Review* 4 (July/December 1979), p. 135.

209 Donovan was to find out: ibid., p. 136.

209 The organization was to invent: Nathan Miller, *Spying for America,* p. 270.

210 "I've never met him. . . .": Nichols, p. 135.

210 With the arrival of Colonel Eddy: ibid.

210 "All their thoughts are centered. . . .": Francis Russell, *The Secret War*, p. 96.

210 "complacently neutral. . . .": Christopher Andrew, *For the President's Eyes Only*, p. 134.

210 Nearly 100,000 troops: Donald A. Walker, "OSS and Operation Torch," *Journal of Contemporary History*, vol. 22 (1987), p. 673.

210 "That place is a sieve! . . .": Burns, *Roosevelt: The Soldier of Freedom*, p. 287.

210 "Don't worry about Cordell. . . .": Andrew, p. 134.

210 Murphy left Roosevelt: ibid.

211 "You know I am not supposed. . . .": Sherwood, p. 633.

211 According to anti-Nazi: Walker, p. 668.

211 The President had taken out: Burns, *Roosevelt: The Soldier of Freedom*, p. 290.

211 The President had it on good authority: ibid., p. 293.

212 The ship count for Torch: Martin Blumenson, *Mark Clark*, pp. 75–76.

212 Murphy communicated Mast's wishes: ibid., p. 77.

212 Attending the meeting: ibid., pp. 77–79.

212 Clark was to try to enlist: ibid., p. 79.

213 "I am leaving in twenty minutes. . . .": ibid., pp. 79–80.

213 He and the men boarding: ibid., pp. 79–81.

213 By 6 a.m. Clark's party: ibid., p. 81.

213 Mast then asked for: ibid., p. 82.

213 Not until the middle: ibid., pp. 84–85.

213 There, Eisenhower decided: ibid., p. 87.

214 "The P. had an awful nightmare. . . .": Suckley, Binder 16, p. 258.

214 "We have landed in North Africa. . . .": Burns, *Roosevelt: The Soldier of Freedom*, p. 292.

214 As the forces landed: Miller, p. 271.

214 General Mast managed: Peter Young, ed., *The World Almanac Book of World War II*, pp. 181–82.

215 Colonel Eddy's team had amassed: Nichols, p. 136.

215 The enemy was where: Walker, p. 669.

215 That enemies could penetrate: Gentry, p. 245.

215 Hitler had revealed his timetable: PSF Box 2; Orville H. Bullitt, ed., *For the President, Personal and Secret: Correspondence Between Franklin D. Roosevelt and William C. Bullitt*, pp. 319–21.

216 He had even braved the disfavor: Richard Rhodes, *The Making of the Atomic Bomb*, p. 525.

216 Roosevelt was already attacked: Lucy S. Dawidowicz, "Could the United States Have Rescued the European Jews from Hitler?" *This World*, Fall 1985, p. 21.

216   Bigots parodied his New Deal: Goodwin, p. 102.

216   In that period, before war broke out: Liva Baker, *Felix Frankfurter,* pp. 200–201.

217   Instead of going to Roosevelt: letter, Rosenman to Berle, Oct. 19, 1939, FDRL.

217   The transcript Bullitt had sent: Joseph E. Persico, *Nuremberg,* p. 282.

217   "The Jew party [was]. . . .": Goodwin, p. 102.

217   "I now think he travelled. . . .": James Roosevelt, *My Parents,* p. 219.

217   A 1938 Roper poll: Goodwin, p. 102.

217   The tight immigration laws: William J. vanden Heuvel, "America, FDR and the Holocaust," *Society,* vol. 34, no. 6 (October 1997), p. 3.

217   Even unfilled quotas: Dawidowicz, pp. 16, 17.

217   A bill introduced in the House: Goodwin, p. 101.

217   The saga of the SS *St. Louis:* ibid., p. 102.

218   Many who landed: vanden Heuvel, p. 5; *Washington Post,* Aug. 2, 1998; Goodwin, p. 102.

218   "The whole trouble is in England": John Morton Blum, *Years of War, 1941–1945: From the Morgenthau Diaries,* p. 208.

218   "some very wonderful. . . .": ibid., p. 207.

218   "I actually would put a barbed wire. . . .": ibid., p. 208.

218   All had turned out: Charles Roetter, *The Art of Psychological Warfare: 1914–1945,* p. 46.

219   "The post-war settlement. . . .": M 1642, Reel 1, Frames 543, 544.

219   "From Midland. . . .": M 1642, Reel 23, Frames 22, 23.

219   One account described: Ernest B. Furgurson, "Back Channels," *Washingtonian,* vol. 31 (June 1996).

219   His agents interrogated: Irwin F. Gellman, *Secret Affairs,* p. 283.

219   "Yesterday's cleansing action in Slonim. . . .": David Stafford, *Churchill and Secret Service,* p. 298.

219   "The number of Jews engaged. . . .": Francis L. Loewenheim, Harold D. Langley, and Manfred Jonas, eds., *Roosevelt and Churchill: Their Secret Wartime Correspondence,* p. 308.

220   The largest number: Goodwin, p. 101.

220   One, the Portuguese: Joseph E. Persico, *Piercing the Reich,* p. 3.

220   Throughout the war: Robert H. Ferrell, *The Dying President: Franklin D. Roosevelt, 1944–1945,* p. 150.

CHAPTER XVI: AN EXCHANGE: AN INVASION FOR A BOMB

222   The President pointed out: James MacGregor Burns, *Roosevelt: The Soldier of Freedom,* p. 235; Jim Bishop, *FDR's Last Year,* pp. 47–48.

222   "vast and conspicuous factories": Eric Larrabee, *Commander in Chief,* p. 646.

222 "when the President said he. . . .": ibid.

222 That matter settled: *FRUS,* 3d Washington Conference, p. 2.

222 Besides, the British considered: Larrabee, p. 645.

222 Two American physicists: *FRUS,* p. 4.

222 What the British had shared: H. D. Smythe, "The Smythe Report," *Library Chronicles,* p. III6.

222 "[I]nterchange on design. . . .": *FRUS,* p. 5.

223 Serving with the Army: *American National Biography,* vol. 5, pp. 284–315.

223 Conant expressed General Groves's position: HH Box 132.

223 Upon learning that FDR approved: *FRUS,* p. 6.

223 "The War Department is asking. . . .": ibid., p. 1.

223 "There is no question of breach. . . .": ibid., p. 2.

223 ". . . entirely destroys. . . .": ibid., p. 5.

223 The Americans had chucked: ibid., p. 3.

224 His government wanted to share: HH Box 132.

224 "impossible [and] dangerous": Brian Loring Villa, "The Atomic Bomb and the Normandy Invasion," *Perspectives in American History* 2 (1977–1978), p. 472.

224 At one point, he told: ibid., p. 499.

224 "never had any intention. . . .": ibid., p. 481.

224 And a conciliatory FDR: ibid., p. 483.

224 "since our program is not suffering. . . .": *FRUS,* First Quebec Conference, p. 631.

224 The secretary of war advised: Villa, p. 478.

224 "I think you made a firm commitment. . . .": HH Box 132.

225 "Dear Van, while I am mindful. . . .": *FRUS,* Quebec, p. 633.

225 "magnificent in reconciliation. . . .": Villa, p. 493.

225 "to bring the Tube Alloys project. . . .": *FRUS,* Quebec, Aug. 19, 1943; Villa, p. 495.

225 "It would be in the best interests. . . .": HH Box 132.

225 Among them was a slight: Norman Moss, *Klaus Fuchs,* pp. 36, 45.

226 "[W]hat you are after is to see. . . .": Richard Rhodes, *The Making of the Atomic Bomb,* p. 314.

226 Still, plenty of brainpower remained: Pamela Spence Richards, "Wartime: The OSS and the Periodical Republication Program," FDRL.

226 "would throw a man off his horse. . . .": Thomas Powers, *Heisenberg's War,* p. 151.

226 "The attached clipping shows. . . .": *NYT,* April 4, 1943; HH Box 132.

226 Heisenberg was a loyal German: Thomas Powers, p. 40.

226 "At every point during the argument. . . .": ibid., pp. 132, 151.

227 "Professor Heisenberg had not given. . . .": Rhodes, p. 405.

227 Of 1,006 bombs dropped: Thomas Powers, p. 212.

227 While Bill Donovan was raining: Robin W. Winks, *Cloak and Gown,* p. 176; Nathan Miller, *Spying for America,* p. 245.

227 Running the scientific smuggling: Richards, p. 262.

228 Within minutes, a mysterious: ibid., pp. 261–62.

228 FDR, whose early law practice: *Los Angeles Times,* Sept. 22, 2000

229 "practically became a member. . . .": Curt Gentry, *J. Edgar Hoover,* p. 303.

229 The young man was soon: ibid.

229 It was from this post: Doris Kearns Goodwin, *No Ordinary Time,* p. 420.

229 Thus investigators opened his mail: Athan Theoharis, ed., *From the Secret Files of J. Edgar Hoover,* p. 59.

229 The general reviewed the CIC record: Gentry, p. 305; Theoharis, p. 63.

229 "indicated quite clearly that Mrs. Roosevelt. . . .": Theoharis, p. 61.

229 "I'm so happy to have been with you. . . .": Goodwin, p. 420.

230 "Subject and Mrs. Pratt appeared. . . .": Gentry, p. 305.

230 Actually, they had played gin: ibid.

230 At the prompting of a furious FDR: Goodwin, p. 421.

230 Marshall ordered the CIC's domestic spying: Theoharis, p. 60.

230 The CIC was supposed to hunt: ibid., p. 62.

230 Eleanor went to her husband: Gentry, p. 299.

230 "This type of investigation. . . .": ibid.

230 "[O]h gosh, Hoover has apologized. . . .": ibid., p. 300.

231 "anybody who knew anything about this. . . .": Theoharis, p. 61.

231 He was to keep the scurrilous: ibid., p. 62.

231 "bosses want me to speak about": John Franklin Carter Diary, Feb. 23, 1943.

231 "Doctors know more about. . . .": ibid.

231 He began spouting: PSF Box 98.

232 Chin lifted, he began dictating: Carter Diary, Feb. 23, 1943.

232 He believed himself utterly unappreciated: PSF Box 98.

232 "When the Hitler regime begins. . . .": ibid.

232 "The Army could really be turned. . . .": ibid.

233 Among his deliveries was the daughter: M 1642, Reel 109, Frame 398.

233 "Probable Mode of Exit of Adolph Hitler . . .": PSF Box 98.

233 "Hitler is familiar enough with ancient history. . . .": ibid.

234 He startled his family: *NYT,* Dec. 31, 1974.

234 On one occasion, the burly envoy: William B. Breuer, *Hoodwinking Hitler,* p. 36.

234 At one dance hall, he listened impatiently: Ladislas Farago, *The Game of the Foxes,* p. 574.

234 State Department careerists were less amused: Breuer, p. 36.

234 The old capital of the Ottoman Empire: Farago, p. 570.

235 "[W]e had a General. . . .": Burns, *Roosevelt: The Soldier of Freedom,* p. 323.

235 "I heard the words. . . .": Anthony Cave Brown, *Bodyguard of Lies*, p. 247.

235 "A gradual break-up in Germany. . . .": Winston S. Churchill, *The Second World War: Closing the Ring*, pp. 573–74.

235 "If you were given two choices. . . .": Brown, *Bodyguard of Lies*, p. 248.

235 "[S]uddenly the press conference was on. . . .": Burns, *Roosevelt: The Soldier of Freedom*, p. 323.

236 A policy of uncompromising total surrender: John Gunther, *Roosevelt in Retrospect*, pp. 332–33.

236 "Of course, it's just the thing. . . .": Richard A. Russell, *Project Hula: Secret Soviet-American Cooperation in the War Against Japan*, p. 29.

236 Stalin believed that leaving the Germans: *FRUS*, Cairo Conference, p. 513.

236 Upon checking into Istanbul's luxurious: Farago, p. 572.

236 He signed the telegram: ibid.

236 Ten days after Earle checked into: ibid., p. 576.

237 "unquestionably a Nazi agent. . . .": MR Box 13.

237 "Earle is cooperating. . . .": ibid.

237 When the Allied troops did invade: Farago, pp. 578–79.

237 One day FDR received a large envelope: ibid., p. 577.

238 "there would be no place. . . .": ibid., p. 576.

CHAPTER XVII: LEAKAGE FROM THE TOP

239 Yet, he had trouble persuading: Christopher Andrew, *For the President's Eyes Only*, p. 143.

239 "I have learned that you seldom. . . .": ibid.

239 "C in C [Commander in Chief] combined. . . .": Norman Polmar and Thomas B. Allen, *Spy Book*, p. 606.

240 While the Battle of Midway: Andrew, p. 138.

241 "Oshima often impressed this observer. . . .": Polmar and Allen, *Spy Book*, p. 417.

241 "I took occasion to ask him. . . .": RG 457 #89076.

241 "Why does Germany have to take . . . ?": RG 457 #92031.

242 "Before long, as things now look. . . .": RG 457 #93120.

242 "Well, it is quite true that these bombings. . . .": RG 457 #94081.

242 In one summary, the ambassador: RG 457 CBOM 76.

243 "Local municipal authorities told me. . . .": RG 457 #94388.

243 "The main reason is failure to close. . . .": RG 457 SRH 111.

243 ". . . [T]he prisoners tell us. . . .": RG 457 CBOM 76.

244 On December 15 the Japanese foreign office: ibid.

245 ". . . [L]ooking at it from the American point of view. . . .": RG 457 #74938.

245 In 1943 over four hundred messages: Polmar and Allen, *Spy Book*, p. 417.

245 "was our main basis of information. . . .": ibid.

245 "[a]n American espionage agency in Lisbon. . . .": RG 457 SRH 113.

245   "would be nothing less. . . .": ibid.

245   "the folly of letting loose a group. . . .": ibid.

245   ". . . that steps be taken immediately to recall. . . .": ibid.

246   "the ill advised and amateurish efforts. . . .": Anthony Cave Brown, *The Last Hero*, p. 305.

246   "used by the Japanese . . .": ibid., p. 306.

246   "Nothing has happened to the code books. . . .": RG 457 SRH 113.

247   ROOSEVELT PROTECTED IN TALKS TO ENVOYS: Ladislas Farago, *The Game of the Foxes*, p. 586.

247   "completed . . . an installation. . . .": ibid., pp. 587–88.

248   "We do not want to propose armistice. . . .": Warren F. Kimball, *Churchill & Roosevelt*, p. 357.

248   "This is incontrovertible evidence. . . .": ibid.

248   Hitler had decided three days before: David Kahn, *Code Breaking in World Wars I and II*, p. 176.

249   ". . . in view of the position which you have taken. . . .": Brown, *The Last Hero*, p. 343.

249   Instead, he signaled that Wild Bill: ibid., p. 344.

249   It was the bureaucratic infighting: Richard Gid Powers, *Secrecy and Power*, p. 226.

249   Donovan pointed out that the OSS: PSF Box 8.

249   Britain's Lord Louis Mountbatten pleaded: Robert E. Sherwood, *Roosevelt and Hopkins*, p. 688.

250   Donovan informed the President that he had: PSF Box 149; Neal H. Petersen, ed., *From Hitler's Doorstep: The Wartime Intelligence Reports of Allen Dulles, 1942–1945*, p. 4.

250   "Espionage is not a game. . . .": Ernest Volkman, *Spies*, p. vii.

250   Dulles was also a ladies' man: Petersen, p. 5.

251   He had the lightbulbs removed: Jim Bishop, *FDR's Last Year*, p. 502; Brown, *The Last Hero*, p. 274.

251   During a diplomatic assignment to Bern: Joseph E. Persico, *Piercing the Reich*, p. 65.

251   Unsuspected by his superiors: William B. Breuer, *Hoodwinking Hitler*, p. 26.

251   "I don't believe you. . . .": Persico, *Piercing the Reich*, p. 64.

251   Aware of the skepticism he aroused: Brown, *The Last Hero*, p. 279.

251   Dansey was described by his own people: Breuer, p. 28.

251   "obviously a plant" whom "Dulles. . . .": Brown, *The Last Hero*, p. 279.

251   However, when Kolbe's purloined messages: ibid.

252   "[S]hipments of oranges will continue. . . .": Persico, *Piercing the Reich*, p. 68.

252   Another foreign office communiqué: ibid.

252 "We have secured through secret intelligence. . . .": Brown, *The Last Hero,* p. 280.

252 The first fourteen messages from Kolbe/Wood's: ibid.

252 Thirteen-year-old Sumner: Irwin F. Gellman, *Secret Affairs,* p. 59.

253 Furthermore, Cordell Hull was suffering: Curt Gentry, *J. Edgar Hoover,* p. 307.

253 Sumner Welles, reserved, soft-spoken: Gellman, p. xi.

253 When the porter declined: Gentry, p. 307.

253 He had made homosexual passes: ibid., p. 308.

253 Hoover, aware that he himself was rumored: Athan Theoharis, ed., *From the Secret Files of J. Edgar Hoover,* p. 346.

253 The results were kept in the FBI's "OC": Gellman, p. 236.

254 According to FDR's son Jimmy: James Roosevelt, *My Parents,* p. 186.

254 Bullitt had somehow managed to get his hands: Gentry, p. 309.

254 Bullitt was further suspected: ibid.

254 In April 1941 the egocentric: Orville H. Bullitt, ed., *For the President, Personal and Secret,* p. 512.

254 "I know all about. . . .": ibid., p. 513.

254 As the general stepped in: ibid., p. 514.

255 He might commit suicide: Gentry, p. 309.

255 "Well, he's not doing it. . . .": ibid.

255 Long ago FDR had had his own brush: Suckley, Binder 18, pp. 230–32.

255 He told Senator Alben Barkley: Gentry, p. 287.

256 Shortly after Welles's resignation: Gellman, p. 2.

256 " *'You-can-go-down-there!'* ": James MacGregor Burns, *Roosevelt: The Soldier of Freedom,* p. 350.

256 Bullitt had fulfilled the description: Gentry, p. 308.

256 "If I go to Moscow. . . .": Sherwood, p. 756; Gellman, p. 317.

CHAPTER XVIII: DISTRUSTING ALLIES

257 "As far as it is known. . . .": Ladislas Farago, *The Game of the Foxes,* p. 655.

257 The Abwehr agreed to a plan: ibid., p. 648.

258 When he smiled he exposed: ibid., pp. 649–55.

258 Koehler was briefed by the Abwehr: ibid., p. 648.

258 They set him up: ibid., pp. 650–51.

258 "This information is being made available. . . .": POF Box 106.

259 As a young Communist in Germany: Norman Moss, *Klaus Fuchs,* p. 12.

259 While engaged in this work: ibid., p. 53.

259 Before the year was out: ibid., pp. 38–40.

259 More important, he possessed: ibid., p. 59.

259 Sonya explained to Fuchs: ibid., p. 40.

259 "Can you tell me the way . . . ?": ibid., p. 47.

259 Gold, a chemist by profession: ibid., p. 48.

260 They were meeting at Berle's: U.S. Congress, *Hearings on Proposed Legislation to Curb or Control the Communist Party of the United States,* February 1948, p. 1406.

260 He had been part of a Communist: ibid., p. 1293.

260 He had broken with the party: Allen Weinstein, *Perjury: The Hiss-Chambers Case,* p. 307.

261 Felix Frankfurter gave the Hisses: ibid., p. 63.

262 "The campaign of calumny against the Soviet Union. . . .": MR Box 8.

262 Secretary of State Hull managed: ibid.

262 "Since the Polish Government. . . .": ibid.

263 "The military and police officers. . . .": Pavel Sudoplatov and Anatoli Sudoplatov, *Special Tasks,* p. 477.

263 "[s]pecial tribunals . . . without summoning. . . .": ibid., pp. 477–78.

263 Documents released following the collapse: ibid., p. 476.

263 O'Malley made clear: Warren F. Kimball, *Churchill & Roosevelt,* vol. 2, pp. 389–94.

263 "[I]n view of the immense importance. . . .": ibid., p. 398.

263 "If," his message ended: ibid., p. 399.

264 "Nevertheless, should you have time. . . .": ibid., p. 389.

264 The President never made: MR, Roosevelt to Stalin, April 26, 1943.

264 A Magic decrypt picked up: RG 457 #85850.

264 "extraordinarily beautiful woman . . .": Allen Weinstein and Alexander Vassiliev, *The Haunted Wood,* p. 4.

264 Duggan, according to Soviet wartime documents: ibid., p. 9.

264 By 1939, Duggan had begun: ibid., p. 19.

264 In March of that year: Henry Wallace Papers, Reel 13, Frame 1149, FDRL.

265 "There's been an awful lot. . . .": Robert D. Graff Papers, Box 3, FDRL.

265 In 1940 the old Bolshevik had been railroaded: POF Box 1.

265 His conviction, however, did not deter: ibid.

265 The feisty La Guardia came to the White House: Graff Papers, Box 3.

266 "They had been engaged in. . . .": James Roosevelt and Sidney Shalett, *Affectionately, F.D.R.,* pp. 50–51.

266 At Tehran, Stalin could be expected: Laslo Havas, *Hitler's Plot to Kill the Big 3,* p. 170.

267 "had been making a certain amount. . . .": PSF Box 153.

267 "had come on a highly secret. . . .": ibid.

267 Because the bombing was destroying: ibid.

268 OSS obligingly arranged the flight: M 1642, Reel 117, Frame 297.

268 "The story he brought back. . . .": PSF Box 153.

268 Hurley, he told FDR, "disclaims. . . .": ibid.

268 "I beg you to read this. . . .": ibid.

269 The idea that Morde's plan: M 1642, Reel 7a, Frame 298.

269 With the President were Mrs. Hull: Day-by-Day, Nov. 10, 1943.

269 Reilly had persuaded friends: Michael F. Reilly, *Reilly of the White House*, p. 28.

269 People like him had no business: PSF Box 153.

269 For anyone else, support of: Jürgen Heideking and Christof Mauch, eds., *American Intelligence and the German Resistance to Hitler*, p. 6.

269 On October 14, Earle sent the White House: MR Box 13.

269 A few months before, in August: ibid.

270 "one half of Rumanian production": ibid.

270 The rest of the planes: ibid.

270 Still, Earle had tapped some valuable sources: HH Box 138.

270 "I ought to let you know. . . .": Winston S. Churchill, *The Second World War*, Vol. 5, *Closing the Ring*, p. 197.

270 "I am personally as yet unconvinced. . . .": ibid., p. 203.

270 "rupturing the Anglo-American plans. . . .": ibid., p. 197.

270 He was dissuaded: F. H. Hinsley, *British Intelligence in the Second World War*, vol. 3, pt. 1, pp. 415, 449.

270 "For this reason," Churchill continued: Francis L. Loewenheim, Harold D. Langley, and Manfred Jonas, eds., *Roosevelt and Churchill: Their Secret Wartime Correspondence*, p. 389.

270 "About June 10, he told. . . .": Churchill, *The Second World War*, p. 197.

271 Over 120 scientists and 600 foreign workers: Loewenheim, Langley, and Jonas, p. 389.

271 On November 5, Roosevelt received: MR Box 13.

271 "We too have received many reports. . . .": Loewenheim, Langley, and Jonas, p. 392.

271 After Peenemünde was struck: ibid.

271 "Stratospheric attack on America. . . .": MR Box 13.

271 The objective, he revealed, was: Hinsley, p. 347.

CHAPTER XIX: DECEIVERS AND THE DECEIVED

272 "A supply of money. . . .": William M. Rigdon, *White House Sailor*, p. 61; Michael Reilly, *Reilly of the White House*, pp. 59–60.

273 On Saturday, November 27: William B. Breuer, *Hoodwinking Hitler*, p. 4; James MacGregor Burns, *Roosevelt: The Soldier of Freedom*, p. 406.

273 "a catalytic agent. . . .": David Stafford, *Churchill and Secret Service*, p. 198.

273 "I think if I give [Stalin]. . . .": William Bullitt, "How We Won the War and Lost the Peace," *Life*, August 30, 1948, p. 94.

273 The Stalin whom Roosevelt hoped: C. P. Snow, *Variety of Men*, pp. 266–67.

273 The burly Irishman: Jim Bishop, *FDR's Last Year*, p. 2.

273   They had two missions: Reilly, p. 175.

274   "There can never be. . . .": William L. Shirer, *The Rise and Fall of the Third Reich,* p. 1027.

274   By the fall of 1943, the SD: Laslo Havas, *Hitler's Plot to Kill the Big 3,* pp. 160, 204.

274   With this intelligence in hand: Breuer, p. 5.

274   Under Skorzeny's tutelage: Pavel Sudoplatov and Anatoli Sudoplatov, *Special Tasks,* p. 130.

274   Its members practiced assassination: Havas, p. 159.

274   By September 10, SS chief: ibid., pp. 160, 204.

274   The mission to murder: Breuer, p. 4.

274   "I like to be more independent. . . .": Rigdon, p. 78.

274   The President chose to stay: Robert E. Sherwood, *Roosevelt and Hopkins,* p. 776.

274   At nine-thirty the following morning: Rigdon, p. 61.

274   Stalin feared, Harriman said: Havas, p. 222.

275   "Assassination": Sherwood, p. 776.

275   The pro-Allied shah, Reza Pahlavi: Havas, p. 80; Rigdon, p. 79.

275   Roosevelt decided to move: Rigdon, p. 80.

275   The legation became a whirlwind: Havas, p. 195.

275   By 3 p.m., a motorcade: ibid., p. 223.

275   The caravan rolled out: William D. Leahy, *I Was There,* p. 203.

275   All but six of the hit men: Havas, p. 218.

275   But the six remaining: ibid., pp. 227–28.

276   The President was lifted: Rigdon, p. 80.

276   Reilly instructed the driver: Breuer, p. 6.

276   The car slid through the gates: Leahy, p. 203; Rigdon, p. 80.

276   Stalin gave up the main residence: Rigdon, pp. 80–81.

276   "The servants who made. . . .": Breuer, p. 6.

276   Along with the comfortable: Havas, p. 223.

276   Stalin wore a plain: Burns, *Roosevelt: The Soldier of Freedom,* p. 406.

276   However lacking in stature: Doris Kearns Goodwin, *No Ordinary Time,* p. 257.

276   "I have tried for a long time. . . .": Burns, *Roosevelt: The Soldier of Freedom,* p. 407.

276   "There was no waste of word. . . .": Sherwood, pp. 343–44.

276   They made an odd pair: Goodwin, p. 257.

277   "Roosevelt was about to say something. . . .": Robert H. Ferrell, *The Dying President: Franklin D. Roosevelt, 1944–1945,* p. 17.

277   The Tehran conference ended: Burns, *Roosevelt: The Soldier of Freedom,* p. 411.

277   Maybe the way to spike: Leahy, p. 243.

277 Back home, holding a press conference: *The Complete Presidential Press Conferences of Franklin D. Roosevelt,* Dec. 17, 1943.

277 "Do you realize what a bad impression . . . ?": RG 457 CBOM 76.

278 "The author of the statement. . . .": ibid.

278 "whatever was said was concerning. . . .": ibid.

278 The six surviving Skorzeny: Reilly, p. 182.

278 "Who will command Overlord?": Burns, *Roosevelt: The Soldier of Freedom,* p. 410.

278 "I do not believe we can wait. . . .": MR Box 165.

278 "We are making preparations. . . .": Francis L. Loewenheim, Harold D. Langley, and Manfred Jonas, eds., *Roosevelt and Churchill: Their Secret Wartime Correspondence,* p. 228.

278 "No responsible British general. . . .": ibid., p. 222.

278 "like carrying a large lump of ice. . . .": Winston S. Churchill, *Memoirs of the Second World War,* p. 619.

279 "especially about our being. . . .": Loewenheim, Langley, and Jonas, p. 237.

279 Though Churchill had finally agreed: ibid., p. 331.

279 At one point, he stood: Sherwood, p. 590.

279 "Germany can be beaten. . . .": *FRUS,* First Quebec Conference, p. 497.

279 "None of these methods. . . .": ibid.

279 Churchill may well have preferred: Sherwood, p. 591.

279 On one errand for the OSS: Churchill, *Memoirs,* p. 463.

279 "Why is the Prime Minister so anxious . . . ?": Ernest Cuneo Papers, Box 108, FDRL.

280 "The importance of the command. . . .": MR Box 17.

280 "I believe General Marshall. . . .": ibid.

280 The choice of Marshall had appeared: Burns, *Roosevelt: The Soldier of Freedom,* p. 392.

280 As Henry Stimson remembered: Henry L. Stimson and McGeorge Bundy, *On Active Service in Peace and War,* p. 441.

280 "to transfer [Marshall]. . . .": PSF Box 83.

280 "You are absolutely right. . . .": ibid.

280 "Ike, you and I know. . . .": Sherwood, p. 770.

281 Ike would be coming back: ibid.

281 "I believe that Marshall's command. . . .": Stimson memo to Harry Hopkins, Nov. 10, 1943, FDRL.

281 But Mrs. Marshall began to move: Maurice Matloff, *United States Army in World War II,* p. 274; Sherwood, p. 761.

281 General Pershing's position: Matloff, p. 294.

281 A Nazi broadcast out of Paris: Eric Larrabee, *Commander in Chief,* p. 149.

281 Though Marshall continued to keep: Sherwood, p. 761.

281 "I was determined. . . .": Leonard Mosley, *Marshall,* p. 265.

282 "The [President] evidently assumed. . . .": ibid., p. 266.

282 "Well, I didn't feel I could sleep. . . .": ibid.; Larrabee, p. 150.

282 "I said frankly that I was staggered. . . .": Stimson and Bundy, p. 442.

282 "The President said he got the impression. . . .": ibid.

282 "I knew in the bottom of his heart. . . .": ibid.

282 "He therefore proposed to nominate. . . .": Winston S. Churchill, *The Second World War,* p. 357.

282 Roosevelt's next stop after Cairo: Sherwood, p. 803.

283 "Dear Eisenhower you might like. . . .": POF Box 8912.

283 "Eisenhower is the best politician. . . .": James Roosevelt, *My Parents,* p. 167.

283 In his report, Oshima described: Stafford, p. 274.

284 What if, before Overlord: Loewenheim, Langley, and Jonas, p. 432.

284 Thus he endorsed: Bishop, p. 289.

284 "to transport the Army. . . .": U.S. Army Historical Manuscripts Collection, file 8-3, 6ACA, FDRL.

284 The closer the May 1944 invasion: F. H. Hinsley, *British Intelligence in the Second World War,* vol. 3, pt. 1, p. 46.

284 ". . . [T]here is an indirect way. . . .": David Kahn, *Hitler's Spies,* p. 483.

285 "Truth is so precious. . . .": Churchill, *The Second World War,* p. 328.

285 "Stalin and his comrades. . . .": ibid.

285 "In particular it was agreed. . . .": Anthony Cave Brown, *Bodyguard of Lies,* p. 389.

285 Beneath the pavements: ibid., p. 1.

285 In December 1943, less than a month: Ladislas Farago, *The Game of the Foxes,* p. 614.

285 London Controlling Section: Brown, *Bodyguard of Lies,* p. 8.

285 "I cannot prophesy. . . .": Samuel I. Rosenman, *Working with Roosevelt,* p. 367.

286 "No doubt some government department. . . .": David Irving, *Hitler's War,* p. 279.

286 "I am inclined to believe. . . .": David Kahn, *Code Breaking in World Wars I and II,* p. 148.

286 All these conditions: Churchill, *The Second World War,* p. 507.

286 "Our object is to get Turkey. . . .": Kahn, *Hitler's Spies,* p. 344.

286 While the ambassador was in his office: ibid., pp. 340–41.

287 The Allies learned of the alarming leak: Breuer, p. 32.

287 Cicero, feeling the approaching breath: Joseph E. Persico, *Piercing the Reich,* pp. 69–70; Kahn, *Hitler's Spies,* p. 345; Brown, *Bodyguard of Lies,* p. 398.

287 The crafty German ambassador: Kahn, *Hitler's Spies,* p. 344.

287 British intelligence operatives: Brown, *Bodyguard of Lies,* p. 402.

287 "the ambassador's valet succeeded. . . .": Norman Polmar and Thomas B. Allen, *Spy Book,* p. 121.

CHAPTER XX: THE WHITE HOUSE IS PENETRATED

288 "all the major railroad stations. . . .": PSF Box 4.

289 "The essential business of Berlin proceeds. . . .": ibid.

289 "that immediate retaliatory action. . . .": PSF Box 83.

289 "It seems to me that such action. . . .": ibid.

289 "Entire train on bridge. . . .": RG 457 Memorandum from General Marshall to FDR, Feb. 15, 1944.

290 The latter, unknown to the Americans: Allen Weinstein and Alexander Vassiliev, *The Haunted Wood,* pp. 240–41; William B. Breuer, *Hoodwinking Hitler,* p. 72.

290 Fitin, blond, blue-eyed, and soft-spoken: Breuer, p. 72.

291 "the boon companion. . . .": Bradley F. Smith, *The Shadow Warriors,* p. 338.

291 As a sweetener, he immediately offered: Weinstein and Vassiliev, p. 241; Smith, *The Shadow Warriors,* p. 338.

291 By the end of the day: Smith, *The Shadow Warriors,* p. 339.

291 The Soviets soon announced: ibid.

291 All that now remained for him: MR Box 163.

291 Hopkins read Hoover's letter: Smith, *The Shadow Warriors,* p. 341; Curt Gentry, *J. Edgar Hoover,* p. 311.

291 "a highly dangerous. . . .": Smith, *The Shadow Warriors,* pp. 340–41.

291 "[m]ilitary advantages accruing to the United States. . . .": MR Box 163.

291 "I don't need to suggest to you. . . .": ibid.

292 "engaged in attempting to obtain. . . .": Smith, *The Shadow Warriors,* p. 341.

292 "Under the statutes. . . .": PSF Box 49.

292 The implication Biddle so delicately raised: Smith, *The Shadow Warriors,* p. 346.

292 "What do we do next?": PSF Box 49.

292 "an exchange of O.S.S. and N.K.V.D. . . .": Eric Larrabee, *Commander in Chief,* p. 171; Smith, *The Shadow Warriors,* p. 344; M 1642, Leahy memorandum, March 15, 1944.

292 He provided the Russians: Gentry, p. 312; Smith, *The Shadow Warriors,* p. 349; Weinstein and Vassiliev, p. 245.

293 Donovan also assured the Soviets: Weinstein and Vassiliev, p. 244.

293 One man who knew immediately: ibid., p. 257.

293 "[O]ur task is to insert there. . . .": ibid., pp. 240, 257.

293 Thirty years old in 1944: U.S. Congress, *Hearings on Proposed Legislation to Curb or Control the Communist Party of the United States,* 1948, p. 717.

293 "[a]verage height, medium brown hair. . . .": Elizabeth Bentley, *Out of Bondage,* Devin-Adair edition, p. 182.

293   Though Lee was not a Communist: *Hearings,* p. 175; Weinstein and Vassiliev, p. 257; Bentley, *Out of Bondage,* Devin-Adair edition, p. 182.

293   Immediately after graduating: *Hearings,* p. 720; Weinstein and Vassiliev, p. 241.

293   By the time the COI: M 1642, Reel 67, Frames 457, 463.

293   Early in 1943, Lee: *Hearings,* pp. 720, 725.

293   "I am the gal. . . .": ibid., p. 529.

293   An FBI agent later described Bentley: Bentley, Devin-Adair edition, pp. 223–24.

293   This product of a stern New England: Weinstein and Vassiliev, p. 88.

294   Bentley and Lee began meeting: *Hearings,* p. 529.

294   ". . . highly secret information. . . .": ibid.

294   "Cables coming to the State Department. . . .": Weinstein and Vassiliev, p. 257.

294   "He was one of the most nervous. . . .": Bentley, Ivy edition, p. 126.

294   On the delicate matter of Poland's future: Robert Louis Benson and Michael Warner, eds., *VENONA,* p. 227.

294   ". . . he told me," she later claimed: *Hearings,* p. 728.

294   Oak Ridge was the site: Richard Rhodes, *The Making of the Atomic Bomb,* p. 486.

294   At one of their drugstore: *Hearings,* p. 727.

294   "I'm finished. They'll come. . . .": Bentley, Devin-Adair edition, p. 260.

295   "According to Kokh. . . .": Robert Louis Benson, *A History of U.S. Communications Intelligence During World War II,* pp. 337–38.

295   He feared Donovan had begun: Weinstein and Vassiliev, pp. 259–61.

295   The Soviets were just as happy: ibid., pp. 260–61.

295   "drug stores with two exits. . . .": Statement of Elizabeth Ferrill Bentley to the FBI, Nov. 30, 1945, p. 66.

295   "memorize the last two numbers. . . .": ibid., p. 67.

295   "to go down one or several. . . .": ibid.

295   "to turn around and start following. . . .": ibid., p. 61.

296   "place a book behind my front door. . . .": ibid., p. 68.

296   "a thin black thread. . . .": ibid.

296   "I was to remove. . . .": ibid.

296   No conversation of substance: ibid., p. 69.

296   "should either use a phone booth. . . .": ibid., p. 70.

296   Either Bentley's training was sound: Norman Polmar and Thomas B. Allen, *Spy Book,* p. 56.

296   Soviet agents like Elizabeth Bentley: Christopher Andrew, *For the President's Eyes Only,* p. 89.

296   The image the President had: ibid.

296   "I have a weakness. . . .": Weinstein and Vassiliev, p. 63.

296   She displayed this penchant: ibid., p. 51.

296 "[M]y father has great influence. . . .": ibid., p. 57.

296 "I have access. . . .": ibid., p. 55.

296 As an NKVD officer put it: ibid., p. 58.

296 She did not hesitate to use: ibid., p. 64.

297 "She should . . . be guided to approach. . . .": ibid., p. 62.

297 Dodd would remain unwavering: ibid., p. 71.

297 There he joined the Communist Party: ibid., p. 72.

297 The usher's log for October 21: Day-by-Day, Oct. 21, 1941, FDRL.

297 The First Lady suggested: Weinstein and Vassiliev, p. 74.

297 "In those places. . . .": ibid.

297 "[O]ne should render assistance. . . .": ibid., pp. 82–83.

298 "I got a very mysterious call. . . .": John Morton Blum, *Years of Urgency, 1938–1941: From the Morgenthau Diaries,* p. 340.

298 White, valued by Morgenthau: John Morton Blum, *Years of War, 1941–1945: From the Morgenthau Diaries,* p. 89.

298 The Treasury secretary continued: Weinstein and Vassiliev, p. xxiv; Benson, p. 322.

298 "ready for any self-sacrifice. . . .": Weinstein and Vassiliev, p. 168; Benson and Warner, pp. 321–22.

298 "Timely receipt by us. . . .": Weinstein and Vassiliev, pp. 163–64.

299 No record of this letter: ibid., p. 226.

299 Roosevelt was highly sensitive: Smith, *The Shadow Warriors,* p. 143.

299 "Bill, you must treat the Russians. . . .": Stanley Lovell, *Of Spies and Stratagems,* p. 185.

299 "Pappy thought American words. . . .": John Franklin Carter Diary, March 25, 1943.

299 "The Soviet people in Moscow. . . .": PSF Navy, Box 62.

300 "[h]aving had my fingers burned. . . .": Adolf Berle Papers, Box 213, FDRL.

300 "The list of the military secrets. . . .": ibid.

300 ". . . [T]he engineers they have wished to let in. . . .": ibid.

300 "The Russian denouement is unpredictable. . . .": ibid.

300 The Army, Navy, and FBI: ibid.

300 It was not until the spring: Bradley F. Smith, *Sharing Secrets with Stalin,* p. 119.

300 "specifications of the latest. . . .": ibid., pp. 119, 140.

300 The U.S. naval attaché in Moscow: ibid., p. 140.

300 Wallace is said to have planned: Christopher Andrew and Vasili Mitrokhin, *The Sword and the Shield,* pp. 59, 109.

CHAPTER XXI: IF OVERLORD FAILS

301 German towns were being incinerated: David G. McCullough, ed., *The American Heritage Picture History of World War II,* p. 418.

301 "all secret and confidential intelligence. . . .": MR Box 164.

301 ". . . [T]here is no substantial evidence. . . .": ibid.

302 "The OSS representative in Bern. . . .": MR Box 73.

302 Speer, a realist, put together: RG 457 CBOM 76.

302 FDR's military staff advised him: F. H. Hinsley, *British Intelligence in the Second World War,* vol. 3, pt. 2, p. 42.

302 "A man who does not. . . .": Martin Blumenson, *Patton,* p. 222.

302 Two weeks before the North African: PSF Box 83.

302 "During the tea some screams. . . .": ibid.

303 "This report must be kept secret. . . .": ibid.

303 On D-Day, Patton: Anthony Cave Brown, *Bodyguard of Lies,* p. 474.

303 Two massive army groups: ibid., pp. 460–61.

303 Its genuine units: ibid., p. 474.

303 "A man must be alert. . . .": Blumenson, pp. 222–23.

303 The Russians even agreed: Bradley F. Smith, *Sharing Secrets with Stalin,* p. 181.

304 ". . . [D]etails for the preparation. . . .": MR Box 104.

304 "Would it not be well for you and me . . . ?": Francis L. Loewenheim, Harold D. Langley, and Manfred Jonas, eds., *Roosevelt and Churchill: Their Secret Wartime Correspondence,* p. 486.

304 ". . . [I]t is our firm intention to launch Overlord . . .": ibid., pp. 488–89.

304 "pay a handsome tribute . . .": ibid., p. 488.

304 "probably the most important. . . .": Smith, *Sharing Secrets,* p. 193.

304 Kept from the D-Day secret: Loewenheim, Langley, and Jonas, p. 487.

304 "We call him Joan of Arc. . . .": Brown, *Bodyguard of Lies,* p. 570.

304 "Personally, I do not think. . . .": Loewenheim, Langley, and Jonas, p. 484.

305 The Prime Minister agreed . . . : James Leutze, "The Secret of the Churchill-Roosevelt Correspondence, September 1939–May 1940," *Journal of Contemporary History,* July 10, 1975, pp. 1498–99.

305 "The resistance army. . . .": MR Box 17.

305 Ike was to lead him to believe: Brown, *Bodyguard of Lies,* p. 582.

305 Early in the war, FDR: Kimball, vol. 8, p. 57.

305 "[A] great deal of information. . . .": Brown, *Bodyguard of Lies,* p. 543.

305 He found particularly disconcerting: ibid., p. 544.

305 "continues to operate in favor. . . .": ibid., p. 543.

305 The note ended: ibid., pp. 543–44.

306 De Valera, as much the politician: Kimball, vol. 8, p. 57.

306 "Now as for the question. . . .": RG 457 CBOM 77.

307 The transcript, delivered to Hitler: Ladislas Farago, *The Game of the Foxes,* p. 591; Kimball, vol. 8, p. 11.

307 "For it is there that the enemy. . . .": David Kahn, *Hitler's Spies,* p. 489.

307 "They would establish. . . .": Hinsley, vol. 8, pt. 2, p. 61.

307 "the Cotentin [Peninsula] would be. . . .": Kahn, *Hitler's Spies,* p. 502.

307 Consequently, two seasoned German: ibid.; Hinsley, vol. 8, pt. 2, p. 61.

307 "What I want to impress upon the people. . . .": MR Box 30.

307 "I brought your No. 341. . . .": ibid.

307 "I have received your message. . . .": ibid.

308 At the same time that FDR: PSF Box 99.

308 "I assume that somewhere here. . . .": ibid.

308 "What do you think . . . ?": ibid.

308 "For a matter of two or three hours. . . .": ibid.

308 "When I think of the beaches. . . .": *Time,* June 6, 1994.

308 "I doubt if I did. . . .": William B. Breuer, *Hoodwinking Hitler,* p. 92.

308 "I am personally. . . .": Loewenheim, Langley, and Jonas, p. 493.

309 ". . . [T]he war cabinet shares my apprehension. . . .": ibid., p. 494.

309 And FDR, unlike Churchill, was disinclined: ibid., pp. 493–95.

309 Both Bodyguard and Fortitude: RG 457 CBOM 77.

309 ". . . [M]ost indications point toward his action. . . .": ibid.

309 Every night, members of the French resistance: Farago, pp. 625–26.

310 If Overlord failed: Breuer, p. 194; *MHQ,* Spring 1998, p. 66.

CHAPTER XXII: CRACKS IN THE REICH

311 The first to express concern: Jim Bishop, *FDR's Last Year,* p. 3.

311 His breathing was shallow: ibid., p. 2; David Brinkley, *Washington Goes to War,* p. 247.

312 On March 27 he called: Bishop, p. 2.

312 For years, part of the physician's job: ibid., p. 3.

312 The President was suffering: ibid., p. 6.

312 His blood pressure: ibid., p. 4.

312 Bruenn estimated the life left: ibid., p. 6.

312 After the examination FDR: ibid.

312 The mid-forties were not a favorable era: Robert H. Ferrell, *The Dying President: Franklin D. Roosevelt, 1944–1945,* p. 44.

313 "He would ask my opinion. . . .": William Leahy, *I Was There,* p. 298.

313 When an aide asked: Ferrell, *The Dying President,* p. 107.

313 "I had a good talk with the P. . . .": Suckley, Binder 17, p. 85.

314 On Monday afternoon, June 5: ibid., p. 118.

314 Grace Tully noted: James MacGregor Burns, *Roosevelt: The Soldier of Freedom,* pp. 475–76; Bishop, p. 63.

314 At five minutes past 11 p.m.: Bishop, p. 63.

314 Sensing the pall: ibid.

314 As he spoke, the mightiest armada: F. H. Hinsley, *British Intelligence in the Second World War,* vol. 3, pt. 2, p. 131; David G. McCullough, ed., *The American Heritage Picture History of World War II,* p. 482.

314   a flotilla one hundred miles wide: *Time,* June 6, 1994.

314   He kept picking up his bedside phone: Eric Larrabee, *Commander in Chief,* p. 624.

315   Allied casualties: Hinsley, p. 131; *Time,* June 6, 1994.

315   For all the elaborate machinations: Doris Kearns Goodwin, *No Ordinary Time,* p. 508.

315   "They will need thy blessings. . . .": Bishop, p. 66.

315   "The Germans appear to expect. . . .": William B. Breuer, *Hoodwinking Hitler,* p. 215.

315   "Not a single unit": David Kahn, *Hitler's Spies,* p. 515.

315   Three days after the invasion: ibid., p. 516.

316   "Rommel had insisted. . . .": PSF Box 149.

316   After Hitler issued an order: F. W. Winterbotham, *The Ultra Secret,* p. 198.

316   On August 7, Kluge conceded: Kahn, *Hitler's Spies,* p. 519.

316   By then, the Allies: McCullough, *American Heritage Picture History,* p. 464.

316   Over two years before D-Day: Adolf Berle Papers, Box 214, FDRL.

317   "I said that in a country. . . .": ibid.

317   On July 10, 1944: PSF Box 149.

317   Donovan's source revealed: ibid.

317   Their rapacity surfaced: RG 457 CBOM 76.

317   "At our last meeting. . . .": RG 457 CBOM 77.

318   However, that the gold ingots: William Slany, "Preliminary Study on U.S. and Allied Efforts to Recover and Restore Gold and Other Assets Stolen or Hidden by Germany During World War II," U.S. Department of State, p. 165.

318   "We would like to warn you. . . .": PSF Box 149.

318   While it was selling Germany: Slany, pp. 165–66.

318   They had allowed American fliers: Joseph E. Persico, *Piercing the Reich,* p. 69.

319   On April 11, 1944: PSF Box 9.

319   The approach was simple: Slany, pp. 166–67.

319   "We ought to block the Swiss participation. . . .": PSF Box 153.

319   And while most Swiss loved: Slany, p. 168.

319   After the American raids: Roger J. Sandilands, *The Life and Political Economy of Lauchlin Currie,* p. 395.

320   "the most valuable of all. . . .": Slany, p. 91.

320   ". . . [R]ush orders given to SKF by the Germans. . . .": M 1642, Reel 79, Frame 513.

320   The Swedish navy escorted: Slany, p. xviii.

320   Over 250,000 of Hitler's forces: *NYT,* June 21, 1998.

320   Theirs was a small country: Slany, p. xviii.

320 Before 1944 was out: ibid.

320 Spain's Blue Division: *NYT,* June 21, 1998.

321 ". . . [W]e Spaniards and Portuguese. . . .": RG 457 CBOM 77.

321 Albert Speer: Slany, p. xiv.

321 He told the President: PSF Box 50.

321 "We certainly want to cut down. . . .": ibid.

321 Ultimately, the shipments: Slany, pp. xxxviii, xiv.

321 In late January 1944: Jürgen Heideking and Christof Mauch, eds., *American Intelligence and the German Resistance to Hitler,* p. 8.

322 He quickly became disillusioned: Persico, *Piercing the Reich,* pp. 49–50.

322 He cited a date for the coup: ibid., p. 58.

322 Still, he continued to send messages: Breuer, p. 33.

322 Several weeks before D-Day: Anthony Cave Brown, *The Last Hero,* p. 531.

322 "The Breakers group wishes. . . .": Heideking and Mauch, p. 231.

322 ". . . is especially concerned. . . .": Neal H. Petersen, ed., *From Hitler's Doorstep,* p. 265.

323 Gisevius informed Dulles: Persico, *Piercing the Reich,* p. 60.

323 "There is a possibility. . . .": *The "Magic" Background of Pearl Harbor,* vol. 1, p. A-224.

323 "A revolution is not to be expected. . . .": PSF Box 149.

323 "Those opposed to the Nazis. . . .": ibid.

323 "We must judge. . . .": ibid.

323 That summer, Eleanor Roosevelt: PSF Box 37.

323 "Large sums of money. . . .": ibid.

324 "the Bolshevik armies are supreme. . . .": ibid.

324 "not on any grounds of principle. . . .": PSF Box 149.

324 On July 20 the conspirators: Heideking and Mauch, p. 234; William L. Shirer, *The Rise and Fall of the Third Reich,* p. 1054.

324 "The developments did not come. . . .": PSF Box 149.

325 "Photographs appearing in the German press. . . .": ibid.

325 Donovan also reported: Heideking and Mauch, p. 9.

325 Days after the failed coup: RG 457 CBOM 77.

326 "The doctor reported," Hewitt cabled: PSF Box 4.

328 "Hitler has often vowed. . . .": PSF Box 99.

328 "Mr. Towell of OSS has requested. . . .": Athan Theoharis, ed., *From the Secret Files of J. Edgar Hoover,* p. 301.

328 In the fall of 1944, Wild Bill: Kermit Roosevelt, *The Overseas Targets,* p. xvi.

329 "Dear Bill, Ever so many thanks. . . .": PPF Box 6558.

CHAPTER XXIII: A SECRET UNSHARED

330 His daylight hours were spent: Ernest B. Furgurson, "Back Channels," *Washingtonian,* vol. 31 (June 1996).

331 "I talked with the Prime Minister. . . .": PSF Box 99.

331 "If it is not the fashion now. . . .": Furgurson.

331 FDR called Hanfstaengl's reports: ibid.

331 "allowed their embryo doctors. . . .": PSF Box 99.

331 The British, he explained: John Franklin Carter Diary, Feb. 4, 1944.

332 "If I can get close enough. . . .": Furgurson.

332 The President dismissed: ibid.

332 "very confidentially, that the State Department. . . .": PSF Box 100.

332 "did not feel it was worthwhile. . . .": ibid.

332 "I thought you would want. . . .": ibid.

332 "My own opinion on the subject. . . .": ibid.

332 Late in the fall: ibid.

332 However, Colonel Davenport: ibid.

333 "The source of this information. . . .": ibid.

333 "Dear George," he wrote: ibid.

333 In launching the invasion: William L. Shirer, *The Rise and Fall of the Third Reich,* p. 829.

333 During delirious celebrations: ibid., p. 824.

333 On April 6, German bombers: Winston S. Churchill, *Memoirs of the Second World War,* p. 428.

333 The punitive diversion set: Anthony Cave Brown, *The Last Hero,* p. 457.

334 Initially Churchill did support him: Gerhard L. Weinberg, *A World at Arms,* p. 524.

334 When one of his staff asked him: David Stafford, *Churchill and Secret Service,* p. 272.

334 ". . . [T]he guerrilla forces appear. . . .": Brown, *The Last Hero,* p. 456.

334 Churchill complained that Donovan: Stafford, pp. 280–81.

334 "We have no sources of intelligence. . . .": PSF Box 153.

335 "We are now in the process. . . .": Francis L. Loewenheim, Harold D. Langley, and Manfred Jonas, eds., *Roosevelt and Churchill: Their Secret Wartime Correspondence,* p. 482.

335 "In view of your expressed opinion. . . .": ibid., p. 483.

335 "The situation," he wrote: PSF Box 153.

335 "[p]lease ask General Marshall. . . .": ibid.

335 He told the British foreign secretary: James MacGregor Burns, *Roosevelt: The Soldier of Freedom,* p. 365.

336 "to be launched against. . . .": Loewenheim, Langley, and Jonas, p. 688.

336 ". . . [I]f the enemy were to take. . . .": ibid., pp. 688–89.

336 One week after D-Day: David G. McCullough, ed., *The American Heritage Picture History of World War II,* p. 420.

336 "Combat experience with this weapon. . . .": Loewenheim, Langley, and Jonas, p. 689.

336 The pilot was: Richard J. Whalen, *The Founding Father,* p. 370; Michael R. Beschloss, *Kennedy and Roosevelt: The Uneasy Alliance,* p. 254.

337 ". . . Hitler was the greatest genius. . . .": POF Box 3060.

337 "Harbors sheltering. . . .": M 1642, Reel 128, Frame 177.

337 The man Donovan chose: Joseph E. Persico, *Casey: From the OSS to the CIA,* p. 449.

337 By June 17, 1944: M 1642, Reel 128, Frame 213.

338 On August 12 the first mission: Whalen, pp. 370–71; Beschloss, p. 256; Norman Polmar and Thomas B. Allen, *Spy Book,* p. 468.

338 "Harry," he snarled: David G. McCullough, *Truman,* p. 328.

339 Yet, the President was disconcerted: *FRUS,* 2d Quebec Conference, p. 492.

339 Lowen had earlier talked himself: Doris Kearns Goodwin, *No Ordinary Time,* p. 621.

339 During a year at Oxford: Liva Baker, *Felix Frankfurter,* p. 4.

339 Eager to exploit Bohr's expertise: Thomas Powers, *Heisenberg's War,* pp. 231–32; Baker, pp. 4–5.

339 Bohr subsequently went to America: Burns, *Roosevelt: The Soldier of Freedom,* p. 457.

339 He told the Americans, incorrectly: Thomas Powers, p. 230.

339 Should Russia learn: Baker, pp. 273–74; Richard Rhodes, *The Making of the Atomic Bomb,* p. 528.

339 The swift pace of work: Baker, p. 275.

339 After leaving Los Alamos: Thomas Powers, p. 241.

340 Bohr returned to England: Baker, pp. 275–76.

340 According to an eyewitness account: Jim Bishop, *FDR's Last Year,* p. 143.

340 "He talked inaudibly. . . .": William Stevenson, *A Man Called Intrepid,* p. 438.

340 Churchill's thoughts, at the time: Bishop, p. 144.

340 The Prime Minister, through his: Norman Moss, *Klaus Fuchs,* pp. 1–2.

340 Anything Bohr required: Burns, *Roosevelt: The Soldier of Freedom,* p. 458; Moss, p. 2.

340 "I did not like the man. . . .": Rhodes, p. 530.

340 Felix Frankfurter, in a "Dear Frank" letter: PSF Box 136.

340 Better Stalin should learn: ibid.

340 He included along with: ibid.

340 "Roosevelt agreed that an approach. . . .": Rhodes, pp. 536–37.

341 Niels Bohr had even been led: ibid., p. 537.

341 Lunch was served immediately: *FRUS,* 2d Quebec Conference, ed. note.

341 Next, the interfering Niels Bohr: Bishop, p. 144.

341 The only reason the Russians wanted: ibid.

341 "The suggestion that the world. . . .": ibid.

341 "Enquiries should be made. . . .": ibid.

342   That day Churchill left Hyde Park: *FRUS,* 2d Quebec Conference, ed. note.

342   "He [Bohr] is a great advocate. . . .": Baker, pp. 276–77.

342   The NKVD code name: Allen Weinstein and Alexander Vassiliev, *The Haunted Wood,* p. 181.

342   The month before Churchill: Dan Kurzman, *Day of the Bomb,* p. 62.

342   Thereafter, Oppenheimer invited: Moss, p. 72.

342   "He worked days and nights. . . .": Norman Polmar and Thomas B. Allen, *Spy Book,* p. 223.

342   "one compartment I allowed. . . .": Moss, p. 200.

343   Even before coming to Los Alamos: Kurzman, pp. 130–32.

343   "I was worried about the dangers. . . .": *NYT Magazine,* Sept. 14, 1997, p. 72.

343   Hall was nineteen: Christopher Andrew and Vasili Mitrokhin, *The Sword and the Shield,* p. 131; *NYT Magazine,* Sept. 14, 1997, pp. 70–73.

344   ". . . [H]e remembers Woodrow Wilson. . . .": Suckley, Binder 16, p. 274.

344   No one, she thought: ibid., Binder 17, p. 96.

344   "[I]f the election were held tomorrow. . . .": ibid., pp. 50–51.

344   He chose Senator Harry S Truman: Goodwin, p. 526.

345   Kolbe delivered the incriminating: Neal H. Petersen, ed., *From Hitler's Doorstep,* pp. 191–93.

345   "The OSS report did not seem. . . .": Ladislas Farago, *The Game of the Foxes,* pp. 348–49.

345   "Stores are closing one by one. . . .": RG 457 CBOM 77.

345   "Living conditions of the people. . . .": ibid.

345   "My Dear Mr. President. . . .": PSF Box Navy 62.

346   "Well," Dewey said: Christopher Andrew, *For the President's Eyes Only,* p. 143.

346   "I am writing to you. . . .": Roberta Wohlstetter, *Pearl Harbor,* p. 177; Andrew, pp. 144–45.

346   ". . . largely result from the fact. . . .": Wohlstetter, p. 177.

346   ". . . Some of Donovan's people. . . .": ibid.

347   A Dewey aide pointed out: Andrew, p. 144.

347   "The President was surprised. . . .": Robert E. Sherwood, *Roosevelt and Hopkins,* p. 827.

347   The Nazi RSHA: David Kahn, *Hitler's Spies,* pp. 339–40.

347   "the Germans were fitting. . . .": MR Box 164.

348   ". . . [O]ur own submarine campaign. . . .": ibid.

348   how hard the Germans continued: John Morton Blum, *Years of War, 1941–1945: From the Morgenthau Diaries,* p. 340.

348   "We have got to be tough. . . .": ibid., p. 342.

348   "left no doubt. . . .": ibid.

348   "I . . . gave him my idea. . . .": ibid., p. 344.

349   ". . . [I]f you let the young children of today. . . .": ibid.

349   "[T]hat is not nearly as bad. . . .": ibid.

349   "This so-called 'Handbook' . . .": ibid., pp. 348–49.

349   "All Junker estates. . . .": ibid., p. 358.

349   "No German shall be permitted. . . .": M 1642, Reel 52, Frames 378–84.

350   Stimson remained adamantly opposed: Stimson to FDR, Sept. 15, 1944, FDRL.

350   He and Churchill then signed: Blum, *Years of War,* pp. 373, 381.

350   By mid-September, Allied troops: Joseph E. Persico, *Piercing the Reich,* p. 8.

350   American GIs, he predicted: Blum, *Years of War,* pp. 378, 382.

350   "I will stay here. . . .": ibid., p. 379.

351   "No one," he told Cordell Hull: ibid., pp. 380–81.

351   Its advantage to the enemy: ibid., p. 382.

351   "According to what American officials. . . .": RG 457 CBOM 76.

351   ". . . feels there is an excellent. . . .": Suckley, Binder 18, p. 169.

352   "I still think he is. . . .": Burns, p. 530; Bishop, pp. 195, 196.

CHAPTER XXIV: "TAKE A LOOK AT THE OSS"

353   By the fall of 1944: Thomas F. Troy, *Donovan and the CIA,* p. 295.

353   ". . . [T]he results achieved by OSS. . . .": Roger J. Spiller, "Assessing Ultra," *Military Review,* vol. 7 (August 1979), p. 239.

354   Through his bookshop contacts: Joseph E. Persico, *Piercing the Reich,* pp. 167–68.

354   His recruits were Communists: Persico, *Piercing the Reich,* pp. 253–58.

354   "a question which will rise. . . .": Donovan to FDR, Dec. 1, 1944, FDRL.

354   "what we are prepared to do. . . .": *FRUS,* 1944, vol. I, p. 566; M 1642, Reel 81, Frame 642.

355   "What do you think?": PSF Box 151.

356   Rosenbaum happily reported back to Donovan: NA Microfilm A3304, Rosenbaum to Donovan, Oct. 12, 1944.

356   "Bill Donovan's Office of Strategic Services. . . .": Anthony Cave Brown, *The Last Hero,* p. 624.

356   "In my opinion, consideration. . . .": PSF OSS Box 153.

356   "I am sending the enclosed to you. . . .": ibid.

357   "I am afraid that the author. . . .": PSF Box 150.

357   Under his proposal, the new service: PSF Box 153.

357   Finally, Donovan's brainchild: ibid.

357   "Though in the midst of war. . . .": ibid.

357   What Donovan was saying to FDR: Brown, *The Last Hero,* p. 623.

358   "civil service regulations. . . .": M 1642, Reel 3, Frames 756–61.

358   The document brashly styled: ibid., Frame 764.

358 Four days after receiving: PSF Box 153.

358 "Such power in one man. . . .": Curt Gentry, *J. Edgar Hoover,* p. 313.

359 Hoover placed her under: ibid., p. 311.

359 Revealing his closeness to FDR: Athan Theoharis, ed., *From the Secret Files of J. Edgar Hoover,* p. 325.

359 "The Germans believe that this station. . . .": POF Box 106.

359 "a rather amusing sidelight. . . .": ibid.

359 "The well known American writer. . . .": ibid.

359 "OSS intends, according to this source. . . .": ibid.

360 The Secret Service first delivered him: David Brinkley, *Washington Goes to War,* p. 165.

360 The truth was: John Gunther, *Roosevelt in Retrospect,* p. 139; Jim Bishop, *FDR's Last Year,* p. 44.

360 "the day the late President. . . .": Troy, *Donovan and the CIA,* p. 282.

360 However seriously, or specifically: Troy, *Donovan and the CIA,* p. 282.

361 "Cadillac automobile is essential. . . .": M 1642, Reel 45, Frame 481.

361 Over the next several months: Stanley Lovell, *Of Spies and Stratagems,* p. 107.

361 And then, on December 16: John Keegan, *The Second World War,* p. 440.

361 Prior to the offensive: Lyman B. Kirkpatrick Jr., *Captains Without Eyes,* pp. 261–62; F. W. Winterbotham, *The Ultra Secret,* p. 254.

361 On the very day the Germans: Bradley F. Smith, *The Shadow Warriors,* p. 279; Doris Kearns Goodwin, *No Ordinary Time,* p. 564; Kirkpatrick, pp. 261–62; Winterbotham, p. 254.

361 On December 19, President Roosevelt: Day-by-Day, Dec. 19, 1944, FDRL.

362 The initial ferocity of the assault: Kirkpatrick, pp. 261–62; Winterbotham, p. 254.

362 "In great stress, Roosevelt. . . .": Goodwin, pp. 564–65.

362 He was a West Pointer: *Academic American Encyclopedia,* vol. 15, p. 154.

362 "the biggest sonovabitch. . . .": Richard Rhodes, *The Making of the Atomic Bomb,* p. 426.

362 As soon as an atom bomb could be ready: Thomas Powers, *Heisenberg's War,* p. 404; Dan Kurzman, *Day of the Bomb,* pp. 106, 107; "FDR," *The American Experience,* PBS, Aug. 3, 1999.

363 Oddly, while worrying about a dud: Kurzman, p. 107.

363 ". . . [W]hen a 'bomb' is. . . .": *FRUS,* 2d Quebec Conference, p. 492.

363 "Following a successful test. . . .": Nat S. Finney, "How FDR Planned to Use the A-Bomb," *Look,* vol. 14, no. 6 (March 14, 1950), pp. 23–24.

363 Sachs also left that day: ibid., p. 24.

364 "Only I know that my father. . . .": James Roosevelt, *My Parents,* p. x.

364 The Argentine reported: PSF Box 1.

364 "We studied the papers by candlelight. . . .": F. H. Hinsley, *British Intelligence in the Second World War,* vol. 3, pt. 2, p. 586.

365 "If we do not keep ahead. . . .": Jim Bishop, *FDR's Last Year,* p. 244.

CHAPTER XXV: SYMPATHIZERS AND SPIES

366 But the ciphers: Robert Louis Benson, *A History of U.S. Communications Intelligence During World War II,* p. xiii.

366 In effect, each message sent: Venona Historical Monograph #2.

366 Colonel Carter Clarke of SIS: Benson, p. xiii.

366 The operation, initially called Bride: ibid., p. vii.

367 Still, the traffic of the NKVD and GRU: Norman Polmar and Thomas B. Allen, *Spy Book,* p. 577; Allen Weinstein and Alexander Vassiliev, *The Haunted Wood,* p. 291.

367 Had the Soviet codes been decrypted: Weinstein and Vassiliev, p. 48.

367 A December 1944 message: Benson, p. 383.

367 Years later, the Venona codebreakers: ibid., p. 337.

367 In a cable: ibid., p. 324.

368 On another occasion: ibid., p. 375.

368 "R expressed doubt. . . .": ibid., p. 299.

368 "an exceptionally keen mind. . . .": ibid., p. 423.

368 *Rulevoi,* the Russian word: Weinstein and Vassiliev, p. 300.

368 "If the election were to take place. . . .": Benson, p. 266.

369 The fact that he: Weinstein and Vassiliev, p. 307.

369 In 1944, Moscow engineered: ibid., p. 301.

369 FDR also admired the man's ability: Roger J. Sandilands, *The Life and Political Economy of Lauchlin Currie,* pp. 96–97.

369 Currie came to the White House: *NYT,* Dec. 30, 1993; Sandilands, p. 390.

369 A fresh assessment: Sandilands, pp. 107, 108.

370 Thus, in January 1941: Robert Thompson, *A Time for War,* p. 306.

370 Currie also deduced: Sandilands, p. 107.

370 "a queer character. . . .": John Keegan, ed., *Who Was Who in World War II,* p. 56.

370 If he really wanted to undercut: Sandilands, p. 110.

370 "I alerted FDR to the inefficiency. . . .": ibid., p. 124.

370 "It appears to me. . . .": ibid., p. 120.

370 Back in 1940, FDR had favored: ibid., p. 115.

370 That scheme had not come to pass: ibid., p. 116.

370 More significantly, it was Currie: ibid., p. 112.

371 "We have respected. . . .": PSF Box 132.

371 Should there be the slightest doubt: ibid.

371 With the border between France: Sandilands, p. 138.

371 "You have not only thwarted. . . .": ibid., p. 139.

372 Puhl, according to Kolbe: M 1642, Reel 21, Frames 168–69.

372 Currie had been a graduate: *Washington Post,* Aug. 14, 1948.

372 When Silverman came to the capital: ibid.

372 Thereafter, Currie continued to see: ibid.

372 Silvermaster was born in Odessa: *NYT,* Oct. 15, 1964.

372 The Civil Service Commission, MID: U.S. Congress, *Hearings on Proposed Legislation to Curb or Control the Communist Party of the United States,* February 1948, p. 618.

373 "A few days ago," it read: Venona Decrypt, National Security Agency, Sept. 2, 1943.

373 Therefore Currie did not regard him: Herbert Romerstein, "Ideological Recruitment of Agents by Soviet Intelligence, in the Light of Venona," Symposium on Cryptological History, National Security Agency, Fort Meade, Maryland, Oct. 29–31, 1992, p. 15.

373 "It's no use fighting. . . .": Elizabeth Bentley, *Out of Bondage,* Devin-Adair edition, p. 173.

373 Silvermaster's productivity had grown: ibid., p. 175.

373 "pull every string you can. . . .": ibid., pp. 173, 174.

373 By now the two men: Sandilands, p. 164.

374 "I have personally made. . . .": *Hearings,* p. 628.

374 "Greg [Silvermaster] was permitted. . . .": Bentley, Devin-Adair edition, p. 174.

374 Vasili Zarubin: Weinstein and Vassiliev, p. 161; Polmar and Allen, p. 578.

374 "a letter from a friend in China. . . .": PSF Box 91.

374 "could find no evidence of graft. . . .": ibid.

374 "I accepted, thinking that I might. . . .": PSF Box 132.

375 "I think Lauch Currie would be good. . . .": John Morton Blum, *Years of War, 1941–1945: From the Morgenthau Diaries,* p. 164.

375 "did not want Currie. . . .": ibid.

375 "T.V. Soong, had opposed Laughlin. . . .": John Franklin Carter Diary, April 14, 1943.

375 Currie informed Harry Hopkins: Michael Warner and Robert Louis Benson, "Venona and Beyond," *Intelligence and National Security,* vol. 12, no. 3 (July 1997), p. 10.

375 The building: David Brinkley, *Washington Goes to War,* p. 36.

375 The beneficiary: Romerstein, p. 16.

375 What Currie had done for Hagen: ibid.

375 On August 7, J. Edgar Hoover: Weinstein and Vassiliev, p. 274.

375 Zarubin was one of those: Warner and Benson, pp. 11, 13.

375 Currie was apparently: Whittaker Chambers, *Witness,* p. 383.

375 Elizabeth Bentley later stated: Statement of Elizabeth Ferrill Bentley to the FBI, Nov. 30, 1945, p. 24; *Hearings,* p. 552.

375   According to an August 1944 NKVD cable: Venona Decrypt, National Security Agency, Aug. 31, 1944.
376   "I have been reliably informed. . . .": *Washington Post,* July 22, 1948.
376   At this time, Bentley: ibid.
376   Currie further reported progress: PSF Box 13.
376   Bentley delivered plans for the B-29: *Washington Post,* July 22, 1948.
376   "Mr. Silverman told me. . . .": *Hearings,* pp. 519, 552–53.
376   It achieves some credibility: Benson, p. xiv.
376   In *The Haunted Wood,* Currie: Weinstein and Vassiliev, pp. 106, 161, 243.
376   One cable sent in 1942: ibid., p. 154.
377   An NKVD message dated April 6: ibid., p. 160.
377   "Find out from Albert. . . .": Venona Decrypt, Feb. 15, 1945.
377   "P. [for Pazh] trusts R. . . .": ibid., March 20, 1945.
377   "The man was not a Communist": Bentley statement to FBI.
377   She was not sure that Currie: *Hearings,* p. 553.
377   Harry Hopkins, before the Tehran conference: Christopher Andrew and Vasili Mitrokhin, *The Sword and the Shield,* p. 111; Weinstein and Vassiliev, pp. xxvii, 239.
378   "No one who talked to the Bureau. . . .": Sandilands, p. 149.

CHAPTER XXVI: A LEAKY VESSEL

379   What Currie had learned: Christopher Andrew and Vasili Mitrokhin, *The Sword and the Shield,* p. 130.
379   In November 1944, Wilho Tikander: Michael Warner and Robert Louis Benson, "Venona and Beyond," *Intelligence and National Security,* vol. 12, no. 3 (July 1997), p. 9.
379   Finland had dropped out: Robert Louis Benson, *A History of U.S. Communications Intelligence During World War II,* p. xviii.
379   Consequently, he recommended: Bradley F. Smith, *The Shadow Warriors,* p. 353.
380   He instructed Tikander to proceed: Christopher Andrew and Oleg Gordievsky, *KGB,* p. 284; Warner and Benson, p. 9; Smith, *The Shadow Warriors,* p. 353.
380   "I wanted you to know. . . .": PSF Box 151.
380   Though Donovan had tried to limit: Smith, *The Shadow Warriors,* pp. 353–54.
380   ". . . [W]e had taken advantage. . . .": PSF Box 49.
380   Of course, Fitin replied: Andrew and Gordievsky, p. 285.
380   Donovan's aide Ned Putzell: Bradley F. Smith, *Sharing Secrets with Stalin,* p. 233.
380   For their part, American cryptanalysts: Warner and Benson, p. 9.
381   The Russian codes sold: ibid., p. 10.

381 However, Putzell: interview, Erwin J. "Ned" Putzell, Nov. 29, 1999.

381 Neither the archives of the OSS: Smith, *Sharing Secrets*, p. 233.

381 For Stalin to suspect: Smith, *The Shadow Warriors*, p. 355.

382 "[W]ith all the tremendous burdens. . . .": PSF Box 131.

382 Roosevelt handed the task over: PSF Earle.

382 "My dear Mr. President, Turkey. . . .": ibid.

382 "Eighty million Germans. . . .": ibid.

382 "There is no vacancy. . . .": ibid.

382 He fired off a warning to the President: MR Box 164.

382 "The fact that this raiding. . . .": James MacGregor Burns, *Roosevelt: The Soldier of Freedom,* p. 73; MR Box 19.

383 Casualties from the V-1s: David Irving, *The Mare's Nest,* p. 295.

383 On December 7, Leahy carried: MR Box 20.

383 Leahy, still skeptical: MR Box 164.

383 "The entire Atlantic Seaboard. . . .": Suckley, Binder 8, p. 237.

383 "the extent of offshore coastal protection. . . .": POF 106.

383 "This development of the [V-2]. . . .": Walter Dornberger, *V-2,* p. 142.

383 Thus German rocket scientists: Gerhard L. Weinberg, *A World at Arms,* p. 564.

384 "Very fast. . . .": Dornberger, p. 143.

384 Indeed, a rocket launch site: Dennis Piszkiewicz, *The Nazi Rocketeers,* p. 184.

384 "The purpose of this," the report: MR Box 164.

384 The German navy's chief: Jim Bishop, *FDR's Last Year,* pp. 82–83.

384 The photo of the U-boat with rails: POF 106.

384 Confirming Admiral Doenitz's strategy: Hoover to Hopkins, Jan. 8, 1945, FDRL.

384 "The capability exists. . . .": MR Box 164.

385 And well over a year had passed: F. H. Hinsley, *British Intelligence in the Second World War,* p. 347; Weinberg, p. 564.

385 In another engineering triumph: Peter Young, ed., *The World Almanac Book of World War II,* p. 471.

385 The reality, however, was: Irving, *The Mare's Nest,* p. 299.

385 The very next day his wife: *NY Mirror,* Feb. 17, 1945; HH Papers, Box 138, FDRL.

385 On his arrival, still trembling: Robert H. Ferrell, *The Dying President: Franklin D. Roosevelt, 1944–1945,* p. 12.

385 "Imagine my shock," he told her: Earle to Boettiger, March 21, 1945, FDRL.

386 "I have read your letter. . . .": MR 171.

386 He wanted it understood: ibid.

386 "I shall issue no public statement. . . .": PSF Box 131.

386 "Your orders to the Pacific. . . .": ibid.

387 Now Hoover was telling him: Hoover to Roosevelt, Jan. 8, 1945, FDRL.

387 "Willy, I suppose about sixteen. . . .": Francis Biddle, *In Brief Authority,* p. 342.

387 He went into the Navy: David Kahn, *Hitler's Spies,* p. 8.

387 They were to be infiltrated: ibid., p. 13.

387 Not only did the SD: ibid., pp. 12–22.

388 The next day, he turned himself: ibid., p. 23.

388 "She stated that. . . .": POF Box 103.

388 "[H]e [Willy] is no relation of mine. . . .": ibid.

388 On Valentine's Day 1945: Kahn, *Hitler's Spies,* p. 26.

389 He feared that the Pacific war: Winston S. Churchill, *The Second World War,* Vol. 5, *Closing the Ring,* p. 569.

389 "When I first got to Tehran. . . .": Suckley, Binder 17, p. 91.

389 "I have received a reply from U.J. . . .": Francis L. Loewenheim, Harold D. Langley, and Manfred Jonas, eds., *Roosevelt and Churchill: Their Secret Wartime Correspondence,* p. 596.

390 "That mountain road had been built. . . .": William Rigdon, *White House Sailor,* p. 145.

390 ". . . [I]f we had spent. . . .": ibid., p. 137.

390 Consequently, Roosevelt supported: Loewenheim, Langley, and Jonas, p. 656; John Gunther, *Roosevelt in Retrospect,* p. 359.

390 Churchill's foreign minister: Burns, *Roosevelt: The Soldier of Freedom,* p. 575.

391 He was ready to meet: Bishop, p. 545.

391 "Ross and Bruenn are both worried. . . .": Ferrell, p. 108.

391 ". . . [T]he President appears. . . .": ibid., p. 105.

391 FDR left frail in body: Winston S. Churchill, *Memoirs of the Second World War,* p. 927.

391 Occupation zones: *FRUS,* 1945, vol. I, p. 579.

391 The tall, patrician Alger Hiss: Norman Polmar and Thomas B. Allen, *Spy Book,* p. 262.

392 "After the Yalta conference. . . .": Benson, p. 423.

392 The jump to an inside page: *Chicago Tribune,* Feb. 7, 1945.

392 "Creation of an all-powerful. . . .": ibid., Feb. 9, 1945.

393 Senate Democrat: Anthony Cave Brown, *The Last Hero,* p. 628.

393 "[T]his document, emanating from an office. . . .": ibid., p. 629.

393 "What is happening here? . . .": M 1642, Reel 3, Frames 788, 789.

393 "The joint chiefs of staff. . . .": *Chicago Tribune,* Feb. 11, 1945.

394 "Comparing the proposal. . . .": *NYT,* Feb. 13, 1945.

394 "Donovan is one of the trail blazers. . . .": *Washington Post,* Feb. 16, 1945.

394　Donovan was soon back in Washington: Smith, *The Shadow Warriors,* p. 400.

394　"was not the result of an accident. . . .": ibid.; Donovan to JCS, Feb. 15, 1945, FDRL.

394　The JCS staff had made changes: *Chicago Tribune,* Feb. 9, 1945; Donovan to JCS, Feb. 19, 1945; National Archives, M 1642.

395　"A reading of these articles. . . .": Donovan to Roosevelt, Feb. 23, 1945, FDRL.

395　Hoover "goes to the White House. . . .": Curt Gentry, *J. Edgar Hoover,* p. 313.

395　By deliberately leaking the documents: interview, Walter Trohan, Sept. 29, 1999.

395　He was also at the time: Gentry, pp. 313–14.

395　"[T]he British were believed to know. . . .": Thomas F. Troy, *Donovan and the CIA,* p. 282.

396　Virgilio Scattolini was a short, fat Roman: Brown, *The Last Hero,* p. 702; Robin W. Winks, *Cloak and Gown,* p. 356.

397　The first delivery to Scamporini: Winks, p. 353.

397　Soon the Vatican reports: *Washington Post,* Aug. 3, 1980.

397　Donovan's front office: M 1642, Reel 119, Frames 2, 3; Brown, *The Last Hero,* p. 689.

397　"This series offers great promise. . . .": M 1642, Reel 119, Frames 2, 3.

397　Scamporini knew only that Settacioli: Brown, *The Last Hero,* pp. 685–86.

397　The informant also had access: Winks, p. 355.

397　What he did not know: ibid.; Brown, *The Last Hero,* p. 685.

397　His office was handling over: Winks, p. 354; Brown, *The Last Hero,* p. 687.

398　On January 11: PSF Box 151.

398　Vessel message 7a: ibid.

398　"The Japanese minimum demands. . . .": ibid.

398　The papal envoy showed a sensitivity: ibid.

399　"On 10 January the Japanese Emperor. . . .": ibid.

399　Along with the White House, Donovan: M 1642, Reel 136, Frame 677.

399　"The Japanese have recently. . . .": M 1642, Reel 11, Frame 4.

399　Using Vessel to cultivate the Navy: Brown, *The Last Hero,* p. 694.

399　Even while the President: ibid., p. 697.

399　Roosevelt's secretary, Grace Tully: ibid., p. 696; M 1642, Reel 119, Frame 71.

399　Thereafter, with Mussolini's acquiescence: William L. Shirer, *The Rise and Fall of the Third Reich,* p. 1005.

399　The widow then fled: Shirer, p. 1005; M 1642, Reel 21, Frames 485, 486.

400　A Vessel message forwarded to the President: PSF Box 153.

400   "... Vessel report was undoubtedly. ...": M 14, Reel 119, Frame 132; Brown, *The Last Hero,* p. 695.

400   "warn all people handling Vessel. ...": M 1642, Reel 119, Frame 88.

400   Both men feared: Brown, *The Last Hero,* pp. 699–700.

401   "We have very good reason to believe. ...": M 1642, Reel 110, Frame 104.

401   Rome was aware of ten: Winks, p. 355.

401   "... suggest you also consider. ...": M 1642, Reel 119, Frame 104.

401   On March 2, Dunn advised: *Washington Post,* Aug. 3, 1980.

401   "Conversation as reported. ...": M 1642, Reel 119, Frame 129.

401   "Dear Jimmie. ...": M 1642, Reel 21, Frame 294.

401   He found it hard to swallow: Brown, *The Last Hero,* p. 686.

401   Angleton, a Catholic: Winks, p. 355.

401   "The procedure of the Papal audiences. ...": *Washington Post,* Aug. 3, 1980.

402   Scattolini had, in fact: ibid.

402   While FDR was en route to Yalta: PSF 151.

403   He wanted to uncover the chain: Winks, p. 356; Brown, *The Last Hero,* p. 701.

CHAPTER XXVII: WHO KNEW—AND WHEN?

404   "We Soviets welcome. ...": Richard A. Russell, *Project Hula: Secret Soviet-American Cooperation in the War Against Japan,* p. 8.

404   Out of this demand was born: ibid., pp. 8–16.

405   General Douglas MacArthur: Douglas MacArthur, *Reminiscences,* p. 262.

405   "From time to time. ...": Dwight D. Eisenhower, *Crusade in Europe,* p. 229.

405   "I did not then know. ...": ibid., p. 443.

405   That army, by now, had grown: James MacGregor Burns, *Roosevelt: The Soldier of Freedom,* p. 456.

405   "I reported as requested. ...": Omar N. Bradley and Clay Blair, *A General's Life,* p. 211.

406   "When I finished, Roosevelt. ...": ibid.

406   "I decided that the President. ...": ibid.

406   "What if the Germans had ... ?": interview, John Eisenhower, May 30, 2000; John Eisenhower, *Strictly Personal,* p. 97.

406   "is the biggest fool thing. ...": Christopher Andrew, *For the President's Eyes Only,* p. 150; Jim Bishop, *FDR's Last Year,* p. 25.

406   "I am not sure how long. ...": Bishop, p. 249.

406   While trusting in Stettinius: Cordell Hull, *The Memoirs of Cordell Hull,* p. 1110.

407   "We now have the discovery. ...": Joseph P. Lash, *A World of Love: Eleanor Roosevelt and Her Friends, 1943–1962,* pp. 125–26.

407 Sensing that this was one arena: Burns, p. 455.

408 He was subsequently removed: Doris Kearns Goodwin, *No Ordinary Time,* p. 621.

408 "A single bomb of this type. . . .": Alexander Sachs Box 1, FDRL.

408 "When he asked about my emotion. . . .": James Roosevelt, *My Parents,* pp. 169–70.

408 J. Edgar Hoover learned of the bomb: Pavel Sudoplatov and Anatoli Sudoplatov, *Special Tasks,* p. 187.

408 Thus, in the spring of 1943: David Dallin, *Soviet Espionage,* pp. 468–69; Robert Louis Benson, *A History of U.S. Communications Intelligence During World War II,* p. xviii.

408 Hoover's rival, Wild Bill Donovan: Anthony Cave Brown, *The Last Hero,* pp. 771–75.

408 His predecessor as vice president: *FRUS,* 3d Washington Conference, p. 188.

409 "Stimson told me. . . .": Harry S Truman, *Memoirs,* Vol. 1, *Year of Decisions,* p. 10.

409 "He does all the talking. . . .": David G. McCullough, *Truman,* p. 328.

409 "[T]he president told me. . . .": Robert Ferrell, *Harry S. Truman,* p. 172.

409 ". . . [H]e's just going to pieces. . . .": ibid.

410 "You remember when we were together. . . .": Robert Ferrell, unpublished draft, undated.

410 As a senator who chaired: ibid.

410 "It may be necessary. . . .": Dan Kurzman, *Day of the Bomb,* p. 212.

410 "is a nuisance. . . .": ibid., p. 213.

410 "the wisdom of testing. . . .": Richard Rhodes, *The Making of the Atomic Bomb,* p. 635.

411 "I do not know the substance. . . .": PPF 7177.

411 "The President . . . had suggested. . . .": Henry L. Stimson and McGeorge Bundy, *On Active Service in Peace and War,* p. 615.

411 "A German espionage agent. . . .": POF 10B.

411 "This information is. . . .": ibid.

412 ". . . [H]ope for a German bomb. . . .": Leslie B. Rout Jr. and John F. Bratzel, *The Shadow War,* p. 480.

412 ". . . [R]espect the right of all peoples. . . .": Burns, *Roosevelt: The Soldier of Freedom,* p. 130.

412 "Let me, however, make this clear. . . .": Robert E. Sherwood, *Roosevelt and Hopkins,* p. 656.

412 He had been particularly irked: ibid.

412 "I imagine it is one. . . .": David Stafford, *Churchill and Secret Service,* p. 284.

412 ". . . [I]f we really believed. . . .": Phillip Knightley, *The Second Oldest Profession,* p. 230.

412 He had confided to his son: Burns, *Roosevelt: The Soldier of Freedom,* p. 379.

413 Bill Donovan had long wanted: Robin Winks, *Cloak and Gown,* p. 176.

413 On February 19, 1945: M 1642, pp. 269–70.

413 "Had we passed this along? . . .": M 1642, Reel 89, Frames 267–70.

413 They offered to conduct: Bradley F. Smith, *The Shadow Warriors,* p. 324.

413 "I do not want to get mixed up. . . .": ibid., p. 323.

413 "OSS personnel not to be employed. . . .": M 1642, Marshall to Sultan, Feb. 9, 1945.

413 "We had been at war with Germany. . . .": Knightley, p. 231.

414 Churchill complained to FDR: Smith, *The Shadow Warriors,* p. 281.

414 "something better to look forward to. . . .": Knightley, p. 231.

414 "I want you to know. . . .": Kermit Roosevelt, *The Overseas Targets,* pp. xvi, xvii.

414 "Morale is very high. . . .": M 1642, Reel 24, Frames 358–61.

CHAPTER XXVIII: "STALIN HAS BEEN DECEIVING ME ALL ALONG"

415 Previously, while moving: Otto John, *Twice Through the Lines,* pp. 188–89.

415 There he told his story: Norman Polmar and Thomas B. Allen, *Spy Book,* p. 300.

416 John was struck: John Toland, *Adolf Hitler,* p. 803.

416 John was especially surprised: Jürgen Heideking and Christof Mauch, eds., *American Intelligence and the German Resistance to Hitler,* pp. 283–85.

416 In an organization chart: Charles Higham, *Errol Flynn,* p. 279.

416 If Speer was coming over: Heideking and Mauch, p. 285.

416 "I heard the radio announce. . . .": ibid., p. 286.

416 "The following information. . . .": ibid., p. 284.

416 Three weeks after the failure: Polmar and Allen, *Spy Book,* p. 300.

417 The Gestapo had indeed continued: Joseph E. Persico, *Piercing the Reich,* p. 82.

417 On January 20, 1945: ibid., pp. 59–60, 152–55.

418 "to destroy Central Information office. . . .": Neal H. Petersen, ed., *From Hitler's Doorstep,* pp. 437–38.

418 "The present situation. . . .": PSF Box 151.

418 He claimed further: Petersen, pp. 438–39.

418 "Wehrmacht officers who contribute. . . .": PSF Box 151.

419 "If the German was permitted. . . .": Persico, *Piercing the Reich,* p. 11.

419 "This whole project seems. . . .": Petersen, p. 417.

419 He had word that the commander: ibid.

420 As Ribbentrop instructed: RG 457 CBOM 77.

421 Dulles put Wolff to the test: Heideking and Mauch, p. 384.

422 Ultra intercepts suggested that Wolff: Richard Breitman and Timothy Naftal, "Report to the Interagency Working Group on Previously Classified OSS Records," NA, p. 3.

422 Wolff managed to get a message: Jim Bishop, *FDR's Last Year,* pp. 503–506.

422 There the matter hung: Heideking and Mauch, pp. 381–85.

423 "It is believed. . . .": Persico, *Piercing the Reich,* p. 289.

423 "I do not believe. . . .": PSF, Donovan to FDR, March 6, 1945.

423 "I say quite frankly. . . .": MR Box 23.

424 "I'd put Stalin. . . .": Persico, *Piercing the Reich,* p. 167.

424 In a remote corner of liberated France: ibid., p. 255.

424 That March, the *Chicago Tribune:* Washington *Times-Herald,* March 13, 1945; *New Leader,* March 17, 1945.

424 "[M]embership in the Communist Party. . . .": M 1642, Reel 27, Frame 572.

424 "I'm simply not in a position. . . .": Persico, *Piercing the Reich,* p. 8.

425 "These people were a bunch. . . .": ibid., p. 24.

425 "These four men. . . .": Washington *Times-Herald,* March 13, 1945.

425 By the time Donovan appeared before: Allen Weinstein and Alexander Vassiliev, *The Haunted Wood,* pp. 257–59.

425 The Iron Cross mission was scrubbed: Persico, *Piercing the Reich,* p. 259.

425 On March 12 he notified: Bishop, pp. 504–505, 508.

426 The Combined Chiefs of Staff: ibid., p. 509.

426 Molotov shot back: ibid., p. 505.

426 On March 24, FDR sent: MR Box 28.

426 FDR also maintained: ibid.

426 "a matter in which Russia. . . .": Leslie B. Rout Jr. and John F. Bratzel, *The Shadow War,* p. 332.

426 "I agree to negotiations with the enemy. . . .": MR Box 28.

427 The Soviet leader understood: Bishop, p. 505.

427 "I must repeat that the meeting. . . .": MR Box 28.

427 Roosevelt was so taken aback: Bishop, p. 509.

427 His fear, he confided to an associate: ibid.

427 "You insist there have been. . . .": MR Box 28.

428 "the Germans on the Western front. . . .": ibid.

428 "I have received with astonishment. . . .": ibid.

428 ". . . [Y]our information," FDR went on: ibid.

428 ". . . I cannot avoid a feeling. . . .": ibid.

428 "I have never doubted. . . .": ibid.

429 He had one more charge to unload: ibid.

429 "will to fight. . . .": MR Box 167.

429 "The Japanese government expects. . . .": RG 457 CBOM 77.

429 "At the time when this treaty. . . .": ibid.

CHAPTER XXIX: "THE FOLLOWING ARE THE LATEST CASUALTIES"

430 He now believed the Soviets: Jim Bishop, *FDR's Last Year,* p. 545.

430 A few days before, on March 29: ibid., p. 520.

430 As the train was pulling: ibid., p. 44.

430 Bruenn had started his White House duties: ibid., p. 18.

431 The doctor well understood: ibid., p. 499.

431 "The Drs. love this little time. . . .": Suckley, Binder 19, p. 14.

431 "I get the gruel. . . .": ibid.

431 "He took half his evening gruel. . . .": ibid.

432 "As you probably know. . . .": PSF Box 153.

432 ". . . [T]he possible advantages. . . .": MR Box 163.

432 ". . . a frank, across-the-table discussion. . . .": PSF Box 153.

432 Grace Tully thought that FDR: Bishop, p. 520.

432 In the meantime, he felt: Anthony Cave Brown, *The Last Hero,* p. 736.

432 "I should think that system. . . .": ibid.

432 Biddle's response: ibid.

433 "I was terribly shocked when I saw him. . . .": John Morton Blum, *Years of War, 1941–1945: From the Morgenthau Diaries,* p. 416.

433 There he began a stream: ibid., p. 417.

433 "A weak economy for Germany. . . .": ibid., p. 419.

433 "three or four times saying. . . .": ibid., p. 418.

433 "I am going there on my train. . . .": ibid., p. 417.

433 The President forgivingly: MR Box 28.

433 "I respectfully request. . . .": MR Box 23.

434 "prepared to do everything in their power. . . .": PSF Box 152.

434 "The redoubt is becoming a reality. . . .": MR Box 152.

434 But if the OSS would deal with him: PSF Box 152.

434 This message would be the last: PSF Index.

434 The intelligence out of Bern: Doris Kearns Goodwin, *No Ordinary Time,* p. 602.

434 "I glanced up from my work. . . .": Suckley, Binder 19, p. 32.

434 Roosevelt had suffered: Bishop, p. 583; Goodwin, pp. 602–603.

434 "Darlings, Pa slept away. . . .": MR Box 14.

435 The first listing read: James MacGregor Burns, *Roosevelt: The Soldier of Freedom,* p. 602.

CHAPTER XXX: AFTERMATH

436 On April 30, eighteen days: *American Heritage,* April/May 1985.

436 ". . . [W]e are wiring various points. . . .": RG 457 CBOM 77.

437 Eleven days before the President's death: James MacGregor Burns, *Roosevelt: The Soldier of Freedom,* pp. 487, 588.

437 ". . . [T]he Americans will not forget. . . .": RG 457 Magic #74923.

437 "I casually mentioned to Stalin. . . .": David G. McCullough, *Truman*, p. 442.

438 The last time his Soviet controllers: Norman Moss, *Klaus Fuchs*, pp. 2, 73, 79, 80.

438 Fuchs was among those present: ibid., p. 81.

438 "Tell Comrade Kurchatov. . . .": Norman Polmar and Thomas B. Allen, *Spy Book*, p. 35.

438 It is estimated that Soviet agents: T. A. Heppenheimer, "But on the Other Hand . . . ," *American Heritage*, September 2000, p. 46.

438 This stolen treasure: Allen Weinstein and Alexander Vassiliev, *The Haunted Wood*, pp. 190–94; Christopher Andrew and Vasili Mitrokhin, *The Sword and the Shield*, p. 132; Pavel Sudoplatov and Anatoli Sudoplatov, *Special Tasks*, p. 211.

438 The first nuclear weapon the Soviets: Andrew and Mitrokhin, p. 132.

438 "At no time from 1941 to 1945. . . .": Henry L. Stimson and McGeorge Bundy, *On Active Service in Peace and War*, p. 613.

439 Between 80,000 and 100,000: Gerhard L. Weinberg, *A World at Arms*, p. 870.

439 A Gallup poll taken just a month and a half: *MHQ*, Spring 1998, pp. 68–69.

439 Still he chose to appease: Doris Kearns Goodwin, *No Ordinary Time*, pp. 427–28.

440 The all-Japanese 442nd: Polmar and Allen, *Spy Book*, p. 395.

440 But, as the cabinet debated: Burns, *Roosevelt: The Soldier of Freedom*, p. 463; Weinberg, pp. 590, 632, 652.

440 "The more I think of this problem. . . .": Goodwin, p. 514.

440 Finally, FDR reversed himself: Burns, *Roosevelt: The Soldier of Freedom*, p. 464.

440 "the worst single wholesale violation. . . .": ibid., p. 216.

440 "[N]ot one plan or proposal. . . .": William J. vanden Heuvel, "America, FDR and the Holocaust," *Society*, vol. 34, no. 6 (September/October 1997), p. 7.

441 Many Jewish accounts had been emptied: *NYT*, Nov. 17, 1999.

441 The compensation agreement: *NYT*, Jan. 19, 31, March 26, Aug. 1, 1999.

441 Seven months after FDR's death: Elizabeth Bentley, *Out of Bondage*, Devin-Adair edition, p. 286.

441 "They made no bones. . . .": *Hearings on Proposed Legislation to Curb or Control the Communist Party of the United States*, 1948, p. 540.

441 On November 30, 1945, Bentley began: Statement of Elizabeth Ferrill Bentley to the FBI, Nov. 30, 1945, pp. 18–28, 34–36, 40, 43, 52, 57, 74–75, 78, 80, 91.

441 In 1948, Bentley became the star witness: *Hearings*, p. 503.

442   She was shaken to find her name: Bentley, pp. 307–309.

442   Between Bentley and Chambers: *Hearings,* pp. 1349–51.

442   Harry Dexter White, Alger Hiss: ibid., p. 1351.

442   A HUAC power, Congressman Karl Mundt: Harvey Klehr and Ronald Radosh, *The Amerasia Spy Case,* p. 160; *Hearings,* p. 862.

442   Further working in Currie's favor: *Hearings,* p. 1351; Klehr and Radosh, p. 111.

442   Currie had submitted: Currie to Truman, April 16, June 14, 1945; Truman to Currie, June 15, 1945, both in Truman Library.

442   In 1950, Currie moved to Colombia: Klehr and Radosh, pp. 160–61; *NYT,* March 27, 1956.

442   He continued to live there: Klehr and Radosh, p. 161.

442   Alger Hiss: Allen Weinstein, *Perjury,* p. 502.

442   Not until three years later: Michael Warner and Robert Louis Benson, "Venona and Beyond," *Intelligence and National Security,* vol. 12, no. 3 (July 1997), p. 6; Polmar and Allen, p. 577.

443   In 1949 another of these "Venona": Polmar and Allen, *Spy Book,* pp. 223–24.

443   The FBI traced ChARL'Z: ibid., p. 577.

443   Fuchs confessed: ibid., pp. 223–24.

443   The Venona decrypts also incriminated: Weinstein and Vassiliev, p. 168.

443   The appointee died: *Time,* Sept. 12, 1955.

443   "I recognize that I could. . . .": *NYT Magazine,* Sept. 14, 1997.

444   "We do not give a damn. . . .": Richard J. Whalen, *The Founding Father,* p. 320.

444   Kent ended his days: Tyler Kent Papers, Box 1, FDRL; Polmar and Allen, pp. 309–10.

444   "Believe me, I was never. . . .": Charles Wighton and Gunter Peis, *Hitler's Spies and Saboteurs,* pp. 29–39.

444   Not until the war ended: *American Heritage,* April 1970, p. 91.

444   William Colepaugh and Erich Gimpel: Francis Biddle, *In Brief Authority,* p. 343.

444   In January 1945: John Franklin Carter Diary, memo to Grace Tully, Jan. 18, 1945.

444   The journalist's facile pen: Ernest B. Furgurson, "Back Channels," *Washingtonian,* vol. 31 (June 1996); letter from Sonia Carter Greenbaum to William Safire, April 18, 1994.

445   "the booby prize. . . .": Christopher Andrew, *For the President's Eyes Only,* p. 132.

445   It was Carter who alerted FDR: John Franklin Carter Papers, Box 98, FDRL.

445   While the Putzi Hanfstaengl operation: Andrew, p. 133.

445 And Carter's well-placed business: Carter Diary, April 24, 1945.

445 "It was a picturesque. . . .": Andrew, p. 133.

445 A more formidable rival for FDR's favor: Polmar and Allen, *Spy Book,* p. 203.

445 Until his death in 1972: Athan Theoharis, ed., *From the Secret Files of J. Edgar Hoover,* p. 64.

446 "authorized me to make. . . .": Thomas F. Troy, *Donovan and the CIA,* p. 282.

446 "the main purpose of this school. . . .": Memorandum from Colonel Richard Park Jr. to President Harry S Truman, Appendix I, p. 2.

446 Park reported that the OSS: ibid., p. 12.

446 "In Portugal," he stated: ibid., p. 13.

446 "Before Pearl Harbor General Donovan. . . .": Park report, Appendix I, p. 26.

446 ". . . [T]here are some examples. . . .": ibid., p. 36.

446 OSS missions into occupied France: Joseph E. Persico, *Piercing the Reich,* pp. 14, 333.

446 "If the OSS is permitted to continue. . . .": Park report, pt. II, p. 1.

446 "It has," Park charged: ibid., p. 2.

447 "Came in to tell how important. . . .": Randy Sowell of Truman Library to author, May 24, 1999.

447 By September 10, Harold Smith's staff: Michael Warner, "The Creation of the Central Intelligence Group," *Studies in Intelligence,* Fall 1995, p. 6.

448 Just a week before his death: PSF Box 153.

448 The horseplay masked: Warner, "The Creation of the Central Intelligence Group," p. 1.

448 "I stopped him. . . .": Curt Gentry, *J. Edgar Hoover,* p. 148.

448 Whether through Hoover's machinations: Polmar and Allen, *Spy Book,* p. 173.

448 "What a man! . . .": Brown, *The Last Hero,* p. 833.

449 He delighted in his midnight rides: William M. Rigdon, *White House Sailor,* p. 18.

449 "Mr. Roosevelt made a fetish. . . .": Eric Larrabee, *Commander in Chief,* p. 624.

449 It was FDR who chose the exotic: William D. Hassett, *Off the Record with F.D.R., 1942–1945,* p. 113.

449 "He had long ago learned to conceal. . . .": Rexford Tugwell, *The Democratic Roosevelt,* p. 355.

449 He did not want anyone to know: Larrabee, p. 624.

449 "[F]ewer friends would have been lost. . . .": Goodwin, p. 78.

449 Roosevelt himself rarely recorded: Brian Loring Villa, "The Atomic Bomb and the Normandy Invasion," *Perspectives in American History* 2 (1977–78), p. 466.

449 "[T]here took place. . . .": *FRUS,* 2d Quebec Conference, vol. 1, p. 481.

449 "There is hardly a dependable record. . . .": Larrabee, pp. 144, 624.

450 The OSS, only temporarily scuttled: Joseph E. Persico, *Nuremberg,* pp. 359, 517.

450 In a generation, the United States: *NYT,* Dec. 5, 1999.

451 Hitler once pronounced accurate intelligence: David Kahn, *Hitler's Spies,* p. 540.

451 Across a report on Russian: ibid., p. 187.

451 "I was," this spy observed: Persico, *Piercing the Reich,* p. 38.

451 "opportunistic in meeting problems. . . .": Burns, *Roosevelt: The Soldier of Freedom,* p. 55.

Index

About the Author

JOSEPH E. PERSICO'S books include *Nuremberg: Infamy on Trial*, which was made into a major television docudrama, and *Piercing the Reich*, on the penetration of Nazi Germany by American agents. He is also the coauthor of General Colin Powell's autobiography, *My American Journey*.

About the Type

This book was set in Times Roman, designed by Stanley Morison specifically for *The Times* of London. The typeface was introduced in the newspaper in 1932. Times Roman had its greatest success in the United States as a book and commercial typeface, rather than one used in newspapers.